Jodie: Now that you have been to Alaska this might help with

Bent Pins to Chains:
Alaska and Its Newspapers

Some background. Enjoy!

Lew Williams Jr.

~~January 2007~~
April 2008

Evangeline Atwood
and
Lew Williams Jr.

Copyright © 2006 by Lew Williams Jr.

Library of Congress Control Number: 2005909552
ISBN 10:   Hardcover   1-4257-0066-7
            Softcover   1-4257-0065-9

ISBN 13:   Hardcover   978-1-4257-0066-9
            Softcover   978-1-4257-0065-2

All rights reserved. No part of this book may be reproduced or transmitted in any form or by any means, electronic or mechanical, including photocopying, recording, or by any information storage and retrieval system, without permission in writing from the copyright owner.

This book was printed in the United States of America.

To order additional copies of this book, contact:
Xlibris Corporation
1-888-795-4274
www.Xlibris.com
Orders@Xlibris.com

Contents

About This Book 7
Prologue 13

Chapters 1-9
Early Alaska Journalism and Southeast Alaska Changed by the Gold Rush

Chapter 1:   First Push for Railroad to Alaska 19
Chapter 2:   First Plea for Statehood in 1885 24
Chapter 3:   Churches Bring the Presses North 34
Chapter 4:   Sitka Loses Capital and Its Journalists 42
Chapter 5:   Miners Found Juneau Journalism 48
Chapter 6:   Bells Ring for Douglas Publisher 56
Chapter 7:   Seattle P-I Story Triggers Stampede 63
Chapter 8:   Dyea and Soapy Lose to Skagway 72
Chapter 9:   Talented Writers Follow Editor Strong 82

Chapters 10-15
Journalists Stampede Next to Nome and Fairbanks

Chapter 10: Early Nome Attracts Dawson City Journalists 93
Chapter 11: Teller, Council, Nome Lose Papers 107
Chapter 12: Fairbanks Attracts Talented Newsmen 116
Chapter 13: Thompson Starts His Miner 125
Chapter 14: Thompson Adds News to His Miner 130
Chapter 15: Thompson's N-M to Lathrop 142

Chapters 16-19
Journalists also Stampede to Southeast Before and After Gold Rush

Chapter 16: Stampeders, Swineford to Ketchikan 155
Chapter 17: Customs Man Founds Sentinel 166
Chapter 18: Controversial Editors in Juneau after Gold Rush 177
Chapter 19: Early Juneau Incubates Libel 185

Chapters 20-26
Prince William Sound and Rural Journalists Reach End of Trail

Chapter 20: Valdez Wins Then Loses 199
Chapter 21: Pinchot Burned at Katalla and Town Dies 207
Chapter 22: Cordova to Chitina 214
Chapter 23: Election Kills Three Valdez Papers 226
Chapter 24: Railroad and Harry Rise and Fall 234
Chapter 25: Seward, a Newsman's Dream 243
Chapter 26: Gold Rush Editors Reach End of Trail 252

Chapters 27-30
Southeast Journalists Report Disasters While Content and Style Change

Chapter 27: Writing Style, Content Change 269
Chapter 28: Hyder Papers, Mines Suffer 277
Chapter 29: Political Disaster Destroys Strong 289
Chapter 30: Dentists Rescue Skagway's Alaskan 296

Chapters 31-32
Anchorage from Knik to Ship Creek to Statehood

Chapter 31: Anchorage, the Late Bloomer 311
Chapter 32: The Atwood Years and Statehood 325

Chapters 33-35
Juneau, Ketchikan Papers Battle Statehood and Gruening

Chapter 33: Rise and Fall of Troy and His Empire 345
Chapter 34: The Rise of the Ketchikan Alaska Chronicle 358
Chapter 35: News Rises, Chronicle Falls 366

Chapters 36-39
Transportation, Military Boost Rural and Fairbanks Areas

Chapter 36: Military, Transportation Boost Rural Papers 381

Chapter 37: The Lathrop Years 389
Chapter 38: Jessen's Years in Fairbanks 396
Chapter 39: The Native Press Appears 407

Chapters 40-44
Sitka, Wrangell and Petersburg
Newspapers Overcome Setbacks

Chapter 40: Navy and Mill Boost Sitka 423
Chapter 41: Wrangell Sentinel's Williams Years 436
Chapter 42: Sentinel Reaches One Hundred Years 446
Chapter 43: The Pilot Succeeds in Petersburg 455
Chapter 44: Petersburg Press Switches to Offset 466

Chapters 45-48
Kodiak, Seward, Valdez and Cordova
Journalists Record Recoveries

Chapter 45: Kodiak Disasters Hit on Sunny Days 479
Chapter 46: Mirror Sparkles with Native Editor 489
Chapter 47: Seward's Fortunes Rise with WWII 497
Chapter 48: Valdez, Cordova Stagger and Recover 512

Chapters 49-51
Southeast Journalists Engage Bureaucrats,
Environmentalists, Lawmakers and the Court System

Chapter 49: Newspapers Battle Bureaucrats, Seattle 531
Chapter 50: Empire Upholds Privilege 545
Chapter 51: Reynolds, to Morris, to Courtroom Photos 557

Chapters 52-54
Peninsula Journalists Lead Fight
on Public Records and Meetings

Chapter 52: Peninsula Journalists First at Seldovia 577
Chapter 53: Frontiersman Triggers '94 Meeting Law Change 591
Chapter 54: Clarion Wins Public Records Ruling 605

Chapters 55-58
New Publishers, New Technology Lead
Newspapers Into Twenty-First Century

Chapter 55: Gregory, McGuire Acquire Nugget 623
Chapter 56: Mukluk Telegraph to Satellite 634
Chapter 57: Fairbanks Publishers Were Technical Pioneers 642
Chapter 58: Dominance Shifts from Times to News 658

Epilogue
Journalism Education Advances in Alaska

Epilogue: Atwoods Promote Journalism Education 679

Appendix
Index 691
Books and Other Sources of Information 715
What is a Newspaper? 723

About This Book

This book began in the mid-1970s, after historian and author Evangeline Atwood finished her sixth book on Alaska. *Fairbanks Daily News-Miner* executive Charles Gray and *Ketchikan Daily News* publisher Lew Williams Jr. urged her to write a history of Alaska newspapers. She finished a manuscript, "A History of One Hundred Years of Newspapering in Alaska, 1885-1985," but died of cancer in 1987 before it could be published.

Evangeline Atwood
-*Photo Courtesy of the Anchorage Daily News*

She gave copies to Gray, Williams, and to her husband, *Anchorage Times* publisher Robert B. Atwood. She asked Williams to edit it and have it published. Copies of her manuscript are in the state library archives in Juneau and in the archives of the University of Alaska Fairbanks and the University of Alaska Anchorage.

After retiring as a Ketchikan newspaper publisher, Williams began updating Mrs. Atwood's manuscript, resulting in an expanded archive copy. That copy is with

Lew Williams Jr.
-*Photo Courtesy of the Ketchikan Daily News*

Terry Miller
Managing Editor

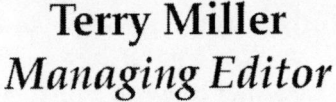

Angie Oaksmith
Graphic Artist

Ketchikan Daily News Photos by Hall Anderson

her original manuscript in the various archives. This book was developed from that updated copy.

Mrs. Atwood was born in Sitka in 1906, the daughter of E. A. and Jenny Rasmuson, who acquired National Bank of Alaska. Her brother, Elmer Rasmuson, and then her nephew, Edward Rasmuson, headed the bank before it was sold to Wells Fargo.

Mrs. Atwood was associated with her husband in *The Anchorage Times* from the time the couple purchased it in 1935.

During her years in Anchorage, she was a founder or president of nine different civic organizations.

Williams began his newspaper career in 1936 as a carrier for the *Daily Alaska Empire* in Juneau. He later operated newspapers with his wife, Dorothy, in Petersburg, Wrangell, Sitka, and Ketchikan, where they retired in the 1990s. He still writes a column that appears in Ketchikan, Juneau, and Anchorage newspapers.

The late Elaine Atwood, daughter of Evangeline and Robert Atwood, and the Atwood Foundation contributed financially to this book project.

About This Book

More than seventy books and other documents, plus the microfilm newspaper files at the state library, were examined to assemble the archive copies and this manuscript. Author Williams's sister, Susan Pagenkopf, retired educator and librarian, researched many microfilm files. The authors are indebted to more than one hundred individuals who provided information for this project, and to R. N. (Bob) DeArmond, William (Bill) Tobin, Christena (Tena) Williams, and Dorothy Williams, for extensive editing of the original archive manuscript and to a dozen others who read and edited various chapters. All are listed in the archive copies.

Final editing was done by prominent Alaska journalist Larry Persily and by *Ketchikan Daily News* managing editor Terry Miller. Retired *Anchorage Daily News* publisher Fuller Cowell performed a final review of the manuscript. Cover artwork is by Roger Maynard, a retired state trooper and freelance political cartoonist in Ketchikan (fiddlestix.biz). All picture layouts are by *Ketchikan Daily News* graphic artist Angie Oaksmith.

If readers find errors of fact, author Williams would like to be informed so that corrections can be inserted in archive copies and in any future publication of this manuscript.

    – Llewellyn (Lew) M. Williams Jr.
      October 2005
      E-mail: *lmwjr@worldnet.att.net*
      755 Grant Street
      Ketchikan, Alaska 99901

Prologue

Alaska Newspaper Industry

Changes with 1980s

Newspaper War

We are under siege . . . It is pretty hard to survive.

– Robert B. Atwood,
Publisher, 1935-92
The Anchorage Times

Competing Publishers
Kay Fanning, above, was publisher of the Anchorage Daily News from the death of her husband in 1971 until she became editor of the Christian Science Monitor in 1983. Robert B. Atwood, left, receiving the Anchorage Chamber of Commerce Gold Pan Award, was publisher of The Anchorage Times from 1935 until he sold it to Bill Allen in 1989. *–Photos courtesy of the Anchorage Daily News.*

Prologue

Early in the afternoon of June 2, 1992, editor J. Randolph Murray climbed on a desk in *The Anchorage Times* newsroom. He called for staff's attention. Bad news. Next morning's edition would be the last one for the newspaper.

The *Times*, founded in 1915 by veterans of the 1898 Gold Rush, was following those pioneers into history.

Thousands stampeded into the Yukon Territory in 1898, seeking to wrest a fortune from the ground. Among them were dozens of newspapermen. Those who arrived in Dawson City after 1897 were disappointed. Corporations had bought up the most promising Klondike claims. Massive dredges dug the treasure. Gold pans and sluice boxes couldn't compete. The stampeders pushed on to Alaska.

That Klondike Gold Rush triggered the development of Alaska, promoted and recorded by gold-seeking journalists. They battled the elements – weather vagaries to Washington politics – to lay the foundation for today's Alaska.

Some found a new gold in Alaska – newspaper circulation. Big corporations finally arrived there, too. One hundred years after the Klondike Gold Rush began, Outside chains own the biggest, most lucrative Alaska circulation "claims" – 65 percent of state's estimated 170,000 newspaper circulation.

The Anchorage Times recorded the most significant change in Alaska journalism after publisher Bill Allen – who had purchased the *Times* from longtime publisher Robert B. Atwood – said his fifty-thousand-circulation newspaper was going out of business. He was leaving the "claims" to the seventy thousand-circulation, chain-owned *Anchorage Daily News*. Alaska's largest, independently owned newspaper had succumbed to a larger, richer corporate competitor.

The big shakeup in Alaska newspapers came in the last few decades of the twentieth century. New technology, electronic competition, and the invasion of newspaper chains dominated the industry.

Anchorage boomed during World War II and after oil was discovered on the Kenai Peninsula in 1957. The boom continued, spurred by congressional passage of the Alaska Statehood Act in 1958 and the discovery of the huge Prudhoe Bay oil reserve ten years later.

The Anchorage newspaper war started eight years after President Dwight Eisenhower signed the proclamation on January 3, 1959, making Alaska a state and after the *Anchorage Daily News* founders, the Norman Browns, sold the paper to Larry and Kay Fanning. When the McClatchy Co., a California-based chain, took over the *News* in 1979, 59 percent of the state's four hundred thousand people lived in or near Anchorage. That circulation gold would be worth the fight.

It was a classic battle. It pitted an afternoon newspaper, the *Times*, against a morning newspaper, the *Daily News*; a locally owned newspaper, the Atwood family's *Times*, against a chain-owned newspaper, McClatchy's *Daily News*; a newspaper that concentrated on serving its local area, the *Times*, against a newspaper with statewide aspirations, the *Daily News*; a pro-development newspaper, the *Times*, against a pro-environment newspaper, the *Daily News*; a newspaper with conservative ideas, the *Times*, against a newspaper with liberal leanings, the *Daily News*; a news staff with a depth of experience, the *Times*, against a staff of young activists at the *Daily News*.

By 1979, Atwood had been publisher of the *Times* for forty-four years. He and his newspaper had been leaders in the battle for Alaska statehood.

The *Times*' top editor, Bill Tobin, had set up the first full-time Associated Press bureau in Alaska in 1956. He joined the *Times* in 1963 and began a column still appearing weekly in 2005.

Although the *Times* went through multiple managing editors and city editors during the newspaper war, all had lengthy experience. Tobin, with the most, was the backbone of the *Times* news department for almost thirty years and continued that role for "The Voice of the Times" in the *Anchorage Daily News* after the *Times* ceased publication.

In contrast to the experience of the *Times*' leaders, Kay Fanning of the *Daily News* had been a newspaper publisher only since the death of her husband, Larry, in 1971. Most of her newsroom staffers were barely ten years out of high school when they won their first Pulitzer Prize in 1976. They won a second in 1989.

The deciding factor was who was willing to spend the most money. Both sides had a lot. The Alaska newspaper war pitted the Atwood millions against, first, the millions of the Marshall Field family of Chicago into which Fanning had been married, and later, the McClatchys of California. The war continued in the million-dollar range after Bill Allen, owner of VECO, an oil service and construction company, bought the *Times* from the eighty-two-year-old Atwood on December 15, 1989.

Allen changed the *Times* to a morning publication, but that long-delayed action came too late. *Daily News* circulation had topped the *Times* in 1984. The gain continued despite Allen's infusion of money.

In the end, Allen sold the *Times'* circulation list, library, equipment and other assets to McClatchy. The *Times'* building was purchased by the Alaska Court System. As part of the dramatic end to the newspaper war, Allen negotiated a ten-year agreement with McClatchy to use the top half of the op-ed page in the *Daily News* to maintain the editorial "Voice of the Times." That provides *Daily News* readers an alternate, and more conservative, editorial opinion. The agreement was renewed in 2002.

As the only city in Alaska with two daily newspapers in the 1980s, and one of the few remaining in the nation, the battle for Anchorage circulation and advertising was intense.

"We're under siege," Atwood claimed. "It's mighty tough competition to have them giving away subscriptions and giving away advertising. It's pretty hard to survive."

McClatchy management guaranteed the *Daily News* staff forty-eight pages of news hole every day, regardless of advertising.

At the height of the battle in the 1980s, each Anchorage newspaper printed more inches of advertising daily – meaning more pages – than the *Seattle Times*, the Portland *Oregonian* or the *Spokane Spokesman-Review* and *Chronicle*. In 1985 the *Anchorage Daily News* printed more pages than McClatchy's flagship *Sacramento Bee*.

McClatchy built a $30 million plant that opened in June 1986 with a press that enabled it to print seventy thousand 144-page papers an hour, compared with the *Times'* capacity of sixty thousand 90-page papers.

The McClatchy victory ended local ownership of major Alaska newspapers. William Morris III, who operates sixty-one newspapers under Morris Publishing Group of Augusta, Georgia, bought the *Juneau Empire* (cir. 8,500) in 1969, the Kenai *Peninsula Clarion* (cir. 7,000) in 1990, the *Alaska Journal of Commerce* and *Alaska Magazine* in 1995, and the *Alaska Star* and the *Homer News* in 2000. Morris also owns several Anchorage radio stations, *The Milepost* and other Alaska businesses.

W. Dean Singleton and Richard Scudder, who also operate more than sixty newspapers under MediaNews Group based in Houston, purchased the *Fairbanks News-Miner* (cir. 21,000) in 1992 and the *Kodiak Daily Mirror* (cir. 4,000) in 1999.

The only Alaska dailies left in local ownership in 2005 were Sitka's *Daily Sentinel* (cir. 3,400), owned by the Thad Poulson family, and the *Ketchikan Daily News* (cir. 5,000), owned by the Lew Williams family.

The grand prize for the winner of the Anchorage newspaper war was the biggest circulation claim and dominance in an area that is home to more than one-half of all Alaskans.

Chapters 1-9

Early Alaska Journalism

and Southeast Alaska

Changed by

the Gold Rush

Gold! Gold! Gold! Gold!

– *Seattle P-I* banner
July 17, 1897

Publisher Governors

–Three Alaska newspaper publishers also served as governor. A. P. Swineford, left above, took a newspaper printing plant to Sitka when he was appointed Alaska's second governor, 1885-89, starting The Alaskan. J.F.A. Strong, right above, started the Alaska Daily Empire in Juneau in 1912 and sold it to John W. Troy, right, in 1913 when Strong was appointed governor. Troy mounted an investigation of Strong in 1918 that led to Strong's resignation as governor. Troy was later appointed governor in 1933-39 while publisher of the Empire. -1. *Swineford photograph from Alaska State Library, 01-140. 2. Strong photograph from Alaska State Library, 01-1981, photo by Backrack. 3. Troy photograph from Alaska State Library, Territorial Governors Collection, 274-2-6, photo by Mercer.*

Chapter 1

First Push for Railroad to Alaska

Ice was forming on the shore of Port Clarence in October 1866, only one hundred miles below the Arctic Circle in westernmost Alaska. It was calm but cold – down in the low teens at night at a Western Union telegraph cable construction camp, twenty miles south of present-day Teller. The whaling fleet used Port Clarence as shelter from winter winds off Norton Sound while it waited for supply boats that also carried its catches back to San Francisco.

A year before Alaska was transferred to the United States from Russia, John J. Harrington, a telegraph line worker at the camp, announced he would publish the first edition of his monthly, *The Esquimaux*, on October 10. He met that first deadline for an Alaska newspaper. The pages were written in longhand and held together by bent pins.

Western Union's Port Clarence station of forty men was commanded by Captain Daniel B. Libby, hence its name, Libbyville.

The Esquimaux was the only journal circulated on the North American continent north of Victoria. Its publication continued for a year, recording local happenings as well as national events. Editor Harrington collected his news from supply ships arriving at Port Clarence.

Work on the telegraph line continued into the summer of 1867. Then a company vessel reported the successful completion of the Atlantic cable, eliminating the need for a cable across Bering Strait.

Libbyville was abandoned and the men were ordered to return to San Francisco.

They arrived in San Francisco in October 1867 – the same month and year the United States took over Alaska from Russia. Copies of *The Esquimaux* were printed and bound in one volume of fifty-two pages. A copy is in the Alaska Historical Library archives in Juneau.

Shipboard newssheets appeared earlier in the North Pacific, but *The Esquimaux* was Alaska's first land-based newspaper.

Railroad to Sitka

The first edition of Alaska's second newspaper, *The Sitka Times*, appeared September 19, 1868, almost a year after Alaska became U.S. territory. It advocated extending a railroad to Sitka, and was the first Alaska newspaper to advocate development and self-government.

Sitka had been the administrative headquarters for Russian America from 1808 to 1867. Alexander Baranov, general manager of the Russian American Co., named the settlement *Nova Arkangelsk* (New Archangel), but the Americans adopted the Native name, Sitka, after transfer from Russia.

New Archangel, the largest settlement in Russian America, was the cultural and business center during Russian control. It boasted a theater on the second floor of the wooden castle; a public library that received quarterly shipments of books from St. Petersburg; a geological institute; a zoological institute; four lower schools; and a seminary.

A reporter for the *Alta California* claimed that no upper-class home was without its piano. The Lutheran Church boasted a German pipe organ.

Those trappings of civilization might be why the Russian America Co. was losing money and why the trappings all disappeared when the United States took over. So did the Russian-established industry.

At the time of the transfer to America on October 18, 1867, Sitka had a population of about one thousand, exclusive of the Natives. Its industries consisted of iron and brass foundries, machine shops, a sawmill, grist mill, tannery and shipyard, with the usual complement of shoemakers, bakers, tailors, and other tradesmen.

A motley group of adventurers arrived in Sitka when the Americans took over – traders, speculators, politicians, harlots, gamblers, and a contingent of two hundred soldiers. Missionaries soon followed.

The Russian-America Co. owned the businesses in Sitka so the newcomers built new buildings and businesses, including a new feature – saloons. The Russian company had ladled liquor out free to its employees, another way to lose money.

Treasury Department agent William Sumner Dodge established a customs office in Sitka. Among the early arrivals was a thirty-year-old Thomas G. Murphy. He was a tailor by trade and newsman by inclination. He began sending dispatches to a Victoria newspaper, *The British Colonist*, signing his pen name, Barney O'Ragen. He was present at the ceremonies when the Stars and Stripes replaced the double-eagle banner of Czarist Russia.

Unsure of women's rights, matrimony

Dodge, the town's first mayor, and Murphy, its first attorney, determined the town needed a newspaper. There was neither type nor press, nor even newsprint in the country, but they had pen, ink, and ordinary foolscap paper. Copyists wrote the news in black ink and underscored and divided the columns in red ink. Each copy consisted of two sheets of paper, handwritten on both sides, and held together with bent pins. It sold for twenty-five cents a copy.

The editorial "we" took the nom de plume of Barney O'Ragen. In his "Introductory," September 19, 1868, the editor outlined the policies of the paper:

> Today we present *The Sitka Times* to the citizens of Sitka and the world at large. It is the first attempt ever made to publish a paper in this vast land of Alaska.
>
> The *Times* will be devoted to local and general news, and we shall, when we deem it advisable, discuss all matters of public interest, touching the affairs about Alaska.
>
> In politics and religion, the *Times* will be neutral.
>
> The Pacific railroad we are in favor of and would like to see it extended to Sitka if possible.
>
> We are strongly in favor of a civil government instead of a military one.

> The *Times*, not having a devil in its shop, will be virtuous.
>
> We will pay proper attention to all fights we may hear of, but do not wish to participate in any ourselves.
>
> Matrimony we believe in and will advocate it, provided, however, it is not carried too far.
>
> In the question of women's rights, at present we are undecided.

In the fifth edition (October 17, 1868), Murphy recalled the ceremony accompanying the transfer of Alaska to the United States. Whenever he referred to the Russians, he lowercased the letter R.

> On the 18th of October, 1867, at 3 o'clock p.m., the U.S. warship *Ossippe* thundered forth the salutes to the russian flag, floating over the governor's house. These were quickly answered from the guns ashore, who (sic) echo resounded over crag and glen, as if to speak the tidings of the last hour, when the imperial banner shall have waved its last.
>
> The Star Spangled Flag of Freedom was ready to wave its glorious folds above the heads of the impatient spectators and at 3:30 p.m. the russian flag was hauled down and amidst the Stentorian (sic) cheers of an admiring people the banner we love so fondly and so well was fluttering in proud defiance to the mountain breeze.

The November 7, 1868, issue of the *Sitka Times* was its last. Murphy and Dodge decided that Sitka needed a printed newspaper. Murphy found a used handpress in Seattle. He returned to Sitka with it, a variety of type and a printer, William C. Calhoun.

The first issue of the *Alaska Times* printed on the press appeared April 23, 1869. It appeared on Saturdays for the next eighteen months. The price per copy was "seventy-five cents greenbacks."

When a subscriber sent him a leg of beef, Murphy thanked the donor publicly, observing that "beef is a rarity, and for weeks you might as well expect to find the grace of God in a lawyer's office as beef in Sitka." (Alaska's first lawyer joke?)

All assumed that the U.S. government would encourage settlement. They were disappointed. The government chose to ignore its new acquisition. The principal industries, which served the West Coast as far as California, were abandoned. The shipyard was demolished. There was no further use for the foundries. The white population dropped to 150 by 1870. Buildings were boarded up, people left.

Murphy suspended publication with his October 1, 1870, edition, departing for Seattle where he resumed publication of the *Alaska Times* on October 30.

A long article appeared in the *Seattle Post-Intelligencer* the following February telling about Murphy being flogged by F. Lampson for a scurrilous story that appeared in the *Times*. Lampson pled guilty to assault and battery and was fined $25.

Murphy sold the *Alaska Times* in May 1871. After going through a succession of owners and name changes, it became part of the *Seattle Post-Intelligencer*.

Army men next journalists

Army enlistedmen William E. Jones and Fred C. Pratz published the *Alaska Bulletin* in Sitka for four months in 1875. Then in 1876-77, there were fourteen issues of *The Sitka Post* published by army men William W. Ward and James J. Daly.

One story told of a bill introduced in Congress by Sen. Roscoe Conkling, R-New York, appropriating $100,000 for a route survey for a railroad to be built by the U.S government from the continental United States, through Canada and Alaska, to a port on the Bering Sea "in order to facilitate the settlement and development of resources of the Territory of Alaska."

For more than eight years after the demise of the *Post* in 1877, the closest thing to an Alaska newspaper was the *Alaska Appeal*, published in San Francisco, 1879-80, by its editor, Ivan Petroff.

Petroff, born in Russia, served in the U.S. Army in Alaska. He was a translator for historian Hubert Howe Bancroft and is alleged to have fabricated some of his material.

The *Appeal* was eight tabloid pages issued semimonthly. Much of the news was about San Francisco firms doing business in Alaska, the growing Alaska fishing industry, and about the placer gold mines in the Cassiar district of British Columbia. In some issues the paper carried business directories of Sitka and Wrangell. The last issue appeared April 15, 1880.

Chapter 2

First Plea for Statehood in 1885

Alaska journalism began in earnest when experienced newspaper publisher Alfred P. Swineford landed at Sitka in September 1885 as Alaska's second governor. He had published the *Marquette* (Michigan) *Mining Journal* for seventeen years, and had served in the Michigan Legislature and as Marquette's mayor. He also had been a delegate to the Democratic National Convention in 1884 and helped nominate Grover Cleveland for president.

Following Cleveland's election, Swineford was rewarded with appointment as governor of Alaska. Whether shipping someone off to the Alaska wilderness at that time could be considered a reward might be debated. But it solved a problem shared by Swineford and Cleveland.

Swineford had been a widower for four years, and his departure for Alaska was an escape from feminine admirers. Among them was President Cleveland's sister, Cynthia, who charged Swineford with breach of promise. She authored a novel in which he was the villain and she the rejected lover. Publication of the book was to coincide with Swineford's marriage to a former reporter, Mrs. Wilhelmina (Minnie) Smith. President Cleveland ordered his sister's book taken out of circulation.

Swineford was expected in Sitka on the August 1885 mail steamer but missed the boat at Portland. While he waited for the next boat, Swineford purchased a handpress, a couple of cases of type, and some newsprint.

The Organic Act of 1884 changed Alaska from a military district to a civil judicial district. It provided for presidential appointment of a governor, district judge, district attorney, marshal, clerk of the court, and minor officials. The first set of officials served through the final months of President Chester A. Arthur's administration. Most of them were described as bibulous and cantankerous. President Cleveland fired them all except Commissioner John G. Brady.

Alaska's first governor, John Henry Kinkead, was among those fired after having been governor for less than a year. Prior to that, he had been governor of Nevada, and before that he had been postmaster and operator of a trading post at Sitka.

Sitka was a quiet little village when Swineford arrived. There were about two hundred whites and Creoles. Some seven hundred Tlingit Indians lived outside the stockade that was left over from the Russian era. The warship *Pinta* was stationed there with sixty Navy men. A small contingent of U.S. Marines lived ashore in a large log barracks.

There were a half dozen merchants, several saloons, two hotels, and two or three restaurants run by Chinese. Federal officials included a postmaster, a collector of customs, a marshal, a few deputies, an attorney, and a commissioner.

Alaskan staff paid by feds

Governor Swineford organized the Alaskan Publishing Co. with nine shareholders. Swineford kept the controlling interest although he did not use the paper in his feuds with missionaries, the Navy and Republican office holders.

The Alaskan made its first appearance on November 7, 1885. It was a five-column, four-page weekly. Swineford was editor. Colonel Mottram D. Ball, the U.S attorney, assisted him. Ball served with the Confederate Army in the Civil War and later as editor-publisher of the *Virginia Sentinel*, in Alexandria, Virginia.

Edward H. Brown, a special deputy collector of customs, was the printer. He was the son of veteran journalist Beriah Brown, editor of the *Seattle P-I*.

Thus, the three men principally involved in producing the first editions of *The Alaskan* – Swineford, Ball, and Brown – were all on the federal payroll.

Governor's Newspaper

–Gov. A.P. Swineford brought a newspaper plant north and started The Alaskan in Sitka when he was appointed governor 1885-89. He later started Ketchikan's first newspaper, The Mining Journal, in January 1901.
-Photo courtesy Alaska State Library, 01-1563.

The Alaskan's initial editorial proclaimed it would be "devoted wholly and solely to the advocacy for Alaska's development, not only as one of the very wealthiest of all the territories but place her in possession of all the elements essential to the endowment of a great and powerful state."

Thus, Governor Swineford became the founding father of Alaska statehood. Others pleaded for home rule but he was the first to suggest statehood.

Territorial status killed

As early as 1888, Governor Swineford persuaded the House Committee on Territories that Alaska should have at least a territorial form of government. But businessmen of Sitka and Juneau signed a petition opposing the proposal and sent it to the committee, killing the idea.

Years later, after Commissioner Brady, a Sitka businessman, became governor, his newspaper opposition asserted it was he who drafted and circulated the damaging petition.

The Alaskan carried advertisements on its front pages during its twenty-two years of publishing. Cohen's Sitka and Juneau breweries advertised pure beer expressly and exclusively for "medicinal, mechanical, and scientific purposes."

The Organic Act of 1884 prohibited the manufacture and sale of alcohol except for the three purposes cited above.

News items reflected the town's frontier character:

> Quantities of venison, wild geese, ducks and grouse are for sale at the meat markets, but there is a shortage of beef.
> Peter French, collector of customs, seized a barrel of Claret, half a barrel and two kegs of whiskey for illegal entry.
> Current market quotations: Grouse and mallard ducks, 60c per brace; herring abundant at 10c per string of 20; wild geese weighing from 12 to 15 lbs., $1 apiece; plovers, 25c a dozen; venison is plentiful but not in as good condition as it was a month ago; flounders are coming in in quantities and are retailed at 2c a pound; fish is of excellent flavor.

One story told of "a most audacious outrage perpetrated on the dignity of the governor of Alaska.:"

While he was alone at dinner a bob-tailed Thomas cat, not having the fear of a strong man in his heart, boldly leaped upon the table and seized from off the platter a roast of venison, which he bore away through an open door into the rear yard.

The amazed official then quietly arose and laying hold of his gun, proceeded to the door and drew a line on the felonious feline. The report of the rifle was the death knell of Tommy, and the executive meal was finished without further interruption – or venison.

On March 13, 1886, *The Alaskan* reported there had been a meeting of the paper's shareholders to reorganize the staff. Governor Swineford notified the shareholders he would be unable to continue with editorial work because of the press of government business. The story did not contain the names of shareholders, but one of them is known to have been Commissioner Brady, a Republican, whom Swineford, a Democrat, grew to detest – a mutual feeling.

About the time of that meeting, Brady wrote to Dr. Sheldon Jackson telling him that he had sold his stock in the publishing company.

Brady had arrived in Sitka in 1878 as a Presbyterian missionary. He later joined Amos T. Whitford in the Sitka Trading Co., Sitka's largest store. In 1884, President Arthur had appointed him U.S. commissioner. Despite Swineford's efforts to have Brady discharged, he served his full term, four years and a little longer.

Caned and whipped

Colonel Ball took over the editorial chores from Swineford. Barton Arkins, a U.S. marshal of a literary bent, assisted him. Ball did not hold the editor's job for long.

Later in the year, William A. Kelly, the superintendent of the Sitka Industrial Training School operated by the Presbyterians, wrote to Dr. Jackson:

"Since Colonel Ball has been deposed from the editorial chair, and the governor being absent, *The Alaskan* has emerged into personalities which caused a shaking up of dry bones yesterday. Mrs. Cowles went to the office of Marshal Arkins and vigorously caned him."

That ended Marshal Arkins's journalistic career. On December 18, 1886, the paper announced, "Mr. Edward Chamberlain, having consented to take charge of our local columns, has also been appointed business manager."

Chamberlain was born in England about 1858 and arrived in Sitka in June 1886. He was a talented artist and painted many Sitka scenes. Sometimes he raffled them off, three chances at fifty cents. (In 1983, the Anchorage Museum of History and Art purchased for $1,500 a ten-inch-by-sixteen-inch watercolor by Chamberlain entitled *Baranof Castle, Sitka, Alaska, April 1889*.)

Chamberlain was ill-prepared for the turbulent role of newspaper editor. One day he was sitting alone in the editorial office when three men entered. One was carrying a cowhide whip in his hand. A six-shooter peeped out of his pocket. The editor recognized him as John McCafferty, the acting collector of customs.

McCafferty had written a letter to the editor, and Chamberlain had published it, prefaced by the statement that McCafferty was "a vagabond and a servile tool of the whiskey ring." McCafferty whipped the editor and left him prostrate on the floor.

When McCafferty first arrived in Alaska from Helena, Montana, he claimed he was a correspondent for The Associated Press. He instigated a riot against Chinese mine workers at Treadwell, across Gastineau Channel from Juneau, resulting in eighty Chinese being shipped to Wrangell. Then McCafferty went south and returned with an appointment as customs collector. The U.S. Senate, however, declined to confirm him, and he was soon replaced.

McCafferty was arrested after his assault on Chamberlain, but the jury acquitted him on grounds he was insane. There were no facilities in Alaska to care for the insane, so he took the next southbound steamer, a free man.

Chamberlain recovered from the beating and remained in the editorial chair until June 1887. Maurice F. Kenealy took over the paper on July 23. He wrote that he had purchased the paper from Governor Swineford and other stockholders.

Maurice Edward Kenealy, like Chamberlain, was born in England. He had been city editor of the *Tacoma Ledger* and had worked on papers in Vancouver and Victoria. He went to Sitka originally as private secretary to Governor Swineford.

With Kenealy as editor, *The Alaskan* expanded its news coverage to the entire District of Alaska and paid more attention to cultural affairs in Sitka. News of other areas came to him through letters, newspapers from Portland and San Francisco, and from magazine articles and government reports.

The paper reported on the growing salmon canning industry, the cod and halibut fisheries, the Arctic whaling fleet and its annual catch, and on the sealing fleet. He reported the controversy over seal hunting in the Bering Sea and the dispute over the Alaska-Canada boundary.

He covered the work of the Coast Survey, the mining industry – including the growth of placer mining in the Yukon River Valley – the Natives of Alaska, law enforcement, the liquor business, and just about every other aspect of Alaska life.

The Alaskan's "society" columns highlighted events held by the officers of the Navy gunboat stationed at Sitka and their wives, and by government officials and local fraternal organizations.

The town was growing, although slowly. The future of the struggling Presbyterian mission seemed assured when it secured a contract to operate an industrial training school for Natives.

A salmon cannery was established at the Redoubt near Sitka. The local halibut fishery was growing. A few months after Kenealy acquired the newspaper, the Alaskan Society of Natural History and Ethnology was organized. It created the Sheldon Jackson Museum, an attraction for the increasing number of tourists visiting Alaska.

Newspaper turnover in '90s

There were many changes in owners and editors of Sitka newspapers in the 1890s.

Republican Benjamin Harrison was elected president in 1888, and that changed government in Alaska. Swineford tendered his resignation as governor in February 1889, but his successor, Lyman F. Knapp, failed to reach Sitka until the middle of June. Knapp, a lawyer, also was the former editor and publisher of the *Middlebury* (Vermont) *Register*.

Another new official was Orville T. Porter, who arrived in September to serve as U.S. marshal. Porter had been a newspaperman in Albany, Oregon, and he brought north with him his son, Walter, twenty-two, also a newsman.

At the beginning of November 1891, Kenealy sold *The Alaskan* to Walter Porter and Christian H. Schaap, who published their first issue on November 7, the sixth anniversary of the founding of the paper.

Schaap had arrived in Sitka in 1883 as a Navy yeoman. He was born in Amsterdam, Holland, son of a wealthy export merchant.

The Porter-Schaap partnership lasted only a month. Schaap purchased Porter's interest in December 1891. To finance the purchase, he borrowed $300 from schoolteacher Cassia Patton, a sister of Mrs. John Brady. Mrs. Brady was the wife of the same local businessman who had a falling out with Governor Swineford and sold his interest in *The Alaskan*. Miss Patton held a mortgage on the equipment.

Walter Porter did not stay out of print for long – about seven months. He started a weekly paper in competition with *The Alaskan*. Volume I, number 1 of his *Alaska Herald* appeared June 27, 1892.

Vitriloic Herald

The *Herald* was an attractive paper, but it did not attract many local advertisers. It was considered Governor Knapp's organ and Knapp was not well liked by most Sitkans. They considered him not only a carpetbagger but a pinchpenny Yankee. In turn, he labeled his detractors the Sitka Mafia.

Porter wielded a sharp editorial pen against what he called "the venal Alaskan press" because of its negative criticism of "carpetbag appointees." He blamed the press for inflaming the populace against these representatives of law and order. He said the "venal press" encouraged "a reign of terror in Alaska ... Newspapers in the hands of criminals and ignorant, unprincipled demagogues" brought about this chaotic state of affairs.

The only press – venal or otherwise – in Alaska at that time, aside from the *Herald,* was its competition in Sitka and the *Juneau City Mining Record*.

Porter's bitterness blossomed in an editorial in which he castigated Frank Myers, a former Sitka printer and educator, who was editor of the Juneau paper:

> This guttersnipe, who bears no resemblance to the human family, if the science of phrenology goes for anything, whose facial resemblance to an African baboon is so like and striking that it would deceive a genuine baboon itself, whose ponderous mouth, square under-jaw

and prominent gullet would put those organs in a full-grown gorilla to the blush, cannot, we are told, be no more a man than the devil can transform himself into an angel of light.

The thing is the lowest form of animal life, a groveling, sycophantic scum of earth, a loathsome reptile wallowing in its *own* ooze and slim. We hate to soil the columns of the *Herald* with a natural description of this dirty vagabond, but forbearance ceases to be a virtue under long continued provocation, and it is full time that the stench of this hideous Ape be hurled back upon himself, and that he be buried out of sight and smothered in his own filth and rottenness.

Although confident that his paper was an avenging nemesis brought forth to right the wrongs of men, Porter's vituperate writing antagonized townspeople. One day while he was out of his office, someone entered and dumped two double galleys of type onto the floor. They had been ready for printing in that week's edition of the paper. That act of vandalism only emphasized his contention that Alaskans were anarchistic.

Grover Cleveland returned to the White House in 1893. Early in 1894 Orville Porter was replaced as U.S. marshal and returned to Oregon. His son soon followed him.

In a "valedictory" in the *Herald* March 19, 1894, Walter Porter wrote that he had sold the paper to E. O. Sylvester, who had recently sold his Juneau newspaper.

Schaap carried on as editor and publisher of *The Alaskan* until May 31, 1894, when he died of a heart attack at age fifty-two. Chamberlain was recruited to return and run the paper until the Schaap estate could sell it.

Near the end of September 1894, E. Otis Smith, who had edited the *Juneau City Mining Record* for a year, purchased *The Alaskan* from the Schaap estate. Smith and Sylvester worked out a deal to combine the papers. Then one paper appeared with the front-page banner *The Alaskan and Herald Combined*, and with Smith and Sylvester on the masthead as publishers and proprietors.

With its issue of June 15, 1895, the paper dropped "and Herald Combined" from the front page.

Vice president visits

A highlight of that summer of 1895 was the visit by Vice President Adlai Stevenson with his wife and two daughters and two of his brothers. *The Alaskan* covered the story in depth, including a public reception for the party and their entertainment by then Governor and Mrs. James Sheakley at the governor's residence. Sheakley, who had been superintendent of schools for Alaska for six years, had replaced Knapp in 1893 after the second election of President Cleveland.

With the issue of October 5, 1895, Chamberlain was added to the masthead again, this time as associate editor.

Sitkan finances Juneau

Meanwhile, prospectors Dick Harris and Joe Juneau made a big gold discovery in 1880 about one hundred miles northeast of Sitka. The two met during the Cassiar gold stampede out of Wrangell in the mid-1870s and later moved to Sitka where they met George Pilz, a mining engineer from San Francisco. Pilz grubstaked the two veteran prospectors "to prospect the mainland of Alaska for gold and silver quartz lodes and placer mines."

Harris and Juneau, financed by a Sitka-area mining engineer, discovered the Silver Bow Basin claims that led to the founding of Juneau. The Juneau-Douglas area boomed, and in twenty-five years it took over not only the journalism and mining lead from Sitka, but also the offices of Alaska's government – its capital.

Chapter 3

Churches Bring the Presses North

Churches and missionaries were among the first to bring printing presses and newspapers to Alaska. Church-related publications appeared first at Wrangell and Sitka, and then in the Yukon River area.

They were especially influential before the Gold Rush of 1898, during a time that professional journalists confined themselves to Sitka and Juneau, the only frontier towns with enough English-literate settlers to support a newspaper. Kodiak, Kenai, and Wrangell were small Russian settlements. Ketchikan was a fish camp. Skagway and Petersburg were yet to be founded in Southeast.

When the Episcopal Church shipped the first printing press to Interior Alaska in 1894, Nome, Anchorage, Fairbanks, Seward, Valdez, and Cordova were nonexistent. The press went to the St. James Mission at Fort Adams, a trading station on the Yukon River, eight miles below the current community of Tanana.

Contempt of press?

The Rev. Jules L. Prevost published the *Yukon Press* at the mission for a few years to serve the Yukon Basin as well as other Interior missions. Later, the press was leased to other publishers. Its final home is the museum at Central on the Steese Highway, between Fairbanks and Circle Hot Springs. How it got there is best described by U.S. District Court Judge James Wickersham in his book, *Old Yukon; Tales, Trails and Trials*, published by West Publishing Co. in 1938:

Some years later (1906) the press and type were leased by an impecunious and convivial editor named (George Hinton) Henry who printed a small paper on it at Tanana, also called the *Yukon Press*. Henry began to criticize and abuse the commissioner, ex-officio justice of the peace, probate judge, recorder and coroner at Tanana (John Bathurst).

This factotum happened to be irritable by nature, a Cockney by birth with an exalted opinion of his own importance, and not inclined to turn the other cheek.

He issued a warrant for Henry's arrest for contempt of court, tried the case before himself, returned a just verdict, of course, and sentenced the jolly scribe to ninety days in jail.

The editor had better food, more regular meals and shorter hours of work in jail than out, and began to enjoy himself. He got a tramp printer to set type for his paper, and from the safety of his cell criticized the justice in the following issue in the most approved radical manner.

The justice thereupon evolved the bright idea of a contempt proceeding *in rem* against the press, and on such process caused it to be torn from its moorings, brought to the jail and put under lock and key in the cell next to that occupied by the editor, which effectively stopped all criticism of the court by that press.

The editor served out his time and then wandered off, leaving his press behind. After a time it was rolled out the back way and dumped upon a refuse heap as a further mark of the court's contempt for its late owner.

Wickersham traveled through Tanana about twenty years after the offending press was dumped. Recognizing its value as the first printing press in Interior Alaska, he rescued it and sent it to the University of Alaska Fairbanks, then known as the Alaska Agricultural College. It was displayed there for years and then loaned to the museum at Central.

Editor next in irons

Henry wasn't through. Neither was Commissioner Bathurst. Henry managed to collect the necessary equipment to start another weekly

The First Printing Press in northern Alaska sits disassembled in a museum in Central, 127 miles northeast of Fairbanks, waiting for an expert in old letterpresses to reassemble it. The Episcopal Church shipped the press in 1893 to the Rev. Jules L. Prevost at the St. James Mission at Fort Adams, a trading station on the Yukon River eight miles below the current community of Tanana, to print hymnals. The church leased it out to early newspaper publishers along the Yukon until it ended up on a trash pile at Tanana in 1907. Judge James Wickersham salvaged it for the University of Alaska, which later loaned it to the Circle District Museum.
-*Photo courtesy of the Circle District Historical Society.*

called *The Tanana Citizen*, and resumed his criticism of officials. It made him popular because the local residents generally disliked federal officials.

A heinous example of official tyranny occurred when Henry was charged with libel for printing a letter to the editor from a man who had been thrown into jail without any charge being explained to him and left to languish there for four days.

Henry, who had printed the man's letter of complaint, was dragged aboard a river steamer for arraignment in U.S. district court in Fairbanks, without being given an opportunity to contact friends to put up bail. He was handcuffed and placed in leg irons in a stateroom. A sign was posted warning passengers he was a dangerous man and they should not talk to him.

The Fairbanks court dismissed Henry's case on the grounds that printing the letter did not constitute "willful publication of false and scandalous matter with intent to defame another." Frederick Heilig, editor of the *Fairbanks Times*, suggested editorially that the official's conduct was so reprehensible that to suggest that it was possible to libel him would be considered a joke.

Episcopal press first in Interior

The history of that first press in Interior Alaska begins in the spring of 1893, when Prevost was waiting at St. Michael for transportation up the Yukon River. He met three trading post operators – Leroy N. McQuesten, Alfred Mayo and Arthur Harper. They brought up the idea of printing a newspaper for the region. And Prevost just happened to have a press coming. Their encouragement and promise of financial assistance – advertising – led Prevost to establish the *Yukon Press*. He enlisted the help of Gordon Charles Bettles and George T. Howard, each with printing experience.

The twenty-five-year-old Bettles first came north in 1884 to work in the Treadwell mines, a teenage immigrant from Canada. He crossed the Chilkoot Pass into the Yukon Valley, stopping at Fortymile, Circle, Koyukuk, and St. Michael. In an interview with the *Seattle Times* in July 1937, Bettles claimed credit for founding the townsites of Tanana in 1891, Rampart in 1892, Circle City in 1894, and Bettles, on the Koyukuk River, in 1898.

Not much is known about Howard except that a couple of years later he froze to death on a trail, an incident frequently reported in early newspapers.

With the combined efforts of Prevost, Bettles, and Howard, volume I, number 1, of the *Yukon Press* appeared January 1, 1894. It consisted of three columns on each of eight pages of typewriter paper held together with the old bent pins.

Most of the news came by "Mukluk Telegraph," meaning that sourdoughs wearing mukluks brought the news in from the hills.

A string of seven trading posts, hundreds of miles apart, supported the paper with ads. Small wood-burning steamers reached these posts when the Yukon River wasn't frozen.

Only six editions of Prevost's *Yukon Press* appeared in three years. Then with the Klondike gold discovery in '97, white settlers deserted Tanana, and it returned to its original status as an Indian village. Prevost decided to establish a mission in the booming new settlement of Circle City, 275 miles down the Yukon from Dawson City. He took his press and planned to resume publication of the *Yukon Press* at the new camp.

Food panic at Circle

Circle City, 130 miles northeast of Fairbanks, was established in 1887 when McQuesten set up a trading post there. Topographers of that day thought it was located on the Arctic Circle, only to learn later that it was forty miles south of the official line.

Prospectors in the Birch Creek district first discovered gold in 1893, forty-five to eighty miles from Circle City. Some 1,500 miners clustered along the streams and Circle boasted of being the largest log cabin town in the world.

By late spring 1897, Circle's population dwindled to fifty when the prospectors headed for the big strikes near Dawson. But with the threat of a food shortage at Dawson, hundreds returned to Circle for the winter. That caused a panic among Circle residents, who feared a food shortage there as well.

Among the winter's residents were two talented writers – Sam Dunham and Joaquin Miller. Dunham arrived in the Yukon River area in 1897 on special assignment for the U.S. Department of Labor to check on conditions in the mining camps. He later wrote a book, *The Alaskan Gold Fields*, that was reissued as late as 1985. Miller came north to cover the Klondike stampede for the *San Francisco Examiner*. A few years later, he gained national fame as a poet and author.

With time on their hands, they decided to put out a local newssheet. Prevost had been delayed in his move from Tanana. Rather than await the mission press, they published volume 3, number 1 of the *Yukon Press* in March 1898 using the hectograph method where copy is typed onto a gelatin-coated sheet and transferred to paper numerous times.

The literary quality of the news made up for the lack of mechanical perfection. It sold for a dollar a copy. In its fourteen pages, stories reported the problems of liquor control, the shortage of food, steamboat movements, and business opportunities.

The marrying press

The Reverend Prevost arrived with his press in time to put out the edition of January 15, 1899. Eight more editions followed at irregular intervals, terminating with the April 20, 1899, number when the reverend returned the press to the St. James Mission near Tanana. There it was leased out several times to other publishers until it landed on the Tanana dump.

But before the press left Circle, three editions of the *Yukon Press* carried a poetic marriage contract that was accepted as legal, inasmuch as there were no church or government officials on hand to perform a ceremony.

In one instance, Aggie Dalton was the bride, Frank McGillis, the bridegroom, and J. Durant (French Joe), the minister:

> Ten miles from the Yukon, on the banks of this Lake.
> For a partner to Koyukuk McGillis I take,
> We have no preacher and we have no ring –
> It makes no difference, it's all the same thing.
>
> – Aggie Dalton

> I swear, by my "gee-pole," under this tree,
> A devoted husband to Aggie I always will be,
> I'll love and protect her – this maiden so frail
> From them sourdough stiffs on the Koyukuk trail.
>
> – Frank McGillis

> For two dollars apiece in Cheechako money,
> I unite this couple in matrimony.
> He be a rancher, she be a teacher,
> I do the job up, just as well as a preacher.
>
> – French Joe

On January 1, 1899, Circle's population of 625, included sixty-five soldiers, thirty-two women, seven children and twenty-six Indians. The rest were prospectors. By September, the population had dropped to fifty-five, the majority having stampeded to Nome.

Publications first at Sitka, Wrangell

Church-related publications appeared at Wrangell and Sitka before they appeared in the Yukon River area. The Rev. S. Hall Young, a prominent Presbyterian missionary, established *The Glacier* in Wrangell in December 1885. It was published at the Tlinkit (Tlingit) Training Academy at the church mission at Fort Wrangel (spelled with one *l* at that time).

Young, a talented writer, frequently contributed to other newspapers after *The Glacier* suspended in 1888.

The Rev. Sheldon Jackson, another prominent Presbyterian missionary, began the *North Star* at Sitka in 1887, the first of three newspapers published by Sheldon Jackson School – later College. It did not attempt to compete with *The Alaskan*, Sitka's local newspaper, for either news or advertising.

Volume IX, number 5 of the *North Star*, in August 1898, announced that it was the last issue. Ten years lapsed after the *North Star* suspended until another church-sponsored paper, *The Thlinget* appeared in August 1908. It started publishing just a month after *The Alaskan* folded, leaving Sitka without a community newspaper.

The Thlinget took on public issues that affected Natives. It expressed opposition to fish traps, recounted other Native concerns and hailed the law that permitted Alaska Natives to again engage in pelagic fur seal hunting. Although the Alaska Native Brotherhood had some of its roots in the Sheldon Jackson School, *The Thlinget* ceased publication shortly before the ANB was formed at Juneau in the fall of 1912.

The Verstovian followed *The Thlinget*, as the third paper published at Sheldon Jackson School. It lasted the longest. Its first issue was in October 1914. The paper took its name from Mount Verstovia, close behind the campus.

It was the only newspaper in Sitka until 1920. After the December 1971 issue, the name was changed to *SJC Today*, the school had changed its name to Sheldon Jackson College. Today the paper is *SJC Adventurers*.

Other church-sponsored publications appeared throughout Alaska before the Gold Rush. One to train young Eskimos in writing and printing was the *Eskimo Bulletin*. It began publishing annually at Cape Prince of Wales in 1893. It was started by W. T. Lopp and H. R. Thornton at the American Missionary Association Missionary School. It suspended publication in 1902.

Father William Duncan left a Church of England post in 1887 at old Metlakatla in British Columbia and founded new Metlakatla on Annette Island near Ketchikan. He immediately put out a newspaper called the *Metlakahtlan*. It was first issued in November 1888. It lasted until December 1891.

Kodiak's first newspaper was the *Orphanage News Letter*. It began in 1899 as a project of the Kodiak Baptist Orphanage on Wood Island under auspices of the Woman's American Baptist Home Mission Society. Curtis P. Coe was editor and retained that post when its name was changed in 1907 to *News Letter* and continued publishing until 1922.

Its most dramatic reporting was that of the eruption of Mount Katmai in June 1912. It was the closest paper to the scene. There was no general circulation newspaper in Kodiak until 1941.

Missionary finances largest paper

Other missionaries were indirectly involved in newspaper publishing in Alaska. John G. Brady, an ordained Presbyterian and later governor, was the financial support for his sister-in-law, Cassia Patton, in acquiring *The Alaskan* at Sitka in 1898. He had been one of the founders of the paper.

Presbyterian missionary Edward Anton Rasmuson was a schoolteacher, postmaster and U.S. commissioner at Yakutat 1904-12. Then he earned a law degree. By 1917 he was president of the Bank of Alaska, which became the National Bank of Alaska and more recently merged with Wells Fargo. Rasmuson and a group of Anchorage businessmen bought *The Anchorage Daily Times* at a marshal's sale in 1924.

Eleven years later, Rasmuson and his associates sold the *Times* to his daughter, Evangeline, and her husband, Robert B. Atwood, who built the *Times* into Alaska's leading newspaper, a position it held for fifty years.

Chapter 4

Sitka Loses Capital and Its Journalists

The Gold Rush of 1898 brought prosperity and changes to Alaska, but it cost Sitka the capital. Ships rushing gold seekers from Seattle, San Francisco, and Portland to the stampede trails at Wrangell, Skagway, and Dyea skipped stops at Sitka. The town, sitting on the outside of Baranof Island, was out of the way on the Inside Passage. Tides in Sergius Narrows sometimes delayed ships going to Sitka. Delays meant lost time and lost revenue.

But first, Sitka and its newspaper had their big day.

A sign of home rule

On July 15, 1897, Sitkans celebrated when John Green Brady, a nineteen-year resident, was inaugurated as Alaska's fifth governor. The Alaska press – three weeklies in Juneau, one in Skagway, and *The Alaskan* at Sitka – lauded his appointment as recognition of home rule, a goal sought by Alaskans ever since the region became a U.S. possession.

Brady was not the first resident of Alaska to be appointed to the position. The previous governor, James Sheakley, had lived in Alaska, but only six years as a federal employee (school superintendent) before he became governor.

Brady arrived in Sitka in April 1878 as a Presbyterian missionary. In 1880, he joined the largest store in town as a partner. He was appointed Sitka's first U.S. commissioner in 1884. He claimed a 160-acre homestead east of town and later donated it as the campus of what is now the Sheldon Jackson College.

Brady's appointment as governor coincided with the start of the Klondike Gold Rush. It and the subsequent gold rushes to Nome and other points brought hordes of men, and some women, to Alaska. Many of the new settlers were antagonistic toward Brady's moral standards and his bias toward law and order, as well as his support for the rights of Alaska Natives. In his inaugural address, Brady said he was aware of that but promised he would try to be impartial and deal justly with all.

Despite that promise, the newspapers in Juneau and the new town of Skagway, after lauding his appointment, dubbed Brady "an old fogy" who was out of step with Alaska's modern needs, hence unfit to remain in office. When he espoused the right of the Natives to vote, the Alaska press unanimously called for his ouster. Despite those protests, he was reappointed governor in 1901 and 1905.

By March 1898, E. Otis Smith either could not or would not pay off the $300 mortgage Christian Schaap signed to finance purchase of *The Alaskan* and Cassia Patton, Mrs. Brady's sister, foreclosed.

On March 5, the paper reported: "At a marshal's foreclosure sale, the fixtures and good will of *The Alaskan* were sold to John Brady, on behalf of Cassia Patton, for $300. Miss Patton, who will continue to teach school, becomes the sole owner of the paper."

Patton quit teaching. She became Brady's secretary and operated the newspaper. A year later, H. H. Hildreth appeared as editor and manager.

Little is known of Hildreth's life before he came to Alaska except that when a Juneau newspaper referred to him as a Democrat he responded with editorial wrath:

> We don't mind being called a Missourian, or a bald-headed bachelor, or almost any old thing, but we certainly draw the line at being called Democrat. That is one thing that has never yet made its appearance in an ancestry that can be traced back to the landing of the *Mayflower*, and from present indications there will never be a person of that religious believe (sic) in the family.

Capital threat arises

Hildreth took the editorial chair at *The Alaskan* at a time when Sitka faced the most serious problem in its pioneering history. Juneau residents were intent upon moving government offices – Sitka had never been officially dubbed the capital – to their growing city.

The Klondike Gold Rush was in full swing. Steamships that once stopped at Sitka now rushed direct to and from trailheads and the States. With Sitka bypassed, Juneau litigants, lawyers, and jurors found it more and more difficult to attend court in Sitka. Court business gradually moved to Juneau.

Mass meetings were held in Sitka, committees appointed and letters written to congressmen. Governor Brady spent a lot of time in Washington. As Sitka's lone spokesman in the nation's capital, he faced a larger, more effective Juneau lobby. What may have been Hildreth's last editorial in *The Alaskan* appeared February 24, 1900:

SITKA AWAKE, ARISE OR BE FOREVER FALLEN

> That a crisis has come in the history of Sitka is a fact that can no longer be ignored. The danger of her losing the seat of government with all the prestige it gives, is imminent.
>
> The forces that are antagonistic to her are gaining the ascendancy.
>
> They are organized, active, alert and pulling altogether. They are leaving nothing undone to accomplish their purposes. They have a powerful lobby in Washington, which is instant in season and out of season, ever insistent and persistent for the removal of the capital to Juneau.

When Hildreth was offered the position of 1900 census taker in Southcentral Alaska, Brady offered to have him appointed postmaster at Sitka. He declined in favor of the census job.

The editor of Skagway's *Daily Morning Alaskan* noted the departure of Hildreth with glee:

> The man who turns the crank of the mangle on which is printed the organ of Governor Brady at Bradyville has received his pay in a political job. He is to be census taker in the Cook Inlet country, and Juneau will probably miss him, like one misses the ephemeral housefly whose buzzing is irritating but whose bite is not feared. He is a terrible fellow

in print, especially on the subject of Juneau as a rival to the Brady cabbage patch and sawmill.

Chauncy Dunn Shaw became the editor and manager of *The Alaskan* April 28, 1900. He introduced a flair that the paper lacked previously. Interesting local news was presented in a lively literary style. Editorials were more frequent and there was a full page of social events.

It shall remain in Sitka until . . . .

It fell to Shaw to record the June 6, 1900, enactment of a law making further provisions for civil government in Alaska. It increased the number of district judges, provided a method for incorporating municipal government. And it also provided that "the seat of government shall remain at Sitka until suitable buildings shall be obtained by purchase or otherwise at Juneau."

The district judge and the marshal moved to Juneau at once. The collector of customs moved a couple of years later. But Governor Brady was not about to find suitable buildings in Juneau. He remained in Sitka, as did the land office under the surveyor general, who was ex-officio secretary of Alaska and acting governor when the governor was away.

Shaw remained as editor of *The Alaskan* through February 23, 1901. He then became associate editor of Juneau's *Record-Miner*. In December he won the contract to carry the mail from Katmai to St. Michael, a two-thousand-mile round-trip over mountains and glaciers. He froze his hands and feet and went to Valdez to join his old friend Hildreth in a variety of enterprises.

When he left *The Alaskan*, Shaw wrote that the proprietor would henceforth edit and manage the paper. Cassia Patton may have done so for a time, but a news story June 28, 1902, listed Chas. H. Scheffler as the editor. The paper had more local news than it had carried for a long time.

Scheffler stayed with *The Alaskan* until July 1904 when he moved to the *Record-Miner* in Juneau. The new city on Gastineau Channel was gradually stealing journalists as well as the capital. In 1908, he was associated with Richard Bushell in publishing *The Interloper* at Skagway, but the paper lasted only eight months. In 1913, Scheffler appeared in Cordova and for many years was associated with the *Cordova Times*.

With the departure of Scheffler, *The Alaskan* began to go downhill. Subsequent editors were not named in either the masthead or the news columns. A lot of boilerplate was used to fill the pages.

Local news coverage was minimal even when a major story perched on the doorstep, such as the arrival in Sitka of Roald Amundsen following his conquest of the Northwest Passage. Some issues were reduced from four pages to two, one of which was boilerplate. The town seemed ripe for another newspaper, although the town was barely supporting one.

The Sitka Cablegram, a four-page paper, debuted on February 2, 1905. William H. Robinson, who had arrived in Sitka with the Marine Corps, was editor and publisher. When his enlistment expired he clerked in the W. P. Mills Store. He apparently had some experience as a printer and a newsman. He persuaded Mills to back him in the newspaper.

The name came from the fact that the submarine telegraph cable had reached Sitka from Seattle the previous August, making telegraph news possible. But *The Cablegram* used little telegraph news and *The Alaskan* none at all, probably because of the cost.

Robinson put out a fair budget of local news. Instead of boiler plate he found some interesting local features. He advocated passage of a bill providing for a delegate to Congress from Alaska and saw the bill enacted into law in May 1906.

Brady forced out

During the nine months *The Cablegram* published, it reported the forced resignation of Governor Brady, just a year into his third term. Brady had been conned by a developer, Henry D. Reynolds, into using his office to promote a scheme to build a railroad from Valdez to the Interior. Reynolds also conned many in Valdez out of money and the city of Valdez out of property before he went bankrupt.

President Teddy Roosevelt named Wilford B. Hoggatt to succeed Brady. Hoggatt announced that he would take the oath of office in Sitka in April 1906 but that he had found "suitable buildings" in Juneau and would establish his office there. Hoggatt was manager of a mine at Berner's Bay north of Juneau before becoming governor.

Robinson recommended in *The Cablegram* that Sitka residents ignore Hoggatt when he arrived in town because of his plan to move the capital to Juneau.

Two months later, Robinson folded *The Sitka Cablegram* and followed the capital to Juneau, taking his press and equipment. There he joined the staff of the *Record-Miner*.

Juneau now had the governor's office. Most of the other government officials were quartered there. But Sitka clung to the last vestige of the "seat of government," the office of the surveyor general with its small land office staff. Then President Roosevelt signed an executive order moving that office to Juneau. So Surveyor General William L. Distin and his staff packed up the last vestiges of the government and left for Juneau.

With the closure of the office of the governor in Sitka, Cassia Patton, the owner of *The Alaskan*, was out of a job. Her post as secretary to the governor also went to Juneau. She went to Oregon to visit a sister.

Miss Patton stopped in Juneau on her way back from Oregon and was interviewed by the *Alaska Daily Dispatch*. She said that she had sold *The Alaskan* and that she expected that it would soon cease publication. The interview was reprinted in *The Alaskan* and whoever was running the paper – it may have been the buyer – denied that the paper would "throw in the sponge." Instead, "the paper will probably, with the plant, be moved to the Westward where it will continue to be published."

The plant of *The Alaskan* did move out of Sitka and quite possibly went to Cordova. A paper, *The Alaskan*, had begun publication there on June 16, 1906. The pages measured nine by thirteen inches. Then on September 21, 1907, a month after the last issue of *The Alaskan* at Sitka, the Cordova paper increased its page size to eleven by eighteen inches with five columns. That indicated acquisition of a larger press.

The last available issue of *The Alaskan* at Sitka is dated August 17, 1907. There is no valedictory in that issue to indicate that it was intended to be the final issue. One of its stories ends with the line "Continued next week."

It was to be a long "week" for newspaper readers in Sitka – thirteen years!

Chapter 5

Miners Found Juneau Journalism

Joe Juneau and Dick Harris discovered placer gold in Silver Bow Basin, five miles up Gold Creek, in August 1880. The camp that sprang up at the mouth of Gold Creek that winter became Juneau. It lacked Sitka's Thomas G. Murphy to start a newspaper, so the growing town was without one during its first six years.

Prospectors soon discovered gold on Douglas Island, across Gastineau Channel and a little south of Juneau. The early placer mining led to quartz veins for which stamp mills were erected to crush the gold-bearing rock. Mines and mills went into operation on both sides of the channel. A Juneau-Douglas ferry system developed, with five daily trips across the channel.

Juneau flourished as a commerce center. Prospectors outfitted in Juneau, disappeared into the hills in early spring, and returned in the fall. Additional gold was found at Sheep Creek south of Juneau, Berner's Bay north of Juneau, and Glacier Bay northwest of Juneau.

The estimated Juneau population in 1890 was 1,567, of which 851 were Indians, 671 were whites, 43 were mixed, one was black, and one was Chinese. Eighty other Chinese had been run out of town, the victims of a riot at the Treadwell mine in 1885.

The remaining Chinaman was Hi Chung, or "China Joe." He moved to Juneau in 1881 where he owned a bakery. Prospectors owed Chung money for bread, and needed more, so he stayed.

The combined populations of the three Gastineau Channel settlements (Juneau, Douglas and Treadwell) reached four thousand during the 1890s while Alaska's total population was only 32,052, of which 25,354 were Natives.

Journalistic emphasis shifted from Sitka to Gastineau Channel in the 1880s and 90s. Newspapers flourished as fast and furious as the Gastineau Channel communities. "Furious" included doses of frontier violence.

Juneau's first paper in '87

Among the early prospectors were J. C. Howard and his sons, Arthur and Frank, who had followed the dual roles of journalists-miners in the Colorado gold fields.

The Howards started *The Alaska Free Press* in Juneau in January 1887. Alaska's only other newspaper, *The Alaskan* at Sitka, then owned by Gov. A. P. Swineford, greeted the newcomer gleefully:

> Whoop-a-la! *The Alaskan* has got a big brother. He is rather large for his age, and in some respects too big for his clothes. It will be observed that he doesn't talk plain – lisps and stutters, but these little vocal impediments will be overcome as he grows older.
>
> So far from being jealous, *The Alaskan* wishes *The Free Press* the most abundant prosperity, and is only too glad in having so efficient a co-worker in behalf of the best interests of Alaska and her people.

The Howards aspired to be the leading newspaper of the Northwest and promised to become an effective tool in publicizing Alaska's riches. They echoed Governor Swineford's plea for self-government.

When spring arrived, Clarke Miller was installed as editor while the Howards went prospecting. The first report of their success came in June. They discovered a rich vein of gold adjoining the Treadwell property. In hailing the good news, the *Free Press* suggested that "possibly the next issue of the paper will be printed on type of solid gold."

In its first anniversary edition, the *Free Press* summarized its role in publicizing Alaska's resources and its needs:

> *The Free Press* was born in a land then unknown, unthought of and uncared for, a country that, until it (*The*

Free Press) began circulating throughout the civilized land in the east, was considered worthless – a pile of mountains capped with ice.

Not until the advent of *The Free Press* were these erroneous ideas corrected, and the country talked of as being rich in minerals, furs, fish, timber and climate.

For the rapid development of the country, it will plead with Congress for that legislation which is absolutely necessary to its advancement. First, the country wants better mail facilities, a service that will enable it to communicate with the outside world oftener than once a month; also a mail route to the northward; the extension of the land laws, that settlers may obtain title to their homes; a representative in Congress that our future wants may become known; aid in opening up routes into the almost impenetrable interior. A full territorial form of government at present is not needed, for reason that the white population is too small, but if that population increases in the next year, it will be asked for at that time.

In January 1891, J. C. Howard sold his interest in the paper to his sons and opened a placer mine at Lituya Bay "where he expects to reap greater and richer returns than the newspaper business affords."

First paper merger

The sons sold the *Free Press* in 1892 to Thomas Nowell, another successful mine operator in the Juneau area. He, in turn, merged it with a second weekly, the *Juneau City Mining Record*, which had made its debut April 5, 1888, with Frank F. Myers as editor and publisher.

Myers had gone to Sitka in 1887 from Port Townsend, Washington Territory, where he had published the *Port Townsend Call*. He edited *The Alaskan* at Sitka for a short time before moving to Juneau.

The *Mining Record* started as a three-column, eight-page sheet, brimming with ads. Myers editorialized vigorously for full territorial government. He opposed "carpetbag" appointees to federal jobs in Alaska, which alienated him from that influential circle. Thus, when he sought the post of collector of customs under President Benjamin Harrison's Republican administration, Swineford registered his opposition, and the post went to Max Pracht, who had been associated with a salmon saltery and cannery at Loring, near Ketchikan.

Myers tasted revenge when he filed charges accusing Pracht of selling whiskey to Indians. That resulted in Pracht being removed from office halfway through his term.

Myers's continuous criticism of "carpetbag" officials netted him repeated arrests on charges of criminal libel. Instead of arraigning him in Juneau's commissioner's court and allowing him to post bail, he was transported to Sitka, where he languished in jail awaiting trial. No grand jury ever indicted him, but the inconvenience of traveling to Sitka and the harassment provided his tormentors with some satisfaction.

From libel to attempted murder

The climax of this feud between Myers and federal officials occurred in the fall of 1892, when he and Charles Coon, a Juneau druggist, were charged with attempted murder.

One evening when the U.S. commissioner was entertaining guests, a messenger arrived at his door, carrying a sack containing two watermelons, compliments of a friend. The following day, members of the commissioner's family who had tasted the melons became ill. Circumstantial evidence pointed to Myers and Coon as the culprits, and a warrant was sworn out for their arrests. They were whisked off to Sitka, where they were held without bail. They were back in Juneau within a month, the grand jury having found "no true bill."

Myers soon concluded that Alaska journalism was an unprofitable enterprise. In January 1893, he sold the *Mining Record* to a group of Juneau businessmen and returned to Port Townsend.

In August of that year, the paper was sold to the Rev. E. Otis Smith. He and his wife arrived in the Juneau area in the early 1890s as Gospel Mission workers.

Third paper appears

E. O. Sylvester, a leader in Juneau's social set, decided to share his literary talents with his fellow townsmen. He established Juneau's third weekly, the *Alaska Journal*, March 1, 1891. He was a native Bostonian and had taught school in New York City.

Soon after arriving in Juneau in 1891, he opened a night school, specializing in commercial courses. He was admitted to the Alaska bar and headed a mining company. He organized a men's literary and debating society and a men's and women's glee club. His suburban home, known as Lemon Creek Ranch, was a social center.

Sylvester's detractors accused him of starting the *Alaska Journal* at the beginning of a Democratic administration in order to regain his status as a bona fide Democrat after having served as a deputy U.S. marshal under a Republican regime. It worked. He was retained in the marshal's post under the new administration.

Dalton's first fame

Sylvester's journalistic integrity came under fire during the murder trial of Jack Dalton, the famous Alaska trailblazer. Dalton, a deputy marshal at Chilkat, was accused of murdering Daniel McGinnis on March 6, 1893. But a Juneau jury acquitted him, ruling that the shooting was an accident.

In covering the trial, Sylvester became so convinced of Dalton's innocence that when the jury returned its verdict, he reported that the spectators in the courtroom noisily demonstrated their satisfaction. Sitka's two newspapers, *The Alaskan* and the *Alaska Herald*, not yet merged, reported to the contrary. They reported that the acquittal created such a sensation that there was public discussion of lynching the liberated defendant.

Dalton was ordered to leave Alaska for his own safety. Instead he returned to guiding fortune seekers out of Haines over the Dalton Trail.

Seven months after the trial, Sylvester sold the *Journal* to George A. Carpenter and Frank H. Ward, California and Oregon newsmen. He moved to Sitka and bought the *Alaska Herald*, one of the newspapers disagreeing with him on his Dalton trial coverage. The Reverend Smith of Juneau's *Mining Record* bought *The Alaskan*, the other Sitka paper disagreeing with Sylvester. The two then merged their Sitka newspapers into *The Alaskan*, sold it, and left Sitka.

In the meantime, Carpenter and Ward changed the name of the *Journal* to *The Alaska News*. In their initial edition on October 26, 1893, they promised to "champion the cause of Juneau, Douglas Island, and Alaska in their struggle for development, prosperity and success."

In championing self-government, the editors contended that Alaskans were being treated like residents of a penal colony, being deprived of their constitutional rights as American citizens. They blamed the disgraceful treatment on misinformation being peddled to the members of Congress by corporation lobbyists and missionaries:

> Until Congress shall give ear and harken to the earnest pleadings of her people, in preference to the willful misrepresentations of hired assassins and missionaries, the former the lobby-members of corporations, and the latter who aim for Alaska no other future than as an Indian reservation and a rich field for missionary labors, who fill the eastern press with rot and infest the national capital during its every session, we have little hope for a redress of grievances or assertion of our rights.

Like most of his contemporaries, Carpenter had his day in court on a criminal libel charge. In the story about missing funds in the office of former marshal Orville Porter at Sitka, the names of two deputy marshals, Sylvester and Max Endelman, and of attorney John Maloney were mentioned without suggesting wrongdoing on their part.

Maloney accused Carpenter of criminal libel. The jury dismissed the charge as just another attempt to muzzle the press.

Carpenter and Ward's more prosperous competitor became even more prosperous when it changed hands in the spring of 1894, and *The Juneau Mining Record* became the *Alaska Mining Record*. Willis Thorpe, a Juneau entrepreneur, formerly of Yakima, Washington, and George B. Swinehart, a newsman from Seattle, became the new owners. Frank Howard, successful miner and formerly of the *Alaska Free Press*, and Eugene C. Stahl, a new arrival who had worked on papers in New York City and Chicago, were hired to run the paper.

Thorpe owned a successful meat and grocery business in addition to his mining operations. And he was the principal stockholder in the Alaska Electric Light & Power Co., which still serves the Juneau-Douglas area.

The *Mining Record* had been the leading journal of Alaska ever since its debut, although that was before the Gold Rush of '98 when there were papers only at Sitka and Juneau. The new owners promised to maintain the same high standards. It opposed self-government for Alaska because of the taxation it would entail.

Meanwhile, Carpenter and Ward were having financial problems publishing the *Alaska News* in competition with the better financed *Alaska Mining Record*. When they bought the paper from Sylvester, they thought there was an understanding that he would not reenter the Juneau journalism field within a year. But ten months after the sale, he was back from his Sitka venture and started the weekly *Alaska Searchlight*.

Discouraged, Carpenter and Ward sold the *News* to Captain Alexander Thomson, who promptly sold it to Stahl, former editor on the *Alaska Mining Record*. Stahl kept the paper for two years and then sold it to William A. Beddoe and took off for Dawson.

When Sylvester's *Alaska Searchlight* appeared on December 17, 1894, Sitka's *Alaskan* described it as the best journal ever published in Alaska. Not a surprising comment, considering the source. Sylvester had just merged his *Herald* in Sitka into Otis Smith's *Alaskan*.

The *Searchlight*'s sixteen pages were printed on fine book paper, specially made for it by an eastern factory and bound like a magazine with colored covers. It was illustrated with steel engravings. It increased to twenty pages within the first year.

Sylvester hired three experienced newsmen to make it the liveliest paper in the district. Theodore R. (Ted) Needham was his associate editor and J. B. Praetor was in charge of the mechanical department, both former Seattle printers. John Timmins was his business manager.

It was more of a literary journal than a news organ. It featured Alaska history, arts, geography, and the mining and fishing industries. News columns from neighboring towns were labeled "Wrangell Glimmerings," "Sitka Gleams," and "Chilkat (Haines) Snowflakes." A local gossip column was titled "Local Rays."

Competition heated with gun

Bitter competition between the three weeklies – the *Alaska Searchlight*, the *Alaska News* and the *Alaska Mining Record* – led to personal hostility among the personnel. One day in 1895, the

Searchlight's business manager, Timmins, found a story in the *Mining Record* uncomplimentary to him, and he set off to punish its editor, Frank Howard.

The offending story told how the previous evening Timmins had arrived at a fire in an inebriated condition. He proceeded to issue orders to the firemen while perched on a nearby roof. The firefighters turned the hoses on him, toppling him to the ground, much to the amusement of bystanders.

When Timmins arrived at the *Mining Record*, he found Howard sitting in the editor's chair. Howard admitted responsibility for the story, whereupon Timmins whipped out a .38 caliber revolver and started shooting. Timmins stalked out, leaving the editor on the floor in a pool of blood, and turned himself in to the deputy marshal.

Timmins drew a seven-year jail sentence while Howard recovered and went back to the safer occupation of prospecting.

With Timmins in jail, Sylvester suspended publication of the *Searchlight* in February 1898, abandoning Juneau for the boomtown of Skagway. He left with a pocketful of cash, having sold his half interest in the Juneau Ferry & Navigation Co., his interest in the Silver Queen gold mine and his interest in a copper property on Prince of Wales Island. He built a wharf in Skagway and served on the city council. But in 1902, he moved on to the newer boomtown of Valdez.

Chapter 6

Bells Ring for Douglas Publisher

The growing town of Douglas, across Gastineau Channel from Juneau, welcomed its first newspaper in October 1896. Ted Needham left the *Searchlight* in Juneau and teamed with George M. Hill, an itinerant printer, to launch the weekly *Douglas City Miner*.

Both men later joined the stampede to Canada's Klondike in 1898, and then returned to Alaska to help build its newspaper industry, Needham as a founder of *The Anchorage Daily Times* and Hill as a founder of the *Weekly Fairbanks News*. Both newspapers also were the first in their respective towns.

By the spring of 1897, Needham and Hill were itching to go prospecting so they sold the Douglas paper to William Arthur Beddoe, the new proprietor of Juneau's *Alaska News*. Beddoe moved the *Douglas City Miner* plant to Juneau in October 1897, consolidating it with his *News*. He called his new weekly *The Alaska Miner*. That left Douglas without a newspaper for a year, until the *Douglas News* started publishing in November 1898.

Beddoe was one of the more colorful miner-journalists. He was a British citizen and claimed to be an heir to the British throne as a son of King Edward of England.

He was known as a "remittance man," a son in exile from an affluent family that sent him checks at intervals. When he was flush with money he invested in mining claims that he hoped would reap him a fortune. At other times, he worked at whatever job was available to provide food and shelter.

Beddoe earned the enmity of Gov. John Brady and Dr. Sheldon Jackson when he supported the election of a delegate to Congress. Those two saw no need for a delegate, believing that they were competent to interpret Alaskans' needs.

In May 1899, Beddoe sold *The Miner* to a group of Juneau businessmen whom he described as "a Democratic syndicate." When the new owners failed to retain him as editor, the paper's employees staged a walkout in protest and launched their own weekly, *The Alaska Truth*. Beddoe helped them get it started and then left for Dawson City, like many others.

Truth Short lived

George E. Riggins became editor of the *Truth*, a six-column, four-page tabloid. Skagway's *Daily Morning Alaskan* called it the best printed and most ably edited of "any weekly in the whole territory. It is also fearless and independent."

The editorials were anti-Brady and campaigned for moving the capital from Sitka to Juneau.

The paper suspended publication November 2, 1900, having been sold to ex-governor A. P. Swineford. The printing plant, accompanied by Riggins, moved to Ketchikan where he and Swineford launched the *Mining Journal* January 5, 1901, Ketchikan's first newspaper.

Meanwhile, Willis Thorpe and George Swinehart heard the "call of the Yukon" and sold Juneau's prosperous *Alaska Mining Record* to Gus B. Leach, one of their employees.

Swinehart set off for Dawson in a party of eight men, including his brothers, Bill and Guy. While waiting at Caribou Crossing for the ice to melt in the lakes, Swinehart set up his printing equipment and published an edition of the *Caribou Sun*, May 16, 1898. Obviously proud of his achievement, he wrote:

> To put together a power press and complete printing plant all of which has been taken apart in every detail and shipped direct from the foundry, prepare the paper stock and publish a paper, in the wilderness of the Arctic regions alongside a trail where only a few tents and not a single wooden structure mark the spot; where a few score people have their temporary abiding place but where in three weeks

hence not a single white man will be encamped, is an undertaking never before accomplished and which can be appreciated only by those who have had such an experience.

When Swinehart got to Dawson, he started the *Yukon Midnight Sun*, with the first issue June 11, 1898. He sold the paper six months later and started organizing the Alaska Telegraph Co., soliciting $60,000 from Juneau businessmen to construct and operate a telegraph cable between Juneau and Skagway. There was already a line between Skagway and Dawson City.

Mining Record goes daily

Back in Juneau, Leach sold the *Alaska Mining Record* to George T. Ulmer in December 1898. Ulmer had recently arrived in Juneau from Dyea where he had been publishing *The Dyea Trail*.

While struggling for survival in Dyea, Ulmer learned from Skagway businessmen what an aggressive newspaper campaign could do to promote the advantages of its hometown. Ulmer saw Juneau as the outfitting center for miners headed for the newly discovered Atlin gold fields via the Taku Trail, thus one of his first editorials was to urge Juneau merchants to establish a publicity bureau in Seattle:

> This needs to be done immediately. Every steamer from now on will be loaded to the guards with passengers, all bound for the new gold fields. The businessmen of Skaguay have men in Seattle talking up the merits of their trail and denouncing the Taku trail.
>
> Citizens of Juneau, you have the shortest, safest, best and cheapest trail to the Atlin gold fields. The distance from Skaguay to Atlin is twelve to thirty-two miles greater than by way of Juneau. This means a great deal to the prospector who is dragging his blankets and provisions on a sled. It means a difference of two days time in the first place and in the second place an outlay of much more money.

Ulmer made the *Mining Record* a daily in February 1899 – Juneau's first daily newspaper. He renamed it the *Daily Evening Record and Weekly Mining Record*. In announcing his plans, he noted that

Skagway, scarcely a year old, had two dailies and one weekly, so why shouldn't fourteen-year-old Juneau be able to support one daily.

Unfortunately, the *Evening Record* was but two weeks old when Ulmer died of pneumonia on March 1, 1899. He was buried in Evergreen Cemetery. The honorary pallbearers comprised the leading lights of the Gastineau journalistic fraternity – his son, George T. Jr.; A. G. McBride, editor-publisher of the new *Douglas Island News*; W. A. Beddoe, editor-publisher of *The Alaska Miner*; and Edward C. Russell, editor-publisher of the new *Weekly Alaska Dispatch*.

Russell, who had published the *Dyea Press* in 1898 at the same time Ulmer published the *Dyea Trail* – two short-lived papers in a short-lived town – became editor of the *Evening Record*. He combined it with his weekly, changed its name to the *Daily Alaska Dispatch*.

From 1900 to 1902, the *Dispatch* was designated the "city's official paper," thus eligible for all municipal printing jobs and legal notices, much to the displeasure of the weeklies. That could have contributed to the *Truth* folding and selling its equipment to Swineford.

Second Douglas paper

On the November 23, 1898, volume I, number 1 of the *Douglas Island News* greeted its readers, with A. G. McBride and Charles Hopp, his brother-in-law, as editors-publishers. Actually, they started the newspaper as the *Fort Wrangel News* in June 1898 and then moved to Douglas with a name change. The three thousand combined population of Douglas and Treadwell promised a likely market for a weekly, although 90 percent of the population consisted of immigrants who could not read English and spent ten to twelve hours a day in underground mine shafts.

McBride accepted the appointment of U.S. commissioner at the new gold camp of Cape York, near Nome, in March 1899, leaving the Douglas paper for his brother-in-law.

The Hopps were active in the Methodist Church and allotted generous space in the paper to church activities. Sometimes sermons were reproduced verbatim and the town's church directory was posted on the front page. The paper was a staunch supporter of Governor Brady and Dr. Jackson.

Hopp enjoyed a community esteem that the Juneau editors lacked. He was elected the town's first mayor in 1902 and was reelected in 1905. He served several terms on the city council and school board, invariably being the top vote-getter in each election.

Hopp weighed more than three hundred pounds, leading Russell of the *Dispatch* to call him the fattest editor in Alaska, an ironic remark inasmuch as Russell's own girth obliged him to wear a trunk strap for a belt.

Juneau's editors were inclined to ridicule their neighbors across the channel, even suggesting that their moral standards were offensive to the finer sensibilities of Juneauites.

Hopp's response was immediate and vehement. He called Russell both stupid and boorish and lacking "a depth of intelligence sufficient to properly construct the simplest sentence."

Hopp was even more virulent in regard to "Gloomy Gus" O'Brien of the *Record-Miner*, who slept with a pistol under his pillow, after that newspaper was established in 1907:

> We know nothing about this fellow's past other than the general belief that he has either escaped from a penitentiary or a lunatic asylum. We only know that since coming to Juneau a few months ago he has done nothing but vomit forth the most villainous rot ever read in this part of the North.
>
> He is not only a man without a friend, but all honest people are his enemies, a fact which he well knows, for when he walks the streets in his hand is clutched a weapon to protect him from the righteous wrath that hangs suspended over his head.
>
> His very name has got to be a curse, and mothers in that town frighten their children by telling them that if they are bad "Gloomy Gus" will get them. This is the man who has attacked the editor of the *News* because he is jealous of the job work given this paper by the Treadwell Company.

After eighteen years of struggling along on a financial shoestring, Hopp's ill health forced him to retire. When he sold his paper in March 1916 to E. J. (Stroller) White, editor-publisher of the *Whitehorse* (Yukon Territory) *Star*, he asked his fellow townsmen to give White their support. Hopp wrote that White "will make the

News a power for progress, a bulwark of defense and a pillar of fire in the march toward that day when Alaska shall stand in the forefront among the nations of the world."

A gala banquet at the Douglas Island Labor Union Hall honored the departing editor. He was presented a gold watch and chain. Hopp planned to retire to a farm he owned near Enumclaw, Washington, but he suffered a heart attack and died at age fifty within a month of leaving Douglas.

On the day of Hopp's funeral in Seattle, all businesses in Douglas closed their doors; flags flew at half-staff and bells tolled on the two fire towers and the schoolhouse. The entire community mourned the man who had done more than any other at that time for the town of Douglas.

Accolades flowed from his fellow journalists. White was the most eloquent when he wrote:

> That "Death loves a shining mark" was never more fully or realistically verified than when the death angel laid his icy hand on Charles A. Hopp and marked him for his own.
>
> Hopp came to Douglas when it was little more than a camp on the beach. He was then less than 32 years of age, young, hopeful, confident. He cast his lot with the embryo city to which he practically gave the remainder of his life.
>
> He was essentially a man of peace and all his official acts were aimed at the promotion of harmony and the advancement of the public good. Of Charlie Hopp it can be truthfully said: "And thus he bore without abuse, the grand old name of gentleman."

Record-Miner evolves

The once prosperous Juneau weekly, *The Alaska Miner*, became Juneau's second daily briefly in October 1899, with E. H. Gough as editor. It reverted to weekly after a few issues with the name changed to *The Alaska Record-Miner*. The following June, the stockholders petitioned Judge Melville C. Brown to appoint a receiver in order to salvage their financial investment.

The paper was sold in February 1901 to the Rev. George M. Irwin, a Methodist minister. He said he bought the paper as a "peacemaker hoping to terminate the editorial feuding, which was giving Juneau a bad name." He had been serving in the Methodist pulpit in Juneau since 1898.

Irwin put out a lackluster paper. His editorials were long-winded, dealing with vague, philosophical matters, not remotely relevant to local issues. However, he exhibited special concern for the welfare of the Native people and supported the election of a delegate to Congress.

After nine months of publishing *The Alaska Record-Miner*, Irwin despaired of bringing peace to Juneau's journalism world. It would take eight more years and grand jury indictments to accomplish that. He accepted appointment as U.S. commissioner in Douglas and sold the paper in late 1901 to John W. Frame, former editor-publisher in Snohomish and Everett, Washington, more recently of Dawson City's gold rush newspapers.

The Juneau and Douglas economies further shrunk with the discovery of gold on the beaches of Nome, following the earlier exodus of miners to Dawson and Atlin. The Gastineau Channel area stabilized as a smaller but prosperous industrial center with large firms owning the mines and mills. However, many of the workers were unable to read English. The free-spending and literate prospectors, the newspaper readers and newsmakers, had stampeded north.

That left Juneau with Ed Russell's daily *Dispatch* and Frame's weekly *Record-Miner*. (The O'Brien-edited *Daily Record* didn't appear until 1907.) Douglas had Charles Hopp's *Douglas Island News*. Three newspapers were still too many papers for the shrinking Gastineau Channel area.

However, Juneau enjoyed an economic boost when Berner's Bay mine supervisor Wilford Bacon Hoggatt was named governor and moved Alaska's capital from Sitka to Juneau in 1906. He served a controversial three years and resigned rather than obey the edict from Secretary of the Interior Richard Ballinger that the governors of the territories – Alaska, Arizona, New Mexico, Hawaii, and Puerto Rico – remain in their territories.

Moving the capital gave Juneau a fledging new industry – government. Sitka lost everything, including any newspaper for another thirteen years.

Chapter 7

Seattle P-I Story Triggers Stampede

On a misty Puget Sound morning, July 17, 1897, a *Seattle Post-Intelligencer* reporter chartered a tugboat to take him to the S.S. *Portland*, as it steamed toward the Seattle docks. He had learned that there were passengers on board who had struck it rich in the Klondike Creek area of the Yukon Territory. He hurriedly interviewed them and then sped back to his paper. An "extra" was on the streets by the time the steamer was greeted by a crowd on the wharf.

"Gold! Gold! Gold! Gold!" screamed the headline.

"Sixty-eight Rich Men on the Steamer *Portland*: Some Have $5,000, Many Have More, and a Few Bring Out $100,000 Each. The Steamer Carries $700,000."

By the time the story reached other newspapers around the world, a new headline shouted: "A Ton of Gold on the *Portland*."

It was that enterprising young reporter's ballyhooed story about a "ton of gold" that really started the stampede to the Klondike area and created Dawson City. That led to major gold finds in Alaska's wilderness and to the founding of Nome, Fairbanks, and a half dozen other communities.

More than forty journalists funneled through Dawson and continued on to Alaska during the few years of the Klondike stampede. Those journalists recorded Alaska's history and established an Alaska newspaper industry that helped build communities and a territory into what became the forty-ninth state. Prior to the stampede there were newspapers in Sitka and Juneau and periodic journals printed on a mission press along the Yukon. But there were no other newspapers because there were no other towns with a literate population large enough to support a newspaper.

Although thirty years had elapsed since Alaska had become a U.S. possession, little was known of the district's geography, climate, or resources. Stateside newspapers referred to it as "a land of ice and snow," inhabited by blubber-eating Eskimos.

That was brushed aside by visions of sudden riches after George W. Carmack's gold discovery on Bonanza Creek in August 1896 was announced to the world. His strike was on a tributary of the Klondike, a small river flowing into the Yukon River near the boundary line between the United States and Canada. It was on the Canadian side but that failed to inhibit gold seekers, or journalists, of any nationality.

One prospector, Joseph Ladue, owned a portable sawmill and profited handsomely. He saw that merchants made more money than prospectors, so he filed on 160 acres of land on the Yukon River bank where the Klondike flows into the Yukon. It became Dawson City.

First he built his home, which also was the town's first saloon. Then he built a warehouse, a building for a newspaper, and a building for a brothel named Ruby's Place. He had a town. He named it for geologist Dr. George Dawson and proceeded to saw and sell lumber to thousands who flocked to the bustling new community.

Newsmen stampede

The Klondike gold strike fired up a group of hungry newsmen. Among those was Captain Richard Roediger, whose *Tacoma Daily News* had gone broke in the 1893 panic. (It was common practice at the time for prominent men to adopt the title captain, major, or colonel, although most had no military experience.)

One of his newspaper partners had been James Wickersham, probate judge for Pierce County preceding his appointment to a federal judicial post in Alaska. Another partner was Franklin K. Lane, who later served as President Woodrow Wilson's Secretary of the Interior during construction of the Alaska Railroad.

Roediger had the vision, and William McIntyre, a printer, the cash to buy *The Tacoma News*. After the paper suspended publication, it was sold by the sheriff to satisfy a judgment held by McIntyre for $14,000. McIntyre bid it in for $3,200, becoming sole owner.

Dawson's first daily

Roediger and McIntyre remained friends and with McIntyre's equipment started the *Dawson News* in Ladue's new building. It started as a weekly in 1899 but soon became the first daily in that part of the world. There were weekly newspapers in Dawson before the *News*. The *Klondike Miner*, the *Klondike Nugget*, and *The Yukon Sun* began publishing in 1898 but lasted only a few years and suspended or sold out to the better-equipped *News*, which continued to publish until 1954, the last few years as a weekly. Moving the capital of the Yukon Territory from Dawson to Whitehorse in 1953 resulted in less government printing for the *News* so the newspaper folded. Parks Canada owns the building and equipment and is refurbishing the plant as a newspaper museum.

At the height of the gold rush, seven newspapers were printed in Dawson at the same time. More than two dozen appeared and disappeared between 1897 and 1907.

When gold fever subsided around Dawson, those Klondike newsmen moved to new strikes in Alaska. They went first to Nome and Fairbanks, then to Cordova and Valdez, down to Southeast and to the many mining camps – Katalla, Rampart, Iditarod, Hyder, and later to Anchorage.

Roediger and McIntyre bought George Hill's *Fairbanks News* in 1904 and five years later they bought the *Tanana Daily Tribune*. They sold their Dawson paper to a group including their city editor, Charlie Settlemier. Settlemier was a successful prospector and successful Klondike and Alaska journalist. He later was editor of *The Anchorage Daily Times* and the *Fairbanks Daily News-Miner*.

While Roediger attempted to build a northern newspaper empire, Tacoma began prospering as the terminus for three transcontinental railroads. On a visit to his old hometown in 1910, Roediger decided to reenter the Tacoma journalism field and invested the modest $40,000 fortune he had accumulated in the north, purchasing the bankrupt *Tacoma Tribune*, only to lose it in short order.

He still owned substantial stock in the *Fairbanks Daily News-Miner* and returned to Fairbanks in the summer of 1912 to arrange for shipment of the defunct *Tanana Tribune* plant to Tacoma. His longtime friend, Secretary of the Interior Lane, appointed him surveyor-general for the state of Washington, but he died May 14, 1913, at age fifty-nine before he could settle in his new job or start another newspaper.

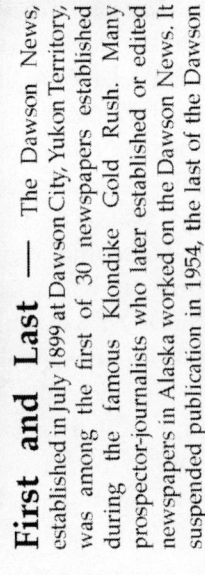

First and Last — The Dawson News, established in July 1899 at Dawson City, Yukon Territory, was among the first of 30 newspapers established during the famous Klondike Gold Rush. Many prospector-journalists who later established or edited newspapers in Alaska worked on the Dawson News. It suspended publication in 1954, the last of the Dawson City newspapers. It started in a log building, right, and later moved to 123 Third Ave. S., Dawson City, where the building was stabilized and is now an integral part of the Dawson Historical Complex National Historic Site of Canada. All of the old printing equipment resides in the building. *–Photos courtesy of Dawson Historical Complex National Historic Site of Canada, Malstrom Collection, 16/131 and 16/134.*

Well Dressed Journalist — This early Dawson journalist dressed up for his picture before his typesetting machine. He is not identifed. Forty prospector journalists worked on Dawson City newspapers before stampeding on to establish newspapers in Alaska. Among the editors who manned the Dawson News' desks at various times, and later made their mark in Alaska journalism, were Harry Steel, J. Harmon Caskey, E. B. Wishaar and Charles Settlemier. -*Photo courtesy of Dawson Historical Complex National Historic Site of Canada, Malstrom Collection, 29/136.*

Names to remember

Miners were panning gold in paying amounts on the beach in front of Nome by 1900. Prospectors and journalists stampeded there from Dawson. Prominent among them was Major J. F. A. Strong. Later he was governor of Alaska after he founded the *Nome News*, the *Nome Nugget*, the *Katalla Herald*, the *Iditarod Nugget*, and the *Alaska Daily Empire* at Juneau.

George Swinehart, George Carpenter, David Tewkesbury, and newspaper cartoonist Arthur Buell left Dawson for Nome in 1900 and started the *Arctic Weekly Sun*. The *Nome Chronicle* absorbed it and became Strong's *Nome Nugget*, still published today. Tewkesbury later was an editor of the *Fairbanks Daily News-Miner*, and the *Ketchikan Times*.

Also heading to Nome from Dawson were George Maynard, later longtime publisher of the *Nugget*, E. B. Wishaar and the Steel brothers, Will and Harry. The Steels joined Strong at the *Nome News* before he sold it and founded his *Nugget*.

Allan X. Grant followed Strong to Nome from Dawson. By 1910, he and Strong were co-publishers of the *Iditarod Nugget*.

Also at the *Nome News* from the Klondike was John J. Underwood, originally from Australia. He went to Council from Nome to start the *Council City News*. Underwood became a correspondent for Seattle newspapers, traveled Alaska extensively. He wrote a book about it, *Alaska, an Empire in the Making* (Dodd, Mead and Co., New York, 1913). He later worked for the Seattle Chamber of Commerce, often taking sides against Alaska on issues – the usual stand for the Seattle establishment over the years.

Eugene C. Allen and his brother, George, founders of the *Klondike Nugget* in Dawson, headed for Nome. Eugene continued on to Teller, seventy-two miles northwest of Nome, and started the *Teller News*.

George stopped in Nome. The November 1, 1900, Nome *Gold Digger* reported that George was caught in a roundup of "thirty thugs, sneak-thieves, stickup men and prize fighters," who were being shipped out of town on one of the season's last boats. However, the judge released him when he proved his identity as a son of former U.S. Sen. John Allen of Washington State.

Bernie Stone, a New Zealand native, went from Dawson to Nome to edit the *Nugget*.

In 1914, when Stone was editor and publisher of the *Seward Gateway*, he sent Ted Needham and L. Frank Shaw north to start Anchorage's first newspaper, the *Cook Inlet Pioneer & Knik News*, which became *The Anchorage Daily Times*. Needham and Shaw not only founded the newspaper but also led the petition drive that resulted in establishing the site for the city of Anchorage.

Stone later teamed with Ed Morrissey to found the *Ketchikan Chronicle* in 1919. He returned for a while to *The Anchorage Daily Times* and was editor of the *Valdez Prospector* before going to Fairbanks to finish his career as editor of the *News-Miner*.

On to Fairbanks

After glitter wore off at Nome, it was back up the Yukon River to Fairbanks and new gold strikes.

Stampeding newsman George Hill, with the help of Frank Mason and George Bellows, skipped Nome and went straight from Dawson to Fairbanks. They founded Fairbanks' first newspaper, the *Weekly Fairbanks News*. Hill had been founder of a Douglas paper with Needham before heading for the Klondike.

James Wilbur Ward and Needham went directly to the *Fairbanks Times* from Dawson.

The Steel brothers beat it from Nome to Fairbanks where Will joined the *Times*. Harry joined its competitor, the pioneering *News*. They later ran the *Cordova Daily Alaskan* with John W. Frame, noted for his caustic editorials. Frame edited newspapers in Juneau, Cordova, Valdez, Anchorage and Hyder after leaving Dawson.

Sam Wall left the *San Francisco Call* to become an editor in Dawson. By 1905 he was city editor of the *Fairbanks News*.

Dawson veteran Bob McChesney ended up running the *Fairbanks Weekly News*, successor to Hill's *Weekly Fairbanks News*. It became the *Fairbanks Daily News*.

W. F. Thompson later merged his *Tanana Miner* with the *Fairbanks Daily News* to form today's *Fairbanks Daily News-Miner* and became that paper's first editor and publisher. Thompson started his northern journalistic career on newspapers in Dawson. So did Henry Roden from Switzerland. He ran competition against Thompson in Fairbanks with his *Chena Times*.

Roden became a prominent Alaska lawyer. He served five terms in the territorial Senate and then was territorial attorney general and territorial treasurer.

Following Hill, Mason, Bellows, Thompson, and Roden from Dawson to Fairbanks was newspaper editor J. Harmon Caskey, who joined the Fairbanks' *Alaska Citizen*.

Roy Southworth, another Dawson veteran, worked on the *Fairbanks Daily Times* then started a newspaper in Anchorage and later became editor of *The Anchorage Daily Times*.

Jack Filbin worked on both the *News* and *Times* in Fairbanks after leaving Dawson and then was a co-founder of the *Alaska Citizen* at Fairbanks.

E. S. Bunch left Dawson to join the *Tanana Tribune* as editor and manager when it started publication in Fairbanks in 1907. One of the owners of the *Tribune* was former Dawson newsman Frank J. Cotter.

Casey Moran started in Dawson where he became famous for his story alleging the remains of Noah's Ark had been found by Indians "three hundred days' walk" from Dawson. He then moved to the *Fairbanks News* as a reporter.

George Garwood, with George Arbuckle, left Dawson in 1906 and started the *Tanana Teller* at Chena, near Fairbanks

Then Arbuckle and Ward started the *Hot Springs Post* in 1908 and later moved it to Tanana.

Arbuckle started the *Iditarod Pioneer* in 1910. Two of his friends, Filbin and Grant, saw the Iditarod economy begin to fade and started the *Ruby Record-Citizen* and urged Arbuckle to join them. But Arbuckle exuded the optimism of many pioneer journalists. He refused to leave Iditarod, believing better days were ahead. He died there in 1920.

Chester Kingsley Snow, with Klondike experience, joined Filbin as owner of the *Ruby Record-Citizen* in 1914. Before that he had prospected in the Nome area and reported for Nome newspapers.

Sam Callahan established the *Yukon Valley News* and published it both at Rampart, 1904-07, and Tanana in 1909. Although he had worked in Dawson, it was as a blackjack dealer, not a newsman.

E. J. (Stroller) White left the *Skaguay News* to edit the *Dawson Free Lance* and *Whitehorse Star*, then moved back to the Juneau-Douglas area. He ended up as a famed columnist and editor-publisher of *Stroller's Weekly* in Juneau.

Three missed the Klondike

Three prominent pioneer editor-publishers missed Dawson but were active with their contemporaries in building Alaska and its newspaper industry. Sydney Dean Charles arrived in Fairbanks from

Tacoma as an editor in 1904. He edited and owned newspapers around Alaska until he joined Ketchikan's *Alaska Fishing News* in 1934. He bought it a few months after its founding by a fishermen's union and gradually turned it into today's *Ketchikan Daily News*. He died in January 1959, after fifty-five years working on or owning seventeen different Alaska newspapers.

John Troy worked in Skagway in 1897 as a correspondent for New York and Seattle newspapers but became ill and returned south. He was back in Skagway in 1902 as editor of the *Daily Morning Alaskan*. A few years later he made his mark in Alaska and Juneau with the *Empire* and as governor of the territory, like newspaper publishers Strong and A. P. Swineford before him.

L. Frank Shaw also missed the Klondike. He stampeded to the Porcupine area instead before he was co-founder with Ted Needham of Anchorage's first newspaper and its townsite. Later, when Shaw was a Fairbanks journalist, he was named as one of the first regents of what became the University of Alaska.

The issues on which Alaska gold rush editors expounded between 1897 and 1912 included: the need for self-government and removal of bureaucratic shackles; opposition to carpetbag appointees; improved roads and trails; opposition to Seattle's intrusion into territorial affairs; cheaper freight rates; better mail service; improved telegraph service; relocation of the capital; and opposition to land withdrawals by the federal government.

The persistent editorial pleas for local autonomy, whether it was called "home rule," "territorial government" or "self-government," succeeded in staving off imposition of an appointed commission to supervise the District of Alaska. Although the pioneering journalists disagreed often, their campaigns led to granting of an elected delegate to Congress in 1906 and to territorial status with an elected legislature in 1912.

Chapter 8

Dyea and Soapy Lose to Skagway

When Klondike gold was discovered, prospector-journalists stampeded out of Juneau faster than they had out of Sitka earlier, joining the swarm from other states and countries. Most chose to reach the gold fields through the new towns of Skaguay or Dyea. (Skaguay was officially designated Skagway in the fall of '98.)

Among the journalists from Puget Sound heading for Dawson City was John Franklin Alexander Strong. He and his wife arrived in the booming tent city of Skaguay in October 1897, too late to reach Dawson that season.

M. L. Sherpy, a printer from Puget Sound, had preceded the Strongs by ten days and was preparing to give the town its first newspaper. When he learned the Strongs were spending the winter in Skaguay, he hired Strong as associate editor of his *Skaguay News*.

Editor Strong leads vigilantes

Strong left his mark in Skaguay before continuing his Alaska newspaper odyssey. He led the vigilantes who rid Skaguay of the notorious outlaw Jefferson (Soapy) Smith.

Smith acquired his nickname of Soapy while living in Denver where he developed an adroit method of selling cakes of soap. He would remove the paper from a bar of soap, wrap a five or ten dollar bill around the bar, replace the original wrapper – all in plain sight of the customer – then offer to sell the soap for a dollar. When the purchaser tore off the wrapper, he invariably discovered that the money was missing.

Despite reports of Soapy's shadowy past, he donated generously to charities and cultivated the goodwill of Skaguay community leaders sufficiently to give the impression that he favored law and order. All the while his gang of con men was relieving returning miners of their gold dust and nuggets.

Soapy served as grand marshal of the 1898 Fourth of July parade and made a handsome picture on his white stallion. Strong was not fooled by Soapy's fine manners. He helped organize a vigilante Committee of 101, together with Frank H. Reid, a surveyor from Oregon, and Josiah (Si) Tanner, who ran a hardware store and later was appointed U.S. marshal. The committee was determined to rid the town of its unsavory characters.

Reports of Soapy's gang preying on returning miners were causing miners to seek a different route to the States from the gold fields. Soapy's operations were bad for Skaguay business.

A crisis flared one day when a construction worker entered a saloon to buy himself a drink. He offered a large bill in payment and when the bartender refused to give him change, the customer objected, whereupon the barman heaved him out onto the street. When the customer returned with the deputy marshal, the bartender fired at them, killing the marshal and mortally wounding the abused customer. Townsfolk demanded that the killer be punished. Realizing that his life was in danger, the barman sought protection of Soapy's gang.

The Committee of 101 insisted that the murderer be brought to trial. Soapy promised to surrender him if assured a fair trial.

The next morning, a crowd of townsmen filed into a local church auditorium to try the killer, surrendered by Soapy's men.

Strong was chosen chairman by acclamation. He appointed ten men to guard the prisoner and twelve more to serve on the jury and question the witnesses. Jury members insisted that Strong act as judge. Just then, one of Soapy's men jumped up onto a bench and shouted, "There's a government boat coming up the bay and this mob will get its deserts."

Strong knew there was no government boat due, but he adjourned the trial and the accused was spirited away to a secret place. That evening, Soapy persuaded the U.S. commissioner to allow the killer to board a steamer for Sitka to await trial. There he served a short sentence in jail and departed on a southbound steamer.

A short time later, a young Australian prospector was robbed while in the back of Jeff Smith's Parlor. When Soapy refused to cooperate in returning the man's nuggets and gold dust, the vigilante committee called a mass meeting on Skaguay's Juneau Wharf to consider how to rid the town of Soapy and his gang.

Editor deported

Soapy tried to crash the meeting. Reid, who was posted as a guard to prevent such disruption, shot it out with Smith and died later of wounds. Smith died at the scene. So passed Soapy Smith, the master con man of his era, at the early age of thirty-eight.

After Soapy's demise, his gangsters were rounded up, placed aboard a southbound steamer and told never to return. Included in the group was Dr. J. A. Hornsby, former editor of *The Daily Alaskan*, a competitor of the *News* in Skaguay.

Hornsby had been fired from the newspaper because he had omitted mention of the robbery that led to the killings, thereby avoided pointing the finger of guilt toward Soapy and his gang. The paper's proprietors apologized to their readers for this faulty reporting, holding Hornsby responsible.

Another journalist also was involved with Smith. When the outlaw's clothing was searched at the morgue a note was found in his pockets from one of his spies in the community. It was signed with the letter "S" and in the handwriting of Billie Saportsa, allegedly a reporter for a New York newspaper. So he was deported with the others.

Hornsby argued vociferously with U.S. Commissioner Sehibrede against being deported. That official told him that he had the choice of leaving or standing trial.

Hornsby did not return to journalism in Alaska but he served as a physician, first for the City of Nome in 1900 and then for the Copper River & Northwestern Railway at Cordova, just as he had for the White Pass & Yukon Railroad in Skaguay.

When Soapy's gang got off the boat in Seattle, many of them were arrested on warrants from other states for earlier crimes that had caused them to flee to Alaska.

The Soapy Smith incident is outlined by Frank. G. Robertson and Beth Kay Harris in the book *Soapy Smith, King of the Frontier Con Men*, published by Hastings House in 1961.

Strong from Canada

Strong was born in Salmon Creek, New Brunswick, Canada, and trained as a teacher. At age thirty, he left for the United States, leaving a first wife and three children behind.

He worked on newspapers in Butte, Montana, Spokane and Bellingham, Washington He owned and published the *Bellingham Independent* for five years. He also edited a paper in Victoria, British Columbia.

Strong was editor of the *Tacoma Ledger* when he married Annie Hall on April 4, 1896. She was teaching at the University of Washington in Seattle after graduating from a four-year course at the Berlin Conservatory of Music. Strong was forty years old and his bride was twenty-six.

Three routes to Dawson

Thousands of stampeders began their arduous overland trek to the Klondike gold fields from one of three ports along the northern shores of Lynn Canal.

The Dyea Trail over Chilkoot Pass and the Dalton Trail over Chilkat Pass had been trade routes of the Chilkat and Stick Indians for centuries. The new port of Skaguay introduced stampeders to the White Pass, six hundred feet less in altitude than Chilkoot Pass and shorter than the Chilkat.

The village of Dyaytahk (later Dyea) was the beginning of a trail over Chilkoot Pass that the first white prospectors hiked to reach the Fortymile and Rampart regions in the 1870s and 1880s. Arthur Harper, Leroy McQuesten and Al Mayo moved their trading post supplies into the Yukon River Basin over Chilkoot Pass.

They carved "stairs of ice" on the side of the pass. The trail descended into British Columbia to Lake Lindeman and Lake Bennett. There crude boats and rafts were built to float the five hundred miles down a chain of lakes and the Yukon River to the gold fields near Dawson City.

Tlingit chiefs had persuaded the Rev. S. Hall Young, a Presbyterian missionary, to establish a mission in 1881 at Dei-Shu, near the mouth of the Chilkat River. The town's name became Haines, named for Mrs. F. E. Haines, a member of the Board of Missions, who helped raise $15,000 for the mission program.

Frank Leslie of *Leslie's Magazine* organized a party in 1890, to explore up the Chilkat River and over the divide into the Interior. One of his guides was a young Jack Dalton who had bargained with the Chilkats for the use of their trading trail. He constructed a haul road to take supplies with pack horses and teams of oxen to Interior miners in the 1880s, hence the name Dalton Trail.

The Dalton Trail had a more gradual ascent but it was 250 to 260 miles longer than the Chilkoot or White Pass. The Dalton was well suited for horses, cattle and sheep. It played an important role in supplying pack animals and fresh meat to booming Dawson. Later, it kept Dalton out of Juneau after he had been acquitted of murder in a trading dispute.

Moore homesteads Skaguay

While veteran trailblazers used the Dyea (Chilkoot) and Dalton (Chilkat) trails, a Stikine riverboat captain, William (Billy) Moore, discovered a third route that he considered preferable to the ones out of Dyea and Haines. It was the White Pass out of Skaguay Bay, a few miles longer than Chilkoot Pass, but easier to travel with hand sleighs.

Moore and his family homesteaded 160 acres at the head of the bay, built themselves a log house and put in a wharf. In the summer of 1896, they started building a pack trail into the canyons leading to Lake Bennett.

On July 29, 1897, they induced their friend, Capt. James Carroll, to tie his steamer *Queen* at their dock and disembark two hundred passengers and their outfits. This was the first large steamer to make Mooresville, as it was called, a regular port of call. From then on, other steamers included it on their regular schedules, and by the first of October the town's population had grown to two thousand and several hundred houses had been built. Many of those first stampeders helped the Moores improve the trail over the White Pass. Then British engineer M. J. Heney began his White Pass & Yukon Railroad between Skagway and Carcross.

Dyea booms, busts

Meanwhile, a post office had been established at Dyea in 1896. On March 25, 1897, the first ocean steamer, the *City of Mexico*, arrived with between six hundred and seven hundred passengers. Four days were spent lightering the cargo from the ship to the beach. Then began the strenuous tramp over Chilkoot Pass. Very few horses were aboard, so most of the outfits were packed on foot with the help of Indian guides.

Dyea's first newspaper plant was set up in a tent on the corner of Fourth and Broadway in a flourishing town of five thousand. Charles D. Ulmer Sr. and his sons, George T. and Ralph, formerly with the *Port Angeles* (Washington) *Tribune-Times*, arrived in Dyea with a printing press in December 1897.

Volume I, number 1 of the weekly *Dyea Trail* appeared January 12, 1898, proclaiming in its initial editorial that "as surely as there was built a San Francisco, so surely will there be built the city of Dyea, the natural gateway to the golden interior of Alaska."

It told of two aerial tramways being completed from Canyon City to the summit and of rails being laid by the Chilkoot Railroad as far as Canyon "and the cars are already here." Within ten days, "Dyea will be able to transport five hundred men and their outfits over the summit each day." There were twenty-seven transportation companies ready to organize pack trains for the newcomers. The tramways would cut travel time from tidewater to the headwaters of the Yukon River from one month to one day, the story claimed.

The masthead listed Charles D. Ulmer Sr. as editor; George T. Ulmer as managing editor, and Ralph Ulmer as business manager. The paper was a four-column, eight-page tabloid that came out on Wednesdays.

Its second edition trumpeted the city as a "hive of industry" with hundreds of new buildings appearing each week. From early morning until dark, the carpenters' saws were heard, and each steamer brought a new group of businessmen ready to embark on a new venture in Dyea. The editors predicted that as soon as their new office building was completed, the *Trail* would publish as a morning daily as well as a weekly. Two new powered presses were en route from Seattle.

By spring, people were pouring in by the thousands; three steamers arrived on one day, unloading 1,200 passengers, with six thousand in one week in March 1898, including several hundred women. By May, it was estimated that twenty-five thousand had gone over Chilkoot Pass since the first of the year.

THE DYEA TRAIL.

VOL. I. DYEA, ALASKA APRIL 3 1898. NO. 12

EXTRA! TEN O'CLOCK EDITION EXTRA!

TERRIBLE CALAMITY!

BIG SNOWSLIDE THIS MORNING NEAR THE STONE HOUSE.

Eighteen Bodies Already Taken out and From Thirty to One Hundred More Buried.

Deadly Avalanche — Prospectors and survivors of the April 3, 1898 avalanche at Sheep Camp on the Chilkoof Trail walk on the snow that covered and killed more than 50 people. That tragedy and the completion of the White Pass & Yukon Railroad between Skagway and Carcross later in the year made Dyea a ghost town and its two newspapers suspended. *-Photo courtesy of Dawson Historical Complex National Historic Site of Canada, R.C.A.F. Collection, #3417, 36/19.*

Two companies of the Fourteenth Infantry of the U.S. Army arrived in March 1898 to maintain law and order. The usual "shell men" were on hand to fleece the unwary and the soldiers brought them before the U.S. commissioner.

A second weekly newspaper, *The Dyea Press*, appeared March 12, 1898, with the Edward C. Russells, a father and son team, as editors-publishers. It was a full-size paper with six columns to each of its four pages. The Russells were experienced newsmen from Portland. The initial edition told about the blowing up of the battleship *Maine* in the Havana harbor, to set off the Spanish-American War.

Both newspapers enjoyed generous advertising patronage. The Dyea Brewing Co. boasted of being the largest brewing firm in Alaska. Dr. T. L. Price had a log cabin drugstore, with an adjoining forty-bed hospital, located on River Street – "all special diseases carefully treated." Clancy & Co. sold pure liquors, wines and cigars. Peterson's Tram hoisted passengers and freight over its rope tramway.

Disaster on the trail

A disastrous avalanche occurred at Sheep Camp on the Chilkoot Trail on Sunday, April 3, 1898. More than fifty people were buried alive. Editor Russell told readers that in a camp of eight thousand inhabitants such a happening was not unduly alarming as accidents as bad or worse happened in much smaller communities in the States.

By May 1898, Dyea had a mayor and city council, a chamber of commerce, an orchestra and a Literary and Social Society. The *Press* put out a special edition of four thousand copies to circulate in the States to advertise the advantages of the Chilkoot Pass route to the Yukon.

In August, the *Trail* printed fifty thousand copies of its "first annual illustrated edition," for stateside distribution and even to the principal cities of Europe, stressing the Chilkoot Pass as the only year-round trail and the least hazardous to the gold fields.

Nearly four-fifths of the Interior-bound freight went by the Dyea route. However, when the White Pass & Yukon railroad out of Skagway reached Lake Bennett in 1898, the Dyea aerial tramway was as dead as the town soon became.

Despite their propaganda efforts, the Ulmers apparently were skeptical about the town's future. They suspended publication of the *Trail* in August 1898. Charles and Ralph returned to Puget Sound but George went to Juneau, where he bought Gus Leach's *Alaska Mining Record* and turned it into a daily.

The Russells followed suit in suspending publication the following December, the father going to Haines and the son to Juneau. Another ghost town was in the making. In June 1902, the Post Office Department closed its station at Dyea, making it necessary for the people still living there to go to Skagway to receive their mail.

One hundred years later, the entire townsite of Dyea, three miles northwest of Skagway, was a tree-covered park accessible to tourists via a narrow dirt road from Skagway. A few rotting piling poke out of the mud in the bay where ships once moored to unload hundreds of Klondike-bound gold-seekers. Remains of a few rusty stoves peek between tall, second-growth trees.

Chapter 9

Talented Writers Follow Editor Strong

Journalists John Franklin Alexander Strong, Elmer John (Stroller) White and John Weir Troy, each starting at Skagway, gave strong guidance to Alaska's evolution. Strong and Troy also became governors of Alaska, following in the footsteps of Alaska's second governor, newspaper publisher A. P. Swineford. White made it to Territorial House Speaker in 1919.

The Strong-edited weekly *Skaguay News* had appeared October 15, 1897. Money was scarce so other legal tender such as gold nuggets and cords of wood were accepted. In less than a year, it boasted a paid circulation of 1,600.

In its initial editorial, the *News* reassured its readers that the town was not as corrupt as the Seattle papers pictured it. Evil reports were attributed to arrivals who were ill-prepared for frontier life and faulted the country rather than themselves.

When a murderer was not immediately hanged, Seattle papers attributed it to the depravity of the town's residents. The *News* called that "a base libel."

But as the hordes continued to pour off the steamers, lawlessness increased and local editors were hard-pressed to defend the town. That situation inspired the Committee of 101, headed by Strong, to successfully boot out the lawless element.

The initial issues of the *News* listed more than 250 offices and businesses, including sixteen hotels and lodging houses, nineteen restaurants, eleven saloons, ten groceries, fifteen general mercantile stores and one bank. There was neither a church nor a school.

Alaska's first daily

Alaska's first daily newspaper, *The Daily Morning Alaskan*, was born in Skaguay February 1, 1898, with Oscar W. Dunbar as editor. He and A. J. Howells, a fellow printer from the weekly *Astoria* (Oregon) *Town Talk*, were the proprietors. In 1904, the name was changed to *The Daily Alaskan* and was generally referred as *The Alaskan* until it suspended in 1924.

Dunbar sold *The Alaskan* in April 1898 to George W. DeSucca, a Skagway storekeeper. DeSucca and his son Charles handled the business end of the operation while hiring editors for news.

Dr. J. Allan Hornsby, a former Chicago physician, was their first editor. He had been practicing medicine in Skaguay, mainly for the railroad, for six months and also dabbled in real estate. He was a popular man – about – town and known to be a personal friend of Soapy Smith. That led to his departure from town with the Smith gang.

Weston Coyney, Alaska correspondent for the *New York Herald*, succeeded Hornsby as editor of *The Alaskan*. He had worked on papers in London, New York, Washington DC and on the West Coast before trekking north. For several years, he was with James Gordon Bennett, publisher of the *New York Herald*, for whom Lake Bennett is named.

In April 1898, Strong left the *News* and mushed over Chilkoot Pass from Dyea and spent the summer prospecting. In the fall, Strong sold his claims and took a job as editorial writer for the *Dawson Daily News*, established by Richard Roediger and William McIntyre from Tacoma.

White succeeded Strong at the *Skaguay News*. At the end of seven months, White and Albert M. Rousseau, a printer, leased the *News* from founding owner M. L. Sherpy. For the ensuing year, the *Skaguay News* took on the colorful character of its editor.

White was an experienced journalist when he arrived in Skaguay in the spring of 1898. He was born on a farm in Ohio and graduated from Muskingum College in New Concord, Ohio. He taught school and worked on newspapers in that state before moving to Florida in 1881. He taught school there for a couple of years and then went into newspapering full-time.

He spent the next eight years working on papers in Florida, Georgia, and Louisiana. In 1889, he migrated to Puget Sound and worked on various papers before heading north.

Introducing himself to the readers of the *Skaguay News*, White said the paper would be run on a "wide open, flatfooted basis, and those who do not like the platform of God, morality, and Skaguay may trot up to our business manager's desk, pay up all arrears and discontinue their patronage."

White became one of Alaska's colorful and respected journalists after stints as editor in Dawson City and Whitehorse. He acquired the nickname "Stroller" from his weekly column. He was editor-publisher of *Stroller's Weekly* in Juneau when he died there in September 1930.

White a fast leaner

Skaguay's busy populace paid little attention to newcomers and it was up to them to learn the rules of the game and to learn them fast. Some of White's lessons are reported in R. N. DeArmond's books, *Stroller White; Tales of a Klondike Newsman* or *Klondike Newsman: Stroller White*. The first was published in Vancouver, British Columbia, in 1969. The second is an updated reprint of the first but with five additional chapters. It was issued by Lynn Canal Publishing in Skagway in 1992.

White was a fast learner. The evening he arrived he stopped at a hotel to ask for a room.

"We have a room," said the clerk. "Gimme a dollar and go up both flights of stairs. The room is at the top of the last flight. Take the first bed that isn't occupied."

White followed instructions, found a cot just inside the door, rolled into it, and went to sleep. The following morning, he discovered that he had seventy-eight roommates, sleeping in tiers of bunks four deep around the walls. The entire floor space, which was big enough to be a skating rink, was thickly sprinkled with cots. Before the next night, he moved into the printing office where he slept on a mattress under the press.

One night a man was killed in the Klondike Saloon. The stranger who did the shooting fled, pursued by a crowd of enraged friends of the deceased. Five shots were fired at the stranger just as he passed the printing office, but none of them connected with their target. Two struck the sidewalk and three penetrated the newspaper building in which White slept. While none of the bullets found their way to his pallet under the press, the next morning White secured several sheets of boiler iron with which to surround his boudoir.

In April 1899, Sherpy sold the *News* to Joseph T. Hayne, secretary of the Methodists' McCable College in Skagway. Hayne assumed the editorship, whereupon White became editor of *The Alaskan* until he departed for Dawson City in July.

Too many newspapers

Dunbar, who had founded and sold Alaska's first daily newspaper early in 1898, reappeared in Skagway to launch the *Skaguay-Atlin Budget* November 25, 1898. He had been living in Oregon since selling *The Alaskan* the previous April. When gold was discovered near Atlin, British Columbia, he visualized it as an economic revival for Skagway.

The *Budget* began as a weekly and changed to a daily, giving the town three dailies. The Klondike gold rush was over and Skagway's year-round population had shrunk to three thousand.

Dunbar sold the *Budget* in March 1900 to C. E. Cole, John Dormier and G. C. Findley. Five months after selling the *Budget*, Dunbar launched the daily *Alaska Travellers' Guide*, a fourth daily competing in the collapsing community! This sparked the demise of all of the newspapers within a matter of months, except for *The Alaskan*.

DeSucca sold *The Alaskan* to Ingvard M. (Ed) Jensen and George S. Towne in December 1901, and two years later Jensen became sole owner.

Jensen and Towne had been employees on *The Alaskan* since 1898 and were aware that the paper had been losing money during the previous year. They shipped the Linotype machine back to Seattle and reverted to setting type by hand.

Troy arrives

Although Jensen and his *Alaskan* enjoyed having the Skagway journalism field to themselves after demise of the *News, Budget* and *Guide*, he had difficulty keeping editors until Troy took charge in 1902. Troy remained until 1907 when Jensen sold the paper to Dr. L. S. Keller, a local dentist.

Troy was born on a farm near Dungeness, Washington, the son of Smith and Laura Troy, pioneers of Washington Territory. His father was a member of the First State Legislature and was state superintendent of schools for fourteen years. John's maternal uncle,

Allen Weir, was a delegate to Washington's constitutional convention and was Washington's first secretary of state.

John entered upon his dual career of journalist-politician at an early age. He was a reporter on Allen Weir's *Port Townsend Argus* at age eighteen, and three years later he was appointed deputy county auditor for Clallam County. At twenty-four, he was elected county auditor on the Democratic ticket and was reelected. Meanwhile, he launched his own weekly *Port Angeles Democrat* and ran it for six years.

John joined the Klondike stampede as a newspaper correspondent for Seattle and New York papers, landing in Skaguay August 19, 1897. Later, he took a job managing J. H. Brooks's packtrain operation between Skaguay and Lake Bennett and worked part-time on *The Alaskan*.

He was stricken with "camp fever," a form of paralysis that had become an epidemic in the frontier town. He was carried aboard a southbound steamer on a stretcher and spent the next three years under the medical care of his father-in-law in Port Angeles. His paralysis was arrested so he was spared the permanent disability that many suffered after contracting the disease.

After Troy returned to Skagway to edit *The Alaskan*, the paper assumed leadership in territorial affairs. Troy was a pioneer in the crusade for self-government for Alaska. He wrote pro-home rule editorials on an average of once a week. The first demanded that Congress grant Alaskans the right to make their own laws. He called for the ouster of Gov. John Brady, who opposed home rule.

Troy opposes timber withdrawal

Troy protested President Teddy Roosevelt's withdrawal from entry of a large block of Southeast Alaska timber land that later became Tongass National Forest. He described it in an August 24, 1902, editorial as "one of the most severe of the blighting blows our government has delivered upon the very vitals of Alaska."

Troy predicted that it would lead to economic stagnation as the prospector and the homebuilder would turn elsewhere when they could not secure title to the mineral properties they discovered.

When ownership of *The Alaskan* passed into the hands of Dr. Keller July 1, 1907, Troy returned to Seattle and was employed in a variety of jobs until 1912 when Strong invited him to join his new Juneau newspaper, the *Alaska Daily Empire*.

Dalton's Porcupine City

After Dyea folded, journalists headed for Skagway or Juneau, except for Ed Russell Sr. He headed for Haines, a town that once welcomed a few journalists with big dreams for that area.

Haines is situated at the head of a natural bay called Portage Cove on Chilkoot Inlet, on the west side of Lynn Canal, sixteen miles southwest of Skagway.

Gold was discovered on Porcupine Creek, a tributary of the Klehini River, about thirty-five miles from Haines, in the summer of 1898. The strike brought one thousand people into the area the following year.

Guide Jack Dalton laid out a townsite of 150 acres, about half a mile below the mouth of Porcupine Creek, calling it Porcupine City.

A year later, rich copper deposits were discovered across the headwaters of the Klehini River within British Columbia, sixty-five miles from Haines. Local residents began dreaming of a railroad carrying the ore to tidewater at Haines

Russell's weekly *Porcupine Quill* prophesied that Haines would become a major port of entry to Interior Alaska and Canada. However, he suspended publication after about six months

Will A. Nash published the weekly *Porcupine Nugget* briefly in 1900.

In September 1902, Capt. Wilds P. Richardson arrived at Haines in charge of constructing a military post on 389 acres one-half mile from the town of Haines. It was named Fort William H. Seward. Troops were assigned there in the summer of 1904.

'Live, Laugh and Love'

Among the troops was Claud Kinney, formerly associated with the *Skagway Alaskan* and the *Cordova Alaskan*. He launched the weekly *Musher* September 21, 1907. It was a two-column, four-page folio measuring five and a half by eight and a half inches.

One page was devoted to Haines news. There were about a dozen ads from Haines merchants. The slogan in the masthead read: "Live, Laugh, and Love; There'll Come a Time When You Can't." Copies of the publication are in the Sheldon Museum & Cultural Center in Haines.

In 1909, deposits of gold, silver, copper and iron were discovered within a mile of Haines. A wagon road was constructed into the Rainy Hollow district, and Haines became a busy port.

Lt. Henry P. M. Birkinbine at Fort Seward launched the weekly *Haines Pioneer Press* May 15, 1909. He started promoting a railroad from Haines into the interior of both Canada and Alaska, his slogan being: "From Puget Sound to Fairbanks via Haines Eliminates the Open Ocean and Saves Three Hundred Miles." His allusion to "open ocean" was meant to denigrate railroad proposals from the towns of Cordova, Valdez and Seward.

Although not an experienced newsman, Birkinbine published such a lively newssheet that *The Pacific Printer*, the principal trade journal of the Pacific Coast, in its April 1910 issue said: "*The Haines Pioneer Press* and *The Nome Weekly Gold Digger* are the two principal weekly papers in Alaska."

Birkinbine resigned from the military and opened a civil engineering office in Haines. His newspaper was an effective tool in winning incorporation for the town, thus making it eligible to receive federal license monies to help pay the expenses of local government.

Bushell Arrives

Meanwhile, over in Skagway, the owners of the *Daily Record* in Juneau helped launch the weekly *Interloper* in Skagway in 1908 in order to counteract *The Alaskan*'s support for Judge James Wickersham and self-government, both of which they opposed. Charles H. Scheffler and Richard Bushell, *Record* employees, went to Skagway to run the paper as part owners.

Scheffler had worked on the *Sitka Alaskan* (1901-04), the *Juneau Mining Record* (1904-06), and briefly on the *Skaguay Alaskan* in 1906. He sold his interest in *The Interloper* after the 1908 general election and returned to his job at Juneau's *Daily Record*.

Bushell was born in Hull, England, in 1876 and arrived in the Pacific Northwest in 1889. He bought the *Snohomish* (Washington) *Tribune* in 1899. He and his wife, Mary, also experienced in newspapering and printing, arrived in Ketchikan in 1905 to work for Walter S. Coutant on his *Ketchikan Mining Journal*.

Looking for more money, Bushell moved from the *Journal* to office manager of the Brown-Alaska Mercantile Co. at Hadley on Prince of Wales Island in 1906. The bottom fell out of copper, closing Prince of Wales mines. So by January 1907, Bushell was back in Ketchikan as business manager of A. P. Swineford's new newspaper, the *Ketchikan Mining News*, running competition to the *Journal*. The following year the Bushells moved to Juneau and the *Daily Record*.

By the time Bushell and Scheffler arrived in Skagway in 1908, Skagway had been bypassed by the gold rush to other ports. Many buildings were boarded up. The railroad controlled the town and was supported by *The Alaskan*. But a faction in the town, opposed to the railroad, Wickersham and self-government, wanted a newspaper. Thanks to Juneau's *Daily Record*, they got their appropriately named *Interloper*.

The paper only lasted a year. After Scheffler pulled out, Wrangell businessmen urged Bushell to buy the *Alaska Sentinel*, which he did. He moved *The Interloper* equipment to Wrangell to supplement the *Sentinel* equipment. *The Interloper* folded. The name of the *Alaska Sentinel* was changed to *Wrangell Sentinel*, its name today.

Hearing news of *The Interloper*'s suspension, the Juneau *Transcript* – which was feuding with Juneau's *Record*, sponsor of *The Interloper* – observed that it must come as a terrible blow to Skagway's residents who had come to love *The Interloper* like "the average man loves his mother-in-law."

Chapters 10-15

Journalists Stampede

Next to Nome

and Fairbanks

> *A newspaper should be fiercely independent. An editorial page that is neutral is harmful to the prestige of the paper, harmful to the community it serves, harmful to the highest requirements of journalism.*
>
> – U.S. Sen. E. L. (Bob) Bartlett (b.1904-d.1968), former reporter and associate editor of the *Fairbanks Daily News-Miner*

William Fentress Thompson founded the Fairbanks Daily News-Miner in May 1909 and was its publisher until he died of pneumonia on Jan 24, 1926 at age 62. *— Photo courtesy of the Fairbanks Daily News-Miner.*

Chapter 10

Early Nome Attracts Dawson City Journalists

The best gold claims along the Klondike were in the hands of big corporations by 1899. Then word circulated that a stormbound party of Swedes and Laplanders were scooping up placer gold at Anvil Creek on the Seward Peninsula.

Within a year, eighteen thousand gold seekers, many from the Klondike, were on the beaches of Anvil City panning for gold. They established a town called Nome and recorded its travails in seven different newspapers in its first decade.

A storm led to Nome's founding. Storms since have plagued the town on its exposed site along Norton Sound.

Alaska's most famous claim jumping was attempted at Anvil Creek but failed to wrest the claims away from the Swedes and Laplanders. A federal judge was removed and his cohorts went to jail for their efforts.

Famed Arizona lawman Wyatt Earp, promoter Tex Ricard and other notables landed in Nome. They avoided trouble because the citizens of Nome organized and sent troublemakers packing on the next boat to Seattle.

The headline over the lead story on the front page of the September 8, 1900, *Nome Daily Nugget*: "'Bad' People Must 'Git.'"

The subheads: "Grand Jury Reports Against the Dissolute Women." And: "Directs the District Attorney to Weed Out the Criminal Classes From the Town."

St. Michael's Aurora

But first, before there was a Nome, the only newspaper in Northwest Alaska was at St. Michael Island. It was the site of an old Russian military stockade, Redoubt Michaelovsk, at the mouth of the Yukon River. It leaped into the national headlines when the first stampeders arrived down the Yukon from Dawson City in 1897, with more than a half a million dollars in gold dust.

The Russians built a fort at St. Michael in 1833 to control the fur-trading traffic on the river that was being infiltrated by the British Hudson's Bay Company. St. Michael was the point where all cargo and passengers transferred between ocean and river steamers.

On June 25, 1897, the river steamer *Alice* arrived at St. Michael from Dawson with twenty-five miners loaded with gold dust. Two days later another party of men came staggering in under pokes of gold valued from $55,000 to $175,000. Still others followed. These were the men who arrived in Seattle and Tacoma in July and were the subjects of the *Seattle P-I*'s famous "ton of gold" story that precipitated the Klondike stampede.

St. Michael's harbor filled with ocean steamers in the following weeks. Riverboats struggled to empty the jammed warehouses and move freight up river before freeze-up. Gangs of gamblers pitched tents along the beach and began plying their trade. The War Department established an army post, Fort St. Michael.

On October 31, 1897, a sixteen-page typewritten newssheet, the *Aurora Borealis*, started weekly publication, with J. P. Agnew as editor and J. B. Bouse as publisher. It, too, was held together with bent pins.

Its expansive staff could have managed a Seattle daily. With managing editor Agnew were Samuel Hubbard as city editor, Lt. Edward Bell as society editor, E. S. Echols as sports editor, H. W. Winde as dramatic editor, George Dunn as police and waterfront editor, B. B. Earle as mining editor, George Belt as livestock editor, H. M. Morgan as telegraph editor, and F. E. Earle, His Infernal Majesty.

Its regular sale price was one dollar. However, currency was scarce, so seal oil, gold dust, blubber, fur, ivory and fish were accepted in payment. A porterhouse steak bought ten papers.

Volume I, number 5, carried a story about the icebound whaling fleet near Barrow. Thirteen men were lost trying to make the edge of the ice, where nine men were finally taken on board a steam whaler and landed at Barrow.

The only known copies of the *Aurora* are in the C. L. Andrews collection at Sheldon Jackson College in Sitka.

Anvil City Becomes Nome

Klondike excitement had hardly subsided when that other sensational gold discovery was made on the beaches of the Seward Peninsula near Anvil Creek. Again the attention of the world was attracted north, and a second stampede, this time to Alaska, occurred in 1900.

In August 1898, a group of six prospectors in a sailboat from Golovin Bay, eighty miles east of the present site of Nome, were washed ashore by a storm. They were on their way to the northwestern coast of the Seward Peninsula to look for gold-quartz deposits.

Landing at the present site of Nome, they passed their time prospecting while waiting for the storm to blow out. On Anvil Creek, a tributary of the Snake River, they found rich deposits of placer gold.

The group, including two Laplanders and two Swedes, returned to Golovin and secured the use of a four-ton schooner owned by the Swedish Covenant Mission and returned to their claims.

They met at the mouth of the Snake River and formed the Cape Nome mining district, thus giving birth to a settlement first known as Anvil City. It was derived from Anvil Creek but shortly thereafter was changed to Nome, for Cape Nome, a point of land on Norton Sound, twelve miles southeast of the present town.

When the news of their discovery reached Dawson in the spring of 1899, thousands of disappointed Klondikers, who were heading down the Yukon en route to the States, stopped at Nome.

In the meantime, gold was found in fine, flaky particles on the beach. It was a "No Man's Land." The government had reserved for wharfage a strip along the shore between the high tide mark and the sea. Mining claims could not be registered, but there was no provision preventing any one from extracting the gold.

A miners' meeting was held. By mutual consent, it was agreed that each man should be entitled to as much ground as he could reach with his shovel from the edge of the hole in which he was working. The beach miners made from $10 to $100 a day. Many of them left in the fall with full pokes.

Future governor brings News

Among the early arrivals in Nome from Dawson were Major and Mrs. J. F. A. Strong, with the equipment to start the weekly *Nome News*. Will Steel, the businessman in the Steel family, owned 80 percent of the stock in the new publishing firm. His brother Harry, the editor, and Strong each owned 10 percent.

The Steel brothers came from Pennsylvania. Their father, Colonel J. Irvine Steel, together with his five sons, owned a chain of fourteen newspapers in the Keystone State in the latter half of the nineteenth century. Each of the sons served an apprenticeship as city editor on at least one of the family's papers.

Tiring of the sedentary security of their family fortune, the two youngest sons, Will and Harry, migrated to the West Coast in the late 1890s. Each found jobs on papers in San Francisco and Seattle. In the spring of 1899, they joined a party of Puget Sound newsmen, headed by Richard Roediger of Tacoma, transporting seventy-five tons of printing equipment and supplies over Chilkoot Pass. They started the *Dawson News*, which became the first daily in the Klondike area. Strong was on the editorial staff of the *Dawson Daily News*. Harry Steel was editor. Will probably counted the money, as he did throughout his years in Alaska.

Their stay in Dawson was short. By the fall of 1899, they were in Nome. A front-page story in the initial edition of their *Nome News* of October 9, 1899, told of $2 million being washed from the sea beach and another $2 million from the creeks during that first summer. There were numerous instances where men rocked from $10,000 to $20,000 each from the seashore, while scores made between $3,000 and $5,000 each in a few weeks, the newspaper reported.

The *News* came out on Saturdays. With the arrival of a steam power plant, the *News* went daily on June 26, 1900, and continued until the close of navigation the end of October. During the winter, it varied between a weekly and a biweekly.

Strong's editorials analyzed local needs and offered solutions. He urged establishment of a school, a pure water supply and proper waste disposal. Typhoid fever reached epidemic proportions that first winter, claiming many lives. Care for the destitute and ill received frequent editorial attention.

Cassius M. Coe, a San Francisco newsman, and his wife, Marie, launched a second weekly, *The Nome Gold Digger*, two weeks after the first edition of the *News*. Both papers carried the same amount of advertising and both indulged in superlative boosterism about the town's future.

When a townsman complained that the two papers lacked "stamina," Strong responded:

> If the newspaper defamer thinks in his verbose grandiloquence that it is the province of a newspaper to incite trouble, create distrust, sow dissension, be the organ of some cheap clique that wishes to get even with some other clique, again it pleads guilty to the lack of backbone; if the *News* is unable to view public questions and men from an extremely narrow, warped and prejudiced standpoint, whose horizon is bounded alone by self and selfish interests, self-aggrandizement or self-glorification, must it be accused of lack of stamina?
>
> If the average man would think more and talk less, such charges concerning newspapers will not sound like the braying of an immortal ass.

Decrying congressional incompetence in governing Alaska, he wrote:

> We are long past the wet nurse period. We have been wearing the cast-off clothes of our sister states long enough. We want a new suit, made to fit us as perfectly as possible. We are American citizens, capable of self-government, independent, honest, in the main; courageous, or we would never have ventured thus far; and enterprising, as our acts, not words, show.
>
> We must act unitedly to get legislation that will make us self-respecting; make us feel that we are a part and parcel of the U.S., and not a foundling eager to accept any crumbs, or cast-off garments that a lot of congressmen, who know nothing of our needs or requirements, may see fit to give us.

Claim jumpers foiled

U.S. District Court Judge Arthur H. Noyes arrived with his court retinue in July 1900, supposedly to establish law and order. Actually his disregard for the law promoted a notorious attempt at claim jumping.

Alexander McKenzie, a Republican national committeeman from North Dakota, hatched a scheme to seize the Anvil Creek claims by alleging that federal law prevented the Swedes and Laplanders – foreigners – from owning them. McKenzie went to Washington and attempted to have that written into law. He failed but succeeded in having his friend Noyes appointed federal judge in Nome.

Noyes appointed McKenzie receiver for the claims after a court case challenged their ownership. The U.S. Court of Appeals in San Francisco reversed Noyes. The appeals court ordered the claims returned to the original stakers, along with any gold taken out by McKenzie.

When Noyes and McKenzie failed to follow the order, they were found in contempt. Noyes was removed from office and barely escaped imprisonment. McKenzie was sentenced to jail but pardoned by President William McKinley. Two of their associates and the district attorney served jail time.

Ladies hold teas in wilderness

While men sought their fortunes by various means, their ladies maintained social patterns in accordance with their status in the community. Marie Coe reported in the *Gold Digger* that wives of the judiciary dispensed Russian tea "in frail and dainty porcelain, suggestive of a London or New York drawing room" at their Saturday afternoon "at homes."

These same hostesses held open house on New Year's Eve to which "all the prominent citizens" were invited. The men arrived in tuxedos and the ladies in elegant gowns.

The Arctic Weekly Sun, Nome's third journalistic venture, was launched on July 18, 1900, by George Swinehart, George Carpenter and David Tewkesbury, all former employees of the *Yukon Midnight Sun* in Dawson. Carpenter and Swinehart also had been publishers in Juneau before going to Dawson.

When the trio first arrived in Nome, Swinehart and Tewkesbury had U.S. commissioner appointments in their pockets – Swinehart for Nome and Tewkesbury for the Kougarok district. Carpenter was general manager of the newspaper.

Accompanying them was Arthur Buell, a cartoonist who also had worked on Dawson papers. His sketches of local personalities and events gave the *Sun* a sprightly character; every page had at least one sketch illustrating a story.

Judge Noyes 'sets' the Sun

The *Arctic Sun*'s demise came when Judge Noyes nullified Swinehart's and Tewkesbury's commissioner posts. Creating vacancies was the judge's technique for filling judicial positions with his handpicked accomplices in the crime of claim-jumping.

The final edition of the *Sun*, less than a month old, appeared on August 4, 1900. Three days later, Swinehart sold it to a group of local attorney-politicians and Walter C. Kurtz, a former *Nome News* printer.

The new owners launched Nome's third daily, *The Nome Daily Chronicle*, on August 11, 1900, in competition with the *Daily News* and the new *Daily Gold Digger*. The *Chronicle* was a four-page tabloid replete with Buell cartoons.

Swinehart moved to Seattle.

Tewkesbury opened a trading post and operated a riverboat transportation business at Mary's Igloo. In 1904, he moved to Wenatchee, Washington, where he published his own weekly for the next ten years and then became night editor for The Associated Press in Seattle.

Carpenter opened a brokerage office in Nome and later a roadhouse on the trail between Nome and Council City. One day he got caught on the trail in a four-day blizzard and almost froze to death. He had to have both his hands and feet amputated. The excruciating pain unbalanced his mind and he was adjudged insane. He was hospitalized at Fort Davis in Nome, where he died on May 10, 1902.

The *Chronicle* was a daily during the summer but became a weekly or a biweekly during the economically depressed winter months. It suspended publication on June 18, 1901, after a strenuous struggle for survival.

Strong had left the *News* and started the *Nome Nugget* with a special New Year's edition January 1, 1900. After the *Chronicle* folded, he bought the *Chronicle* plant and launched *The Nome Nugget & Chronicle*

Society Editor, Alaska Style– This photo courtesy of the Carrie M. McLain Memorial Museum in Nome is labeled simply "Bell." The only Bell in the newspaper business in northwest Alaska during the gold rush was Lt. Edward Bell, listed as society editor of the Aurora Borealis at St. Michael in 1897. The hat, the shirt and tie and the high button shoes indicate this is a society editor examining an issue off the old hand press to the left. -*Photo courtesy of the Carrie M.McLain Memorial Museum in Nome, photo by Arthur L. Bell of a well dressed printer examining his product in one of Nome's newspaper plants betwven 1903-1909.*

EARLY NOME ATTRACTS DAWSON CITY JOURNALISTS

The Nome Daily Chronicle

NOME, ALASKA, MONDAY, AUGUST 20, 1900.

MYSTERIOUS SEA TRAGEDY

SCHOONER EDITH COMES INTO PORT SHORT TWO OFFICERS.

Dan Woo Shot On the Siberian Coast.—The Other Was Knocked Overboard and Drowned.

LAWYER HALL IS MISSING

HIS FRIENDS ENTERTAIN GRAVE FEARS OF FOUL PLAY.

Left Port Clarence With Two Unknown Men Who Returned and Said They Lost Him.

THE NOME NEWS
SEMI-WEEKLY

CITY OFFICIAL PAPER

NOME, ALASKA, WEDNESDAY, AUGUST 14, 1901   PRICE 25 CENTS

TELEGRAPH LINE TO NOME
Communication with Outside Next Year.
PROGRESS OF WORK

JUDGE NOYES INTERVIEWED
Denies That He Ever Disobeyed Orders of Circuit Court.

NEWS FROM FAIRHAVEN
Country North of There Showing Up Well.
GOLD COMING OUT

If you must have the News you must subscribe for the Gold Digger.

Nome Daily Gold Digger.
FOURTH YEAR

The Gold Digger is Not Controlled by Any Corporation or Company.

VOL III NUMBER 1   WEDNESDAY, JULY 24, 1907   PRICE TWENTY-FIVE CENTS

VICTORIA, B. C. NEARLY DESTROYED BY FIRE!

District Mile long and Half Mile Wide in Victoria wiped Out in Conflagration---Loss $250,000---Tenderloin Section Destroyed and Half of Chinatown.

EXPECT TO FIND THIRD BEACH LINE IN COUNCIL

Prospectors Discover Gravel Deposit 3 Miles Long and 2 Wide Between Bear and Fox Creeks---Company of Nome and Council Men Organized to Prospect Ground---Good Colors Found at 6 Feet Depth.

July 9, 1901, publishing two times a week. The words "& *Chronicle*" were dropped after a few weeks.

E. B. Wishaar had succeeded Strong as editor of the *Nome News*. He had been editor of the *Daily Morning Alaskan* in Skagway briefly in 1899. Then he was editorial writer for the *Dawson Daily News*. Several editors followed Wishaar until the *Nome News* suspended publication in May 1906 when *News* editor Harry Steel was enticed to move to the *Nugget*. A group headed by Harry Steel's new father-in-law had purchased the *Nugget* from Strong.

Suspension of the *News* reduced Nome newspapers to the *Gold Digger* and the *Nugget*.

Strong's strong editorials

Before Strong sold out and left Nome in 1906, he had modernized the plant's equipment. He wrote editorials that were articulate, thought provoking and strong. His commitment to the Alaskan lifestyle was evident:

> Because a man wears furs in Alaska, he is not necessarily a barbarian; because he has his habitation here, he is not necessarily untutored. It is pleasant to touch elbows with "civilization," we suppose, once in a while, if only for the purpose of being enabled to see what a farce and humbug this modern alleged civilization is.
>
> We fail to see wherein those who are "permitted to dwell in the concourses of the civilized" are a whit more to be envied than are those who live on the frontier. There one is "cribbed, cabined and confined"; if he is not rich he is a white slave, a mere automaton, who follows a groove, and the mind and body both suffer in consequence.
>
> Here he is free, and therefore, we say a better man, because his environments are more amplified, so to speak, his opportunities greater, and unlike the white slave of this delectable "civilization" which is measured nowadays by the weight of a poke, he may feel, if he wants to, that he is not a "brother to the ox."

When it appeared likely that Alaskans would be accorded the right to elect a delegate to Congress, Strong stressed the importance of northwestern Alaskans presenting a united political front, rather than be torn apart by partisan strife. He helped organize a nonpartisan political club and served as its first president. In accepting the office, he promised to "shun the partisan path. The time for drawing party lines and cracking the party whip has not yet arrived. It will come soon enough, and in the meantime the people of this portion of the district should be united."

Seattle selfishness noted

Resentment against the way Seattle businesses treated Alaskans inspired frequent editorial tirades. Strong abhorred Seattle's selfish attitude toward Alaska, "the goose that lays the golden egg for Seattle," and yet scarcely a dollar of Seattle money is invested in the northland:

> Last year Seattle's commercial transactions with Alaska reached the magnificent total of $20 million, yet if an Alaskan were to approach a Seattle capitalist with a bona fide mining proposition, he would be turned down with scant courtesy. Yet they are investing their money in mines in Nevada towns, many of these stocks of doubtful value.
>
> They are not farsighted enough to see that the development of Alaska's resources means added growth and prosperity for Seattle. Seattle's attitude toward Alaska has always been of the mean-spirited kind.

Denouncing Congress's outrageous treatment of Alaska, Strong suggested that "the men behind the revolution of 1776 had not a tithe of the legitimate grievances against the British parliament that the people of Alaska had against the Congress of the U.S." Alaskans were being taxed while deprived the rights of self-government.

Papers unite against whalers

The Nome papers disagreed on a number of issues, but on one there was unanimous agreement: the practice of whalers abducting Eskimo girls must stop.

Marie Coe's *Gold Digger* published a list of the whaling vessels and the number of girls kidnapped and brought aboard each vessel. It gleaned its information from deserting crewmembers.

For years, it had been the custom of the whalers to trade whiskey to parents for girls. Or the whalers would get the entire village intoxicated and then kidnap the girls.

The Nome press called on the federal government to put a stop to this practice of "making these whaling ships floating harems." The practice soon stopped.

Marie Coe had held on to the *Gold Digger* after her husband, Cassius Coe, died in December 1901. She continued to publish it for the next three years. Then she sold it to S. H. Stevens, her general manager, and moved to San Francisco.

Strong's literary talent far surpassed that of his peers. His pen was an important factor in shaping the destiny of the new country. By 1905, the *Nugget's* circulation was four times greater than the combined circulation of all other newspapers published on the Seward Peninsula.

Strong resorted to florid rhetoric when heaping scorn upon the foibles of puffed-up politicians. When Judge James Wickersham and Gov. John Brady quarreled publicly, Strong wrote:

> The roll of the battle drums, the snort of the war horses, the noise of the captains, and the shouting, are heard from Baranof Island to where rolls the turgid Tanana, and hears no voice save the war cry of General James Wickersham and his valiant personal bodyguard of federal office-holders hurling the defiance across moor and mountains, rippling rivulet and roaring river; on across the mighty Gulf of Alaska, on whose boisterous bosom is borne even to Sitka the anathemas of the doughty General Wickersham's devoted henchmen.
>
> For Governor Brady has seized an inkpot, and General Wickersham has unsheathed his tongue from its scabbard, and a war of voices is heard in the land.
>
> Let them wade to their necks in their inkpots, and when their tongues shall have again been sheathed and the smoke of battle cleared away, let the president of the U.S. give the people of Alaska a taste of that "square deal," which he talks about, and make the Tanana solon and the Sitka satrap private citizens.

Strong sold the *Nugget* on June 1, 1906, to the Nome Cooperative Publishing Company, headed by Dr. H. C. Wilkinson, Harry Steel's father-in-law, and moved to California.

The new publishing company's $30,000 capital stock was subscribed to by practically all of the businesses of Nome. Harry Steel was named general manager. His brother Will sold the *News* equipment to the new firm and the plants merged with the *Nugget* name retained. Will moved to Fairbanks to become editor of the *Fairbanks Times*.

Harry Steel remained with the *Nugget* only briefly and then left for the *Fairbanks News*. Bernard M. Stone, a native of Auckland, New Zealand, succeeded Harry. Stone had practiced the printer's trade in the South Sea Islands before migrating to the United States in 1898. He hit the trail to Dawson and later joined the gold rush to Nome.

The *Morning Pioneer Press* appeared in Nome on October 24, 1907, as a tri-weekly with L. C. Denny and Allen X. Grant as publishers. It was printed in the *Nugget* shop. Both men had worked as printers on the *Nugget* and had owned stock in the paper.

The forty-five-year-old Grant, a native of Detroit, Michigan, joined the Klondike stampede in 1898 and worked as a printer on the *Dawson Daily News*, the *Dawson Nugget* and the *Yukon Midnight Sun*. He accompanied the Strongs to Nome and worked on both the *Nome News* and the *Nome Nugget*.

The *Pioneer Press* became a daily during the following summer but suspended publication in September, when the last steamer of the season departed, leaving fifteen hundred winter residents.

In December, Grant purchased the *Nugget* plant and published the paper for a year. Then he sold it to E. C. Devine, George Maynard and F. Whittren. Devine had been a printer on the *Gold Digger* and the other two had been printers on the *Industrial Worker*, a strange newspaper. It was a nonunion shop started by a union.

Union starts 'scab' shop

The Western Federation of Miners Union, a member of the Industrial Workers of the World (IWW) established the weekly *Industrial Worker* on July 5, 1907, with J. W. Walsh, an IWW national organizer, as editor. But he departed a month later, turning over the editorial reins to Paul Turner, a union member.

Its editorials preached that the employer and the employee had nothing in common; labor produced all the wealth hence the wealth belonged to the workers. The IWW was committed to world revolution until the workers got their fair share of the wealth. The *Gold Digger* and the *Nugget* were viewed as capitalistic organs.

Stevens responded in the *Gold Digger* that his was a union shop and paid its employees the highest salaries in Alaska. His paper supported pure unionism, but he did not "advocate labor agitators or socialistic disturbers of the public peace."

The printers at the *Industrial Worker* did not receive union wages, so the Nome Typographical Union labeled it a scab shop. In the spring of 1908, printers Maynard and Whittren quit and sued the paper for unpaid wages. When an explosion occurred in the back shop, an editorial "pointed the hand of suspicion unerringly toward those two printers who have turned traitor and gone over to the enemy (capitalism)." Maynard, who had moved to the *Nugget* as a printer, sued for libel but the case ended in a hung jury.

The *Gold Digger* was forced to suspend publication on July 27, 1910, when the U.S. marshal took possession of the plant. Two lawsuits were filed against editor Stevens, one for wages and another for legal fees. Stevens contended that the litigation was staged in order to suppress the paper's support of Wickersham for delegate to Congress.

Devine, one of the owners of the *Nugget*, was the plaintiff in the wage case and his paper was promoting the candidacy of Edward S. Orr for delegate.

After *The Gold Digger* folded, the *Nugget* and the *Industrial Worker* had the Nome journalism field to themselves. The *Industrial Worker* lasted only eight more years. The *Nugget* survives today as Alaska's oldest newspaper, dating from January 1, 1900.

Chapter 11

Teller, Council, Nome Lose Papers

While Nome journalists enjoyed the gold boom, nearby communities of Teller and Council hosted less spectacular journalistic ventures financed by the *Nome News* – less spectacular but just as optimistic. One editor predicted a railroad tunnel crossing Bering Strait.

It had been at Libbyville, close to the townsite of today's Teller, seventy-two miles northwest of Nome, that Alaska's first newspaper, *The Esquimaux*, appeared October 14, 1866. It lasted a year.

Thirty-five years later the *Teller News* appeared for two years. At Council, sixty miles northeast of Nome, the *Council City News* lasted four years.

Teller became an important shipping port when gold was discovered in the Kougarok region in 1900. It had a population of more than five thousand between 1900 and 1903. There were eighteen saloons and several large trading posts. As many as twelve six-horse teams loaded with supplies left Teller daily for the Kougarok.

Eugene C. Allen, former business manager of Dawson City's *Klondike Nugget*, started the weekly *Teller News* on April 1, 1901, with a grubstake from Harry and Will Steel and J. F. A. Strong at the *Nome News*. Allen lost his own equipment in a storm while crossing Norton Sound.

Eugene Castle Allen was born in Oak Park, Illinois, in 1868. After graduating from the University of Kansas, he moved to Seattle in 1888, where he published the suburban *Green Lake News*. He also was a printer at the Metropolitan Printing & Binding Company. He, his brother George and a fellow printer, Zack Hickman, joined the Klondike stampede in 1898 and started the *Klondike Nugget* at Dawson.

The four-page weekly *Teller News* garnered most of its news stories via the Mukluk Telegraph. There were accounts of parties stranded without food and others suffering frozen limbs in blizzards.

Sometime during the summer of 1901, George Maynard, who was working as a typesetter on the *Teller News*, took it over for back wages. Maynard formerly worked as a printer in Nome.

Allen returned to Nome where he worked on the *Nugget* and became a co-owner. Later he worked on the Steel brothers' *Cordova Alaskan* and on the *Valdez Prospector*, before going south in the 1920s.

Maynard's proprietorship of the *Teller News* came to an abrupt end when Max R. Hirschberg, manager of the Arctic Mining & Trading Co. and the Northwestern Commercial Company, fired him in April 1902. Hirschberg had lost a libel suit against Maynard, so he purchased the mortgage on the paper from the *Nome News* so he could get rid of Maynard.

The latter started another paper called *The Teller Musher* but it proved to be a futile effort, so Maynard returned to Nome. Teller was gradually changing from a boomtown to a ghost town.

Teenager reports father's death

The town of Teller decreased in population after 1903 until the 1920s when a mini-boom occurred with the discovery of tin and copper in its vicinity. The U.S. commissioner's fourteen-year-old son, Walter John Marx, decided to publish a newssheet as an exercise in cultivating his writing and typing skills.

The Marxes formerly lived in Nome where Walter was born in 1906. They moved to Teller in 1916. Recalling in later years how he was inspired to launch *The Pioneer Scout* in Teller on July 24, 1920, he said:

> We had no radio or telephone, no high school, doctor or dentist, no wireless. In winter our mail came once a month by dogsled from Nome – it took the mailman three days to cover the ninety miles. There was no road.

My father bought me a simple device called a hectograph and I could grind out almost a hundred copies from one master copy made with a special typewriter ribbon. I gradually acquired subscribers, mainly from Nome, where the merchants were interested in the goings and comings of the various traders who defied both American and Soviet law to trade with the Siberian Eskimos.

In winter the news was terribly dull – what can happen in a snowbound village of some thirty people, half of them children? We did have an almost annual tragedy as some white man froze to death when lost on the trail. When I was sixteen my little paper had to report the death by freezing of my own father on the Shishmaref-Teller route – there was no staked trail.

Walter issued the four-page *Pioneer Scout* every two weeks during the winter months and weekly during the summer. It bore the heading: "The Best Newspaper in Teller."

The summer issues were full of exciting news – a running gun battle between an American schooner and the Soviet Coast Guard, shipwrecks, and the arrival of new mining outfits.

The *Pioneer Scout* suspended publication in February 1925 after Walter's mother decided he should go to Seattle to continue his education. At its peak, he had sixty subscribers.

Underwood to Council

The *Nome News*, undaunted by failure in Teller, dispatched John Jasper (Jack) Underwood and Leo Dumar with a small outfit to start a weekly at Council City in 1902. Council was where gold was discovered on Niukluk River in the fall of 1897.

Underwood was born in Sydney, Australia, in 1875. He was initiated into the printer's craft and into the wanderlust of a prospector at an early age. Unsuccessful in his prospecting ventures, he became a correspondent for Australian and London newspapers in New Zealand.

This background served him well when he joined the Klondike stampeders in 1897, followed by stampedes to the Fortymile and Nome. He once explained what made men forsake the comforts of home to tackle the treacherous life of a prospector:

> It is not the lust for gold – the mere acquirement of money – that attracts miners to Alaska, but the joy experienced in actually taking from the ground a piece of virgin gold.
>
> Endowed with physical courage and initiative, brought together from all parts of the world, unfettered by traditions or conventions, unhampered by personal vanities, the gold hunter stands in a new mining community as God created him, and he is surrounded by fellows of his own kind.
>
> Around the campfires one hears tales of men who have wandered in every out-of-the way corner of the world; stories of fortunes just missed, of lost mines and lost creeks, of competencies made and dissipated or lost again.

When funds ran low on his prospecting treks, Underwood served as a mail carrier or a deputy U.S. marshal. He was mechanical foreman on the *Nome News* when he was dispatched to Council City, which had burgeoned to fifteen thousand restless miners and associates. In the initial edition of the *Council City News*, March 15, 1902, Underwood praised the local residents for their warm hospitality, contrasting it to the "gimme" attitude of Nomeites.

A local story told about five tons of mail lying at Fort Yukon awaiting transportation because the mail carrier between Fort Yukon and Rampart had his feet frozen and then amputated.

Scarcity of currency was a major problem in the town's commercial transactions and the *News* chastised the "bodies corporate," who employed "the public be damned" policy of substituting checks for hard cash. Miners were paid with checks. They used gold dust to make purchases, both methods causing financial woes for everyone. Thousands of dollars were drained from the economy when people were obliged to go to Nome to get cash. Underwood accepted ivory, gold dust, or furs in exchange for his paper, which sold for twenty-five cents a copy.

In October 1902, Underwood welcomed a new partner, Frances E. Fitz, who bought a half interest in the paper. Her brother, Albert H. Fitz, served as business manager. The Fitzes owned valuable mining claims on nearby creeks. The following July, the Fitzes became sole owners of the *News*. Underwood spent the remainder of the summer searching for gold.

He spent the winter in Seattle and from then on commuted between Seattle and Alaska. He worked a while on the *Nome Nugget* in 1907 when Bernie Stone was in charge. He was a reporter for the *Seattle Times* in 1909 and remained associated with that paper for the next twelve years, serving as its correspondent in Washington, DC, the last three years.

Underwood wrote a series of articles on Alaska for *Leslie's Weekly* and *Harper's Magazine* in 1913-14. Dodd, Mead and Company published his 440-page book entitled, *Alaska, an Empire in the Making*, in 1913.

In his book predicting Alaska's potential, he wrote:

> It is, therefore, not improbable that at some time in the not-too-remote future, engineers and financiers will join in forces in the construction of a tunnel under Bering Straits, and with the aid of a few hundred miles of railroad in Alaska and Siberia, make it possible to ride from New York to Paris on wheels.

In 1921, when Warren Harding won the U.S. presidency, C. B. Blethen, publisher of the *Seattle Times*, lobbied in Washington to have Underwood appointed governor of Alaska.

Ironically, the appointment went to Scott C. Bone, a former editor-in-chief of the *Times*' competitor, the *Seattle Post-Intelligencer*.

After owning the *Council City News* a year, the Fitzes sold the paper to Neville H. Castle, a local attorney, and devoted themselves wholly to mining.

Castle ran a lively paper, with both local and world news. There were correspondents in the area's mining towns of Solomon, Teller, Candle, Nome and Fairbanks. But editor Harry M. Moreno was given to castigating prominent local citizens. That resulted in the major merchants withdrawing their advertising patronage. The paper suspended publication January 5, 1907 for lack of community support.

In calling it quits, Moreno wrote: "Upon our next journalistic venture (may God forbid) we will confine ourselves strictly to a diet of oxtail soup and beef tongue – thus making both ends 'meat'!"

Following the *Council City News* suspension, and that of the Nome *Gold Digger* in 1910, only the *Nugget* and the *Industrial Worker* served

Northwest Alaska where nine papers had shared in the Northwest area – Teller, Nome, Council – in the previous ten years. The gold seekers were moving on.

Nome destroyed

A dozen years after fortunes were picked up off Nome beaches, the town was no longer the glamorous "City of Golden Beaches." Icebound for seven months or longer each year, only the stouthearted, or those without the price of a southbound steamer ticket, remained after the last ship departed in the fall. Corporate dredges replaced the pick and shovel miner as they had on the Klondike.

Nome residents were not only isolated but they were subject to severe windstorms that wrecked their town. A one hundred-mile-an-hour storm crushed the buildings on the entire south side of Front Street in the fall of 1913, reducing them to kindling wood. Five were washed out to sea. Fire broke out in the remaining debris and residents were reduced to living in tents with a scant supply of food and clothing. The newspapers suspended publication for several weeks.

George and Mary Maynard, by then publishers of the *Nome Nugget*, had participated in the Klondike stampede of '98 as teenagers with their parents. George was from Pennsylvania. Mary was from Oregon. He learned the printing trade on the *Dawson News* and *Nugget*. He later worked as a typesetter on each of the Nome papers, becoming a part owner of the *Nugget* in 1909.

Mary was a native of Kansas City but her family moved to Portland, Oregon, in 1897. The following year they moved to Skagway where they operated a dairy farm and chicken ranch. They moved from Skagway to Cordova, to Valdez and finally to Nome in 1904, engaging in the dairy and chicken business in each locality. Mary married Maynard in 1906. The couple had two children, Russell and Mildred. Russell followed his parents into the newspaper business.

Flu hits

More than seven hundred people died during the 1918 flu epidemic across Northwestern Alaska. The disease was particularly virulent among the Eskimos; 200 of the 250 Nome Eskimos perished.

Nome almost disappeared during World War I as miners were drafted into military service. The *Nugget* and the *Industrial Worker*

Devoted To The Interests Of Nome And The 2nd Division

Member of Associated Press — Oldest Newspaper in Alaska

THE NOME NUGGET

GLACIER PRIEST REPORTS FIND
SCHMELLING ON CHAMPIONSHIP COMEBACK
MAKES FLIGHT NEW YORK TO NOME IN 8 DAYS

Devoted To The Interests Of Nome And The 2nd Division

Member of Associated Press — Oldest Newspaper in Alaska

THE NOME NUGGET

RELIEF PARTY CONTACTS BYRD
2ND ASS'T POSTMASTER GEN. COMING NOME
BOMBERS PREPARING FOR HOP TO STATES

had agreed to publish triweeklies on alternate days to preserve labor and supplies during the war. Printing costs had skyrocketed nearly 400 percent.

A brisk fur traffic operated between the Siberian coast and Nome, with American and Russian schooners shuttling back and forth. A banner above the paper's name on the front page of the *Nugget* read: "Nome is the Distributing Center & Gateway to Northern Alaska and Siberia."

In 1920, Maynard bought the equipment of the *Industrial Worker*. It had suspended after battling a shortage of workers, a shortage of supplies, the flu epidemic, storms and the exodus of miners to other areas. Maynard consolidated its equipment with that of the *Nugget*.

Diphtheria epidemic hits

On January 28, 1925, a news dispatch reported worldwide that Nome was suffering a diphtheria epidemic. Several deaths occurred and new cases were reported daily. Schools closed and the town was quarantined. The majority of the patients were Eskimos.

There was only one doctor and the nearest source of antitoxin was one thousand miles away in Anchorage. The Public Health Service ordered a million units of antitoxin from Seattle to go via Seward and the Alaska Railroad to Nenana and then to Nome by dog team.

Delegate to Congress Dan Sutherland was unsuccessful in getting an airplane to fly from Fairbanks to Nome. *Fairbanks Daily News-Miner* publisher W. F. Thompson editorialized in favor of using an airplane and he just happened to have one handy. He was one of the owners of Fairbank's only flying service.

The successful dog team relay run to Nome was commemorated in a rerun seventy-five years later. It inspired the annual Iditarod sled dog race from Anchorage to Nome.

Maynard calls judge a 'lemon'

Maynard was not given to editorializing on controversial local issues but when the Democratic administration sent a Tennessee man to take a judgeship instead of an Alaska resident, the *Nugget* called it a "bombshell of political miscarriage":

> Alaska is unalterably opposed and will remain so forever to the appointment of non-residents to any federal positions in Alaska. We have been fighting for the past 25 years for self-government. We are entitled to the privilege of governing ourselves by our own representatives and lawmakers.
>
> Adding insult to injury is this latest "lemon" which the people of the Second Division will have to stomach. Why should some person be sent to Nome from one of the remotest states in the Union, when within our own Division we have men who are just as capable?
>
> We looked up Cumberland Gap – it has 400 people and is situated right up amongst the "Hill Billies."

On September 17, 1934, fire destroyed every business in town except two lighterage operations. The *Nugget* plant and the Maynards' living quarters upstairs over the plant were uninsured. The fire originated in the three-story Golden Gate Hotel. Nome's horse-drawn fire wagon proved wholly inadequate to control the flames. The *Nugget* appeared as a one-page mimeographed sheet distributed free of charge until new equipment arrived in November.

The guardhouse at Fort Davis, an abandoned army camp, was dragged about one and one-half miles to Nome's main street to be the headquarters of the *Nugget*, a building it still occupies today.

Russell Maynard was running the paper at the time of the fire. His father and mother were in the States vacationing for the first time in eighteen years.

On August 27, 1939, Maynard died in a Portland, Oregon, hospital from complications following a tonsillectomy. In accordance with his wish, he was buried in Nome. His widow continued to publish the *Nugget*.

Mary Maynard forced out

The *Nome Nugget* was one of the newspaper casualties of World War II. Mary Maynard, plus one employee, had put out the triweekly after her husband's death. But on November 27, 1942, she closed the doors and moved to Juneau where her son, Russell, was director of the territory's Department of Public Welfare and her daughter, Mildred, was a U.S. district court stenographer.

Failure to receive supplies, rising prices and a dwindling civilian population, coupled with the fact that Nome was rapidly becoming an armed camp equipped to wage war, compelled Mrs. Maynard to suspend publication.

The following August, the suspended paper was sold to Wilfred and Emily Boucher, daughter and son-in-law of Antonio Polet, pioneer Nome merchant.

Chapter 12

Fairbanks Attracts Talented Newsmen

Not all stampeders headed downriver to Nome after the Klondike offered no more riches. Some stopped en route at a new mining camp on the Chena River, Barnette's Cache. Some traveled on the Tanana and Yukon rivers to Hot Springs, Rampart, Ruby, Innoko, or Iditarod. Then from Nome and other strikes they gravitated back to Barnette's Cache. There they built the city of Fairbanks.

Through catastrophic fires, floods and a major bank failure, Fairbanks matured into Alaska's second largest city. After shaky starts, Fairbanks' newspapers merged and matured into the *Fairbanks Daily News-Miner*.

Barnette grounded

Most Alaska towns owe their existence to a strategic location but Fairbanks' birth was an accident, or at least unplanned. Situated on the bank of a shallow slough, deep in the wilderness, miles from anywhere, the setting would not normally lure settlers. But when a riverboat captain got stuck on a sandbar and ordered his passengers to disembark with their possessions, Fairbanks was born.

It was August 26, 1901. Captain Charles Adams started up Chena Slough with his riverboat *Lavelle Young* to bypass Bates Rapids in the Tanana River

Elbridge Truman Barnette, a wandering adventurer from Montana, had chartered the boat to take him to Tanacross, where the Valdez-Eagle trail crossed the Tanana River. He planned to establish a trading post there and make a fortune because the trail was a shortcut to the Klondike gold fields. Instead, he and his wife Isabelle found themselves stranded on a bank overlooking little Chena Slough on that chilly August evening.

Their bad luck soon changed. Two prospectors in the nearby hills, running low on supplies, spied smoke from the stern-wheeler in Chena Slough. They went to investigate and became Barnette's first customers. They bought their supplies and disappeared into the hills.

They reappeared at Barnette's Cache the following summer with the exciting news of a major gold discovery only fifteen miles away. On July 22, 1902, Felix Pedro and Tom Gilmore started an Alaska gold rush second to the rush to Nome's beaches.

United States District Court Judge James Wickersham designated Barnette's Cache court headquarters after he was ordered to move his court from Eagle to a place in the Tanana Valley. It was to be either Chena or Barnette's Cache. Chena, at the confluence of the Tanana and Chena rivers, ten miles southwest of present-day Fairbanks, was a prosperous shipping point. It provided a convenient transfer point for large riverboats unable to traverse the Chena at low water.

When Barnette agreed to rename his Barnette's Cache for Sen. Charles Warren Fairbanks of Indiana – who had been instrumental in getting Wickersham appointed a federal judge – it was the beginning of the end for Chena. Even with Chena's strategic location and the fact that it was the terminus of the narrow gauge Tanana Mines Railroad, Fairbanks became court headquarters and headquarters for everything else in the valley. By the end of 1904, about eight thousand people were in the area. Chena, in a few years, went the way of Dyea in Southeast.

Among the earliest arrivals in Fairbanks from Dawson City were three printers – George M. Hill, George Lafayette Bellows and Frank Mason. Although their *Weekly Fairbanks News* was Fairbanks' first bona fide newspaper, three short-lived, typewritten publications preceded them.

Fairbanks Miner came first

G. Carlton Woodward and his brother, Harry, Philadelphia Business College graduates, distributed a few typewritten copies of the *Fairbanks Miner* during the summer of 1903.

Some original copies of the *Miner* exist in the library of the University of Alaska.

A second, one-issue *Fairbanks Miner* appeared on May 19, 1903, as a fund-raiser for Judge Wickersham's ascent of Mt. McKinley. Wickersham wrote the entire copy, which covered eight legal size pages.

Thirty-six ads were sold at $5 apiece and the paper sold for $5 a copy. George A. Jeffrey typed seven copies that were read before audiences, usually assembled in a saloon, for an admission fee of $1 per person. Enough funds were collected to grubstake the mountain climbing expedition.

Judges selling ads, copies of their newspaper and charging admission would be considered unethical conduct today, but not in "the good old days." A copy is preserved at the University of Alaska Fairbanks.

A third single-edition typewritten "newspaper" was *The Fairbanks Gazette*, appearing on July 17, 1903, with Alfred L. Smith as editor and proprietor. It was a six-page tabloid and asked in its lead editorial, "Does Fairbanks Need a Newspaper?" Answering in the affirmative, the editor apologized for launching the *Gazette* "with such slender equipment as a typewriter" but he felt the need was so urgent that he could not await the arrival of a full-fledged newspaper plant. For Smith it never came.

Then came the News

Two months later, Fairbanks journalism started in earnest when the Hill-Bellows-Mason trio issued the *Weekly Fairbanks News* on September 19, 1903.

According to the history of the *Fairbanks Daily News-Miner – Adventures in Alaska Journalism since 1903*, by Paul Solka Jr. – George M. Hill hauled a newspaper press and type through four hundred miles of wilderness between Dawson and Fairbanks.

While in Dawson, Hill had interspersed his prospecting forays by working as a printer on George Swinehart's *Midnight Sun*. Later, he operated his own print shop and published the *Monthly Mining Review* and the *Morning Bulletin*.

George Bellows had worked for several months on the *Skaguay Alaskan* in the winter of 1897 before continuing to Dawson. He learned the printing trade in his native New York City.

Little is known of Frank Mason, who was the first editor of the *Weekly Fairbanks News*.

The News started with ten 9"x12" pages and later changed to four 17"x24" pages. Hill was listed as proprietor and Bellows as mechanical foreman. In the salutatory, the hope was expressed that they might "acquire public confidence and esteem, and become a power for good." They subscribed to a weekly telegraphic summary of world news.

Fairbanks had a population of approximately one thousand, with additional hundreds along the creeks. It was a wide open mining camp where men scooped up a fortune by day and threw it away at night.

Prostitutes and gamblers enjoyed a heyday. Town government subsisted on license fees collected from them, even though both were illegal operations. Who cared what the city licensed as long as city officials refrained from assessing a property tax?

Chena hosted early newspapers

The *News* trio parted company as each sought additional income. Bellows moved to Chena in the spring of 1904 where he started the weekly *Chena Herald* on June 10, 1904. Hill went into real estate and Mason hung on at the *News* until selling out in 1905

E. J. Hutmacher arrived in Chena a month after Bellows, establishing the weekly *Chena Times*. After a few issues, he sold the paper to another late arrival, Henry Roden.

Roden, a Swiss immigrant, renounced a career as a concert pianist to participate in the Klondike stampede. He was studying in Paris when he read about the gold strike and bought a ticket direct from London to Skagway, with a stopover in Juneau. He arrived in Juneau on Christmas Day, 1897. The following February, he mushed over the White Pass Trail from Skagway to Dawson.

Roden was a disillusioned miner after Dawson and shifted to journalism when he arrived in Chena. He started studying law on the side. He and Bellows consolidated their printing equipment, with Bellows in charge of the mechanical department and Roden in charge of editorial and advertising.

On July 18, 1905, they put out an "extra" celebrating the driving of a golden spike on Falcon Joslin's Tanana Mines Railroad, marking its completion between Chena and Fairbanks. Isabelle Barnette, co-founder of Fairbanks, wielded the sledge hammer, and Judge Wickersham delivered the main address.

By the fall of 1906, Roden was ready to go into law practice in Fairbanks, so he left the *Times*. He eventually became Wickersham's law partner, when the latter left the bench. Over the years, Roden was active in law and politics throughout Alaska. He retired in 1955 and died in Seattle eleven years later, the last of the Klondike stampede journalists.

Bellows continued publishing the *Times* until June 1907, when he merged it with the newly established *Tanana Miner* published in Chena by Will F. Thompson and George Arbuckle, recent arrivals from Fairbanks.

In the meantime, Mason had sold the *Weekly Fairbanks News* to Richard Roediger and William McIntyre, the Dawson newspaper magnates, originally from Tacoma.

Robert J. (Bob) McChesney, who had been mechanical foreman for Roediger and McIntyre at the *Dawson Daily News*, was made general manager of their Fairbanks acquisition. Roediger and McIntyre then purchased the plant of the defunct *Yukon Morning Sun* in Dawson and sent it to Fairbanks so that the *News* could become a daily.

When the *Fairbanks Evening News* appeared on May 1, 1905, it was the only paper in Fairbanks, competing against only Bellows' *Times* at Chena.

McChesney had worked on Roediger and McIntyre's Tacoma papers before joining the Klondike stampede in 1898. He chose the Stikine River route, stopping in Wrangell long enough in the spring of '98 to help Ted Needham, a Tacoma colleague, put out a special edition of his *Stikeen River Journal*.

Fairbanks News hires talented team

McChesney hired a group of livewire newsmen to staff Fairbanks' first daily. He became sole owner within a matter of months and added new, modern equipment, including a complete photoengraving setup so he could feature local pictures. He was setting a trend Fairbanks newspaper publishers have followed for more than ninety years, installing the most modern equipment and hiring talented staff.

McChesney's first recruit for managing editor was a former Tacoma colleague, Sidney Dean Charles. According to Charles's autobiography, found in later newspaper columns, he "first saw the light of day on September 6, 1870, in St. Cloud, Minnesota, as the son of John B. and Agnes (McPherson) Charles."

Sid's journalism career began at age seventeen, as a reporter on the *Portland* (Oregon) *Telegram*. His first publishing venture was in Medford, Oregon, where he started *The Southern Oregonian*. He then worked on a dozen newspapers between St. Louis and Tacoma.

He was on the *Tacoma Daily News* when McChesney tapped him for the Fairbanks post. Having to go north in midwinter, Charles left his wife and childen in Tacoma,. They joined him the following summer.

Charles's arrival in Alaska was the beginning of a fifty-five-year career as reporter, editor or publisher on Alaska newspapers. He is best known as founder of the *Ketchikan Daily News*.

In a series in the *Alaska Fishing News*, "Memoirs," Charles recalled in detail that trip to Fairbanks in February of 1904:

> Our trip to Valdez was made on the old *Santa Ana*. She was loaded to the guards with humans, horses, lumber and mingled smells.
>
> Valdez was a strange collection of people and outfits; everyone thought he was going places. Many of them never got beyond Thompson's Pass. There were man fights, dog fights, people dressed in all colors of the rainbow, dogs of all breeds, from the small Irish setter to the great St. Bernard, with malemutes and huskies predominating.
>
> The gambling halls were crowded, with the sky the limit, with the rattle of chips, the hum of talk and swearing and in between times the orchestra and dancing and singing and the inevitable dance hall girls – glamorous and otherwise.
>
> I went over the trail to Fairbanks with a mail carrier. It was Arctic twilight; frosted steam arose from men and dogs. The fine string of malemutes was eager to go. I was piled on top of the mail, wrapped in a fur robe, the carrier grabbed the handles of the sled in the rear, yelled "mush" and we were off in a swirl of flying frost and singing steel sled

runners. We went around several outfits. One was pulled by oxen, the idea being to slaughter them at trail's end.

At Copper River, Sid decided to remain a day or two and sent the mailman on ahead, deciding he'd hike the remaining distance to Fairbanks. He was warned that the roadhouses were sometimes forty miles apart. The first one, fortunately, was only twenty-two miles and his feet were sore and swollen when he arrived that night.

After nineteen days on the trail he arrived at Fairbanks.

Edward Miller, business manager of the *Tacoma Daily News*, wrote Judge Wickersham asking him to extend a hand of friendship to young Charles, describing him as "enterprising and ambitious. He goes to Alaska to win wealth and fame if that be possible," according to the *Wickersham Diaries*. It was an endorsement that came in handy later.

Brash Wall joins staff

McChesney hired Sam Wall, another Tacoma newsman, as city editor under Charles. Wall had won national laurels and was noted for his brash, adventurous personality. During his ten years in the editorial field in Tacoma, his exploits threatened his survival. Tacoma was a boomtown and there was bitter rivalry between the newspapers.

One day, after reading a spiteful article in a rival paper that he regarded as an attack upon his character, Wall pocketed a small-bore revolver, strode to the office of the competition, and shot the editor. Fortunately for all concerned, a piece of metal in the editor's cravat deflected the bullet and perhaps prevented a murder. In the scuffle to disarm Wall, the editor's assistant suffered a bullet wound. Wall was charged with assault but was never brought to trial. Most Tacomans thought he had taken the proper course in defense of his honor.

As an editor on the *San Francisco Call*, Wall pulled a stunt that won him national headlines. He received a letter from confidence men in New York who offered to sell $10,000 in money "like the real thing" for $500. Wall took the bait and impersonating a Rube, made the trip from San Francisco to New York.

He met the crooks at a cheap hotel. When everything was in readiness for the transfer of the spurious money, Wall suddenly flashed two guns and covered the men. He marched them downstairs and turned them over to the police, who had been searching for them for months.

Wall joined the Klondike stampede as a correspondent for the *San Francisco Call* in 1898, spending the winter of 1898-99 in Skagway. When he got to Dawson, he was so fascinated with the excitement of the area that he remained for two years as editor of the *Dawson Daily News*.

Wall arrived in Fairbanks in the spring of 1905 as a correspondent for the *San Francisco Chronicle* and again became so enamoured with the local scene that he accepted the city editor post at the *Fairbanks Evening News*.

Moran discovers Ark

The inimitable Casey Moran filled a reporter's slot on the *Evening News* between 1904 and 1907. Born Bernard B. Moran, Casey first showed up in Juneau in 1894 at age twenty-one. There are several versions of how he made a living while there, one being that he sold suspenders. But in reality – those were the days of prohibition in Alaska "except for medicinal purposes" – he sold liquor to anyone who would keep it a secret. He wore a loose-fitting coat and in the pockets he carried liquor bottles that supplemented, and probably exceeded, his suspender sales.

E. J. (Stroller) White, with whom Casey worked as a reporter in Dawson, told how Casey went into the ice business during his early days in Juneau. Casey noticed that the local saloons needed ice, so he borrowed a rowboat and went down the channel until he sighted an iceberg from which he chipped off a couple hundred pounds and returned to town. He borrowed a wheelbarrow and peddled the ice to the saloons for ten cents a pound.

In 1896, Casey joined a party of mail carriers who were leaving Juneau for Circle City and Fort Yukon. He was in Dawson when that camp opened and in 1900 he worked on the *Klondike Nugget*, where White also was a reporter. One winter morning, when the telegraph line had been down for a week and there had been no mail for almost a month, Casey set out to find a news story. The one he wrote brought him international fame.

He reported he encountered some Indians who told him about a wonderful house that was resting on a great mountain, three hundred days' walk from Dawson. It was a house bigger than any in Dawson and had at one time been used to float on the water. It was very large. It was very old.

Casey was reminded of the Bible story of Noah's ark so he took the Indians to his hotel room and showed them a picture of the ark in his Bible. They assured him that absolutely was the building they had seen resting in the Koyukuk Mountains. His story of the discovery of Noah's ark in the northland was a sensation.

He reported for the *News* for three years and then was appointed publicity director of the Alaska-Yukon-Pacific Exposition in Seattle. Later, he published *Moran's Weekly Alaskan* in Seattle.

In 1910, he advocated home rule for Alaskans in testimony before a congressional committee in Washington DC. That same year, he wrote a series of articles on Alaska for *Collier's Weekly*.

In 1914, he was in California promoting investments in Alaska oil wells, claiming his proposition was greater than anything thus far developed in Calgary, Canada. A man ahead of his time.

His son, also named Casey, also was a visionary and promoter. He was the marine pilot who pioneered bringing large cruise ships to Alaska after statehood.

McChesney, Young end war

Other literary talent McChesney recruited included Dr. S. Hall Young, the Presbyterian missionary known as "the mushing parson" because he traveled about establishing missions in Canada and Alaska. He had written for church publications at Wrangell and Sitka.

McChesney and Young became acquainted in Dawson so when Young spent the winter of 1904-05 in Fairbanks he agreed to write occasional editorials for the *News*.

Recalling those journalistic efforts, Dr. Young wrote in later years: "Together we managed the Russo-Japanese War and brought it to a successful conclusion."

Chapter 13

Thompson Starts His Miner

The luxury of having the Fairbanks newspaper field to himself ended for Bob McChesney shortly after he launched his *Fairbanks Evening News* in 1905. A controversy swirled around Judge James Wickersham because one of his rulings on mining was contrary to the wishes of some influential citizens. So they sought a journal to oppose the judge.

Wickersham had declared that an actual discovery of gold was necessary to stake a valid mining claim. And the discovery must be made within ninety days of staking the claim. This decision eliminated the "power of attorney" device whereby one individual could stake an unlimited number of claims on behalf of his friends without any assessment work being done on them.

Miners generally were dismayed by Wickersham's decision as they were accustomed to staking a whole creek, swearing that they had made discoveries and were holding it back from development.

Adding to that, Capt. E. T. Barnette was a major stockholder in the *Evening News*. So, when Judge Wickersham decided a claim dispute in Barnette's favor, the *News* came under severe attack. Capt. L. B. Anderson was the opposing claimant. Barnette and Anderson had been close friends until that decision.

Anderson was a native of Alabama, who in Judge Wickersham's opinion was "'po' white trash." He derived his "captain" title from supervising a railroad section gang in Texas.

Anderson had nothing when he arrived in Fairbanks and begged Barnette to help him get a job. The latter got a woodchopping job for him with the Northern Commercial Company and hired him to build a home. Barnette also pulled political strings to secure Anderson the job of road overseer. It was from that job's earnings that Anderson invested in mining claims on Dome Creek.

Anderson used the profits from his mining property to start a second newspaper to counteract the *News'* support of Wickersham. He organized the L. B. Anderson Publishing Company and started the weekly *Fairbanks Times* on September 3, 1905. It appeared thereafter on Sunday mornings, the one day that the *News* did not publish. James Wilbur Ward, recently from Dawson City, was editor and general manager.

Ward's only newspaper experience had been as a reporter for the *Dawson Daily News*. He and his father went to Dawson in 1899 when Jim was eighteen years old, moving from Grand Rapids, Michigan

The five-column, four-page *Times* took up the fight of the miners against Judge Wickersham. It became so popular that Ward was sent outside to buy equipment to make it into a daily.

During Ward's absence, Ted Needham, former Dawson, Juneau, Douglas and Wrangell newsman, and a *Times* stockholder, took charge. Fire struck in the spring of 1906, destroying the building and a portion of the equipment along with most of downtown Fairbanks. But the plant of the new Fairbanks Printing Company in the Riverside Hotel was saved so that the initial edition of the *Fairbanks Daily Times* could be produced the day after the fire. Thus was born from the great conflagration of May 22, 1906, Fairbanks' second daily paper. The older paper wasn't so lucky.

McChesney had sold his interest in the *Evening News* to Capt. Barnette just three days before the *News* plant went up in flames in that same community disaster. McChesney got $20,000 cash for his original $4,000 investment. The McChesneys became world travelers for the next two years.

The fire left Barnette and his fellow stockholders with only goodwill for their substantial purchase price. They put up another $20,000 to buy an old printing plant in Olympia, Washington, to restart the *News*.

Thompson starts third paper

It was at this point that William Fentress Thompson appeared on the scene. The forty-one-year-old Thompson had more than twenty years' experience in the newspaper business, the last five in Dawson. But whiskey and poker had taken its toll. His initials, "W. F.," evoked the nickname of "Wrong Font," a font being an assortment of type.

In May 1906, Thompson was walking the streets of Seattle, jobless, in debt, and twice divorced. He had been fired from his last editorial post in Dawson because his fiery editorials during a political campaign embarrassed the owners of the newspaper.

He was in a dejected mood when he met former Dawson colleagues, Los Bernard and E. S. Bunch, and Fairbanks businessman, Roy Brombaugh. All had just arrived from Fairbanks. They vowed that Fairbanks "was a new Klondike and greater than the old Klondike in every way, and that the man who could land there with a modern newspaper plant and fight Wickersham, as Thompson had fought the government leaders in Dawson, would get rich quick."

Impressed with their story, Thompson promoted a complete newspaper plant, including the cost of freighting it north, without investing a dollar of his own, of which he had none. Just before Thompson left Seattle for the north, E. W. Griffin, trading post operator at Chena, bought a half interest in Thompson's operation. J. Harmon Caskey, who had worked with Thompson on the *Dawson News*, offered to construct a building to house the newspaper plant.

Thompson arrived in Fairbanks in June 1906. His plant followed but not as ordered. The Mergenthaler Linotype machine had been destroyed in the San Francisco earthquake and an old typesetting machine from a defunct Seattle shop had been substituted, without the brass matrixes necessary to cast lines of type.

Despite this disappointing mechanical mix-up, Thompson found the spare parts and type he needed and launched a third daily paper in the little community of four thousand.

On August 8, 1906, seven thousand copies of Thompson's sixteen-page *Tanana Daily Miner* were distributed free throughout the area. The *Miner* and the *Times* were morning papers and the *News* continued to come out in the evening.

Thompson admitted later that launching a third daily was a bluff. He was confident that Barnette and his *News* would have to seek an alliance with the *Miner* if they were to survive. He was right. Barnette offered to consolidate his operation with the *Miner*.

Thompson news career starts early

Through the years, Thompson provided an autobiography in his column, "In Our Town," that described his career before he started Fairbanks' third daily. He was born in New York on June 11, 1865, the son of Will H. Thompson, an attorney. The family was active in the Church of Jesus Christ of Latter-day Saints. Although he was not a regular churchgoer as an adult, Thompson often quoted from the Mormon scriptures.

Thompson began "riding the rods" as a tramp printer at age eighteen. He edited the *Exposition Magazine* in New Orleans in the early 1880s. Then he worked on newspapers from Texas to Washington State. He started the *Des Moines News*, the *Steilacoom News*, the *Roslyn News* and the *Westport-On-The-Sea News* in Washington, all at the same time. One was a Democratic paper, another was Populist, and the others independent – not a Republican one in the lot. He had three libel suits on his hands at one time.

In 1895, Thompson moved to British Columbia where he published three different papers simultaneously – *The Nelson Daily Miner*, *The Trail Creek News* and a third one in Rossland.

Thompson heads north

Thompson was still married to his first wife when he joined the Klondike stampede in the fall of 1897. Accompanying the Thompsons north were her teenage son by a previous marriage, and the son's friend, Raleigh (Los) Bernard, who had been living in the Thompson home, and who went on to be a prominent Southeast Alaska journalist.

Choosing the Stikine River route to Dawson, the Thompson party got as far as Glenora, British Columbia, where freeze-up forced them to spend the winter. Thompson landed a job editing the *Glenora News*. Glenora was a town a few miles below Telegraph Creek, British Columbia, on the Stikine River. It was created for the start of a railroad north to Teslin Lake and the headwaters of the Yukon, and down the Stikine River Valley to Wrangell. The project was abandoned with completion of the competitive railroad out of Skagway to Whitehorse.

Editor J. H. McKeand of the *Stikeen River Journal* at Wrangell, described the *Glenora News* as "an extremely bright and spicy paper, and shows Thompson to be a man of mean ability."

Thompson and Bernard continued to Dawson in the spring while Mrs. Thompson and her son went back to Seattle. The Thompson family was reunited in the fall and spent the winter in Nelson, British Columbia, where Thompson managed the *Daily Miner*.

The following spring, the call of the north started Thompson on his way again. He got as far as Whitehorse when he ran out of money and wired Bernard for a loan.

In recalling the incident, Bernard said, "Thompson was apt to run out of money at any time. He had a proclivity for good whiskey and never lost his desire to chance a few dollars on the turn of a card."

During the next five years, Thompson led a frenetic career in Dawson journalism. First, he was editor and part owner of the *Yukon Morning Sun*, also known as the *Yukon Midnight Sun*. It was supposed to represent the provincial government. But under his editorship, political factionalism developed to the point that he was arrested several times for criminal libel, and once for inciting a riot. His marital relations deteriorated, ending in divorce and marriage to Maude Stone, the daughter of a successful miner.

After a honeymoon to New York, Thompson resumed the editorship of the *Yukon Sun*. After a bitter political campaign in which his candidate lost, he suspended publication of the *Sun* in January 1905 and joined his wife in southern California, vowing never to return to Dawson. They did return in March, however, and resumed publication of the *Sun*, until October when he was fired by his backers and landed – divorced again, out of work and dejected – in Seattle.

That was the spring of '06 when Thompson talked his way into support for a newspaper attempt in Fairbanks. The town's third daily, the *Tanana Daily Miner*, was born that August. He merged his *Miner* with Barnette's *Evening News* the next month, and still faced an uphill struggle against the financially stronger *Fairbanks Times*.

Chapter 14

Thompson Adds News to His Miner

Competition was tough for W. F. Thompson and his new daily because one of his two competitors, the *Times*, had installed a new Linotype and new press in July 1906, a month before Thompson's *Tanana Daily Miner* appeared.

The *Times* upgrade enabled it to increase its size and its circulation along the creeks, leaving the *Evening News* far behind. Also, some of the most prominent civic and political leaders of the region held stock in the *Times*. And Capt. L. B. Anderson's Dome Creek mines were producing well for him and his *Times*.

The *Times* published both daily and weekly editions, the latter being primarily for distribution in the outlying camps.

Charles starts newspaper

When Bob McChesney sold the *Evening News* to E. T. Barnette just before the May 1906 fire, editor Sid Charles was out of work. He took a job as "shovel stiff" at a mine near Manley Hot Springs, but by fall he was back in Fairbanks. He launched the weekly *Northern Light*, together with J. M. (Kirk) Latimer, from the *Skagway Alaskan*. The new newspaper, the first of about one-half dozen Charles would start over the next fifty years, quickly went through a succession of editors and owners in the highly competitive Fairbanks market.

Latimer left the paper after a couple of months and was succeeded by Roy Gratton Southworth, a native of Stockton, California, who mushed over the Dyea Trail in 1898 at age twenty-two. Southworth spent his first two years in Dawson City prospecting for gold. Then he became a printer's apprentice and worked on various newspapers before moving to Fairbanks in November 1906.

The chances for survival of another newspaper in Fairbanks appeared nil, particularly because its owners were endowed with more optimism than money but also because of its editorial crusades for social reform. In harmony with the national "muckraking press," the *Northern Light* charged that the *News* and the *Times* were spokesmen for corporate interests and predicted their early demise. That was not a popular viewpoint among the independent pioneers.

During its year-long existence, the *Northern Light* boasted a weekly printing of five hundred copies. It favored home rule and castigated both Judge James Wickersham and Gov. Wilford Hoggatt.

The *Northern Light* was sold in September 1907 to Dan H. Jonas, a local entrepreneur, who changed its name to *The Tanana Tribune*. E. Struthers Bunch, a Thompson acquaintance from Dawson, was hired as editor and general manager. Charles and Southworth moved over to the *Times*, the object of their editorial criticism a short time before, as reporters.

Thompson fired again

Meanwhile, Thompson merged his *Miner* into the *Evening News*, dropping the *Miner* title, and acquired three Mergenthaler Linotype machines to meet the *Times*' competition. His was the only straight union shop in the camp for a while, with the men working eight-hour shifts, earning $250 a month. Others shops followed the practice so Thompson is credited with beginning the practice of an eight-hour day in Interior Alaska. Nine and more hours a day had been the norm.

His *Evening News* was an eight-column daily with eight to sixteen pages, plus a twenty-four-page weekly.

The spring of 1907 found Thompson "invited to step out" of the editor's chair at the *Evening News* by his backers, mainly Barnett. The paper had acquired a $13,500 debt under Thompson's management. J. Wilbur Ward, former *Times* editor, took over the editorial reins and the name was changed to *Fairbanks Daily News*.

Nine months of Thompson's strident editorials criticizing prominent individuals and businesses cost the paper valuable advertisers. His greatest sin was to label the Northern Commercial Company "A Big Monopoly" just because it furnished "the light, water, power, heat, supplies, freight,

Fairbanks Daily Times

FAIRBANKS, ALASKA, WEDNESDAY JANUARY 9, 1907

DICTS EARLY RUSH TO TANANA

tions Are That Stages Will be
ed With Passengers From
Latter Part of This Month

GRIFFIN, CHIEF OF FISH CAMP TRIBE

Big Man of N. A. T. & T. Co. Installed in
Blanket-Tossing Ceremony---Hiyu
Potlatch Effects

PARISIAN VAN PLIES H

Claiming to Be Savun
Women Into Being
Plunges Knife I

Fairbanks Daily News

FAIRBANKS, ALASKA, WEDNESDAY, AUGUST 15, 1908

MES WICKERSHAM ELECTED DELEC

Incomplete Returns Show Him Leading Chilberg With More Than
1,000 Majority---Total of Votes Reported 8,107, With Many More
to Come---Cordova and Fairbanks Districts Only Ones Winner Did
Not Carry---Big Demonstration In Fairbanks Last Night.

Fairbanks Sunday Times

FAIRBANKS, ALASKA, JANUARY 27, 1908

EARTHQUAKE SCARE IN SOUTHERN SPAIN

Reported Yesterday Morning That the Southern Coast Had
Been Submerged---Avalanche at Romara.
Italy Shaken Again.

GRAND JURY THROWS LIBE

transportation, religion and society for the town, allowing the rest of the town to furnish the money therefore." Such a situation was intolerable to this "righter of wrongs" and he refused to tone down his editorial "straight talk."

Thompson admitted that there were too many newspapers in town for anyone to make a profit. As he put it, "with presses enough to print five thousand papers an hour, in a field that is fully covered by five hundred papers a day, there is no hope aside from the sheriff's sale or committal to the asylum."

Another pet peeve of Thompson's was Juneau's efforts to dominate the rest of the territory:

> The disreputable little town of Juneau is chronically afflicted with an idea of its importance that the remainder of the world cannot entertain, and its newspapers are every day "knocking" their betters, and peddling "the Juneau idea" of Alaska, which is that all there is to this great territory is Juneau.
>
> Why Juneau should ever have conceived such an idea of its importance is a matter that passes all human knowledge. It is about the most disreputable looking burg that can be found in Alaska. Its newspapers are the poorest newspapers in the territory. It is a measly little trading post that is mostly made up of saloons and dancehalls, which seem to be about its only industry. But for the Treadwell mines on Douglas Island, and the money the government dumps at Juneau, that town would starve.
>
> The *Record-Miner*, which is composed of all the poor parts of two of the poorest papers Juneau ever possessed, is especially jealous of Tom Cale, our member of Congress. Juneau possesses Governor Hoggatt, and his political pull dragged the decayed old capital of Alaska away from Sitka and to Juneau, and the Juneau idea is that no other man from Alaska must receive a press notice save Governor Hoggatt. Therefore, when Cale is spoken of favorably, which is oftener than is Governor Hoggatt, the Juneau *Record-Miner* rears up on its hind feet and brays.
>
> Some of these days, the people of Alaska will stick a pin in the Juneau bubble, and it will go up like a toy balloon.

After Thompson lost his job at the *News* for his fiery editorials and newspaper debt, he teamed up with his former Dawson colleague, George (Buck) Arbuckle, to again publish his *Tanana Miner* weekly in Chena.

Wickersham wins, newspapers lose

The three Fairbanks dailies played active roles in the 1908 delegate campaign. In June of that year, Henry Roden, Zack Hickman and Judson Harmon Caskey bought the *Daily News* from Thompson's backers. They did so with the understanding that the *Tribune* would merge with them. When that did not materialize, the trio became financially vulnerable to political donations and accepted the offer of John Corson, the Republican candidate, to buy a third interest in the paper. Corson hired veteran newsman Harry Steel to be his campaign manager and also to manage the *News*.

The owners of the *Times* were equally intent on defeating Wickersham. The Democratic Party subsidized the paper in order to elect John Ronan. Local attorney Tom Marquam, who had served as editor since June 1907, was replaced by Harry Steel's brother, Will, for the duration of the campaign.

The Tanana Tribune supported Wickersham, and when he was victorious, its owners expanded the paper into a daily on September 1, 1908. The financial "angels" of the *Times* and the *News* disappeared and advertising patronage declined. The Steel brothers departed for Cordova and the two papers faced an uncertain future.

The *Times* reorganized from within, turning management over to three of its department heads – Frederick Heilig, editorial; Arthur G. Bell, circulation and advertising; Roy Southworth, mechanical.

The *Fairbanks Daily News* suspended publication on March 18, 1909.

News-Miner is born

Thompson decided the time and events were right to return to Fairbanks and prove to his friends that he could make a success of a paper in that town. He persuaded a group of his cronies at the Tanana Club to finance his takeover of the defunct *News* plant, from which he had been fired two years before, and combine it with the *Tanana Miner* he was publishing at Chena. Thus four days after the *News* suspended, the *Fairbanks Daily News-Miner* appeared on March 22, 1909, and is still on the scene more than ninety-six years later.

The *News-Miner* was a crusading organ under Thompson's leadership, reaching emotional heights during political campaigns. It zealously attacked its enemies and defended its friends. Thompson was a political maverick – he was as apt to support a Republican as a Democrat or a Socialist.

The daily masthead proclaimed the paper's editorial guidelines: "Policy – uninterrupted progress; Politics – antigraft; Nationality – Arctic Brotherhood; Religion – Tanana."

Through the years, Thompson repeated annually his "Declaration of Faith" in how he ran a newspaper:

> The Greatest Good for the Greatest Number.
>
> The same identical consideration for Bridget O'Grady and the Captain's Lady.
>
> The same criticism for the Pauper and the Prince.
>
> Half-century of strenuous pioneer existence and consort with both basement and second-story workers has taught us that there is so much good in the worst of us and so much bad in the best of us, and
>
> Play the game, and to hell with the Opposition, wherever or whatever it may be In Our Town.

One of Thompson's first customers was Frank E. Becker, a local attorney who said he had a mammoth newspaper plant on its way in over the ice, but would like space in the *News-Miner* to inform the public of his proposed editorial goals. He said there were already so many papers in town that another could not hurt the situation much.

Thompson sold him one page on Mondays, which Becker titled *The Fairbanks Weekly Palladium & Local Regulator*. In the first edition of April 26, 1909, Becker proclaimed:

> We fling our banner to the breeze between the skirts of that great and fearless little palladium, the *News-Miner*, on

each Monday. We chose the name of *Fairbanks Palladium* because we don't know what it means and it certainly does sound fine. On second thought, we added that part about the *Local Regulator* 'cause that's our chief business. We're going to regulate all over the place. It's lots of fun and we do hope you will enjoy it.

Becker's journalistic enthusiasm apparently dissolved by fall. He next turned up as editor of Arbuckle's weekly *Iditarod Pioneer* where he remained for two years and then went Outside. He returned north in 1928 and was a reporter for the *Seward Gateway* when he suffered a heart attack and died at his desk in February 1931.

First joint operating agreement

By January 1910, the Fairbanks economy was reeling from the exodus of its residents to other gold strikes. The *Tribune* was absorbed by the *News-Miner* on January 8, 1910. Two days later, the *News-Miner* signed a contract with the *Times* to combine their plants. Both papers were printed in the *Times* plant; the editorial and news departments of the two papers remained independent of each other.

Despite the shrinking economy, three local printers launched a new weekly titled *The Alaska Citizen* on March 2, 1910. One was George Bellows, a co-founder of the original *Weekly Fairbanks News*; another was Jack Filbin, a Linotype operator on both the *News* and the *Times*; and the third was J. Harmon Caskey, who traveled to Fairbanks in 1906 with Thompson.

A year after its founding, the *Citizen* plant was wrecked by the spring flood in 1911 that inundated most of the low-lying business district along Chena Slough. But the paper recovered to become a principal competitor of the *News-Miner* for the next seven years.

Filbin, a native of Cleveland, Ohio, worked in Portland, Oregon, for several years before going to Dawson in 1899. He worked on the *Klondike Nugget* until he migrated to Fairbanks.

Caskey was born and reared in Ohio, where his maternal uncle, Judson Harmon, served two terms as governor and lost the Democratic nomination for the U.S. presidency to Woodrow Wilson in 1912.

Caskey had moved to Seattle in the late 1880s, where he established two newspapers. He went to Dawson with the Roediger-McIntyre party in 1899 and was general manager of the *Dawson Daily News*. In

Fairbanks, he had been elected chairman of Alaska's Fourth Division Democratic Committee. He promised that the *Citizen* would support Democrats in their bids for political office.

In the 1910 delegate race, four Fairbanks papers – the *Times*, the *News-Miner*, the *Citizen* and the *Miners' Union Bulletin* – opposed the re-election of Wickersham so his friend, Ward, started the *Tanana Daily Star* in support of Wickersham's candidacy. The $5,000 required to put the plant into operation allegedly came from a group of Valdez leaders, headed by O. P. Hubbard, an attorney who was trying to get a government subsidy for a railroad from Valdez to Fairbanks. The *Star* was published from July 1 to August 8, and then died a natural death.

Thompson takes a rest and a wife

By the fall of 1911, Thompson decided he needed a rest and departed on a six-month vacation, turning over the editorial reins of the *News-Miner* to O. P. Gaustad, a successful local mine operator, who had published a newspaper in North Dakota before moving to Alaska. Thompson sold him some of his newspaper stock in order to finance his vacation.

En route through Skagway, Thompson told a reporter he was going to Europe for six months. But a visit to his sister, Mrs. Edmund G. Tennant, in Yakima, Washington, changed all of those plans. It was there that he married Nellie Mulrooney Noble, his third wife, on November 2, 1911. He had known the Mulrooney family in both Dawson and Fairbanks.

After a honeymoon to the East Coast, Thompson and his bride arrived in Fairbanks in February 1912. This marriage changed Thompson's whole attitude toward life. He became a devoted husband and father. Nothing was too good for his family and his two sons, William Fentress and Harry Richard, and daughter, Beulah Marian, even if it meant going into debt to buy them luxuries.

The Fairbanks economy was at a low ebb in 1912. Gold mining was in a slump. Low prices, government neglect and prohibitive transportation costs dealt what seemed a death blow to the industry. The town's population, which once had reached twenty thousand, had dwindled to 1,200, and property was almost valueless.

Nevertheless, the *News-Miner* predicted growth and prosperity. In 1912, Alaska had changed from a district to a territory with its own legislature. Congress passed legislation in 1912 directing the president to investigate feasible railroad routes from tidewater to the Interior.

Remittance man enters the field

The 1912 elections were a boon to the struggling journalists. Political campaigns meant a boost in the newspapers' revenues as competing candidates sought editorial support through financial donations – advertising.

Wickersham was at a disadvantage under these circumstances because he was a political maverick, not a recipient of organized party funds that could be funneled to the media.

The *Daily News-Miner* supported Nome attorney William Gilmore, the regular Republican candidate for delegate to Congress; the *Daily Times* favored Juneau attorney Bob Jennings, the Democratic machine candidate; and the weekly *Citizen* promoted Martin Harrais, a Tanana Valley miner also running on the Democratic ticket. Delegate Wickersham was running as a Teddy Roosevelt "Bull Moose" Republican and no local paper supported his successful re-election.

The Socialist Party headquarters in Chicago sent professional organizers to the Tanana Valley to campaign for Ketchikan attorney Kazis Krauczunas, the Socialist candidate. The Socialist Labor Party was actively recruiting members in the mining camps, where there was a preponderance of alien labor.

A new editorial voice joined the already loud journalistic chorus, when Louis Klopsch, the son of the publishers of the *Christian Herald* magazine of New York City, launched the daily *Alaskan World* on May 23, 1912. He had mushed into town over the Circle trail the previous November and worked awhile as a reporter on the *News-Miner*.

Klopsch's *Alaskan World* lasted for only seven issues and he was back on the street looking for a job. Then on August 27, 1913, he started a weekly titled *The Fairbanks Facts*. In his salutatory he promised "to attack from time to time the public character of prominent men in order to keep the public informed as to the inner workings of certain 'higher ups.'"

Local meat merchants were the targets of his first expose. He charged them with selling cholera-infected hogs. The grand jury indicted them but they were not prosecuted.

Klopsch's fearless efforts to reveal the truth subjected him to unpleasant consequences. When he accused U.S. District Court Judge Frederick Fuller of mishandling the Washington-Alaska bank failure case in Fairbanks, he was arrested for contempt of court. Four of the town's top attorneys – Tom McGowan, Tom Marquam, Mort Stevens and Louis Pratt – defended him without charge, such was the general feeling in Fairbanks about the bank case.

During the course of the trial, the courtroom was packed with Klopsch's sympathizers – after all, 1,400 Fairbanks people had lost their savings in the bank closure. When the guilty verdict was read, the bailiffs cleared the courtroom quickly in order to prevent a demonstration. Klopsch was sentenced to six months in jail and fined $300, which meant the demise of his *Fairbanks Facts*.

Klopsch acquires, kills Times

Two years later, Klopsch's mother sent him enough money to buy Southworth's interest in the *Fairbanks Daily Times*. Southworth's former partners Bell and Heilig had sold out earlier. So Klopsch became sole operator the *Times*.

Klopsch's initial editorial reflected unusual self-restraint:

> If there is anything we hate it is a coward, but if there is anything we hate more it is a meddling fool. An editor, like every other man, should face courageously the work set out for him, but he should not get into the habit of hatching troubles for himself. It is not his job to reform the world, nor is he to be a scapegoat for all sinners and cranks of the community.
>
> A newspaper should not take itself too seriously, carry a chip on its shoulder, a knife up its sleeve, or dignity in its heels; but it should be self-respecting and speak, if it speaks at all, with authority.

He published an eight-page daily seven days a week in addition to a *Weekly Times*. He obtained exclusive rights to United Press reports in Interior Alaska. He subscribed to a special feature service from the American Press Association and had his own Seattle correspondent.

Despite these improved services, the market could not support two dailies and the *Times* suspended publication on September 30,

1916 when former owner Southworth foreclosed on his mortgage for lack of payments.

Henry back, boosts Socialists

The cause of socialism got a boost with the arrival of George Hinton Henry, of *Yukon Press* fame, in the fall of 1913. For years, Henry beat the socialist drum with vigor, between his frequent incarcerations on charges of criminal libel.

His weekly organ started as *The Free Press* and later changed to *The Socialist Press* and still later resumed its original title. He was expelled from the Fairbanks Socialist Club when he made unflattering comments about Socialist candidates.

Usually Henry was acquitted of the criminal libel charges because the complaining witnesses were of such dubious reputation that the editor could do little to worsen them.

In one instance, the father of a fourteen-year-old girl, who had testified as a victim in a series of rape cases, charged that the editor of *The Socialist Press* had reflected badly upon his daughter's character. Henry had reported how the girl had accosted a man in the district attorney's office, during one of the rape trials, and promised she would not tell on him. After an hour's deliberation, the jury acquitted the editor.

But, as Henry's addiction to booze worsened, his supporters deserted him. Editor Caskey of the *Alaska Citizen* called him "a travesty on the name of newspaper editor." In an editorial titled "Rottenness Personified" Caskey recommended him for a tar and feather party:

> This creature is the living personification of the rottenest conglomeration of filthy material that it would seem possible to stuff around the framework of a human being, normal or abnormal. The "thing" needs a bath badly. Not an ordinary soap and water bath, but one made up of special ingredients such as are usually used to cure festering sores on dumb brutes or on the human race.
>
> The remedy which has been suggested is the liberal application of a plentiful amount of tar heated to the right temperature and applied by hands willing and able. If the unusual treatment is fatiguing to him, a bed of feathers

might be added that he may obtain a muchly needed rest and give decent citizens the long sought opportunity of ridding themselves of a public nuisance.

Henry made his exit from Alaska journalism in June 1918 when he received a one-year sentence in a federal jail for writing a letter to the U.S. Attorney General during World War I charging that the local U.S. district attorney's associates were all pro-German.

With the death of the *Times* in 1916 and the death of the socialist and union press, Thompson's *News-Miner* and the *Daily Alaska Citizen* had the promising Fairbanks market to fight over, which they did for the next four years. It was a promising market with the new college campus and the prospects of a railroad connection to saltwater at Seward.

Chapter 15

Thompson's N-M to Lathrop

The W. F. Thompson family spent the winter of 1915-16 in the States. Ole Peter Gaustad, a Cleary Creek mine operator, took charge of the *Fairbanks Daily News-Miner* just as he had when Thompson went on vacation previously. Gaustad also operated a sawmill, a bank, and a twelve-mile railway at Cleary Creek.

Thompson fights feds, wins

Thompson made national headlines during his vacation, with a story of how he saved an Alaska railroad owner from having to pay a $100,000 fine levied by the federal government. The story illustrated the extent to which government red tape could harass anyone trying to develop anything in Alaska.

The Interstate Commerce Commission informed Falcon Joslyn, president of the forty-five-mile Tanana Valley Railway running between Chena and the nearby gold camps, that he must pay $100,000 in fines and spend 363 days in jail. Joslyn went to Thompson for help. The editor wrote his friend, Franklin K. Lane, chairman of the commission, describing the silliness of the agency's regulations:

> Dear Frank: When you and I used to work together on the old *Tacoma News*, a generation and more ago, you used to be a good fellow, but today you are not, and if you don't change your system something bad is apt to happen to you.

For instance, you threaten to put our little railway out of business unless it hauls dynamite ten car-lengths from the engine. In the first place, the blamed railway hasn't ten cars and in the second place it hasn't an engine that could haul ten cars if it had them.

The only way they can comply with your demands is to hitch the car of dynamite unto the engine with a ten-car-length of rope. Do you care to be responsible for what happens to the engine and the crew thereof when the train starts down hill?

He went on to explain how the dinky little narrow-gauge railway was financially bankrupt and was not equipped to comply with regulations applicable to stateside railroads. Three weeks later, Lane replied assuring both him and Joslyn that the commission would make no more trouble for the little railway.

In due time, Congress remitted the $100-a-mile tax it charged on all Alaska railroads "for all time to come," according to the October 31, 1915, *Valdez Miner*.

Thompson fights Caskey

When Thompson returned to Fairbanks, he and Harmon Caskey of the *Citizen* resumed their editorial feuding. Thompson had Caskey arrested on a charge of criminal libel. Caskey had accused Thompson of resorting to blackmail while collecting funds for construction of a local armory and getting "a good commission from the deal." When the case went to trial, both gentlemen were exonerated and the charges dismissed.

When asked why he had taken Caskey to court, Thompson said he wanted to show up the "gossips and slanderers in this community to whom Caskey had mistakenly listened." He was hurt to think his longtime colleague and Klondike peer would believe such malicious gossip.

He recalled that nineteen years earlier he had hustled transportation to take Caskey and seven other newsmen from Seattle to Dawson City. The two of them worked in the same shop or in the same town for seventeen years.

"I don't believe he (Caskey) would deliberately try to hurt me; outmaneuver me in the paper business, yes," Thompson was quoted in the August 17, 1917, *News-Miner*.

Thompson excelled in a common journalistic practice of his day of leading telegraphic news dispatches with multidecked headlines. Always short of cash, editors could afford only abbreviated dispatches so they would embellish them with sensational headings, sometimes designing pyramids eight lines deep. Headlines also were cheaper to typeset and took up space more quickly in a column than setting regular text. The following examples illustrate Thompson's innovative presentation:

HIS TUMMY IS HURTING HIM

Pres. Wilson Suffering from Troubles in the Interior
and is Denying All Visitors An Audience

HE EATS TOO MUCH

The Rich Foods of the People in High Places Are Not
the Kind for a Straight Presbyterian Stomach

Washington, D.C. – Suffering from indigestion, Pres. Wilson today adjourned the regular Friday cabinet meeting and returned to the White House where he is denying himself to all callers

* * *

MAJOR STRONG HOGTIES A CINCH

President Today Intimated That He Will Name the
Juneau Newspaperman as Governor Very Soon

"JUST FLOP ALONG" Wins

He Ought to Know Alaska, and Should Make a Good Governor If He Does Make a Good Governor

Washington, D.C. – Pres. Wilson intimated today that within a few days he would name Major J. F. A. Strong of Juneau as governor of Alaska.

"Just Flop Along" was a nickname for J. F. A. Strong, sometimes called "Major."

One famous headline was attributed to Thompson – "Jerked to Jesus." He disclaimed authorship in these words:

> We have no recollection of anything like that ever happening in this paper. It is copyrighted by Willie Semple, who presided over the destinies of a newspaper in Dawson in the early days.
>
> The writer does not remember a time when he ever sent a murderer along to The Perfect Judge in any heading in his paper via the jerking route.

Then he went on to describe the one and only hanging he attended in Dawson:

> O'Brien, the Clayson murderer who murdered wholesalely in the Yukon country and paid the penalty therefor, is the first and last man we ever saw hanged. We were with him in his cell the night before his hanging and at his request walked with him to the scaffold, he being of the opinion that our paper was the only one on earth which had given him a square deal through his trial.

He died gamely but his last words were addressed to Jesus. He called down the Blessing of the Virgin Mary upon the *Yukon Sun*, our paper, and the Curse of Christ upon the *Dawson News* and the *Klondike Nugget* – the *Yukon Sun* died first.

Thompson was vociferous on the subject of prohibition. As a reformed alcoholic, Thompson sympathized with those lacking the willpower to abstain from the stuff. Caskey enjoyed needling Thompson about his bifurcation on the subject.

Stroller White of the *Douglas Island News*, a prohibitionist, said he had personal knowledge that Thompson was employed by the California Liquor Dealers' Association to write articles opposing prohibition. Mrs. Cordelia Hatcher, the Women's Christian Temperance Union campaigner in Alaska, said she understood that $3,500 was the price paid by the liquor dealers for the efforts of Thompson's pen.

Thompson's contradictory viewpoints on the pending prohibition referendum was revealed in his editorials:

> We cannot "drink or let it alone" as some men can. Drinking with us makes of us a periodical drunkard. We have tended bar and sold gallons of liquor, and drank almost as much as we have sold; we have taken the Keeley Cure twice and have been treated for excessive drinking probably a hundred times. It is a condition that no man of family or right impulses cares to endure, and no man or men ever were more sincere in their hope that they have touched, tasted and handled the drink which intoxicates for the last time than we are today.
>
> Yet, Alaska would suffer more than twice as much under prohibition as any state in the Union as about all the loose money we have for schools, charities and public improvements come from the liquor traffic, therefore I am opposed to it (the prohibition referendum).

Caskey burned out

Caskey's *Citizen*, the *News-Miner*'s competition, became a seven-day-a-week paper in September 1916. It had the sole franchise to The Associated Press news service for the Fairbanks area. During the winter months the paper shrank in size and became a twice-weekly publication.

On January 30, 1920, a fire started in the composing room of the *Citizen* and destroyed the plant, a loss of about $60,000 with little insurance. The Caskeys' apartment was above the plant.

The Caskeys left Alaska, spending the remainder of their lives in the Los Angeles area where he edited the *Seal Beach Post*, the *Belvedere Citizen*, the *Venice Vanguard*, and the *San Clemente Herald*. The end of the trail for that Klondike stampeder came May 19, 1937, in Los Angeles.

Following the demise of the *Citizen*, the *News-Miner* had the field to itself for the next fifteen years.

In 1921, the *News-Miner*'s circulation was down to 241 paid subscribers in the Fairbanks area and an additional 154 in street sales and out-of-town subscribers. Times were tough in Fairbanks. Though it had survived its competition, the *News-Miner* barely made ends meet.

Sometimes, instead of giving his employees their salaries in cash, Thompson gave them outstanding accounts to collect and apply to the salaries owed them.

Still clinging to dreams of better days to come with the completion of the government railroad, Thompson persisted in putting out a daily, contending that it would be a terrific blow to the people's civic pride if they were obliged to accept a weekly in the place of a daily newspaper. When the first train arrived from Seward on June 15, 1923, the townsfolk took a new lease on life.

An historic event transpired in the *News-Miner*'s plant on July 16, 1923. The President of the United States, Warren G. Harding, walked in, sat himself down at a typecase and proceeded to set a line of 36 Alternate Gothic: "W. G. H." The printers presented him with a solid gold makeup rule.

Harding had been publisher of the Marion, Ohio, *Star* before going to Washington DC. He bought the *Star* as a weekly. While he dabbled in politics, his wife Florence turned the *Star* into a profitable daily in a manner many women have been successful in publishing or in co-publishing Alaska newspapers.

The *News-Miner* put out a sixteen-page special edition celebrating the president's Fairbanks visit.

Thompson invests in aviation

Although newspapering was his first love, Thompson was fascinated with the potential of developing the territory through aviation. He and his banker friend, Dick Wood, organized the first aviation company in Fairbanks in 1924, and helped Carl Ben Eielson, a local schoolteacher, become one of Alaska's first bush pilots.

Thompson was one of Eielson's first passengers when he flew off of Week's Field in his OX-5-powered Jenny for which he charged $25 a ride. Thompson then hired the aircraft to deliver newspapers to outlying camps, the first such newspaper delivery and a method that was to become common in the next seventy-five years. That Jenny is on display in the terminal of Fairbanks International Airport.

Also in 1924, Thompson made an unsuccessful bid for a seat in the territorial Senate, as an Independent candidate. Then his failing health forced him to take a four-month vacation in the States.

He was back in Fairbanks in early 1925 to lobby strongly for using an aircraft to take serum from Nenana to Nome to combat the diphtheria epidemic. He reminded readers and public officials he knew exactly where there was an airplane in Fairbanks, stored in a barn with its wings folded until summer weather. The dog teams beat out the airplane for the last time in Alaska history.

Thompson's trail ends

The town's failing economy weighed heavily on Thompson's well-being. He reduced his paper to a triweekly and sometimes a semiweekly as his advertisers curtailed their patronage. He "roasted" the merchants for adopting an "every man for himself" attitude, predicting dire consequences for the town.

On January 22, 1926, Thompson collapsed at his desk, the victim of pneumonia. He was taken to the hospital. Two days later, the Klondike veteran was dead at age sixty-two.

Fairbanksans packed the Eagles' Hall for the funeral. Many stood outside in below-freezing temperature to pay tribute to their longtime editor-publisher. All government offices, private businesses, the public school and the college closed their doors on the afternoon of his funeral. The Pioneers' Igloo conducted memorial services. Thompson was buried in the Clay Street cemetery. Only Douglas publisher Charles Hopp, among other Alaska publishers, has been so honored by his community upon his death.

Thompson's city editor, Hjalmar Nordale, eulogized his mentor in the following editorial:

> W. F. Thompson was a fighter, a soldier of fortune with a pen in his hand. He had no fear and he knew no quarter – his battlefields were wherever chance or fate landed him. May it be said that when his battles were won his thoughts were sympathetic; the purpose accomplished, the cause was dropped.
>
> Children claimed his deepest interest, for his was the heart of a child.
>
> Picture the man as you may remember him. Immaculately dressed in street attire, head tilted back and shoulders squared, his measured tread always paced with a cane. No matter whether shoulders were weighted with care or feet weary, the posture and tread were always the same. Even in the shadow of death there was work to be done that caused him to steal from his bed and return to his desk. His was an unbroken will.
>
> Thompson was tall and slender with a thick shock of gray hair which more often than not, hung down over his forehead while he concentrated on his work. He had a close-cropped gray beard and invariably wore glasses over his sharp and discerning eyes. He was slightly deaf and used this to ignore that which he considered not worth listening to.
>
> He was always immaculately dressed, generally in gray herringbone tweed with vest. He wore the high "hard-boiled" collars of his day, with a tie and large diamond stickpin. His shirts were pin-striped almost always. When he discarded his suit coat to go to work at his desk or in the composing room, he pulled over his cuffs and sleeves the long black "sleeve protectors" which clerks of that era favored. He had a black ribbon watch fob with the gold initials "WFT" in flowing script at least an inch high. His shoes were always polished, summer or winter, rain or shine.

In the summer he wore a black or gray hat and matching topcoat. In the winter he exchanged these for a coonskin coat and marten fur cap.

He walked with a slight limp and always with a black, silver-mounted cane. In those days, when traffic was almost nil on Cushman, the office staff always knew when "WF" was approaching by the "tap, tap, tap" of his cane on the board sidewalks.

Thompson invariably arrived at the office about eight and after a walk about the shop, sat down to his typewriter. A steady stream of copy poured forth, most of it conceived in his fertile brain. At 2 o'clock he left his typewriter, read the galley proofs and came into the composing room where he "made up" the front page and perhaps more of that day's paper. He often "hand-spiked" one or more display heads, making up the words as he went along.

He was blessed with a real sense of humor as well as an acid wit and often turned a joke on himself if the occasion warranted. I recall that after working long and hard on a special Shriners' Edition, he donned one of the cone-shaped green electric lamp shades then in vogue and sat in his office to receive his red-fezzed visitors.

Like many gifted individuals, Thompson had little regard for the value of money and his business suffered as a result. Toward the end of his career, the *News-Miner* was on a strictly cash-on-the-barrelhead policy as far as the supply houses were concerned. I remember it was a common practice for him to write out a check, send me to the bank with it, where the cashier issued a release for a single bundle of newsprint which I then picked up from the warehouse – just enough paper for that day's edition.

Mrs. Thompson continued to publish the paper with Nordale as managing editor. Nordale had been Thompson's assistant, beginning as a roving reporter in 1919.

Nordale had difficulty keeping the paper afloat after Thompson's passing because it was deep in debt and the Thompson family depended upon it financially.

Mrs. Thompson sold the paper in November 1929 to Austin E. (Cap) Lathrop, and then moved to Seattle, where she died of cancer in November 1935.

Nordale, who had worked for Democrat Thompson, left after four months. The new owner had announced that the newspaper henceforth would be Republican-oriented.

Chapters 16-19

Journalists also Stampede

to Southeast

Before and After

Gold Rush

> *There is a legend prevalent in governmental circles at our national capital that Alaskans are a cantankerous lot . . . This idea can best be refuted by the sincere and general regret which will be caused by the death of (Governor) A. P. Swineford . . . . He left office with the respect and admiration of the people he was sent to rule.*
>
> – John W. Troy, editor
> *Daily Alaskan*, Skagway

First Publisher Governor—When Alfred P. Swineford, a Michigan publisher, was appointed Alaska's second governor in 1885, he took printing equipment with him to Sitka and started The Alaskan. Later, as a prospector, he started Ketchikan's first newspaper, the Mining Journal, in 1901.
-*Photo courtesy of Ketchikan Museums.*

Chapter 16

Stampeders, Swineford to Ketchikan

The Klondike, Nome and Fairbanks gold rushes are famous in Alaska history, 1897-1903. Juneau, Sitka and Wrangell earned fame earlier in the search for gold. Those mining stampedes – plus local prospecting – also built Ketchikan. It was the first city in Alaska visited by stampeders on their way north. That traffic provided an economic boost to a community that adopted the title "The First City."

The *Mining Journal*, Ketchikan's first newspaper, began publishing in January 1901. Its pages were a solid mass of type expounding the great potential of Alaska's mining industry, particularly in the Ketchikan district. Its editor-publisher, sixty-four-year-old A. P. Swineford, also former governor, was the first and most vociferous journalist advocating self-government for Alaska.

He waged uncompromising editorial warfare against the "bastard government with which Alaska was shackled." He made frequent trips to Washington and attended national conventions at his own expense to plead for full rights of American citizenship for Alaska's residents.

Early Ketchikan

In the early 1900s, Ketchikan was the busiest place in Alaska, barring only the town of Nome. Northbound stampeders stopped in Ketchikan to buy supplies. Disappointed prospectors stopped southbound and discovered deposits of copper, gold and silver on islands neighboring Ketchikan. A post office had been established in 1898. The city was incorporated two years later.

The first mines in the area were developed on Prince of Wales Island, within forty miles of Ketchikan. At one time before the First World War, twenty-one mines were active or being developed on Prince of Wales. A copper smelter operated at Hadley. In later years, marble and even uranium were mined on Prince of Wales.

By 1906, Ketchikan had a population of approximately 1,500 whites and two hundred Indians. As mining declined, salmon fishing became the major industry, earning for the town the slogan: "The Canned Salmon Capital of the World." Fourteen canneries operated in the area in the early 1930s.

When fishing wound down in the forties and fifties, the timber industry came to the rescue with the opening in 1954 of Ketchikan Pulp Company's mill at Ward Cove, six miles north of town. It closed in 1997 just as cruise ship traffic was increasing dramatically, bringing to town more than eight hundred thousand visitors a season.

Swineford first

Before Swineford came to Alaska, he had been publisher of the Marquette, Michigan, *Mining Journal*. He brought a printing plant north with him and started *The Alaskan* at Sitka in 1885.

When Grover Cleveland won a second term as U.S. President in 1893, Swineford hoped for reappointment as governor. But his journalistic crusade for self-government earned him powerful political enemies among nonresident owners of mining and fishing corporations, who opposed home rule for Alaskans.

He also alienated two prominent Presbyterian churchmen, Dr. Sheldon Jackson and John Brady. They opposed self-government for Alaskans and opposed Swineford's reappointment. Brady was appointed Alaska's fifth governor in July 1897.

As a consolation prize, Swineford was appointed Inspector General of Surveyors. He resigned from his federal job in December 1897, to devote all of his time to his Alaska mining operations. He also took time to write a travelogue entitled *Alaska, Its History, Climate and Natural Resources*. It was published by Rand, McNally & Co. in 1898.

His writing was flowery, the sentences long, as was common among journalists at the time. In describing the founding of Metlakatla he wrote in a fifty-four-word sentence:

Here, with appropriate speeches, song and prayer, the new settlement was inaugurated, the Native people there and then declaring allegiance to the starry emblem under which, for the first time, they were assembled and to which they accorded three as hearty cheers as ever came from the throats of the most loyal American assemblage.

Of Ketchikan, he wrote in two sentences that would never pass a current copy editor:

From Metlakahtla (sic) the steamer plows her way into Tongass Narrows, which is a narrow passageway between the islands of Gravina on the west and Revilla Gigedo (sic) on the east, stops at the village of Ketchikan, where there is a post office and a Native population of perhaps two or three hundred. Both the Presbyterian and Episcopal denominations have established missions and schools in the immediate vicinity of Ketchikan, while a few miles to the northward some of Mr. Duncan's people operate a steam saw-mill (sic), passing which, the steamer next calls at Loring, on Revilla Gigedo Island, where there is a salmon cannery post office and store, and in addition to the white residents, a Native settlement.

In 1900, Swineford was appointed recorder of the Ketchikan mining district, where he was a partner in copper and gold claims. It was not long before this veteran newsman was back in his second vocation, journalism. He persuaded George Riggins to move the plant of the defunct *Alaska Truth* from Juneau to Ketchikan, and the two established the *Mining Journal*, with Volume I, number 1, appearing on January 5, 1901. It was Ketchikan's first newspaper. It came out on Saturdays and sold for a dime.

Riggins returned to Juneau, after a month's stay in Ketchikan, to edit the *Juneau Journal*, and Swineford became editor-in-chief of the *Mining Journal*.

Swineford vs. 'Bastard Government'

Swineford's low esteem for Governor Brady was reflected in such references as: "his most exalted incompetency, the not altogether

A Ketchikan First

–Ex-Governor Alfred P. Swineford, right, stands outside the plant of the Ketchikan's first newspaper, The Mining Journal. Swineford started the newspaper in January 1901. This photo was taken in March 1904. *-Photo courtesy of Ketchikan Museums.*

ornamental figurehead of Alaska's bastard, ill-shapen and half-made-up civil government," and "his most excellent incompetency, who for some inscrutable reason Providence, through the instrumentality of President Roosevelt, retains as the figurehead of the bastard government begotten by Congress."

Brady aroused Swineford's wrath when he was quoted in stateside papers to the effect that the movement for a territorial form of government in Alaska was dead. Referring to the governor's "senseless twaddle, which was making him the laughing stock of all intelligent Alaskans," Swineford wrote:

> To what shall it be ascribed – ignorance or a natural impediment in veracity for which he cannot with propriety be held responsible?
>
> It is hardly to be supposed that the figurehead of the ship should have accurate information of what is really going on among the crew and passengers she carries, nor can a person immured in the solitude of the deserted village once known as the capital of Alaska be supposed to have any considerable knowledge of the general public sentiment of the district.
>
> Instead of being dead, the movement has but fairly been started.

No to statehood, ever

U.S. Sen. Charles H. Dietrich, R-Nebraska, sponsored legislation providing for an appointed commission to govern Alaska. One clause declared that the bill "shall not be understood as indicating the purpose of Congress ever to admit Alaska as a state."

Although President Theodore Roosevelt and Governor Brady testified in behalf of the bill, Swineford rallied his editorial forces and contributed to the defeat of the measure:

> The measure is totally monstrous and the *Mining Journal* does not hesitate to opine that if this bill is enacted into law, any Alaskan resident supporting it will deserve the scorn of all true Alaskans, and to be burned in effigy in every town and mining camp where there are a sufficient number of them to kindle the blaze.

Swineford, in a lengthy editorial in the *Mining Journal* of September 8, 1904, took on Judge James Wickersham for a speech in Fairbanks in which the judge threw out the following feeler for public reaction:

> It is intended, as in the case of the Philippines, that Alaska shall not be permanently annexed as an integral part of the United States.

In response, Swineford threw out his own feeler:

> Shall the people of Alaska be required to organize here a sovereign independent nation... shall the Republic of Alaska be divided into four or more states... Sitka, with its capital at Juneau; Alaska, with its capital at Valdez; Sumner, with its capital at Nome; and Tanana, with its capital at Fairbanks?

On April 1, 1905, Swineford and his partner, James (Jake) Rice, sold the *Mining Journal* to Walter S. Coutant and Walter A. Wyatt for $4,262 for the plant, lot and building, goodwill and subscription list. Swineford set up a law practice in Ketchikan and Rice went into the poultry business.

Seattle seeks to bury dissent

Coutant and Wyatt were financed by a Seattle group with interests in Alaska that opposed Swineford's crusade for self-government. One member of the group was a former U.S. district judge in Alaska, Melville C. Brown, who was practicing law in Seattle. Their strategy was to buy three leading newspapers in Alaska and drown out the self-government propaganda.

Colleagues mourned sixty-nine-year-old Swineford's retirement from active journalism when he sold to Coutant and Wyatt. Editor J. F. A. Strong of the *Nome Nugget* called him "the nester of Alaska newspapermen, whose forceful mind and vigorous style is needed in this stage of Alaska's development in its struggle for real freedom."

Editor John Troy of the *Skagway Alaskan* called him "the ablest writer in the north. The stoppage of his sledgehammer blows in the battle for right and justice will be sadly missed by a people struggling to secure the God-given right of self-government."

Editor Charles Hopp of the *Douglas Island News* wrote:

> As a writer he has no peer in the district. He wrote fearlessly and forcibly, and every sentence bore the stamp of wisdom and truth.
>
> His converts to his theory (self-government) are numbered by the thousands from Ketchikan to Nome. When the day comes that the right of self-government is granted to Alaska, the first act of the Legislature should be some fitting recognition of the man whose untiring efforts in the behalf of this much abused people opened the way for the light to shine in.

Such recognition never occurred.

Coutant, formerly of Laramie, Wyoming, had gone to Juneau in 1900 as private secretary and court reporter for Judge Brown. Brown's distinguished career included the chairmanships of both the Wyoming and Idaho constitutional conventions, membership in the Idaho Legislature, and mayor of Laramie, a town he helped organize. However, Brown's Alaska career was tarnished by charges of corruption, so President Roosevelt refused to nominate him for a second term.

When Judge Brown departed Alaska in 1904, Coutant became editor of the *Alaska Record-Miner* in Juneau. Then he moved to Ketchikan and the *Mining Journal* in 1905. He hired Richard Bushell on the sole qualification that Bushell and his wife were nondrinking printers.

What earthquake?

Bushell also was a good reporter. One day early in 1906, a salesman disembarked from a ship and asked, "Had we any late news on the San Francisco disaster?"

There was no cable or wireless into Ketchikan at that time so no one had heard about the great San Francisco earthquake and fire on April 18, a couple of days earlier. The salesman had heard an early news flash just before his ship left Juneau.

A group of Ketchikan business leaders assembled to discuss the news. They were worried because J. R. Heckman, the town's leading store owner, banker and cannery operator, was in San Francisco ordering supplies for the summer season. His wife and his foreman, Capt. Jimmie Sayles, were with him.

Ketchikan residents were so concerned they took up a collection and chartered a boat to take Bushell to Port Simpson, British Columbia, the closest cable station, to seek some news.

Bushell described his first trip through choppy waters in a small boat as unsettling. It took eight hours. But he got the information that the three from Ketchikan had survived the earthquake and fire. They lived in a tent, but were otherwise okay. They had to reorder their supplies before returning home. Bushell also obtained a Canadian Associated Press report on the disaster and returned to Ketchikan.

Bushell had written bulletins on his way home and hoped to post them in the Stedman Hotel lobby. But half of the town met him at the dock and insisted on an immediate verbal report. Several hoisted him up on an upended fish tierce (large wood barrel) for the report.

"I got so excited when I was telling them that I stomped harder than the tierce would stand, breaking the top. Down I went into it, but fortunately it was empty," he wrote in his memoirs.

Swineford the victim

A hot political issue early in the century was whether Alaska should have an official delegate in Congress. Affirmative bills had passed the U.S. House several times but were killed in the Senate, where Sen. Orville H. Platt, R-Connecticut, was serving his fifth term. He was committed to the "taxable interests" in Alaska and vowed he would never let it pass. He died in April 1905 and was succeeded as chairman of the judiciary committee by Sen. Clarence D. Clark, R-Wyoming, who was sympathetic to Alaska's needs.

The delegate bill passed both houses of Congress on May 7, 1906, and an election was scheduled in Alaska for August 16. The Democrats nominated Swineford as delegate. But a strong coalition of miners on the Seward Peninsula and in the Interior nominated Frank Waskey, a Nome miner and also a Democrat. Waskey was elected after a bitter campaign, but served only a year.

During the election campaign, Ketchikan's *Mining Journal* referred to Swineford, its founder and former owner, as "senile" and a "fanatic." That caused Skagway editor Troy to ascribe the "indecent assaults on Governor Swineford to Coutant's spirit of revenge for the governor's opposition to Judge Brown's reappointment."

Douglas editor Hopp called on Ketchikan residents to not "allow a remnant of that dethroned gang of carpetbaggers to slander a noble citizen who was devoting the last years of his life in an effort to benefit the condition of his fellow citizens."

When Coutant and Wyatt took over the paper, they announced that they planned to make it into a daily as soon as a cable was laid between Seattle and Ketchikan so they could receive daily world news dispatches. The first edition of the *Daily Miner* appeared on December 26, 1906.

It was the first daily newspaper in the Ketchikan mining district. Wyatt had left the paper. Bushell had taken a higher-paying job as paymaster at the copper mine and smelter at Hadley on Prince of Wales Island. That left Coutant as editor and proprietor. He continued the *Mining Journal* as the weekly edition of the *Daily Miner*.

Ketchikan was enjoying a healthy economy with a thriving year around mining industry. Coutant was relieved to have the newspaper field to himself, having come from Juneau where three dailies were fighting for survival. His good fortune ended when seven of the twelve local saloonkeepers withdrew their advertising.

The revolt was the result of a U.S. census giving Ketchikan a population of 1,260. The annual federal liquor license jumped from $500 to $1,000 when a town's population exceeded one thousand. When Coutant refused to give his editorial support to the saloonkeepers' claim that the town's population was under one thousand, they pulled their ads.

Saloonkeepers flex muscles

The liquor dealers formed a combine and raised $6,000 to start a second newspaper, with the elderly Swineford as editor. Swineford's son-in-law, Allen Shattuck, a Juneau insurance man and former journalist, shared in financing the venture. The initial edition of the *Ketchikan Mining News* appeared on January 18, 1907. It was a four-page weekly tabloid.

Two months later, Coutant sold the *Mining Journal* and the *Daily Miner* to Swineford's Ketchikan Printing Company and returned to Juneau.

Swineford suspended publication of the *Mining Journal* and merged the *Daily Miner* with the *Mining News*, changing the name to the *Ketchikan Miner*. It came out both as a daily and as a weekly by the same name. The weekly was devoted to a discussion of public affairs, while the daily covered telegraphic and local news.

Swineford's unswerving support for increased self-government caused him to cross swords with Gov. Wilford Hoggatt, Brady's successor, who declared that only "politicians, loafers and the saloon element favored territorial government, while the businessmen were all opposed to the plan."

Hoggatt's blatant attack on the concept of home rule made him so unpopular in Alaska that he spent most of his time in the States. When Secretary of Interior Richard Ballinger, a former Seattle mayor, ordered him to stay in Juneau, he tendered his resignation.

Failing health forced Swineford to relinquish his editorial duties in September 1908, whereupon he and his wife moved to Juneau to be near their daughter, Mrs. Allen Shattuck. Swineford died on October 26, 1909, at age seventy-three. That was a long life in an era when life expectancy was about fifty years. He was buried in Juneau's Evergreen Cemetery. But his daughter by his first wife had him reinterred a year later beside her mother in Park Cemetery, Marquette, Michigan

In an editorial obituary, titled "Alaska's Friend Is Gone," Skagway editor Troy wrote:

> There is a legend prevalent in governmental circles at our national capital that Alaskans are a cantankerous lot, that the general criticism directed at the carpetbaggers who are sent to rule us is not caused so much by the actions of those men as from the general cussedness of the people of Alaska. This idea can best be refuted by the sincere and general regret which will be caused by the death of A. P. Swineford.
>
> Swineford was governor of Alaska, but he left office with the respect and admiration of the people he was sent to rule, and had the people been enfranchised, Swineford would not have been succeeded when he was.
>
> While governor, Swineford fathered the territorial government idea by recommending it in his first report and he has always championed the cause of home rule in Alaska, advancing eloquent and cogent reasons why Alaska was entitled to political freedom.

The news 'fit to print'

W. C. Curtis was editor of the *Ketchikan Miner* after Swineford and until January 1909. During his tenure, a reader wrote asking if the paper always told the whole truth about a local event and Curtis answered in the negative, going on to explain why it was necessary to select "the news fit to print":

> If the newspapers publish half the stuff they hear there would be ten divorce suits to one now. There would be social ostracism of many who now shine in the "400." There would be shotgun matinees, lynching bees, hatchet parties, imprisonment, desolation and misery.
>
> An editor learns of nearly all the sin and hypocrisy of life, and it is a wonder he believes in man or woman, witch or devil, heaven or hell. Many people are continually finding fault with the newspapers when as a matter of fact they owe their very standing in the community to the editor's waste basket.

Saloonkeepers will drink to that.

Chapter 17

Customs Man Founds Sentinel

While Alaska's first professional journalist, A. P. Swineford, was founding Ketchikan's *Mining Journal*, a former deputy collector of customs at Sitka, A. V. R. Snyder, prepared to start the *Alaska Sentinel* in Wrangell. Snyder had previous newspaper experience in Oregon.

Under three flags

In 1834, Russia built a fort, Redoubt St. Dionysius, near the mouth of the Stikine River, which extends 330 miles into Canada, to prevent the British Hudson's Bay Company from encroaching on their fur trade with the Indians.

Wrangell and Wrangell Island in Southeast – not to be confused with Wrangell Island in the Russian Arctic – were named for Admiral Baron Ferdinand Petrovich von Wrangel. He was general manager (governor) of Russian America at the time. Some members of his family spelled their surname with one *l* and others with two *l*s. The spelling of both the island and the nearby river underwent changes through the years, ending with the official spelling being "Wrangell" and "Stikine."

When Russia leased its fort to the Hudson's Bay Company in 1839, the fort's name was changed to Fort Stikine. When the United States purchased Alaska, it became Fort Wrangel and a company of U.S. soldiers was stationed there for ten years. Wrangell residents boast that it is the only Alaska town to have existed under the flags of three different nations – Russia, Britain and the United States.

Others say four, counting the Tlingit Indians. But the dominant Indian village of the area, Kotzlitzna, was located thirteen miles south of Wrangell. It has been abandoned for many decades.

First gold rush in '74

A major gold stampede occurred in 1874 when strikes were made on creeks running through the Canadian Cassiar country northeast of Wrangell. The stampeders went by way of the Stikine River and the trail from Telegraph Creek to Dease Lake and to Teslin Lake. Hundreds of prospectors spent the summers on the creeks running into those lakes.

They returned to Wrangell for the winter. In the spring, they outfitted themselves and returned to their claims. An estimated thirty thousand prospectors used Wrangell as a transfer point and a total $5 million worth of gold was taken from the Cassiar Mountains over a twelve-year period, ten to twenty years before the Klondike stampede.

In 1898, some gold seekers reached the Klondike and Yukon gold fields via the Stikine to Teslin Lake, which drains into the Yukon River. The Teslin route avoided the arduous passes out of Dyea and Skagway. Wrangell boomed again from the '98 stampeded.

During the 1897-98 winters, an estimated five thousand adventurers disembarked from steamers at Wrangell. In the spring they took riverboats to the headwaters of the Stikine and mushed inland, heading for the Yukon country. The British Columbia government promised to build a wagon road and a railroad to Teslin Lake from Glenora, on the Stikine near Telegraph Creek.

During the optimistic winter of 1898, there was a newspaper at Glenora, the *Glenora News*. W. F. Thompson, who was on his way to Fairbanks to become a legend in Alaska journalism, ran it. Glenora became a ghost town after the competitive railroad was completed from Skagway to Whitehorse.

Despite the influence of early missionaries in Wrangell, former *Council City News* editor Jack Underwood wrote in his book, *Alaska: an Empire in the Making*, that "Wrangell in those days (1897-1899) was one of the most lawless towns I have ever seen, either in Alaska or anywhere else. A member of a noted family of Arizona outlaws acted as deputy U.S. marshal. Holdups were common occurrences. Many bullet-pierced bodies were found in the bay."

Years after the gold rush, Wrangell residents bragged that Wrangell was too tough for Colorado badman Jefferson R. (Soapy) Smith. He had stopped briefly but continued on to Skagway where he was shot.

Stikeen River Journal

Local merchants decided Wrangell needed a newspaper to publicize the advantages of the Stikine route to the gold fields, to compete with Haines, Dyea and Skagway. They pooled their resources and hired Ted Needham, a former Juneau-Douglas editor, who had spent the summer prospecting for gold on Admiralty Island south of Juneau.

Needham purchased the necessary equipment in Seattle. The initial issue of his *Stikeen River Journal* appeared on New Year's Day, 1898.

Needham recruited Angus G. McBride, a local attorney, as his associate editor. McBride had lost his bid for re-election as assistant prosecuting attorney for King County, Washington, so joined the Klondike stampede in the fall of 1897. He started too late to make it to Dawson before freeze-up and remained in Wrangell for the winter. He formed a law partnership with Willoughby Clark, who had the distinction of being the first of his profession to practice in Alaska.

Clark had married Georgiana Choquette, the daughter of Buck Choquette, who with Henri Thibert, staked the claims that started the 1874 Cassiar Gold Rush.

The *Journal* was a five-column, four-page weekly, printed on book paper. The merchants were generous advertisers. Weekly features included a directory of federal officials, lists of missing persons, and names of those for whom letters were waiting at the post office

Needham sold his interest in the *Journal* in July 1898, returning to Admiralty Island. McBride had already severed his connections. The stockholders hired T. G. "Tug" Wilson, formerly of the *Tacoma Globe*, and J. H. McKeand, a stampeder from Houghton, Michigan, to keep the paper operating. But by the fall of 1899 they decided it was hopeless and suspended publication.

Meanwhile, McBride had launched the weekly *Fort Wrangel News* on June 8, 1898. Associated with him was his brother-in-law, Charles A. Hopp, a printer from Oberlin, Kansas. Their wives were sisters. After four months, they, too, concluded that Wrangell was an unprofitable place for a newspaper. They moved their plant to the new boomtown of Douglas. Hopp became a popular Douglas publisher. McBride went on to the Klondike and Nome.

Wrangell was without a local newspaper for the next three years. The failure of the Canadian government to construct a railroad from Glenora to Teslin Lake changed Wrangell from a boomtown to a quiet, conservative community, unlike what Underwood experienced earlier. Its population dropped from three thousand to five hundred.

Sentinel for statehood early

Two newspapers appeared in Wrangell in the fall of 1902. The weekly *Wrangell Standard* appeared in September, with W. G. Beattie and Adolph Stark as editors and publishers. It was a four-page, tabloid. There are no known copies in existence and only a few issues were published, according to the September 26, 1902, *Skagway Alaskan*.

Snyder's weekly *Alaska Sentinel* appeared on November 20, 1902, and continues today as the *Wrangell Sentinel*, the oldest continuously published newspaper in Alaska.

Snyder had lived in Alaska for two years, serving as deputy collector of customs in Unga, Sitka and Wrangell. He was born in Illinois about 1850 and began his newspaper career at seventeen as an apprentice printer on the *Ogle* (Illinois) *County Reporter*. He moved to Oregon and was associated with newspapers in Yamhill and Polk counties before leaving for Alaska. He was married and had two grown sons and two daughters. His oldest son, George Curtis Lee Snyder, joined his parents in Wrangell.

The father and son put out a lively four-page weekly. It was brimming with ads and spirited editorials on local issues. Skagway's *Alaskan* welcomed its debut:

> Wrangell need no longer be conceived to be a historic graveyard, interesting only for the glamored memories of the Russian occupation, the Cassiarers, her interesting totem poles and weird rancheries. The *Sentinel* makes a splendid showing of live business advertisements and the job office is running a night and day shift to keep up with its orders

At first, Snyder disapproved of the pleas for self-government. But after a couple of years, he was ready to advocate full statehood for Alaska. He scorned the objection of Sen. Orville Platt, R-Connecticut, to Alaska having a delegate in Congress on the grounds that it might be an opening wedge to its being granted statehood.

Snyders outspoken

Snyder crusaded for laying a submarine cable from Ketchikan to Juneau via Wrangell and for dredging Dry Straits on the Stikine River flats so that steamers could avoid the rocks and reefs of Wrangell Narrows. He opposed Outside hiring of workers by the fish canneries, thus depriving Alaskans of a livelihood.

When Snyder was appointed U.S. commissioner for Wrangell in September 1905, he turned the paper over to his son. George followed in his father's footsteps writing forceful editorials. He criticized Gov. Wilford Hoggatt for opposing home rule, predicting that "the juggernaut of popular opinion" would crush the governor if he continued to oppose Alaskans being given their rights as free American citizens.

He wrote a scathing editorial condemning the governor for summoning the military from Fort William H. Seward at Haines to quell a strike at the Treadwell mines.

Hoggatt's response was to remove the senior Snyder from his post as U.S. commissioner, despite the latter's insistence that he had no control over the paper's editorial policies. Wrangell residents circulated a petition demanding Snyder's reinstatement, which was accomplished five months later.

Son George continued to deplore working conditions at the Treadwell mines. One day he met a husky Swede mine worker and called him a "Treadwell scab," whereupon the miner blacked both of George's eyes and cut a gash on his head.

The first fire in '06

The *Sentinel*, its building and much of its stock and equipment were destroyed when a fire swept the business district about four o'clock Saturday afternoon, March 24, 1906. The post office building, four stores, two hotels, some warehouses and homes were among the thirty-one buildings destroyed.

The Snyders were able to salvage enough printing equipment to distribute a weekly edition five days later, printed on butcher paper with red ink. The headlines: "Almost Entirely Destroyed." "Peaceful Little Village Visited by Fire."

It was inevitable that young Snyder's judgment and his bold stands stirred divided opinion among his subscribers. He insisted that his was a straight forward newspaper and not an "organ of a special interest," hence would not be swerved from its path.

"If a paper cannot live pursuing these lines," he said, "it had best die and die early."

When he exposed a man practicing medicine in Wrangell without a doctor's certificate, he called for federal legislation forbidding such practice. The following day, a score of businessmen withdrew their ads, declaring a boycott of the paper and threatening to start another paper.

Snyder announced on February 24, 1909, that he would be returning to his home in Salem, Oregon.

Bushell to rescue

Richard Bushell had worked in Ketchikan for the *Mining Journal* and in Juneau for the *Record* before going to Skagway to start *The Interloper* in 1908. He was in Juneau attending a political convention in 1909 when he met Wrangell businessmen John Grant and Peter McCormack. They guaranteed that Wrangell businessmen would buy $150 a month in advertising if Bushell took over the *Alaska Sentinel*.

It was a good deal, compared to his competitive situation in Skagway. He closed *The Interloper* and headed to Wrangell. The name was changed to *Wrangell Sentinel* when it first appeared on May 20, 1909, with Bushell as editor. The last issue of the *Alaska Sentinel* had appeared the week before. Bushell's editorials reflected his business supporters' sentiments; namely, pro-Hoggatt, anti-Wickersham, pro-mine operators, anti-self-government.

After two years in Wrangell, Bushell and his wife went back to Puget Sound to look for a newspaper.

The *Sentinel* was turned over to Harold F. Dawes. He had arrived from Chicago with his physician brother, Dr. Leonard P. Dawes. Harold had no previous newspaper experience and it showed in his news judgment, although he produced a livelier and more interesting paper than the conservative Bushell.

Dawes avoided controversial editorials but dug up local news items that attracted his readers even if he failed to research them to assure their validity. He revealed, for example, that through a clever diplomatic maneuver at the time the treaty of cession was signed between Russia and the United States that Natives affiliated with the Greek Catholic Church were granted the right to vote in Alaska elections. Alaska history researchers have found no reference of that. Also, there were no legal elections in Alaska until 1900, thirty-three years after the transfer of Alaska.

Dawes featured Indian lore, such as brief histories of the totem poles, for which Wrangell was famous. He told his readers that Dave King was the real name of Rex Beach, the famous author of Alaskan novels. However, *Who Was Who in America* and *Cyclopedia of American Biography* lists no other name for Beach or his parents.

Good times at Wrangell

Wrangell enjoyed a mini-boom in the early decades of the twentieth century. There were new gold strikes in the Cassiar and along the Stikine River. Vermont and San Francisco firms were developing marble quarries at Tokeen on nearby Prince of Wales Island. The area's timber resources were attracting sawmill men and commercial fishing looked promising.

Dawes sold the *Sentinel* back to Bushell on May 15, 1913, and began chartering boats. Bushell induced Needham to return north from Goldfields, Nevada, to run the paper.

During Needham's fifteen-year absence from Wrangell, he had been pursuing a dual career of prospector and journalist, with mining gaining top priority. Hence, it was no surprise that, when he began writing stories about the exciting new gold strikes in the Cassiar that he convinced himself that he should head for the hills.

Bushell replaced Needham with Paul Stanhope, who had been a printer on the *Sentinel* previously and was Bushell's associate editor on the *Ketchikan Miner* the previous two years. The Bushells had been attracted back to Ketchikan from Puget Sound by J. R. Heckman to take over the *Miner*. The paper had gone downhill during the illness of Swineford and after his death.

The twenty-one-year-old Stanhope, a native of Green Forest, Arkansas, was so happy to get back to Wrangell that he immediately accepted Bushell's offer to sell the paper to him.

Stanhope found himself a lone voice crying in the wilderness among Southeastern editors when he voiced support for the reelection of James Wickersham and for immediate statehood for Alaska:

> This country is now knocking at the doors of Congress for full and complete statehood. No half measures will do. It demands the right to regulate its own affairs. The issue is one that cannot be sidetracked nor can the people be fooled. Statehood or nothing is the persistent, insistent Alaska cry.

Stanhope put out an attractive paper – graphic art illustrations, bold, black headlines, syndicated features, and good coverage of local happenings.

Stanhope also served as city clerk. After three years, though, he sought wider horizons for his family. He sold the paper to Jim Pritchett, mechanical foreman of Skagway's *Alaskan*, whose sister taught school in Wrangell.

The Stanhopes moved to the state of Washington. They spent the next two years working on the *Aberdeen Herald*, the *Bremerton News* and operating their own paper briefly, the *Cosmopolis Times*. They returned north to a Ketchikan newspaper job, where Paul died at age twenty-six in the 1918 influenza epidemic, leaving a widow and two children.

Editor Prichett also clerk, mayor

James Wesley Pritchett was born in Fayette, Alabama, on December 28, 1878, the son of a Confederate Army officer. His father died when Pritchett was still a young lad, so he had to quit school to help support his mother and sister. He learned the printing trade and worked on newspapers along the Mexican border and in Guadalajara, Mexico.

He headed north in 1914 to be near his sister. He worked on Skagway's *Alaskan* and made occasional visits to his sister. In taking over the *Sentinel* on September 30, 1916, he said he did so "with a slight trembling of the knees, but with great pleasure at the opportunity."

According to one of his employees, "the man with the green eyeshade was a gentleman. He had a quiet and fine sense of humor that all who knew him appreciated. He could be exasperated but never driven to using bad language. He would, instead, stamp about the shop doing his work and singing at the top of his lungs, 'Nearer, My God to Thee.' That seemed to be a relief to him."

He married Mrs. Sarah Eleanor Edmunson, the principal of the Native school in Wrangell on July 18, 1918. She and her teenage son, Robert, had arrived in Alaska in September 1912.

Jim Pritchett was Wrangell's town clerk for many years and served as mayor from 1919 to 1923, being on hand to greet President Warren G. Harding when Harding visited in the summer of 1923.

Pritchett was a good public citizen during his fourteen years in Wrangell but his paper changed from a lively, interesting organ into a dull one. The six-column, four-page, folio resembled a bulletin board.

Cable news was presented like a laundry list. The pages were a solid mass of tiny print, with no story captions. Local news was limited almost totally to arrivals and departures on steamers. Editorials were usually "boiler plate" from feature services. When he did comment on local issues, it was in a whining, peevish voice.

He did modernize the plant, replacing the handset type with a Linotype. The job and news presses were soon driven by electric motors, abandoning the Pelton water wheel.

Wrangell's economy blossomed during the 1920s as gold strikes continued in the Cassiar region, resulting in lively riverboat traffic between Wrangell and Telegraph Creek.

Wrangell Lumber & Power Company built the largest sawmill in the territory. Lumber was shipped as far as the East Coast. A lot of lumber went into wooden boxes for shipping the summer's canned salmon pack.

Pritchett was stricken with liver disease in the spring of 1929. After a month's stay in the local hospital, he went to New York City for treatment. He made a partial recovery but fell acutely ill a year later. He was aboard a southbound ship, en route to New York again, when his condition worsened and his nurse had him admitted to a hospital in Vancouver, British Columbia. He died there on September 8, 1930. Mrs. Pritchett had reluctantly remained in Wrangell to run the paper.

Funeral services and burial were in Boise, Idaho.

Woman publisher for Wrangell

Mrs. Pritchett remained in Idaho for six months, leasing the *Sentinel* to a young bachelor, Linden B. Pentz. She resumed management of the paper in April 1931 as the only woman editor-publisher in Alaska at the time. She held that post for the next eight years, assisted part of the time by her son.

She enlivened both the appearance and content of the paper. Her stories carried catchy headlines. She introduced a column, "Fifteen Years Ago This Week," starting with her husband's takeover of the *Sentinel*. "The Mukluk Trail" column chronicled happenings in the nation's capital, authored by Delegate Tony Dimond's administrative assistant, Bob Bartlett, a former associate editor of the *Fairbanks Daily News-Miner*.

Bartlett was later delegate himself and one of the state of Alaska's first two U.S. senators. Bartlett also married a Wrangell schoolteacher in 1930, Violet Marie (Vide) Gaustad. Miss Gaustad, like Bartlett, was from Fairbanks where her father had operated the *News-Miner* while W. F. Thompson was on vacation

In 1931, the Bureau of Indian Affairs built Wrangell Institute, a boarding school for Indian boys and girls. It started with an enrollment of seventy students. The *Sentinel* carried a weekly column of "Institute News."

Tells off Juneau

Mrs. Pritchett editorialized zealously against fish traps, Outside control of Alaska labor unions, and conservationists who wanted to keep Alaska "locked up." When the 1933 territorial legislature appropriated funds for a new Pioneers' Home, invitations were issued by a building commission to various towns asking what they had to offer should they want the institution. Mrs. Pritchett made a strong pitch to have it in Wrangell and chastised Juneau's *Empire* for advocating it remain in Sitka:

> Juneau very generously reasons that since Sitka has had the Pioneers' Home for nineteen years, it has a sort of vested interest in that institution. Right you are, Juneau, but that argument was not very popular with you when you wrested the capital from Sitka, which for more than a quarter

of a century had been the capital of the territory. But scenery and vested interest, notwithstanding, the capital was removed from Sitka and taken to Juneau.

Mrs. Pritchett's son deserted the printing presses for gold mining near Tanana in 1937. She found a buyer for the paper in October 1939, when Lew Williams Sr. was terminated from his job as associate editor of the *Daily Alaska Empire* in Juneau.

In her farewell editorial, before retiring to Boise, Idaho, the modest but effective early Alaska woman publisher thanked her friendly neighbors for their support.

She said she had been keenly aware of her limitations when she took over the paper but was determined to stand on her own feet and not ask for favors because she was a woman.

Chapter 18

Controversial Editors in Juneau after Gold Rush

John Frame and Ed Russell – controversial editors of the Gold Rush era – dominated Juneau journalism after the stampede expired and until J. F. A. Strong founded the *Empire* in 1912.

Frame a crusading Democrat

John Wesley Frame saw himself as a Jacksonian Democrat standing for God, party and the common man; fighting prostitution, special privilege, Republicans, bankers, industrialists and Chinese. He wanted to crush evil with a club, to persecute wickedness with a sword. One of his Washington state colleagues called his Washington paper the most ably edited but the "most anarchist sheet in the state."

Tired of scraping a living from that "anarchist sheet," the *Snohomish County Democrat*, Frame joined the Klondike stampede in the spring of 1897 with a small army press and a few fonts of type.

In later years, Frame recalled how he succumbed to "Klondike Fever":

> I sold a timber claim we had in Washington for $50 in order to get away quick, before others hogged the best claims.
>
> We had a lot in Everett and owned a cow. We sold the lot to a man for $100 but we couldn't sell the cow, and, as the fellow who bought the lot couldn't read, in making out the deed we slipped the title to the cow in with the lot – so we could get to Dawson "quick."

After two years in Dawson, Frame joined the stampeders to Fortymile, Nome and Valdez, trying his luck at sluicing for gold along the way with little success. In Valdez, he was reduced to washing dishes to earn enough money to buy a ticket to Juneau.

In Juneau, Frame's old friend, Judge Arthur K. Delaney, offered to help finance the purchase of a local paper if Frame would stay and publish it. Delaney had been a practicing attorney in Everett when Frame published one of Everett's papers.

Soon after taking charge of Juneau's *Record-Miner*, Frame initiated an investigation of Judge Melville C. Brown, U.S. district court judge for the First Judicial Division. Frame soon was convinced "that things judicially were rotten, very rotten." He began writing exposes of the judge's activities. An investigator arrived from Washington, DC. On the basis of his report, Brown was not reappointed.

The other Juneau newspapers, friendly to the judge, castigated Frame but he stood his ground.

Frame transformed the *Record-Miner* from a feeble twice-weekly into a robust daily. Within a month of his purchase, the circulation doubled and advertising patronage trebled. Chauncy Shaw, former editor of the *Sitka Alaskan*, was his associate editor. The initial edition of the daily appeared on January 2, 1902.

Pet editorial targets were federal carpetbag appointees who Frame labeled "pettyfogging officialdom." His was the lone editorial voice in the Gastineau region supporting increased home rule. The other editors joined the mining and fishing corporations in opposing it.

By June 1904, Frame decided to quit the daily field and sold the paper to a couple of young court reporters, Louis T. Gillette and Walter S. Coutant. A little over a year later, Gillette and Coutant sold the paper to a group of local businessmen, headed by John B. Denny, a local attorney and city magistrate. Denny was the son of the first white family to settle on the present site of Seattle.

Gillette went into private law practice in Juneau. Coutant moved to Ketchikan where he and Walter Wyatt bought the *Mining Journal*.

In the meantime, Frame re-entered Juneau journalism with a weekly, the *Alaska Transcript*, three months after he sold the daily. For the next four years, Frame's inflammatory language was weekly fare. His rival editors rebuked him. Frame displayed his raucousness in his assessment of Southeast newspapers, printed in his *Alaska Transcript* on July 13, 1907:

Ketchikan Miner – much about territorial government, with a flavor of "all-damn-fools-but-me," ex-Governor Swineford tells good, humorous stories; *Record-Miner* – a lot of "sameness," an occasional good editorial; *Skagway Alaskan* – Troy's writing is quite formal and on many subjects quite able, but not sufficiently interesting, too statistical; *Douglas News* – Hopp always has something that cheers you up, makes you feel like pressing onward and upward; *Alaska Sentinel* – editorially rather prosaic, the colonel (A.V.R. Snyder) does not write them as he used to; *Sitka Alaskan* – its editorials are sometimes quite good, but more generally they treat of subjects not concerning many of its readers; *Dispatch* – a medical sheet published by Eddie Russell. It is devoted to diseases of the human body, gonorrhea, sore nipples, eczema, etc., its editorials are written almost wholly by outside parties, has no standing.

Record-Miner sold

Denny and his associates sold the *Record-Miner* in April 1906, to a new stock company, headed by Captain John J. Johnston, a Juneau realtor and mining broker. The name was changed to the *Alaska Daily Record*.

Johnston's partners included some of Juneau's financial and political luminaries: Robert A. Kinzie, manager of the Treadwell mine; Clem M. Summers, president of the First National Bank of Juneau; Gov. Wilford B. Hoggatt; and law partners Louis P. Shackleford and Thomas R. Lyons.

Editors' names did not appear in the masthead during the ensuing two years; the turnover was so rapid. It was the only Juneau paper with a Linotype machine; the only one with a modern cylinder press. It had the only power stitching machine that could handle books or pamphlets. It boasted the largest circulation of any Alaskan daily. It provided lively competition for Ed Russell's *Daily Dispatch* and Frame's weekly *Transcript*.

Frame abandoned the crowded Juneau newspaper field in the spring of 1908, going to the boomtown of Cordova. There the Guggenheim's Copper River & Northwestern Railway soon would be transporting millions of tons of copper ore to the coastal terminal en route to a Tacoma smelter. Frame sold the *Transcript* to a couple of former printers on the *Daily Record*'s staff – Will C. Ullrich and Claud H. Dech. Dech and Ullrich changed the name to the *Alaska Weekly Transcript.*

Frame got out and Ullrich got in just in time for the 1909 Juneau grand jury that indicted three Juneau editors, a Douglas editor and a Skagway editor for criminal libel, some of it in reaction to Frame's bombast. (Details in chapter 19.)

Ullrich became sole owner the following October when Dech left for Whitehorse to be mechanical foreman on Stroller White's *Whitehorse Star.*

Third daily for Juneau

On May 6, 1909, Ullrich launched Juneau's third daily, converting his weekly to *The Morning Transcript.* The *Daily Record* and the *Daily Dispatch* were evening papers. Although physically handicapped as a deaf mute, Ullrich was regarded as one of Alaska's ablest editors.

There was some question as to where he got his financial backing. The *Daily Record* contended that Sewald Torkelson was the real owner, despite Ullrich's denial. Torkelson was a union activist, a member of the Western Federation of Miners, who had started the *Industrial Worker* in Nome in 1907, and who staged strikes at the various mines. Ullrich championed the unions. That disturbed some of his advertisers.

The paper had the support of Mayor Emery Valentine and John Maloney, both Wickersham supporters, thus providing an official organ for the third of the three political factions in Juneau. The *Daily Record* was a Governor Hoggatt supporter and the *Dispatch* was aligned with the Louis Shackleford wing of the Republican Party.

Considering the spheres of influence behind the *Record* and the *Transcript*, it was obvious that Russell's *Dispatch* was the weakest of the three. He tried to sell his paper to the *Record* stockholders but failed. Being a hustler and a fiery fighter by nature, he persevered and two years after the 1909 grand jury, his was the only newspaper left in Juneau.

Eddie Russell pops out

Little is known of Edward Crawford Russell before he arrived in Dyea in March 1898, from Portland, Oregon, with his wife, Margaret Stewart, and their infant son, Edward, his parents and a sixteen-year-old brother, Allen. Frame's acid pen described Russell as being from "the slums of Portland" where he was known as "Scar-Faced Charley."

Russell's detractors credited him with introducing yellow journalism to Alaska when he arrived in Dyea. His arrival surely inspired yellow journalism. Frame wrote that Russell was a "poor addlepated nincompoop" or an "egotistical nincompoop" or just plain "jackass." One day he devoted an entire editorial to "Russell's Origin":

> In the beginning God created the heavens and earth, then the editor and the liberal advertiser, which was very well. The next day it snowed and he created the man who does not believe in advertising, and another who doesn't take the home paper. And that night the devil got into the molding room and created the man who takes the paper for several years and fails to pay for it.
>
> After he had completed that sorry job and having a few lumps left, he threw them into the hopper, and, adding thereto; the hind leg of a cur, one jackass ear, a whale's gall bladder, and a gross package of cigarettes, he said, "Let come what will," and out popped Eddie Russell.

Coutant called Russell "a knave of the blackest die" and "pusillanimous Ed, the blackmailer." He said Russell was "too bewilderingly ignorant, so addlepated and generally unstrung mentally" that it might seem unfair to question his judgment:

> Why, Russell, you poor silly fool, if I could only borrow for you some untutored Siwash's brains for one short hour, I'd like to have you see yourself, just once, as others see you – as every other newspaperman in Alaska sees you – a jackass is too good a name for you.

It was Russell's ill manners that subjected him to ridicule. According to the *Cordova Alaskan*, when a river steamer purser doubted the validity of Russell's newspaper pass because of his crude behavior, Russell told him to telegraph Skagway's *Alaskan* for verification.

"Man aboard representing himself to be editor *Juneau Dispatch* presents Russell's pass. Think he is a fake. Looks more like a tough and uses the language of the dive. Says 'has went' for 'has gone' and shows general marks of an illiterate."

Back came the answer: "That's him," and Russell's pass was honored. Or so the *Cordova Alaskan* reported. Frame was a partner in the *Alaskan* at that time.

Russell was equally insulting toward his peers. He called the editor of Skagway's *Alaskan* "an acrocephalic youth," which the dictionary defines as congenital deformity of the skull. Almost daily he referred to Coutant as a "contemptible liar" or "little pimple" or "little runt" Coutant.

When Gov. John Brady visited Juneau, the *Dispatch*'s front-page headline blared: "Siwash Brady Comes to Town" in scornful recognition of the governor's efforts to have the Indians admitted to full citizenship. Later he called Governor Swineford "a general all-around ass." Besides being anti-Brady, and anti-Swineford, he was anti-Hoggatt, anti-church, and anti-mine operators.

Down to two Republicans

However, by 1912 Russell's *Daily Alaska Dispatch* was the only daily paper in the Juneau area. He had outlasted his vociferous critics in journalism at the *Record* and the *Transcript*, which had suspended. The only other publication was the weekly *Douglas Island News*. It and the *Dispatch* were Republican-oriented.

When a split in the Republican Party resulted in former President Theodore Roosevelt forming the Progressive (Bull Moose) Party to challenge William H. Taft and Democrat Woodrow Wilson in the November 1912 election, it was assumed that a Democratic administration would take over the White House in March 1913. That meant a new slate of appointees to territorial offices.

In 1912, six of the world's richest gold quartz mines were operating on both sides of Gastineau Channel. Some workings were entirely under the bed of the channel. Between four thousand and five thousand men were employed in the underground tunnels.

The choicest political plum in Alaska after the 1912 national election would be that of governor. One man stood out as the Alaskans' choice for that position – sourdough editor-publisher John Franklin Alexander Strong. Alaska Democrats had repeatedly begged him to seek the office through the years, recognizing his widespread popularity, but he had declined.

When the Strongs returned to Seattle in the spring of 1912, after closing his Iditarod newspaper, he was besieged by friends to seek the nomination as Alaska's governor. Strong attended the Democratic National Convention in Baltimore in June. He returned to Alaska to campaign for the election of Robert Jennings, the Democratic candidate for delegate to Congress. Jennings was opposing the incumbent, James Wickersham, a Progressive Republican.

Strong launches Empire

As an initial step in his campaign for governor, Strong launched the *Alaska Daily Empire* in Juneau on November 2, 1912, three days before the national elections. He had taken his Iditarod printing plant out of storage and shipped it to Juneau.

In his initial editorial, Strong reiterated his support for home rule for Alaskans, a cause for which he had been fighting ever since his arrival in the northland in 1897.

He promised that the paper would be politically independent, "reserving the right to honestly commend or fairly criticize any political party that may be in control of the federal or territorial administrations":

> The people of Alaska ask for and expect a square deal from the Congress and government of the U.S. We believe they have seldom received it, but in the coming years conditions may change, and wrongs inflicted be redressed, with a more intimate and comprehensive knowledge of this territory and its needs, on the part of our national lawmakers.
>
> Notwithstanding the many disabilities under which Alaska has labored for years past, partly due to politics and partly due to ignorance, misinformation and misdirected zeal on the part of the national school of ultra-conservationists, the growth and development of this great commonwealth has been greatly retarded, if not absolutely prohibited in important sections.
>
> A change of policy by the federal administration we believe to be indispensable to the end that the people of Alaska may be permitted to enjoy the fruits of their labors, in developing its great latent natural resources. The land is

the people's, and the fullness thereof; the treasures of the sea should be for the benefit of all, not the few.

The *Empire* received its name because of the fact that Alaska is an empire within itself, and as such this territory is fairly entitled to imperial treatment at the hands of the federal government.

Strong led the editorial chorus urging the selection of nonpartisans for the First Territorial Legislature. A caucus of summertime-Alaskans was held that winter at the Arctic Club in Seattle. It nominated fourteen so-called nonpartisans for the legislature, but they actually were associated with Outside corporations.

President Woodrow Wilson summoned Strong to Washington in February 1913, a month before the legislature convened, where he was offered the post of governor. Strong invited a former colleague in the Pacific Northwest, John Troy, to run the *Empire* during his absence.

Capital relocation arises in First

Relocation of the capital precipitated a hot argument in the First Territorial Legislature. The argument started when Rep. Arthur Shoup of Sitka, letting bygones be bygones over loss of the capital to Juneau, introduced a memorial asking Congress to appropriate funds for the construction of a federal building in Juneau.

Rep. Hunter Ingram of Valdez called the idea preposterous and the thought of spending the money in a place like Juneau was "still more outrageous. If we must have a new capital building let us build it in the central part of the territory. Build it in Valdez."

Reps. Tom Gaffney of Nome and Ernest B. Collins of Fox favored Fairbanks as the proper place for the capital. Gaffney referred to Southeast as an "insignificant strip of hard rock preempted by fish trap owners."

Despite these oratorical outbursts, the memorial for funds for a federal (capitol) building received unanimous approval.

But Alaskans returned only eight of twenty-four members of the First Legislature to the Second, favoring instead, home-rule candidates over the corporations' anti-home rule, so-called nonpartisans.

Chapter 19

Early Juneau Incubates Libel

Prospectors and miners who founded Juneau provided the literate population to be both the birthplace and the graveyard of more newspapers than any other town in Alaska – more than all other major towns combined. It gave birth to thirteen different newspapers in the last thirteen years of the nineteenth century, starting with the *Alaska Free Press* in 1887. It spawned eighteen more newspapers in the twentieth century. Only the *Juneau Empire* and the *Capital City Weekly* survive into the twenty-first century.

The maze of similar titles is confusing but reflects how the town evolved from a mining camp. The first newspapers had *Miner*, *Mining Record*, or *Record* in their flags. After Juneau became the capital in 1906, the word *Capital* began appearing.

With that many newspapers, most of Alaska's early journalists spent some time on Juneau newspapers before or after working in other towns, or participating in the Klondike stampede.

If there is confusion about the number of publications and titles in Juneau, there is no confusion about the competition. It was fierce to the point of being physical. It put Juneau journalists in the forefront in court cases deciding libel.

Criminal libel first

Journalists were charged with criminal libel in days before those who were libeled discovered it was more profitable to file civil lawsuits seeking money. Criminal libel was based on Oregon law of the 1890s.

In Alaska, a story, advertisement, letter to the editor or editorial could be presumed injurious and criminally libel if there was no justifiable end or good motive for printing it.

There have been no charges of criminal libel filed against an Alaska newspaper since the law was amended in 1949 and no cases at all since the Alaska Supreme Court ruled the law unconstitutional in 1978 in a case not involving a newspaper.

Even after Juneau acquired the final pieces of the capital from Sitka, supposedly bringing an awareness of law and order to the new capital, journalism was a rough business. Juneau's newspapers constantly snipped at each other.

Banker shot

One day late in 1908, Clem Summers, president of the First National Bank and a stockholder in Juneau's *Daily Record*, marched into the *Daily Dispatch* office. He demanded the retraction of a story, or else he "would knock the editor's block off."

Robert L. Colby was acting editor of the *Dispatch* while editor-publisher Ed Russell was vacationing in Seattle. Colby had alleged that the editors of the *Record* were "hired to do the dirty work of Louis Shackleford and Summers."

When no retraction appeared the following day, Summers paid a second visit to the *Dispatch* office. That confrontation is described in the November 7, 1908, issue of Juneau's third newspaper, the *Weekly Transcript*:

> Williams, the foreman of the office, attempted to prevent Summers from entering, but was shouldered out of the way by Summers, who is a tall, powerfully built man. Reaching Colby, Summers proceeded to put his threat into effect, and chased Colby around the office, striking him on the head a number of times. Colby, who is a comparative small man, finally dodged past Summers and seized a revolver from a table near by. The sight of the gun cooled Summers' ardor for battle, and he made a flying run for the door, being followed by a couple of shots.

The newspaper reported that the banker suffered two bullets in the chest – barely missing his heart – and one in the shoulder as he fled out the door. There is no explanation of how he got shot in the chest running for the door.

Colby was not arrested. It was generally accepted that he acted in self-defense and that Summers was looking for trouble and found it. Colby finished the day's work at the typesetting machine with the doors locked and the revolver hanging by his side.

Three months later, Summers accosted Colby on the street and hit him on the head as he passed by. A third assault took place a few months later, involving Summers, Henry Shattuck, editor A. R. O'Brien of the *Record*, and Ed Russell, editor-publisher of the *Dispatch*.

Taking exception to another article in the *Dispatch*, Summers, Shattuck and O'Brien searched for Russell and found him seated in a billiard hall playing cards. O'Brien went up to him and gave him a glancing blow with brass knuckles. Summers and Shattuck stood by to ward off interference.

The night marshal appeared and sought to arrest O'Brien, whereupon Shattuck snatched his club and together with Summers, prevented O'Brien from being taken into custody. Owing to the crowd of spectators, the marshal hesitated to draw his gun.

He finally managed to place O'Brien under arrest because by then, according to the *Transcript*, the heavyset Russell had O'Brien down and was rubbing his face on the floor. Summers put up $200 cash bail and O'Brien was released.

The incident was headlined in all three papers, with each editor offering his interpretation.

The continual squabbling between the editors brought them, plus Douglas and Skagway editors, grand jury indictments in 1909 for criminal libel – W. C. Ullrich of the *Transcript* (by then a daily), Russell of the *Dispatch*, O'Brien of the *Record*, C. A. Hopp of the *Douglas Island News*, and even Dr. L. S. Keller, a dentist and editor-publisher of Skagway's *Alaskan*. Each was brought to trial but the juries found them not guilty, except for O'Brien, who was fined $200 plus court costs.

Complicating the judicial proceedings was that Shattuck was clerk of the court and Summers was U.S. jury commissioner. They, too, were indicted, along with one of their friends who tried to break up the fight, pharmacist C. F. Cheek. All were charged with trying to rescue a prisoner, O'Brien, from custody. All charges were dismissed.

It is surprising more Alaska newspaper editors were not indicted for criminal libel. Editors from Ketchikan to Cordova had been calling each other names as long as they had been in business. The real physical fights had started after *Dispatch* editor Colby accused *Record* editors of being hired to do dirty work. He was irritated with the *Record* for reprinting an acrid editorial from John Frame of the *Cordova Alaskan* that "cast a slur" upon Mrs. Russell, wife of Colby's boss.

Also, indicating the extent of the newspaper feuds, editor Russell commented in a column after the indictments: "Torn with jealous rage at not being invited to the 'grand jury party,' the editors of Wrangell and Ketchikan are acting real devilish."

The editor of the *Skagway Interloper*, Richard Bushell, whose paper was backed by the *Record* owners and who had joined in the verbal skirmishes, missed indictment because he suspended publication early in '09 and moved his equipment to Wrangell, where he purchased the *Sentinel*.

Another factor that led to the feuding was labor unrest at the Treadwell Mine on Douglas Island. One investor in the *Record* was the superintendent of the mine. The *Transcript* supported the mine workers. The *Douglas Island News* defended Douglas against criticism from Juneau's *Dispatch*.

When the criminal libel cases were over, editorial comments were notably absent except that Dr. Keller accused the grand jury of acting "with unwarranted zeal." Hopp admitted resentment, saying, "that should any member of that grand jury ever fall into evil ways and get caught, his sentence may be to run a newspaper for one year without making a mistake."

The aftermath

The *Transcript* suspended publication that fall, with the *Dispatch* buying its circulation. That reduced the number of Juneau area newspapers and the tension.

O'Brien, a twenty-seven-year-old bachelor, had become editor of the *Alaska Daily Record* in August 1908, less than a year before his grand jury indictment.

Details of his past remained a mystery as he refused to discuss it. He was ever ready for trouble. He kept a revolver in plain sight on his desk and it is reported that he slept with a gun under his pillow.

The *Record*'s stockholders called it quits with the May 8, 1911, edition. The paper had lost nearly $20,000 in three years.

Commenting on the suspension, Stroller White, who was at the *Whitehorse Star* at that time, wrote:

> After several years of "bucking" public sentiment in the matter of home rule for Alaska, the *Record* has turned its toes to the daisies and the mocking bird is singing over her grave. As a newspaper, it was first-class and up-to-date, being without a superior in Alaska, but in its attempts to coerce rather than mold public opinion, it sounded its own death knell.

The plant was shipped to Marshfield, Oregon, where O'Brien waited to start a weekly.

The *Record* suspension left only the *Dispatch* in Juneau until the *Empire* came along the next year.

Editorial freedom wins

George Knapp of Sitka, son of Alaska's third governor, Lyman Knapp, brought the first civil libel action against a newspaper in Alaska in 1890. He sued the newspapers in Juneau, Sitka and Seattle for printing a story that he had abused his wife, Gertrude, while she was confined in childbirth. His suit failed and he left Sitka. Gertrude was the sister-in-law of Sitka businessman John Brady, who would become Alaska's fifth governor.

The *Empire* won a civil libel suit in 1921, a decision upholding editorial freedom to criticize politicians. John Rustgard, territorial attorney general and candidate for delegate to Congress, had brought the action. Publisher John Troy criticized Rustgard in an editorial for belonging to a dissident faction in his political party and for "speaking egotistically" about himself.

The federal court ruling (there were only federal courts in Alaska when it was a territory) concluded that the editorial failed to bring public contempt, ridicule or scorn upon Rustgard but was merely newspaper humor and not actionable when said of a candidate for public office.

The *Fairbanks Daily News-Miner* also won protection for editorial comment when Golden North Airways sued in 1955. The editorial supported action by the Civil Aeronautics Board to discourage competition to scheduled air carriers by nonscheduled carriers. Although the editorial referred to nonscheduled airlines as a group, Golden North alleged it was aimed at it. The court disagreed.

The editorial was fair comment in an area of public interest, the court said, and Golden North failed to show the editorial was directed at that specific firm.

The unltimate defense

The ultimate defense of editorial comment occurred in 1910 after Judson Harmon Caskey and George Bellows of Fairbanks' *Alaska Citizen* were indicted by a federal grand jury for criminally libeling Peter Steil, even though his name was not mentioned in the editorial.

The newsmen's attorney argued, and won dismissal, on the grounds that if Steil asserted that the editorial referred to him, he thereby acknowledged that he was a professional "tunnel-site staker," a "pencil miner," and a "would-be hold-up." In that case, the article was truthful and not libelous. On the other hand, if he denied those terms described him, he could not claim to have been the person libeled.

The *News-Miner* was indirectly involved in an action over an advertisement when it owned the *Valdez Vanguard* in the 1980s. A firm selling urethane insulation brought an action against the city and the owner of the city's newspaper. The city bought an ad in the newspaper to warn residents about fly-by-night building companies selling such insulation without a building permit. It also cited the danger of using such insulation.

The court ruled that truth was the defense in one statement (no building permit) but not another (insulation dangerous). However, "common law privilege pertaining to matters of public interest protected the city's issuance of the warning in question."

The *Anchorage Daily News*, when owned by Northern Publishing Company, was targeted in two libel actions that it successfully defended. In *West vs. Northern Publishing*, the newspaper reported in 1971 that illegal distribution of liquor occurred in Nome; that the city was dominated by the liquor merchants and cab companies who distributed liquor to minors.

The court said the story was of public interest and it was not shown that defamatory falsehoods were published with the knowledge that they were false or that they were published with a reckless disregard of whether they were false.

In the other, *Green vs. Northern Publishing*, in 1982, the court decided that a doctor who provided services to five jails in the Anchorage area was a public official – his qualifications and performance were of public interest – and therefore he must prove actual malice by the newspaper in its criticism of him, which he failed to do.

Journalists are public figures insofar as the issues on which they write are concerned and also have to prove malice to collect in a libel action. That was the decision in *Rybachek vs. Sutton*.

Rose Rybachek wrote a natural resources column for the *Fairbanks Daily News-Miner*. A reader, Larry Sutton, wrote a letter to the editor of the paper accusing Rybachek of water quality violations. The letter writer produced several letters from the Environmental Protection Agency that suggested the letter writer's statements might be true. The columnist failed to prove otherwise so, in the opinion of the court, there was no malice.

The case of the 'Gooey Goose'

The "Gooey Goose," the "Garbage Man of the Fourth Estate," and the "Mystery Man of the Drug Corridor" joined with the *Juneau Empire* in a significant libel case in March 1995. The result was an opinion from the Alaska Supreme Court that pulled all of Alaska's civil libel decisions together in one opinion favoring newspapers.

Especially helpful was awarding the *Empire* some of the attorney fees that it ran up defending itself. The court said that awarding 50 percent of fees is a good start but given the "unreasonable discovery" undertaken by the plaintiff, which was unnecessary, 60 percent was a fair figure. So the *Empire* was awarded $31,250 in the "Gooey Goose" case.

It began when Juneau businessman Charles Keen, his Alaska Trams corporation and his associates in Mount Juneau Enterprises, sued the *Juneau Empire* in 1991. They alleged that the *Empire* libeled them in two news stories about their efforts to build a tram from downtown Juneau to the top of Mount Juneau. They lost in superior court and appealed the case to the Alaska Supreme Court. That court upheld the lower court in an opinion based on all previous Alaska libel decisions, effectively pulling them together in one decision.

In one story, the *Empire* had reported that when Alaska Trams was in bankruptcy that Keen attempted to continue the tram project through his Mount Juneau Enterprises, until stopped by the bankruptcy trustee. The second story reported that children saw a goose fly into an oil storage tank on property owned by Keen. The tank had sixty thousand gallons of "gooey" fuel in it. The goose was rescued by raptor volunteers but died after several washings.

There were minor technical inaccuracies in the stories such a misidentifying the title of the attorney advising the bankruptcy trustee; in calling a violation of the migratory bird act a felony instead of a misdemeanor, and in saying the tank was owned by Keen instead of his Alaska Trams. Keen and associates charged that the paper acted with malice and negligence in printing the stories.

In upholding the superior court decision, and awarding attorney's fees to the *Juneau Empire*, the Alaska Supreme Court affirmed: (1) that Keen was a public figure because he sought city (public) support for his project and inserted himself into negotiations with the city; (2) under the U.S. Supreme Court decisions *New York Times vs. Sullivan* and in *Gertz vs. Robert Welch*, a public figure has to prove malice; (3) that the *Empire* reporter depended upon reliable sources for her story so that under *Gay vs. Williams*, an Alaska case, there was no malice, and; (4) the "Gooey Goose" article is protected under freedom of expression on matters of public interest. The justices cited the case of *Pearson vs. the Fairbanks Publishing Company* for its last point, "matters of public interest."

Keen had contended there was malice because the *Empire* reporter was not told by anyone to check her facts before writing the stories; that she conducted an inadequate investigation; that she was given the assignment despite a lack of training or understanding of legal matters; that she assumed without question that whatever people told her was true; and that there was no rush or deadline so there was no reason for failing to adequately investigate and ascertain the true facts.

The Arizona connection

The high court opinion said that "assuming that these contentions are true, they alone do not establish actual malice." Citing *Gay vs. Williams*, the court said that failure to make a prior investigation into the accuracy of published statements does not itself constitute sufficient proof on whether the statements were published with reckless disregard – malice.

In *Gay vs. Williams*, an Anchorage air charter company owner, Al Gay, sued Lew Williams Jr., representing his *Ketchikan Daily News*, and sued the *Juneau Empire* and The Associated Press for a story that described Gay as "the mystery man of the drug corridor."

Gay owned most of Lukeville, an Arizona border crossing into Mexico on the way to the resort town of Rocky Point. Following the car bombing death of *Arizona Republic* reporter Don Bolles in June 1976, a team of reporters from newspapers around the United States descended on Arizona to expose crime and corruption in that state.

The team called themselves Investigative Reporters and Editors. Their series of stories with a lot of innuendo were sent back to their papers. The Associated Press picked up some of the stories for the wire.

The story describing Gay as the mystery man of the drug corridor was sent to Alaska where it was printed in the Ketchikan and Juneau papers.

The case against the *Ketchikan Daily News* was the most difficult to defend because a reporter, inexperienced at editing, was acting editor that day and wrote a headline "Alaska bush pilot accused in Arizona drug trafficking." Gay had not been accused of anything in the story except with using his private plane to fly between Lukeville and Rocky Point to go fishing. Gay dropped his case after a judge ruled that there is no actual malice when a newspaper prints a story from a national wire service without independent investigation.

A political battle

The case of *Pearson vs. Fairbanks Publishing Company* is more a story of dirty politics.

Drew Pearson was an influential Washington DC-based columnist from the 1930s through the 1960s. His column, "The Washington Merry-Go-Round," later taken over by his protégé Jack Anderson, appeared in six hundred newspapers around the world, including the *News-Miner* and the *Empire* in Alaska. With his radio show, it is estimated Pearson had sixty million readers and listeners, according to a report that *News-Miner* columnist Dermot Cole wrote in 1976.

Cole reported that Pearson used tipsters and any information he could lay his hands on without regard to accuracy. That resulted in as many as 275 libel suits filed against him over the years, seeking more than $200 million. It is reported Pearson lost only two lawsuits, the one he filed against the *News-Miner* and another he filed against Hearst's conservative national columnist, Westbrook Pegler. Pearson's favorite targets were conservatives.

As a liberal Democrat, Pearson had known Ernest Gruening since before Gruening went to Alaska in 1939 as governor. After Congress approved Alaska statehood June 30, 1958, Alaskans had to hold an election to accept it and elect state officials. Former *News-Miner* reporter and editor E. L. Bartlett, a Democrat and Alaska's last territorial delegate to Congress, was conceded to win one of the U.S. Senate seats. The race for the other seat pitted Gruening, a Democrat, against Mike Stepovich, a Fairbanks Republican who resigned as territorial governor to run for the seat. *News-Miner* publisher C. W. Snedden supported Stepovich.

A week after Congress approved statehood, Pearson wrote, "A lot of Johnny-come-latelys such as Gov. Mike Stepovich are now claiming credit for making Alaska the forty-ninth state in the Union. But the man who unobtrusively, but consistently, badgered senators, buttonholed congressmen, maneuvered in smoke-filled rooms to bring statehood to Alaska is an ex-newspaperman named Ernest Gruening."

Snedden was in Washington when he heard about the column criticizing Stepovich and wired *News-Miner* editor George Sundborg to cancel Pearson's columns immediately. Sundborg was a longtime friend of Gruening and diplomatically suggested in a return wire to his employer that to kill the column would do more harm than good. He suggested that they run the column, write an editorial in response and then cancel Pearson at the end of the month. Snedden agreed.

In an editorial responding to the Pearson column, and in defending Stepovich and criticizing Gruening, Snedden's editorial concluded: "for the time being we'll get a clothespin for our editorial nose, while we decide what to do about this freewheeling garbage man of the fourth estate."

Snedden said he got the idea for that line when he heard a Washington reporter say as Pearson approached, "Here comes the garbage man."

After Stepovich out-polled Gruening in the August primary election in which each was unopposed, Pearson came up with the idea of suing Snedden for libel, according to records Cole uncovered. Pearson reasoned that if they could get Stepovich in court to testify how little he had done for statehood, compared with Gruening, it would discredit Stepovich.

Pearson must have realized that courts don't move that fast but was satisfied that publicity alone was enough. Gruening won in the November general election by a close margin. But before the election, and while the case was pending, Sundborg had been asked to resign from the *News-Miner*. He did and went to work for Gruening.

It wasn't until November 1964, five years later, that the case finally came to trial. Superior Court Judge Everett Hepp ruled in favor of Snedden. Pearson appealed to the Alaska Supreme Court and lost. The Supreme Court confirmed Pearson was a public figure, that he invited public judgment by what he wrote, and like a person who submits a book or work of art for public approval, he should be in no position to complain if the comment is adverse.

Also in the court's decision on Pearson, the Supreme Court cited decisions in two other *News-Miner* cases: in the 1962 case of *Fairbanks Publishing vs. Pitka*, the assertion that a person (a schoolteacher) has been fired was ruled not defamatory; and in the 1964 case of *Fairbanks Publishing vs. Francisco*, it was ruled that a newspaper is privileged to publish the report of a public official even if the report contains inaccurate or defamatory material.

Despite Snedden winning the case, the *News-Miner* was denied recovery of its legal expenses. Sundborg claimed later that it was because at first Snedden denied the exchange of telegrams between him and Sundborg over the Pearson column. Then Snedden was forced to admit in court that the exchange had occurred.

Journalists warned

Although the Juneau case of *Keen vs. the Juneau Empire* brings together all previous civil libel decision in a concise package concerning newspaper privilege in reporting, Dan Riviera, a Seattle attorney who conducts libel seminars for the Pacific Northwest Newspaper Association, to which Alaska newspapers belong, said:

"Certainly this status of the law is not a license to libel. And if I were going to pass on a word to newspaper people, it would be a word of caution. The privileges and the freedoms which the courts have laid out were not made to be abused. If some maverick goes too far, then the courts will start to go the other way and hedge these freedoms with limitations that may be very difficult to live with."

Chapters 20-26

Prince William Sound

and Rural Journalists

Reach End of Trail

In time a Moses will be born to lead us out of the wilderness, but until this time comes the children of Alaska must labor ever as those of Israel, without hope, without recompense, and without escape.

– Harry Steel, editor
Seward Gateway, 1923

John Edmund Ballaine was an experienced newspaper man when he envisioned a railroad from Resurrection Bay to Interior Alaska. He sent a survey crew north in 1902 to survey his project and lay out a townsite that became Seward. The first spike for the railroad was driven in 1904, the same year he and his brother Frank launched the Seward Gateway to report the railroad's progress.

-Photo courtesy Resurrection Bay Historical Society, Seward.

Chapter 20

Valdez Wins Then Loses

The gold rush to Interior Alaska highlighted the need for an all-American route from tidewater. Existing trails all crossed parts of Canada before reaching the Interior. Seward, Cordova, and Valdez could be jumping-off places for an all-American route.

Cordova and Valdez vied for Alaska's first major economic development, the Kennicott copper mine, and its Copper River & Northwestern Railway. Cordova won. When Alaska's last major economic development came along in the 1970s – North Slope oil with its trans-Alaska pipeline – Valdez won. In between, Seward beat them both to win the terminus of the all-American railroad route to the Interior.

Alaska's Switzerland: Valdez

The first settlers landed in Valdez in 1897, nine years before one of M. J. Heney's railroad men nailed a board to a tree with the word "Cordova" on it.

Spanish Explorer Don Salvador Fidalgo in 1790 named Valdez Bay, an arm of Prince William Sound, for Spanish naval officer Antonio Valdes y Basan. It was relatively unknown until the Klondike gold discovery was headlined around the world.

Early Alaska adventurers sought the quickest route to the gold fields. The Copper River route appealed to many, starting in Valdez harbor.

Entrepreneurs were attracted northward with visions of riches from establishing a townsite. Once within the safe anchorage of

Valdez Bay, the question was where along the shoreline was the best place to create a debarkation point. The first band of argonauts spent the winter where the Pacific Steam Whaling Company had established a trading post on the delta of Valdez Glacier.

Other potential settlement sites came to be known as Swanport, Bloomerville and Hazeletville. Their Seattle agents promoted their respective sites at the expense of the whaling company's trading post, claiming that its site was dangerous because great blocks of ice might loosen from the glacier and swamp boats.

Hazeletville, located about three and a half miles northwest of the trading post, almost came out first choice except for two things. First, prospectors objected to carrying their supplies over a wide expanse of mudflats in order to reach the trail into the Interior; and second, although land was cleared and buildings constructed as a terminus of the Copper River & Northwestern Railway, its owners had abandoned it for the new town of Katalla.

Ironically, sixty-seven years later, the town was moved to that original Hazeletville site following the 1964 earthquake because it had more stable ground.

The first forty-two men to arrive at Valdez in the fall of 1897 were known as the La Ninfa Company, named for their vessel. The following spring, 1898, vessels of every description, from tiny sailing craft to good-sized steamers, arrived at Valdez, loaded beyond their legal capacity. By the first of June, an estimated two thousand people had arrived and half of them had begun their trek over the glacier toward the Interior

That same spring, the War Department dispatched Capt. William R. Abercombie to Valdez to survey a route for a wagon road from the coast to the Interior. Construction began in 1899. It eventually became the Richardson Highway, terminating in Fairbanks.

The post office department inaugurated a mail route from Valdez to Circle City via Eagle before there was a Fairbanks. The War Department began stringing a telegraph line along the same route to connect the military installations in the district. Valdez was the starting point for all of these facilities. With them came dreams of economic growth.

Copper was found in abundance. Valdez boomed. In 1900, placer diggings on Chisana and Slate creeks struck gold, and for several years brought prosperity to Valdez. In the fall of 1900, a military installation named Ft. Liscom was established about four miles across the bay from Valdez.

Valdez News first

When the town's first newspaper started in the spring of 1901, four thousand to five thousand persons wintered in Valdez. There was no wharf, so supplies and outfits were landed on the beach above tidewater. Then there was a five-mile trek over mudflats to the foot of the glacier.

Outfits were hoisted up to the first 250-foot bench; then up several more benches, to the five thousand-foot summit; then down a crevasse to Klutena Lake. After whip-sawing the lumber for a boat, they traveled down swift waters to the Copper River. There, some went upstream, others downstream. Many just went down – drowned.

There were outfitters of all kinds in Valdez, selling everything from a deck of cards to a steam boiler. According to newspaper advertisements, there were eight saloons, seven restaurants, nine general mercantile stores, six attorneys and three doctors. The Grand Hotel, with pioneer Adam Swan as proprietor, offered lodging for twenty-five and fifty cents a night and regular meals for thirty-five cents, or three meals for $1. It boasted a private dining room for "Ladies and Escorts."

The *Valdez News* appeared on Saturday morning, March 1, 1901, with Albert W. Rochford as editor, assisted by Lucy DePew. Miss DePew was reported to be the only female printer employed in Alaska at that time, although Marie Coe of the Nome *Gold Digger*, 1899-1904, probably was competent in the printing department, as were most editor-publishers of small newspapers.

J. F. Hielscher, formerly of Dyea, and now operating a meat market in Valdez, grubstaked Rochford in the venture. The whole outfit cost less than $1,500. The two men met originally in Skagway when Rochford worked on the *Skagway News* and Hielscher was transporting livestock over White Pass to Dawson.

Five steamship lines ran between Seattle and Valdez. It was conceded at that time that Valdez was the natural gateway to Alaska's Interior. It was just a matter of time before a railroad would be built, making Valdez the metropolis of Alaska. The optimistic press assured its readers "that the sounds of a locomotive whistle will be echoing among the hills surrounding Valdez Bay before snow flies."

The initial issue of the *News* carried an account of the first wedding to be solemnized in Valdez, that of Captain Austin E. Lathrop and Mrs. Cosby McDowell of Seattle on February 18, 1901. Lathrop later was publisher of the *Fairbanks Daily News-Miner*, had extensive other business interests and was sometimes dubbed "Alaska's first millionaire." At that time he was captain of a steam schooner plying the waters of Cook Inlet and Prince William Sound.

Prospector next

H. H. Hildreth, former editor of Sitka's *Alaskan*, together with two other local businessmen, Joseph Bourke and Will H. Crary, launched the weekly *Alaska Prospector* on February 13, 1902. The masthead listed Hildreth as Quill Pusher, Crary as Ink Slinger, and Bourke as Walking Delegate. John Goodell, an attorney and deputy customs collector, was assistant editor.

It started with a weekly run of five hundred copies.

Front-page stories gave glowing reports of rich strikes in the Tanana Valley. The Richardson Trail was crowded with packers, with their dog teams and horse-drawn sleds, bound for the Interior.

The government's telegraph line to Eagle was completed on August 24, 1902. Hildreth sent the first wire to the *Yukon Sun* in Dawson City and the mayors of Valdez and Eagle exchanged greetings.

When summer came, Hildreth's prospector's feet got itchy and he took off for the hills, leaving Crary to run the paper.

Both the *News* and the *Prospector* received generous advertising patronage. They refrained from abusive criticism of one another except on the home rule issue.

Duel over home rule

Rochford advocated territorial government, which included the election of a delegate to Congress and an elected territorial legislature. He believed that home rule was essential to the opening of Alaska "which is destined to be the mineral storehouse of the world and an important addition to the American Union."

Those who opposed home rule on the grounds that it would cost too much, he called "un-American," arguing that "our forefathers did not stop to count the cost when they placed their honor and their property on the altar of high principle."

The *Prospector* called home rule supporters "anarchists and fools who should be imprisoned for treason," whereupon the *News* retorted that "this hysterical shrieking would be amusing were it not known that it emanates in all seriousness from a gray-haired old man for whom the community has the greatest pity."

In reply, editor Crary noted that he was on the editorial staff of the *New York Herald* before the *News* editor was born.

The two papers carried on in a desultory fashion, waiting for the day when Valdez would burst into the northland's shining star.

First a boom

Four major copper claims had been staked in the Copper and Chitina rivers' watersheds in 1899 and 1900. That, with the Bering River coal deposits and gold prospects, all accelerated the demand for a railroad.

The *Valdez News* and the *Valdez Prospector* in 1901 and 1902 – before there was a Cordova – had run frequent items speculating that Valdez was the natural starting place for a railroad from tidewater to Eagle on the Yukon River, the major camp for American gold miners and judicial headquarters.

The *Valdez News* finally reported construction was to start on the Copper River & Yukon Railroad out of Valdez and then was disappointed. A lawsuit among mineral claimants stopped everything until 1905 when the suit was settled and the Alaska Syndicate was formed and bought up the copper claims in question.

The Alaska Syndicate consisted of the House of Morgan, the Guggenheim brothers, the Havemeyer financial house, and Kuhn, Loeb & Company. The House of Morgan was headed by J. Pierpont Morgan. Meyer Guggenheim, who died in 1905, had seven sons, all working in his mining and smelting empire. The Syndicate went into other businesses in Alaska, including transportation and fisheries. The Guggenheims ran the mining sector of the Syndicate and were frequent targets of editorial and political comment.

The *Valdez Prospector* hailed the Syndicate's appearance.

> Now the copper magnates from the interior are beginning to appear, and one can hear talk of bornite, 600-foot ledges and millions on every corner. One prospector

says that there is so much copper where he was this summer that even the water in the swamps carries a green stain and the grass was also tinged with green.

In selecting Valdez as headquarters for his proposed Copper River & Northwestern Railway, a Guggenheim was quoted by *The Alaska Monthly* in April 1906:

> We want to go into the territory and build railroads and smelters and mining towns and bring men there and populate the country and do for it what the earlier figures of American railroad building did for sections of the great West.
> The American Smelting and Refining Company will not only build a railroad but will build smelting works at Valdez for the reduction of the ores.

Docks were built and the right-of-way graded for twelve miles into Keystone Canyon, where a tunnel was started. At about the same time, Col. A. W. Swanitz started construction on his Valdez & Yukon Railroad, to go from Valdez to Eagle.

Both papers became so excited about the town's future that they changed from weeklies into dailies. The *Valdez Daily News*, a morning paper, started on November 6, 1906. A week later, the *Prospector Daily Bulletin* appeared afternoons.

In the meantime, oil had been discovered at Katalla, one hundred miles southeast of Valdez. That and the Bering coal fields nearby attracted two railroad companies to Katalla.

Then a bust

Events then transpired to quash Valdez's dreams. The Alaska Syndicate began negotiating for the purchase of M. J. Heney's railroad at Cordova and began building a railroad from Katalla to tap the newly discovered coal and copper deposits.

With the Cordova and Katalla railroads under construction, railroad work at Valdez shut down. Valdez merchants realized they must retrench financially and the two daily papers consolidated their plants, publishing one daily and one weekly. Both bore the name

Prospector. The first issue of the merged sheet appeared on April 14, 1907, with Will Crary as editor.

The town had scarcely recovered from its disappointment when a promoter named Henry D. Reynolds appeared promising Valdez residents that he would build them their very own railroad, the Alaska Home Railway.

The city council granted Reynolds a ninety-nine-year franchise to the entire townsite and offered to build and operate a wharf at the foot of Broadway. Reynolds bought the *Prospector*, as well as a sawmill, a bank and the largest mercantile store. He went around town soliciting stock subscriptions. The Reynolds-owned newspaper gave an exuberant hurrah when the $150,000 mark was reached.

Reynolds promised to take Valdez residents over the summit in Alaska Home Railway cars "before the snow flies." Editorials noted that Alaskans were being rescued from the stranglehold of Eastern corporations intent upon monopolizing Alaska's economy.

A typical editorial in the *Prospector* entitled "Let Us Stand Behind Reynolds," reflected the local mood:

> Since the first small party arrived in 1897, on the beach of what has since been Valdez, we have been sorely afflicted with what is familiarly known as a bunch of knockers. For at least seven years, we have had to contend with proposed rival townsites and whenever a railroad has been proposed, it has never been from Valdez.
>
> Now, when a man comes here and says he is going to build a road, commencing in the center of the town of Valdez, and shows his own faith in his ability to do so by buying large amounts of real estate in the heart of the city; hires every man possible to aid in the construction of the road and by his own tireless energy stimulates every man associated with him – asks nothing at the hands of the people except that they voluntarily subscribe – it seems as if the "Knockers' Club" must be out of a job.

By October 1907, the town's holiday spirit turned to despair. Reynolds was bankrupt and five hundred unemployed workers roamed the streets begging for tickets on the next southbound steamer. Reynolds was arrested in his hometown of Boston for fraudulent use of the mails but escaped imprisonment by pleading insanity. After a few months in a mental hospital, he was set free.

Alaska Gov. John G. Brady had supported Reynolds's questionable promotion, which forced Brady's resignation one year into his third term as governor.

Porcupine stampeder takes over

Elmer E. Ritchie, Seward attorney and former editor of the *Seward Gateway*, arrived in Valdez in January 1908, to serve as receiver for the bankrupt Reynolds businesses, which included the *Prospector*. He replaced Will Crary with L. Frank Shaw as editor of the *Valdez Weekly Prospector*.

Shaw joined the gold stampede to the Porcupine region from Haines in 1898 and went on to Siberia before returning to Alaska.

Around Nome, the rocker and hand sluicing method of mining was yielding to the hydraulic dredge, so the independent miners and journalists headed to Seward as well as Fairbanks. At Seward, they hoped the Alaska Central Railroad would open a field of valuable mineral lands.

While waiting for the railroad out of Seward, Shaw went to Valdez and the *Prospector*. He stayed there less than a year and then exchanged editor posts with Elliott Stewart, who was editor of the *Seward Gateway*.

Valdez began to recover from the Reynolds fiasco. New quartz discoveries and the successful operation of the Cliff Creek and Slate Creek mines contributed to a stable economy. Automobile travel was initiated later on the Richardson Trail to Fairbanks. It was designated a highway in 1923.

Valdez became headquarters of the Third Judicial Division in 1909 with a federal judge when the number of federal judicial districts was increased to four. That brought a steady government payroll to the town until Third Division headquarters moved to Anchorage in 1940.

Chapter 21

Pinchot Burned at Katalla and Town Dies

British railroad engineer M. J. Heney, who built the White Pass & Yukon Railroad out of Skagway, 1898-1900, a few years later filed with the federal land office for a route out of Eyak. It was a Native village and the site of an Alaska Packers cannery near where Cordova was later established.

Heney landed a construction crew and supplies at Eyak in mid-March 1906 to start construction of his Copper River Railroad. Three months later the *Cordova Alaskan* appeared and reported:

> The Copper River Railroad Company is rushing work right along. They are working 500 men ... the company's sawmill which was completed and started last week is kept running to its full capacity ... The railroad was projected to run to the great Katalla coal fields which are only 75 miles from Cordova ... the Copper River Railroad will be hauling coal and copper ore from this great river valley long before any of the projected railroads which are being constructed in Alaska, because M. J. Heney who has the contract to build this railroad is known all over Alaska as having built the White Pass & Yukon.

Then the Alaska Syndicate bought out Heney and his associates, stopped railroad construction at both Valdez and Cordova and switched to Katalla. A new newspaper, *The Katalla Herald*, trumpeted "Katalla, Where the Rails Meet the Sails."

First Alaska oil discovered

Following the discovery of oil near Katalla in September 1902, the Alaska Petroleum & Coal Company laid out the townsite. Katalla was located in Katalla Bay, fifty miles southeast of the site that later became Cordova.

Oil had been discovered at the mouth of the Bering and Copper rivers at a depth of 365 feet. A gusher spouted a nine-inch column of oil eighty feet into the air.

The Bering River coal fields and the Copper River copper deposits were near Katalla. These rich mineral lands suggested a brilliant economic future for the area, but the dreamers did not reckon with the federal bureaucracy.

Anti-slavery attorney first editor

Katalla seemed like a bright spot to attorney Willoughby Clark, when he launched his newspaper, *The Catalla Drill*, on December 21, 1903. Clark had been hopping from one boomtown to another ever since he arrived in Sitka in 1885. Although he was a native of Ottawa, Canada, he claimed to have practiced law in forty-two American states and territories before arriving in Alaska.

But before that, Clark won the Sah-Quah case in 1886 in which he secured the freedom of an Indian slave from another Indian. The U.S. district court decision in that case outlawed slavery in Alaska and the mutilation of slaves.

Clark was disbarred in 1892 on a charge of larceny by bailee. Soon thereafter, he moved to Wrangell and was reinstated to the bar in 1896. In Wrangell, he married the daughter of famous Cassiar prospector Buck Choquette.

By 1899, Clark was in Nome amidst the turbulence over judicial corruption. He served as chairman of various miners' protest meetings, at least one of which was broken up by the military. Rex Beach adapted the incident for his novel, *The Spoilers*.

Moving to Valdez, Clark and some associates tried to "jump" the military reservation of Fort Liscum. They built a house in the street and under cover of darkness moved it to the reserved area. The commanding officer sent a squad of soldiers to demolish the structure, tossing the debris back into the street. Clark filed a complaint in the district court, but it, too, was tossed aside.

Having worn out his welcome in Nome and Valdez, Clark then launched his newspaper and a law practice in Katalla. "Catalla" was the Tlingit word for the bay. The Tlingits had traded there for decades with the Eyak and Chugach people. *The Catalla Drill* was a mimeographed sheet of two pages on standard typewriter paper. He had a column titled "Seepages," devoted to news about oil activities.

The paper's faulty spelling, grammar and punctuation raised a question about the quality of Clark's education. The seventh issue of the *Drill*, appearing on February 8, 1904, was his swan song. Early in 1905, Clark was back practicing law in Wrangell. He died there on October 9, 1906.

Roosevelts' big resource freeze

The U.S. mining laws were amended in 1904, limiting coal claims in Alaska to 160 acres, which made coal mining impracticable.

Two years later, President Roosevelt withdrew all coal lands in Alaska, terminating any further staking of claims and stopping development of already staked ground. The order cancelled some 1,100 claims upon which large amounts of money had been spent, representing the life savings of many claimants. Soon after, timber and oil lands also were withdrawn.

The withdrawal order was supposed to be temporary, giving Congress time to evaluate the best means of handling Alaska's resources. The "temporary" status encouraged the Alaska Syndicate to go ahead with its plans for constructing a railroad from tidewater to the mineral deposits.

Three different railroads were under construction at Katalla in the summer of 1907, heading for the Bering River coal fields, a distance of about fifty miles. The Alaska Syndicate even had locomotives on hand. Rail spurs were planned to the copper deposits. Plans envisioned smelters soon to be in operation. Between five thousand and ten thousand people poured into Katalla – construction workers, prospectors, oil men, and coal miners.

All of this excitement was a magnet for journalists. The J. F. A. Strongs left Greenwater, California, and returned north. Their *Katalla Herald* made its first appearance on August 10, 1907.

Two weeks later, O.M. Kinney and his son Claud moved from Cordova to launch the weekly *Diamond Drill*. Claud left after a few

SEWARD DAILY GATEWAY

VOL. I — SEWARD, ALASKA, THURSDAY EVENING, NOVEMBER 23, 1905 — NO. 94

SELL CROW CREEK MINING PROPERTY

Company Given $200,000 Option on Famous Hydraulic Claims Which Will be Taken up December 15—Arrangements for Transfer Made by Representative Now in Seward.

WILL SEEK TO SHOW CONGRESS

Convention Proceedings to be Sent to Members—Protest Against Humphrey.

By Cable to The Daily Gateway.

Seattle, Nov. 23—The full official account of the proceedings of the Alaska convention is being prepared, and copies will be sent to the President, to all members of both houses of Congress, and to leading newspapers all over the country.

A fight has been started against the seating of Capt. Omar J. Humphrey,

WITTE STRICKEN WITH PARALYSIS

Russian Statesman Believed to be in State of Physical Collapse.

By Cable to The Daily Gateway.

St. Petersburg, Nov. 23—Count Witte is in a state of physical collapse. This morning he fell forward in his chair while reading a petition from workingmen. It was found that his right arm and shoulder were partially paralyzed.

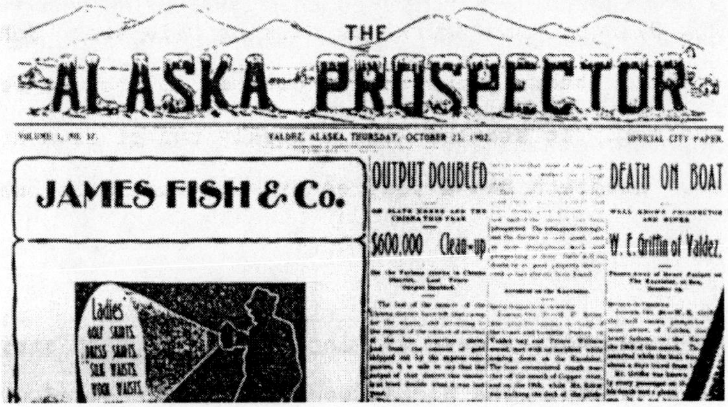

THE ALASKA PROSPECTOR

VALDEZ, ALASKA, THURSDAY, OCTOBER 23, 1902. — OFFICIAL CITY PAPER.

JAMES FISH & Co.

OUTPUT DOUBLED

$600,000 Clean-up

DEATH ON BOAT

W. E. Griffin of Valdez.

THE KATALLA HERALD

KATALLA, THE COMING METROPOLIS OF ALASKA, WHERE THE RAILS MEET THE SAILS

VOL. 1. No. 43. — KATALLA, ALASKA, SATURDAY, MAY 30, 1908. — PRICE TEN CENTS

Are Ready to Start the Work—But When?

SURVEY OF PORT

Katalla Strategic Point of Importance

TALKED OF WIRELESS

At the Meeting of Chamber of Commerce

weeks to enlist in the U.S. Army at Fort Seward near Haines. There he started the weekly *Musher*.

Strong resumed his crusade for local autonomy, which he had initiated as a Nome editor. He argued that Alaskans were entitled to the same self-government that in the past had been extended to other states and territories. He wrote in *The Katalla Herald* on September 27, 1907:

> Alaska, the greatest of all the possessions of the U.S., has withstood the jeers and banters of outrageous fortune, for the most part with unexampled patience and fortitude, buoyed by the hope that justice will yet be done them by those placed in authority over them.
>
> Alaska is the land of opportunity for all, the rich, the poor, the bonded, the free – all who have in them the courage to do right and assist in the upbuilding of what is destined to be one of the greatest of stars in the galaxy of states.

Nature took a hand in determining Katalla's destiny. Fierce windstorms wrecked the breakwater and piers in the fall of 1907. The multimillion-dollar sea wall built by the railroad companies was washed out to sea. Ships could not land so mail and cargo had to be relayed by small boat from Cordova. The railroads terminated construction. The builders of the Copper River & Northwestern Railway then selected Cordova as its terminus instead of Katalla.

After the storms, Katalla was cut off for two months and the *Cordova Alaskan* reported that Katalla residents were living on "snowballs, love and hope, with an occasional stray porcupine for a banquet . . . . The sails have not connected with the rails of late."

Fed's action shuts down Katalla

More and more buildings were boarded up as people left Katalla following the federal land withdrawals of 1906 and the storm of 1907.

Unemployment was rampant. Laid-off workers lacked money to buy a steamer ticket. Katalla was without meat – except for porcupines – for two months. Then a steamer managed to land fresh provisions at the harborless settlement.

The *Diamond Drill* gave up in December 1907. O. M. Kinney headlined: "To Move to Cordova." The story said: "The new location is not yet known . . . no one, except perhaps officials of the Morgan-Guggenheim Syndicate, have any idea where the town will ultimately land – if it lands anywhere." That was in reference to Heney's original site at Eyak, near Cordova, being considered too small for a railhead.

Strong hung on with his *Herald*, writing on March 22, 1909:

> Oil to the right of us – oil to the left of us sizzles and sputters, and that's all it does. Coal, coal, by the hundreds of millions of tons in the adjacent hills and not an ounce of it to burn. The winter of our discontent will soon be over, but we don't know what summer will bring.

He was optimistic that with "coal in a thousand hills and its vast oilfields, Katalla's time will come as surely as waters run, grasses spring or flowers bloom." He was willing to take his chances with the community a little longer.

But by July 1909, Strong conceded that what he had described as the "Pittsburgh of the North" was dead. The Strongs traveled north to Iditarod to start a paper, then to Juneau in 1912 where he founded the *Empire*.

No coal for residents

A bonfire blazed on the beach of Katalla in May 1911. Gifford Pinchot, the arch conservationist and President Theodore Roosevelt's chief forester, was burned in effigy. A copy of President Roosevelt's "temporary" withdrawal order also was tossed into the fire amid cheers from the crowd.

Pinchot's credentials as a conservationist, who advocated locking up Alaska resources, especially coal, were tarnished when it was reported in the Portland *Oregonian* that he held a substantial interest in Pocahontas Coal Company on the East Coast. Alaska coal represented competition to that company.

The flamboyant, outspoken, publicity seeking Pinchot, later fired by President William Howard Taft, also was criticized by Alaskans for visiting communities wearing a gun on his hip. Alaskans frowned on that practice and considered it an insult that Pinchot felt he needed protection from Alaskans.

When Secretary of Interior Walter L. Fischer, also a conservationist, visited Katalla later in the summer, the residents begged permission to dig enough coal to heat their homes. They were rebuffed.

Katalla not dead yet

Katalla experienced a brief rebirth in the 1920s when oil leasing was in effect. A thousand barrels a month were produced, all of it used in Cordova and vicinity. On Christmas Day 1933, the oil refinery burned, and Katalla joined the ranks of forgotten ghost towns. It was alleged that the caretaker at the refinery left his longjohns hanging too close to a stove and they caught fire.

Strong's optimistic predictions still might be realized. Early in 2001, an exploration company began drilling on private and Native land in the area. The Chugach Native Corporation had until 2005 to prove up on oil reserves under ten thousand acres of its land, or lose its subsurface rights.

Chapter 22

Cordova to Chitina

"Cordova, Alaska's Gateway, Where the Rails Meet the Trails." That was how *The Alaskan*, Cordova's first newspaper, described its community. It might have been the inspiration a year later for *The Katalla Herald* to proclaim: "Katalla: Where the Rails Meet the Sails." Eventually "Trails" won over "Sails."

M. J. Heney triggered Cordova's birth on March 21, 1906, at the head of Orca Bay, on the eastern shore of Prince William Sound. That was the day that Heney sent word to his survey crew, which had arrived the previous week, to start work. He had secured official title to the right-of-way for his Copper River railroad. He told them the new town would be called "Cordova" in honor of his favorite town in Spain.

Heney's railroad was by then one of seven under construction in the area – three at Katalla, one out of Seward and two at Valdez, all aimed at transporting rich mineral ores to tidewater.

The Alaska Syndicate, which owned the Kennecott copper mine in the Copper River Valley, had dispatched its engineers earlier under George C. Hazelet to investigate the Copper River route. Hazelet reported negatively on the problem involved in bridging the river between Miles and Child's glaciers. Therefore, the Syndicate chose Valdez as its terminal.

That did not dissuade Heney. He went ahead with the backing of the same British financiers who had built the White Pass & Yukon Railroad. They planned to tap both Copper River coal and copper, working from Eyak.

Kenney, Hillary start Alaskan

The Alaskan debuted in Cordova on June 16, 1906, with Claud Kinney and Tad Hillary as editor-publishers. Both were former printers on Skagway's *Alaskan*, having come north as teenagers with their parents in the Klondike stampede. Claud's father, O. M. Kinney, at one time published the *Skagway Guide*.

The main story in the initial issue of *The Alaskan* was a report on clearing the roadbed for the railroad. Heney hired sixteen former Skagway residents who had worked for him on the White Pass line.

The first spike on the Copper River Railroad was driven on August 28, 1906. Work languished after the Alaska Syndicate bought out Heney and moved railroad operations to Katalla but they were back in Cordova in 1908, blown out of Katalla by storms.

With that shift in plans, a new townsite was surveyed a mile north of Eyak, on the shores of Orca Inlet. By the end of the summer of 1908, a frontier city had replaced the colony of tents at the site Heney called Cordova.

Between two thousand and three thousand railroad workers arrived for the summer's work. Riverboats were busy moving passengers and freight on the Copper River. Cordova was heralded as the "San Francisco of the North" and even the future capital of Alaska.

Veteran newsmen arrive

In June 1908, control of *The Alaskan* passed to the Cordova Publishing Company comprised of local businessmen George Hazelet, Tom Donohoe and Sam Blum. John Frame, the outspoken former publisher of Juneau's *Alaska Record-Miner*, owned a third interest and served as editor. Eugene Allen, former editor of the *Teller News* and former business manager of the *Klondike News* was a staff member.

Cordovans soon learned that they had a fighting editor in their midst as Frame swashbuckled his way through the 1908 delegate race. Judge James Wickersham was making his first bid for delegate to Congress as an Independent. His principal campaign issues were home rule for Alaska and opposition to Guggenheim-Morgan control of Alaska's natural resources. Cordova was a one-company town, owing its existence to the Syndicate's railroad. Wickersham was anathema to Syndicate supporters, who included *The Alaskan*'s chief stockholders.

According to historian Lone E. Janson in *The Copper Spike*, Wickersham "nursed the wounds from his own 1907 job refusal from the Guggenheims," which inspired his campaign to win election by hammering the Syndicate.

The Alaskan supported John W. Corson, the Republican candidate, who was a Seattle attorney with mining interests at Nome. John Ronan, a Fairbanks mine operator, was the Democratic candidate.

Vote fraud fails

A characteristic Frame editorial fusillade was fired at Ed Russell, editor of Juneau's *Alaska Dispatch*, who was supporting Wickersham's candidacy. Under the title of "The Juneau Nincompoop," he wrote:

> For the benefit of those who do not have personal acquaintance with Eddie Russell, the ostensible author of the vile balderdash appearing in the Wickersham sheet of Juneau, let us say that he is one of the most disreputable of the slum class of Portland (Oregon).
>
> The paper that Russell pretends to publish in Juneau is only the sewerage channel through which the sore heads of the capital city spew their slime at Governor Hoggatt and every other official of Alaska who does not dance to their music in a manner that will permit them to rob and plunder the people and the government.
>
> Russell tried very hard to get Corson to subsidize his sheet while in Juneau, but Corson has some acquaintance with the knave and would give him nothing for he knew Russell would not "stay bought."
>
> Poor John Ronan did not know the crooked shyster and put a good purse in his hands. After this, the traitor was one of Wickersham's most zealous boosters. Russell is a cross between a pistareen and a nincompoop with a good dash of knavery and cowardice in his make-up.

On Election Day, railroad workers were brought into town on flatcars to vote for Corson, resulting in a Cordova vote of 925, of which seven hundred were for Corson. A one-year residence in Alaska was a voting qualification and those workers were there for only the summer season. Most were aliens as well. Despite this obvious voting fraud, Wickersham won handily.

The Alaskan became a daily on October 26, 1908. A deep sea cable had been installed connecting Cordova with Seattle, making national and world news readily available. The following spring, Hazelet paid Frame $3,000 cash for his interest in the paper, which probably reduced tension within the newspaper because Frame disagreed with his partners in attitude toward big business. During the next year, Frame alternated between prospecting for gold and operating a restaurant.

Glowing reports of Cordova's economic future attracted Robert J. (Bob) McChesney, former editor-publisher of Fairbanks' first newspaper, the *Weekly Fairbanks News*. He and his wife had returned from a world tour, after having "secured a handsome fortune from his two years of newspapering in Fairbanks." He had sold the Fairbanks paper for $20,000 in a day before income or capital gain taxes – and three days before it went up in flames.

Charles, McChesney, Steels at Cordova

The McChesneys arrived in Cordova in March 1909, with a complete newspaper plant to launch a second daily. It made its debut on April 24, 1909, under the name of *The North Star*.

Fred M. Brown, a Valdez attorney and former Valdez mayor, was his partner. Sid Charles, who had worked for McChesney in Fairbanks, was hired as city editor.

The *Star*'s support of Wickersham angered the owners of *The Alaskan*. *The Alaskan* called the *Star* "the enemy of Cordova and the neighboring country" when it echoed Wickersham's condemnation of the Guggenheim Syndicate's monopolistic policies.

The *Star* said it did not object to Guggenheims' constructive capitalism but to its agents becoming political lobbyists.

Will and Harry Steel, pioneer newsmen from the Klondike, Nome and Fairbanks, bought *The Alaskan* in September 1909. Harry assumed active management of the paper while Will lived in Seattle, where he conducted a press clipping service for several Alaska newspapers.

Harry Steel took seriously the slogan that ran across the top of the front page: "Cordova, Alaska's Gateway, Where the Rails Meet the Trails." He campaigned vigorously on the superiority of the trail from the Chitina rail head to Fairbanks, rather than the Richardson Trail from Valdez via the hazardous Thompson Pass. The Chitina route also was sixty miles shorter than the one from Valdez.

Steel put out a lively journal, filled with news of the whole region, including weekly columns from Katalla, "The Coal and Oil City," and Valdez, "The Glacier City." He envisioned Cordova as the inevitable tidewater terminus for Interior Alaska rather than either Valdez or Seward. He envisioned the Copper River railroad extending to Fairbanks, with branch lines to the Bering River and to the Matanuska coal fields.

Steel favored President William Howard Taft's commission form of government for Alaska as opposed to Wickersham's home rule, supported by *The North Star*.

Steel contended that almost everyone coming to Alaska intended to ultimately return to where he or she came from, with never an idea of making it a permanent home. With such a transient population there was no point in extending home rule to the people. He wrote dozens of editorials hammering on the unstable aspect of the population – Alaska towns were here today and gone tomorrow.

Steel's crusade against home rule concurred with the point of view of the railroad officials, some of whom owned large sections of the townsite and feared future property taxes. Steel also jumped into the national controversy between conservationists and developers within the Taft administration. Chief Forester Gifford Pinchot was spokesman for the conservationists, and fired by Taft. Secretary of Interior Richard Ballinger represented the developers' point of view. Although supported by Taft, Ballinger resigned and was replaced by Walter Fischer, who turned out to be a conservationist.

President Taft favored the development of Alaska's natural resources but he feared that Alaskans could not stave off rampant exploitation, hence his recommendation of a presidentially appointed commission to rule the territory.

Wickersham, on the other hand, trusted Alaskans more than he did members of Congress sitting four thousand miles away, with lobbyists and more pressing concerns on their minds.

Frame wins, landowners lose

Steel wanted Outside investors to develop an industrial base for Alaska's economy, so he resented Wickersham's faulting the Guggenheims as enemies of Alaska. During the delegate's campaigns for re-election, Steel wrote as many as six separate editorials in a single issue of his paper, damning Wickersham and everything he stood for.

Such exciting controversy was too much for Frame sitting behind the counter of his restaurant. He re-entered the newspaper field in the spring of 1910 with a weekly called *The Truth* in order to "rout out a gang of highbinders and pimps who were running Cordova." His muckraking sheet succeeded in ousting the Sam Blum crowd from city offices, including the defeat of the prominent George Hazelet for the city council.

Frame's primary targets had been the big landowners, whose commercial enterprises were located on land outside the city boundaries, thus depriving the city of much-needed tax revenue. Those same individuals owned the waterfront property, thus blocking its development by the city for commercial use. The situation inflamed Frame's sense of fairness and he was able to transmit that concern to the electorate.

The new city council appointed Frame city clerk and magistrate as a reward. It also extended the city's boundaries to include the big land holdings and passed an ordinance limiting ownership of the waterfront by private interests.

Frame's boldness in challenging the conduct of the town's economic elite made him a social outcast in some circles. In later years, he reminisced about his Cordova experience:

> *The Truth* was considered "an awful sheet" by the nasty nice. At that time there were men in Cordova who were making a regular business of shipping women from Seattle to "supply the market" while the railroad was building.
>
> The same men who were in this line of work were running for councilmen and others wanted to be school directors. *The Truth* came out boldly and denounced the whole business and for so doing was excoriated by "the leaders of society" most bitterly. The paper was declared by them to be unfit to go into a decent man's family, and yet some of the heads of these families were the chief revelers down in the restricted district.
>
> The press over the country, even all the way down to Portland, was denouncing *The Truth*, declaring that it should not be admitted to the mails. The local press was horrified, but the editors of some of the same paper were such degenerates that even the women of the district would not permit them inside their parlors.

But what a change in two short years. You cannot pick up a paper in any home today but you will see column after column on the horrible practice of "white slavery" – and they talk a great deal plainer about it than ever *The Truth* did three years ago, for at that time the publisher had a hard time of it to keep out of jail.

The greatest menace to the country today is the hypocrisy and prudery of those who try to be the "society" of the community in which they live, for they as a rule will stoop to most anything if they can make a little money out of it. Money, money, that is their God.

The Truth published only from spring to fall of 1910, during the election campaign.

Chitina celebrates with paper

The Steels started a weekly in the new town of Chitina, Mile 132 on the Copper River & Northwestern Railway, calling it *The Chitina Leader*. The first edition on September 14, 1910, was part of the celebration of the railroad's completion to that junction. Will Steel and Governor and Mrs. Walter Clark were among the dignitaries on the first train from Cordova.

The Chitina Leader was printed in *The Alaskan*'s shop in Cordova and the latter's city editors commuted between the two towns in their editorial assignments. Identical editorials appeared in both papers, stressing the advantages of the new Chitina trail connecting with the Richardson Trail to Fairbanks.

An early slogan of the *Leader* was "Where the Team Meets the Steam, via Chitina and Cordova." This backed up a *Fairbanks Daily Times* slogan "Eight Days to the States" and *The Alaskan*'s "Where the Rails Meet the Trails." A special edition of one thousand copies of the *Leader* heralded the opening of the new trail from Chitina to Willow Creek on the Richardson Trail on November 1, 1910. Travelers from the Interior could spend a comfortable night at the new Hotel Chitina and then board a steam-heated coach the next morning for Cordova.

Harry Steel's editorial brimmed with boosterism on December 10, 1910:

When the frigid blanket of conservatism, as exemplified by Pinchot shall have been thrown aside, the fires of industrial prosperity shall flame in their wonted glory. The gold, copper and coal will develop a large industrial population of over 20,000 for the metropolis of Cordova.

When the carcasses of ungenerous detractors of the Copper River way have long since been consumed at the banquet of the worms, the Copper River way shall blossom forth in a splendor undiminishable. The star shall attain the zenith, but shall never wane. It shall poise serene and uneclipsable.

The Ed Orr stage headquarters moved from Valdez to Chitina, with its monthly payroll of $3,000. A matched team of six white horses met the northbound trains from Cordova and carried passengers, mail and freight to Fairbanks.

Frequent editorials urged the federal government to build a railroad from Chitina to the Matanuska coal fields rather than from Seward as it would afford easier construction at less cost. Cordova and Chitina residents kept hoping that the government would choose Cordova as the marine terminus for its proposed railroad. If not, they hoped that a rail spur would be built from Mile 38 to the Bering River coalfields.

The Alaska Syndicate offered to sell its railway to the government at whatever price the latter considered fair but its pleas were ignored because Washington politicians feared association with the "robber barons" so widely maligned at that time in the Outside press.

When Seward was chosen the terminus of the government railroad and there was little likelihood of the Copper River & Northwestern Railway extending further north, prospects for Chitina faded. The *Leader* was suspended after an eighteen-year run.

Kids' view on booze

Steel suspended publication of the *Chitina Leader* on November 24, 1928. The town's population dropped to 116 by 1930 but journalism wasn't dead yet. Actually, it gained national recognition. Steel, who liked to imbibe, might have even appreciated the stand of Chitina's second newspaper.

Three youngsters, twelve, eleven and nine years old, launched the weekly *Chitina Herald* on January 18, 1931. William Alfred Moore, twelve, was editor-in-chief; Adrian Clough Nelson, eleven, was editor, and his brother Philip Clough Nelson, nine, was business manager and reporter. In a letter to *Time* magazine, in May 1931, Adrian described their journalistic enterprise:

> At the first we made our newspaper entirely by hand on an old second hand typewriter of our father's and used carbon paper. But its circulation increased so fast we bought a mimeograph on installment. It is a $131 machine, but we got it at wholesale. At present we use the typewriter only just to print our stencils. We do it for fun. We have had fine support for our paper from all the sourdoughs and oldtimers for miles around and out the trail too.
>
> You will be glad to know that we have eighty-seven paid subscribers on our out-of-town mailing list. And that we sold 220 copies this week. We think that is good because there are not that many population in this town. Billy, Philip and I are the only boys in town except for babies.
>
> Our mother says she could correct our newspaper work and censor it each week, but she does not. The reason: the Alaskan people and Sourdoughs all like it better just exactly the way we get it out. They say they don't want it changed from the way we make it.
>
> All three of us boys are real Alaskans. Sourdoughs, as they say, as Billy was born at Cordova; I was born at the Kennecott Copper camp; Philip came up here when he was only five months old. We have all had a trip Outside one summer. All three to visit relatives. Billy's Daddy is a foreman on the Alaska Road Commission and our Daddy runs the water system here and the hydroelectric plant and is the U.S. commissioner.

The young editors were undaunted in editorializing on controversial local issues. For example, a lengthy editorial dealt with a bootlegger selling liquor to Indians. After describing in detail a drunken brawl that took place in the bootlegger's cabin during which he was badly beaten, the editor commented:

> Selling booze to Indians leads to lots of accidents. Mr. Read sold some to Lloyd Bell last fall and Lloyd got in jail for six months while his wife got on as best she could. He sold it to Tom Bell and Tom ran over a bank and wrecked his car and nearly killed himself. Tom has a wife and two children. Mr. Read got in jail himself for six months and paid a fine of $500.00 and he still likes to sell booze to the Indians.
>
> The Indians are foolish to buy Mr. Read's booze because they have wives and children that need the money and these Indians mostly work for the Ry. and A.R.C. and when they get drunk they lose their jobs and then the Gov't has to feed them if it can. Mr. Read is a very nice man to meet and he works hard on his farm and keeps it looking fine and neat. He raises lots of nice strawberries and vegetables and hay and other things beside booze. He has lots of friends because he always behaves like a gentleman when he is sober and when he is not selling booze to Indians.
>
> People seem to have different ideas about Indians. Some people think they should be treated as though they had no rights and no feelings. Some people would give them all the rights and privileges that they ask for and would not hold them responsible for anything. And some people would give the Indian and would demand of the Indian just the same that they would a white person under the same circumstances. Some people think that the worst thing that can happen to an Indian is for people to act toward him as though he were a fool or a child who is not and never can be responsible for what he does.

When the eldest of the trio drowned in an accident, the two remaining boys enlisted volunteer help from a couple of girls their same age, but the Nelsons worried about their sons not getting enough outdoor recreation. When the boys regretfully suspended publication with the January 22, 1933 edition, their circulation had reached 357, with copies going to six foreign countries and thirty-nine different states. Their project was written up in twenty-two magazines and metropolitan newspapers.

McCarthy Bee buzzes

When the Syndicate started operating the Kennecott Copper Corp. mine in the Wrangell Mountains, the little town of McCarthy sprang up as a lusty rest and recreation resort for the miners. It was first known as Shushanna Junction.

Although the mine operators provided first-class recreation facilities for their workers, the men liked to take a railroad speeder to the settlement just 3.5 miles away. There they could find "wine, women and song" without restrictions. Moonshine was readily available in contrast to strict prohibition at Kennecott.

The Copper Bee was McCarthy's first newspaper, appearing on February 19, 1916, with J. P. Hubrick, editor-publisher, promising to provide all the news about "Alaska's resources and all the latest war dope and scandal." But there were only three issues before Hubrick announced that he was leaving on an expedition to photograph Alaska brown bears. That was the last heard of him.

On August 5, 1916, a weekly titled *The Avalanche* made its appearance with M. V. Lattin as its editor-publisher. It, too, expired after a few issues.

A year later, on September 17, 1917, the C. F. M. Coles launched *The McCarthy Weekly News*. Frank Cole was listed as manager and his wife, M. M. Cole, was editor.

The *News* was a four-column, four-page sheet that changed ownership frequently during the ensuing years.

The hope of continued railroad service kept the editors optimistic about the town's future. McCarthy was a supply center for prospectors, placer miners, hunters and trappers. The June and July 1926 editions were filled entirely with notices of mining claims staked and applications made to patent land; good income but not much of a newspaper.

April 20, 1927, was the final edition that is on file in the University of Alaska Anchorage archives.

McCarthy was without news attention until 1992, when Rick and Bonnie Kenyon began publishing the *Wrangell St. Elias News* in

Glenallen. It is a twice monthly publication that covers news of McCarthy.

McChesney equipment to Valdez

McChesney had begun his *North Star* as an afternoon daily in Cordova in April 1909 but soon dropped it to weekly publication.

He owned mining property at Port Wells. One day in February 1911, when he was felling trees, his foot was crushed. It took his partners a day and a night to get him to medical help. For a while, it was feared the foot would have to be amputated. Although that was not necessary, he suspended publication of the *Star* so that he could go to Seattle for medical treatment.

McChesney asked Frame, a newspaper colleague since their days in Dawson, to negotiate the sale of his printing plant to a group of Valdez businessmen. Frame had quit publishing his *Truth*, giving his equipment to his son Ira to use in his job printing business. Frame quickly concluded the deal with the Valdez group, resulting in their launching the weekly *Valdez Miner* in March 1911, the fourth in the field of Valdez newspapers battling through the 1912 election campaign.

Chapter 23

Election Kills Three Valdez Papers

Valdez, with a population of 750, had four newspapers when the campaign for the 1912 election began in 1911. When the election was over, only one plant remained in operation. Each of the four had its favorite candidate for delegate.

The Weekly Miner supported William A. Gilmore, the Republican. *The Daily Prospector*'s favorite was Democrat Bob Jennings. Al White, city councilman and saloonkeeper, launched the weekly *Valdez News Letter* on behalf of James Wickersham. And John Frame reintroduced the weekly *Truth*, with which he had luck in Cordova, to further the candidacy of Martin Harrais, a second Democratic candidate. After the election, which Wickersham won, the *News Letter* and the *Truth* ceased publication. The *Prospector* and *Miner* merged.

Bob McChesney held a chattel mortgage on the *Miner*, which was publishing on the old Cordova *North Star* equipment. When installment payments fell in arrears and the paper was $1,700 in debt, McChesney had the U.S. marshal seize the plant.

The equipment was sold to the creditors. Those included Elmer Ritchie, McChesney, Elliott Stewart and Ray G. Day.

After McChesney recovered from his accident and returned from Seattle, he became editor of the consolidated *Prospector* and *Miner* until he went to Juneau as manager and shop foreman of the *Alaska Daily Empire*.

Ritchie had arrived in Valdez in 1908 as receiver for the bankrupt railroad of Henry Reynolds. Ritchie was the *Prospector*'s frequent editorial writer. He was active in local and territorial affairs, serving on the city council and two terms as mayor.

No 'mechanical poll parrot'

When Ritchie was accused of using the paper for political purposes, he replied that it was the job of a newspaper to help mold public opinion for the betterment of the community; otherwise it would be but "a typographical phonograph or a mechanical poll parrot."

He noted that the record of government before newspapers was of tyranny and unjust privilege. It was only in the light of publicity that human rights grew.

"There never was a bribe-taking judge ousted from the bench, a corrupt politician retired to private life, a governor or mayor who sold out to corporations and was exposed, that did not hate newspaper reporters above rattlesnakes," Ritchie wrote.

Alaska papers regularly referred to Seattle as the "Spirit City" without being explicit in the meaning. But the *Miner* side of the *Prospector-Miner* gave a full explanation in an editorial titled "Shell Game Spirit" on June 1, 1913. It called Seattle a "beast of prey," having an instinct for "commercial graft."

It noted that at the time of the Klondike discovery, a busted real estate boom had left Seattle "stranded on the shoals of time. Seattle was so hungry that the first meals it bought with the money of Klondike stampeders dropped to its shoes and swelled its feet":

> In those days the Seattle Spirit went after the pilgrims within its gates with the methods of the bunko shark.
>
> During all the succeeding years Seattle has continued the shell game. It holds a drag net for Alaska money but it never gives anything back. Seattle business houses never pay a cent to Alaska for advertising. They think they have a stranglehold on everything Alaskan and they lack the sporting spirit that makes the upper class gambler give back a small stake to the player who has lost his entire wad.

Frame beats establishment again

When the Democrats came back into power nationally in 1913, Frame, a lifelong Democrat, expected to receive some appointment.

When none came his way, he launched a weekly in Valdez through which he vented his exasperation. He called it *The Commoner*, in honor of a newspaper of the same name published by his idol, William Jennings Bryan.

In the initial issue of March 8, 1913, Frame said his mission was to support the interests of the laboring man as opposed to the "monied class." He noted that the majority of newspapers of the day supported the interests of the well-to-do, helping management "fleece the common herd" even though the laboring people "earn all the profits of the rich and produce all they eat and wear."

What irked Frame was that the Alaska delegation to the Democratic National Convention in Baltimore had voted on all forty-six roll calls for Alton B. Parker, an attorney for J. P. Morgan, for the presidency. Yet, when Woodrow Wilson was elected, those same Democrats were the recipients of the political plums.

Emulating his idol Bryan, Frame launched a campaign to discredit the Democratic Party machine in Alaska, charging it with conspiring with the ringleaders of the Republican machine. It didn't matter which party was in office, he wrote, the same Juneau attorneys were running the show and in charge of dispensing political patronage. He referred to them as the "Dirty Dozen," listing ten Juneau attorneys plus two fellow travelers. He urged his readers to fight them to a finish. He criticized Gov. J. F. A. Strong for appointing Republicans in his administration.

Frame organized his supporters into the Progressive Democratic Party and was chosen its territorial chairman. It opposed the John Troy Democrat faction. Frame's party held a convention in Valdez in June 1914, nominating Wickersham for delegate to Congress, while the regular Democratic Party convention in Skagway nominated Charles Bunnell, a Valdez attorney and businessman.

Frame attacked Valdez's socially elite Tillicum Club for selling liquor without a liquor license. He called the members "bootleggers" for dispensing liquor without paying the annual $1,000 license like any public saloon. His expose led to law enforcement officials closing the club's doors until a license was procured.

Just as he had in Cordova, Frame objected to major local businesses operating outside the city's boundaries, thus avoiding paying taxes. For example, Jim Lathrop's dock, assessed at $71,000, paid not one penny in taxes and yet profited from every dollar of cargo shipped in by the town's residents. Frame vowed to right these wrongs so that no longer would "the lawyers, bankers and steamship men run Valdez for their own selfish interest and aggrandizement."

Frame organized a ticket for the city council in opposition to incumbent Mayor Ritchie and his supporters. A hot campaign ensued, with the *Prospector-Miner* and *The Commoner* castigating each other. An editorial in the *Prospector-Miner* said the chief issue in the election was whether the voters wanted as their political dictator "a tramp newspaper blackmailer, a professional deadbeat and tinhorn grafter":

> For two years, John Frame squirted ungrammatical vilification through his measly little rag upon men in Valdez whose personal, business, professional and financial reputation is above reproach; men to whom any decent prospector or laborer with at least half a reputation for honesty can go and get aid any time he asks; men who are now carrying the laboring classes of the town for thousands of dollars.
>
> No decent man cares to engage in a hand-to-hand contest with a skunk, but when the skunk gets on your front porch you have to get him off even at the cost of personal contact.
>
> It is sometimes alleged that all things have their uses, and it may be the Almighty tolerates John Frame as an autoptic preference of total depravity, as an illustration of what an anthropoid freak can do among men. And so John keeps going – a pithecan monster, repulsive as a gorilla, with the manners of a stevedore and the morals of a pirate. His venality is fully equaled by his hypocrisy and both are exceeded by his ossified effrontery. He keeps his dinky weekly libel on the town afloat because he is too lazy to work and he is buoyed along with the hope, occasionally realized, that somebody will pay him $5 for support or $10 for silence.
>
> And yet it is alleged that John Frame was rocked in a cradle once, and went to school, and played on town lots with the boys, and was suspected of having human instincts.

A typical Frame rejoinder to such a tirade was: "Poor, pusillanimous nincompoops! May the Lord have mercy on their think tanks."

Frame got even. His ticket won and he was appointed town clerk and magistrate, as he had been in Cordova. In due course, the "mudflats" section of town was incorporated into the townsite boundaries and the property owners were obliged to ante up their share of property taxes, as business property owners had been forced to do at Cordova.

In June 1915, the U.S. marshal seized the plant of *The Commoner* at the instigation of attorneys Ritchie and Lyons. The plant's owner, Charles M. Day, local hotel operator and territorial legislator, had failed to make payment on an overdue note. Thus, Frame's editorial voice was silenced again, at least for a while.

On July 18, 1915, a fire destroyed the entire Valdez business district, including the plant of the *Prospector* and *Miner*. *The Commoner* had gone out of business the month before. Publication of the *Miner* continued in a limited fashion on a job press until new equipment arrived from the States.

Selbys take over

Hal B. Selby, a former printer from Bellingham, Washington, joined Elliott Stewart as owner of the *Prospector* and *Miner*, serving as editor. Stewart was business manager. After a couple of years, Selby became sole owner.

Selby had spent the best years of his life in the States before realizing his dream of moving to Alaska. He was born in Jerseyville, Illinois, on March 28, 1868. After learning the printing trade in his father's shop in Hardin, Illinois, he went to Fort Myers, Florida, where he worked several years as a printer. He married Alice Haskew on February 14, 1896. They had two sons, Tom and Harry, and a daughter Ruth, all later active in the newspaper and printing business.

Selby and his wife set off for the Klondike in 1898 but stopped at Bellingham to recoup their finances. They stayed there for eighteen years. Selby worked most of the time on the *Bellingham Herald* and the *Morning Reveille*.

After its fire, Valdez began losing population to the new railroad town, Seward. Its remaining residents feared for the town's future. Hometown boosterism was needed to dissuade people from deserting Valdez. Selby's editorials envisioned "a smelter on Valdez Bay, a fish cannery on the city dock, and a stamp mill pounding away on our waterfront."

Although the Third Division's two territorial senators were Valdez residents and ardent statehood advocates, the *Prospector* and *Miner* remained neutral on the subject.

After six months of silence, Frame was back in type with his weekly *Forty-Ninth Star*, promoting statehood. He was backed by John S. Heckey, a Valdez merchant and deputy U.S. marshal. In the initial issue of December 5, 1915, Frame promised that the *Forty-Ninth Star* would "twinkle continuously and everlastingly until statehood is secured for this grand and glorious country of the North. There is no country in the world where the government of the people is in the hands of those who have been so overwhelmingly rejected by those governed as is poor old Alaska."

He said Alaskans were being peonized rather than colonized.

Frame moved his plant to Anchorage in the spring of 1916, joining forces with Robert and Hazel Hunter, who were publishing *The Weekly Alaskan*.

Valdez's *Daily Prospector* suspended publication in May 1918, primarily because its staff had been drafted for World War I and replacements were unavailable. That was the end of daily newspapering in Valdez. The weekly *Miner* continued publication.

Newspaper syndicate fails

When the Republicans returned to power in 1921, Selby and Harry Steel of the *Cordova Times* planned to form a syndicate of Republican-oriented newspapers in Juneau, Cordova, Valdez, and Seward, to promote the candidacy of George Hazelet of Cordova for governor, in opposition to Wickersham. As a first step, they bought the *Seward Gateway* and Selby moved to Seward to become the editor.

The syndicate scheme fizzled when Scott C. Bone, a *Seattle P-I* editor, was appointed governor instead of either Wickersham or Hazelet.

The *Miner* continued publication under the editorship of Charles Herbert Wilcox, a mining engineer who had lived in the Valdez area since 1898. At one time he had been co-publisher of the *Cordova Times*.

Wilcox urged moving the capital from Juneau to Seward, writing almost daily editorials on the subject. He compiled a list of reasons for the relocation.

"It is impossible to do business with the capital as far away as from Chicago to London; the logical site for the capital was in central Alaska," he wrote in the *Miner* February 26, 1921.

Wilcox received political appointments whenever the Democrats were in office. He was deputy and chief clerk of the district court for the Third Judicial Division from 1917 to 1920 and deputy clerk and chief deputy U.S. marshal from 1933 until 1940 when the court's headquarters moved to Anchorage.

When Wilcox became clerk of the district court, the editorial reins of the *Miner* passed from one to the other of local scribes, including Alaska Egan, brother of William A. Egan, Alaska's first state governor.

Its stockholders suspended publication in the fall of 1934 for a three-month overhaul of the mechanical equipment. Hal Selby, who had been south for medical attention, arrived back in town in December when the plant was ready to resume operation. He took over as editor.

Despite his efforts to inspire optimism, Selby blamed the town of Anchorage and the Alaska Railroad's general manager, Col. Otto F. Ohlson, for Valdez's decline. He wrote a heated editorial March 13, 1936, titled "The Rape of Valdez," after Secretary of Interior Harold Ickes levied a toll on all freight trucked over the Richardson Highway between Valdez and Fairbanks to discourage competition with the railroad.

When Dr. Ernest Gruening, director of the Division of Territories and Insular Possessions, returned to Washington from a visit to Alaska in the summer of 1936, he reported that "it was like turning the clock back a quarter of a century – the towns were the vintage of '98."

Selby responded in an editorial June 26, 1936, titled "Who Made Alaska Behind the Times?"

> If Alaska is a quarter of a century behind the States, who made us that way? Who made us living curios for the rest of America? Who has consistently pulled our caudal appendage and caused the hirsute facial adornments to grow longer year by year? The Government!
>
> We have been steamrollered, carpetbagged, taxed and retaxed to a standstill. Our fisheries, our game, our minerals

and our timber have been bureaucrated to death. Rule from Washington by a set of officials who have gutted the Territory repeatedly, can one wonder that we look like something the cat dragged out of the woods?

We are forced to use British Columbia coal, with mountains of coal of our own; we use British Columbia newsprint with forests dying of old age – some of the finest pulpwood in the world, and are charged from 20% to 50% more for everything we buy in Seattle, because we are Alaskans.

In July 1936, Selby was out driving with friends one evening when their car went over an embankment and Selby suffered a fractured skull. That forced him to slow down. His son Tom and daughter Ruth helped put out the paper in order to lighten his load.

The paper reached a paid circulation in 1939 of 1,600, larger than any other weekly paper in Alaska. The majority of subscribers were former Valdez residents living Outside. Although the annual subscription was only $2, about three hundred subscribers were in arrears in their payments, a financial burden for the one-man operation.

Assailed by wartime shortages in help, supplies and business, Tom Selby suspended the *Miner* as a newspaper in 1943. He moved the *Miner* equipment to Juneau and began a commercial printing shop, Miner Publishing Company. That operation lasted until the mid-1990s, the last forty years owned and operated by Jack and Jeannie Gucker, who closed it when they retired.

Valdez was without a newspaper for twelve years after the *Miner* suspended. Then Helen L. Long introduced the *Valdez Breeze* in the summer of 1955.

Chapter 24

Railroad and Harry Rise and Fall

Katalla residents were hunting their last porcupines; Valdez residents were recovering from the Reynolds fiasco – thankful for a wagon trail to Fairbanks – when the Copper River & Northwestern Railway was completed out of Cordova in March 1911. Cordova bustled with anticipation of ore shipments.

Despite that, Robert (Bob) McChesney suspended Cordova's *North Star* after crushing his foot in an accident. He sold his equipment to some Valdez businessmen. That left the Steel brothers, Harry and Will, unopposed with their *Cordova Daily Alaskan*. Will was business manager but lived in Seattle. Harry ran the paper.

Their monopoly didn't last long. When it appeared that the Democrats were likely to win the national election in 1912, Cordova's Democratic leaders decided the time had come to launch a Democratic organ to counteract the Republican-oriented *Alaskan*.

A group of local businessmen organized the Alaska Times Publishing Company with A. Judson Adams as president, Charles H. Scheffler as treasurer and James Flynn as secretary. Charles Wilcox bought in later.

U.S. Commissioner Adams was one of the original townsite planners. Scheffler, a longtime Alaska printer, had recently arrived from Juneau. Flynn was a Cordova businessman. Wilcox was a mining engineer.

On May 4, 1913, the weekly *Alaska Times* appeared with Flynn as editor and Scheffler in charge of the mechanical department. It was a seven-column, four-page, standard size sheet that came out on Sunday mornings.

On December 2, 1914, it became a daily with – surprise – Harry Steel, hired away from the *Alaskan*, as editor, reminiscent of Harry's newspaper switch in Nome eight years earlier.

Harry Steel's teaming up with the Democrats after being such a staunch Republican all of his life, struck some of his newspaper peers as strange. John Frame wrote in the Valdez *Commoner*:

> Something has happened to Ole down in Cordova. Harry Steel, the man who was made postmaster under Taft by recommendation of L. P. Shackleford, has joined with Charlie Scheffler and Charlie Wilcox who have been publishing *The Alaska Times* as a Murphy Democratic organ, and the fusion trio have started the *Daily Times* while Willie Steel has his name at the head of the editorial column of the *Daily Alaskan*. It seems that these Taft Republicans and Murphy Democrats don't care who they sleep with as long as they can hang on to the post office and play goat during the political campaigns.

Steels tangle

A rift developed between the Steel brothers due in large part to Harry's heavy drinking. Although an able writer when he was sober, Harry went on binges that lasted for days. Will came north to take charge of the *Alaskan* after Harry switched papers.

Cordova's future looked bright. Two million dollars worth of copper a month was shipped through its port to a Tacoma smelter. The Copper River & Northwestern Railway planned to extend a branch line to the Katalla coal fields and the federal government had allotted $100,000 for a new federal building for the town

The big question at the time was which town would be the coastal terminus of the government railroad – Cordova, Valdez or Seward. Harry Steel ran front-page slogans such as "When Alaska's Coal Fields are Unlocked Cordova will Become the Permanent Metropolis" and "Construction of Trunk Line from Cordova to Fairbanks with Coal Branch to Soon Start."

When Congress passed the railroad authorization bill, Cordovans celebrated with the city's brass band marching down the main street.

They lit a huge bonfire. Passage of the bill was regarded as the dawn of a brighter day for Alaska and Cordova.

It was expected that coal from the Bering field would be brought to Cordova and a smelter established, using cheap local coal to process the rich copper ore. Press dispatches reported that the Alaska Syndicate offered to sell or lease the Copper River & Northwestern Railway to the government for its proposed railway system.

Acrimonious bickering became daily fare as the Steel brothers battled for the community's support. Will referred to the *Times* as the "Weakly Joke," contending that it had come into existence solely to put the *Alaskan* out of business and advance the political ambitions of Commissioner Adams.

Cordova had its "establishment" and its "proletariat" and George Hazelet was the leader of the former. He moved to Alaska from Nebraska during the 1898 gold stampede and helped organize the railway for the Syndicate. He platted Cordova's original townsite and served as its first mayor. He owned all of the town's utilities – water, electricity and telephones – and he was a Republican leader in territorial affairs. Whenever there was a local or territorial election, there were two tickets in the field – Hazelet's and the other one.

When the Steel brothers first arrived, they were allied with the Hazelet faction. But as the years passed, Will supported issues which he perceived as benefiting the majority of the citizens, sometimes colliding with the biggest taxpayers and prominent politicians. Harry sided with the "establishment" viewing it as essential to the town's economic stability.

Bad year for Harry

The year 1915 was a bad one for Harry Steel. His wife divorced him. He lost his jobs as postmaster and as editor of the *Alaska Times*.

It was a bitter disappointment for Cordovans when word came that Seward had been chosen as the coastal terminus for the government railroad. The Bering River coal fields were still withdrawn from development and the Syndicate was hesitant to expand its operations.

The town's economy was at low ebb. Its population had fallen below one thousand. Both papers were losing money. Will Steel closed *The Alaskan*. In a farewell editorial on May 31, 1915, he wrote that it was necessary for him to be absent for two or three months and he had been unable to find a replacement.

Harry Steel had edited *The Anchorage Daily Times* for his friend Charlie Herron during the summer of 1916. He was rehired that fall at the *Alaska Times*, by then called the *Cordova Times*.

During World War I, the *Times* became a four-page tabloid, with canned editorials and very little local news. The front page was filled with war news and the rest of the paper was primarily Associated Press features. Local politics was so humdrum that only forty-three voters turned out in a city election in April 1919.

Herron chain hits Cordova

For ten months in 1918-19, Cordova enjoyed the luxury of two daily newspapers. Cordovans owed this marvel to Charlie Herron's political dreams. Herron had visions of becoming Alaska's governor and decided that a chain of newspapers would help. He also wanted to get on the James Wickersham bandwagon – after years of opposing him – by launching a Wickersham organ in opposition to the Harry Steel-edited *Times*.

The Cordova Daily Herald appeared on July 1, 1918, with Klondike and Fairbanks veteran James Wilbur Ward in charge. Ward was transferred by Herron from his *Anchorage Daily Times* where Ward was the *Times*' business manager.

"Why the *Herald* Is Here" was the caption of the initial editorial:

> *The Cordova Daily Herald* is owned entirely by private capital and its establishment is purely a business venture. The owners have no wrongs to right, no grievances to adjust, no axes to grind, but come into the local field with the kindliest feelings toward every man, woman and child in the city, willing to share a just burden of the responsibilities and labors necessary for the support and upbuilding of the community.
>
> With the exception of adherence to the Republican party, the principles of which will at all times be supported, the *Herald* is affiliated with no faction, group or clique.

It was a bright, newsy paper brimming with ads. It came out seven mornings a week. It appeared at a time when the War Industries Board laid down strict rules because of an acute newsprint shortage. It limited printings and forbid free promotion copies. The

LOYALTY TO TOWN IS THE LUBRICANT THAT MAKES THE WHEELS OF TRADE GO ROUND

Cordova Daily Alaskan

CORDOVA, ALASKA, SATURDAY EVENING, JULY 9, 1910.

J. S. NAVY YEARNS FOR ALASKA COAL

IGHT AGAINST FOREST FIRES

On Account of Withdrawal of these Lands and Lack of Transportation Facilities Government is Seeking Fuel on the Pacific Coast.

FOREST FIRES IN MICHIGAN

DOVA THE COPPER GATE OF ALASKA

The Alaska Times

CORDOVA, ALASKA, SUNDAY, OCTOBER 12, 1913.

TTLE DRYDOCK PLANT IS BURNING

ATHLETICS ARE WORLD CHAMPS | **SHIPBUILDING PLANT IN DANGER OF DESTRUCTION** | **DESTRUCTIVE FIRE TREADWELL**

Cordova Daily Herald

CORDOVA, ALASKA, FRIDAY, JANUARY 3, 1919.

TTLE FIRM MAY FINISH RO

BMIT ITS OR TAKING | **GERMAN GOTHA WAS BUILT TO ACCOMMODATE** | **TRANSPORT NOW IS IN** | **SUFFRAGETTES ARE ATTACKED;** | **EBERT CABINET FORMED: UNITY**

paper was a financial loser from the start and ceased publication April 26, 1919.

In the fall of 1920, Harry Steel became sole owner of the *Cordova Times*.

Harry Steel remarried in the fall of 1922 but his wife chose to live in Seattle where he visited her several times a year. Norman Brown, Steel's associate editor, recalled that the Browns often had Steel to dinner in their small apartment on the top floor of the *Cordova Times* Building and that Steel spent many holidays with them. They never met Steel's wife but he would refer to her as "my little wife in Seattle."

The job printing shop at the *Times*, with its Kelly automatic press, was a money maker. It was the only job press of its kind in Alaska in the early 1920s. A list of its publications in 1923 indicated a large volume of business for the town's lone print shop, especially from the Alaska Syndicate's Kennecott Mines and its railroad.

Steel took frequent two-month vacations, relying on his employees to turn out the paper and commercial printing during his absences.

Klondike veteran a gentleman

Harry died in the Virginia Mason Hospital in Seattle on July 11, 1936, at age sixty-eight. Norman Brown, who had been associate editor during Steel's five final years and later founder of the *Anchorage Daily News*, recalled their association in a letter to author Evangeline Atwood in June 1982:

> I recall my first day on the job after arriving from Valdez. My predecessor, Allan Faith, greeted me with the news that Harry had been taken suddenly ill and would likely not be in his glassed-in front office for several days. Faith had booked passage on the southbound steamer the next day so after a rapid-fire trip through the plant and a very cursory preview of my duties, I was on my own.
>
> I was too naive to realize at the time what had caused Harry to become ill. Even after anxiously checking his swivel chair in front of his roll-top desk for the next ten mornings I failed to recognize the obvious and only came to realize, after many weeks of association with him, that Harry was a confirmed alcoholic.

But the first-time greeting with him during that harrowing week or more was a most gracious and impressive one. Here standing before me in my office was a dapper man, about 5'10" tall, in his late sixties, in a well-pressed business suit, starched cuffs protruding, a felt hat worn slightly at an angle, a lighted cigar in his left hand. His face was ruddy, pleasant and smiling. He introduced himself. There were no apologies, no references to his health.

There were to be many more unexplained absences on the part of the publisher of the *Cordova Daily Times* over the next five years. They ended one summer day in 1936 when Kelly Robinson, the justice for the Cordova area, came to my office to tell me it had been decided to send Harry Outside for treatment. He was to leave the next day. (At that time boats were coming and going in and out of Cordova four times a week making the Kennecott copper haul.) With several others, I went to the dockside. Harry arrived a few minutes later by taxi. He was in very bad shape. After two or three attempts at mounting the gangway, Earl Means, owner of Cordova Transfer, a six-footer, stepped over, lifted Harry in his arms much like cradling a small child and carried him up to his stateroom. That was the last I ever saw of Harry Steel, a gentle man, who even in the fairly "mod" days of 1936 invariably stood with hat in hand in the presence of ladies.

Perhaps Blanche and I avoided Harry when he was on one of his terrible binges and no doubt Harry made it a point never to appear in our presence when he was drunk but I can say we never saw him except as the perfect gentleman he was.

Your reference to the Steels' background in the Keystone state as their having come from a well-to-do family of long practiced traits of good breeding recalls a habit of Harry of changing his suit jacket when he came to his office each morning and slipping into a hunting-type, loose fitting coat with leather patches at the elbows.

He would then sit down at his desk and write in longhand his contributions for the day. Then he would prowl around the shop, stepping over to the stones to rearrange some type or set a running head from a type case. Satisfied, he would change back to his suit jacket and leave, usually for the day. His pieces were usually editorials or an interview with someone who had just arrived on a stopover trip. His editorials were no longer the red-hot type you described although now and then he would go after the chamber of commerce or the council, usually remonstrating one or both for failure to promote this or that project for Cordova.

One morning I recall, he came in, rushed immediately to his desk and dashed off three or four pages of handwritten copy and brought it to me with instructions that it should have prime righthand space on the front page with a 6-column banner. Later the glow must have faded from his "scoop." He called in and ordered the story held up. Mostly without attribution, it was an account of a huge new mining venture for Cordova in which millions were to be invested – another Kennecott.

Immediately following this non-announcement there was once more a prolonged absence from his swivel chair and roll-top desk.

His reporting style was convincing and usually quite clear despite the fact that it was well-sprinkled with flowery words and idioms, the influence of his newspapering that had started closer to the Victorian traditions. I used to pencil it somewhat, but not enough to offend him.

A column heading I never changed, however, was one that he had written apparently in the early days of his Cordova editorship. It was this: Breezy Items Wafted Down from Chitina.

To me this was another Harry Steel, free from that horrendous burden on his back, enjoying the freedom and pleasure of editing and stylizing his own newspaper. The message to me was that Harry had had happier days, thank goodness.

Ranks of Klondike newmen were thinning. Cremation followed Steel's funeral service and his sister, Annette Steel Ladd, of Washington, DC inherited the paper.

Commenting on his passing, Juneau's *Empire* said: "During his forty years in Alaska, he fought honestly and sincerely for what he considered the best interests of the territory. A crackerjack newspaperman and an Alaskan of the first water."

Mrs. Ladd offered to sell the paper to Brown, but he declined. He could see that the Kennecott operations were phasing out. Instead, Brown accepted the job of managing editor of *The Anchorage Daily Times* in January 1937.

Everett Howard Pettyjohn, a *Cordova Times* printer, took charge when Brown moved to Anchorage. He had been with the paper for five years.

In August 1939, Pettyjohn and James A. Nelson, another *Times* printer, bought the paper from Mrs. Ladd. Pettyjohn became sole owner shortly thereafter.

The last train from Chitina

At a hearing before the Interstate Commerce Commission on January 16, 1939, the Copper River & Northwestern Railway was granted permission to abandon its operations. It sold its Alaska Steamship Company in 1944 to the Skinner & Eddy Corporation of Seattle for $4,290,000.

The *Cordova Times* recorded the movement of the last train from Chitina to Cordova on November 11, 1938, with the caption:

"Iron Trail Ends Twenty-Seven-Year Career; Last Train In."

The Alaska Syndicate estimated having spent more than $40 million in surveys, purchases and construction of the railroad. At times, more than six thousand men were employed during the three-and-a-half years of construction.

Cordova was not affected unduly by the closing of the railroad, because it was riding high on fisheries. Its population varied between 1,500 in the winter and two thousand in the summer.

Salmon fishing was at a record high level and razor clam production was booming. There were nine canneries in its vicinity. The average annual catch of salmon in Alaska between 1934 and 1938 was 104 million fish. That record stood until the 1990s.

But four ghost towns, their newspapers and editors a memory, resulted with the end of Copper River mineral development and closing of the railroad – Katalla, Kennecott, Chitina and McCarthy.

Chapter 25

Seward, a Newsman's Dream

John Edmund Ballaine envisioned unlocking Alaska's mineral wealth by building a railroad from tidewater into the Interior before railroad visionaries at Valdez, Cordova, Katalla and Haines. Although he didn't finish his railroad, it progressed far enough under later owners that the federal government bought it as a start for the Alaska Railroad from Seward to Anchorage and Fairbanks.

Ballaine was born in Iowa on September 2, 1868, and traveled west with his parents and six brothers over the Oregon Trail at age eleven. After attending Whitman College, he taught briefly. He was a reporter for the *Spokane Spokesman* and later published the *Colfax* (Washington) *Gazette*. He was managing editor of the *Washington* (DC) *Post* in the late 1890s.

He returned from the Spanish American War, a veteran of thirty-four battles, with a grand idea – a railroad stretching from the shores of ice-free Resurrection Bay, through the undeveloped wealth of Southcentral Alaska, to the riches of the Tanana Valley.

Resurrection Bay, an estuary off the Gulf of Alaska on the southeast coast of Kenai Peninsula, received its name from Alexander Baranov, who visited it on Easter Sunday, 1792, Russian Resurrection Day. The Russians built a shipyard just below what is now known as Lowell Point, and launched a number of ships there between 1792 and 1799.

Ballaine's surveyors went north in the summer of 1902. He and his first construction crew landed from the steamer *Santa Ana* on August 28, 1903, three years before the Alaska Syndicate started its railroad out of Valdez and M. J. Heney started his railroad out of Cordova.

Seward's townsite was laid out in blocks and 1,273 lots were registered in the names of John and Frank Ballaine. John Ballaine christened the town "Seward" in honor of William H. Seward, the secretary of state who negotiated the purchase of Alaska from the Russians in 1867.

First railroad, first newspaper

The first spike of the Alaska Central Railroad was driven April 16, 1904, and its first locomotive arrived nine days later. By July 4, track was laid to Mile Seven.

The Ballaine brothers launched the weekly *Seward Gateway* on August 19, 1904, with Randall H. Kemp as editor. He had been a mining engineer for thirty years and worked on a number of stateside newspapers. The *Gateway* started as a tabloid, five columns to each of the four pages and sold for a dime. The staff included three veteran Alaska newsmen – Walter Wyatt from the *Ketchikan Mining Journal*, Elliott Stewart from the Valdez *Alaska Prospector*, and Tad Hillary from Skagway's *Alaskan*. Claud Dech, a Juneau printer, completed the staff.

A front-page story told of Ballaine's arrival in Seward on August 1, 1904, with the top officials of the Alaska Central Railroad and how the party traveled to the Chickaloon coalfields. They traveled the seventy-five miles from Seward to Sunrise by horse-drawn carriage and there they boarded the steamer Tyonic that landed them at Knik. From there they proceeded up the Matanuska River on horseback to the mines.

The Alaska Central was expected to employ about two hundred during the winter and between fifteen hundred and two thousand during the summer. Seward's resident population was four hundred.

The *Gateway*'s October 21, 1904, edition published the Seward telephone directory – all fifteen numbers. Birth and death notices were published free, but marriage announcements were printed according to the generosity and financial standing of the bridegroom.

Feds interfere again

John Ballaine sold controlling interest in the railroad at the completion of the first twenty miles but retained his real estate holdings in town. The railroad's new stockholders renamed it the Alaska Northern and spent $6 million extending the line another fifty-one miles to Turnagain Arm. Then they, too, went bankrupt, in part because the federal government withdrew coal lands, compelling them to import coal from Canada to fuel their locomotives.

When the federal government bought the Alaska Northern as the first leg of the Alaska Railroad in 1915, the Ballaines hoped to recoup their real estate investment if government officials made Seward the railroad headquarters. When that failed to materialize, John Ballaine became an embittered man and spent much of his time and energy criticizing the government railroad, even to the point of trying to obstruct congressional appropriations for its completion. Eventually, the Ballaines' real estate reverted to the City of Seward for nonpayment of taxes.

Gateway goes daily

The *Gateway* became a two-page daily on August 7, 1905. It was printed on only one side of a sheet and sold for a nickel. After three months, it increased to four pages by printing on both sides of the sheet and folding the sheet to tabloid size. The price went up to a dime.

Kemp left the paper in October to become recruiting officer for the railroad. Wyatt became general manager of the *Gateway* and Elmer E. Ritchie, a local attorney, took over Kemp's editorial duties.

When U.S. District Court Judge Silas Reid appointed Ritchie receiver for the bankrupt H. D. Reynolds estate, Ritchie moved to Valdez. He turned over *Gateway* editor duties to Stewart.

Stewart was editor from January 1908 until April 1909, when he returned to Valdez, trading editor jobs with L. Frank Shaw of the *Valdez Weekly Prospector*.

Shaw's editorials gave the *Seward Gateway* a spirit it lacked previously. The town's morale was low, following two railroad bankruptcies. Commenting on the meager advertising revenue, Shaw wrote: "It's a good thing this writer has a small appetite, has prospected sufficiently to enable him to sleep under a tree, or any other old place, sells a gold mine occasionally, and is a remittance man."

Seward's economic future brightened with news that President Wilson had instructed his Secretary of Interior to locate the government railroad "on a route from the best available point on the southwest coast through the Susitna Valley to the Tanana." That could only mean either Seward or Portage Bay.

But with no assurance, editor Shaw was fed up with Seward and ready to move elsewhere. His exasperation with conditions in Seward was reflected in an editorial:

> This town is cursed with a set of lazy, contemptible idlers, by courtesy called men, who appear to think that it is their privilege to criticize, adversely, about everything worthwhile in Seward.
>
> These loafers, who avoid work as they avoid the plague, times without number, have cast their senile and impotent reflections on this paper, which they borrow from some place of business. The *Gateway* has borne this abuse from these relics of humanity as long as it proposes to. The next specific instance that comes under our observation will subject the cur to a rebuke that he will long remember, and no words will be minced in expressing our opinion either.
>
> These gentlemen of leisure are the same that unjustly criticize our public utilities, such as light and water plants. They burn nothing but candles and steal their water from a neighbor's faucet. They are of no benefit to the town and the sooner they are driven, by force of public opinion, from it, the better the community will be.

Judge Fred Brown appointed Shaw U.S. commissioner for the Nelchina district, the new Matanuska placer camp. The Nelchina gold camp was short-lived. Most of the people left in August 1914, including the Shaws, who spent the winter Outside.

Needham from Wrangell to Seward

Ted Needham succeeded Shaw at the *Gateway*. Needham had edited papers in Juneau, Wrangell, Douglas and Fairbanks. He moved to Nevada in 1906 and returned north in 1913 to again edit the *Wrangell Sentinel*. He was there only briefly before prospecting for gold, then going to Seward.

When Dawson City veteran, Bernard (Bernie) Stone, leased the *Gateway* from the Ballaines in the spring of 1914, Needham resigned and started his own paper, *The Seward Tribune*, on May 9, 1914.

Needham was a busy man. Besides publishing a weekly newspaper, he operated a movie theatre, served as town clerk and magistrate, and did a little prospecting on the side. He sold the *Tribune* to the *Gateway* in October 1914, and assumed the editorship of *The Cook Inlet Pioneer & Knik News*, Anchorage's first newspaper, which Stone was launching. It became *The Anchorage Daily Times*.

Stone and partners bought the *Gateway* from the Ballaines in June 1914 and hired E. O. Sawyer Jr., to share in the editorial responsibilities. Sawyer had come north the previous year as a correspondent for the News Enterprise Association, which sold features to newspapers.

Stone expands Gateway

Stone and partners built the *Gateway* into one of the most influential dailies in the territory. He modernized the equipment and took strong editorial stands. He subscribed to The Associated Press news service.

On April 10, 1915, the front-page headlines exclaimed:

"Hurray! Hurrah! Seward-Fairbanks is route chosen by Secretary of Interior Lane."

Franklin Lane, a former Tacoma newsman, also announced the government's purchase of the Alaska Northern Railroad for $1,150,000. Stone bought Charlie Herron's and James Wilbur Ward's interest in the *Gateway*, becoming its sole owner.

Stone soon had problems with the *Gateway*. When the city council refused to give him a municipal printing contract at twenty cents a line, he gave them such a roasting that they raised $3,500 to start a second daily paper, *The Seward Evening Post*. They hired Sawyer way from the *Gateway* as their editor and general manager. They also had a weekly edition called *The Alaska Weekly Post*.

Two dailies in a town of 1,200 population meant bitter competition. The *Gateway* had the support of the big merchants and the Guggenheims, who by then controlled a steamship company as well as their Kennecott mine and railroad. The *Post* was patronized by the smaller stores and the so-called "common folks."

The *Gateway* and the *Post* merged in January 1917 with Harry V. Hoben, owner of the Alaska Transfer Company, and Frank Ballaine as the principal stockholders. Stone was out. Sawyer was still the editor. The daily was the *Seward Gateway* and the weekly was *The Alaska Weekly Post*, appearing on Sunday mornings.

The Stones moved to Anchorage where he worked for a few months reporting for *The Anchorage Daily Times*. Then he went to work for the *Valdez Prospector*.

Storm hits Seward

A fierce wind and rain storm hit Seward in the fall of 1917, flooding the newspaper office and many residences. Editor and Mrs. Sawyer were stranded on a train from Anchorage during the storm because of washed-out tracks. Upon their return to Seward they found that their home had been washed away and their children were staying with friends. They decided to head for the States.

Elmer E. Friend, with the *Alaska Daily Empire* in Juneau, succeeded Sawyer. Friend was born in Eau Claire, Wisconsin, and attended public schools in Seattle. He worked for the United Press, the *Seattle Post-Intelligencer*, and the *Seattle Star* before going to Skagway in 1900, where he was a reporter for both the *Skagway Alaskan* and the *Skagway News*.

The Friends returned to Seattle in 1906, and for the next ten years he worked for United Press, the *Seattle Star* and the Alaska United Press Service, a clipping service for Alaska papers. Friend joined the *Empire* in 1916 as news editor but for only a year before joining the *Gateway* in 1917.

Under Friend's editorship, the Seward paper became dull and lifeless. He avoided editorializing on local issues. Local stories were scarce. In the place of an editorial, he frequently summarized the Methodist minister's Sunday sermon or filled the space with a syndicated feature.

Friend returned to Juneau after a year at Seward. He became advertising and circulation manager for the *Empire*, and later city editor. He stayed there thirty-three years, retiring in 1951.

F. B. Camp, a well-known soldier-poet and globetrotter, succeeded Friend at the *Gateway*. He left after four months and Harry Steel took charge. The Gateway Publishing Company went into bankruptcy in 1920 and was sold by the U.S. marshal to Harry Steel and Hal Selby, who planned to form a newspaper chain. Although the paper's content improved markedly under the experienced Steel, Seward could not support a daily. It became a weekly.

Times were lean and frequent editorials blamed the conservationists who "branded every capitalist investing in the territory as an unscrupulous, rapacious scoundrel."

In the 1920s, there were fewer than fifteen thousand white residents in Alaska. Many settlers became discouraged over government restrictions and departed. Alaska was set back fifty years, in the opinion of the *Gateway*. In a 1923 editorial Steel wrote:

> In time a Moses will be born to lead us out of the wilderness, but until this time comes the children of Alaska must labor ever as those of Israel, without hope, without recompense, and without escape.

When the vision of a newspaper chain dimmed, Steel sold his interest to his partner Hal Selby and the Selby's son, Tom. Steel then concentrated on his *Cordova Times*. Selbys sold the *Gateway* in 1926 to Ernest F. Jessen and William A. Wolfgram, former Anchorage printers, and returned to Valdez. Jessen and his wife soon were sole owners.

Ernie Jessen starts publishing

Ernest Forrest Jessen was born in Seattle on June 11, 1890. At age fifteen, he decided to visit his brother, Maurice, who was operating a restaurant and bakery in Fairbanks. Ernie worked his way on a freighter from Seattle to Valdez and then started hiking the 471-mile trail to Fairbanks because he didn't have enough money to take the overland stage. Every forty to sixty miles he found a roadhouse where he could eat and sleep.

He arrived at Paxson's Lodge, two hundred miles from his destination, flat broke and hungry. He washed dishes, cleaned a stable and did other odd jobs. At the end of two weeks, he was given a $20 gold piece for his work.

A miner with a dog team offered him a ride to Fairbanks if he would help drive the team, a trip that took eleven days. Thirty-five days after his arrival in Valdez, Jessen mushed into town only to find that his brother had sent him a ticket to ride the stage, a ticket he never received.

Jessen started a messenger service, saving enough to return to Seattle to finish his schooling. Then with a wife and two daughters, he went to Cordova in 1912, intent on going into crab fishing, but financial arrangements fell through. He went to work in the sign shop of the Copper River & Northwestern Railway nights and reported for the *Cordova Times* days.

Jessen's talent as a cartoonist gave him the title of Alaska's leading newspaper cartoonist. In addition to illustrating stories for the *Times*, he drew cartoons for *The Pathfinder*, the Pioneers' monthly magazine, published by John Frame in Anchorage.

Jessen had been a reporter for *The Anchorage Daily Times*, 1919-23 and editor and general manager of the *Anchorage Alaskan*, 1923-24. He managed the Wilson-Jessen Company that handled all advertising for the Alaska Railroad.

The *Seward Gateway* was a two-person operation, with Jessen as reporter, editor, and business and circulation manager. His wife Catherine was in charge of the composing room. The paper was known as a fighter for social causes. As the town's economy slackened, subscribers resorted to barter payments in lieu of cash. One man sent thirty pounds of smoked salmon that the Jessens pronounced excellent.

On to Fairbanks

In January 1938, the Jessens moved to Fairbanks where Ernie Jessen became editor of Cap Lathrop's *Alaska Weekly Miner*. Lester Busey, a staff reporter, took over the *Gateway*, which by then was published twice weekly.

The Jessens remained in Fairbanks the rest of their lives and were successful founders and longtime publishers of *Jessen's Weekly* between 1942 and 1968.

Busey urged road building to connect Seward with the rest of the Cook Inlet country, and joined a long list of Alaska editors critical of conservationists' opposition to development. He pooh-poohed the conservationists' "wheeze that heavy traffic would disturb and deplete the wildlife," adding that "after all, the human element should take first place in the minds of intelligent men."

He opposed a unicameral legislature on the grounds that "two judgments weighed one against the other will produce better laws than will single action." But the issue that aroused Busey's harshest response was Col. Otto Ohlson's suggestion that the Alaska Railroad's terminus be transferred from Seward to Whittier as an economy move.

Ohlson was manager of the railroad. Busey joined the Seward businessmen in organizing the Kenai Peninsula Defense League to fight the proposal.

Busey was one of the few Alaska editors who opposed abolition of fish traps. The paper carried good-sized ads by the Alaska Canned Salmon Industry.

Klondikers going

Newspaper people, the Ballaines, founded Seward. A newsman, Interior Secretary Lane, gave it prosperity with a railroad. And many pioneer journalists from the Klondike – Stone, Ward, the Steels, Needham – followed to provide Seward with a community voice.

Klondikers were reaching the end of their trails in the twenties, thirties and forties. A new generation of journalists would be successful in a push for statehood, and an even newer generation finally established Alaska's first successful newspaper chain, the Native-owned Alaska Newspapers, Inc., which started in Seward in the early 1990s.

Chapter 26

Gold Rush Editors Reach End of Trail

While many prospector-journalists headed for the coast or Southeast Alaska after the glitter of Dawson City, Nome, and Fairbanks gold dimmed, a few wandered Alaska's wilderness still looking for the big strike. George (Buck) Arbuckle and Sam Callahan were among the first and last who wandered the most.

According to fellow journalist Stroller White, Buck had his equipment on steamboats more than half the time during the open season, trying his luck at one gold camp after the other.

However, before Buck, Sam and other Klondike veterans took journalism into the wilderness, James B. Wingate and William R. Edwards leased that famous little Tanana mission press to publish the weekly *Alaska Forum*.

Little is known of Edwards, but Wingate was a native of San Francisco. The twenty-six-year-old survived two shipwrecks en route to St. Michael in the spring of 1898. A mail carrier's route along the lower Yukon River supplemented his meager prospecting income.

In the fall of 1899, he wrote his fiancé in San Francisco, asking her to come north to be his wife. She started north, traveling by way of Skagway and Whitehorse, arriving in Dawson too late to go downriver to Tanana.

The 400-mile honeymoon

After mushing over the ice from Fortymile to Eagle, she sent word to her Jim that she had enough. He should come and get her. He snowshoed the four hundred miles from Tanana to Eagle. They were married in the Episcopal log church at Eagle on January 19, 1900. Traveling the four hundred miles back to Tanana on snowshoes was a rigorous honeymoon for the newlyweds.

The Wingates and Edwards moved from Tanana to Rampart that summer, where Wingate landed a job as mining recorder. The initial issue of their *Alaska Forum* appeared on September 27, 1900. It was Rampart's third newspaper.

Rampart, a supply point on the Yukon River, sixty miles northeast of Tanana, was established in 1896. Gold had been found in the nearby creeks in 1893.

Early in 1898, Sam Hubbard Jr. of California put out the first newspaper, a mimeographed sheet called *The Rampart Forum*. It carried advertisements, telegraphic dispatches, as well as regional and local news. It had a short life.

In January 1899, Mrs. Clara E. Wright started a monthly news organ, *The Rampart Whirlpool*. The sixteen-page mimeographed sheet, held together by bent pins, contained both world and local news, poetry, and lots of ads. She produced five issues and then quit.

Then came the Wingate-Edwards' *Alaska Forum*. It deplored the absence of law and order but vowed to "publish the news regardless of whose toes are trodden upon." One day, as editor Edwards was walking along the street, a man hit him over the head with a revolver because a story criticized the man's behavior.

When Edwards was appointed receiver and special disbursing agent for the U.S. Land Office in January 1901, he sold his interest in the paper to Wingate. Later that fall, Edwards started *The Rampart Miner* in competition to Wingate. A year later, he suspended the *Miner* and left Alaska.

With the field to himself, Wingate began advocating a variety of social reforms and criticized government officials. He accused the U.S. commissioner and the U.S. marshal of czarist behavior and succeeded in getting them transferred elsewhere. He censured a U.S. Signal Corps officer for refusing shelter to travelers at telegraph stations when the thermometer registered 60 below zero. He called the Episcopalian minister "a relentless missionary." He asked for stricter control on the sale of liquor to Indians.

These bold stands alienated him from influential local residents to the point that the missionaries demanded the return of their press in July 1904. He refused to relinquish it, claiming that he had a verbal lease for another year. But the U.S. commissioner ruled in favor of the mission. It took the press back to Tanana.

Thus, an intrusive press was silenced in Rampart, but not for long. Wingate went Outside for a new plant and had it assembled in Rampart after two months' suspension. The plant was a combination of a foot-powered platen press and a Washington handpress. In some manner Wingate rigged the platen to be run by dog power. It was called the "five-dog-power" press, according to Dora Elizabeth McLean in her unpublished manuscript, "Early Newspapers on the Upper Yukon Watershed: 1894-1907."

Mission leases press again

When the mission people got their press back from Wingate, they leased it to Samuel E. Heeter and Sam Callahan, two Rampart entrepreneurs who owned a barge line, a pack train, sawmill, saloon and restaurant. They started Rampart's fifth newspaper.

Callahan served as editor of the new weekly *Yukon Valley News*. The first issue appeared on August 3, 1904.

After a few months, the mission people requested the return of their press and the *News* was obliged to buy a new plant.

Then the mission leased the press for a last time in 1906 to George Hinton Henry to use at Tanana. That was when Henry got himself and the press locked in adjoining jail cells.

Rampart was a prosperous community. Hydraulic machinery had replaced the old sluice box and new gold discoveries were occurring along the tributaries of the Yukon. Despite this economic well-being, the *Forum* and the *News* were editorial enemies, primarily because they were aligned with opposing mining factions in the community.

Wingate was a stockholder in one of the mining corporations, so in August 1906, he decided to devote full-time to his mining interests. He sold his printing equipment to the mission in Tanana, which needed it by then to replace its jailed press.

Callahan suspended publication of the *Yukon Valley News* on August 7, 1907. It had become a burdensome one-man operation. He spent the next two years as a prospector.

It was "30" for Rampart journalism.

Buck stops briefly at Innoko, Hot Springs

After leaving Dawson, Buck Arbuckle and George Garwood established the *Tanana Daily Miner* at Cleary City near Fairbanks in 1906. That didn't work out, so in '07, Buck joined W. F. Thompson in establishing the *Tanana Miner* at Chena. Buck lasted there less than a year.

He and James Wilbur Ward next joined the brief stampede to Innoko and put out several issues of the *Innoko Miner* in July 1908. Then it was on to Hot Springs to establish the *Post*.

In 1902, J. F. Karshner, a prospector, discovered hot underground springs in an area about thirty-five miles southeast of Tanana and about one hundred miles northwest of Fairbanks. The water was near 136 degrees Fahrenheit. He located a homestead and began raising a garden, furnishing vegetables to the nearby mining camps. It was first known as Baker Hot Springs after nearby Baker Creek.

In 1907, Frank Manley, a successful mine operator from Fairbanks, built a three-story, sixty-room log hotel as a health resort for fatigued miners. The hotel was heated by the springs. The area was renamed Manley Hot Springs.

Gold was located nearby, attracting several hundred fortune hunters. It also attracted journalists such as Henry from a Tanana jail cell, and Arbuckle from Innoko.

On July 20, 1907, Henry's *Hot Springs Echo & Tanana Citizen* appeared as a four-column, four-page weekly tabloid. The "*& Tanana Citizen*" was dropped after the first issue.

Henry's initial editorial described the garden produce that grew outdoors due to the warm underground waters – cucumbers, tomatoes, asparagus, watermelons, muskmelons, and various kinds of berries. Manley also was in the livestock business with breeding sows, a herd of cattle, thousands of chickens and a stable full of horses.

Arbuckle and Ward showed up to published the *Hot Springs Post* from October 1908 to February 1909.

Catching up with Buck

Then Buck dragged his well-worn press over the trail and river ice from Hot Springs to Tanana in February 1909. There he introduced the weekly *Tanana Leader* in February 1909. That is where Callahan caught up with Buck, late in the summer of '09.

Callahan started the weekly *Yukon Valley News* at Tanana, the same name he used when publishing in Rampart. He suspended publication after the second issue because he was summoned to Fairbanks for jury duty. After he returned to Tanana, instead of resuming publication of his *News*, he and Arbuckle consolidated their plants. The combined product came out as *The Tanana Leader* with Callahan as editor and Buck as business manager.

This arrangement continued until the following spring when Buck, with the restless feet, mushed off to the new strike at Iditarod. There he launched the *Iditarod Pioneer*.

Callahan carried on with the *Leader* until August 25, 1910, when he told his readers that he was "unable to make the paper a benefit either to himself or the town of Tanana and was quitting."

A third Yukon Valley News

Albert Gustavus Stamm, a staff member of the *Fairbanks Times*, bought the *Leader*. Callahan stayed on as a printer briefly and then went prospecting. Stamm resumed the paper's former name of *Yukon Valley News*, labeling the initial edition of September 22, 1910, as start of a new series. Thus, for a third time, the *Yukon Valley News* appeared as Volume I, number 1.

In addition to publishing a newspaper, the *News* operated a circulating library, an old magazine exchange and a free employment bureau, the latter being an adjunct to the paper's want ads. Anyone in Alaska could place a classified ad for twenty-five cents a day and if no job developed, the price of the ad would be refunded.

Stamm put out a lively sheet. Tanana had its society leaders who dictated the proper social etiquette. As "society editor," Stamm tried to cover the more important social affairs. Calling cards were in vogue and he kept a stock of them on hand.

Democratic informality reigned for the annual community party on Christmas Eve. Every man, woman and child in the area was invited as one large family. The invitation was extended through the columns of the newspaper:

> If you haven't any Sunday clothes, wear your overalls, parkeys, or any other Alaskan attire. Bring the presents you intended for your friends and have them distributed

with the rest. Don't fail to be there for there will be a present called out for you.

The ladies in town and at the post have perfected all the details and will be disappointed if you are not on hand. Over 400 stockings have been made and filled. The immense Christmas tree will blossom out in its yuletide splendor; festivities will begin promptly at 7:30.

George Hill, one of the co-founders of Fairbanks' first newspaper, the *Weekly Fairbanks News*, became editor and publisher of the *Yukon Valley News* in November 1911 when Stamm moved to Valdez to take charge of the *Valdez Prospector & Miner*.

Hill suspended publication of the *News* in January 1913. He placed the equipment in storage and headed south over the Valdez Trail, hoping to find a printer's job in one of the coastal towns. Times were slow in the Interior and the severe climate aggravated his rheumatism.

He was a printer on Juneau's *Alaska Daily Empire* when he died of bone cancer in July 1919.

Hill had no surviving relatives. So a co-founder of Fairbank's first newspaper, George M. Hill – who dragged printing equipment four hundred miles through the wilderness from Dawson to Fairbanks – reached the end of his trail in Juneau's Evergreen Cemetery.

Buck's last stop

It was on Christmas Day, 1908 that William A. Dikeman and John Beaton, a pair of wandering prospectors, struck gold on Otter Creek, a tributary of Haiditarod River. That led to the Iditarod country stampede, the next to the last important gold stampede in Alaska. Ruby was to be the last.

After eighteen months in Tanana, veteran gold camp journalist Arbuckle launched *The Iditarod Pioneer* on July 10, 1910. It came out on Sundays. The first edition had seventy ads for local businesses.

Then *The Iditarod Nugget* began publication on September 3, 1910, with pioneer newsmen J. F. A. Strong and Allen X. Grant as co-publishers.

By freeze-up there were about 1,500 people in the Iditarod district, mostly men but an increasing number of women and children.

Papers Are Ready–Jack Philbin, publisher of the Record-Citizen, stands behind a stack of newspapers folded and ready for sale at Ruby, Alaska in 1916. -*Photo courtesy of the Alaska State Library, Wickersham Collection, 277-4-116, photo by Basil Clemons.*

Buck Was Big–The man leaning on the job press, right, is presumed to be George Arbuckle, noted for his girth and for being publisher of the Iditarod Pioneer 1910-1920. -*Photo courtesy of the Alaska State Library, Wickersham Collection, 277-4-110, photo by Clemons & Koon.*

THE RUBY CITIZEN

SECRETARY FISHER ALASKA'S FRIEND

THE RUBY RECORD-CITIZEN

U. S. COAL MINERS STRIKE APRIL 1

Request for Increase of 10 Per Cent Is Refused by the Operators—Six Hundred Thousand Men Will Quit Work.

Appalling Conditions Result From British Coal Strike

THE KUSKO TIMES

TROUBLES OF M'CORD — He Is Named Defendant In Suit Under Grubstake Agreement.

CONVICTION AFFIRMED — Forbes and Thompson Must Serve 2-Years Prison Term.

Deaf, Dumb, Man, 42, Through Radio, Hears Sound 1st Time in Life

AGAINST ALASKA — Congressman Treadway Deplores Extravagant Government Policy.

ALASKA'S DELEGA[TE] — Introduces Bill for Election of Governor & Secretary by People

Iditarod was seen as the hub of Alaska, a future trade center for a vast area, because it was 484 miles from Nome, 499 miles from Fairbanks and 489 miles from Seward.

It was expected that a railroad would soon be built from Seward to Iditarod. The two towns were already linked by a winter trail that was constantly being improved with the construction of new roadhouses at convenient stopping points.

Buck finally stays put

Although between $200,000 and $400,000 worth of gold was deposited weekly in the two local banks, Iditarod could not support two papers. Strong and Grant suspended publication of the *Nugget* August 10, 1911. The Strongs stored some of the equipment and went on a European tour. Grant shipped some of the plant to the new boomtown of Ruby.

The Iditarod boom was over but there were still new gold discoveries. Iditarod's population had dropped from thirty-five hundred to five hundred as prospectors left for the strikes near Ruby.

Buck remained optimistic about the region's future so he added a new Model 8 Linotype to his *Iditarod Pioneer* plant. National and international news was available through the telegraph services of the Washington and Alaska Military Communications System (WAMCATS), later called the U.S. Army Alaska Communications System (ACS). Buck boasted that his paper was "the leading religiophilosophical journal and fireside companion of this Interior empire."

Other veteran newsmen-miners arriving to get in on the new strikes lent him a hand at the newspaper office. Charlie Derry showed up in time to put the Linotype into operation and former publishing partner Callahan worked in the editorial department for a couple of years, before mushing on to Ruby. Callahan won a set of the Encyclopedia Americana in a raffle held by the local Kennel Club. That provided the paper with a reference library.

Buck stayed in Iditarod, refusing to be lured by the glowing reports of Alaska's last great gold rush in the *Ruby Record-Citizen* that his longtime friends, Jack Filbin and Chester Snow, were publishing. Callahan left for Ruby to become part owner of the *Record-Citizen* in 1915 and Derry left for Ruby to work in the mechanical department.

On to Ruby

Miners and journalists began abandoning Iditarod for Ruby a year after the Iditarod stampede of 1910. Ruby's stampede was the first Buck had missed since hitting the beach at Skagway in '98.

Gold was first discovered in 1907 on Ruby Creek, which flowed into the Yukon about 120 miles west of Tanana. But the Ruby stampede did not take place until 1911, when gold was discovered on nearby Long Creek.

Ruby, on the Yukon River, became a major trading and transportation center for the gold camps in the Yukon Valley hills.

Two newspapers blossomed within a week of each other. *The Ruby Citizen* appeared on October 1, 1911, with Jack Filbin, formerly with the *Alaska Citizen* in Fairbanks, as publisher and W. F. Harrison as editor.

The Ruby Record started on October 7, 1911, with Allen X. Grant as publisher and Jack McGrath as editor. Both had worked on Nome papers together. After four months, these four experienced newsmen merged their operations into one weekly called *The Record-Citizen*.

The paper exuded the usual boosterism, prophesying a glowing future for all of Alaska, even predicting the North Slope petroleum potential. According to whaling captains, "oil was boiling up through the sea near Point Barrow and was so plentiful that it could be taken in buckets from the surface of the water."

When the government railroad was in the planning stage, the paper lobbied to make Ruby the Yukon River terminus.

The Ruby Record-Citizen hailed what it called Ruby's Golden Jubilee, celebrating the district's "accession to the throne of Success. With the haunting phantom of Doubt banished forever, and with the heroic figures of Victory residing in the minds of all, the men and women of Ruby joined in a banquet followed by dancing. To speak in confident terms of Ruby's outlook now would be like gilding refined gold or painting the lily." Or, so the *Record*'s editor proclaimed on February 3, 1912.

Passage of the railroad bill in 1912 was partially responsible for the euphoria of the townsfolk. They were confident that Ruby was the logical Interior terminus. A commercial club was organized to promote the idea.

Grant sold his interest in the *Record-Citizen* to Filbin in the spring of 1914 and went prospecting. He went Outside for a vacation in the fall, the first since coming north in 1898. He returned the next year to work briefly as a printer for Juneau's *Daily Alaska Dispatch* and Seward's *Gateway*. Grant joined *The Anchorage Daily Times* as a printer in 1916, where he stayed until 1921.

Chester Kingsley Snow became Filbin's new partner. Snow had been a stampeder ever since crossing the Chilkoot Pass in 1898.

After two years of successful prospecting around Dawson, Snow went to Fortymile and then to Nome. He interspersed his prospecting with reporting for the *Nome Nugget* and the *Nome Gold Digger*.

He stampeded to Ruby in 1911, remaining there until 1917, during which time he owned half interest in the *Record-Citizen*.

Prohibition pushed

Snow was elected twice to the territorial House, 1915 and 1917, first on the Non-Partisan ticket and the second time as an Independent. He promoted referendums on liquor prohibition, which Alaska adopted in 1918, two years before the Lower 48, and the eight-hour work day. He considered those two issues essential to the general welfare of the territory. A "dry" Alaska would spell an end to ruin and destruction in the wake of booze consumption, according to stories in the *Record-Citizen* in 1914.

Snow went to visit his parents in Alliance, Nebraska, but was never able to return because of illness. He died there on July 30, 1918, from cancer and Bright's disease.

Meanwhile, in September 1917, Filbin had been taken to the Nulato hospital with an undiagnosed illness and died shortly thereafter. Ruby was without a paper until the following spring when Gus Lynell leased the equipment from the Filbin estate. Lynell had worked as a Linotype operator on Alaska newspapers for twelve years, including at Nome's *Industrial Worker*. He had been a newspaper printer for forty-five years.

While Lynell operated the mechanical department, U.S. Commissioner Thomas DeVane and bank manager A. J. (Bert) Day took care of the news and editorial departments. Filbin left several thousand dollars in debts, a small portion being due the bank as payment on the Linotype.

DeVane and Day said they were running the paper as a Democratic organ, backing the territorial Democratic machine. In suspending publication on August 3, 1918, the editors boasted that they had rid the town of unpatriotic pro-German citizens. No mention was made whether Day had recovered the bank's money.

'30' for Buck

Still in Iditarod when the United States entered World War I, Buck Arbuckle closed up his shop, promising to return when the war was over. Gold mining was at a standstill because manpower was drafted for military service. He resumed publication of the *Pioneer* in the summer of 1919 but after a few issues he became ill. In September he called it "30," terminating a fifty-year career in the printing business. He was confined to his bed most of the following winter and died in June 1920.

In an editorial in his *Douglas Island News*, Stroller White recalled his friendship with Buck since the "Soapy Smith" days in Skagway in 1898:

> No better, no more eccentric, no bigger groucher (when things went wrong in the "front" room) and no bigger-hearted man than Buck ever joined the everlasting throng in the early-day rush to Alaska – or since. He was true blue and lacked but a few inches of being a yard wide.

Will Steel observed in his *Alaska Daily Capital* in Juneau in 1920, that Buck was a humorist who took life as a sort of game to be played with an open hand and square dealing. He was essentially a man of the frontier, impatient of conventions and more careless of the value of money than most newspapermen.

Iditarod was almost deserted at the time of Arbuckle's passing. Only five women and about a dozen men lived in the town and they were planning to leave before the end of the season.

The U.S. Army rescued Buck's abandoned printing equipment at Iditarod on May 14, 1973, and took it to Anchorage where it was placed in the Transportation Museum. It comprised a Washington handpress, a Gordon job press, a 350-pound paper cutter, and type and type trays found inside the aging press shop.

McGrath and Takotna

A small trading post had been established on the bank of the Kuskokwim River, opposite the junction of the Takotna and Kuskokwim Rivers, in the spring of 1907. It served the new placer diggings on the Innoko River. The town was named for the local U.S. Deputy Marshal Peter McGrath. The village was on the old dogteam trail from Seward to Nome via Iditarod. Its roadhouses did a flourishing business with overnight mushers.

It was ten years after the last gold rush that Allen X. Grant, fresh from Anchorage, launched the bimonthly *Kusko Times* in McGrath on January 19, 1921. He obtained the press of the suspended *Ruby Record-Citizen*. He had it hauled by dogteam from Ruby to Ophir and by riverboat from Ophir to McGrath.

The *Times* was a four-column, four-page sheet selling for twenty-five cents a copy. Joe Blanchell, proprietor of the Pioneer roadhouse on the south fork of the Seward-Iditarod Trail, advertised that "antelope and ibex meat were always on tap" and he had plenty of dog food.

Grant missed editions occasionally in the spring when the Kuskokwim overflowed its banks and flooded the printing office, located only a few feet from the riverbank. He moved his plant to Takotna, fourteen miles west of McGrath, in June 1923, changing from a twice-weekly to weekly

The seventy-two-year-old Grant began losing his eyesight. He suspended publication with the March 10, 1934, edition. He sold the equipment to G. V. Rosander, a placer miner in the Flat country. Grant returned to his native city of Detroit where he died on October 3, 1937, another of the Klondike newsmen reaching the end of his trail.

So long Sam

Sam Callahan, Buck's old partner, worked on *The Ruby Record-Citizen* until it suspended in 1918 and then went prospecting. He went Outside in the early 1920s.

In April 1932, Callahan showed up in Seattle after having hitchhiked seven thousand miles, he said, in order to return to Alaska. He wanted to check on a claim he found twenty years earlier on Lonesome River, sixty miles from Ophir.

He made it to Lonesome River, poling a boat part of the way, and then was given a tow by three other prospectors. They went on their way after helping him unload his supplies at an old cabin.

They returned several days later to give him a hand in getting settled for the winter and found his body just inside the cabin door. They reported to the U.S. commissioner at Ophir then returned to bury Sam. No lumber was available so they buried him in his poling boat. He was seventy-six years old.

A verse that Sam wrote to mark the death of a little girl at Marshal during the winter of 1918-19, "Sigrid of the Alders," was revised slightly by George Kilroy for Sam's service:

> On the bend of Lonesome River
>   They dug a simple grave
> And lowered old Sam into it
>   And loving tribute gave.
> Now he rests among the alders,
>   Undistressed among the alders,
> With all Honor and all Glory
>   That any King might crave.

After the *Nome Nugget*'s George Maynard died in August 1939, and John W. Frame died in Ketchikan in November 1939, more than forty desks in Alaska newsrooms that had been occupied by veterans of the Klondike were vacant. Only David Tewkesbury at the *Fairbanks News-Miner* and Charles Settlemier at the *Alaska Weekly* in Seattle were still editing after 1940. Tewkesbury died in 1945, Settlemier in 1947. Jack Underwood and Henry Roden had switched to different but longer trails than journalism before Underwood died in 1960 and Roden in 1966.

Those Klondike-stampeding journalists and their contemporaries left behind many brilliant pages of Alaska's history.

Chapters 27-30

Southeast Journalists

Report Disasters

While Content

and Style Change

> *Every bed was filled with men of all ages, all dressed in the usual cotton hospital gowns. And not a single one of them spoke English!*
>
> – June Allen, reporter
> *Ketchikan Daily News*, 1965

Alaska's Deadliest Accident—Canadian Pacific Navigation Company's Princess Sophia sits on Vanderbilt Reef 40 miles north of Juneau on Oct. 25, 1918. During the night it slipped off the reef taking 353 people below the waves. According to Juneau's Daily Dispatch, most of the victims were smothered in oil that spilled from the ship's broken bunkers. -*Photo courtesy of the Alaska State Library, Winter & Pond Collection, 87-1702.*

Chapter 27

Writing Style, Content Change

Alaska newspaper style changed over the years. A. P. Swineford, with fifty-four-word sentences never seen today, was a practitioner of a verbose Victorian Era writing style when he founded Ketchikan's first newspaper, the *Mining Journal*, in 1901.

Words and phrases commonly used one hundred or more years ago are avoided today. For example, *The Glacier*, a church-sponsored newspaper in Wrangell in 1886, reported: "In the spring, Mr. X and Miss Y, half-breeds married in January . . . ." The term "half-breed" is frowned upon today. Creole is used in this manuscript to describe people of mixed race.

A thirty-six-point headline in the February 19, 1908, Juneau *Dispatch* asked: "Is There a Nigger in This Special Woodpile?" The story was innocuous but the headline included the "N" word.

When Gov. John Brady visited Juneau in 1905, the *Daily Dispatch*'s front-page headline blared: "Siwash Brady Comes to Town," in scornful recognition of the governor's efforts to have the Indians admitted to full citizenship.

"Half-breed," "nigger," "siwash," and "squaw" once appeared regularly. All are insulting today. There was even a popular Alaska song, "Squaws along the Yukon." Conversely, seldom used in print were words seen in today's stories: "sex," "rape," or even "panties." It was ladies' "unmentionables" in ads of the Victorian Era.

"Jap" appeared frequently in headlines during World War I and II referring to Japanese. "Huns" and "Krauts" referred to Germans. Those terms are avoided today.

Early writing style when referring to Ketchikan's Creek Street, where prostitutes plied their trade, is found in the 1905 *Ketchikan Miner*: "An alarm of fire last Sunday night, about nine o'clock, called the fire brigade to the east side of Ketchikan Creek... where fire had been discovered on the roof of a house occupied by one of the scarlet women of the town." They were "scarlet women" in those days.

Modern writing style occasionally gets the writer into conflict with sensitive readers. An Alaska Airlines jetliner crashed approaching the Juneau airport on the Labor Day weekend in 1971, killing 111 people. It was Alaska's worst air disaster. The Associated Press correspondent in Juneau reported on recovery efforts. He was criticized when he quoted a doctor at the crash scene: "I expected to see an airplane, but this looks like a sanitary landfill."

Relatives of those killed thought the reference, even if a quote of another person, was too insensitive to be used in a news story.

A new literary style appeared in Ketchikan when Bert Howdeshell of Palo Alto, California, bought the *Ketchikan Miner* in early 1909.

Skagway editor John Troy called Howdeshell one of the cleverest and most versatile writers in the north. A. B. Callaham of the *Weekly Capital* in Juneau disagreed. He said Howdeshell suffered from rheumatism and high living.

Whoever struck closest to the truth, Howdeshell introduced levity to his literary style. One time he related "a pipe dream" he had while rocking on the porch, with a mug of beer in his hand – a corncob reverie he called it. He imagined himself going into a trance in which shadows took form and began to speak to him about his wrecked ambitions.

Another mood reverie hailed the approach of winter, likening the mountain top snows to "gray hairs upon the brow of age" and "the frost whiskering the trees created a regiment of Ancient Mariners standing sentinel over the treasure of the sea."

News content also changed

Content also has changed. Until the 1970s, small Alaska newspapers listed local hotel guests and the passengers arriving and departing on steamships and airlines. Hospital admissions and births were printed.

In 1972, Alaskans approved an amendment to the state constitution. It reads: "The right of the people to privacy is recognized and shall not be infringed. The Legislature shall implement this section."

The legislature closed access to death certificates until fifty years after the death. Birth records are closed for one hundred years after the birth, although parents can request publication of a birth announcement.

There were good reasons to drop publication of some lists. Occasionally a man would fight with his wife and move to a hotel. Publishing his name as a local hotel guest caused neighbors to talk and increased animosity between the man and wife, who both turned on the editor.

Logistics as well as privacy rules shut off passenger lists to the media. Applications for marriage licenses are part of the public record but the marriage certificate is closed to the public (media). Publishing the comings and goings of residents has been dropped by even the smallest weekly for a practical reason: it alerts burglars to vacant houses.

Although not required by law, but observed to keep on good relations with the justice system, and to encourage public participation in jury duty, lists of jurors are no longer published.

Bylines for reporters are relatively new. Going back forty or more years, there were few bylines. They were unimportant on early Alaska newspapers because the publisher often was the editor and reporter and the readers knew it. It took only five people to operate Ketchikan's first daily newspaper, the *Ketchikan Miner*.

Bylines were reserved in the early part of the century for exceptional reporting or for editorial comments, now called "news analysis." By 2000, bylines appeared on almost anything running longer than six column inches.

Increased byline usage coincided with the social activism of the 1960s and 1970s. That resulted in editors and reporters exerting more independence. Fortunately, the majority are better educated in journalism and ethics.

A cynical old-time publisher such as Bernie Stone of the *Ketchikan Times* might have said, "Giving a byline line is cheaper than money." Reporters such as Bob Bartlett, who was given a title instead of a raise by editor Stone when both were on the *Fairbanks News-Miner*, might respond: "Both money and bylines were scarce in Bernie's day."

Bushell returns

Howdeshall and Swineford were examples of early publishers who also were editors, reporters and editorial writers.

The *Ketchikan Miner* became a weekly on March 1, 1910. Howdeshall sold the paper on May 24, 1911, and replaced John Troy as editor of Skagway's *Alaskan*.

The *Miner*'s new owner was Richard Bushell, back in Ketchikan where he had worked as editor of the *Mining Journal* 1905-07. He had taken a Hadley mine job in '07 and left that for newspapers in Juneau and Skagway before buying the *Wrangell Sentinel*. He had just sold the *Sentinel* when the *Miner* came on the market.

Bushell continued to carry the torch for the "Tory Press" just as he had at Juneau's *Daily Record*, the *Skagway Interloper* and the *Wrangell Sentinel*.

The "Tory Press" referred to those editors who sided with the absentee-owned businesses that opposed home rule, likening them to the American colonists, Tories, who remained loyal to England's King George during the American Revolution.

Bushell carried on his opposition to home rule until he moved back to Washington State in 1915, even though Ketchikan voters were electing to the legislature such home rule advocates as Charles Ingersoll, J. R. (Bob) Heckman and Charles Sulzer.

Socialist in Ketchikan

One of Alaska's early Socialist papers, *Modern Methods*, was published in Ketchikan during the 1912 election campaign, with E. A. Heath and sons as its proprietors. It appeared in June 1912, promoting the candidacy of Kazis Krauczunas, a Ketchikan attorney, for delegate to Congress.

James Wickersham was running for his third consecutive term as delegate to Congress in 1912 as a "Bull Moose" Progressive Republican. Bushell's *Ketchikan Miner* sought Wickersham's defeat and the election of nonpartisan candidates to the legislature.

Editor Howdeshell of Skagway's *Alaskan* warned that Bushell's endorsement of the so-called nonpartisan ticket was proof that it comprised anti-home rulers inasmuch as he "has fought home rule at every opportunity ever since he graduated from the Gloomy Gus School of journalism."

Heath takes over Mail

Martin S. Perkins started *The Morning Mail* in July 1913. He left Ketchikan in October to become a reporter for the *Alaska Daily Empire* in Juneau, whereupon Socialist Heath took over the *Mail*. Heath wrote lively and incisive editorials. He was a strong Wickersham supporter in the 1914 delegate's race against Charles Bunnell, a Valdez attorney and later the first and longest serving University of Alaska president.

"That Bunnell is a good man may be true," Heath wrote, "we used to have a hired girl who was a real good girl, but as Alaska's delegate to Congress she would have proved a sad Miss Fit."

Battle over development, capital

Heath engaged in a verbal battle with Troy of Juneau's *Empire*. Troy was set on ousting Wickersham by whatever means and wrote volumes of words condemning him.

The feud went back to when President Theodore Roosevelt created forest reserves in Alaska and withdrew coal land from entry. The action was taken supposedly to block the Guggenheims and Morgans of the Alaska Syndicate from controlling Alaska resources.

The Syndicate built the Copper River & Northwestern Railway out of Cordova in 1907-11 to serve the Syndicate's Kennicott copper claims. The Syndicate had no coal claims. A more likely reason for withdrawing the coal from entry was to protect stateside coal mines from competition.

Wickersham campaigned against the Alaska Syndicate. Troy favored development of Alaska's resources and specifically editorialized against creation of the forest reserves in 1902.

Heath's antipathy toward Troy, and the town that he dominated, led Heath to suggest that the capital be moved to Cordova, Valdez, Seward, or whatever point was decided upon as the terminus of the government railroad. Heath contended that Juneau was "so graftingly dirty that it would be cheaper to move than to clean up."

Next the Progressive

Ketchikan became a three-paper town for the first time when Jeffrey E. Rivard started the weekly *Progressive* on October 24, 1914, having moved his plant from Petersburg. The already established papers were *The Morning Mail*, with a weekend edition called *The Saturday Mail*, and Bushell's *Ketchikan Miner*.

It did not take long for Rivard's competition to realize that he had come to Ketchikan to stay and it was equally clear that the town could not support three newspapers. In February 1915, Rivard bought the *Mail*, which had become an afternoon paper. He turned it into a weekly. Eight months later, he bought the *Daily Miner* from Bushell, naming his consolidated trio *The Daily Progressive Miner*, with his weekly *Progressive* continuing publication. He had the field to himself for the next three years.

Surrender Southeast to Canada?

Rivard started a campaign to partition Alaska so that the southeastern section would be relieved of supporting "the other unproductive areas." Calling it Alaska's paramount issue, he argued that if the rest of the territory could be detached "from our natural progressive kite, the First Division could achieve statehood, a goal to which it is entitled."

Rivard predicted that the Second (Nome) and Fourth (Fairbanks) divisions had no possible economic future and it was ridiculous to believe "that the government railroad will ever reach Fairbanks as there is nothing there and was too far from the world markets to ever develop a stable economy."

Whereupon, the *Fairbanks Daily News-Miner* responded that "it may become necessary for the other divisions to adopt some retaliatory measure such as holding up the appropriation for a capitol building at Juneau, or perhaps moving the same to Fairbanks, where it ought to be."

The *Alaska Citizen* in Fairbanks, lamenting the "hoggishness" of the First Division, suggested that inasmuch as the First Division is the most insignificant subdivision of Alaska, the rest of Alaska would be very willing to have the towns along the panhandle annexed by Seattle.

The newly established *Anchorage Daily Times* added its editorial voice by recommending that "if the First Division wishes to withdraw from Alaska, by all means let it do so as it comprised no particular element of strength to the territory as a whole." Then adding, that if Congress should pass supportive legislation, then "it is up to Anchorage to become the capital of the remaining territory. It is only a question of time when this result will be brought about anyway, but it would happen earlier with the First Division becoming a separate territory."

This agitation by the First Division to secede from the rest of the territory inspired some congressional leaders to suggest that the Alaska panhandle be given either to England or to Canada as a gesture of international goodwill.

Early anti-smoking campaign

Rivard had strong personal convictions that he did not hesitate to share with his readers. He opposed prohibition on the grounds that then the property owners would have to foot the tax bill, but seeing women smoking cigarettes aroused his righteous wrath:

> Just because women are wearing pants is no sign they should have the gall to smoke a pill in public. It's disgusting; in fact, it's hell. Let's go back to the primitive men. Let's get a big stick and become cave men. As Billy Sunday would say, "a damn good licking is what some people need."

Content of Alaska newspapers definitely has changed.

Rivard suspended publication of the weekly *Progressive* with the August 15, 1917, issue but continued publishing *The Daily Progressive Miner*. He faced some tough competition in July 1918, when two veteran Alaska newsmen, Ted Needham and Paul Stanhope, former *Wrangell Sentinel* editors, showed up with the weekly *Alaska Pioneer*.

When Rivard called the Alaska Railroad "Alaska's White Elephant" and a waste of taxpayers' money, Needham, who had worked on papers in the north, told him he didn't know what he was talking about.

Needham urged Uncle Sam to finish the railroad "and as soon as the main lines are completed, start some of the laterals into the Kuskokwim and other rich portions of Alaska."

He likened Rivard's ignorance to "the numerous pests that invade this country through the summer months, who know no more about Alaska than the ex-Kaiser knows about Snohomish."

The 1918 influenza epidemic decimated the struggling one- and two-man newspaper operations in Ketchikan and elsewhere in Alaska. Stanhope died on October 31, 1918, after a week's illness.

Rivard's Linotype operator succumbed to the flu, leaving the aging publisher alone to put out the paper. Both papers ceased to be literary productions, becoming instead mere bulletin boards of telegraphic dispatches, but neither publisher was willing to quit.

The *Pioneer*, though edited by Needham, was owned by a group of local businessmen, headed by F. J. Furnival, owner of a general mercantile store. The group had formed a stock company to issue a daily paper to discount Rivard's product.

The inevitable thinning of ranks took place in the spring of 1919 when the Needhams retired to California and Rivard sold his plant to the *Pioneer's* owners. The latter consolidated the two plants, launching a brand new publication called *The Ketchikan Times* on May 1, 1919.

They picked veteran gold rush newsmen Bernard M. Stone as publisher and Edward G. Morrissey as editor. Morrissey, then a special writer for the *Seattle Post-Intelligencer*, had been a newsman at Dawson City and secretary to Charles Sulzer, Prince of Wales Island mine owner. Sulzer served in the territorial Senate and was a candidate for Alaska's delegate to Congress.

The new daily was headed for trouble from the start. The antiquated equipment caused Stone and Morrissey so many problems that they resigned and left for Seattle to buy new equipment with which to start their own daily. That left the stockholders in the lurch and Furnival took charge of the business end while Linotype operator W. M. Dynes became editor.

When Stone and Morrissey returned in July with new equipment, they started the *Ketchikan Alaska Chronicle*. That paper was to last thirty-seven years and at one time was Alaska's leading newspaper, especially in the early 1930s when Ketchikan was Alaska's largest town.

The *Times* couldn't survive and went bankrupt within a year. The *Chronicle* lasted until 1956 when its last publisher-editor, William L Baker, lost a decade-long newspaper war against pioneer journalist Sid Charles's upstart *Ketchikan Daily News*. The battle was every bit as acrimonious as the later Anchorage newspaper war won by the upstart *Anchorage Daily News*.

Chapter 28

Hyder Papers, Mines Suffer

Interior Alaska had its boom and bust gold camps – Iditarod, Ruby, Innoko, Tanana, Hot Springs, Circle, Eagle, Teller, Council and McGrath. Southeast has Dyea near Skagway and Hyder near Ketchikan.

Both Dyea and Hyder are near sites of major mining disasters. Fifty Klondike-bound prospectors were buried alive by a snow slide on the trail out of Dyea in April 1898. Twenty-six miners were killed when a slide wiped out a camp at Granduc mine near Hyder in February 1965. Another mining disaster at Douglas in 1910 killed 37.

Southeast journalists reported those and other deadly disasters – slides, ship wrecks, air crashes, fires, storms and earthquakes.

Portland City to Hyder

Hyder abuts the boundary with Canada at the head of Portland Canal. It was first known as Portland City. When a post office was established in 1915, the U.S. Post Office Department rejected that name. The village was named Hyder for Frederick Hyder, a Canadian mining engineer who was sent to Portland City in 1914 to examine mineral claims.

Ketchikan was the closest American port to Hyder.

There is a good paved highway into Hyder from British Columbia's Highway 16 that serves Prince Rupert and a terminal for the Alaska ferry system. Also, the highway out of Hyder connects to British Columbia's Highway 37 that goes north to meet the Alaska Highway at Watson Lake.

Metal-bearing lodes, chiefly of gold and silver, were found on the Canadian side of the international boundary near Portland Canal in 1898. Similar discoveries were made on the Alaska side by 1901. But no serious work was done until after World War I.

Meantime, the town of Stewart, British Columbia, two miles from Hyder, was established and some twelve miles of railroad were laid from Stewart into the mining camps in the Salmon River Basin. The Salmon River flows out of Canada through Hyder on its way to Portland Canal.

The richest ore lodes were on the Canadian side, the chief one being the Premier Mine with both gold and silver deposits. To reach the Canadian mines by road it is necessary to cross the border and drive through Hyder, up the Salmon River Valley and back across the border into Canada. That keeps Hyder alive today with about 120 residents.

The Guggenheims' American Smelting & Refining Company bought a 40 percent interest in the Premier in 1919, which gave the region a boom lasting about a decade.

The Riverside Mine near Hyder on the American side of the border produced gold, silver, copper, lead, zinc and tungsten from 1924 until 1950. By 1956, most major mining in the area had closed except the Granduc Mine on the Canadian side. It closed in 1984, leaving only the Westmin Resources, Ltd., mine still operating in 2000.

In 1928, the portion of Hyder built on pilings over the water and its dock to deep water were destroyed by fire. All that was left in 2000 were a few of the abandoned pilings on the mud flats. The town now is located above the tideline and along the road paralleling the Salmon River. Maritime activity is through the nearby Canadian port of Stewart.

Miner and Silver Dollar

Hyder's future looked so promising after World War I that the weekly *Hyder Alaska Miner* appeared on October 24, 1919, with W. R. (Rube) Hull as editor-publisher. It was a six-column, four-page publication. Hull had worked on newspapers in British Columbia and the state of Washington.

Hyder Papers, Mines Suffer

HYDER WEEKLY HERALD

Hyder — First Alaska Town That Can Be Reached by Pacific-Yukon-Alaska Highway

Hyder, Alaska, Saturday, March 31, 1934.

HYDER ALASKA MINER

Published at the Gateway to the Salmon River, Alaska - British Columbia, Mineral Area

Hyder, Alaska, Oct. 27, 1929

HYDER WEEKLY MINER

Hyder, Alaska, Monday, December 10, 1923

The initial edition proclaimed that Hyder was the gateway to the Alaska-British Columbia mineral area so rich in minerals that Hyder was the "fastest growing town in the North."

Before a wharf was built in 1922 to handle ore shipments, scows landed and loaded all freight on the beach at high tide. Hyder had a twice-weekly gas boat service from Ketchikan, a distance of 155 miles. Stewart had steamer service with Prince Rupert, British Columbia, 135 miles away. There were no roads.

Hyder had a population of three hundred when U.S. Commissioner John W. Frame published two editions of *The Hyder Silver Dollar* in March 1922, boosting the area as a great opportunity for investors. That's the same Frame who had been an outspoken editor in earlier decades in Dawson City, Juneau, Nome, Anchorage, Cordova and Valdez.

His publication promoted wildcat mining prospects but was mainly a publication used to promote, unsuccessfully, his political ambitions.

Hull suspended publication of the *Miner* with the March 26, 1923, issue, pleading ill health. Seven months later, Charles F. Sandford leased the plant, publishing *The Hyder Weekly Miner*. Sandford had come north in 1900 and was associated with the *Gold Digger* and the *Nugget* in Nome for several years.

Sandford echoed his colleagues' support for secession of Southeast from the rest of Alaska as it would lead to solid development and progress, "leaving the less progressive sections to the care and support of the federal government, where it rightfully belongs."

He condemned the Jones Act, the Merchant Marine Act of 1920 named for Sen. Wesley L. Jones of Washington State. He labeled that act as the most un-American piece of legislation imaginable. The law, revised several times since, prohibits the carrying of passengers and freight (ore) between American ports, such as Hyder and Tacoma, in foreign built vessels, such as Canadian vessels that called at Stewart.

Sandford suspended publication of the *Weekly Miner* on April 7, 1924, to spend the summer prospecting and resumed publication in September, changing the name to *Hyder Weekly Herald*.

For the next ten years, Sandford's boosterism kept Hyder's residents optimistic about the town's future. He received generous advertising patronage. In editorials he urged Canadian railroads to build an extension to Hyder and Stewart to link Alaska with the States. He also promoted the Portland Canal district as a tourist attraction.

In addition to publishing the weekly, he ran a job-printing shop and served as U.S. commissioner, deputy clerk of the district court, and recorder. He was president of the chamber of commerce and chairman of the library board.

On December 1, 1934, he announced that he would suspend publication at the end of the month due to failing health. His wife had died, so he was moving to Seattle to make his home with his daughter, Mrs. Charles Smith, whose husband was with the U.S. Army Signal Corps' Alaska Communications System.

Mine disaster

The first news of a disaster at the Granduc Mine was picked up in Ketchikan, February 18, 1965, via a radio message requesting help and emergency supplies. Although the mine was on the Canadian side of the border, the impact was felt in Ketchikan, which became the headquarters for rescue operations and for the news media from throughout the United States and Canada. The mine was isolated in the Canadian wilderness, seventy air miles east of Ketchikan and thirty miles north of Stewart and Hyder.

The *Ketchikan Daily News* reported that a dozen of the 140 men at the mine had just entered the camp's cook shack for a coffee break when a slide swooped down and wiped out most of the camp. It had been built on the side of a mountain near Le Duc Glacier. Those in the cook shack and tool shop were killed. Most of the camp buildings were smashed and shoved a half-mile down the mountainside.

The slide also covered the mouth of the mine tunnel that was being drilled under the glacier for access to the copper ore. Rescuers from Ketchikan and from Prince Rupert dug them out. One man survived after being buried for seventy-seven hours.

A base camp was set up on the Alaska side of the border at the Chickamin River from which one hundred rescue workers worked – members of the Alaska Troopers, the Ketchikan Volunteer Rescue Squad, the Ketchikan medical community, the U.S. Coast Guard and Canadian agencies.

The *Daily News* reported that twenty-six were killed in the slide; twenty-two were seriously injured and treated at Ketchikan General Hospital.

News media representatives from all over the country made themselves at home in the *Daily News* offices.

Recalling the excitement years later, *Daily News* reporter June Allen said:

"Yes, I was in the thick of it. Sticky rings and empty whisky bottles on my desk every morning, the waste baskets full of bottles. Reporters from all over the world here! The wirephoto thing on the empty desk across from me turning and whirring every hour of every day.

"There was one story of a pushy woman reporter who got off the Coastal-Ellis amphibian plane, ran out to the curb, jumped into a cab and yelled, 'Take me to the mine!'

"Then after the injured men had been brought to town, Albro (editor Albro Gregory) sent me out to the hospital to get interviews. Me and about thirty others from who knows where. None of us were allowed in the door. I was on the verge of tears.

"Sister Terrence (hospital administrator) peeked out the ER door, saw me, and beckoned me in. She took me up to interview the men. I had my steno pad out and was just shaking.

"Every bed was filled with men of all ages, all dressed in the usual cotton hospital gowns.

"And not a single one of them spoke English!"

The mine recovered and operated until 1984. It was owned by a consortium of Newmount Mining Corp. and Hecla Mining Co. The ore was trucked to Stewart and shipped to America Smelter and Refining in Tacoma. Shipping between a foreign port (Stewart) and an American port (Tacoma) in a foreign hull is not prohibited by the Jones Act.

1910 mine blast kills 37

A dozen years after fifty people were buried alive in an avalanche at Sheep Creek on the Chilkoot Trail, two-inch-high letters on the front page of the March 3, 1910, edition of Juneau's *Alaska Daily Record* screamed: "Twenty-Four Miners Killed." The subhead: "Powder magazine on the 1,100-foot level explodes as men are grouped to enter cage at the Mexican Mine."

It was Alaska's worst mine disaster. The avalanche April 3, 1898, at Sheep Creek had killed an unknown number of potential miners, among others, on the trail to the Klondike.

The Mexican Mine explosion occurred at 11:30 the night before the paper went to press, as men in the mine were going off shift. The Mexican Mine was one of the properties of the Alaska Treadwell Gold Mining Company located on Douglas Island, across Gastineau Channel from Juneau.

The March 4 issue gave a final count of the dead at thirty-seven with eleven seriously injured out of one hundred in the mine at the time of the blast. Mine management allowed a reporter for the *Record* to accompany a coroner's jury and a mine official to view the scene.

At one point in the story (no bylines in those days), the reporter wrote: "Within twenty-five feet of where the group of bodies was found were two horses. One of them had been knocked down and doubtless never moved, while the other, whose position must have been within a foot or two further away from the magazine, was calmly nibbling oats a half hour after its mate had been killed."

Juneau had a second mine disaster on April 22, 1917, when water from Gastineau Channel broke into and flooded three mines under the channel. No one was killed but the Treadwell mines never reopened.

Juneau the disaster area

A rain-induced disaster occurred in Juneau early Sunday evening, November 22, 1936, four days before Thanksgiving. The soggy hillside of Mount Roberts, site of the Alaska-Juneau Mine, above South Franklin Street, gave way. Mud smashed two houses, a boarding house and an apartment house. There were twenty-three people in the buildings. Fourteen of them died. The others seriously injured.

South Franklin was closed by a pile of debris twenty feet deep and seventy-five feet across. It smashed into the cold storage building, leaving debris against the building more than twelve feet high. It was a concrete structure on the waterside of South Franklin and didn't move. But debris spread alongside the building going out the alleyway toward the end of the dock.

The *Empire* reported that in the first twenty-two days of November, 20.38 inches of rain had fallen.

ALASKA DAILY RECORD

JUNEAU, ALASKA, THURSDAY, MARCH 3, 1910

24 MINERS KILLED

POWDER MAGAZINE ON 1100 FOOT LEVEL EXPLODES AS MEN ARE GROUPED TO ENTER CAGE AT THE MEXICAN MINE.

Daily Alaska Dispatch

MEMBER OF THE ASSOCIATED PRESS

JUNEAU, ALASKA, SATURDAY, OCTOBER 26, 1918

SOPHIA'S MASTS APPEAR ABOVE SEA

Complicating the disaster was that Standard Oil Company's bulk fuel tanks were south of the slide area. It had to barge heating oil to the main part of town until the roadway could be cleared.

Juneau had been warned of the unstable hillside with less disastrous results seventeen years earlier, according to *Empire* files. On New Year's Day 1920, a nine hundred-foot long area slid down Mount Roberts, across Gastineau Avenue and down to what was then called Front Street, later South Franklin. Six buildings were destroyed, including one rooming house with fifteen men inside. Three men died.

The 1920 slide was stopped by buildings along Front Street so the street wasn't blocked but Goldstein's general merchandise store was flooded with mud.

The Juneau *Empire* quoted officials as blaming slide conditions on rain and melting snow.

Juneau newspapers have had more disasters to report upon in their vicinity than papers in other parts of the state, probably because Juneau is the oldest of the major communities.

Deadliest disaster; smothered in oil

Alaska's most deadly disaster occurred on the night of October 25, 1918, when the Canadian Pacific Navigation Company vessel *Princess Sophia* slipped off Vanderbilt Reef, carrying three hundred and fifty-three people below the waves. Vanderbilt Reef is in Lynn Canal, forty miles north of downtown Juneau. The ship hit the reef the night before. Rough weather postponed removing passengers. However, they were believed safe.

The vessel broke loose while rescuers awaited calmer weather. Lost were seventy-five crewmembers and two hundred and seventy-eight passengers, many of them Alaska and Yukon residents going Outside for the winter. Some were Canadian and American government officials. Early in the twenty-first century, a memorial was dedicated in Dawson City, capital of the Yukon Territory at the time of the disaster, as a tribute to the dead.

The *Daily Dispatch* had reported in a small front-page story October 24: "*Princess Sophia* on the Rocks of Vanderbilt Reef. Goes aground at 2 a.m. – Injuries to vessel are probably very slight ... vessel is not taking water ... small boats have gone for passengers."

A large two-line banner screamed across the front page two days later, October 26: "*Princess Sophia* Sinks and 350 Souls Probably Perish."

The three column subhead told the story: "Terrific storm drives Princess Sophia over reef, on which she had spent two days, and she sinks with all on board; empty lifeboats indicate that a chance that any survived the disaster is very remote"

Subsequent issues of the paper listed the names of the victims and the efforts to recover the bodies. The newspaper also reported the coroner's opinion that most of the victims were smothered by the oil spilled from the ship's bunkers when the vessel broke up, rather than drowning or freezing.

The only survivor was a dog.

The next deadliest Alaska disaster was the Good Friday Earthquake and tidal wave of 1964 that claimed one hundred and thirty-one lives, one hundred and fifteen of them Alaskans, followed by the jetliner crash at Juneau in September 1971 that killed one hundred and eleven.

More shipwrecks

The second most deadly shipwreck in Alaska history was that of the *Star of Bengal* on September 20, 1908. The *Star* was part of a fleet of steel sailing ships owned by Alaska Packers Association. It left Wrangell with a load of canned salmon and one hundred and forty persons, mostly Chinese cannery workers, returning to San Francisco after the salmon season. Such vessels were towed out to the ocean by tugs before they found sailing room. A storm hit and the tugs were unable to keep the *Star* off the beach of Coronation Island, one hundred and sixty miles south of Juneau.

The *Dispatch* headlined the story with a subhead that read: "Captain Warner, one of the survivors, raving mad but will recover." The *Ketchikan Miner* explained that the captain was not "raving mad," but was very angry at the tug operators. The captain said his ship split in three pieces before a rescue line could be put ashore and one hundred and ten were killed by storm-tossed salmon cases and debris. Canned salmon was packed in wooden boxes at that time

Mystery of the Clara Nevada

Mystery surrounds a sinking February 5, 1898. The steamer *Clara Nevada* blew up, burned and sank near Eldred Rock, fifty-five miles north of Juneau. There is no mystery about the accident. It occurred. The mystery is what caused it, how many were killed and what happened to nine hundred pounds of gold it carried.

The Associated Press Stylebook for Alaska says forty people perished. *The Alaskan* at Sitka reported two weeks after the accident that seventy-five died. Canadian historian and author Murray Lundberg says all sixty aboard died. A state Web site and Mike Burwell, who compiled Alaska shipwreck statistics for the Department of the Interior, says one hundred and four died. Author Pam W. Randles, writing the most recent in the *Alaska Southeaster*, says about seventy died, but she also says her research indicates four people survived, a fireman, two stowaways and the skipper, Charles H. Lewis.

Two Seattle newspapers debated the wreck, Randles reports. *Seattle Times* editor and publisher Col. Alden J. Blethen charged negligence by maritime inspectors for allowing the *Clara Nevada* to leave port in its rundown condition. Beriah Brown, publisher of the *Seattle P-I*, wrote that the ship had been inspected. The story was reported in the *New York Times*. Randles wrote that the debate over the shipwreck landed in Congress where it precipitated appropriations for building navigation aids in Lynn Canal.

She says she found evidence that Capt. Lewis survived because he was a flamboyant individual who sought newspaper publicity long after the *Clara Nevada* sinking.

Randles and her former husband, Slim, published the *Susitna Valley Chronicle* 1976-77. She is a retired teacher living in Haines.

Ship sinks in three minutes

On August 13, 1913, as many as twenty-four people died when the liner *State of California* hit a rock in Gambier Bay sixty miles south of Juneau and sank in three minutes.

Earlier in the century, on August 15, 1901, Canadian Pacific's *Islander* hit the beach on the south end of Douglas Island, near Juneau. Thirty-nine of the one hundred and eighty-eight on board perished. The *Juneau Empire* has reported unsuccessful attempts over the years to salvage what was believed to be a large amount of Klondike gold aboard the *Islander*. It was on its way south from Skagway.

Don't feed the bears

Other communities have had their deadly plane crashes, shipwrecks, fires, floods and epidemics on a larger scale than Hyder, but the little town, even with less mine activity today, still has an occasional disaster. And like other Alaska gold rush towns whose paystreak ran out, Hyder residents depended upon a newspaper in a nearby town for their information. For Hyder that is the paper in Stewart.

In 2000, the Stewart paper, the *Border Times*, was a locally owned mimeographed paper of sixteen standard typewriter paper pages. Bent pins had given way to more modern staples for holding it together. A front-page article on July 18, 2000, reported that a Ketchikan man, a frequent visitor to Hyder, was killed and partially eaten by a grizzly bear.

He was camping near the Hyder landfill. Unofficially, it was reported that he was caught literally with his pants down.

On page five of the same issue, a notice informed residents:

"Under the (Canadian) Wildlife Act it is an offence (sic) for a person to feed bears . . . People who fail to comply may face penalties of up to $25,000."

Chapter 29

Political Disaster Destroys Strong

The foundation for a political disaster was laid when J. F. A. Strong, who had been governor of Alaska for seven months on January 20, 1914, passed ownership of the *Alaska Daily Empire* to John Troy and Troy's partners, John M. Cramer, Carl C. Johnson and I. M. Jensen. Troy was designated as president and general manager. Jensen had been owner of the Skagway *Alaskan* when he employed Troy as editor in 1902.

Ten days after the *Empire* ownership changed, the weekly *Alaska Sunday Morning Post* appeared to compete with the *Empire* and the *Alaska Daily Dispatch*. A. B. Callaham, a Socialist attorney, was the *Post*'s editor and manager.

Callaham had covered the First Territorial Legislature's session for the *Dispatch* until he was excluded from sessions because of his biased coverage. Speaker E. B. Collins forbade him to come onto the House floor. The Senate held an executive session to consider punishment.

Callaham serialized his controversial legislative reports after he started the *Morning Post*. John Frame, editor-publisher of the Valdez *Commoner*, described them as "rich and racy" because they revealed to the general public what the legislators did both in and out of working hours. Unfortunately, those issues were not preserved.

Callaham and fellow Socialist attorney John W. Noland staged a mass meeting in the Juneau City Hall on April 25, 1914, where resolutions were adopted critical of the legislators. The *Empire* and the *Dispatch* did not cover the meeting, allegedly at the request of the legislators. So the attorneys circulated a handbill listing the resolutions.

Paper free to unemployed

When the *Morning Post* was less than three months old, it boasted of having "the largest circulation ever attained by any newspaper on the Gastineau Channel" and also that a large number of its subscribers were not reached by any other newspaper. Unemployed workingmen received the paper free. It sold for a dime on the street.

Post stories dealt with management's unfair treatment of workers. The federal government was urged to probe into the "condition of peonage that existed among the cannery workers throughout Alaska."

In October 1914, Lena Morrow Lewis, national organizer for the Socialist Party, came north to run the paper. The party had a full slate of candidates for the legislature in all four judicial districts. Callaham bid for a House seat, and Socialist John Brooks challenged James Wickersham for delegate to Congress. All Socialists trailed far behind the Republicans and Democrats in the election.

Mrs. Lewis ran the paper for a year and then Callaham resumed management until it folded in December 1915.

Callaham made a brief reappearance, together with another Juneau attorney, Alexander C. Young, in the publication of the weekly *Alaska Spokesman*, with Young as editor. It was printed in the *Douglas Island News* plant. It lasted from March 25 until May 20, 1917, suspending when U.S. District Court Judge Robert Jennings ordered both attorneys disbarred.

The grounds for disbarring Young are unknown, but Callaham was disbarred for criticizing the judge's handling of Young's case. Callaham was suspended from practicing law for two years.

Six political editorials a day in Empire

With the demise of the *Post* and *Spokesman*, the *Empire* and the *Dispatch* were left to feud between themselves.

Politically, the two editor-publishers were complete opposites. Russell joined the Republican Party in 1914 and two years later he became a James Wickersham disciple. From then on, Wickersham could do no wrong, while Democrat Troy raged at the mention of Wickersham.

The *Empire* was then the most politically partisan newspaper in Alaska. During campaigns, it ran as many as six editorials in a single edition lambasting Republicans or Wickersham. Two editorials consisted of a half dozen paragraphs each. Then to fill out two columns on the editorial page, one-sentence editorials were added.

When Delegate Wickersham promised to introduce legislation providing for Alaska statehood, the *Dispatch* "nailed the statehood sign" to its masthead:

> Alaska is over-ripe for statehood. The time has come when its affairs should be handled by its own people and when the people and their interests should no longer be made the political chopping block for hordes of federal officials. We want to paddle our own canoe. With all the energies we possess we shall work for that for which the people of Alaska are entitled – statehood for Alaska.

The *Empire* scoffed at "the preposterous idea of statehood," calling it "so absurd, so utterly foolish, that one is sorry for its perpetrators." Subsequent *Empire* editors and publishers opposed statehood until the final vote in Congress June 30, 1958, approved the Alaska Statehood Act.

The *Empire* was tough competition for Russell. Before its debut, Russell had the inside track to all of the government printing during the Republican administrations. That changed when the Democrats came into office.

In order to maintain his competitive edge, Russell decided to build a modern plant and buy new equipment both for the newspaper and the job-printing department. He incorporated the Dispatch Publishing Co., capitalized at $30,000.

The *Dispatch* shifted from an evening to a morning paper starting May 12, 1914. It came out every morning except Monday. The *Empire* was an evening paper. The Secretary of War agreed to open the Army Signal Corps' Seattle-Juneau cable to newspapers so that nighttime news dispatches were available. Russell had been able to obtain The Associated Press news franchise, which was available exclusively to only one newspaper in a town at that time. The *Empire* obtained news from other sources.

Russell ran for a seat in the Territorial Senate in 1918 but lost. This disappointment, coupled with martial problems and a manpower drain brought on by World War I, convinced him that he should leave Alaska.

Russell leaves field to Troy

On October 5, 1919, the Russells left for Seattle, taking with them their plant and two printers. On November 7, 1919, Russell launched the weekly *Alaska Dispatch* in Seattle.

With departure of the *Dispatch*, the *Empire* had the daily field to itself. It had moved into its own new building on Main Street in the summer of 1916 with all new equipment including a Model 19 Mergenthaler Linotype, the first of that improved typesetter on the West Coast. Its Duplex newspaper press was the first of its kind in the territory.

Troy had married Ethel Crocker Forgy, the superintendent of schools in Seward, in 1916. She worked side by side with him at the *Empire*, serving as business manager. She became Alaska's first Democratic National Committeewoman, serving from 1920 until 1928.

After a few years living in Juneau, Mrs. Troy's doctors advised her to move to a drier climate. The high humidity irritated her sinuses. Troy announced that the *Empire* was for sale. He wanted to accompany his wife south. However, he needed a substantial down payment. That did not materialize. He had to remain in Juneau and be content with occasional visits to his wife in Hollywood, California.

Troy's knowledge of Alaska affairs gave him a strong editorial voice. He blamed the territory's slow progress on "pernicious federal meddling." He contended that President Theodore Roosevelt's withdrawal of coal, oil and timber lands – in keeping with the Pinchot doctrine of conservation – destroyed private enterprise's interest in the territory.

Troy played a major role in one of the most vicious political feuds in the territory's history, centered on Wickersham. The degree of vindictiveness indulged in by Troy and fellow Democrats haunted Troy for years.

Troy mounts attack on old mentor

In the months before the 1916 election, every edition of the *Empire* was filled with ugly accusations. Troy called for the ouster of his old friend and mentor Strong as governor because he supported sometimes-Republican Wickersham for delegate to Congress over Democrat Charles Sulzer, a miner from Prince of Wales Island.

After the election, Attorney General George Grigsby, a partisan Democrat, ruled that there had been irregularities in voting in some Westward precincts so those votes should not be counted. Two of the three Democrats on the canvassing board – Governor Strong and his lieutenant governor, Surveyor General Charles Davidson – said they should be counted. That gave the election to Wickersham by thirty-one votes. (Collector of Customs John Pugh, who later lost his life in the *Princess Sophia* disaster, was the third member of the canvassing board.) Grigsby appealed to the U.S. district court, which ruled in his favor. This historic political turmoil left Alaska without a delegate to Congress for two years, 1917-1919, until the U.S. House of Representatives seated Wickersham.

No man had taken office as Alaska's chief executive with a wider base of popular support than Strong. He was especially popular with the oldtimers. He had grubstaked many of them and in some instances shared in their good fortunes. He pioneered community journalism at Skagway, Dawson City, Nome, Katalla and Iditarod before going to Juneau to establish the *Empire*. His refusal to join in a move to "exterminate the Wickersham dynasty" united the Democratic Party bosses in one common goal – get rid of Strong.

It was at the end of Strong's first four-year term as governor, May 22, 1917, when he was up for reappointment, that the episode occurred that brought his downfall.

Troy, Grigsby and other Democrats had lobbied for Strong's original appointment as governor, and then turned on him when he would not juggle the vote tallies in favor of Democrat Sulzer. Troy used his *Empire* to support the appointment of Thomas Riggs as governor, replacing Strong. Riggs had been a newspaper reporter in Tacoma before joining the Gold Rush of '98 and becoming a civil engineer.

Riggs was chief engineer on the Alaska-Canada Boundary Commission, 1903-13, and the engineer in charge of the Alaska Railroad's northern construction section.

Had Strong any idea of the acrimony he faced, he probably would have declined renomination. His health was poor and he did not enjoy the politician's role. But as the attacks increased, he became angered enough to fight back.

At first the Democrats' strategy was to discredit Strong so that he would not be renominated. That strategy was abandoned when they discovered Strong had political strength in Washington.

Their next step was to delve into his past in hopes of finding some personal scandal that would destroy his political career. Although the Democrat inner circle knew at the time of his original appointment that Strong was Canadian-born, it was assumed that he had become a naturalized American citizen. By hiring a special investigator, Troy learned that Strong was still a Canadian citizen, hence ineligible to be governor.

The information was turned over to the Interior Department to investigate. When it was determined a fact, Secretary of Interior Franklin Lane requested Strong's resignation and Riggs was appointed his successor on March 7, 1918.

Troy vindictive

That should have been the end of it, but ousting the man from office was not adequate punishment, in Troy's opinion. A month later the *Empire* ran a front-page story on Strong's citizenship.

Troy alleged that Strong had deserted a wife and three children, leaving them penniless; that he had remarried without securing a divorce from his first wife; and that he had been a habitual drunkard. Troy emblazoned this litany across the front page of the *Empire* in big, bold, black type on April 13, 1918.

The whole situation sickened Wickersham when he recalled how the Strongs had befriended Troy, who had been nothing more than a itinerant newspaperman, and never could have owned a newspaper had not the Strongs extended him credit. Of Troy, Wickersham wrote in his diary: "If there is no hell there ought to be for a dog of that kind."

Wickersham traveled to St. John's, New Brunswick, to verify the facts with Strong's brother, Charles. He did indeed leave a wife and three children thirty years before and had failed to get a legal separation from his first wife. At no time, though, did he have a drinking problem. His wife was still living in New Brunswick at the time and had never obtained a divorce or remarried.

Troy and the *Empire* were criticized for exposing Strong's past after he left office. As long as eight years later, Troy responded in his editorial columns to criticism that his expose had hurt Mrs. Strong.

Troy denied he had even mentioned Mrs. Strong and denied that Strong had helped him acquire the *Empire*. He said he was backed by his newspaper associate from Skagway, I. M. Jensen, and that he had paid Strong more for the *Empire* than it was worth.

Obit on page 8

After leaving Alaska, the Strongs spent their winters in Los Angeles and their summers in Seattle. They traveled extensively, going on two world tours and living a year in India. Strong suffered a heart attack and died in Seattle on July 27, 1929. His obituary appeared on page eight of an eight-page issue of the newspaper he founded. There was no mention of his citizenship, his wife and three children in Canada; no mention of the scandal that brought him down.

Mrs. Strong continued to travel all over the world, making several trips to Russia. Upon her returns to Seattle, she lectured on her travels. She died in Seattle on April 23, 1947.

A complete file of correspondence relating to Strong's ouster as governor can be found in the Strong and the Bunnell papers in the University of Alaska Fairbanks archives.

Chapter 30

Dentists Rescue Skagway's Alaskan

As the economy of a town shrinks, so does its newspaper. Traditionally, newspapers have used their equipment to boost income by doing commercial printing – letterhead, envelopes, brochures and even other newspapers. The *Petersburg Pilot* and the *Skagway News* have expanded further, going into publishing books by local authors on historic aspects of their communities.

Another, but most unusual, way of keeping a newspaper alive is to support it with proceeds from another profession, such as being the town's dentists. Dr. Louis S. Keller and his wife, Martha, both were practicing dentists from Idaho when they rescued Skagway's *Daily Alaskan* by purchasing it in 1907, when Skagway faced economic disaster with the end of the Klondike stampede.

That was just in time to be caught in the 1909 Juneau grand jury probe. It brought criminal libel charges against three Juneau editors, a Douglas editor and Louis Keller. One of the Juneau editors, A. R. "Gloomy Gus" O'Brien, had just left the *Alaskan* for Juneau and was the only editor convicted.

O'Brien had succeeded John Troy as editor of *The Daily Alaskan* after Ingvard M. (Ed) Jensen sold the paper to the Kellers. O'Brien stayed only six months.

Both Kellers were active civic leaders. They established the Christian Science Church in Skagway and led its worship services. He was a top vote-getter when he ran for the city council and served several terms as mayor.

The current *Skagway News* and its publisher, Jeff Brady, are leaders in local events and in local book publishing. After the gold rush wound down and mining went into a slump, Skagway suffered. Now those mining days provide material for books. On the *Skagway News* Web site, http://*www.skagwaynews.com*, more than a half dozen titles are listed.

The Kellers had been prominent in Republican politics in Idaho. He served a term in the state senate before they moved to Skagway.

Louis Keller was born in St. Paul, Minnesota, in 1859. His brother, Herbert, served as a U.S. senator from the state of Minnesota. Another brother, Jack, operated a drugstore in Skagway and later helped out at the newspaper.

Louis Keller's nephew, Harold Louis Cogswell, a student at the University of Washington, filled in as editor after O'Brien left and until Sam Wall, former editor of the *Fairbanks Daily News*, was hired.

Wickersham boosted

The top political issue during Wall's tenure was Judge James Wickersham's first race for delegate to Congress in 1908. Louis Keller was among the judge's admirers.

Wickersham won garnering 3,802 votes out of a total of 9,625, carrying every division and taking Skagway 164 to John Corson's 27.

Skagway's *Interloper* campaigned against Wickersham and for Corson, a Republican and a Guggenheim attorney. *The Interloper* folded soon after the election. Editor-publisher Richard Bushell took his equipment to Wrangell where he bought the *Alaska Sentinel*.

Wall resigned after a year to join his wife and son in Los Angeles. In January 1921, word came to Skagway that he had dropped dead of a heart attack on a Los Angeles street. So ended the journalistic trail of another flamboyant Klondike newsman.

Skagway slips

By 1912, Skagway had slipped to eighth place in population in Alaska, with eight hundred year-around residents, but Skagway's *Daily Alaskan* remained among the strongest editorial voices in the territory. It proudly boasted of being the oldest Alaska daily newspaper still being published.

The town's good fortune in having such a superior journalistic product was due to the civic-mindedness of the Louis Kellers, who derived a profitable livelihood from their dental practices, and of the Jack Kellers, whose drugstore was the only one in town.

Bert Howdeshell, former publisher of the *Ketchikan Miner*, was the *Alaskan*'s editor when the First Territorial Legislature was to be elected. He cautioned against electing anyone who had previously opposed home rule because that candidate would owe his allegiance to Outside bosses rather than to resident Alaskans.

He wrote in an October 21, 1912, editorial that the most important point to be settled by the voters was whether this was to be a government by Alaskans or a government by absentee corporate bosses:

> We tell you that the real fight for Alaska home rule has just begun. It did not end with the granting of a territorial form of government. What good will it do us if we have a territorial form of government when that government itself is in the hands of Alaska's enemies?
>
> Will the cannery men sit down and permit the Legislature to abolish fish traps? They will not and you know it.
>
> Will the big mines who exploit labor, allow their elected legislators to pass an eight-hour law? They will not and you know it.

Voters were warned against the First Division's nonpartisan ticket, calling it "the rankest political frame-up pulled off in Alaska or any other country." On the surface they appeared to be fine, upstanding citizens, but beneath the scene they were in hock to their masters in Seattle and San Francisco, Howdeshell claimed.

But the editor's advice went unheeded and the nonpartisans made a clean sweep of the First Division's two Senate seats and the four House seats. The voters caught on by the Second Legislature. Only Art Shoup of Sitka was returned to the House and J. M. Tanner of Skagway returned to the Senate.

Howdeshell resigned as editor of the *Alaskan* in the spring of 1913 to join the stampede to the Teslin gold fields in the Yukon Territory. Later that fall, he went to work as a printer for Juneau's *Empire*.

When Howdeshell went to work for the *Empire*, editor John W. Frame of *The Commoner* in Valdez observed:

> If he is to take Troy's place, the readers are to be congratulated, for Howdeshell is one of the best writers in the north. He is as far above Troy in ability as the eagle in his most lofty flight over Mt. Juneau is above the woodpecker drumming on a spruce log at the mouth of Jackass Slough.

Jack Keller took over the editorial reins of Skagway's *Alaskan* when Howdeshell left, retaining them for the next three years. The paper shrank in size and most of the editorials were "canned." Although it retained the word "daily" in its title, it appeared as a triweekly much of the time.

Louis Keller died of cancer in Seattle on Thanksgiving, 1922. His widow continued publishing the paper until July 1924 when she sold the plant to the Alaska Native Brotherhood, which moved part of it to Petersburg and part to Ketchikan.

Sparse journalism after Kellers

With the departure of the Kellers, Skagway's population of only four hundred residents had to be content with sporadic journalistic efforts during the summer tourist season. In the summer of 1927, Gurden J. Farwell, bookkeeper for the White Pass & Yukon Railroad, published a *Skagway Alaskan* twice a week.

In the fall of 1936, Lois Hudson Allen, a newspaperwoman from Colorado, launched the weekly *Skagway Cheechako*, a four-page mimeographed tabloid.

Mrs. Allen published a weekly in Denver, Colorado, for several years before deciding to pull up stakes for an adventure in the North Country. After putting two sons through college, the fifty-seven-year-old widow wrote to Governor Troy asking about journalism opportunities. He advised her to go to Skagway. Troy, of course, was enjoying his monopoly in news and printing in Juneau.

The *Cheechako* was a chatty, friendly sheet reporting on meetings of the bridge and sewing clubs, the Eastern Star, the Woman's Club, hiking and picnicking parties, Eagles and Elks dances, and individual nightly bowling scores at the Elks Club.

There were cooking recipes by local housewives, jokes, bits of Alaska history and commentary about spectacular Northern Lights displays. One front-page column gave a digest of world news received through the Army Signal Corps' ACS office.

After about eighteen months, Mrs. Allen bid her readers "Au Revoir but Not Goodbye," departing for western Alaska:

> With this issue the *Cheechako* dies with its boots on, i.e., with all bills paid. The editah of the papah is off to the Westward for the same reason that the bear came over the mountain.

Between 1938 and 1942, Mrs. Allen published the *Moose Pass Miner* in Southcentral Alaska.

During the summer of 1939, brothers John and Bert Poling put out *The Alaskan* in Skagway, a mimeographed, eight-page weekly, appearing on Sunday mornings. The first issue, on June 25, was a twelve-page special edition celebrating the visit of the National Editorial Association.

In suspending publication with the September 2 edition, the Polings thanked the community for its enthusiastic support, the school board for use of typewriters and a mimeograph machine, and the twenty-seven advertisers.

Haines seeks railroad

Early in the twentieth century, while Skagway struggled to survive without Klondike stampeders, the *Pioneer Press* across Lynn Canal was promoting Haines. It launched a campaign to convince federal officials that Haines was preferable to Seward, Valdez, or Cordova as a terminal port for the railroad authorized by Congress in 1912. One argument was that Haines was closer to the major Pacific Coast ports through which Alaska cargo was shipped.

For years, Haines residents had visualized trains whistling down the main street, loaded with ore for steamers waiting at dockside. They also witnessed how the railroad was keeping neighboring Skagway alive after the Klondike Gold Rush. One of the earliest railroad dreams was the Haines Mission & Boundary Railroad in 1906. It was to go from Haines to the international boundary at Pleasant Camp and eventually on to Fairbanks, according to the December 13, 1906, Skagway *Alaskan*.

Another was Falcon Joslin's Alsek & Yukon Railroad going from Haines to Fairbanks. He had secured a charter for the right-of-way across Canadian territory, according to the November 26, 1909, *Pioneer Press*, and was operating a pioneer railroad in the Fairbanks-Chena area.

John Rosene's Alaska Midland Railroad also was to go from Haines to Fairbanks and eventually on to Nome.

The Alaska Syndicate's Copper River & Northwestern Railway from Cordova had penetrated to within a few miles of White River. The *Pioneer Press* reported in three articles in 1912 that mining men at White River said that the easiest grade to tidewater was via Haines.

When the federal railroad commissioners visited Haines in the summer of 1913, editor H. P. Birkinbine escorted them over the wagon road to the Porcupine-Rainy Hollow region to display the advantages of the route. The chamber of commerce wrote an open letter to President Wilson urging the Haines route. Had they been successful there might never have been an Anchorage.

In an editorial May 18, 1912, titled "We Will Crow and Grow" celebrating the third anniversary of the *Pioneer Press*, Birkinbine prophesied that if Haines got the government railroad, it would be destined to be the major metropolis in Alaska:

> If Haines gets her railroad and we think she will, we may grow as big as the *New York World*, and when the cars on the railroad come into town loaded with thousands of tons of that rich ore which is only a little way up the valley, we will grow again and we will just keep on growin' and crowin' for Haines.

However, when it became obvious that the government railroad would go to one of the western coastal towns, Birkinbine suspended publication with the July 19, 1913, issue and devoted himself to civil engineering.

Personnel at Fort Seward, adjacent to Haines, published a mimeographed weekly titled *The Fort Seward News* starting on November 18, 1921. Wanting to endow it with more local flavor, the name was changed to *The Chilkat Post* in 1922 and a year later to *The Chilkoot Post*, when the post's name became the Chilkoot Barracks. It carried a page of "Haines Items." The four-page weekly suspended on June 25, 1926, and for the next four decades Haines was without a local newssheet.

The paperless 1940s

The Lynn Canal towns of Skagway and Haines were without their own newspapers during the 1940s. Both communities experienced boomtown conditions during World War II, especially when the Alaska-Canada Highway was under construction. Skagway expanded in population to twenty-five hundred from its usual four hundred residents. Work crews and materials for construction of the highway passed through its port. But the future was too uncertain to encourage establishment of a newspaper.

When the Japanese struck Pearl Harbor on December 7, 1941, Chilkoot Barracks at Haines, Alaska's oldest active military installation, consisted of eleven officers and three hundred men, equipped with World War I Springfield rifles. No road then connected Haines and its military post with the rest of the territory. So, more than two thousand men and women poured into Haines. Chilkoot Barracks and all available local rooms were occupied by construction crews working on the Haines Cut-off, to connect with the Alaska Highway.

'50s and '60s bring new newspapers

The weekly *Haines Herald* and weekly *Skagway Alaskan* were launched in 1952. The *Alaskan*, a subsidiary of Juneau's *Empire*, first appeared on August 28, 1952. Publisher Helen Troy Monsen and her editor, Elmer Friend, printed it until July 1954, and then merged it with the *Haines Herald*, titling the new venture *The Lynn Canal Weekly*. It suspended publication a year later when plans for an aluminum mill in the area collapsed. For the next eleven years, Lynn Canal residents garnered their news from the Juneau newspapers.

The state ferry system and the summertime cruise ships rescued Skagway and Haines from the postwar economic doldrums. The ships' passengers and crew revitalized a tourist industry that had almost disappeared with the end of U.S. commercial passenger ship service to Alaska in October 1954.

The White Pass & Yukon Railroad was still Skagway's economic backbone. The faltering timber industry worried Haines residents. Skagway's year-around population had dropped to three hundred and fifity and Haines' to two hundred and fifty.

North Wind blows in

After a lapse of eight years without a year-round newssheet, Cyril A. (Cy) Coyne, one-time Skagway mayor and state legislator, launched the mimeographed monthly *North Wind* in May 1963. It consisted of eight pages of legal size paper. During the summer tourist season it appeared as a biweekly. It was well-patronized by local advertisers. In later years, it was a printed publication, complete with local pictures.

A twenty-page special edition appeared on June 4, 1977, to commemorate the dedication of the Klondike Gold Rush National Historical Park. Under the supervision of the National Park Service, the historic buildings in downtown Skagway along Broadway were renovated as tourist attractions. After fourteen years of irregular publication, Coyne retired to southern California.

Raymond R. Menaker started a biweekly in Haines on January 3, 1966. The first issue appeared without a title but listed eighteen suggested titles from which his readers were to make a choice. *Chilkat Valley News* won. The paper was printed in Bill Hartmann's Chilkat Press shop at Fort Seward. It was a four-column, four-page, 8 1/2x 11 sheet.

William Jeffrey Brady started the biweekly *Skagway News* in 1978. It was a four-column, eight-page tabloid. It carried only local and Skagway-oriented state news.

On January 31, 1979, the *Skagway News* and the *Chilkat Valley News* merged their operations. The consolidated product was renamed the *Lynn Canal News*. It was printed in Hartmann's shop and he became the third partner in the newly organized Lynn Canal Publishing Co.

A fire destroyed Hartmann's shop in June 1981 and he dropped out of the partnership. The paper was printed thereafter by the *Empire*. A year later, the two papers ended their joint operation, the Haines paper retaining the name of *Lynn Canal News* and Brady returning to *Skagway News*.

In July 1984 Menaker reverted to the original name of *Chilkat Valley News*. It no longer was an upper Lynn Canal paper, but identified itself solely with Haines and Klukwan. It was a healthy, eight-page tabloid weekly with Menaker as publisher and Janis Marston as editor.

A twenty-four-page annual Visitors' Guide to the Chilkat Valley area, called *The Haines Sentinel* was published by the *News* and distributed free of charge, being supported in part by a grant from the Haines chapter of the Alaska Visitors Association. It was rich in history and offered recreational tips for visitors.

Menaker sold the paper in 1986 to Marston and Bonnie Hedrick. A year later Marston sold her interest to Hedrick, who was still operating the newspaper in 2005.

Menaker was a retired Haines schoolteacher and had served fifteen years on the borough assembly. He also was active in the Lynn Canal Conservation Council and in Lynn Canal Players. He stayed in Haines in his retirement.

Hedrick, originally from Ohio, visited Alaska in 1980 on a backpacking trip while a biology student at Cornell. She returned north in '81 to work for the Forest Service and later with the Alaska Department of Fish and Game before going into the newspaper business.

Hedrick's staff included reporter Tom Moffitt, who had been with the *Chilkat Valley News* for fifteen years by 2000. (He has since left for a government job.) Before that he was with *The Anchorage Times*. A second reporter, Steve Williams, had been with the paper three years in 2000. With Hedrick and a part-time darkroom assistant, the paper had a steady staff.

Haines book author Heather Lende, who contributes to the *Anchorage Daily News* and National Public Radio, also writes the "Duly Noted" column for the *Chilkat Valley News*.

The Haines economy fell flat after its sawmill closed in the 1990s. Cruise ships cut back their stops in 2000 in response to a head tax that the borough imposed on visitors. Some visitors take a forty-minute catamaran trip from Skagway while ships are in port in the nearby city. The Haines attraction is the eagle reserve.

New paper less 'green'

Despite the economy, Haines had two weekly newspapers for a while. A group of Haines business owners started the weekly *Eagle Eye* in 1997. They were dissatisfied with the *News*, claiming it was too "green," too aligned with environmentalists' goals. John Florske, a Juneau developer with business interests in Haines, headed the group.

The first *Eagle Eye* editor was Peggy Ormasen. She served from April 1997 until January 1, 2000. Carol Waldo replaced her for 2000 and then Robert Jump was hired as editor March 1, 2001.

Jump was the most experienced newsman to hold the post. He was a graduate of Fresno State with ten years of daily newspaper experience, first at the *Hanford* (California) *Sentinel*, owned by the Scripps League, and then at the *Coos Bay* (Oregon) *World*, a Pulitzer Co. newspaper.

One example of how the two newspapers differed on economic and environmental issues was illustrated by the April 2000 visit of a Juneau magazine publisher to the Haines Chamber of Commerce.

Dave Fremming published *Alaskan Southeaster* magazine and was frequently critical of the actions of environmentalists who oppose economic development projects. The *Eagle Eye* not only gave front-page coverage to Fremming's visit, it also ran his speech in full over the next three weeks.

In contrast, the *Chilkat Valley News* ran a single story on page 9 about Fremming's visit under a headline, "Publisher blames 'malcontent idiots' for economic problems." The story elaborated, "His speech was unusually vitriolic for the luncheon, referring eight times to 'malcontent amateur idiots' he called 'economic bigots' who oppose development and support regulation and whose influence on government action is disproportionate to their numbers..."

But continued business recession hurt Haines. Ben Williams closed his grocery store in the summer of 2002, eliminating one owner-advertiser for the *Eagle Eye*. Other owners said they were unable to continue their support so it was announced on November 11, 2002, that the paper was closing.

Papers at Gustavus

Icy Passages is a monthly "Newspaper of Gustavus" published in a community of three hundred and fifty people fifty miles south of Haines. Gustavus is better known as the entry to Glacier Bay National Park. Editor and owner Chris Spute arrived in Gustavus in May, 1993, as the bride of Gustavus resident John Spute.

Chris had previous experience putting out a newsletter for a club in Minneapolis. So a resident suggested that she start a newspaper. She collected information from people around town and took those handwritten notes to the library and created a newspaper. The first issue of *Icy Passages* was off the press in December 1993.

The current issues, running twenty-four letter-size pages, includes local news, letters to the editor and a healthy amount of advertising.

Chris Spute
Editor/Publisher
Icy Passages

Icy Passages Photo

Over the years, she installed her own computers. Computer problems terminated publication for several months late in 2004. However, the January 2005 issue came out on time.

With *Passages* down for several months, a retired state worker, Carolyn Edelman, started the eight-page *Fairweather Reporter* in January 2005. The *Reporter* claims a circulation of two hundred and fifty.

The *Icy Passages* circulation is two hundred and seventy-five during the winter and three hundred and twenty-five summers, with copies going across the United States and as far as Europe and Australia.

Skagway News survives two hits

Brady's *Skagway News* suffered two economic hits in 1982. First, the printing partnership with the Haines paper was dissolved after the 1981 fire. And second, the White Pass & Yukon Railroad closed down in the fall of 1982. Brady said he was committed to sustaining local morale following the railroad's closure.

Brady had worked as sports and features writer and on the copy desk of *The Tarheel* at the University of North Carolina. He visited Skagway summers, working in the tourist business. He also helped Cy Coyne with his paper in 1977 before Coyne closed it.

After the Haines and Skagway newspapers split in 1982, Brady printed every other week for a while and for three years he printed

Skagway News Publisher Jeff Brady stands before his recreation of a Gold Rush Era newsstand. He holds a copy of "Klondike Newsman: Stroller White," from which he reads to elderhostel groups visiting Skagway in the winter and to tourists in the summer. -*Skagway News photo.*

only once a month in the winter. Then the highway from Skagway to Whitehorse and the Alaska Highway opened in 1986, giving the community and its newspaper a boost. Brady expanded his publishing business. He provided a visitor guide and expanded into book publishing. He also hired Dimitra Lavrakas, formerly of Anchorage, as his newspaper's editor.

The railroad revived in 1988 as one of the most popular tourist attractions in Southeast Alaska, carrying more than three hundred thousand passengers a summer to Lake Bennett and Carcross.

Brady moved his operation into a new and unusual building at 264 Broadway in the historic district on April 1, 1987. The building was built originally in Dyea as Boa's Tailor Building. It was moved to Skagway during the Gold Rush, when everyone was abandoning Dyea for Skagway. The building was among those refurbished by the National Park Service and leased to private businesses.

The *Skagway News* business offices are on the second floor. On the first floor, Brady set up an old-time newsstand and print shop, called the Skaguay News Depot, after a similar business in Skagway during the Gold Rush. He sells antique wood type and souvenirs with famous headlines and stories of the Soapy Smith era printed on t-shirts, mugs, aprons, and totes. He also prints a newspaper page with a space for visitors' names in the headline above reprints of old stories from the Gold Rush papers.

The walls are decorated with photographs of newspapers, print shops, newsboys, and newsstands from the old days. It's a museum of newspaper history from the days when there were five newspapers in Dyea and Skagway.

Among the most interesting books published by Brady and his *Skagway News* is a compilation of police reports that have appeared in his newspaper over the years. Contrasting Skagway's early days, when editor Stroller White dodged bullets fired at an escaping murderer, a current item in the *Skagway News* police report said: "Police received a call from the Skagway Inn in reference to disposing of some type of 'hazardous material.' Upon arrival, officers disposed of leftover chocolate pie with whipped cream and coffee."

Thereby avoiding a "disaster?"

Chapters 31-32

Anchorage from

Knik to Ship Creek

to Statehood

> *The people of Anchorage are so enthusiastic about Anchorage that they consider it reasonable for every person of sound mind to come here. We have heard it said that arrangements have been made to have the Second Coming in Anchorage, too.*
>
> – Robert B. Atwood, publisher
> *The Anchorage Daily Times*, 1945

Eager Alaskans watch President Dwight Eisenhower, seated center, sign a proclamation on Jan. 3, 1959 making Alaska the 49th state. Also seated is Vice President Richard Nixon, left, and House Speaker Sam Rayburn. Standing, left to right, Alaska's first state congressional delegation: Congressman Ralph Rivers, former Alaska territorial attorney general; Senator Ernest Gruening, territorial governor 1939-1953; and Senator E. L. Bartlett, the territory's last delegate to Congress. Next is Interior Secretary Fred Seaton; Waino Hendrickson, the territory's last governor; an unknown White House clerk; Mike Stepovich, who resigned as territorial governor to run unsuccessfully for the Senate against Gruening; and Robert B. Atwood, publisher of The Anchorage Times, and chairman of the Alaska Statehood Committee. Gruening had been a Maine editor and publisher before going into politics. Bartlett had been a reporter and editor for the Fairbanks Daily News-Miner. Seaton owned a chain of newspapers in Kansas and Nebraska. -*Photo courtesy of the Fairbanks Daily News-Miner.*

Chapter 31

Anchorage, the Late Bloomer

Kodiak, Kenai, and Sitka were more than 115 years old before Anchorage was born. Dozens of daily and weekly newspapers had come and gone in Alaska towns and mining camps before the weekly *Cook Inlet Pioneer & Knik News* began publishing in 1915 at Ship Creek, the site that became Anchorage.

Other Alaska towns were founded near resources or military posts. Anchorage was different.

> During a year when hundreds of European towns were being wiped away by war, an American wasteland became, as if by white magic, a prosperous and busy town. Not even the records of Colorado and California, when the soil first revealed its precious ore, furnish any complete parallel to this amazing development.
> For Anchorage came suddenly into being, not because of the deceptive lure of gold, but as a result of that sure herald of commerce and civilization, the government railroad.
> – *New York Times Magazine*, August 1915

Why Anchorage?

On March 12, 1914, Congress authorized the president to construct and operate government railroads in Alaska for developing Alaska's resources. Alaskans celebrated.

President Woodrow Wilson chose Franklin K. Lane, a Tacoma newspaperman, for his Secretary of Interior and directed him to proceed with railroad construction. The Alaska Engineering Commission was appointed to supervise the project.

William C. Edes of the Southern Pacific Railroad, with thirty-five years of railroad experience, was appointed AEC chairman. Army Lt. Frederick J. Mears, who had been a construction engineer with the Great Northern Railroad and on the Panama Canal Railroad, and Thomas C. Riggs Jr., a geologist and chief engineer with the Alaska International Boundary Survey, completed the AEC.

Survey crews spent the summer of 1914 investigating possible railroad routes. The Alaska Syndicate offered to sell its railroad out of Cordova but was ignored. Instead, the defunct Alaska Northern Railroad, extending seventy-one miles north from Seward, was purchased as the first segment of a government road to extend 470 miles to Fairbanks.

When construction began in the spring of 1915, Edes established his headquarters in the old Alaska Northern Railroad offices at Seward; Mears was assigned to Ship Creek and Riggs to the northern section, headquartered at Nenana. Railroad headquarters were later established at Anchorage.

Journalists were on the scene at each of the three sites from the beginning of construction – the *Seward Gateway* at Seward, the *Cook Inlet Pioneer* at Ship Creek and the *Nenana News* at Nenana.

Paper starts at Knik

George Palmer established a trading post at Knik, on the west side of Knik Inlet, in 1903 to serve miners of the Matanuska-Willow Creek district. A post office opened there in 1904. It was there that the *Knik News* was established in October 1914.

A place down the inlet, at the mouth of Ship Creek, became known as Knik Anchorage, because that was as far up the inlet as big steamers could go. After railroad construction started, it became known simply as Anchorage.

Bernie Stone and Ted Needham, veterans of Klondike journalism, met again in Seward in the spring of 1914. Needham launched the weekly *Seward Tribune* in competition with Stone's older and better-established *Seward Gateway*. The *Tribune* was soon absorbed by the *Gateway* and Stone sent Needham to Knik to establish a newspaper there.

When the Seward Gateway Publishing Co. established the weekly *Knik News*, the town had a winter population of approximately five hundred.

The *News* was a four-column, four-page tabloid, appearing on Saturdays. Almost two full pages of advertising in each issue showed generous community support.

Needham left Knik in March 1915 to go to the bedside of his ill wife in Juneau. L. Frank Shaw, who was working as a reporter for the *Seward Gateway*, was dispatched to Knik to take charge of the paper.

Shaw had worked on newspapers in Nome and Valdez before going to Seward.

Knik began losing its residents when railroad workers developed a settlement on the Ship Creek mudflats. So when Needham returned after his wife's recovery, he and Shaw moved the newspaper plant to Ship Creek.

In May 1915, they pitched a tent along the creek's bank and readied themselves for a new journalistic venture. They found themselves immediately amidst discord and confusion.

Anchorage born

Within weeks after the arrival of Lieutenant Mears and his party at Ship Creek in April 1915, two thousand people were living in tents and ramshackle structures on the banks of the creek.

The railroad builders were hindered in their efforts to get construction started. Squatters were in their way. Nonrailroad personnel were equally frustrated in their attempts to establish their various businesses. It was obvious that an area needed to be set aside for a townsite.

The two newsmen, Shaw and Needham, circulated a petition requesting the federal government to provide a townsite along the railroad right-of-way. Washington responded by authorizing Mears to plat a townsite on a bluff south of the railroad yards. The newsmen put out an "extra" on May 27, describing the commission's plans, distributing it free of charge.

Their paper was brimming with ads from five rooming houses, a blacksmith shop, four general mercantile stores, a fish market, two marine transportation companies, a meat market, a barber shop, a physician-surgeon, a jeweler, a dressmaker-milliner (who also made mosquito nets to order), a motion picture house, two combination restaurants and bakeries, a grocery store, a drugstore, and a couple of pool and billiard parlors where meals were served.

The newsmen called their new publication the *Cook Inlet Pioneer & Knik News*, with regular weekly publication beginning on June 5, 1915. A copy of the initial edition was mailed to Secretary Lane, thanking him for starting construction of the Alaska Railroad.

After the auction of townsite lots on July 10, the newsmen built a log cabin on the bluff, moving in during the first week of August.

They purchased the equipment of the defunct *Cordova Daily Alaskan* and began publishing a daily edition in October, continuing to publish a weekly simultaneously. Allen X. Grant, former co-publisher of the *Nome Nugget* and the *Ruby Record*, ran the Linotype.

Both the weekly and the daily were six-column, four-page papers. They sold for ten cents a copy and were the first newspapers for the settlement that became Anchorage.

Subsistence an early issue

An editorial in the initial weekly edition warned against wanton slaughter of wild game, recalling the aimless killing of wild game during construction of the Alaska Central Railroad out of Seward:

> The wild game must be preserved for the man in the hills, the prospector and miner, and the Native population. Those who live in settlements where fresh meats may be obtained at markets are not dependent on game animals.
> – *Cook Inlet Pioneer & Knik News*, June 5, 1915

At the end of the twentieth century, subsistence hunting and fishing still was an unresolved, eighty-five-year-old issue in Alaska.

It was not long in 1915, before newspaper competition from an unexpected source challenged the *Pioneer*. Dissatisfaction arose among the hundreds of foreign, unskilled railroad laborers over their low wages. A wage of thirty-seven and one-half cents an hour, with $1 deducted for board, made a net of $2 a day, a dollar less than the Alaska Road Commission paid for similar work. The mood was ripe for a social-reform-oriented journalist to battle on behalf of the laborers. The *Pioneer* was viewed as management's friend.

Socialists were prominent at that time in politics and journalism in other Alaska towns – Valdez, Nome, Cordova, Fairbanks, Juneau, and Ketchikan.

'Gravy Bob,' activist editor

Robert R. and Hazel Hunter had lived in Alaska intermittently since the Klondike Gold Rush. His friends called him "Gravy Bob" because, as a camp cook, he made delicious country gravy. He was hired by the AEC in June 1914 as the railroad's chief cook.

Hunter had never worked on a newspaper but he was known as a labor activist. He was so upset by what he viewed as unfair treatment of the railroad's laborers that he quit his chef's job. He went to Valdez and bought *The Commoner* plant from the U.S. marshal and shipped it to Ship Creek.

The Hunters were obliged to print the first two issues of *The Weekly Alaskan* (December 4 and 11, 1915) on wrapping paper because their newsprint order was unloaded at Seward by mistake. They had to forward it over the trail to Anchorage by dog team.

In his introductory editorial, Hunter said he aimed at "helping those who have no public press to air grievances piled high on their already-overburdened and stooping shoulders. We are going to advocate a wage for all who labor that will enable them to at least put a few dollars away for future emergencies, not a wage that barely enables one to exist."

The new weekly was greeted with mixed reactions. The *Seward Gateway* prophesied on October 9, 1915, "an agitation is about to be started that will do the country no good . . . there ought to be a law to license newspapers like dogs. It would save decent ones."

John W. Frame, the outspoken ex-editor of a half dozen journals, including the recent *Commoner*, was running the *Forty-Ninty Star* in Valdez. He welcomed Hunter, "that warhorse of Democracy," and predicted he would enjoy a wide readership.

The *Record-Citizen* of Ruby also welcomed Hunter's "radical press" because, it said, the radical press was a thinking press while conservative papers were too smug and self-contained to think.

"Right now, the one newspaper in Alaska that above all others stands conspicuous in editorial ability is a Socialist-Labor organ. Will the ultra-conservatives heed the lesson of the facts?" the Ruby newspaper asked in a December 11, 1915, editorial.

Alaskans disregarded

Hunter railed against the AEC's policies and attacked Mears for his insensitivity to the working conditions of his employees and his disregard of resident Alaskans' welfare. He condemned the AEC for hiring foreign laborers – who sent their earnings to their native lands – while refusing to hire longtime Alaska settlers. He noted that the government railroad was being built to develop Alaska's natural resources and not to destroy "the wage earning power of a people who have blazed the trails of this new and unexplored portion of the U.S."

Hunter labeled the railroad's commissary as unfair competition to the local merchants. He criticized the shoddy quarters provided for the workers and the horses:

> The horse "barns" are tents open at both ends, thus allowing the wind to sweep through at 30 degrees below zero at Matanuska Junction. There they are tied and compelled to suffer because of the stupidity and lack of horse sense in providing the proper equipment for the dumb but faithful animals.
>
> The men at the Eagle River bridge camp are about as well housed as the horses. They have to hire someone to keep the fires going at night to keep them from freezing to death.

The paper was instrumental in encouraging the organization of a militant Alaska Federal Labor Union, whose leaders were members of the Industrial Workers of the World.

Ownerships change

Anchorage journalism underwent a general overhaul in the spring of 1916. Stone, Shaw, and Needham sold the *Pioneer* to Charlie Herron, a sourdough mining engineer. The Hunters sold their *Alaskan* to John S. Heckey, a former Valdez businessman who had recently moved to Anchorage and backed *Forty-Ninty Star* publisher Frame.

Herron was not an experienced newspaperman, but he had the money to be a successful publisher. He was one of Alaska's first entrepreneurs to reinvest his fortune in the territory rather than taking it Outside.

The first issue of the *Pioneer* under Herron's ownership appeared on May 1, 1916. Harry Steel, a pioneer journalist who had been fired from the *Cordova Times*, became editor.

On May 24, the paper's name was changed to *The Anchorage Daily Times & Cook Inlet Pioneer*. A year later, *Cook Inlet Pioneer* was dropped. *Daily* was dropped from the title in 1976. By June 15, the paper, barely three years out of Knik, had a paid circulation of 2,500. It had grown to a six-column, twelve-page paper. On July 1, 1917, The Associated Press began delivering news to it by telegraph.

Anchorage then was the newest and largest town in Alaska, with a summer population of six thousand and one-half that number during the winter months.

Frame and Heckey had moved the *Forty-Ninth Star* plant from Valdez to Anchorage, consolidated it with Hunter's equipment, and put out the *Daily Alaskan*, in competition to the *Times*. They also continued publishing the *Star*. The *Alaskan* first appeared in June 1916 and folded in July 1917.

Alaska 'peonized'

In advocating immediate statehood through the columns of his *Forty-Ninth Star*, Frame dwelt on the curse of absentee rule by federal agents and foreign corporations, tirades he had been famous for in Juneau, Cordova, and Valdez. He said Alaska was being "peonized rather than colonized, by the rule of a pack of corporate wolves who are as devoid of any regard for civic pride and duty as their four-legged prototypes."

In reply to the opposition's contention that Alaskans could not afford statehood, Frame wrote:

> Alaska has copper mines that are producing a revenue to their owners that astonishes the world and yet they do not pay a cent of taxes. Under the law of Arizona, the Bonanza copper mine, if located in that state, would pay $600,000 taxes annually to that commonwealth.
>
> Canneries are being built everywhere and our bays and rivers are being depleted of fish and no one pays enough tax to build a log school house on Hogan's Gulch. But still these "resident agents" of the cannery people and tools of

the copper magnates say that we cannot have self-government for the reason that we are too poor.

The Democrat appears

Frame and Heckey sold the *Forty-Ninth Star* in February 1917 to Fred Martin and Jeremiah Murphy, leading Anchorage Democrats. It became the official organ of the Democratic Party under the title of *Anchorage Weekly Democrat*.

Martin and Murphy were 1897 gold stampeders. Martin once owned Al White's famous California Saloon in Fairbanks. Murphy served as deputy U.S. marshal in Hot Springs, Fairbanks, Fort Gibbon, Iditarod, Ruby, Koyukuk, and Knik before moving to Anchorage to open a law office.

The *Anchorage Weekly Democrat* made its initial bow to the public on March 4, 1917. It was printed in *The Anchorage Daily Times* plant. It ceased to appear weekly after a few issues and came out irregularly into the 1920s. At times it appeared as *The Sunday Democrat*.

With money in his pockets from sale of his weekly, Frame decided to take a breather from both journalism and politics. He and John F. Coffey, an attorney, formed a partnership as real estate brokers. Frame helped organize the Anchorage Booster Club, serving as its first president. He also worked gold claims in the Broad Pass country. He said he was so disillusioned with the Wilson Administration's appointment of carpetbaggers that he became a Republican.

As historian of the Grand Lodge of the Pioneers of Alaska, Frame published the monthly *Pathfinder* magazine, from 1919 until 1921. Then he relinquished it to a group of Valdez Pioneers, headed by Anthony J. Dimond, an attorney who was later elected Alaska's delegate to Congress. Frame headed for Hyder and Ketchikan to finish his career.

Times expands

Meanwhile, Herron's operations were expanding. In addition to his *Daily Times* and *Weekly Times*, his shop printed the *Alaska Labor News* and the *Alaska Railroad Record*.

The *Labor News* was the official organ of the Alaska Labor Union. It lasted from September 30, 1916 until August 1917.

Herron terminated his printing contract with the union when Industrial Workers of the World activists dominated it and the weekly assumed an anarchistic tone. Instead, the *Times* allocated one page in its weekly edition to labor news, with Charles H. Packard, a former union president, as editor.

The *Railroad Record* was published from November 1916 until June 1920, when the AEC suspended publication as an economic move. It had been distributed free to railroad employees and sold for $1 a copy to the general public.

It reported weekly progress on construction of the railroad, dates of steamer sailings, contract settlements, land specials, train schedules, weather data, contracts awarded, missing men, and activities of the railroad YMCA. Charles W. Jones, David Tewkesbury, and John F. Coffey edited the eight-page tabloid.

The *Times* was the primary source of news along the railbelt from Seward to Nenana. Every evening the men congregated in the mess halls for supper and someone in the Anchorage telephone office read excerpts from the paper to the assemblage.

Finding capable editors for his papers posed an ongoing problem for Herron. Harry Steel had returned to the *Cordova Times* after three months.

Times editors turn over

Shaw succeeded Steel as editor and served intermittently until August 1919 when he moved to Seattle. Sid Charles, later founder of the *Ketchikan Daily News*, took charge in 1917 for a few months. David Tewkesbury, then the townsite manager, followed him. In April 1918, Tewkesbury resigned from the *Times* to become editor of the *Railroad Record*.

Shaw became editor of Ed Russell's *Alaska Weekly Dispatch* in Seattle from 1919 until 1923. Then Russell sold the paper to Herron, who changed the name to *The Alaska Weekly*. Shaw became a stockholder and served as news editor until his death on March 14, 1931.

The *Anchorage Times* published a sixteen-page Sunday edition from July 1917 to July 1918 when it ceased at the request of the Federal Trade Commission due to a newsprint shortage during World War I.

Herron tried to hire Alaska Gov. J. F. A. Strong to be editor of the *Times*, when the latter was battling Democrats trying to oust him as governor. In declining the invitation, Strong wrote:

It may be that later I will be glad to consider becoming identified with your most excellent newspaper, which is far and away the very best newspaper in the Territory. The narrowness and political crookedness of the *Empire* is in strong contrast with the broad-mindedness, patriotism and intelligence of *The Anchorage Times*. I shall ask you to consider this communication as confidential for the time being.

James Wilbur Ward succeeded Shaw as editor and general manager of the *Times*. He had been a partner with Herron in the *Seward Gateway*. When Herron bought *The Anchorage Daily Times* in 1916, Ward was business manager.

First Alaska chain attempt

Herron dreamed of becoming Alaska's governor. To reach that goal he established Alaska's first newspaper chain. In addition to the daily and weekly in Anchorage, he started the *Cordova Daily Herald* in 1918, making Ward its editor.

Two years later, Herron launched the *Alaska Daily Capital* in Juneau, with Ward as its business manager. And he had *The Alaska Weekly* in Seattle that circulated in Alaska, with Shaw as editor.

When Ward moved to Juneau, Edgar L. (Ted) Bedell became editor of *The Anchorage Daily Times*. Bedell was an avid sports fan, having played tournament tennis and professional baseball. His first journalistic experience was as sports editor for the *Times*.

The *Times* was one of the territory's most innovative newspapers during Bedell's tenure. It employed its own staff artist, who sketched a daily cartoon for the center of the front page. It experimented with a weekly called the *Anchorage Alaskan*, devoted to industrial and agricultural interests. It started on August 5, 1920, with Clarence J. (Jack) Lincke as editor and suspended three months later.

Lincke was transferred to Herron's *Daily Capital* in Juneau. When it suspended publication in 1923, he returned to Anchorage.

Economic slump hits

The Anchorage economy suffered a setback during the 1920s, as did the rest of Alaska. Construction on the railroad had slowed to a halt during World War I. Sentiment developed in Congress that the railroad was a bad deal and should be scrapped.

Many young men who had been drafted for military service did not return north when the war ended because employment was plentiful in the States. The 1920 census showed a 15 percent loss in the territory's population. Anchorage's population slid from six thousand to 1,856.

Despite this exodus of residents, ex-Klondike journalists Roy Southworth and Bernie Stone, along with Ernie Jessen, launched a second Anchorage daily on December 1, 1923, called *The Anchorage Daily Alaskan* with Lincke as editor. It lasted until February 1925.

The *Daily Alaskan* was a six-column, eight-page paper published by the Alaska Miners' News Publishing Co. The trio also published a weekly summarizing the week's events previously recorded in the daily, similar to the *Times*' weekly. The plant equipment belonged to Southworth. He had used it publishing the *Fairbanks Times* and the *Nenana News* until each folded.

It was obvious that a town of fewer than two thousand people could not support two dailies and their two weeklies. It was a matter of which one would fold first. Herron's political dreams were waning. He had failed to interest wealthy Republicans on the East Coast in financing a strong Republican press in Alaska. He was defeated in his race for Republican National Committeeman.

Herron moved to Seattle, leaving unpaid a $21,000 promissory note to the Bank of Alaska in Anchorage.

New newspaper owners

The end came on December 27, 1924, when both papers were sold at auction; the *Alaskan* to satisfy a mortgage held by the First National Bank of Anchorage, and the *Times* to cover Herron's bank note.

Two different groups of local businessmen bid for the newspapers. Dr. Beeson, president of the First National Bank of Anchorage, representing a group of Alaska Railroad employees, bought the *Alaskan*. Edward A. Rasmuson, president of the Bank of Alaska (now Wells Fargo), bought the *Times* on behalf of a group headed by J. B. Gottstein. Dr. Beeson also offered $5,000 for the *Times*, but Rasmuson upped his bid to $10,000 and got it.

Gottstein was elected *Times* board chairman, Arthur A. Shonbeck, president, and Oscar Anderson, vice president. They called their firm the Times Publishing Co. Ray O. Scott, who had worked as a

Linotype operator on the *Times* since 1917, was promoted to business manager. He had managed the *Port Townsend* (Washington) *Leader* before coming north.

Both newspapers resumed publication following the sales, but the *Alaskan* folded after a month's trial. It was Jack Lincke's third and final fling as editor. Lincke was described by his colleagues as one of the most versatile writers in the north. But after being associated with three failing newspapers – *The Anchorage Alaskan*, the *Daily Capital*, and the *Anchorage Daily Alaskan* – he deserted journalism to become a real estate broker in Anchorage.

The stockholders sold the *Alaskan's* equipment to the *Times*. Southworth replaced Bedell as editor of the *Times*.

For the next two decades, *The Anchorage Daily Times* had the field to itself. It varied in size according to available advertising revenue. Ownership shifted from one group of local businessmen to another, with the Bank of Alaska extending loans as needed.

Chief among the stockholders were Capt. A. E. Lathrop, who owned theaters and office buildings and ran a transfer business; Ike Bayles, a men's clothier; and Z. J. Loussac, a pharmacist and drugstore owner. Bayles was president of the Times Publishing Co. from 1931 to 1951. Lathrop later owned the *Fairbanks Daily News-Miner*.

In 1927, Charles J. Fisk became editor of the *Times*, and Southworth handled the advertising and did most of the reporting.

Fisk began his newspaper career on his father's Townsend, Montana, paper. He worked both as a Linotype operator and on the editorial staffs of Montana and Seattle newspapers.

In 1919, Fisk moved to Alaska to be a Linotype operator on the *Ketchikan Alaska Chronicle*, and serve later as its editor. Still later, Fisk was associate editor and Linotype operator on the *Cordova Daily Times*. Then he moved to Anchorage where he was editor of *The Anchorage Daily Times* until March 1931.

Capital move again

Fisk editorialized from time to time on the advantages of Anchorage as a site for the territory's capital city. Memorials were introduced at almost every session of the legislature to move the capital from Juneau to the westward. The House passed the memorials several times only to have them defeated in the Senate. The idea became dormant for a few years following construction of the Federal Building in Juneau in 1929-30.

"Anchor with Anchorage – Your Ship of Hope will Never Strike Shoal Water" was the *Times*' front-page slogan during the early 1930s. The city's population in 1930 was 2,268, up from 1,856 in 1920.

Southworth resumed editorship of the *Times* in 1931 when Fisk left for Seattle.

Southworth's vacation

In January 1933, Southworth decided to go Outside for a vacation, the first since he came north in 1898. Charles Settlemier, a colleague from his Dawson City newspaper days, was passing through Anchorage on his way to the States. Southworth persuaded him to take over as *Times*' editor while Southworth went on a short vacation.

Southworth's vacation turned into a six-year stay. He bought an interest in a commercial print shop in Portland, Oregon. He was editor and manager of the firm's weekly organ, *The Montavilla Times*. He wrote Settlemier in the summer of 1934:

> The Great Outside has not yet "got me down" although I do not mind admitting to you right here and now that the "call of the North" is everything we editors of the North ever claimed for it. I am not saying how long I am going to be able to fight it off but for the present I am getting a living out of our print shop.

Southworth succumbed to the "Call of the North," returning to Anchorage in 1939 when the *Times* was again under new ownership, this time headed by Robert B. Atwood.

Southworth and Roy Lee, a *Times* Linotype operator, started the weekly *Alaskan*, a five-column, sixteen-page tabloid. Upon receipt of its first issue, Sid Charles of the *Alaska Fishing News* in Ketchikan congratulated its editors for having the temerity to enter into competition with the *Times*, which, Charles wrote, "has had things its own way too long":

The Alaskan existed from July 14, 1939 until May 15, 1942. With its demise, Southworth abandoned his journalism career and became secretary of the Anchorage Elks Lodge.

The Settlemier years

Charles Settlemier was one of the few newsmen who enjoyed financial success in the dual careers of journalism and mining. He was a native of Albany, Oregon, and learned the printing trade on Tacoma papers. He came north in 1898 as a correspondent for *The Oregonian*. He was city editor of the Skagway's *Daily Alaskan* from 1899 to 1900. Then he moved to Dawson City.

Settlemier became part owner of the *Dawson Daily News* and the *Dawson World* when Richard Roediger and William McIntyre, the Tacoma tycoons, sold the papers.

Settlemier retired from newspapering in 1924 to devote fulltime to mining. By the time Settlemier took over as editor of *The Anchorage Daily Times* in 1933, so Southworth could go on his extended vacation, he was a widower and weary of mining and traveling. He loved the northland, frequently editorializing about it being the best possible permanent home. He was enthusiastic about Anchorage's future.

Settlemier noted that "Alaska has been milked of her wealth for decades" and it was time "she put a stop to this life-sapping process, kept her gold and her money at home, and began the great adventure of developing her resources to the maximum – the time is now."

Shortly after Atwood took over the *Times* as editor and publisher, Settlemier moved to the *Fairbanks Daily News-Miner* until 1941 and then to *The Alaska Weekly*, where the gold rush pioneer reached the end of the trail in 1947, the last Klondike veteran still active in journalism.

Chapter 32

The Atwood Years and Statehood

The Anchorage Daily Times headline on January 3, 1959, read: "Stroke of President's Pen Makes It Official":

> The ceremony took place in the Cabinet room. The President took his high back black leather chair at the center of the table, placed House Speaker Sam Rayburn in a chair to his left and Vice President Nixon to his right.
> Interior Secretary Fred Seaton stood just behind the President. Fanned out to his right were senators-elect Bartlett, Gruening and Representative Rivers. To Seaton's left were Acting Territorial Governor Waino Hendrickson, Ex-Governor Stepovich and Robert Atwood.
> A battery of movie and TV cameras whirred furiously recording the historic event. After Ike distributed the six pens used in signing the proclamation, he went back to the flag and watched for it to be unfurled. The 49-star flag becomes the official ensign on July 4, 1959.

The Robert Atwood in the cabinet room when President Dwight Eisenhower officially signed the proclamation making Alaska the forty-ninth state was the publisher of *The Anchorage Daily Times*. He was there in recognition of his twenty-four-year editorial battle for Alaska statehood, during which he headed the eleven-member Alaska Statehood Committee appointed by Alaska's governors Ernest Gruening and Mike Stepovich.

Twenty-four years earlier . . . .

On June 15, 1935, a young reporter, Robert Bruce (Bob) Atwood of Chicago arrived in Anchorage. It was obvious that he was destined to be editor and publisher of *The Anchorage Daily Times*. He was married to the daughter of the banker who was an owner of the *Times*. So Charles Settlemier, a former Klondike newsman who had been editor for two years, moved to Fairbanks to edit Austin E. (Cap) Lathrop's *Fairbanks Daily News-Miner*.

Statehood was Atwood's crowning achievement in a career of campaigns that successfully pushed for local government reform, for making Anchorage an air crossroads, for constructing the Ted Stevens Anchorage International Airport, and for attracting military bases to Anchorage. He pioneered the use of the Port of Anchorage. He supported education by sending participants to the national spelling bee, by helping finance Alaska Pacific University, and by providing an annual grant to the University of Alaska Anchorage's Journalism and Public Communications program. He was a leader in organizing Alaska newspaper organizations and in improving the newswire service to Alaska.

Back in 1935, coming to Alaska for the twenty-eight-year-old reporter was the realization of a dream, the result of listening to tales about the last frontier from two uncles who had spent a portion of their early years in Alaska.

A paternal uncle, Dr. Wallace W. Atwood, professor of geology at the University of Chicago, spent the summers of 1903 to 1908 conducting surveys for the U.S. Geological Survey on the Alaska Peninsula. In 1908, he surveyed the Matanuska and Bering coal fields for a group of Chicago capitalists.

A maternal uncle, Andrew Stevenson, in 1916 established the first branch banking system in Alaska, known as the Bank of Alaska (later the National Bank of Alaska until merging with Wells Fargo), representing a syndicate of New York investment brokers. The headquarters were in Skagway and branches were opened in Wrangell, Cordova and Anchorage. Edward A. Rasmuson, who had been serving as the banks' attorney since its inception, succeeded Stevenson in 1918 in the presidency of the bank chain.

Robert Atwood was born to Burton Homer Atwood and Mary Stevenson Atwood in Chicago on March 31, 1907. He attended public and private schools in Chicago and Winnetka, Illinois. He went east to Worcester, Massachusetts, to major in geography at Clark University, where Dr. Wallace Atwood had become president. He graduated in 1929.

At Clark, Atwood was managing editor of the *Clark News* and on weekends he reported for the *Worcester Telegram*. His first job after graduation was with the *Telegram*. Then he moved to Springfield, Illinois, to be court reporter for the *Illinois State Journal*.

It was during his years with the *Journal* that he married Rasmuson's daughter, Evangeline, who was a children's caseworker in Springfield. After their marriage on April 2, 1932, the Atwoods moved to Worcester where Bob worked as court reporter on the *Telegram*.

When word came that a little daily newspaper was for sale in Anchorage, the young reporter and his Alaska-born wife jumped at the opportunity.

Starts with staff of three

When Settlemier departed for Fairbanks, Atwood was left with two printers and a woman in the office to run the newspaper. In addition to writing news stories and editorials, Atwood went up and down Fourth Avenue soliciting advertising and pinch-hitting in the composing room, including running the Linotype.

The *Times* was an eight-page tabloid when Atwood arrived, but within a month he secured enough advertising to warrant increasing its size.

In later years, Atwood was fond of recalling what the town was like when he first arrived:

> Anchorage was a tiny island of people surrounded by a sea of wilderness called Alaska. The community had one radio station and one newspaper. The two thousand people who lived here depended on those media for their news and entertainment. Ken Laughlin was responsible for entertainment by radio. The editor of *The Anchorage Times*, of whom this writer had the honor of being, was responsible for providing the news.
>
> All was not always happy between the radio and the newspaper. When the editor and his four employees worked all day to produce their newspaper and came home for

dinner and relaxation, they were not happy to hear Laughlin reading the paper for free, but the paper survived and so also the radio station, thanks to the merchants of the tiny town.

Electrical outages were a continuing problem. Ice jams would throw the Eklutna power plant out of commission. The Alaska Railroad plant provided emergency electricity. Cooperating with the city in conserving electricity during the daytime, *Times* employees occasionally worked nights, with the paper delivered to the homes before sunrise.

Fifty years later, Atwood refused to follow the industry trend and switch to morning publication, although he had pioneered it in Anchorage out of necessity.

Settlers arrive

In May 1935, only a month before the Atwoods arrived in Alaska, the federal government transported two hundred drought-stricken Midwestern farm families to the Matanuska Valley, forty-five miles northeast of Anchorage. They were settled on forty-and eighty-acre tracts of land, with all expenses covered by thirty-year loans. They came to make new homes for themselves, thus introducing a permanency not prevalent previously in Alaska.

Before then, many accumulated a comfortable nest egg during the summer months, went Outside for the winter and returned in the spring with empty pokes. Editors urged people to reinvest in the territory to help it develop instead of scattering their earnings Outside. Atwood wrote during his first fall in Anchorage:

> As soon as Alaska learns to keep her hard-earned wealth at home, the sooner will she get underway as a land of permanent wealth. And one of the best ways to do this is to stay with the country, make this a homeland and apply every cent of available funds to the opening of latent resources summer and winter.

As problems arose during the settling-in period in the Matanuska Valley, the disgruntled wrote their stateside friends about their troubles. The Outside press bemoaned the fate of those poor unfortunates "who were consigned to a U.S. Siberia." Even the Alaska press, especially in Southeastern, home of Alaska's longer-established and more conservative journalists, doubted the feasibility of the project. But not the *Times*. It praised the efforts of the colonists and predicted ultimate success.

Norman Brown arrives

Atwood hired Norman Cole Brown, associate editor of the *Cordova Daily Times*, as managing editor of *The Anchorage Daily Times* in January 1937. Brown had spent his early years in Valdez, where his father had gone in 1903 to prospect for gold.

In 1926, young Norman left the University of Washington in his senior year of journalism to take a cannery job in Valdez. For the next six years, he worked at a variety of jobs not associated with newspapers. He married Blanche Sutherland, a Valdez schoolteacher. Their daughter Susan and a son, Norman Jr., later worked in the newspaper and printing businesses.

From 1932 through 1936, Brown was associate editor of the *Cordova Daily Times*. After its publisher, Harry Steel, died in 1936, the executor of his estate offered to sell the paper to Brown. He chose to move to Anchorage instead. The Kennecott copper mining operations were winding down near Cordova, a blow to the town's economy.

War boom

When rumors circulated that officials in Washington contemplated establishing a military headquarters near Fairbanks, *The Anchorage Daily Times*, in cooperation with the Anchorage Chamber of Commerce, waged a campaign to sell Anchorage as a preferable location. A list of twenty-two reasons favoring Anchorage was forwarded to Washington.

When President Franklin Roosevelt signed an executive order on April 29, 1939, withdrawing a fifty-thousand-acre tract of land between Anchorage and the Chugach Mountains from settlement, Anchorage residents had won their argument.

The 1940s heralded an era of large-scale federal defense projects in Alaska – airports for Anchorage and Fairbanks; navy bases at Sitka and Kodiak. To connect the Lower 48 with Alaska's Interior, the United States and Canada built a 1,400-mile highway between

March and November 1942. The Civil Aeronautics Administration installed radio beam stations and airfields throughout the territory.

When a troop train arrived in Anchorage in June 1940, with the first contingent to start work on the military base four miles from town, townspeople were at the depot to greet it. The *Times* put out a sixteen-page welcoming edition. Anchorage's population was 3,445.

The sudden emergence of a neighboring community – the military base – of thirty thousand population triggered severe social and economic problems for the small town. Merchants found their stocks depleted and craftsmen left town jobs for better-paying ones on the military reservation.

The *Times* occupied the main floor of the Odd Fellows Building on Fourth Avenue between F and G streets, presently known as the Reed Building. A Goss Duplex press was installed in the summer of 1941. The new press allowed the *Times* to expand to a full-size seven-column, eight-page paper.

A war-induced newsprint shortage forced the *Times* to cease publication of its weekly edition in May 1942. A manpower shortage and lack of housing precipitated the following notice in the *Times*:

> Alley Oop Lovers: If any more printers are compelled to leave the *Anchorage Times* for lack of housing accommodations in the city, we will be compelled to eliminate two pages from the paper and one of them will be the comic page.

The response was immediate. One printer, who was sleeping on a davenport, was quartered in a comfortable room. Another, who was en route north from the States, was provided with a room.

When the war wound down in 1945, the *Times* and the *Fairbanks Daily News-Miner* began receiving national and international news service from The Associated Press via Teletype, which typed out the entire story instead of the former skeletonized telegram version. Transmission of news from the Seattle bureau was still through the U.S. Army Signal Corps' Alaska Communications System that had provided the telegram service. It operated Alaska's long distance telephone and telegraph service until sold to RCA in 1970.

City manager proposed

City councilmen were hard-pressed to divide their attention between their own businesses and the city's expanding problems during the war boom. To Atwood, the answer was hiring a professional municipal staff. He sent for literature from the International City Managers' Association in Chicago and acquired an expertise on the city manager form of government.

In addition to writing dozens of editorials urging its adoption, he appeared before any group willing to listen. With books and pamphlets piled at his side, he advocated securing trained personnel to run the city's affairs. After a four-year crusade, the voters approved the city manager plan and the council hired a city manager in 1946, the first in Alaska.

News established

At war's end, Atwood decided to resume the *Weekly Times*. He offered the editor post to Brown, but the latter decided he wanted to strike out on his own.

Brown and two local printers, Alvin DeJulio and Earl Bramble, organized the Northern Printing Company and started the weekly *Anchorage News*. The first edition of the *News* appeared on January 13, 1946. It was a twenty-four-page tabloid issued on Sunday mornings and distributed through the post office.

Another weekly, titled *Anchorage Hi-Life*, appeared briefly in 1947. It was printed at the *Anchorage News* plant and its editor-publishers were Hal Gates and the *News*' sportswriter, Wallace Graves. It folded in October 1947 after having two libel suits filed against it – one by the entire police department and the other by a woman accused of running a bawdy house.

Statehood push

Four years after Atwood's arrival in Anchorage, Ernest Gruening, who had edited newspapers in Boston and was a founder and editor of the *Portland* (Maine) *Evening News*, was appointed Alaska's governor. The two became friends. They agreed that Outside interests, especially those headquartered in Seattle, were thwarting the territory's development and something had to be done. The ultimate answer: statehood.

Atwood resurrected the name *Forty-Ninth Star* when he resumed publishing a weekly after the war. It, too, came out on Sunday mornings. Its title signified a new statehood push.

Edward J. Fortier, a Minnesota newspaperman who had served three years in Alaska in military intelligence during World War II, was hired as editor of the new weekly. He had traveled extensively throughout the territory, thus was aware of its problems.

The *Star* made its debut on February 10, 1946, as a twenty-four-page tabloid, including a colored comic section. A local scene or personality was featured on the cover of the magazinelike publication. The first cover picture was of a lifeboat filled with passengers being rescued from the SS *Yukon* which ran aground in Johnstone Bay a few hours after leaving Seward southbound.

As a golden anniversary salute to the Klondike stampeders of '98, the 1948 series of cover portraits were close-ups of Anchorage's pioneer community leaders.

Prior to the 1946 referendum on statehood, the *Star* published a series of articles narrating the territory's struggle for self-government.

The *Star* made its final appearance on June 24, 1951, the victim of another newsprint shortage, this one caused by the Korean War. The *Times-Star* newsprint quota was insufficient for the *Star's* circulation of five thousand and the *Times*' circulation of twelve thousand. The *Times* also stopped all mail subscriptions and limited display advertising to accommodate its eight-page limit.

City of 100,000 envisioned

In 1945, Atwood recommended Anchorage as a suitable site for the United Nations because "it is the most central spot in the world and it has all the necessary physical resources readily available."

His chauvinism at times irked other towns who blamed their lack of progress on Anchorage's greediness. Atwood's reply:

> People in Anchorage are too busy building a better city to concern themselves about taking anything away from other Alaskans.
>
> The people of Anchorage are so enthusiastic about Anchorage that they consider it reasonable for every person of sound mind to come here. We have heard it said that

arrangements have been made to have the Second Coming in Anchorage, too.

Whereupon, the *Fairbanks Daily News-Miner* observed:

> We must express admiration for the spirit of Anchorage. We don't begrudge them their growth and expansion, but, if they get the Second Coming, too, that will be too much. Loyal Fairbanksans should go to church and protest those arrangements.

In the summer of 1946, the *Times* initiated construction of its plant at 820 Fourth Avenue, now occupied by the Alaska Court System. It started as a one-story structure.

Atwood's faith in Anchorage's future constituted an unbroken editorial melody through the years. In an editorial in 1948 titled "An Enchanted City," he predicted that the town's future was so "pregnant with possibilities that dreams of a city of fifty or a hundred thousand persons cannot be dubbed impossible."

The Columbus Expedition

In June 1946, twenty-one Alaska businessmen staged an event that promoted Anchorage as the international aerial crossroads.

Learning that the Civil Aeronautics Board was studying future Alaska air service patterns and a new route between the United States and the Orient via the Arctic, they chartered an Alaska Airlines DC-3 to fly a proposed route to Chicago. It was dubbed the "Columbus Expedition" because they were searching for trade routes to the East. In the party were Governor Gruening and editors Atwood and Bill Baker of the *Ketchikan Alaska Chronicle*.

They took thirteen days off from work and paid all of their own expenses. Seattle groups raised a war chest of $250,000 to oppose the proposed route, which would bypass Seattle. Siding with Seattle were Southeast Alaska editors of Juneau's *Daily Alaska Empire* and the *Ketchikan Daily Alaska Fishing News*, forerunner of the *Ketchikan Daily News*. (The *Empire* had changed its name in 1926 from *Alaska Daily Empire* to *Daily Alaska Empire*.)

Preceding the expedition, and as president of the Anchorage Chamber of Commerce, Atwood flew to Seattle hoping to explain

Anchorage's position to that city's chamber. He was denied an opportunity to appear before their chamber. He was told that Seattle was only trying to protect what was "historically and rightfully ours."

The Alaskans stopped at Edmonton, Great Falls, Fargo, and Minneapolis on the way to Chicago. They were entertained at banquets at each place. They took with them a hindquarter of moose and a stock of smoked salmon with which to treat their hosts.

The response at each stop was so favorable that when they reached Chicago, their original destination, they voted unanimously to continue on to the nation's capital to tell their story to the top federal officials, including President Harry Truman.

On August 1, 1946, the *Times* headline read: "City Hits Air 'Jackpot.'" The Civil Aeronautics Board designated Anchorage as the port for international air travel operating the North Pacific routes from the continental United States to the Orient. It also designated Northwest Airlines to operate nonstop between Anchorage and Minneapolis-St. Paul, Chicago, and New York.

Airport next

The following year, the Anchorage Chamber of Commerce sent its president, Fred Axford, and Atwood to Washington to testify to the need of a new and larger airport to accommodate the stepped-up air traffic.

Ten months later, President Truman signed a bill funding an $8 million international airport at Anchorage. The bill was supported by the army, navy, and air force, and by the interior, commerce, and state departments on the grounds that up to 75 percent of all air traffic between the United States and the Orient would pass through Anchorage. From then on, the *Times* touted Anchorage as the "Air Crossroads of the World."

Anchorage port pushed

Aggravating the newsprint shortages following World War II were frequent West Coast shipping strikes. After the Korean War, when Anchorage's economic boom demanded larger papers, tie-ups in maritime shipping forced shrinkage rather than expansion.

On one occasion the *Times* ordered one thousand tons of Norwegian newsprint with the stipulation that it must be delivered at the Anchorage dock. Crown Zellerbach Paper Corp. chartered the Norwegian freighter

Trolleggen to make the delivery. Atwood wanted to publicize the Anchorage port as an alternative to Valdez or labor-troubled Seward.

Other Times promotions

The *Times* launched an annual statewide spelling bee in 1959, open to all sixth-, seventh- and eighth-grade pupils. The grand prize was an all-expense-paid round-trip for the state winner, accompanied by an adult, to Washington DC to participate in a national spelling bee sponsored by Scripps-Howard newspapers.

The same year, the *Times* launched the International Airlines Ski Races at the Alyeska Ski Resort to publicize the accessibility of the Anchorage area to Europe and the Orient, as well as the Lower 48. The event grew in popularity to the point that twenty-six airlines with more than 350 individual participants competed annually in the races. Alyeska became so well known in international ski circles that the *Times* terminated its sponsorship in 1980, having accomplished its original purpose.

As the town grew, so also did the need for modernizing the *Times* plant. In 1951, the ten-year-old, eight-page Goss press was replaced by a new thirty-two-page Hoe rotary press, which produced papers at a rate of up to thirty-six thousand an hour. It did the same job in twenty minutes that the Goss did in nine hours. A new wing was added to the building in 1951, a second floor in 1956, and a third floor in 1968 to accommodate expanding staff.

When the Richfield Oil Company struck oil on the Kenai Peninsula in July 1957, the impact on Anchorage was immediate. Seventeen of the eighteen major companies that were engaged in some phase of oil exploration in Alaska established headquarters in Anchorage. Anchorage Natural Gas Corporation installed eighty miles of pipe from the Kenai gas fields to provide natural gas to Anchorage residents.

Six years after Richfield's discovery, the Swanson River field had fifty-two wells producing an average of 28,500 barrels of oil a day. Atwood and other Anchorage businessmen profited from interests they held in oil leases.

250 statehood editorials

Statehood became the *Times*' paramount editorial issue through the 1940s and '50s. Atwood had written more than 250 editorials on the subject by the time Alaska was admitted to the union on January 3, 1959.

His first editorial advocating immediate statehood for Alaska appeared in 1943. It was a lonely stand at a time with the war on. Also, bankers, politicians, and others with authority didn't think joining the union was a good idea. Even if they did, they didn't say so because Seattle business interests opposed it. Seattle banks were the only ones who could lend Alaskans money when assets of local banks were insufficient.

Atwood testified before congressional committees both in Washington and in Alaska. His first statehood hearing was in Washington in 1947 and from then on he spent several months of each year in the nation's capital. C. W. (Bill) Snedden, who purchased the *Fairbanks Daily News-Miner* in 1951 from statehood opponent Austin E. (Cap) Lathrop, supported statehood and joined Atwood lobbying in Washington in the fifties.

Retention of Gruening as Alaska's governor was viewed as essential to the statehood fight. The territorial governor and secretary of Alaska (lieutenant governor) were presidential appointees. When Gruening came up for reappointment after President Truman was reelected in 1948, statehood foes lobbied strenuously for his rejection, partially because he advocated a tax program to support statehood.

Drew Pearson, author of the syndicated newspaper column "Washington Merry-Go-Round," wrote on February 11, 1948:

"They don't like his drive for lower maritime freight rates, and for higher taxes on fishing, canning, and shipping. Gil Skinner, president of the Alaska Steamship Company, is a skillful backstage operator for the lobby."

In an editorial titled "Gruening Should Stay," Atwood wrote, "from the Alaskan point of view, Gruening is irreplaceable and invaluable. He is the spearhead of the great statehood movement."

Gruening was reappointed and confirmed by the Senate. So was his secretary of Alaska, Lew M. Williams Sr., publisher of the *Wrangell Sentinel*.

Atwood was appointed chairman of the Alaska Statehood Committee financed by the Territorial Legislature in 1949. The committee's responsibility was to organize the statehood effort both inside Alaska and nationally. Bill Baker, publisher of the *Ketchikan Alaska Chronicle*, was vice chairman of the committee.

CONGRESS APPROVES ALASKA STATEHOOD

WHAT A PARTY! WOW!

The eleven-member organization waged a crusade, enlisting Alaskans and stateside groups to lobby members of Congress. This meant organizing planeloads of citizen lobbyists to fly to Washington. Atwood wrote hundreds of letters to newspaper editors in the States, urging their support. He had personal interviews with each of the U.S. presidents during the fifteen-year campaign.

Alaska Statehood Association chapters throughout the territory helped stem the anti-statehood propaganda appearing in the editorial columns of the *Empire*, the *News-Miner* (before Snedden bought it), the *Anchorage Daily News*, the *Ketchikan Daily News* and the *Daily Sitka Sentinel*. Two other Alaska newspapers split on Alaska statehood but did not editorialize extensively. The *Kodiak Mirror* opposed statehood and the *Nome Nugget* supported it.

Lew Williams Sr. of the *Sentinel* supported statehood at first. As the years wore on, he became an opponent, but his son and daughter-in-law, Lew Jr. and Dorothy Williams of the *Petersburg Press*, supported it through final victory. The elder Williams's switch was due to his dismissal as secretary of Alaska in 1951 by President Truman on the recommendation of Gruening.

The *Empire*, *Anchorage Daily News*, *Ketchikan Daily News*, *Wrangell Sentinel*, and *Sitka Sentinel* also opposed ratification of the Alaska Constitution and opposed the adoption of the Alaska-Tennessee Plan for sending pseudo members of Congress to Washington to promote Alaska statehood.

The *News-Miner* had become a statehood supporter in time to welcome the constitutional convention to the University of Alaska Fairbanks in 1955-56.

Wrangell and Ketchikan were the only towns in Alaska where the majority of voters were against ratification of the constitution.

Famous headline

On June 30, 1958, the *Times* put out an "extra" proclaiming in a seven-inch headline "We're In" with a smaller subhead: "64-20 Vote Makes Alaska Forty-Ninth State," followed by a third subhead: "Historic Vote Ends Six Days of Debate":

> Alaskan Statehood forces won their most historic congressional battle tonight by pushing the Statehood bill

through the Senate in a whirlwind finish. Opposition forces utterly collapsed tonight after six days of debate.

The historic moment came at 8 o'clock EDT (2 p.m. Anchorage time.) Victory came on the vote of 33 Republicans and 31 Democrats. Opposing it were 12 Democrats and 8 Republicans.

Then followed a story of how Anchorage residents celebrated the victory, under the caption "Anchorage Blows Its Lid":

Alaska's largest city rocked and rolled as the air was split by the sound of sirens, horns, bells, firecrackers, guns – and everything else that could be used to make a noise. Employees streamed from their places of business and an immediate holiday was declared.

Although most of the activities were uncontrolled, there was some with a definite purpose. Members of the Elks Lodge hurried with their huge American flag to the federal building. There, Fur Rendezvous Queen Rita Martin placed a large, 49th golden star on to the flag as it was hung across the front of the building.

Amid the din and the roar of celebration were prayers and expressions of thanksgiving that the long-awaited celebration was now a reality.

The celebration included a 49-gun salute by the 207th Infantry Battalion of the Alaska National Guard.

Similar celebrations were held in other major Alaska towns, even in those where statehood had been opposed by the newspapers such as in Ketchikan, Wrangell, Sitka, and Juneau.

Several hundred copies of statehood special editions of the two Anchorage dailies and the *News-Miner* were placed aboard an Air Force bomber headed for the nation's capital. They arrived there in five hours and twenty-five minutes from Anchorage's Elmendorf Air Force Base. The plane had been scheduled to fly to Andrews Air Force Base near Washington DC, and the Alaska newsmen were granted permission to include one thousand pounds of newspapers in its bomb bay. Copies were delivered to all members of Congress, and some were placed on sale on Washington newsstands.

-Photo courtesy of the Anchorage Museum of History and Art and the Anchorage Daily News

Then on January 3, 1959, Atwood was on hand in the White House to acquire one of the six pens President Eisenhower used to sign the proclamation making Alaska the forty-ninth state. Ike commented to the publisher, "Now you're in."

Chapters 33-35

Juneau, Ketchikan

Papers Battle Statehood

and Gruening

Comparing accomplishments of the Territorial Legislature with the accomplishments of the annual convention of the Alaska Native Brotherhood and Sisterhood at Kake, it might be a good idea to turn Alaska back to the Indians.

– Sid Charles, editor-publisher
Alaska Fishing News, 1945

Sidney Dean Charles worked on a dozen newspapers in the other states before joining the Fairbanks News in 1904 and beginning a 55-year career as reporter, editor and publisher of newspapers throughout Alaska. He is best known as founder and publisher of the Ketchikan Daily News. -*Photo courtesy of the Charles family*

Chapter 33

Rise and Fall of Troy and His Empire

John Troy's *Alaska Daily Empire* lost its Juneau newspaper monopoly when Charlie Herron, publisher of *The Anchorage Daily Times*, launched his *Alaska Daily Capital* on March 5, 1920.

Empire publisher Troy did not welcome this new competition. Originally, it was planned that the *Capital* would be a morning paper just as the *Dispatch* had been before it departed for Seattle. However, the *Empire* subscribed to both the morning and evening Associated Press services. It grabbed the morning service on departure of the *Dispatch* in 1919. When the AP directors asked Troy to surrender the morning service to the *Capital*, he refused.

So Herron made his an evening paper and subscribed to a private news service in Seattle. After nine months' publication, the name was changed to *The Juneau Daily Capital*, and in June 1921, it became the weekly *Sunday Capital*.

Charles among Juneau editors

Herron employed some of the territory's best newsmen as editors – Will Steel, Sid Charles, James Wilbur Ward, and Earle Jameson. Steel and Ward were especially experienced, having started their northern careers more than twenty years earlier in Dawson City. Charles had fifteen years of newspaper experience in Canada and the States before joining the *Fairbanks News* in 1904. He had been working on Alaska newspapers since.

It was an uphill struggle. Herron was the outsider while Troy was the hometown boy.

Six weeks after the *Capital* was launched, it was struck with a $50,000 libel suit filed by George C. Hazelet, Cordova attorney and Republican aspirant for governor. The paper had accused Hazelet of being responsible for a murder that took place during the Keystone Canyon riots near Valdez during railroad construction. The case was settled out of court, and Herron issued an apology retracting statements implicating Hazelet.

Will Steel became managing editor of the *Capital* in 1921, and the paper livened up. He warned his readers that an effort would be made in the next legislature to move the capital to Seward.

"The tail cannot continue to wag the dog and the panhandle cannot continue the wagging of Alaska," Steel wrote. "It does not take one wiser than Solomon to see the handwriting on the wall."

He warned city leaders that unless they took positive action in getting a congressional appropriation for a much-needed federal building to house the legislature and territorial offices, they would lose out.

For eleven years, such an appropriation lay dormant because Juneau landlords preferred receiving rent from government tenants. But with the scare of losing the capital to a northern site, Juneau leaders supported the appropriation.

Herron left Alaska in 1923 after folding his *Juneau Sunday Capital*. He stopped in Seattle where he bought Ed Russell's *Alaska Dispatch*, changing its name to *The Alaska Weekly*.

By the following year, Herron's dream of an Alaska newspaper chain faded. His *Cordova Herald*, started in 1918, had lasted only two years. His *Sunday Capital* folded in July 1923. His *Anchorage Daily Times* was seized and sold at a marshal's sale in December 1924. So he sold his interest in *The Alaska Weekly* to Frank Cotter and E. W. Knight and moved to California.

Charles, out of a job when the *Daily Capital* went weekly, launched the weekly *Juneau Spirit* on March 19, 1921. Admitting that Juneau was already overrun with newspapers, he said he had to start his own as a means of livelihood. Then Stroller White moved the *Douglas Island News* to Juneau as *Stroller's Weekly* three months after Charles launched his venture. That further crowded the field, so Charles suspended publication and headed for Sitka.

White moves to Juneau

White's *Douglas Island News* was having a difficult time surviving in Douglas after the closure of the Treadwell mines. On Sunday morning, April 22, 1917, waters of Gastineau Channel broke into the underground workings of three mines in the Treadwell complex, flooding them out of existence, throwing a thousand workers out of their jobs. No lives were lost, but more than $10 million worth of machinery was destroyed.

Gov. Thomas Riggs appointed White as Alaska's publicity director in 1918. White also was elected to the territorial House, serving as speaker in the 1919 session. After White moved the *Island News* plant to Juneau in 1921, he ran for delegate to Congress and was defeated by the Republican incumbent, Dan Sutherland. From then on, he shunned active politicking, preferring to offer editorial comment.

White's talent as a columnist set him apart from his fellow editors. In his "Bedtime Story for Juneau Children" he interwove streets and residents' names familiar to the children into his columns. That also attracted their parents. His "Heart-to-Heart Talks with Mothers" offered advice to "disconsolate females who wept out their sorrows on his shoulders"; and in his "Stroller Column" he commented on current affairs. Alaska historian and journalist Robert N. DeArmond assembled a book of White's best writing, *Klondike Newsman: Stroller White*, which came out in second edition in 1997. DeArmond had been a reporter for White.

Relative harmony reigned in Juneau's journalistic circles when the pioneer editors – Troy, Charles, Will Steel, and White – shared the market. They also shared conservative views on a majority of issues, if not political parties.

Troy's editor, John Edouard Pegues, joined his peers in editorial commentary. He was Troy's loyal teammate in promoting Democrats during the Republican administrations. He went to work for the *Empire* when his job as managing editor of the *Citizen* in Fairbanks terminated with the plant's destruction by fire in 1920.

White's monument a mountain

White terminated all of his columns at the end of 1929. He was tired and ill, wanting to sell out and return to the States where he hoped to do some feature writing. While seeking a buyer for his weekly, however, illness overcame him. He died in Juneau on September 28, 1930, another Klondike newsman reaching the end of the trail.

A five-thousand-foot mountain northwest of Mendenhall Glacier, thirteen miles from Juneau, was named Mt. Stroller White a year after his death.

White's widow, Josephine, continued to publish the weekly, with the assistance of Hal Selby, former editor of the *Valdez Miner* and the *Seward Gateway*. In July 1931, Selby and Latimer (Dolly) Gray, a Juneau printer, bought the paper.

Gray served his printer's apprenticeship on the *Laramie* (Wyoming) *Republican*. He arrived in Juneau in 1904 as a typesetter for Juneau's *Record-Miner* and was employed on Juneau papers from then on. In 1912 he was a city councilman and was elected mayor in 1920. He was chief of the fire department for fourteen years.

In December 1932, E. S. (Bill) Evans purchased Selby's interest, and the *Weekly* was incorporated as the Capitol Publishing Co. Gray served as vice president of the firm.

Evans became both editor and general manager. The name of the paper was changed to *The Alaska Press* on March 10, 1933. It was a semiweekly.

Evans first moved to Juneau with his parents in 1897. They later traveled to Dyea and then to Fairbanks. The Evanses were among the original residents of Fairbanks.

After Evans took over, he inaugurated an annual tradition of allowing the Juneau Woman's Club to put out a special edition of the paper each spring. The women solicited the advertising as their major fund-raiser and split a percentage with the paper; the edition ran about fifty pages.

A popular feature was a personal evaluation by Mrs. Russell (Mildred) Hermann, the club's president and an attorney, of each legislator's performance during the preceding session. After the Alaska Statehood Committee was created in 1949, she was appointed to that body and named its secretary.

FDR selects Troy

When Democrats, led by Franklin D. Roosevelt, took over the national administration in 1933, the *Empire* was recipient of a real

Empire Staff Lineup–John W. Troy, publisher of the Alaska Daily Empire 1913-1942 (in derby hat in center) and his staff pose for a photo in front of the Empire's Main Street building. Elmer Friend, city editor, is second from left. Arthur Bringdale, head Linotype operator, is at the right wearing an apron. -*Photo courtesy Alaska State Library, Winter & Pond Collection, 87-1265.*

boost over its competition. President Roosevelt chose its publisher to be Alaska's governor.

Troy was sworn into office on April 19, 1933, before a joint session of the territorial House and Senate, with Sen. Thomas J. DeVane, D-Ruby, administering the oath. Later that evening, the Juneau City Band serenaded under the governor's windows at his apartment above the *Empire* at 138 Main Street, just below Telephone Hill. The *Empire*'s city editor, Elmer Friend, pounded the bass drum.

Troy acknowledged the greeting from his window. When band members returned to their headquarters in Ed Garnick's grocery store, two blocks away on Seward Street, they were treated to refreshments dispatched by the governor.

Empire managing editor Pegues also was rewarded for his loyalty to the Democratic Party. He was appointed Federal Housing Administrator for the territory, and later territorial director of the National Emergency Council.

Troy's son-in-law, Robert W. Bender, succeeded Pegues at the *Empire*. Bender was born in Tacoma on September 12, 1896. After graduating from the University of Washington, he was assistant business manager of the *Everett* (Washington) *Daily News*. It was while a student at the university that he met Helen Troy, who graduated from the school of journalism in 1921. They were married in Everett on January 20, 1922.

Press goes daily

The Alaska Press stepped up its competition against the *Empire* when it became a daily on July 24, 1935. It installed two multiple-magazine Linotypes. A new two-revolution cylinder press and Dexter folder enabled the *Press* to produce a full size eight-page paper almost as fast as the *Empire* with its eight-page Duplex. The *Press* subscribed to the United Press news service. It was an afternoon paper going head-to-head with the afternoon *Empire*, The Associated Press member.

A special edition of the *Press* commemorated dedication of the new Juneau-Douglas Bridge on October 13, 1935. The 2,701-foot span was built with a $255,000 grant from Roosevelt's public works administration. It was a dream realized after thirty years of promotion.

Despite lauding construction of the bridge with New Deal funds, the *Press* was anti-New Deal. "Creeping socialism" was its tamest term for Roosevelt's programs. Its criticism included the Matanuska Valley colonization project near Anchorage. Referring to the colonists as "the New Deal's 'Chosen Children,'" the paper called the project the "screwiest" of all the "dizzy games" brought forth by the national administration. It resented that the project had absorbed almost the entire road-building appropriation for Alaska. It ridiculed equipping colonists with such luxuries as electric washing machines, radios, and overstuffed furniture.

Press defends press freedom

The *Press*'s vigorous defense of the freedom of the press helped defeat a bill introduced in the legislature by Rep. Art Chamberlin, D-Deering, himself a former reporter with the *Seattle Post-Intelligencer* and The Associated Press.

Chamberlin's bill would mete out a one-year sentence and a $1,000 fine to anyone "who would utter, write, print or publish anything which was considered opprobrious, insulting, disrespectful, defamatory or contemptuous of any civil or military officers of the territory, which includes legislators." The measure would be an amendment to the sedition law then in existence. In an editorial titled "Muzzle Freedom of Speech," Evans wrote:

> Plainly, we have disrespect and contempt for Chamberlin's measure. It is inconceivable that certain peanut politicians who became important public figures purely because they registered as Democrats in 1932, should become immune from accountability to the citizenry. After all, the public official is the servant of the man who pays his wages – and if the servant cannot take a deserved "calling down" it is time for him to quit and get a new boss.

The bill died a quick death on the House floor. A veteran senator, Andrew Nerland, R-Fairbanks, branded it as "vicious" and another testified that "when I need a bill like that to protect me, it will be time for me to retire."

During the extended maritime strikes in the 1930s and 1940s, both the *Empire* and the *Press* supported the merchants who denied credit to local longshoremen who refused to unload steamers sent north with emergency supplies and perishables. The two papers also objected to those unemployed longshoremen receiving welfare checks. The *Empire* was a Democratic organ, but Troy belonged to the party's conservative wing and did not subscribe to the New Deal's social welfare programs.

Although partisan politically, Troy was an excellent businessman and community booster in the twenty-five years he actively ran the *Empire* from 1912 to 1937. In addition to putting in the latest equipment in a new building in 1916, he used new technology in other fields. In 1935, he assigned his reporters to provide fifteen minutes of news each evening to the new Juneau radio station, KINY. The *Empire* also sponsored newsreels at the Capitol Theater.

Among the reporters reading the news on station KINY were Lew Williams Sr., later publisher of the *Wrangell Sentinel*, and Robert Henning, who bought the *Alaska Sportsman* in 1956 and converted it to the *Alaska Magazine*.

Williams filled in temporarily for managing editor Robert Bender when Bender went Outside for medical care in the winter of 1937, fighting alcoholism. Bender was found dead in his hotel room in Phoenix, Arizona, the day after Christmas.

After Troy was confirmed for a second term as governor, his daughter, Helen Bender, took charge of the editorial department of the *Empire*, hiring a series of editors to assist her. The Empire Printing Company was reorganized with Mrs. Bender as president, Los Bernard, vice president, and J. A. Cooper, secretary-treasurer.

Bernard, the veteran Klondike journalist, had been with the *Empire* from 1917 to 1919 and a co-owner and business manager of the *Empire* from 1926 to 1932. Then he sold his interest to Bender and joined the *Ketchikan Alaska Chronicle* briefly.

Bernard returned to Juneau and joined the staff of the *Alaska Daily Press*, resigning in February 1938. He rejoined the *Empire* in April as business manager and vice president.

Williams was terminated as managing editor and headed south. He stopped in Wrangell when he heard that the *Wrangell Sentinel* was for sale and made the purchase. He was financed by E. A. Rasmuson of the Bank of Alaska who had purchased *The Anchorage Daily Times* in a 1924 marshal's sale and later sold it to his daughter and son-in-law, Robert and Evangeline Atwood.

Ickes gold tax disaster

Troy's ill health was given as the reason for his resignation as governor on August 29, 1939. But his refusal to support an 8 percent tax on gold mining, as requested by Secretary of Interior Harold Ickes, was the main reason he was forced to resign. Ernest Gruening later wrote that Ickes threatened Troy, if he didn't resign, with a conflict of interest charge for failure to report that his newspaper did business with the territory while he was governor. Secretary Ickes was the father of Harold Ickes who served as adviser to President William J. Clinton and his wife Hillary in the 1990s.

In his annual report to Secretary Ickes, Troy termed the 3 percent additional gross tax on top of the 5 percent on gold production an "adverse factor" in the development of mining. Ickes replied: "These statements are contrary to the view of the Department of Interior and with your approval I shall arrange to have them eliminated." The report was revised and published over the governor's signature.

Troy won unanimous support from his Alaska newspaper colleagues in standing up for the mining industry. Typical of that sentiment was an editorial in *The Anchorage Daily Times*:

> Since when was a governor told what he could report? Since when did the Interior Department obtain authority to dictate the attitude of the Alaska governor?
>
> Governor Troy would betray Alaska if he followed the commands of Ickes. The governor is an oldtime Alaskan and has first-hand information on conditions here. If the governor failed to make those statements in his annual report, he would be derelict in his duty.
>
> Instead, the vituperous Secretary of the Interior closed his eyes to facts and virtually commanded the governor that he must heed Mr. Ickes' crackpot theories.

After his resignation as governor, Troy made his home with his daughter in Juneau until the spring of 1941 when he moved to St. Ann's Hospital. When Mrs. Bender remarried on October 18, 1941, to Pan American pilot Alf Monsen, the ceremony was held in her father's hospital room.

A mountain and a ship for Troy

Troy died on May 2, 1942, and was buried in the Elks plot in Evergreen cemetery. On January 11, 1944, a World War II Liberty ship was named in Troy's honor, and on July 7, 1951, a mountain on Douglas Island was named for him.

With the passing of Troy, an era in Juneau politics and journalism ended. Although the *Empire* remained in the ownership of his daughters, Helen Monsen and Dorothy Lingo, thirteen more years, its influence beyond the city's boundaries was limited as the economy of Alaska changed.

With the end of World War II, the Montana Creek and Duck Creek army installations near Juneau closed. The Alaska Juneau gold mine, which was closed during the war as nonessential, failed to reopen. The sawmill burned. Federal mismanagement led to declining salmon fisheries, hurting most of Alaska's coastal towns, including Juneau. There was little economic boost from the limited territorial government compared with the later state government.

Newspapers were hurt by shortages of manpower and newsprint and by price controls brought on by the Korean War. Juneau's economy lagged in the late 1940s and early 1950s, which hurt the local newspapers. *The Alaska Daily Press* was bought out by the *Empire* and run as a weekly until folded in 1951. The *Empire*, even without competition, began losing money in 1950. Meanwhile, opening of the Alaska Highway and construction of military bases expanded the economy of the northern part of the state.

A new brand of Democratic politics had been introduced by Troy's gubernatorial successor, Ernest Gruening, with his background as East Coast editor, publisher, and writer.

When Gruening first arrived, the *Empire* welcomed him. But soon the conservative Democrats, Troy and Monsen, who defended the mining, fishing, and transportation industries, clashed politically with the liberal Democrat Gruening, who sought to increase taxes paid by industries. Gruening also battled Alaska Steamship Co. over its freight rates.

Empire publisher Monsen grew so antagonistic toward Gruening in later years that she ordered that the name Ernest Gruening never appear in the *Empire*. When necessary, the *Empire* just referred to "the governor."

Civil rights debate covered

The *Empire* was still friendly enough with Gruening to use his name in a story when he signed the historic House Bill 14 in 1945, outlawing racial discrimination in Alaska.

The *Empire* reported the debate about the legislation in detail, especially when the House bill hit the Senate floor on February 5, 1945. Reports since, including an *Anchorage Daily News* editorial forty-six years later, list Sen. Allen Shattuck as leading the opposition. Shattuck was the son-in-law of former governor A. P. Swineford, who had founded the first newspapers at Sitka and Ketchikan.

During debate, the Anchorage editorial said Shattuck asked, "Who are these people, barely out of savagery, who want to associate with us whites, with five thousand years of recorded civilization behind us?"

Elizabeth Peratrovich, Grand Camp president of the Alaska Native Sisterhood, was in the gallery and asked to be heard. She was granted the floor.

"I would not have expected that I, who am barely out of 'savagery,' would have to remind gentlemen with five thousand years of recorded civilization behind them, of our Bill of Rights," she began.

The United States was engaged in a battle against a self-styled super race in World War II when the legislature met in 1945. So the only news outlet covering the lawmakers was the *Empire*. It missed the Shattuck statement, if it had been made, but under headlines: "*Super Race Theory Hit in Hearing.* Native Sisterhood President Hits at 'Rights Bill Opposition,'" a non-bylined *Empire* story reported:

> Opposition that had appeared to speak with a strong voice was forced to a defensive whisper at the close of yesterday's hearing on the "Equal Rights" issue. Mrs. Roy Peratrovich, Grand President of the Alaska Native Sisterhood, the last speaker to testify, climaxed the hearing by wringing volleying applause from the galleries and the Senate floor alike, with a biting condemnation of the "super race" attitude.
>
> Reciting instances of discrimination suffered by herself and friends, she cried out against a condition that forces the finest of her race to associate with "white trash."

Opponents to the bill alleged that its passage would increase hard feelings between Natives and whites. They were defeated 11-5, and the bill was before Gruening for his signature eleven days later. He signed it on February 16, 1945, a date now designated in Alaska as Elizabeth Peratrovich Day.

Heaping more insult on the lawmakers, Sid Charles wrote in his *Alaska Fishing News* a week later:

> Comparing accomplishments of the Territorial Legislature with the accomplishments of the annual convention of the Alaska Native Brotherhood and Sisterhood at Kake, it might be a good idea to turn Alaska back to the Indians.

Empire loses on layout

The *Empire*'s criticism of Gruening climaxed with the 1952 libel action, which the *Empire* lost partly because of careless makeup of its front-page – a lesson for journalists.

Mrs. Monsen had hired James Beard as *Empire* managing editor soon after he retired from the U.S. Army Alaska Communications System in Juneau. He lacked newspaper experience.

On September 25, 1952, the *Empire* ran a banner across the front page, "Reeve Raps Graft, Corruption." In the right-hand column was a political story reporting that Republican candidate for Delegate to Congress Robert Reeve had charged there was corruption in the Democratic Party. And in multiple left hand columns under the banner, complete with artwork of a check, was a story that implied irregularities in the handling of revenue from the territory's ferry that ran between Juneau (Tee Harbor) and Haines. This time the *Empire* used Gruening's name with secondary headline proclaiming "Gruening, Metcalf, Roden Divert Chilkoot Cash to Private Bank Account."

This was during days of hot-metal newspaper production when newspapers such as the *Empire* printed column rules and cutoff rules around stories. But on this front page, the *Empire*, whether by mistake or on purpose by the editor or makeup man, failed to put a cutoff between the "corruption" banner head and the story about the ferry revenue. It could be inferred that the banner also concerned the ferry bookkeeping.

What really hurt the *Empire* was a reference in the story likening the ferry bookkeeping to the case of former territorial treasurer Oscar Olson, who had gone to prison for embezzling territorial funds. The *Empire* editor and publisher had second thoughts about that and apologized in the next day's paper. It was too late.

Governor Gruening, Highway Engineer Frank Metcalf, and Territorial Treasurer Henry Roden, a pioneer Klondike and Alaska journalist, had created a separate bank account for the ferry funds that was later found all in order. So they sued the *Empire*, probably also a little fed up with the *Empire*'s constant criticism of the Gruening administration. A jury in Ketchikan decided against the newspaper, which also lost on appeal. The three libeled men won $5,001 each in actual and punitive damages.

While the case wended through the court system for five years, publisher Monsen was faced with competition from the *Juneau Independent* and labor unrest that eventually led a to a printers' strike.

Monsen had enough. She sold the *Empire* in 1955 to flamboyant Colorado and Texas publisher William Prescott Allen. Allen was called before Judge Walter Hodge while the lawsuit was being tried in Ketchikan and admonished to desist from publicly proclaiming he would accept bets on the outcome. He was willing to bet that the *Empire* would win.

In its 1957 decision against the *Empire*, the appeals court said: "What a newspaper actually says or carries to its readers must be judged by the publication as a whole, and headlines alone may be enough to make libelous per se an otherwise innocuous article, or the article may become libelous by juxtaposition with other articles or photographs."

Chapter 34

The Rise of the Ketchikan Alaska Chronicle

Former Klondike journalists Bernard Stone and Ed Morrissey, who had quit the *Ketchikan Times* soon after it was created in May 1919, arrived in Ketchikan two months later with new newspaper equipment. They launched a daily, the *Ketchikan Alaska Chronicle*. Morrissey was editor, and Stone the business manager.

Stone already had launched what had become *The Anchorage Daily Times* for a seventy-seven-year stay. The *Chronicle* was to last thirty-seven. In both cases, Stone failed to stay with each paper after he helped start it. He had the itchy feet that plagued Klondike stampeders.

Morrissey became sole owner of the *Chronicle* in the fall, and Los Bernard, another old-time Alaska newsman, joined Morrisey in the *Chronicle*.

Although the overall economy of Alaska was in a slump after World War I, Ketchikan enjoyed a boom. A report from U.S. Customs said that in 1919, Ketchikan was the busiest port in the territory. Import of goods in Ketchikan exceeded those of the Second Division (Nome) and Fourth Division (Fairbanks) combined; more than Juneau, Douglas, and Treadwell combined.

"Not only as to imports, but also to population, as to number of vessels registered, it is shown that Ketchikan leads all other communities, with the outlook for 1920 even brighter," the *Chronicle* reported.

Ketchikan was to keep that lead until the early 1930s. The 1930 census listed Ketchikan as the largest city in Alaska with 3,800 residents.

Competition was keen between its two daily newspapers, leading to personal feuding between the editors. The *Chronicle* was favored by the politicians and the canned salmon industry. It landed contracts to print thousands of labels each spring for the salmon canneries. The *Times* was well patronized by advertisers, with lively editorials on local issues, extensive local stories as well as Alaska and world news.

Ketchikan's boom led to it becoming wilder than other pioneer outposts during the "Roaring Twenties." Bootlegging and prostitution flourished.

The *Chronicle* urged the law-abiding citizenry to protest the lawlessness, claiming that upward of twenty open bootlegging places were conducting thriving businesses. The *Times* ridiculed the *Chronicle*'s "gallant knight bearing aloft his shield of shining civic purity."

Apparently, Ketchikan residents favored the *Chronicle*'s position. The Times Publishing Company filed for bankruptcy and suspended publication on May 26, 1920. The *Chronicle* had the field to itself for the next two years. Then those who considered it the mouthpiece of the fisheries corporations persuaded Jeffery E. Rivard to return to the newspaper field so that the townspeople could read a viewpoint other than that of the *Chronicle*.

Rivard slams reserves

Rivard and Ernest Blue started *The Ketchikan Daily News* on March 6, 1922, with Rivard as editor and Blue as business manager. It was the first of two newspapers of that name in Ketchikan, but unrelated.

In his initial editorial, Rivard wrote that he had "a very very strenuous fight against certain private interests" who tried to prevent him from starting a rival paper. But he believed that the time had passed when Ketchikan should submit to one man "calling the tune." He stood ready to challenge such autocratic rule.

Ketchikan's alleged autocratic one-man ruler was J. R. (Bob) Heckman, president and chief stockholder of the Miners & Merchants Bank, owner of a general mercantile store and a mortuary, and who held investments in fisheries and mining enterprises.

As a member of the Territorial Senate, Heckman's voting record showed him to be a protector of the canned salmon industry. He is credited with inventing the floating fish trap. Any editor critical of the fishing industry risked cancellation of industry advertising, no small item in a fishing community.

The Ketchikan Daily News was a lively sheet, full of local, national, and world news. It was well patronized by businesses. It was an eight-page, six-column tabloid, selling for a nickel a copy. On page two of the initial edition was a picture of its new Model 14 Mergenthaler Linotype, the most up-to-date typesetting machine manufactured at that time.

Rivard referred to the *Chronicle* as "the local organ of the would-be 'Mighties.'" He condemned bureaucratic control by the federal government that created extensive reservations. He attributed Alaska's economic poverty to that excessive "conservation" policy.

Five months after the birth of the *Daily News*, Rivard suspended publication due to poor health. He claimed more than five hundred subscribers when he announced that his final edition would appear August 9, 1922. Louis Hanson, owner of the Bon Marche mercantile store and a competitor of Heckman, purchased the newspaper plant, which had been operating in the basement of his store. He hired Elbert Bennett of Seattle to be his editor and manager.

The paper continued to attack the "fish trust" and crusaded for the rights of the local fishermen. Delegate Dan Sutherland wrote the Fishing Vessel Owners' Association and the Deep Sea Fishermen's Union, urging them to give their financial support to Hanson. He said the fishermen needed a good editorial writer to present their case to the public and counter the fish trust that had its news organs scattered throughout the territory. The paper condemned the use of floating fish traps for their "wanton destruction of one of our greatest natural resources."

After three months' operation, Hanson decided he did not have the time to run both a department store and a newspaper, so he sold the paper to Charles R. Berry and Edward G. McKean, who assumed control on April 1, 1923. Rivard was again recruited to become its editor.

A hot political issue during the Sixth Territorial Legislature, March to May 1923, was the Foster Literacy Bill, introduced by a Republican Cordova attorney, Rep. Frank H. Foster. The bill required that "no person unable to read the Constitution of the United States and write the English language shall be eligible to vote." It was aimed at disenfranchising more than one thousand Indians in Southeast

Alaska. Voting as a bloc, they could affect the balance of voting power in the territory.

Supporters of the bill contended that these Indians were prey to the machinations of political charlatans. Alaska editors, including the *Chronicle*'s, were generally supportive of the bill's passage. The *Ketchikan News* was an exception, contending "better a dumbhead voter than a political schemer." The *News* cautioned against allowing racism to color the issue. The bill was killed in the Senate by a tie vote.

Splitting Alaska fails

Completion of the government railroad from Seward to Fairbanks exacerbated the capital relocation issue. Northern and western residents were almost unanimous in advocating Seward as a preferable capital site to Juneau.

To some Southeast residents, secession was the only solution. Then there could be two capital cities – one in Juneau and the other in Seward. The *Chronicle* and the *News* opposed Juneau losing the capital and agreed that splitting the territory would benefit all Alaskans.

An idea originated in Ketchikan in 1923 to have residents of Southeast vote on whether they wished to split off from the rest of the territory. It was promoted in news stories and editorials by both daily newspapers. A vote on November 7, 1923, overwhelmingly favored splitting. The vote in Ketchikan, then Alaska's largest town, was 441 in favor and 39 against. All of Southeast favored the idea. And Cordova residents asked to be included with Southeast.

Former Juneau Mayor R. E. Robertson took the idea to Congress, where it was given no consideration.

Despite its economic leadership in Alaska, Ketchikan could not support two dailies. The *News* quit June 8, 1923, before the election on the above issue it supported. Rivard resumed his law practice and his commercial printing business.

Frame, Charles, Paul arrive

Failure of Ketchikan to support two dailies did not deter three veteran politician-journalists from entering the Ketchikan arena – John W. Frame, Sidney D. Charles, and William L. (Bill) Paul. Frame and Charles had been hopping from one mining camp to another in search of another bonanza. Paul had been fighting for the Indians' civil rights.

In 1924, federal legislation extended citizenship to all Indians born within the territorial limits of the United States. Before then, only those who could prove that they had "severed all tribal relationships and adopted the habits of a civilized life" were qualified to vote in Alaska elections.

The enfranchisement of the Indians worried political candidates outside the Panhandle, where influential Indians lived. A voting bloc ranging from 1,500 to two thousand could swing the election of a candidate for territorial office. Paul, an influential Native leader, controlled that influential Southeast Indian vote.

Bill Paul was born on May 7, 1885, in Port Simpson, British Columbia, the son of the Louis Francis Paul Pyreau and his wife, Matilda (Tillie), both Presbyterian-trained Alaska missionaries. His mother was one-half Tlingit and one-half Scottish, and his father was one-half Tlingit and one-half French.

With a law degree, a wife and four children, Bill Paul moved to Ketchikan in 1920. In 1923, he negotiated the purchase of the Skagway's *Daily Alaskan* plant on behalf of the Alaska Native Brotherhood. Part of the plant went to Petersburg. Paul transported a portion to Ketchikan where he established the monthly *Alaska Fisherman*. His editorials were a continuous din against the canned salmon industry and its use of fish traps.

Bill and his brother Louis published the monthly *Fisherman* in Ketchikan until 1931. Then it moved to Petersburg where Louis was printing the *Alaskan* as the official organ of the Alaska Native Brotherhood.

One political coup for which Bill Paul could claim personal credit was the election of Frame to the office of Republican National Committeeman for Alaska in 1924.

After a lengthy journalism career in other towns in Alaska, Frame served as U.S. commissioner and newspaper publisher at Hyder, 1922-23. He then moved to Ketchikan, where he launched the weekly *Alaska Examiner*, to further his candidacy for Republican National Committeeman. It was published from January to June in 1924.

Prior to 1924, national committeemen for both major political parties were chosen in party caucuses. After that, they were elected in the territorial primary elections. Longtime Republicans were aghast at Frame's effrontery to seek the office after he had been a partisan Democrat editor and publisher all of his life.

The Anchorage Daily Times called him "a mugwump of many colors, a social parasite that exists by betraying the confidence of those who trust him," and "a disgruntled office seeker without a party."

The *Times* supported his opponent, Anchorage attorney Arthur Frame (no relation), a lifelong Republican, who had served in both houses of the legislature.

John Frame came out the winner with 2,511 votes to Arthur Frame's 2,281. John had the active support of Wickersham, Delegate Dan Sutherland, and Bill Paul, who could deliver Southeast's Indian vote. The Indians used their voting franchise for the first time. Widespread illegal voting was reported. It was alleged that some six hundred Canadian Indians voted.

Republican Party leaders were dumbfounded at the election returns and vowed to take their case to the National Committee to prevent the seating of John Frame. Gov. Scott C. Bone, U.S. district attorney Arthur Shoup and Harry Steel, editor-publisher of the *Cordova Times*, led a delegation to the Republican national convention in Cleveland, Ohio. The National Committee refused to seat John Frame, appointing George Sexton, a Seward hotelman, in his place.

Frame continued to make his home in Ketchikan, where he published a little booklet, *Frame's Alaska Pocket Pilot*, in which he answered one thousand questions about Alaska.

In 1932, Frame ran for Democratic National Committeeman but lost.

Mrs. Frame made her home with her sons in the Seattle area while John lived by himself in Alaska, struggling with alcohol in his last years.

When he died in Ketchikan on November 8, 1939, at age eighty-two, another stampeder had reached the end of his trail.

Charles arrives from Skagway, etc.

Sid Charles, who had been an Alaska newsman since 1904, arrived in Ketchikan in 1924 with his wife and family. He had been editing Skagway's *Alaskan* for six months after selling his *Petersburg Herald* and *Sitka Tribune*. He went to work for the *Ketchikan Alaska Chronicle*, where he had previously relieved Ed Morrissey when the *Chronicle* editor was on vacation.

Charles's Alaska newspaper trail started in Fairbanks, extended to Anchorage, Skagway, Cordova, Chitina, Juneau, Petersburg, and Sitka before ending in Ketchikan

It was in Sitka that Charles succumbed to the boat fever. He sold the *Sitka Tribune* to C. F. M. Cole and bought a gasboat named *Belle*. An explosion occurred in March 1926 when Mr. and Mrs. Charles were aboard their boat, moored at the city float in Ketchikan. Charles sustained burns on his face and hands. His wife was less seriously injured. During his father's convalescence, Paul (Bud) Charles dropped out of high school and worked at the *Chronicle* as a Linotype operator, a job he held for eleven years.

Competition appeared briefly for the *Chronicle* when Walter T. Neubert, a Seattle printer, put out a weekly called *The Ketchikan Tribune* in October 1930. After nine months, Neubert sold his equipment to the *Chronicle* and returned to Seattle.

Chronicle co-founder Morrissey died of influenza in April 1931. Two of his employees, Thomas K. Smith and Roy Anderson, bought the paper from Mrs. Morrissey with the backing of some local businessmen.

Sid fired

Sid Charles rejoined the *Chronicle* after recovering from his injuries. But the new owners fired him. They alleged Charles was too old. However, Charles stuck around Ketchikan for another twenty-five years. He was not too old to build the weekly *Alaska Fishing News* into the new *Ketchikan Daily News* and run the *Chronicle* out of business by 1956.

Tom Smith handled the advertising and business end of the *Chronicle's* operation until his friendship with a woman living on Creek Street caused problems with his family. He resigned, sold out and moved to New York.

Anderson, who took over the editorial reins of the *Chronicle*, put out a lively paper, writing editorials on local issues. He authored a front-page column captioned "Fins & Tails" giving random observations of local happenings. There was a four-page comic section. Numerous syndicated feature articles enlivened the paper.

An annual "Fish & Game" special edition came out simultaneously with the opening of the fall hunting season. A Sunday edition appeared from 1934 to 1937, with the slogan across the top of the front page.

"More Canned Salmon Is Packed in Ketchikan Than in Any Other City in the World."

First Alaskan editor

When Anderson became editor of the *Chronicle*, he was the first Alaska-born editor-publisher of a daily newspaper in the territory. He was born in Ketchikan on September 21, 1905, the son of Adolph and Andrea Anderson. After graduating from high school, he worked a year as a reporter for the *Chronicle* before entering the University of Washington.

After a year of study, he worked on various papers in Seattle and in Olympia, Washington, Portland, Oregon, Stockton, California, and New York City. He was associate editor of Fawcett Publications in Minneapolis, Minnesota, when he quit in 1930 to return to his hometown to work on the *Chronicle*. He married Oleta McDaniel, a Ketchikan schoolteacher, in August 1932.

Owners of the *Chronicle* with Anderson at that time were Ketchikan businessmen W. C. Arnold, A. W. Brindle, M. J. Heneghan, and W. F. Schlothan. Arnold was an attorney representing the fishing industry. Brindle headed of Ward Cove Fisheries. Heneghan owned a bakery, and Schlothan owned a shipyard.

The last and most dramatic story Anderson covered in his final years at the *Chronicle* was the survival of four men for thirty-three days in freezing weather, two thousand feet up the side of a mountain in Boca de Quadra, south of Ketchikan, after their plane crashed on January 10, 1943. The Morrison-Knudsen Co. twin-engine aircraft was piloted by a pioneer Alaska bush pilot Harold Gillam of Fairbanks. A woman passenger perished after the crash, and pilot Gillam froze while hiking out for aid.

While reporting daily progress in the search for the plane, the *Chronicle* also headlined that British Columbia and Southeast Alaska were cloaked in cold with Ketchikan area temperatures between 9 and 34 degrees, the lowest January temperatures in eight years.

Chapter 35

News Rises, Chronicle Falls

Sid Charles, recently fired from the *Ketchikan Alaska Chronicle* because of his age, became part of the team that ended the *Chronicle*'s monopoly status. In July 1934, the Alaska Trollers' Marketing Association started the weekly *Alaska Fishing News* with A. W. Sherman as publisher and Charles as its one-man editorial staff.

The salmon trollers organized a cooperative in the summer of 1934 in order to bargain for higher prices for their catches. They wanted their own newspaper to tell their side of a price dispute. The *Chronicle* invariably took the processors' side. One of the *Chronicle*'s investors was an Alaska Canned Salmon Industry's lawyer, W. C. Arnold.

The *Chronicle* contended that fish traps were not responsible for unemployment of Alaskan fishermen. It was a matter of Outside unions controlling the job market. It also defended the importation of nonresidents to work in the canneries during the summer months because of a lack of local labor.

In December 1934, Charles became sole owner of the *News*, by then a biweekly. The following spring, he contracted for United Press news service. Charles's daughter-in-law, Mildred Sutter Charles – wife of son, Paul (Bud) Charles – was his business manager until her death from cancer in 1939. Her family members were trap and cannery owners.

The *News* began publishing three times a week on May 26, 1939. Bud Charles quit his job as a Linotype operator on the *Chronicle* in 1941 and joined his father as partner in the *Fishing News*.

The birth of the News

Alaska's First City enjoyed relative harmony in its local press between 1935 and 1944; especially in the years that hometown boy Roy Anderson owned the *Chronicle* and Charles the *Alaska Fishing News*. Both shared mutual respect and appreciation for the Alaska Canned Salmon Industry and its role in the town's economy. Both viewed the new "socialistic" governor, Ernest Gruening, with distrust.

This journalistic euphoria vanished when the *Chronicle* was sold to William L. (Bill) Baker, a thirty-year-old Oregon newsman. Baker was an active Democrat. His views contrasted to those of seventy-four-year-old Republican Charles, whose conservative views had strengthened during his forty years on the Alaska frontier.

Baker sold the *Sitka Sentinel* to the Harold Veatches in July 1944 in order to make a down payment on the *Chronicle*. Baker was backed only briefly by former *Chronicle* owners Anderson, Arnold and W. F. Schlothan, whose support of the salmon industry contrasted to Baker's criticism of the industry.

Baker put out a lively, eight-column, six-page paper with lots of ads. The *Chronicle* was a member of The Associated Press, and carried Drew Pearson's Washington Merry-Go-Round column. Baker's column of local news was captioned "Around the Town with the Whirligig."

Baker's managing editor in the mid-1950s was Richard L. Whittaker, later a Kodiak publisher briefly and then a Ketchikan attorney and state legislator. Editorials appeared almost daily on local issues. Encouraging new industries was a common theme.

The Charleses were operating in the basement of the Bon Marche building on Mission Street. It was a shop built by Bon owner Louis Hanson in 1922 to house the first *Ketchikan Daily News* that lasted only a little over a year. The Charleses were able to use some of the old *Daily News* printing equipment.

In addition to the *Fishing News*, Emery Tobin's monthly *Alaska Sportsman* magazine (now *Alaska Magazine*) was produced in the basement shop.

In September 1945, the Charles expanded the *News* into a daily, the *Alaska Daily Fishing News*. It was incorporated as the Pioneer Printing Co., with Sid, Paul, and Paul's second wife, Patricia, the major stockholders.

Charles Family Publishers–Sid Charles, above right, converted his Alaska Fishing News to a daily in 1945 with the help of his son, Paul (Bud) Charles, left above. In 1947, with the help of Bud's wife, Patricia, left, the name was changed to the Ketchikan Daily News. After publisher Sid died in 1959, Patricia became editor as well as co-publisher with her husband. -*Photos courtesy of Ketchikan Museums and the Ketchikan Daily News.*

They bought the former post office building at 501 Dock Street and upgraded the equipment. The old flatbed, hand-fed press was retired and a webfed Duplex installed. The tabloid page was expanded to a regular eight-column sheet. A new Linotype and a new Kelly job press were installed for printing the *Alaska Sportsman*.

On August 1, 1947, the name of the paper was changed to the *Ketchikan Daily News*.

Robert N. DeArmond, who had worked for the *News* as a reporter since December 1944, was named managing editor. He resigned from the post in 1949 to go into the printing business in Sitka.

Starting with when he was still editor in Ketchikan, DeArmond covered several legislative sessions. His column, "Northern Notebook," was syndicated among the "Axis Press," as the anti-Gruening and anti-statehood Alaska newspapers, including the *Daily News*, were sometimes called. DeArmond's conservative views coincided with the publishers of those newspapers.

After DeArmond left, Gene Brice was editor of the *Daily News* until 1958. Gene Brice and his brother, King Brice, grew up in Ketchikan. King owned a shoe store and Gene worked for the *Ketchikan Alaska Chronicle* as a reporter before joining the *Daily News*. When Gene left Ketchikan for a Portland, Oregon, newspaper job, Patricia Charles succeeded him as editor.

Papers disagree on three things

The *News* and the *Chronicle* took opposing positions on the three major issues of the day – Gruening, fish traps and statehood. Baker backed Gruening and statehood and opposed fish traps. Sid Charles opposed statehood, the governor and supported fish traps.

In labeling Gruening a "liberal," Sid likened him to other "liberals" such as Hitler, Mussolini and Stalin. Sid's anti-Gruening news slant so upset the governor that he complained that Charles must be tampering with the United Press news dispatches. The news agency warned the newspaper against such a practice. The *News* later dropped UP service and moved to The Associated Press. It won a lawsuit filed by UP for termination of the contract.

Sid's two personal columns "Grins and Groans" and "Observations At Random" gave him two opportunities daily to criticize the governor and his supporters. Sid's son Bud helped him on occasion, writing columns directly on the Linotype.

Sid's dislike for the governor was so all-consuming that he ignored the opportunity to push for pulp mill development in the vicinity of Ketchikan, dismissing it as fantasy because of Gruening's tax program. Sid accused Baker of lying to his readers when Baker reported pulp development "is a certainty for Ketchikan."

Fed up with Sid's criticism, twenty-three of the twenty-four House members of the Nineteenth Territorial Legislature in 1949 took time out for a little "horse play." They sent him a "valentine" picturing the tail end of a horse with a legend reading, "The minute I saw this I thought of you." Sid was so proud of it that he ran it on the front page of the *News* after enlarging it to four columns, complete with the signatures of the twenty-three legislators. The one legislator who refused to sign it was a Native, Rep. Frank Johnson of Kake.

Sid's colleagues at Juneau's *Empire*, the *Fairbanks Daily News-Miner* and the *Anchorage News* expressed shock at such "a boorish stunt" by lawmakers. Norm Brown of the *News* called it "a low-water mark in the annals of the august body of the Legislature." Bill Strand of the *News-Miner* observed that there wasn't a member of the House with "the integrity, courage, and strength of purpose as a legislator which Mr. Charles displays each day in the operation of his newspaper."

That Nineteenth Territorial Legislature, which met for seventy-seven days (a seventeen-day special session plus the sixty-day regular session) is most famous for providing Alaska with a basic tax program to convince members of Congress that Alaska could afford statehood. The plan, pushed by Governor Gruening, created Alaska's first income tax, enacted a territorial property tax and a business license tax. It enacted the first tobacco tax and put a tax on punch boards and slot machines. It quadrupled the tax on fish traps and increased the license fee for nonresident fishermen. The property tax was repealed in 1953 as too costly to collect and the nonresident license hike was declared unconstitutional by a court. Slot machines were illegal and soon shut down. Lawmakers also passed legislation authorizing communities to levy a sales tax.

That legislature created the Alaska Department of Fish and Game and the Alaska Statehood Committee, which was chaired by *Anchorage Daily Times* publisher Robert Atwood and included *Ketchikan Alaska Chronicle* publisher Baker.

News editor DeArmond covered that Nineteenth Legislature before going to Sitka. At the same time, covering Alaska issues from Washington DC for United Press, to which the *News* subscribed, was Albro Gregory, who later became managing editor of the *News*.

Dewey next . . . oops!

Sid's zealous Republicanism led him to share honors with the *Chicago Tribune* in the headline error of the century when it proclaimed on November 2, 1948: "Dewey Next U.S. President," based on early scattered returns. Harry Truman won and the following day the *News*, in equally large print, proclaimed: "We're Wrong; It's Truman."

While Gruening's Senate confirmation was pending for reappointment as governor, Baker ran a front-page "Greetings to Members of the U.S. Senate." It was entitled, "Gaining and Growing with Gruening for the Sake of Alaska, America and Posterity." Sid proclaimed "Alaska Gasping and Groaning under Gruening" and listing twelve reason why he should not remain as governor. He called Baker's newspaper "The Daily Comical." Baker responded by referring to the *News* as the "Ketchikan Fish Wrapper."

As the Gruening and fish trap feud heated up between the *Chronicle* and the *News*, the Alaska Canned Salmon Industry and Alaska Steamship Co. pulled their ads from the *Chronicle* and doubled their space in the *News*, a severe financial blow to Baker.

Sid called statehood "a dangerous step into the unknown." He accused the Alaska Statehood Committee of misusing public funds when it hired lobbyists in Washington.

Sid's numerous anti-statehood editorials stressed that it would be a disservice to Alaska, that the territory could not afford such a luxury. He was especially critical of proposed statehood legislation in 1949 that would grant the new state only four sections of land from each township (thirty-six sections), or about forty million acres, retaining the rest with the federal government. (The statehood bill that became law in 1958, granted Alaska 104 million out of Alaska's 365 million acres.)

In another editorial, referring to the pittance of a land grant, Sid wrote that old-timers fought for forty-five years to widen self-governing powers. "And now, when their hopes are about to be realized for statehood, they find that a political machine is trying to give them a mere shell."

Bent Pins to Chains: Alaska and Its Newspapers

KETCHIKAN DAILY NEWS
A FREE PRESS FOR A FREE PEOPLE
VOLUME X, NO. 2427 — KETCHIKAN, ALASKA, TUESDAY, NOVEMBER 2, 1948 — TEN CENTS — MEMBER OF UNITED PRESS

DEWEY NEXT U.S. PRESIDENT

KETCHIKAN DAILY NEWS
A FREE PRESS FOR A FREE PEOPLE
VOLUME X, NO. 2428 — KETCHIKAN, ALASKA, WEDNESDAY, NOVEMBER 3, 1948 — TEN CENTS — MEMBER OF UNITED PRESS

WE'RE WRONG; IT'S TRUMAN

While Sid was preaching caution on statehood, Baker extolled its virtues and assured his readers that only in statehood would the territory ever achieve its rightful goals in development.

No, to dividing Alaska

A review of Sid's editorials revealed an assortment of pet dislikes – liberal Democrats, government spending, the Bureau of Indian Affairs, the Civil Aeronautics Board, foreign aid, and Communists.

However, in a 1954 editorial, Sid took issue with Republican Gov. B. Frank Heintzleman for suggesting that Alaska be divided, with part of it becoming a state. It was an idea entertained once by President Dwight Eisenhower. Sid also criticized Alaska Democrats for calling for Heintzleman's removal for the suggestion.

"First, last and all the time the *Daily News* is for statehood for all of Alaska and doesn't want it divided piecemeal ... the *Daily News* has taken the stand that immediate statehood, in absence of year-around self-supporting industries, might prove too much of a burden on taxpayers. We hope the government would remove a lot of present restrictions which are handicapping industrial development, leaving no question as to our ability to fully support statehood later," he wrote in April 1954.

To bolster his argument against dividing the state, the veteran journalist recalled the special election in November 1923, when Southeast residents voted overwhelmingly, 11-1, for splitting off from the rest of the territory, but was rebuffed by Congress.

Sid wrote a signed column when Interior Secretary Douglas McKay toured Alaska in 1954 accompanied by aide William Strand, a former anti-statehood editor of the *Fairbanks Daily News-Miner*, and Governor Heintzleman.

Sid advocated easing rules so mining could again prosper and so that hydroelectric power could be developed. He wrote that fishing would be aided by splitting its management from game. He concluded that "It is important, extremely so, for Alaska development, that Indian claims, if any there be, be settled immediately." His long support of Indian claims settlement might be why Rep. Johnson from Kake refused to sign the famous valentine from the Alaska House.

And Sid was progressive on some issues such as giving strong editorial support for a road bypassing Ketchikan's main artery before the Water Street tunnel was built in 1954. Such a bypass became a reality fifty years later.

On August 8, 1947 the *Daily Alaska Empire* in Juneau proclaimed on its front page: "S.E. Alaska May Secure Five Mills." The story reported that President Truman had signed legislation that put the money from timber sales in escrow until Native land claims were settled, allowing pulp mills at Ketchikan, Wrangell, Petersburg, Sitka and Juneau.

Only Ketchikan and Sitka secured mills.

Timber, fisheries, mining boost town

The $52 million pulp mill at Ketchikan, on which construction began in 1952, created employment directly for an average of eight hundred in the woods and plant and released into Ketchikan's economy approximately $1 million monthly in wages and in purchase of supplies and services.

After Ketchikan Pulp Co.'s mill went into production in Ward Cove in 1954, the Charles printed a special edition celebrating the event. They did it again when Ketchikan was named an All-American City in 1958.

With the upturn in the town's economy, it might appear that two dailies could have survived at a modest profit. But the editor of the *Chronicle* developed a brashness that weakened his standing. His editorial outbursts at times lacked factual basis and his blind devotion to Governor Gruening cost him financially. He suffered costly boycotts because of his uninhibited editorial style, criticizing whomever or whatever. He also lacked competent business management compared with the *News*.

In the mid-1950s, Baker suffered a rash of libel suits, some of which he won and some he lost, but they meant costly outlays in legal fees. Even a Presbyterian minister filed a libel suit charging that an article "had been greatly injurious to his good name, fame and reputation" and asked $12,500 in punitive damages.

Taxing newspaper income okay

In October 1955, Baker challenged the territory's right to tax newspapers on their gross income, contending that it was a violation of the First Amendment to the Constitution, freedom of the press.

The territory was seeking to collect $1,600 in back taxes from the *Chronicle*. He lost the case.

The judge ruled that the territory's business license act was a revenue measure and did not violate any constitutional privilege because its purpose was not to regulate any business.

Baker was obliged to suspend publication for about two months while he collected accounts and sought loans to pay his taxes. When he resumed publication on December 9, 1955, he converted the *Chronicle* to a five-column, twelve-page tabloid. His editorial voice became shriller toward his competition.

In March 1956, Baker was named a defendant in a civil suit that threatened to terminate his career in journalism. It was filed by minority stockholders in his printing company, demanding repayment of loans they had made to him when he was compelled to pay his back taxes. The Bakers were the majority stockholders. The case ended in an out-of-court settlement, ordered by the judge. Baker lost the case and his wife, who moved back to Oregon.

Chronicle suspends

The thirty-seven-year-old *Chronicle* suspended as a daily on April 23, 1956, but resumed six days later as a weekly, coming out on Sundays. Much of the daily equipment was sold to *The Northern Sentinel* in Kitimat, British Columbia. The weekly survived about a year, suspending on March 10, 1957.

Baker turned to radio and television after quitting newspapering. He ran unsuccessfully for mayor of Ketchikan. Then in November 1958, he sued the *Ketchikan Daily News* for $83,500, listing six causes of action, five for libel and one charging conspiracy in alleged restraint of trade. The libel counts resulted from the *News*' coverage of the mayoral election. Baker claimed the paper published falsehoods about his career.

The conspiracy count charged that the Charles put pressure on another Ketchikan print shop to restrain it from providing type to Baker's *Sunday Chronicle*, forcing it to suspend publication. That was discounted because Baker had been getting his paper printed in Prince Rupert. For his final few issues, he was getting his type set by the *Petersburg Press*. Baker won his libel action but went out of business because the money collected went to his wife and his and her attorneys.

Baker printed a mimeographed visitors' guide for Ketchikan and had a smoked salmon brokerage business before his death in Ketchikan in 1988, paralleling the downward spiral of Klondike Gold Rush editor John W. Frame in Ketchikan fifty years earlier.

Sid Charles bows out

In his final column after Alaska became a state in 1959, Sid objected to the new state legislators giving themselves a $3,000 annual salary plus $40 a day per diem. He cautioned them against relying on legalized gambling and easy divorces as quick revenue sources, noting that "people have and will continue to come to Alaska without such dubious attractions."

Eight days later, and three weeks after Alaska became a state, something he had opposed, Sidney Dean Charles died at age eighty-eight. Thus ended an unequaled seventy-year newspaper career, fifty-five of them on Alaska newspapers.

Bud continued his father's "Observations at Random" column minus the concluding biblical quotation that had been his father's identifying signature. Bud's column reflected a continuation of his father's conservative points of view.

Admitting his opposition to statehood, Bud said he was willing to bow to the will of the voters and would "help make Alaska the biggest and most prosperous state in the Union." He put out a twelve-page special edition as a salute to statehood.

Bud urged the legislators to adopt an austerity program and criticized their pay bill as an effort to loot the new state. "Are you going to sell the people of Alaska down the river for a few paltry dollars to line your pockets, or are you going to act like Alaskans, with the interest of Alaska and its people foremost in your hearts?"

The Alaska press generally disapproved of the allegedly high salaries that the legislators voted for themselves.

In summarizing the action of the First State Legislature, Bud noted that the lawmakers had been captives of Anchorage labor unions. No consideration was given to industrial development, he wrote. The three major bills were the legislators' pay bill; workmen's compensation; and employment security compensation.

"The latter penalizes stable industry and year-round working people," Bud wrote, "so that the defense worker, who earns ten thousand dollars and more in six months, can rock for six days a week all winter. On the seventh day he is required to pick up his unemployment check."

No lights for caribou

When one of the state's new U.S. senators, Ernest Gruening, urged building a huge power dam on the Yukon River at Rampart, Bud ridiculed it for attempting "to light the tundra for the caribou."

Chapters 36-39

Transportation, Military

Boost Rural and

Fairbanks Areas

> *I see the future of this territory opening out like a great scroll. Alaska still has vast undiscovered treasures, especially in minerals. We need the right people in Alaska, the kind who will do the impossible things we have only dreamed of doing. Too many restless fools with itching feet trek up here because they failed in the states or because they're running away from responsibility. We want those who will stay and work and open up the Territory.*
>
> – Ernie Jessen, editor-publisher
>   *Jessen's Weekly* in *Reader's Digest*, December 1950

The Arctic Sounder

BARROW — Arctic explorers — Page 3
KOTZEBUE — Summer challenges — Page 5

Vol. 19, No. 34 • Serving the Northwest Arctic Borough and the North Slope Borough • August 11, 2005 • 75¢

---

n **Inside:**
- Calendar 2
- Opinion 4
- Classifieds 11

n **Communities in Crisis:** Platinum's tax troubles. Page 5

n **Fish Factor:** Bering fleet donates part of catch to feed sea lions.

The Bristol BayTimes

"Spawned weekly in Southwest Alaska"

Page 4

Serving Dillingham, Naknek, King Salmon and surrounding villages   75¢ • Vol. 25, No. 34 • Thursday, August 11, 2005

The Cordova Times

In Memory: Former Gov. Jay Hammond.
Page 3

Cordova, Alaska   Volume 91, Number 25   Thursday, August 11, 2005   75 cents

---

4 Hammond remembered
Former Alaska governor's legacy.

6 New niche in town
Business supply shop opens..

Now online
www.alaskanewspapers.com

The Dutch Harbor Fisherman

Unalaska, Alaska   Vol. 13, No. 36   Serving the Aleutians and Pribilofs   Thursday, August 11, 2005   75 cents

The Seward Phoenix LOG

Get the bear facts — Page 3
Silver Salmon Derby — Inside

Thursday, August 11, 2005   Volume 39, Number 50   Seward, Alaska   75 cents

---

The Tundra Drums

The Beat of the Yukon-Kuskokwim Delta

First flight for Samson. Page 2
Fishermen report good summer catches. Page 3

Volume 33, Number 22   75¢   Bethel, Alaska   Thursday, August 11, 2005

Chapter 36

Military, Transportation Boost Rural Papers

The *Nenana News* helped inaugurate Nenana's annual Ice Classic in the spring of 1918. The classic was still going strong in 2005 among Alaskans hoping to win up to $300,000 for guessing the time and date that the ice moves in the Tanana River.

Nenana, a transportation town, is located at the confluence of the Tanana and Nenana rivers, forty-five miles southwest of Fairbanks. It's named for the nearby stream and the Indian word meaning "a good place to camp between the rivers." The town's motto, "Where Rails and Rivers Meet," developed from being a construction base for the Alaska Railroad in 1916.

The modern city rising rapidly in 1916 on the banks of the Tanana attracted Roy Southworth, who recently had sold his interest in the *Fairbanks Times*. When the *Times* folded some months later, he foreclosed his mortgage on the equipment and transported it to Nenana where he established the *Nenana News* on September 24, 1916.

The *News* became a daily on April 1, 1918. Fully two-thirds of the paper was given over to war news. Above the paper's name were slogans such as:

"We Must Save, Serve & Sacrifice to Win the War"; "Climb on the Honor Roll, Buy a Liberty Bond"; "Uncle Sam Needs Your Help to Beat the Kaiser."

Southworth and some of his old cronies recalled the Dawson City ice pools beginning in 1899, marking the breakup of the Yukon River. At Nenana, a post was frozen into the ice in the middle of the

Tanana River and it was connected by wire with the whistle in the Alaska Engineering Commission's engine room. The regulated clock of the local jeweler was accepted as the governing timepiece. The winning time was when the moving ice pulled the wire taut enough to blow the whistle.

The whistle proclaimed a celebration because once more the icebound inhabitants of the North Country had free access to the great Outside before the railroad was completed.

The *News* became a triweekly in the fall of 1920 when the railroad construction payroll began to shrink. Mrs. Southworth took the print shop equipment to Anchorage, where she established the Quick Printshop and issued the weekly tabloid *Town Topics*. Her daughter Margaret assisted her. The newspaper equipment remained in Nenana with Roy.

When President Harding arrived in Nenana in July 1923 to drive the golden spike, marking completion of railroad construction, he was initiated into the Pioneers' Igloo. As Grand President of the Pioneers of Alaska, Southworth had the honor of presenting the president with a gold watch fob emblematic of the order.

With the exodus of construction workers, Southworth ceased publication on August 2, 1923, moving his plant to Anchorage. There he launched the *Anchorage Daily Alaskan*, together with veteran newsmen Bernie Stone and Ernie Jessen.

As Nenana shrunk, so did journalistic efforts in the area. There were two more short-lived attempts at publications. Tim Bradner, Wally Olson, Karen Fredericks and Carol Phillips published the *Roadrunner* infrequently between 1963 and 1966. Then Jane Pender continued the publication as the *Nenana Valley Roadrunner* for a short time as a biweekly.

Robert Turk published the *Nenanan* between 1988 and 1991 as a monthly, more magazine than newspaper.

Last gold rush paper folds

While transportation and the military were attracting journalists to rural areas, the last small town gold rush newspaper folded at McGrath. G. V. Rosander suspended publication of the *Kusko Times* during the summer months so that he could pursue his mining operations. He sold the paper in February 1937 to Alaska Egan and Theodore R. McRoberts, former printers on Jack Allman's *Matanuska Valley Pioneer* in Palmer. Their first issue of the *Kusko Times* was a five-column, six-page sheet. A twenty-five-watt radio transmitter was installed in the *Times* shop.

McRoberts sold his interest in the paper to Frank M. Egan in June 1938 and went into the river freighting business and mining. Alaska Egan was the editor and Frank handled the business end. The Egan brothers were from Valdez. Their brother William later became Alaska's first state governor. The paper suspended publication in December of 1938.

After three years, McGrath welcomed a snappy new newspaper, *The McGrath Weekly*. It first appeared on September 27, 1941. It was edited and published by local schoolteachers Herb and Patrice Brazil. It consisted of six typewritten pages reproduced on the school hectograph; thirty copies were produced.

In the salutatory editorial, the editors expressed the hope that the paper would "provide a little pleasant diversion for the long winter hours." It had a humor column titled "Kusko Whims."

The first edition told of the arrival of a river steamer with winter supplies and the signing of a contract for furnishing wood for the school's winter supply.

The second edition, on October 4, told of the arrival of McGrath's first and only motor vehicle – a truck for the Civil Aeronautics Administration. The paper was a community service distributed free by the Brazils to the town's three stores, two roadhouses and to the residences of "prominent McGrathans."

It suspended publication in March 1942. McGrath was without a newspaper until January 1973, when Sally Jo Collins started the *McGrath Bulletin*. After eight months, the name was changed to *Kusko Courier* and it continued publication until January 1989.

Eagle Tribune to View

The historic village of Eagle on the banks of the Yukon River was almost a ghost town after Judge James Wickersham moved the district court to Fairbanks, and especially after Fort Egbert was abandoned eight years later.

Charles C. Carruthers printed a few issues of the *Eagle City Tribune* in 1898. M. D. K. Weimer published the *Eagle Reporter* briefly in 1899. Typewriter newssheets called the *Eagle Gee Pole* and the *Eagle's Eye* appeared briefly in 1903-04. After the fort closed, Eagle's population hovered around fifty for the next sixty years.

Longtime Alaskans who had spent most of their life in rural villages as schoolteachers or Federal Aviation Administration employees rediscovered Eagle in the 1970s as a northern Shangri-La. The outside world held no appeal for them so they built themselves comfortable homes in this deserted riverside hamlet where they could escape urban stress. In the 1980s, the population was up to approximately 174.

Charles and Karen Preston launched the mimeographed weekly *Eagle View* on May 13, 1971. It was one sheet with writing on both sides and sold for a nickel a copy. The Prestons moved to Fairbanks and Anton and Esther Merly took over on June 10, continuing publication until September 25, 1974.

Folksy stories depicted the quiet lifestyle of the townspeople. Salmon bakes and potluck suppers followed church services, with most of the residents participating. Members of the Historical Society conducted tours for tourists during the summer months.

Big Delta and Delta Junction

The Delta area has a long history as the gateway to the Interior. The U.S. Signal Corps established Big Delta, located at the junction of the Delta and Tanana Rivers, ninety miles southeast of Fairbanks, in 1902. It was a waystation during the stringing of a telegraph line from Valdez to Eagle. It was the "end of the line" for river transportation on the Tanana and a trading center for the miners during the Tenderfoot gold strike in 1917-18.

The building of the Alaska Highway, which started in March 1942, simultaneously from Big Delta and Dawson Creek, British Columbia, brought people into the area and shifted the trading center from Big Delta to Delta Junction, at the junction of the Alaska and Richardson Highways, ten miles farther south.

Big Delta was the site of a radio station that began to provide communications for the Big Delta Air Base on June 19, 1942. It also became the site of a communications repeater station along the Alaska Highway the following year. The communication facilities were opened to the public for commercial traffic in April 1947, along with the opening of the Alaska Highway.

The Department of the Army created the Arctic Test Branch at Big Delta Air Force Base after World War II.

The first commercial newspaper to appear in the Delta region was *The Delta Weekly News*, a mimeographed sheet. It appeared in

Big Delta in March 1954, with Paul and Trilby Lott as editor-publishers. It lasted about a year.

The *Delta Midnight Sun*, also a mimeographed weekly, was launched at Delta Junction on January 8, 1955, and continued until 1973, when the word "Delta" was dropped. W. Don Nilsson, Sid Flesser and Emil Blahut were editors and publishers at various times in those years.

It ceased publication on April 10, 1975.

Ed and Frances Walker started another mimeographed weekly on March 17, 1955, called *Walker's Weekly*. The Walkers owned the Civilian Trailer Court near Fort Greely. Their paper served as a shopping directory for the convenience of newcomers at Fort Greely and Big Delta.

The August 6, 1955, issue described the impressive dedication ceremonies for changing the name of the Big Delta Air Force Base to Fort Greely, honoring Major Gen. Adolphus Washington Greely, who spent three years in the Arctic gathering scientific information for the army.

"Throughout the impressive ceremonies, jackhammers could be heard in the distance as contractors continued construction of the handsome new base. Following the ceremonies, a formal reception and dance was held at the Officers' Club. Alaska wild game of goat, bear, caribou, moose, grayling, salmon and ptarmigan were served at both the Officers' Club and the NCO Club."

The Walkers moved to Valdez in the early 1960s where he went into the construction business. They opened the first motel in the new Valdez townsite after the March 27, 1964, Good Friday Earthquake. After the earthquake, they also published the *Valdez Earthquake Bulletin* as a special edition of *Walker's Weekly*.

Jane Pender began the *Delta Weekly Gazette* in March 1965, and published it for a little over a year.

Loretta Schooley, Patti B. Dull, Susan Swensen and Karen Heffen established the *Delta Paper* on April 14, 1976. They incorporated in 1979 as TriDelta, Inc. with Schooley as publisher.

Schooley came to Alaska in July 1961 to work on the *Fairbanks Daily News-Miner* after working on newspapers in Evansville, Indiana. In December of that year she married the owner of a highway express service that operated in competition with the *News-Miner*'s highway service. She was discharged from the *News-Miner* and moved to Delta

Loretta Schooley one of the founders of the Delta Paper in 1976, is now founder, editor and publisher of the Delta Wind, established in 1992. -*Photo by Janet Boyer.*

Junction. She stayed out of the newspaper business until she and her three associates founded the *Delta Paper*, a mimeograph weekly.

In 1991, the *Delta Paper* was sold to John Lindauer, who owned a string of rural, free-distribution newspapers. Lindauer's chain collapsed on the death of his wife Jacqueline in 1992, so Schooley sued and got her equipment back.

Then she changed the name of the *Delta Paper* to the *Delta Wind* and resumed publication on October 28, 1992. The *Delta Wind* is a tabloid-sized newspaper printed by Dragon Press in Fairbanks. It is distributed every other week as this is written.

The Mukluk News

One of the newer towns in Alaska, Tok, has a newspaper with a name that goes back in history, *Mukluk News*. The "Mukluk Telegraph" was famous in Alaska for passing news along the trails long before the Alaska Road Commission established a camp at Tok in 1942. So much money was expended to build the camp to serve the new Alaska Highway that it was also called "The Million-Dollar Camp."

Tok had been the customs station for highway travelers before the station was moved to the border in 1947. It was a pump station

Publishing Mukluk News–Beth (above) and George Jacobs (right) started the Mukluk News at Tok in 1976 and are still publishing it more than 29 years later. Their hottest story was the threat to Tok by the famous 1990 forest fire. They reported that the town was saved by a "Miracle Wind." *-Photos courtesy of the Jacobs.*

for the fuel pipeline from Haines to Fairbanks until 1979. The Coast Guard constructed a Loran-C (Long Range Aids to Navigation) station there in 1976.

The first attempt to start a Tok newspaper was by Lavelle and Catherine Wilson. When their *Spieler* started is unknown. It was in volume 12 in 1972. But it suspended about the time John T. Nelson tried publishing the *Tok Bugle* in 1974. The *Bugle* was gone when the George and Beth Jacobs family began the *Mukluk News* on February 3, 1976.

The Jacobses publish their paper twice a month and serve, according to their masthead, "Eastern Interior Alaska – Tok, Tanacrosss, Dot Lake, Chicken, Boundary, Eagle, Tetlin, Northway, Border and Mentasa."

And they were still serving their area in 2005, despite one close call. A forest fire in the summer of 1990 threatened the town to the point plans were made for evacuation. More than a one thousand firefighters battled the blaze that cost $20 million before it was under control.

Lightning started the fire on July 1, 1990. After it burned for three weeks, the *Mukluk News* quoted headlines from other newspapers: "Fire Blocks Main Road to Alaska," the *Yakima* (Washington) *Herald* proclaimed. "Residents Stay Ready to Evacuate," the *Fairbanks Daily News-Miner* reported.

By August 20, the fire was dying down and the *Mukluk News* was out with a special fire edition.

The town was saved by what residents call "The Miracle Wind." It diverted the fire just as it reached the first building. The fire burned the rest of the summer, eventually consuming more than one hundred thousand acres of timber.

Chapter 37

The Lathrop Years

When the *Fairbanks Daily News-Miner* press run ended November 11, 1929, it ended the first chapter – its Thompson Years – in the evolution of Interior Alaska's most influential newspaper. The *News-Miner* represented the consolidation of seven pioneer dailies and weeklies into one publication with territory-wide influence. Founder and longtime publisher W. F. Thompson had been fond of reciting the paper's whole name: *The Fairbanks News – Tanana Tribune – Tanana Miner – Chena Miner – Ridge Top Miner – Daily Alaska Citizen – Weekly Alaska Citizen – Fairbanks Daily News-Miner*; *News-Miner* for short.

Multimillionaire Austin E. (Cap) Lathrop, the new publisher, brought vitality to the pioneer publication after acquiring it from Thompson's widow. He had the money to invest in the plant and staff. Its economic future was secure. Its staff exuded optimism. Not only did he own the town's only newspaper, but also its only radio station.

Lathrop was a tall, handsome man. His heavy shock of wavy, white hair gave him an air of elegance, especially when he was dressed up. He liked to go around in a woolen mackinaw and a sloppy hat, to play down the millionaire image his friends bestowed on him. He had a debonair manner with the ladies. But he also was known for frequent temper tantrums during which he indulged in four-letter words.

Austin Eugene Lathrop was born on a farm near Lapeer, Michigan, on October 5, 1865. His formal education came to an abrupt end at age fifteen when he was expelled from high school because he refused to reveal the name of a classmate who had committed a misdemeanor.

He bought a team of horses from his father and struck out on his own as a contractor, stump grubbing for sawmills in Wisconsin. In 1889 he read of the disastrous fire that destroyed much of Seattle. He decided that was where he should go to make his fortune in contracting. He did make a fortune in the Pacific Northwest, but he lost it in the national panic of 1893.

Three years later, he set sail for Alaska, having borrowed funds to buy part-interest in a 110-foot steam schooner. He used it to freight supplies to the mining camps along Cook Inlet.

Regaining solvency, Lathrop began a career involving him in a variety of commercial ventures – oil, movie theaters, night clubs, apartment houses, mercantile stores, banks, transfer companies, newspapers, radio and television stations, fish canneries, the Olympia Brewing Company and the Healy River coal mine. He moved from Valdez to Cordova, to Anchorage and finally to Fairbanks in 1923.

Lathrop had two matrimonial ventures; his second wife died in 1910. He dabbled in politics, winning a seat in the territorial House in 1920 and served as Republican National Committeeman, 1928-32 and 1949-50.

Klondiker Stone hired

Bernie Stone, most recently a co-founder of the *Anchorage Daily Alaskan*, succeeded Hjalmar Nordale as managing editor of the *News-Miner* after the newspaper was sold to Lathrop.

Stone was among a group of New Zealanders who took a printing plant into Dawson during the gold rush. Their newspaper venture never materialized so they stampeded into Alaska. Stone had left Alaska after extensive Alaska experience. He was working on a weekly in Las Vegas, Nevada, when Lathrop offered him the Fairbanks editor post.

Two employees who worked with him – Paul Solka Jr. and Paul Lien – recalled Stone's five years with the *News-Miner*. Solka remembered him as "a short-stepping New Zealander who wore a patch over one eye and looked a bit like Barney Google, the comic strip character at the time. He was adept with the spoken word to a far greater degree than the written phrase. As a consequence, supplying copy for the paper fell almost entirely to associate editor Bob Bartlett."

Stone's prowess as business manager won Lathrop's praise but, according to Solka, Stone "was aided and abetted by the cigarette manufacturers' aggressive national advertising campaign." The *News-Miner* carried full-page ads in almost every issue. Also, the Fairbanks Exploration Company was patenting its mining ground. That meant two or more pages daily of legal advertising.

Lien recalled Stone as "a likeable fellow who liked to imbibe." His editorials were ridiculous but he was a go-getter in advertising and that pleased Lathrop. Stone kept the title of editor and business manager; however, "the later was the burden of Mrs. Lovina Lund, who did a remarkable job in the business department."

Bartlett was a reporter when he asked Stone for a pay raise because he took himself a bride. Stone responded with a promotion in title to associate editor and a listing in the masthead, but no pay raise.

Stone remained with the paper until the fall of 1935 when illness forced him to retire. On January 3, 1937, in San Francisco, he joined Thompson and many of his Klondike peers in the eternal newsroom.

During Stone's tenure, the *News-Miner* took a strong anti-Wickersham editorial stand. When James Wickersham was running for delegate to Congress in 1930, editorials called him a racist because he said the Indians of Southeast Alaska were entitled to financial remuneration for the land appropriated by the federal government. Condemning "the dastardly effort to incite the Natives to hostility against the whites," the editorial commented:

> One of the most deplorable occurrences in Alaska since it came under American rule is the effort of Wickersham and (William L.) Paul to make the Indians believe that all the lands and waters of Alaska were their personal property and that of this they have been robbed by the government.
>
> That these lawyers will be successful in establishing such a claim no one believes. But in instilling dissatisfaction, venom and hatred in the hearts of the Natives, they will be eminently successful. It will take generations hereafter to disabuse the minds of these people to the idea that they have been ill-treated and that their rights have been ruthlessly trampled under foot.

Charlie Settlemier, another Klondike and Alaska newspaper veteran, succeeded Stone as editor in 1935, having transferred from *The Anchorage Daily Times*. Robert B. Atwood, the new owner of that newspaper, was doing his own editing.

During Settlemier's tenure at the *News-Miner*, Lathrop built a new concrete and steel building to house the newspaper plant, which included a new newspaper press.

In 1938, Lathrop decided to publish a weekly in addition to the daily, aiming its circulation at the outlying mining camps. *The Alaska Weekly Miner* started on February 15, 1938, with Ernest Jessen as editor. It did not prove profitable and was suspended on January 28, 1941.

Stone to Settlemeir to Twekes

The New Deal Democratic national administration was anathema to the crusty, Republican newspaper owner. Lathrop particularly opposed its new governor for Alaska, Ernest Gruening. Lathrop worried Democrats were threatening his private empire.

Settlemier lacked the gusto Lathrop sought to produce fighting editorials. So associate editor David (Tewkes) Tewkesbury replaced him in the fall of 1941. Settlemier joined *The Alaska Weekly* in Seattle.

World War II turned Fairbanks into a war camp. Soviet military fliers were ferried into town to pick up fighters and bombers flown up from the Lower 48. They flew them across Siberia for use against the Nazis. Military censorship regulated the media; prices and wages were frozen. But the *News-Miner* prospered.

Tewkes was another veteran of Klondike and Alaska newspapers. He had been on the copy desk at the *Seattle Post-Intelligencer* in 1933 when Lathrop hired him to be associate editor of the *News-Miner*. Bartlett had resigned and left for Washington DC to be secretary to Delegate Anthony J. Dimond.

Tewkes's long years of experience in the newspaper business gave him confidence in embellishing the skeleton AP news dispatches so that his readers gleaned a greater comprehension. He also followed the Hearst principle of centering the front page with a pretty girl's picture whenever possible. His Saturday column titled "Dragline" was a popular feature.

On August 9, 1945, Tewkes complained of feeling ill when he returned to his desk after lunch. In a few moments, he announced that he was unable to continue his work. He gave instructions for completing the edition and headed toward his apartment, a few doors from his office. A heart attack overtook him on the apartment stairs and he died at age seventy-eight in an ambulance en route to the hospital. That left Settlemier in Seattle at *The Alaska Weekly* as the last Klondike veteran still on a news desk. Sadly, Fairbanks hardly noticed David Tewkesbury's funeral because everyone was celebrating V-J Day, the end of World War II.

People began pouring in over the Alaska Highway after World War II and the statehood movement gained momentum. Lathrop's editors dutifully supported their publisher's unrelenting opposition to the entire concept.

Arthur S. Bremer succeeded Tewkesbury as managing editor of the *Fairbanks Daily News-Miner*. Bremer, a former United Press bureau chief in Oregon, had been with the *News-Miner* as a reporter and ad salesman for two years before becoming editor.

He began his newspaper career in Klamath Falls, Oregon, in 1936 as a reporter and joined United Press in 1942, becoming their capital bureau chief in Salem, Oregon, before moving to Fairbanks during the war.

Airmail opposed

Important changes took place in Alaska during the *News-Miner*'s Lathrop years, progressive changes Lathrop opposed. He opposed the inauguration of airmail because it interfered with the established custom of "kiting" checks – issuing checks before the money was in the bank knowing it would take a week or more before the check came back to Alaska to be charged against an account.

He opposed opening of the Alaska Highway because it would bring an influx of "Oakies" detrimental to the country. He socialized primarily with Seattle businessmen whose interests were usually diametrically opposed to those of year-around Alaskan residents.

He was an object of adulation to many Alaskans, however, because he reinvested a major portion of his profits in Alaska, which was a rarity in those days when most financially successful men took their money Outside.

Governor Gruening's statehood crusade was the ultimate in abhorrent change, in Lathrop's opinion. Determined to fight it with all his might, Lathrop recruited as editor William C. Strand, a *Chicago Tribune* correspondent in Washington DC.

The *Tribune* had sent Strand on a couple of trips in 1947 to investigate the statehood issue, and on the basis of his reports, the *Tribune* had taken an anti-statehood stand. The paper was known for its strong anti-Roosevelt sentiment. It viewed Alaska statehood was just another crackpot New Deal concept.

Bremer returned to the advertising department when Strand became the *News-Miner*'s managing editor in February 1948. Bremer later left the newspaper business. He returned to the *News-Miner* in 1974 as a proofreader and edited Solka's history of the *News-Miner: Adventures in Alaska Journalism since 1903*.

Strand was born in Chicago in 1912. His first newspaper job was a three-year stint with Chicago's City News Bureau, before joining the Tribune in 1938.

He started with the *Tribune* as a police reporter and during World War II he was the *Trib*'s correspondent in Europe. When the war was over, he was assigned to the *Trib*'s Washington staff.

Republican Strand was a joy to Lathrop as he lashed out editorially against every move made by Governor Gruening. He vied with Juneau's *Empire* in hurling insults at the governor. Within weeks of his arrival in Fairbanks, an editorial appeared titled "Governor Gruening," signed by Austin E. Lathrop. It urged the U.S. Senate to reject President Truman's nomination of Gruening for another term as governor of Alaska.

The *News-Miner*'s anti-statehood campaign suffered a setback when Lathrop was killed in a train accident at his Healy River coal mine at Suntrana, 112 miles south of Fairbanks, on July 26, 1950. He was standing on the railroad tracks when a loaded coal car backed into him, knocking him beneath the train's wheels and killing him outright. He was eighty-four.

Will sell cheap

Just before his death, Lathrop had become concerned about the future of the *News-Miner*. It had been losing money at a rate of $2,000 a month. Lathrop wanted to sell it or turn it into a profitable operation. He sought the advice of a Portland, Oregon, newspaper consultant named Charles Willis (Bill) Snedden.

When Snedden visited the plant in the summer of 1950, he found a clutter of small job presses, trays of handset type, three Linotype machines and a Goss press that could print only eight pages at a time. The newspaper had outgrown its equipment because of the war boom and the opening of the Alaska Highway.

Snedden submitted a fifteen-page report that recommended buying modern equipment.

"Cap Lathrop didn't get any further than the bottom of the second page, where it recommended that he invest $200,000 in new equipment," Snedden recalled. "He said he didn't need anybody to tell him how to spend money, and he'd sell it for ten cents on the dollar. I told him I'd give him a dollar on the dollar."

Snedden didn't take the conversation seriously and left for a visit to Mount McKinley National Park. Two days later, word came that Lathrop had been killed in the rail yard accident. Snedden was offered the paper by the Lathrop estate at a bargain basement price. He accepted. His first steps were to buy new equipment and construct a new building, just as he had advised Lathrop to do and as Lathrop had done himself fifteen years earlier.

Chapter 38

Jessen's Years in Fairbanks

The first edition of *Jessen's Weekly* appeared in Fairbanks January 23, 1942, despite shortages of manpower and supplies from the United States entering World War II less than two months earlier. Austin E. Lathrop had suspended his weekly *Alaska Miner* in 1941. Ernie Jessen, its editor, joined Lathrop's *Fairbanks Daily News-Miner* staff briefly before striking out on his own.

Jessen began his long Alaska newspaper career in 1912 as a cartoonist and part-time reporter for the *Cordova Times*. Then he helped veteran journalists Roy Southworth and Bernie Stone start the *Anchorage Daily Alaskan*.

The *Alaskan* was absorbed by *The Anchorage Daily Times* in 1925. Jessen reported for the *Times*, and then bought the *Seward Gateway*. He ran the *Gateway* until 1938 when he joined Lathrop's operation in Fairbanks as editor of the *Miner*.

Jessen beats predictions, setbacks

Jessen's Weekly provided a strong editorial voice in Alaska affairs for its twenty-seven years, despite numerous crises.

In the salutatory editorial, Jessen declared modestly: "It is not our intention to set the world on fire or to begin an unnecessary crusade. When the occasion arises to carry the torch for the common cause, *Jessen's Weekly* will come to the front, and until such time, it is our policy to print the news, without fear or favor."

Pioneer Fairbanks Publishers–Ernie Jessen, above left, watches his printers turn out an issue of his famous Jessen's Weekly. Publisher of the Fairbanks Daily News-Miner 1929-1950 was millionaire businessman Austin E. (Cap) Lathrop, shown here at his Healy coal mine. – *Photos from the Reuel Griffen Photograph Collection, 59-845-1022, Ernie Jessen, Archives, University of Alaska Fairbanks and the Fairbanks Daily News-Miner.*

The weekly tabloid started with a staff of three. Henrietta McKaughn, a journalism major from the University of Kansas, was the reporter. Jessen tended to the business end and he and his wife Catherine operated the Linotype.

At the time Jessen launched his weekly, Alaska was bracing for an invasion by the Japanese in World War II. Friends predicted his paper wouldn't last six weeks. Businesses were closing their doors. Men were sending their families Outside. Nightly blackouts were in effect. Labor problems became critical as the young men entered the service. Eventually, Ladd Field commanders permitted servicemen to work part-time in local print shops.

After the war and heading into the statehood battle, both the *Fairbanks Daily News-Miner* and *Jessen's Weekly* supported retention of fish traps, preceding the referendum on October 12, 1948.

Just when the Jessens were pulling themselves out of debt from the start-up, a former mental patient set fire to the newspaper plant on Thanksgiving Eve in 1948. It represented an $80,000 loss. They had no insurance.

"It looked pretty blue," Jessen recalled, "but we never missed an issue. During the six weeks it took to restore the plant, the paper was printed on *News-Miner* presses. We moved into a Quonset hut, and within a few weeks we were back to our usual forty-six-page edition."

The plucky newsman wasted no time in grief but went out and solicited enough job printing to rebuild his weekly operation. He printed the army's official paper, *The Midnight Sun*, and the university's student paper, *The Farthest North Collegian*.

Jessen's Weekly, rising like a phoenix from its own ashes, was the subject of an article in *The Reader's Digest* magazine for December 1950. In it Jessen was quoted:

> I see the future of this Territory opening out like a great scroll. Alaska still has vast undiscovered treasures, especially in minerals. We need the right people in Alaska, the kind who will do the impossible things we have only dreamed of doing.
>
> Too many restless fools with itching feet trek up here because they failed in the States or because they're running

away from responsibility. We want those who will stay and work and open up the Territory.

Jessen grows into new plant

Jessen built a new plant in the Graehl district of Fairbanks and occupied it in 1952. He had shared editorial duties with John Edouard Pegues, and Paul Solka, former *News-Miner* employees, during the *Weekly*'s formative years. Pegues also had been with John Troy and his *Empire* in Juneau. By 1952 Jessen's staff had grown to thirty and Maurice (Maury) V. Smith was editor.

Maury, the son of Dr. O. H. Smith, professor emeritus of physics at DePauw University in Indiana, arrived in Fairbanks in 1937 to prospect for gold.

Maury's first association with *Jessen's Weekly* was as a reporter. He advanced to managing editor, serving a total of eleven years. In November 1958, he deserted the print media for the electronic, becoming general manager of the late Cap Lathrop's KFAR television and radio station. He served a term in the state House (1963-65) and a two-year term in the State Senate (1967-69).

Cancer strikes

Changes took place at *Jessen's Weekly* in the fifties and sixties. Mrs. Jessen discovered in 1957 that she had cancer. The Jessens began looking for a buyer for their paper so that she could go Outside for medical treatment. Following Maury Smith's departure in 1958, Jessen took the editorial reins himself until December 1959, when he hired Albro Gregory, a former United Press correspondent, as managing editor.

Jessen arranged for the sale of his weekly in the fall of 1960 to a grandson, Edwin J. Sandbeck, and a granddaughter's husband, Donald Van Cleave, both of whom had worked on the paper in various capacities. A third partner was Robert Giersdorf, general sales manager for Alaska Airlines in Fairbanks.

Jessen wrote "30," the traditional end of a story, hung up his apron, put aside his green eyeshade, and closed out more than forty years of newspapering in Alaska. He observed that it was time for young blood to take over and make their own mistakes, just as he and his wife had done in their time.

Giersdorf announced that there would be many "progressive changes." The paper changed from a tabloid to a standard-size page. It came out on Sundays instead of midweek. Nationally syndicated columnists and a color comic supplement were added.

Gregory remained as editor for a couple of months under the new owners and then departed to become editor of the *Ketchikan Daily News*. Richard J. Greuel succeeded Gregory in April 1961.

Greuel arrived in Fairbanks in 1947 as a nineteen-year-old army private stationed at Ladd Field. While still in service, he began broadcasting for radio station KFAR. After discharge from the military service, he was program director for the Midnight Sun Broadcasting network, owned by Lathrop.

Greuel had become something of a boy wonder in politics during this period. At age twenty-three, he won a seat on the Fairbanks City Council and served for six years. He also served three terms in the territorial House of Representatives, being elected speaker in 1957. At age twenty-eight, he was then the youngest speaker in Alaska history. He was a delegate to the Democratic National Convention in 1960 when John F. Kennedy won the nomination for the presidency.

Jessen was so impressed with Greuel's performance at the paper that he wrote him a note of commendation that the young editor did not hesitate to print:

> You have breathed life into J-W. Please accept my sincere congratulations. Am confident your editorials – and they are far above the average – will focus considerable attention on *Jessen's*. Your humorous column (Sluice Box) is fresh and well done. The news content is so far ahead of what we have had in the past that there really can be no comparison. I'm proud of the paper. Good luck!

Greuel fades

Jessen's happy expectancy suffered a setback when he discovered that the business end of the paper's operations resulted in a pile of debts forcing him to repossess the property. He dropped the features and went back to the successful format he had used previously.

Jerome Fife Sheldon succeeded Greuel at the newspaper. Sheldon was drafted into the U.S. Army in 1942, after graduating from the University of Washington. He served with the Corps of Engineers on Shemya Island in the Aleutians and was field correspondent for the army newspaper, *Yank*.

Sheldon was news editor on the *Fairbanks Daily News-Miner*, 1954-55, and public relations officer for the Alaska Railroad, 1955-57. He was number two man in the editorial department of the *News-Miner*, 1958-61.

He spent a year with the *Ketchikan Daily News* before joining *Jessen's Weekly* in 1963. He left Alaska in 1965 for an editorial position on the *Toledo* (Ohio) *Blade*.

Snapp, fire and flood arrive

Thomas Aubrey Snapp succeeded Sheldon at *Jessen's Weekly*. He was a former court reporter and special features writer for the *News-Miner*.

Snapp was fresh out of the University of Missouri when he visited his sister, Colleen Redman, in Seward in the summer of 1960. That fall he joined the staff of the *News-Miner*.

While covering rural Alaska for the *News-Miner*, Snapp became acquainted with Native leader Howard Rock, who asked his help in starting a newspaper for the Natives. Snapp left the *News-Miner* to spend a year teaching Rock the fundamentals of journalism before returning to the University of Missouri for graduate work.

Following his graduate program, Snapp returned to Fairbanks in January 1965 to become editor of *Jessen's Weekly*. He remained in that position until April 1968; thus being on deck for the great Chena River flood.

On the morning of August 14, 1967, Fairbanks was nearly a submerged city. A once-in-a hundred-year rain in the headwaters of the Chena drainage sent a wall of water down the Chena Valley. It was also the year Alaskans observed their centennial – one hundred years since purchase of Alaska from Russia. The flood poured up to ten feet of water over a wide area of Interior Alaska. Seven people died and the property damage was estimated at $200 million.

The *News-Miner* suffered minimal damage compared with *Jessen's* because valuable newsprint and office records were moved to a higher level before the water crested a few inches above the first floor of the *News-Miner* building. However, the press pit and the furnace room were lower than the first floor and flooded. The press was easily repaired when the water dropped but the electrical transformers were in the furnace room. Power to the building had been shorted out. The *News-Miner* suspended publication for a week.

It took Jessen three months to get back into operation after the flood wiped out his plant and his and his wife's home. Both Snedden and Jessen secured 3 percent, thirty-year loans from the Small Business Administration to finance rebuilding.

The daily disaster

Jessen's spirits were so revived by the SBA loan that he decided to go daily, a lifelong dream of his. *Jessen's Daily* appeared as a morning paper on December 4, 1967, in competition with Snedden's afternoon *News-Miner*. Jessen's initial press run of his forty-page tabloid was ten thousand and was distributed free. With a population of twenty thousand, Fairbanks was the smallest city in the nation with two independent daily newspapers.

Concurrent with his decision to go daily, Jessen agreed to sell the paper to Charles Willis Jr., president of Alaska Airlines, as part of a newspaper chain Willis and his associates were building. Snapp continued as editor and Al Phelps, editor of the *Nome Nugget* and a Willis associate, became general manager. The paper had a staff of thirteen employees. An expanded commercial print shop employed additional people. The daily had an estimated circulation of six thousand with the Sunday edition, *The Sunday Observer*, reaching seven thousand.

The discovery of oil at Prudhoe Bay in February 1968 was an economic bonanza to the flood-weary Fairbanks residents. New businesses blossomed, increasing advertising for local media.

Jessen's put out the first of what was intended to be the annual *Jessen's Historical Edition*. In its eighty pages, it traced Alaska's history through stories taken from old newspaper files from all parts of Alaska. It sold for a dollar a copy.

But the town was unable to support two dailies and *Jessen's* was financially the weaker of the two. On September 6, 1968, the Internal Revenue Service padlocked the paper's offices, seizing its assets in lieu of payment of $39,000 in back taxes, and put the seized equipment up for a sealed bid sale. The state commissioner of labor filed suit asking for $40,000 in back wages owed employees.

Jessen issued a four-page mimeographed newspaper explaining his predicament, distributing it free in downtown Fairbanks.

Members of the International Typographical Union volunteered their services and nine local businessmen came to his rescue. Jessen cancelled Willis's option to buy the paper and resumed active management himself on November 25.

He struggled for ten months to wipe out the debts accumulated during the Willis regime but pressure from the creditors proved too much for him. The IRS padlocked the doors again on August 27, 1969, after the Mt. McKinley Mutual Savings Bank of Fairbanks filed a $92,363 civil action, claiming priority over other creditors, including the SBA, and state and federal liens totaling more than $50,000. The Jessens filed a $1.5 million suit against Willis and Alaska Airlines, claiming fraudulent and negligent mismanagement.

Ot Hampton, former *Anchorage Daily Times* political reporter, was managing editor of *Jessen's Daily* at the time of the final suspension.

Hampton, forty-four, a native of Grandview, Texas, had served in the U.S. Army Air Corps during World War II. He joined *The Anchorage Daily Times* from a public relations agency in Texas

After nine months with *Jessen's*, Hampton returned to Anchorage to serve briefly as editor of the *Alaska Business Magazine*. He then went south to become special assignments writer for the *Dallas Times Herald*, where he was the third *Herald* reporter to be stabbed to death in nine years.

The Pioneer next

Following suspension of *Jessen's Daily*, Jessen, Snapp and Paul Lien launched *The Pioneer All-Alaska Weekly* on July 3, 1970. Snapp quit his news editor's job at KFAR radio-television station to team up with Jessen in the new venture. Lien had been Jessen's former advertising manager. Their *Pioneer Weekly* was a twenty-four- to thirty-two-page tabloid patterned after the original *Jessen's Weekly*. It was printed in the *News-Miner*'s Commercial Printing Co. shop

The first run was five thousand copies, with three thousand going to subscribers and the remainder distributed free. The editorial offices were in the Northward Building. It carried only state and local news. Its masthead slogan read: "As free and independent as the birds for the cause that lacks assistance, for the wrong that needs resistance; for the future in the distance and the good that we can do."

Jessen suffered a heart attack and died at his home on March 26, 1971, at age eighty-one. He was scheduled to meet with his attorney the next day about his lawsuit against Willis and his airline. Mrs. Jessen decided not to pursue the suit after her husband's death. She entered the Pioneers' Home in Fairbanks where she spent her remaining years.

Snapp carries on

Snapp continued publishing the *All-Alaska Weekly*. The sixteen-page tabloid enjoyed a healthy circulation. He wrote spirited editorials on local and state issues. He gave his front-page news stories a sensational twist and used bright colors for his "flag" to attract attention on the newsstand.

Crime increased notably during construction of the trans-Alaska oil pipeline in the seventies. Slain bodies were found on remote sideroads, and police investigations were fruitless. Crime got so out of control that special investigators were dispatched from the state attorney's office in Juneau to assist the Fairbanks police. Sample front-page headlines were:

"Corpse Found Stuffed Down Gold Dredge Hatch"

That was followed by two subheads:

"Man, Visiting Mother-in-law Finds Murder Victim" and
"Cook Shot Twice, Body Upside Down in 8-Ft. Hole."

Another headline blared:

"Two Murders Here in Three Days"

Two pages in each weekly edition were devoted to the "Police Blotter."

Snapp's sister, Colleen Redman, formerly of Seward, was listed as assistant publisher in the 1970s. In the 1980s, her daughter Linda was listed in the same capacity.

Assails federal land lockup

The weekly was more of an advocacy organ than a straight newssheet. Starting with his own front-page byline story, Snapp invited guest writers with advocacy pitches. Among his editorial crusades were advocating a change in the grand jury system away from a secret presentation of a one-sided case by the prosecuting attorney; advocating a just settlement of the Natives' land claims; advocating an all-Alaska route for transporting Arctic oil and gas; advocating retention of the state subsistence law; and condemning the Carter-Andrus land grab (when President Jimmy Carter and his Interior Secretary Cecil Andrus used the Antiquities Act to lock up land until passage of the Alaska National Interest Lands Conservation Act in 1980).

> Not only does the federal government appear hell-bent on putting most of Alaska in a deep freeze, but it also appears hell bent on forcing most Alaskans to live in the same tight squeeze as those in the smog-filled skyscraper jungles of the lower states' concrete cities.
>
> This is not the first time that the federal government has run roughshod over Alaska. Alaska was raped for its fur. It was raped for its fish. It was raped for its gold. And now it's being raped for its oil and gas. And to make sure that the resources will be reserved for future rapings, the federal government, in violation of Alaska's policy of multiple land use, is withdrawing more than a third of the state and putting it into single purpose non-use.
>
> We maintain the federal government has no right to a vast land domain with which it can enslave the people; and to allow it to do so is a colossal usurpation of states' rights. The federal government is entitled only to that land within a state's boundaries which it has purchased for a military installation or building with the concurrence of that state's legislature. Nothing more, nothing less. This Carter-Andrus land grab is a monumental act of illegality and immorality that should be challenged in any possible way.

During Snapp's newspaper career, he clipped newspapers and kept extensive files of clipping by subjects such as oil, accidents, education, and so forth. He also trained many young journalists, in addition to Howard Rock of the *Tundra Times*. For twenty-five years he was active in the Farthest North Press Club, believing it provided a forum, aside from the chamber of commerce, for interesting speakers.

He tape recorded many speakers. His sister turned over about four thousand tapes of those forums to the University of Alaska Fairbanks after Snapp's death.

Snapp sold the newspaper December 31, 1987, to Tom Alton, later a University staffer, and a group of Fairbanks investors under the name Northern Light Publishing Co. Alton ran it for about a year and a half and ran out of money.

In May 1989, four of the investors bought the paper – Jim and Mim Dixon and Brian Rogers and his wife, Sherry Modrow. They ran it until November 1990 when they sold to Andy Williams. Just before selling to Williams, the *Weekly* published jointly for several months with John Lindauer's rural free newspaper chain – Northern Light staff provided the outside eight pages, and Lindauer's staff did the inside six pages. For most of the time that the investors ran the paper, no one had the title editor – it was somewhat of a shared responsibility.

Williams lasted for about a year, and then sold the *Weekly* to Joe Sitton. The paper folded on October 1, 1992 when the paper's landlord at the Lavery Building locked the door for failure to pay rent. Sitton, who also had served a term in the state legislature while running the paper, left for California.

Snapp and Redmen were unable to collect the clippings and old files in the newspaper office when it closed. But Snapp had continued clipping the *Fairbanks Daily News-Miner* and *Anchorage Daily News* after he sold the paper and until the day before he died, September 8, 1995. Mrs. Redman says she expects those files to go to the university.

Chapter 39

The Native Press Appears

The Paul brothers, William L. and Louis of the Tee-Hit-Ton clan of Wrangell, founded and operated in the 1920s the first Alaska newspapers for Natives.

Howard Rock's *Tundra Times*, started in Fairbanks in 1962, was the most influential Native publication. The e-mail weekly *Chickaloon News*, started in 1995 and edited for the Village of Chickaloon by Patricia Wade, is the latest. The Calista Corp.'s Alaska Newspapers, Inc., is the largest successful Native-owned newspaper operation. But the Paul brothers were first.

How it began

William L. Paul Sr. started the monthly *Alaska Fisherman* in Juneau in February 1923. He moved it to Ketchikan in May. Then William and Louis started the weekly *Alaskan* in Petersburg in 1926, both were published for the Alaska Native Brotherhood

The weekly *Petersburg Herald* suspended publication in February 1926 when its shop foreman, Henry E. Phillips, left for Skagway to dismantle the equipment of the defunct *Daily Alaskan* and ship it to Petersburg for the Pauls. Their new *Alaskan* first appeared in Petersburg on July 16, 1926, with Louis as editor but William always involved. Louis Paul was a teacher at the Native school in Petersburg and was assisted at the paper by Phillips.

The *Alaskan* and the *Alaska Fisherman* were the first newspapers edited and published by a minority group in Alaska with the expressed aim of furthering the group's political and economic well-being. The

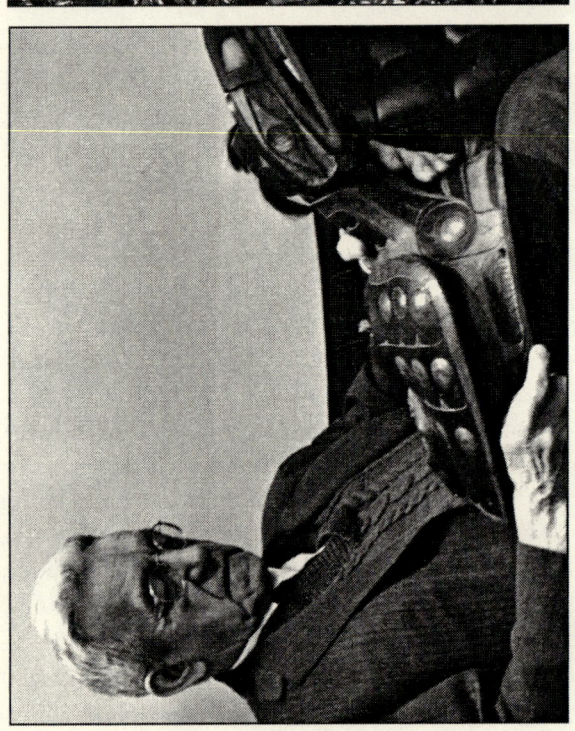

Prominent Native Publishers—William L. Paul, Native leader and attorney, started The Alaskan in Petersburg in 1926 as the first Alaska newspaper dealing with Native issues. He also served in the Legislature and as Grand Camp president of the Alaska Native Brotherhood. Patricia Wade, right, is the editor of the latest Native newspaper, the Chickaloon News, begun for the Village of Chickaloon in 1995. -*Photos courtesy of the Ketchikan Daily News and Patricia Wade.*

Indians of the Southeast Panhandle were operating in Alaska's economic mainstream, while the Eskimos, Athabascans and Aleuts in the rest of Alaska were still subsisting in separate isolated communities.

The Southeast Indians organized the Alaska Native Brotherhood in 1912 and within three years added a women's auxiliary, the Alaska Native Sisterhood. By the mid-twenties, nearly every Indian community in Southeast had a local branch known as a camp. The central organization was the Grand Camp, which met annually.

The purpose of the ANB and ANS was to encourage assimilation of the Natives into the white man's culture. Winning citizenship was a primary goal. Secondary goals were education for themselves and abandonment of aboriginal customs that were seen by whites as uncivilized. In later years, this changed to a strong movement to preserve their Indian culture, along with succeeding in a modern economy.

Of paramount concern was protecting ownership of Native land and fisheries. The Paul brothers believed that the Indians needed their own press in order to make headway in promoting Native claims. The *Alaskan*'s vigorous editorial crusades won several significant goals: an integrated school system; inclusion of Natives in welfare programs; special hospitals for Native patients.

The Paul brothers contended that there were no public lands in Alaska. The whole territory belonged to the Natives. They sparked a land controversy that carried on long after the life of their newspapers, and led to the Alaska Native Claims Settlement Act in 1971.

A corollary of the land controversy was the plight of Alaska seine and gillnets fishermen – which included the Native fishermen – in competition with cannery owned fish traps. Canneries were mostly owned by white-dominated Outside interests. The problem was illustrated in 1928 when 71 percent of the salmon harvested in Alaska waters were caught in traps.

The *Alaskan* and the *Alaska Fisherman* accused the federal fisheries commissioner of favoring the cannery interests in devising regulations detrimental to the local fishermen. Bitter resentment also was voiced against the importation of Oriental labor to work in canneries instead of hiring Alaska Natives.

The 'most dangerous man'

Although the general circulation *Herald* had suspended in Petersburg, the Pauls' *Alaskan* faced local competition a month after its start-up with appearance of the *Petersburg Press*.

When A. O. Elstad was editor of the *Petersburg Press*, he and the Pauls resorted to name-calling and satirical criticism of one another, especially during political campaigns when they were supporting opposing candidates.

In 1921, William Paul was the first person of Native blood admitted to the practice of law in Alaska and in 1924 he was the first person of Native blood elected to the legislature – the same year Congress granted citizenship to all Indians. In the 1926 campaign, when Paul was running for re-election to the territorial House, the *Press* asked:

> Will you cast your vote for William L. Paul, organizer of the Native bloc, the breeder of racial hatred; the man who has made the Indians a political question by inducing them to vote for him and his supporters by making promises which he knows can't be kept either legally or morally; the man who has been described as "the most dangerous man in Alaskan politics" because he threatens to dominate Alaska and to rule the territory by and for the Indians who have placed him in power?
>
> Is not Paul the man who told the Natives that it is not a crime to rob a fish trap and did not two of his friends who believed in him rob a trap and were sentenced to serve three years each in a federal penitentiary?

Paul won re-election in 1926 but was defeated in 1928 and in 1930 in his bids for a House seat. He met defeat again in 1932 when he ran for territorial attorney general as an Independent.

The Pauls' *Alaskan* denounced the incumbent territorial attorney general, John Rustgard, a Republican and a former longtime personal friend of William Paul's. Paul further alienated the Republican Party leaders by demanding that they finance his campaign, promise him a political job, and put the *Petersburg Press* out of business. Otherwise, he would see to it that the Indian vote would not go to Republican candidates as it had in the past.

James Wickersham was running for re-election as delegate to Congress and he made a substantial contribution to the support of the *Alaskan*, according to 1932 entries in his diaries.

On September 30, 1932, there was a fiery front-page editorial in the *Alaskan* titled "Shoot and be Damned, Whom the Gods Would Destroy They First Make Mad," denouncing Attorney General Rustgard. The following week, the U.S. marshal seized the *Alaskan*'s plant on a complaint of Hogue & Tveten, local merchants to whom the ANB Publishing Co. had been in debt for several years.

That action silenced a raucous editorial voice during the final month of a bitterly fought political campaign. It was a landslide victory for all of the Democratic candidates. William Paul suffered defeat together with his former Republican friends. It also spelled the end to the Paul brothers' journalistic career. Both Paul newspapers were printed in Petersburg by then. The newspaper plant was sold to the plaintiffs for $100.

Louis Paul moved to Wrangell and William Paul to Juneau where he instituted court suits against the U.S. marshal and the district judge involved in closing down the papers. They were futile gestures. His conduct in and out of court earned him several contempt charges. He was disbarred in the midthirties. However, that failed to silence William Paul. He remained politically active and outspoken for many years, promoting Native issues, particularly land claims.

Land settlements start

The Indian Reorganization Act (also called the Wheeler-Howard Act) was enacted in 1934 to provide protection through the Department of Interior by establishing reservations. Both Natives and whites in Alaska objected to reservations.

William L. Paul and his attorney son, Frederick L. Paul of Petersburg, filed the first of 17 tribal lawsuits with the U.S. Court of Federal Claims in September 1941 asking $10 million for loss of land and fishing rights. All of the suits were rejected by the court for being improperly filed.

Then in 1944, Secretary of the Interior Harold Ickes joined the fray. He ordered hearings held in Southeast and Seattle to determine the validity of Natives' claims. He envisioned putting 80 percent of Southeast in a reservation controlled by Interior's Bureau of Indian Affairs.

Indians in the Juneau area filed claims to all of the City of Juneau, plus land of the A-J Mine. Douglas, Wrangell, Sitka, Klawock, Kake, Saxman, Hydaburg and Ketchikan Indians filed similar extensive claims, according the September 28, 1944, *Ketchikan Alaska Chronicle*.

Representatives of the white-dominated Southeast communities protested. The *Chronicle* published a forty-four-page special edition supported by advertising from the communities, chambers of commerce, the fishing industry, the timber industry and the mining industry, outlining arguments against Ickes' proposal. Copies were sent to newspapers nationwide. It was part of the debate in the 1944 presidential election campaign because Ickes proposed other controversial land lockups in Western states.

Alaska newspapers editorialized against the claims. Secretary Ickes was accused of fomenting unrest among the Indians in order to seize control of Southeast land from the U.S. Forest Service in the Department of Agriculture, and from private owners.

The *Wrangell Sentinel* bemoaned the hearings: "Most unfortunate reaction arising from the hearings is the revival of racial prejudice which had in recent years largely been overcome."

The *Alaska Fishing News*, forerunner of the *Ketchikan Daily News*, called the secretary's proposal the "Ickes Blight." Editor Sid Charles, representing the opinion of most Alaska and Seattle editors, wrote: "No one objects, least of all the Alaska Fishing News, to Indians recovering any legal rights. For such they should be properly compensated through the United States Court of Claims."

Charles also accused Ickes of using the Indian claims as a stalking horse to kill Alaska development and Alaska statehood, which Ickes opposed.

Newspapers from Honolulu to Witchita, Portland, San Francisco and Seattle joined in the criticism of Ickes. The secretary was sent a strong message December 10, 1944, when the U.S. House overwhelmingly cancelled his proposed Jackson Hole Wyoming National Monument. He announced four days later, exhibiting his arrogance, that he would "let" Congress solve Alaska Native claims.

When Ickes said that he would be resigning after completing a few more projects, President Harry Truman accepted his resignation immediately.

Timber claims settled

A partnership including the *Los Angeles Times*, looked at Thomas Bay near Petersburg in 1946 as the site for a pulp mill, but dropped the idea after William Paul reminded them of unsettled land claims.

Then on August 8, 1947, President Truman signed House Joint Resolution 205, later known as the Tongass Timber Act. It authorized the Forest Service to offer fifty-year Tongass timber sales. Without that resolution, the investment in pulp mills at Ketchikan and Sitka would not have been feasible.

Under the resolution, timber receipts were held in escrow until a future settlement of Native claims because the Tee-Hit-Ton Indians of Wrangell, led again by William Paul, had filed suit with the U.S. Court of Federal Claims for loss of the timber.

The court rejected the claim and the U.S. Supreme Court upheld the Court of Federal Claims in 1955. But in doing so, the Supreme Court confirmed that aboriginal title did exist in Alaska and had not been extinguished. That then was the basis the Alaska Native Claims Settlement Act in 1971 passed by Congress to extinguish aboriginal titles.

Back before the Court of Federal Claims in 1959, the claim of the Tlingits and Haidas of Southeast was recognized but they were not awarded $7.5 million for eight years, until they organized the Tlingit-Haida Central Council to handle the award.

William Paul's advocacy and newspapers were the early impetus for ANCSA and the T-H claim.

Later William Paul moved to Seattle and died there on March 4, 1977, at age ninety-one. Before his death he was reinstated as a practicing attorney in Alaska. And a building at the Ketchikan campus of the University of Alaska Southeast was named in his honor.

Another ANB-ANS paper

Another successful effort to publish a newspaper for the ANB and ANS was carried on for twenty-two years, 1954-76, by Cyrus Peck, and his sons, Cyrus Jr., and Ray. They published and edited the *Voice of the Brotherhood*. It was distributed out of Juneau.

It was a monthly publication established to be a voice on issues important to all Alaskans, especially Natives. Later, the publisher's

The Voice Of The Brotherhood
–A successful effort to publish a newspaper for the Alaska Native Brotherhood and Alaska Native Sisterhood was carried on for 22 years, 1954-76, by Cyrus Peck, right, and his sons, Cyrus Jr., and Ray. Cyrus is shown here with a Juneau Empire pressman. They published, edited, and distributed The Voice of the Brotherhood out of Juneau. -*Photo courtesy of the Peck family.*

statement said it was a subsidiary of the Tides People, Inc., "a corporation dedicated to the promotion and preservation of the values and cultures of the original peoples of Alaska. And the opinions expressed do not necessarily reflect the views of the Alaska Native Brotherhood and Sisterhood."

Artist Rock switches careers

While covering rural Alaska for the *Fairbanks Daily News-Miner*, reporter Tom Snapp became acquainted with Native leader Howard Rock, who asked his help in starting a newspaper for the Natives. Snapp left the *News-Miner* to teach Rock the fundamentals of journalism.

Rock was born in Point Hope on August 11, 1911. He attended a grade school there, pioneered by the Episcopal St. Thomas Mission. He attended high school at White Mountain Industrial School, operated by the Department of Interior.

He worked his way south on the government supply ship *North Star*, to study art under Max Siemes, a Belgian artist, in the little town of Trail, Oregon He attended the University of Washington for three years, majoring in art. For years thereafter, he worked for a jewelry firm in Seattle, engraving Alaska scenes on ivory. He was drafted into the U.S. Army Air Corps in 1942.

Rock mustered out in 1945 and went back to ivory engraving in Seattle. It was on a vacation visit to his family in Point Hope in the summer of 1961 that he became aware of the critical need for his people to have a media voice to lobby for their interests. He moved to Fairbanks that fall and held a one-man art show; selling half of his paintings, one going for as high as $1,000. He gave up his career in art so that he could devote full-time to journalism.

His immediate concern was to help organize Eskimo opposition to Project Chariot, the Atomic Energy Commission's plan to blast a harbor out of the coast near Point Hope by means of nuclear explosions. The Eskimos succeeded in having the project scrapped.

Under Snapp's tutelage and with a grant from the American Association of Indian Affairs, Rock established the biweekly *Tundra Times*. Its first edition rolled off the press on October 1, 1962. The front-page banner read:

> Interior Secretary Udall Visits Alaska – Historic Rights & Claims Settlement Is Number One Problem, Declares Official.

In the initial editorial, Snapp wrote:

> Long before today there has been a great need for a newspaper for the northern Natives of Alaska. Since civilization has swept into their lives in tide-like earnestness, it has left the Eskimos, Indians and Aleuts in a bewildering state of indecision and insecurity between the seeming need for assimilation and especially in Eskimo areas, the desire to retain some of the cultural and traditional way of life.
>
> With this humble beginning we hope, not for any distinction, but to serve with dedication the truthful presentation of Native problems, issues and interests.

Grant boosts paper

The paper needed money to continue. Snapp wrote a forty-five-page letter to Dr. Henry Forbes of Milton, Massachusetts, the wealthy president of the Association of American Indian Affairs, describing the need for a newspaper devoted to promoting the interests of Alaska's Native people. Snapp recounted his frustration in reporting news on Natives issues for the *Fairbanks Daily News-Miner*, which led to his quitting the *News-Miner* to assist Rock.

Dr. Forbes telephoned Snapp, offering to guarantee $35,000 for the newspaper's first year, with Rock as editor and Snapp as assistant.

In 1965, the Eskimo, Indian, Aleut Publishing Co. was formed. Shares of stock were sold as a financial base for the paper's operation as a weekly. It started as a nonprofit corporation, later found infeasible as the paper went deeper into debt. A major source of income was the annual banquet held in conjunction with the Alaska Federation of Natives convention in Anchorage each fall.

Under the Statehood Act, Alaska was granted the right to select from the public domain 104 million acres over twenty-five years. When the selection process began, the Natives were worried that they would lose large tracts of land that they considered an inheritance from their forefathers. They also felt insecure over stepping from a subsistence hunting and fishing lifestyle to the space age in only a matter of a few years. Rock was determined to try to interpret their points of view to the wider Caucasian society that was planning the state's future.

Speaking For Alaska Natives—Howard Rock, left, founder and publisher of the Tundra Times, and Tom Snapp, a Fairbanks journalist and consultant to Rock, explain the newspaper's layout to photographer Theodore Hetzel. -*Photo from the Alfred R. Ketzler Collection, 1961-1974, UAF 1992 202 11, Howard Rock, Tom Snapp, Theodore Hertzel, Archives, University of Alaska Fairbanks.*

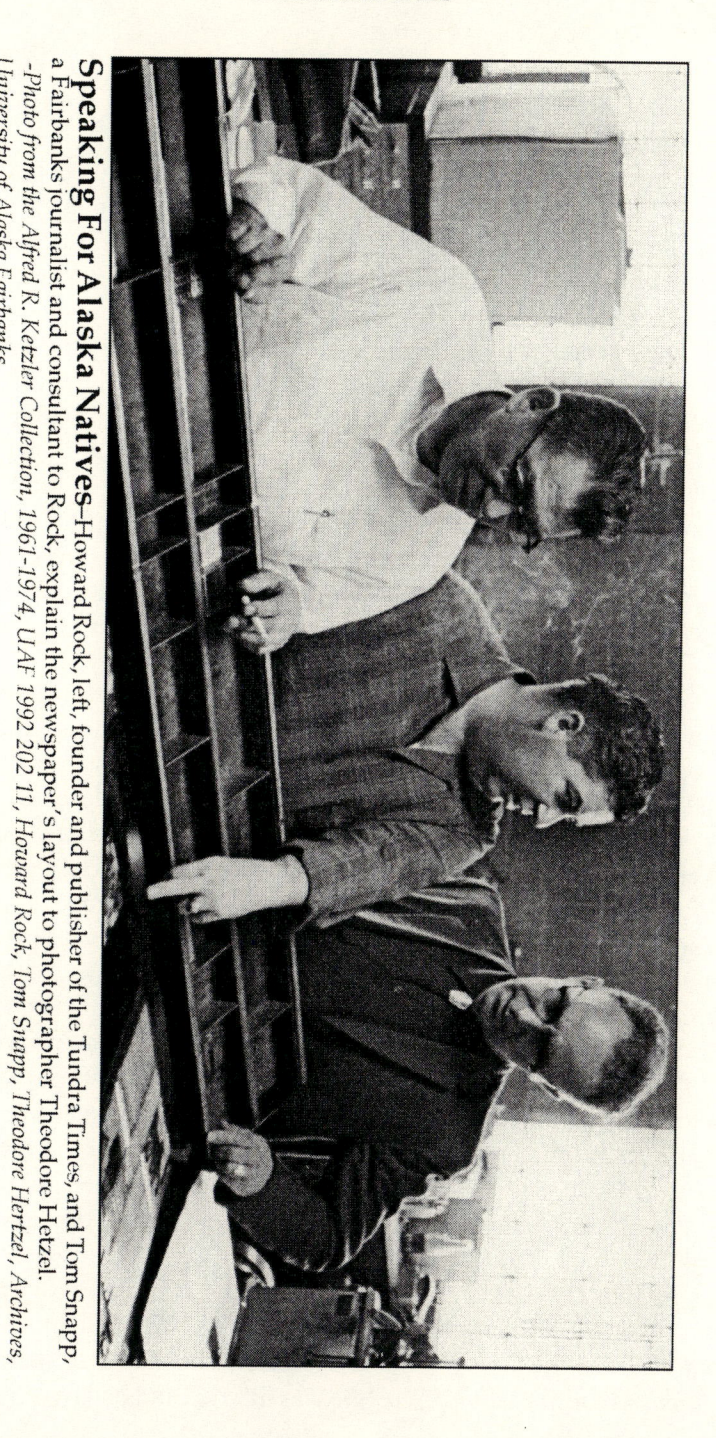

The *Tundra Times* played an instrumental role in the fight for the Alaska Native Land Claims Settlement Act of 1971. It provided a direct Native voice during legislative deliberations.

Rock's service on behalf of the Native people was recognized in March 1974 when he shared the "Alaskan of the Year" award at an Anchorage banquet, along with U.S. Sen. Ted Stevens. Rock died of cancer on April 20, 1976, at Basset Army Hospital, Fort Wainwright. He was buried at Point Hope.

During his prolonged illness, Rock trained two young Eskimos, Sue Gamache and Tom Richards Jr. to continue the *Tundra Times* after his departure. Richards served as publisher from 1976 to 1979.

The paper's headquarters moved from Fairbanks to Anchorage in September 1978, primarily because the Alaska Federation of Natives and the Alaska Native Foundation, plus five of the twelve Native regional corporations, were headquartered there. Those corporations assumed the financial support of the paper. The circulation jumped from 3,400 to six thousand in a year's time after moving to Anchorage.

With the paper on solid financial footing, veteran Alaska newsman Jim Babb was hired as managing editor and two full-time people were hired to handle the advertising and business end of the operation. Babb took charge of the *Tundra Times* on March 21, 1979.

Besides the twelve-page weekly editions, the *Times* put out twenty-four-page special editions every two months. They were real money-makers, selling six times the number of the regular weekly issues. Each special carried a full-color cover and developed a particular theme. Most of the advertising revenue came from Anchorage businesses.

Staffers estimated the *Times* reached forty-two thousand readers in two hundred villages. Around 350 copies were sold off the newsstands in Anchorage and seven hundred through subscriptions. Roughly 20 percent of the papers went to Washington DC and New York City and to international cities where scholars and officials considered it a valuable source of information about Alaska's Arctic region and its Natives.

In January 1982, Linda Lord-Jenkins, a thirty-two-year-old newswoman from Florida, took over as editor. She had a journalism degree from the University of Wisconsin and had worked on the *Orlando* (Florida) *Sentinel Star*. She was married and had two children.

Her husband, Paul Jenkins, worked for The Associated Press in Anchorage and later for *The Anchorage Times* and for "The Voice of the Times."

The *Trunda Times* folded with its final issue May 14, 1997, after the Native corporations withdrew their support. By then the Natives had won a claims settlement and were operating thirteen successful regional corporations and many village corporations. They were well assimilated into modern Alaska politics, its economy and lifestyle, except for one thing. As Alaska moved into a new century in 2001, subsistence fishing and hunting rights were unresolved with the state.

Chickaloon News carries on

Other unresolved issues concerning Native rights are reported weekly by e-mail from the *Chickaloon News*. The newspaper is distributed to more than three hundred subscribers, many of whom forward it to friends. A printed copy is distributed about four times a year summarizing subjects covered in the e-mail editions.

Editor Patricia Wade was born in Palmer and graduated from Palmer High School. Her mother was born in Chickaloon, about twenty-eight miles north of Palmer on the Glenn Highway. Wade tried various occupations including running her own catering business, before joining the staff of the Village of Chickaloon in 1995.

Her newspaper takes strong pro-environment stand as well as defending Native rights.

In addition to editing the *News* and doing other work for the village, Wade teaches Native culture and history.

With the newfound economic and political power of Alaska Natives, the general press is reporting more on Native issues. The Calista Native Corp.'s chain of six weekly newspapers reaches many Alaska villages and small towns. Although owned and operated by Natives, ANI papers serve all Alaskans living in the rural communities, regardless of race. The papers are *The Arctic Sounder, The Bristol Bay Times, The Dutch Harbor Fisherman, The Seward Phoenix Log* and *The Tundra Drums*.

ANI owns and operates its own printing plant in Anchorage to print its weeklies and to do commercial printing for others. In July 2002, ANI started the weekly *Anchorage Chronicle* to serve Alaska's largest Native community but suspended it at the end of 2004.

Shortly after ANI was formed by merging with Edgar Blathchford's Seward and Valdez papers in 1992, one of ANI's editors, Christopher Casati, was promoted to publisher. He organized the management of the chain for more efficiency and saw that the company purchased its own newspaper press. When he retired in 1999, Jim Schwankl, former production manager for *The Anchorage Times*, who actually installed ANI's press, became publisher. Publisher and editor-in-chief of ANI in 2005 was Heidi Bohi with a background in marketing and management

ANI has competition for its *Tundra Drums* at Bethel. On September 1, 1999, Ted Horner, a former editor of the *Drums*, produced the first issue of his weekly *The Delta Discovery*, a tabloid newspaper of five thousand circulation serving Bethel and the villages of the Yukon-Kuskokwim Delta. It is printed at Anchorage Printing Company.

Horner came to Alaska as a bush pilot, became a producer for the public television station at Bethel and then served two and one-half years as editor of the *Drums*.

Lifelong Alaskans Greg and Kelly Lincoln bought the *Discovery* from Horner and Carl Grille January 1, 2005, although neither had journalism experience.

Greg was born in Bethel in 1968 and raised in Toksook Bay. He attended the University of Alaska Fairbanks and is skilled on computers, including designing Web pages.

Kelly was born in Anchorage in 1971. Her grandfather, John Fredson of Fort Yukon, is among the first Gwich'n Athabascans, earning a college degree, which he did in 1933. Her mother, Alice Fredson, is a Yup'ik Eskimo and a linguist translating the Old Testament into Yup'ik. Although English is Kelly's first language, she learned Yup'ik from her grandparents, James and Betty Samson of Kipnuk.

Kelly has been winning writing prizes since the eighth grade. She graduated cum laude with a degree in elementary education from the University of Alaska Fairbanks and taught for ten years in Tooksook Bay.

The Kellys, like many working for ANI, represent a new generation of Alaska Native journalists.

Chapters 40-44

Sitka, Wrangell and

Petersburg Newspapers

Overcome Setbacks

No paper today – editor gone fishing.

– Bob Wahl, editor
Sitka Sentinel, 1940

THE SKAGWAY ALASKAN

"GROWING WITH SKAGWAY"

SKAGWAY, ALASKA, THURSDAY, NOVEMBER ... 1955

School Problems Taken Up

The Superintendents Advisory Commission met in Juneau the week of October 28 with R. V. Shell of Skagway in attendance. The Commission, composed of administrators from the entire Territory, was concerned with a number of problems involving the schools of Alaska. The findings of this Commission are presented in the form of recommendations to the Territorial Board of Education.

Mrs. Deborah Towne, James Armstrong Are Married Here

Mrs. Deborah Towne became the wife of Mr. James Armstrong in a quiet ceremony performed by the Rev. Bertram Buhner in the Presbyterian Church Sunday evening at 8:30 o'clock.

The bride was lovely in a gunmetal faille dress trimmed in silver with a silver and grey hat and silver sandals. Her jewelry consisted of two gold Italian bracelets which had belonged to her mother. For "something old" she wore a slip trimmed with rose point lace taken from her mother's wedding dress. She wore an orchid corsage.

Dividing It Up

Taxes, Oth Items Up At Counci

PETERSBURG PRESS
SERVICE TO THE COMMUNITY

THE PETERSBURG PRESS, PETERSBURG, ALASKA

Blind Slough Hydro Project Postponed to 1955 As Plans For Larger Power Plant Develop

Petersburg's hydro-electric installation at Crystal Lake which was orig inally scheduled for 1954 has now been booked for 1955 in order that the full potential of this power undertaking might be realized under construction terms now favorable to the city...

Hoop Opener With Sitka This Evening

here's Hoping
PEACE 1954

Local Delegates To Attend Seattle Halibut Hearing

New Hospital Pushed for Ju

Daily Sitka Sentinel

and The Arrowhead Press
Member of Associated Press

SITKA'S HOME-OWNED PAPER

VOLUME XIII

Tuesday, September 2, 1952

10c a Copy

Eisenhower Opens Up With Demand For House Cleaning

Pulls No Punches In First Campaign Speech In South

Atlanta, (AP) Gen. Dwight D. Eisenhower today called the Democratic administration a mess of corruption and scandal deliberately not to fire his ammunition too soon.

He said the cost of the "Washington mess" was being taken out of every American through higher taxes, higher prices and by "cutting down the value of every dollar you have put away for the future."

Cordell Hull In Critical Condition At Naval Hospital

Washington, (AP) Cordell Hull remained on the critical list Tuesday at the Bethesda (Md.) naval hospital. A bulletin said "Cordell Hull continues to show slight improvement this morning. His condition, however, remains critical."

The 80 year old former secretary of state entered the hospital Friday for treatment for cerebral thrombosis.

Stevenson "Satisfied" His Swing Thru Michi

Outlines Position On Labor Relations Plans Other Talks

Springfield, Ill., (AP) Gov. Adlai Stevenson said today he is "very well satisfied" with the results of his sweep through...

Chapter 40

Navy and Mill Boost Sitka

After Alaska's capital and Sitka's journalists moved to Juneau, the old Russian capital languished with intermittent newspaper attempts. Then in 1939, the navy established an air base on Japonski Island in Sitka's harbor. That attracted construction workers and service personnel – a population base that would support a newspaper. Several appeared, the twice-weekly *Sitka Sentinel* among them. It survives today as the *Daily Sentinel*.

After World War II, Sitka's economy further stabilized when part of the Japonski base was converted to a Native boarding school and a Native hospital. The U.S. Coast Guard moved its air base to Japonski from Annette Island near Metlakatla. Later, a branch of the University of Alaska Southeast opened on the base and a bridge was built from Sitka.

Alaska Pulp Company opened its pulp mill at Silver Bay in the early 1960s for a thirty-year run. The *Sentinel* grew into the five-day daily of 3,400 circulation.

Sun shines after 13 years

After *The Alaskan* suspended in 1907, newspapers started and failed in Sitka for thirty-two years, despite the best efforts of experienced newsmen such as Sid Charles.

Sitkans had gone thirteen years without a commercial newspaper, when they welcomed the weekly *Sitka Sun* on October 30, 1920. The sincerity of welcome was questionable because it was an inferior product, due largely to the inexperience and lack of education of the editors. The editorials were disorganized and devoid of established rules of grammar and punctuation.

The managing editor was William Richter Hanlon; the assistant editor was his half sister, Margaret Hanlon. His son, William Hanlon Jr., was the reporter.

William Hanlon was born in Sitka in 1879, the son of F. W. and Anna Richter. F. W. was a German-born baker and brewer, his wife a member of a Russian Creole family. After Richter died, Anna married John Hanlon, who had arrived in Sitka in 1879 as a petty officer on the USS *Jamestown*. William Richter eventually adopted his stepfather's name.

The four-page tabloid paper was printed in the Russian orphanage on an old Chandler Price job press owned by the Russian Church. For its first two months, the *Sun* was published weekly. But with monthly expenses of $300 and only $100 in income, it was changed to publishing on the first Saturday of each month. It suspended publication in 1922, but resumed briefly in 1927 and 1928 when Hanlon used it in his unsuccessful bid for a seat in the Territorial House of Representatives.

Kill all of the bears

The *Sitka Sun*'s editorials championed the right of the Natives to full citizenship and the right of Native children to attend the city school rather than the federal one; praised the work of Russian and Presbyterian missionaries; favored the abolition of fish traps; and advocated the extermination of brown bears because they killed salmon and deer and were dangerous to humans.

On April 1, 1924, Hanlon was elected mayor of Sitka, and reelected to six successive terms, plus another term in 1942. His administration was marked by cronyism, favoritism and reckless expenditures of public funds. The mayor and three of his city council were indicted by a grand jury in 1927 on charges of conspiracy to defraud and cheat the citizens of Sitka. A politically sympathetic judge dismissed charges.

Charles shows up at Sitka

After the *Sitka Sun* ceased publication for the first time in the spring of 1922, veteran newsman Sid Charles arrived in Sitka, took over the plant in the Russian orphanage – today known as the Bishop's House – and began publishing *The Sitka Tribune*. The first issue was on May 12.

The Tribune gave Sitkans a good budget of both local and wire news and was well supported by Sitka advertisers. But Charles remained at the helm of the paper for only a year. In May 1923, he sold the paper to C. F. M. Cole and his wife, Mary, who had arrived from McCarthy.

Cole had started the *McCarthy Weekly News* in 1917, and remained its publisher and editor until shortly before moving to Sitka.

They moved the newspaper shop from the old Russian orphanage to the first floor of the Bayview Hotel. Their paper had less local news and more features clipped from other papers, and it might have had less advertising support. *The Tribune* ceased publication with the issue of December 12, 1924.

Charles took back the paper but it did not resume publication until May 19, 1925. Charles was publishing the *Petersburg Weekly Report* by then and sent his daughter, Elaine, to run the Sitka paper

A young man, Clarence LeMaster, was working in Petersburg that fall. He bought *The Sitka Tribune* from Charles and published its last issue on December 18, 1925. He moved the plant to the Bohm Building, on Maksoutoff Street, and on Christmas Day published the first issue of *The Sitka Progress*.

In April, his brother, Kelmar, joined LeMaster. The paper's masthead reported it was published by the LeMaster Brothers, with Clarence as general manager and Kelmar as editor.

The paper suspended publication with the July 30, 1926, issue in which it was announced that the publisher had gone south to buy a typesetting machine. The first issue with machine-set type was on October 8, 1926.

The LeMasters put out a handsome paper, usually of six pages, with clean type, lots of pictures, and loads of ads. Usually there was a piece of poetry in the center of the front page, expressing some lofty moral precept. The paper carried wire news. Local news coverage was comprehensive.

LeMasters crosses Hanlon cronies

Clarence LeMaster tackled controversial issues in his editorials. He was pro-development and censured Dan Sutherland, Alaska's delegate in Congress, for deploring the moral character of the town to the point that investment capital might be scared away. He criticized the Paul brothers for stirring up racial prejudices in the columns of the *Alaskan*, the Alaska Native Brotherhood's newspaper.

LeMaster wrote several editorials titled, "What Is the Matter with Sitka?" – borrowing a theme from prominent Kansas publisher of that day, William Allen White, and his famous "What Is the Matter with Kansas?"

In one of his editorials, LeMaster said that there was too much personal hatred expressed by feuding factions. He suggested that the continued squabbling kept new industry from coming into Sitka. Another time he answered his question by claiming that there was too much haggling in the city council between whites and Natives. That criticism led to the exclusion of LeMasters, and any reporters he might recruit, from meetings of both the city council and the Commerical Club, both dominated by Hanlon cronies.

Inasmuch as the fishing industry was Sitka's primary economic base, LeMaster contended in an August 12, 1927, editorial that the town could not afford to lose fishing vessels to Canadian ports:

> The fishermen cash their checks, buy supplies, and after a shave, haircut and a bath, they go to the picture show and later drink a little Scotch. Then they are picked up by the U.S. marshal and the judge gives them 10 days in jail and a $25 fine.
>
> One time a $21,000 halibut schooner was tied up for ten days at the height of the fishing season because the crew had been thrown into jail for being hilariously drunk on their way back to the ship. It is holding back the development of the territory, as well as a loss to our own businesses.

Soon after the above editorial appeared, LeMaster suspended publication of the *Progress* and left town. The editorial, perhaps, was not the cause. The town was still having difficulty supporting a newspaper. Unable to meet the installment payments on the typesetting machine, LeMaster shipped it back to the manufacturer.

Sun rises briefly

After *The Sitka Progress* and its editor departed, Mayor Hanlon revived the *Sitka Sun* for three issues: November 30, 1927, January 30, 1928, and March 30, 1928. He appropriated some of the display type and even entire advertisements that had been used in the *Progress*. He used the *Sun*'s pages to tout the accomplishments of his administration, and promised industrial development for Sitka.

During the twelve years following the demise of *The Sitka Progress*, the town saw a number of newspapers, none of which was able to continue long. The first was *The Sitka Weekly*, a mimeographed eight-page tabloid produced by William Lindquist and Victor Hanlon from January until May 1929. Five years after that, *The Arrowhead* began publishing every other week with Victor Hanlon and artist Ritchie Lovejoy as editors and publishers.

A woodcut appeared in most issues of the paper, showing local scenes: Mount Verstovia and Arrowhead Peak, Sugar Loaf Mountain, the National Cemetery on Memorial Day. Hanlon dropped out of the partnership in May and Lovejoy carried on alone.

The final issue of *The Arrowhead* was on June 22, 1935. Lovejoy sold the printing plant to Jack Calvin and his wife, Sasha Kashevaroff Calvin. Calvin was operating a photograph studio in Sitka and added a job printing plant to it. He and Sasha also took over the newspaper but changed the name to *Sitka Shopping News*, published once a week with free distribution. The last available issue of that publication was No. 32, on February 28, 1936.

Navy base draws a crowd

Reports that a U.S. Navy Base would be established on Japonski Island attracted people to Sitka in 1938 and 1939. By the end of 1939 some 250 men were at work on the base. When the census was taken in 1940, the count was 1,939, up from the 1,056 of ten years earlier

Among the new arrivals were several newsmen. Three different mimeographed newspapers started. Benjamin Mainhart was first in the field with the weekly *Northern Star*, a six-page weekly tabloid selling for a nickel a copy. The first issue was on September 7, 1939. The paper lacked literary flare.

With the issue of April 26, 1940, Mainhart sold his equipment to Richard A. Ramme, who changed the name of the paper to *Sitka Alaskan* and reported innocuous local news.

He also printed Associated Press and United Press dispatches, increased the number of advertisers, and built the paper up to ten pages in each issue. At the end of a month, however, the paper ceased publication.

Sentinel appears

The third of the trio of mimeographed newspapers was the *Sitka Sentinel*, and it stayed. It began publication on August 16, 1939, appearing on Tuesdays and Fridays. Two Oregon newsmen were its publishers: William L. Baker of the *Coos Bay* (Oregon) *Times* and Robert A. Wahl of the *Pacific Coast Pulp & Paper Mill News*.

They hired Mr. and Mrs. Homer Graham, journalism graduates of the University of Oregon, to operate the paper. It usually ran sixteen pages and sold for a dime. They subscribed to a news service and received letterpress-printed supplements containing syndicated feature stories, pictures and editorials. The Grahams published their last issue on April 2, 1940, and returned to Oregon.

Wahl became the *Sentinel*'s editor with the issue of Friday, April 5. His name appeared in the masthead as Bob Wahl and he had a fiery introduction to Sitka. The Columbia Lumber Co. sawmill burned on the day of his first issue.

Wahl was thirty years old, a native of Whcaton, Illinois, and a journalism graduate of the University of Chicago. His first issue of the paper sported a new banner and was greeted by several advertisers as the "new" *Sitka Sentinel*. It continued as a mimeographed sheet, however, until the issue of Friday, July 19, 1940, when it appeared as a printed four-page tabloid newspaper.

The partners had installed a Model 5 Linotype and a Pony Miehle press. The paper changed to publication on Fridays.

In the issue of October 19, the day after Alaska Day, Wahl had an editorial, "To the People of Sitka," in which he wrote that he had come to the end of his patience with writing "hush-hush" editorials about the sins of Sitka. He said he was disgusted with the way city officials closed their eyes to the undercover gambling, drinking and prostitution. He disavowed moral crusading but felt things had gone too far.

Soon after that, Wahl hung a sign on the newspaper office door, "No paper today – editor gone fishing." That unusual means of announcing that he was severing himself from the paper was noted in several national news magazines.

Baker sends in Harold Veatch

Baker was now the paper's sole owner. He was a native of Fairfield, Iowa, and attended Parsons College where his father was a professor of education and psychology. He worked on various Iowa newspapers to finance his way through college and spent his 1929 summer vacation on a construction job at Sheldon Jackson School in Sitka.

In 1935, he moved to Oregon and graduated from Willamette University at Salem. In the summer of 1939 he revisited Alaska as a member of a National Editorial Association's tour of the territory and saw the potential for a newspaper in Sitka.

Baker sent Harold A. Veatch to Sitka to replace Wahl at the *Sentinel*. Veatch was another Oregon newsman and had learned the trade working on his father's papers. His father, E. A. Veatch, owned weeklies in Montesano, Washington; Rainier, Oregon; and Colville, Washington. Veatch was a bachelor when he arrived in Sitka but he married Ernestine Crandall at Sitka on June 29, 1941. Her name appeared in the masthead of the *Sentinel* on June 1, 1942, as business manager. She also was the newspaper's principal reporter.

One of Veatch's first editorial campaigns was in opposition to the colonization of Alaska with Jewish refugees from Europe. Rep. Samuel Dickstein, D-New York, had introduced a bill proposing the settlement of five hundred thousand nonquota refugees in Alaska, because the territory lacked population. Delegate Anthony J. Dimond opposed the importation of aliens. His successor, E. L. Bartlett, took the same stand in 1944. They contended that if the federal government would change its restrictive policies toward Alaska development there would be plenty of American citizens interested in moving north.

The Department of the Interior had proposed various colonization plans for Alaska, including even a penal colony in the Aleutians. In each instance, Alaskans objected, fearing the colonists would become a drain on the resources of the territory.

In May 1943, the Veatches resigned from the *Sentinel*. Hale Tabor arrived by plane on Sunday, May 30, to take over as editor and publisher. In the paper the following day under the heading "Veatch Leaves Sentinel Staff," Veatch wrote:

> After 30 months as editor and publisher we are glad to surrender the reins and management to another. The hours are long, the work arduous. We withdraw to devote our entire time to the management of Arrowhead Press, recently purchased from Jack Calvin.

Tabor was an operating partner with Baker. He also had attended Willamette University and had served as a reporter on the *Oregon Statesman* at Salem and the *Sheridan Press* in Wyoming. He left the position of city editor on the *Coos Bay Times* at Marshfield, Oregon, to move to Sitka.

Veatches buy back in

Tabor changed publication from three times a week to twice a week, on Tuesdays and Fridays, with the Friday edition occasionally appearing on Saturday. Tabor remained in charge of the *Sentinel* until the end of July 1944. Baker was negotiating to buy the *Ketchikan Alaska Chronicle* and needed cash for a down payment. To get it he sold the *Sitka Sentinel* to the Veatches. They took over again with the issue of August 1, 1944.

Veatch seldom wrote editorials on local issues, but he protested vigorously in 1945 when the Army Quartermaster Corps proposed that the Sitka National Cemetery be moved to Juneau. The Sitka City Council, the chamber of commerce and local veterans' organizations joined Veatch's bandwagon and succeeded in killing the proposal. Veatch also carried on long campaigns for a boat harbor and a pulp mill at Sitka. Both eventually attained.

On June 26, 1946, Veatch initiated an editorial comment column titled Veachcombing. It first appeared at the top of the front page but later migrated to the bottom of that page in either the right or left corner. In it he set forth his opinions on a variety of subjects and gave his sometimes innocuous views of events:

> Truman tells Congress the "State of the Union" and now Congress will tell him what they intend to do about it.
>
> It is three weeks past New Year's and discarded resolutions are a dime a dozen.

Veatches take a rest

At the end of July 1948 the Veatches leased the *Sentinel* to Julius H. Ferney. He had grown up in Walla Walla, Washington, where his father had a newspaper and a commercial printing business. Ferney had most recently been owner of the *Highlands*, a weekly in the Seattle area. For twenty-five years he had worked on newspapers, including the *Post-Intelligencer* in Seattle and the *Oregonian* in Portland.

After leasing the paper, the Veatches went south on vacation. They returned a year later and on August 1, 1949, resumed publication of the *Sentinel*. Ferney moved to Wrangell where he had leased the *Wrangell Sentinel* for a year.

At the end of 1949 the Veatches announced that commencing on Tuesday, January 3, they would begin publishing five times a week, Monday through Friday. The paper was quartered in a very small building at 41 Lincoln Street where it had been since the early 1940s. It might have been the smallest quarters in the country for a five-times-a-week newspaper.

Veatch acknowledges statehood

Despite their personal opposition to statehood, the Veatches put out an "extra" on June 30, 1958, when the U.S. Senate approved the statehood bill by a vote of sixty-four to twenty. The city's fire sirens sounded four long blasts and then nine more. That was followed by the ringing of the bells of St. Michael's Cathedral and St. Peter's by the Sea and the carillon at Sheldon Jackson Junior College. A community bonfire was lit in the old ballpark and four hundred free hot dogs were served, followed by dancing on Lincoln Street.

Appearing in the extra edition was an ad surrounded by a heavy black border suggesting mourning. It read: "Phooey! As of today, everything I have is for sale, cheap. Signed, J. H. VanHorn, a Sitka pioneer."

Steps to remedy the cramped quarters at the *Sentinel* were taken at the end of January 1959. A one-story former garage and automobile sales building was purchased and plans were announced to remodel it and add a second story. Hope was expressed that the paper could move by April 1 but that proved to be too optimistic. The masthead change from 41 Lincoln Street to 112 Barracks Street was not made until August 19.

Daily production was greatly enhanced in January 1960 with the installation of a new Cox-O-type newspaper press, which printed on a web instead of on single sheets. It would print eight full size or sixteen tabloid size papers and would turn out up to 3,500 copies an hour.

Tragedy strikes

The Cox-O-Type had a relatively short life. During the noon hour on Monday, January 22, 1968, a fire started in the sterotype room at the paper and exploded through the building. The business office escaped with only severe smoke damage. The rest of the building was gutted and the combination of high temperature and cold water ruined the typesetting machines and presses. The loss was in excess of $100,000.

The *Sentinel*, however, missed only a week of publication. A local office supply store loaned a Gestafax Duplicator, which was in several ways superior to the old mimeograph. A typed edition of the paper was on the streets on January 29.

It was decided to convert to the new offset printing process so a Goss Community press and Linoquick typesetting equipment were installed.

William (Bill) Weiss, shop foreman at the *Ketchikan Daily News*, and Lew Williams Jr., *Daily News* editor, took turns going to Sitka for a few weeks to assist the Veatches in learning the offset process. The Ketchikan paper had switched to offset two years earlier. The first edition off the new press was on March 8.

The trauma of the fire and learning a new production process may have decided Harold and Ernestine Veatch to get out of the newspaper business. Harold, especially, had spent a quarter of a century lifting sixty-pound type-filled page forms off and on letterpresses, and was now leveraging nine hundred-pound newsprint rolls on to the new offset press. He was a small, wiry man who, like Ernestine, believed in doing as much as he could himself. So they hired little help and the heavy physical part of publishing was telling on a man in his early sixties.

The circulation of the newspaper had dipped to eight hundred in a population area of seven thousand. In the edition of February 3, 1969, it was announced that the paper had been sold to Lew and Dorothy Williams of the *Ketchikan Daily News*. The Veatches started a travel agency but soon retired to Arizona.

The Williams stayed in Ketchikan where Lew was editor and Dorothy was business manager of the *Daily News*. They hired Thad and Sandy Poulson to run the *Sentinel*. Thad Poulson, thirty-two, was The Associated Press correspondent in Juneau; his wife, Sandy, a part-time AP writer.

Before going to Juneau for the AP in January 1968, Poulson was with the AP in New York City and Salt Lake City. Previously, he was on the staff of the *Daily Oklahoman* in Oklahoma City. Mrs.

Poulson was a reporter for the *Oklahoma City Times* before her marriage. She had a sister, Dee Longenbaugh, wife of Dr. George Longenbaugh, living in Sitka.

Enter the Poulsons

The Poulsons bought the *Daily Sentinel* from the Williamses in December 1975. The Williamses needed the money to buy out the Charles family in the Ketchikan paper, which they did in June 1976.

The Poulsons also bought out a local printer and merged his operation into that of the *Sentinel*. They bought a third unit for their newspaper press to increase its capacity to twelve pages from eight. They also finished the second floor of the *Sentinel* building that the Veatches had planned but never finished.

Poulsons campaigned editorially in favor of unification of the city and borough governments. That occurred on December 2, 1971. Thad was elected to a term on the new borough assembly.

The Poulsons wrote editorials infrequently. Sandy Poulson's sister, Dee, and Dee's husband were active environmentalists, which brought criticism against the Poulsons from pulp mill workers, loggers and their supporters for not being more supportive of the timber industry.

But the Poulsons waged a vigorous crusade in the 1980s to save the pulp mill from closing its doors because of prohibitively expensive Environmental Protection Agency restrictions. Boxes were placed around town to collect letters from residents requesting a variance from the additional requirements for effluent treatment. School children were encouraged to join the letter-writing campaign. An essay and poster contest was conducted on the general theme "How would the closure of ALP affect my home, my family and me," with prizes of $100.

The mill survived that threat, but in 1993 the U.S. Forest Service cancelled a long-term timber contract, forcing closure. After the mill closed the town's population dropped from just over 9,000 in 1993 to 8,600 in 1999. Poulsons say their circulation of 3,100 dropped slightly, but by 2000 was back up near 3,400. The paper made money and allowed the Poulsons to invest in boats and real estate. Their son, James, joined them in the operation. Their daughter, Catherine, a Sitka teacher, assists occasionally.

The *Daily Sentinel* and the *Ketchikan Daily News* are the only two daily newspapers in Alaska independently and locally owned

Modern Sitka Plant–Thad and Sandy Poulson today enjoy the modern plant they completed for the Daily Sentinel after they purchased the newspaper in 1975 from Lew and Dorothy Williams of Ketchikan. They began operating the newspaper for the Williams in 1969. -Photo *courtesy of the Daily Sentinel and James Poulson.*

in 2005. Thad Poulson said he deplores the trend toward national chain ownership. Although approached about selling, Thad says no. They are expanding their plant in order to do more color printing.

Sitka survived two major losses in the twentieth century, moving of the capital to Juneau in 1906 and closing of the pulp mill in 1993. Its first newspaper succumbed to the first loss. Its latest newspaper, the *Daily Sentinel*, survives the second handily as Alaska prospers from statehood.

Chapter 41

Wrangell Sentinel's Williams Years

New publishers for the *Wrangell Sentinel*, Llewellyn (Lew) Morris Williams Sr., and Winifred Eugenia Dow Williams, arrived in Wrangell from Juneau on October 27, 1939, with their two daughters, Jane and Susan, and son, Lew Jr. The husband-wife team introduced a higher standard of journalism than Wrangell knew before. Their expertise derived from years of newspapering in the Pacific Northwest.

Lew Williams was born on May 23, 1895, in Fedora, South Dakota. He attended Oregon State University in Corvallis, Oregon, when it was known as Oregon Agricultural College. He served in the U.S. Navy during World War I.

He married Winifred E. Dow in Seattle on April 14, 1923, when both were employed as reporters by Tacoma newspapers. They had met when the publisher of the Tacoma newspapers, Frank Baker, hired Winifred, a radio amateur, to operate a commercial radio station and assigned Lew, a former navy radioman, to assist her.

Following his military service, editorial rooms in Tacoma, Spokane and Olympia knew Lew for twelve years as a reporter, city editor and political writer. He was with the *Tacoma Ledger*, the *Tacoma News-Tribune*, the *Spokane Chronicle* and *Spokesman-Review* and the *Daily Olympian*.

He also operated a couple of weeklies in Oregon, the *Hermiston News* and the *Tillamook Headlight*.

Williams was political writer for the *Tacoma Ledger* when Robert Bender, managing editor of the *Daily Alaska Empire*, invited him to join the *Empire* staff as legislative reporter and editorial writer. He was offered the job on Christmas Day 1934, a real present for a reporter with a wife and three children during the Depression when all reporters in the Tacoma area were reduced to working only three or four days a week.

Political Periscope rises

In his first editorial in the *Sentinel*, Williams predicted that Alaska's ultimate goal of statehood would require years of slow and determined work.

He opposed the various colonization plans by government agencies to deposit special interest groups in Alaska, such as refugees from Europe, to help settle the territory.

Williams also inaugurated in that first edition a personal column titled "Through the Sentinel Periscope." A great title for an ex-navy man. It was destined to become one of the most discussed and cussed columns in Alaskan journalism during the next twenty-five years.

The *Sentinel* took on a pizzazz it never had before. The Williamses made an agreement with The Associated Press whereby the *Sentinel* and the *Petersburg Press* shared a membership, enabling those papers to print news from the AP. They were allowed to copy news from AP's San Francisco radio station, KFS, which distributed news to members around the Pacific Rim via Morse code.

The Williamses were experienced radio operators and copied the latest news on Thursday night for the Friday edition. The *Press* publishers, the Claire Wilders, hired an off-duty Alaska Communications System operator to copy their news.

The *Sentinel*'s front-page headlines became exciting and challenging. The editorials had a punch to them. During World War II, Wrangell watched the war booms hit Ketchikan, Juneau and Anchorage but bypass it. The sawmill had gone broke and was unable to find a buyer.

The people of Wrangell were among the earliest supporters of statehood, due in part to the *Sentinel*'s editorial emphasis. After Delegate Anthony (Tony) Dimond introduced a statehood bill in Congress on December 3, 1943, Wrangell's Mayor Fred G. Hanford organized a local statehood committee. It sponsored Alaska's first statehood banquet in the town's civic center on February 7, 1944, with Secretary of Alaska Bob Bartlett as the featured speaker.

Sentinel Publishers

–Lew Williams Sr., left, standing at his Country Campbell newspaper press, and his wife, Winifred, setting type on a Model L Linotype, were publishers of the Wrangell Sentinel from 1939 until 1965.
-*Photos courtesy of the Wrangell Sentinel.*

Urging unconditional support for immediate statehood, Williams editorialized shortly after Bartlett's visit:

> Of course, if Alaskans do not want to vote in the affairs of this republic, if they want to continue to send a non-voting delegate to Congress, and continue to be a stepchild of the federal government, all well and good. The thing then to do is to join with the obstructionists, who dodge the issue of statehood by saying this is not the time – the Shattucks, the Rodens, the Zieglers, the federal agencies and reactionary thought generally. Now is the time to beat the drum. Remember statehood is not a party issue.

In June 1944, on the recommendation of Gov. Ernest Gruening, President Franklin D. Roosevelt nominated Williams to be secretary of Alaska – the title formerly used for Alaska's lieutenant governor. He replaced Bartlett who had been elected delegate, replacing Tony Dimond who had accepted appointment as a U.S. district court judge in Anchorage. During Bartlett's visit to Wrangell he had approached Williams on the idea at the instigation of Gruening. Williams was sworn into office in Juneau on June 30.

Then the Williams family, minus Lew Jr., who was in the army, moved to Juneau, leasing their paper to Spencer and Ann DeLong. The DeLongs were on the *Empire*'s staff when Williams lured them, although at one time Spencer had been a printer for the *Sentinel*.

When the DeLongs left Wrangell and went to work for the *Fairbanks Daily News-Miner* in the spring of 1945, Mrs. Williams and the two daughters returned to Wrangell, where she took charge of the paper. She relinquished the editorial reins to Lew Jr. upon his return home from military service early in the following year.

During the ensuing three years, Lew Jr.'s infrequent editorials suggested that he was well informed about territorial political affairs. However, Lew Jr. depended upon his father's Periscope column for most of his editorial comment. It was popular because the senior Williams, as secretary of Alaska, was on the inside in Alaska politics.

Sentinel leased again

In August 1949, the Williams family leased the *Sentinel* again while Lew Jr. and his sister Jane went Outside for more education.

Lew Jr. took a business-journalism course in a California business college and returned north in the summer of 1950 to manage the *Alaska Sunday Press* in Juneau. Jane took a Linotype operator's course in Louisville, Kentucky.

Julius H. Ferney was in charge of the *Sentinel* during Williams' absence. He had been editor of the *Sitka Sentinel* during the previous year. Ferney put out a lively paper during his year's tenure.

The Williamses had to return to the *Sentinel* when Ferneys left for Juneau. By then Jane was a competent Linotype operator. Her term as editor was only five months because she was diagnosed with tuberculosis and entered a sanitarium in Seattle. Lew Jr. gave up his *Sunday Press* post and took charge until his parents returned to Wrangell in 1951.

Jane recovered from her bout with tuberculosis and bought a weekly paper in Orting, Washington, with her husband, Valentine (Tiny) Ferguson, also from Wrangell. When Jane became ill again, they suspended the paper and Valentine returned to sea on tugs and fishing boats.

Truman fires Williams

A bitter estrangement developed between Secretary of Alaska Williams and Governor Gruening. In 1949, when both were up for reappointment, Williams was reappointed without controversy despite a "bad report" that Gruening told him had been filed with the Secretary of Interior.

But Gruening's confirmation was held up. A planeload of Alaskans opposed to statehood flew to Washington to block his reappointment. Another planeload of Alaskans supporting statehood and Gruening flew to Washington and successfully lobbied for his reappointment.

The relationship between the two men continued to deteriorate. Gruening was absent from the territory for extended periods in his battle for statehood. During those absences, Williams was acting governor and made decisions displeasing Gruening, such as appointing Neil Moore as territorial auditor on the death of Frank Boyle. Gruening had promised the job to someone else.

Another source of irritation was the frequent negative criticism of the governor's programs that appeared in the *Sentinel*'s Periscope column.

Gruening also was upset with Williams' drinking and partying. But the Williamses complained that Gruening frequently dumped minor visiting dignitaries on Williams to entertain without an expense account.

On September 14, 1951, the top, front-page story in the *Sentinel* read: "Truman Fires Lew Williams as Secretary of Alaska" and the following explanation was given to its readers:

> Henchmen of the governor's attempted to block Williams reappointment two years ago without success and since that occasion the fat has been more or less in the fire. The governor is a very potent man in Washington and it was inevitable that ultimately he would prevail.
>
> The governor declined to comment to the *Sentinel* relative to the dismissal except the usual "I regret" etc. He says he hasn't anything to do with it.

Williams' only comment was: "Hell, I'm fired, and that's that. It's taken them a heck of a long time to get around to it. I always figured Ernest was a faster worker than that."

In subsequent weeks, Williams used his weekly column to narrate a series of incidents, which led to the estrangement between him and Gruening. Williams' ouster from federal office did not diminish his hometown popularity. He was elected mayor the following year, and again and again, serving three terms altogether.

Later, his son, Lew Jr. also served three terms as mayor of Petersburg, thirty miles north of Wrangell, after he and his wife, Dorothy, bought the *Petersburg Press* in 1956. At one time, both Lews were town mayor and the local editor-publisher at the same time.

Second Fire in '52

Fire struck Wrangell's business district again in 1952 on the water side of Main Street. The upland side had been destroyed in 1906. The '52 flames destroyed buildings across the street from the *Sentinel* office. Heat from the flames broke the *Sentinel* widows, forcing the staff to hang a tarpaulin across the front of the building in order to continue its printing operation. A special edition of the *Sentinel* was issued the day after the fire.

Wrangell's economy enjoyed a boost with the establishment of a new lumber mill six miles south of town in the fall of 1957 by the Pacific Northern Timber Co. of Portland, Oregon, the old mill in town had been leased and put in operation a few years earlier by a Japanese company, Wrangell Lumber Co.

Pacific Northern had a contract with the U.S. Forest Service for 750 million board feet of timber in the Wrangell region. Two years later, the company was sold to the Japanese firm owning the in-town mill. The same Japanese business interests also created Alaska Pulp Co. to build and operate a pulp mill at Sitka.

Williams column influential

Lew Williams Sr. resumed active editorship of the *Sentinel* on his return from Juneau. His son helped part-time until he and his wife, Wrangell schoolteacher Dorothy Baum, bought the *Petersburg Press* and moved to Petersburg in May 1956.

Lew Sr. turned lukewarm on the issue of immediate statehood as he joined the anti-Gruening forces. He called the Tennessee Plan of electing state "senators" and a "congressman" to go to Washington to lobby for statehood "the all-time high in political phonies 'sold' to Alaska voters."

Williams' strong influence in molding local public opinion was evident when his fellow townsmen rejected the proposed state constitution, following Williams' negative criticism of it. But when Congress offered to give Alaska statehood, Williams recommended that the Alaskans accept it and Wrangell voters cast a five-to-one favorable vote. He conceded that home rule was preferable to federal bureaucratic control despite his lack of confidence in the new state's leadership potential.

The Periscope column exuded Williamsian humor as he tackled the political issues of the day. For instance, when the "move-the-capital" issue resurfaced in 1959, he expounded on the attributes of the Stikine Flats as a likely site for a new capital city:

> The Stikine Flats, widely populated at this time of year by white geese, ducks, jack snipes and other waterfowl, is located approximately halfway between the International Date Line and the national capital in Washington, D.C. With the construction of the Stikine road, Anchorage, up on the

spur, will have opportunity to get on the main highway and buzz right into the state capital.

There are other advantages. Imagine a beautiful $20 million state capitol building with its golden dome pointing skyward from the heart of Brown's Island, one of the compact group comprising the famed Stikine Flats. Around the base of the dome would be an artistic walkway on which the government workers could take their airing. The governor, with guests for dinner, would be able to take his shotgun out on the walkway and pick off a few green-winged teal for the dinner piece de resistance. Such activity could well build a tradition comparable with Big Ben for Londoners.

Then, too, the channel ways, better known as sloughs down this way, would afford opportunity for the gondoliers, such as harassed office workers, to take their favorite secretaries for leisurely rides in the cool of a summer evening.

The Williamses had an apartment in town and a beach home eight miles south of Wrangell. At their beach home was a frog-designed yard ornament that Williams used in his Periscope column by ending his column with "The Frog Sez." For example, in commenting on the "Alaskan Counties Report," offered to the legislature shortly after statehood, the Frog sez: "Two strikes against it. First it is free, a tremendous handicap. And secondly, no provision for salaries. Gotta have a pay angle or you can't hire statesmen."

Lumber capital proclaimed

"Thank God, they've adjourned," wrote Lew Sr. when Alaska's First State Legislature concluded its sixty-five-day session, after passing a $74-million-dollar budget. "Seventy-four million smackeroos is a substantial figure for a state with a population of two hundred thousand," Williams observed.

Williams' column, "Through the Sentinel Periscope," continued to appear in the far left column of the front page. The paper's flag carried the slogan "Lumber Capital of Alaska." The mill created nearly two hundred jobs for Wrangell residents.

Williams was adamantly opposed to moving the capital from Juneau to the Cook Inlet-Railbelt area. Preceding the referendum on August 9, 1960, Williams' Periscope fairly sizzled in its satirical condemnation of *The Anchorage Daily Times*' editorial support for the relocation:

> Wheel horse for the move-the-capital crowd is *The Anchorage Times* which editorially takes the "whole hog" attitude; blot out Southeastern Alaska and to heck with the rest of the state providing everything is in Anchorage or its environs – that self-important great city of Anchorage which was built and is still maintained by government dollars. If it had not been for Uncle's cash in the defense effort prior to World War II, during that struggle and ever since, Anchorage would still be a wide spot on a road leading to a couple of mining camps.

And a few days before the referendum in 1960, across the top of the front page:

> Vote against Initiative No. 1:
> Make the Southeast vote unanimous against moving the capital. A unanimous vote will tell the world that Alaska is not a land of tinhorns and morons but one of sound-thinking Americans capable of handling their own affairs in a business-like manner and not prone to toss fifty million bucks, they haven't got, down a rat hole because some lightweight promoter came up with a phoney notion.

Wrangell and the Stikine precinct resoundingly defeated the initiative in 1960 and again in 1962, but Lew Sr. lost a bet to Lew Jr. in one of the races. The editors of the Wrangell and Petersburg newspapers bet a new hat on whose town would turn out the fewest votes for moving the capital. Lew Sr. bought Lew Jr. a new so'wester when four Wrangell residents voted for the move but only one in Petersburg.

Senior Williams retire

Ill health forced Lew Williams Sr., seventy, and Winifred, sixty-two, to retire from active management of the *Sentinel* in February 1965. The paper was sold to his son and wife at the *Petersburg Press*.

Thomas C. Johnson, a twenty-five-year-old Petersburg man, who had been associated with the *Press* for the previous seven years, was sent to Wrangell to take charge of the *Sentinel.* Lew Sr. continued to write his Periscope column.

On May 12, 1965, the *Sentinel* appeared in a new format, having switched from a Campbell drum cylinder press to a new offset press. In switching to offset, the paper page was reduced in size to tabloid but the number of pages was doubled. It was the third Alaskan paper to switch from hot metal to offset, being preceded by the *Petersburg Press* and the *Southeast Alaska Empire* in Juneau.

Illness and a fire in an apartment on the second floor of the *Sentinel* ended Johnson's editorship after one year. After discharge from a Juneau hospital, where he had been sent for observation, he killed himself.

Nelson Phillips, a Washington State newsman who attended Skagit Valley Community College and Renton Community College, took over from Johnson. He had worked on the *Mt. Vernon Argus*, the *Edmonds Tribune-Review*, the *Skagit Valley Herald* and the *Burlington Farm Journal*.

The Williamses sold the offset equipment to the new *Seward Phoenix Log* and began printing the *Sentinel* in the Petersburg plant. The *Sentinel*'s circulation was 985.

Phillips left the *Sentinel* in June 1966 and on July 1, Lew Williams Sr. and Winnie Williams returned to operate the paper until Lew Jr., and Dorothy sold it and the *Petersburg Press* to the Nome Nugget Publishing Company in August 1967.

Williams Sr., seventy-seven, died at his Wrangell home on December 29, 1972, and Winnie continued to make her home in Wrangell until 1989, when she moved to the Ketchikan Pioneers' Home, where she died September 21, 2000, at age ninety-eight.

Chapter 42

Sentinel Reaches One Hundred Years

Alaska Airlines President Charles Willis also was president of Nome Nugget Publishing Co. in the mid-1960s. The manager of his Nome, Petersburg, Wrangell and Fairbanks newspapers was former *Nome Nugget* publisher Al Phelps. He hired thirty-one-year-old Robert C. Weaver as managing editor of the *Wrangell Sentinel* after purchasing it and the *Petersburg Press* from Lew Williams Jr. and Dorothy Williams.

Weaver held the post from September 1967 through December 1968 when he transferred to the *Petersburg Press*.

A native of Kokomo, Indiana, Weaver had been a newsman for eleven years when he moved to Wrangell. He started as a reporter for the *Livingston* (Montana) *Enterprise*. In 1948, he moved to southern California where he became editor of the *Brawling News* and the *Victor Press*. He worked three-and-a-half years for the *San Diego Union* prior to moving to Fairbanks in 1966. He was news editor on the *Fairbanks Daily News-Miner*, which competed with Willis' *Jessen's Daily*.

Weaver put out a lively paper in Wrangell – lots of local news and local pictures. He built it into a ten-page paper by the spring of 1968. His initial editorial described the local paper as the "mirror of a community":

> Its news gathering must be the most important phase of the operation. It must keep its readers informed and must strive to educate the reader. It must also strive to be

> the spokesman for the citizen. It should seek out every side of an issue, not just the most popular and vocal.
>
> It is a town crier and a bulletin board, providing the citizen with a method of selling his wares or telling of his service.
>
> In its editorial page, the newspaper is the community's tool for progress. It has a basic responsibility to support or oppose what is happening within its community, the state and the nation. Its support or opposition should be clear cut and issued only after a thorough consideration of whether a movement will benefit a community.

During his final weeks with the *Sentinel*, his editorials portrayed a personal frustration with the provincialism of the townspeople. Their failure to provide adequate recreational facilities for youth was one of his chief complaints. He and his wife Carol had four children. He resented readers' complaints about his running stories that "don't do anyone any good":

> We're not in the business of doing good for people. And if a story offends someone that is unfortunate. The people's right to know is more important than someone's feelings. Suppressing news because someone might not like it or might feel hurt is a second-rate approach to newspapering.

When Weaver was transferred to the *Petersburg Press* in January 1969, Paul Estus succeeded him. He, too, wrote forthright editorials, never mincing words in discussing controversial issues. He took the preservationists to task on several occasions. Their efforts to eliminate the logging industry brought the severest censure.

"We think it is time for the preservationists to wake up and consider the future – all of it. People, too, are a natural resource and they deserve some protection," he wrote.

The NBC television program picturing Alaskans as "bloodthirsty, raw-wolf-meat-eating savages unable to slake our lust for the kill," irritated him:

> What really irks us is being told by the spoilers of the South 48 – that country of polluted streams, smog-clogged

air and all the other assets of civilization – that we are squandering our resources.

Where are the wolves of the Midwest? If these armchair defenders of the great Alaskan resources are really serious, our hunters could crate up some wolves and send them there. And who knows, after a couple hundred years, the wolves might prosper and take over the smaller states. The wolves are killing the deer in Southeastern Alaska.

Estus objected to the Native land claims settlement legislation on the grounds that Alaska's land and its rich resources belonged to all present-day residents – not to the sons or ancestors of any specific ethnic group.

"It is the Alaskan who is building this state today – not the Aleut, the Anglo-Saxon, the Eskimo or the German, the Indian or the Oklahoman – who is working toward Alaska's future. Alaska is in the hands of those who are living here today, whether they have been born here or moved here of their own volition."

Ed Barker of Eagle River succeeded Estus in November 1969. He had been editorial assistant until his promotion. He, in turn, was succeeded in May 1970 by Jamie Bryson of San Diego as Willis went through a quick succession of editors in Wrangell and Petersburg.

Bryson takes over

Thirty-five-year-old Bryson had spent fifteen years in news reporting in San Diego, following a journalism course at San Diego State College. He had been assistant city editor on the *San Diego Union*. He and his wife, Linda, had six children.

The *Sentinel*'s circulation had grown to 1,108. It was still being typeset and printed in the *Petersburg Press* plant and bad weather conditions interfered with scheduled deliveries. So, typesetting equipment was installed in the Wrangell office and the finished pages were sent to Petersburg for the presswork only.

The Brysons bought the *Sentinel* in March 1971 from Nome Nugget Publishing as the Willis' newspaper chain collapsed from financial difficulties. Those difficulties were trying to run a daily, *Jessen's Daily*, in competition with the established and better-equipped *Fairbanks Daily News-Miner*.

Jamie was editor and Linda was business manager of the *Sentinel*. Tragedy struck the following year when Linda was killed and Jamie injured in the crash of their single-engine seaplane as they were returning home from Victoria, British Columbia.

Bryson operated a flying school in Wrangell as well as editing the *Sentinel*. He carried on with his paper and his flying school while Jamie's mother came north to care for his children. It was difficult to operate the paper without Linda. Despite that, when the *Petersburg Press* folded in January 1974, Bryson launched the *Petersburg Pilot* immediately, using his airplanes for communications between the two towns, and to Ketchikan where he had both papers printed. The last operator of the *Press*, Glenn Luckie, had taken his offset press and left town.

Loss of Linda too much

But transportation and weather problems proved too expensive, and the extra work without Linda made it too stressful, so Bryson sold the Petersburg operation in March 1975 to Von Braschler, a former advertising manager for the *Ketchikan Daily News*.

Bryson continued with the *Sentinel* through the following summer and then decided to complete his studies for a journalism degree at the University of Alaska Fairbanks. Carl Sampson, twenty-two, a journalism graduate from the UAF, ran the *Sentinel* during Bryson's absence.

Sampson had come from Philadelphia two years previous. He was editor of the Fairbanks campus paper and a staff writer for the *News-Miner* during his summer vacation.

Bryson returned to Wrangell in January 1976 and married a local teacher. Wrangell's economy started slowing that winter. One of the paper's columnists referred to Wrangell as a "dull, cruddy, little one-horse town."

Spring brought surcease from cabin fever, known locally as "shack-nastiness," when the Alaska Airlines inaugurated twice daily jet service. But for the Brysons, wider horizons were beckoning. They sold the newspaper and in his swan song to his readers, Bryson wrote on May 26, 1976:

> Dear Reader: There are a few stuffed shirts we'd like to roast, but since a stuffed shirt knows he is one, and we are the epitome of the restrained editor, we won't.

What we will do is to say that most Wrangellites are simply great. They have served to prove wrong a prophecy delivered to us when we took on the *Sentinel* six years ago. "Don't buy it, kid. Don't, because they'll break your bloody heart," they warned. The message was that the weekly newspaper business is tough, the hours long, the work demanding, the criticism constant, brutal and sometimes unfair and the rewards few.

We didn't find it so. We found it a wonderful time of challenge and clean, hard work. We learned plenty and we made hundreds of new friends. And at the end we feel we accomplished as much as could be expected with our limited abilities and the troublesome need to sleep at least five hours out of twenty-four.

We think the *Sentinel* has grown up a bit in the six years, that it has developed a polish and a reputation as a quality community newspaper. We think the new owners, Larry and Leslie Persily, will make it even better.

Bryson flew briefly for Stikine Air Service in Wrangell. Then he and his wife and their infant child set off on an around-the-world cruise in their sailboat.

Persily, Murray take over

Larry Persily and his wife, Leslie Murray, were native Chicagoans. Larry received a bachelor's degree from Purdue University in 1972 and was Sigma Delta Chi's outstanding journalism graduate that year. Leslie earned her bachelor's in philosophy from Lake Forest (Illinois) College in 1969; she graduated Phi Beta Kappa.

The Persilys were senior editors for the Lerner newspapers, a chain of weeklies in suburban Chicago in 1976, when they read a "for sale" ad for the *Wrangell Sentinel* in *Editor & Publisher* magazine. They were intrigued with the idea of publishing their own newspaper so decided to move north for "two or three years."

Their first edition of the *Sentinel* appeared on June 2, 1976. It was a lively, six-column eight-pager. It was printed in Ketchikan.

It had numerous pictures of local residents and scenes. It was placed in subscribers' mailboxes rather than delivered to homes by

New Sentinel Plant —Larry Persily, below, puts up a sign on the new Wrangell Sentinel office that he and his wife, Leslie Murray, built in 1982 when they owned the newspaper (1976-84). Leslie interviewed Gov. Jay Hammond, above, while Larry looks on in their comfortable new quarters. -*Photos courtesy Larry Persily.*

juvenile carriers, as had been done for years. Most weeklies were making the same shift to postal delivery.

The Persilys put out forty-page Christmas editions and held open house at the paper's office for the general public. Their editorials urged a diversified economy, stressing tourism as a valuable new industry. They supported the timber industry's legal battles with the environmentalists. They campaigned for voter approval of a 1983 bond issue for construction of a new high school gym and swimming pool; for hiring an economic development director for the town. They aroused higher voter turnouts in local elections.

Their scholarship and experience in journalism was reflected in the high quality weekly they published. Many news stories initiated by the couple scooped larger Alaska newspapers, especially on timber issues. The paper was enough of a financial success that the Persilys built a two-story building for it on the fill area. "Fill" refers to the waterfront side of Wrangell's Main Street that was filled in with harbor dredge tailings after the 1952 fire destroyed structures on that side of the street. The Persilys also equipped the plant with modern computers for setting type and making up pages.

Wrangell suffered a severe economic shock when its Japanese owners closed the sawmill doors in February 1984, throwing more than one hundred employees out of work. Later in the year, a Ketchikan firm reopened the mill on a lease-purchase arrangement but required only half of the former employees, and at a reduced wage rate. That didn't last. The mill closed again when its parent company, Alaska Pulp Corp., closed its Sitka pulp mill in 1993.

By 2000, the sawmill was sold and reopened by an Alaska company, Silver Bay Logging, that employed about forty people. Staying open was a fight, because the administration of President Bill Clinton supported environmentalists' push to close logging in roadless areas of national forests, including Alaska's Tongass National Forest.

In the meantime, the Persilys had sold the paper in September 1984 to Alvin Bunch and his wife, Ann Kirkwood, of Anchorage. The Persilys moved to Juneau where Larry became legislative correspondent for *The Anchorage Times* and Leslie became a reporter for the *Juneau Empire*. Leslie was killed in an auto accident near the *Empire* one month before publication of the *Empire*'s seventy-fifth anniversary edition that she was editing. The edition was dedicated to her.

Larry later worked at the *Empire* but quit to start his own weekly, *The Paper*, which lasted from November 1995 to January 1997. Persily then took various government jobs and was Alaska's deputy commissioner of revenue in 2004 when he became Juneau correspondent and government affairs editor for the *Petroleum News* and later legislative correspondent for the *Anchorage Daily News*. In October of '05 he became editorial page editor.

Bunch to bankruptcy

Bunch had been a copy editor at the *Anchorage Daily News* and his wife a publications consultant for Norgaard Consultants. They moved to Anchorage in 1983 from Boise, Idaho, where Bunch had been with the *Idaho Statesman* for four-and-a-half years and Kirkwood was a reporter and editor for United Press International.

Wrangell's population was estimated at 2,500 and the *Sentinel*'s weekly circulation was posted at 1,400 in 1984.

The change of ownership took place amidst a stormy dispute that threatened to split the self-proclaimed "Friendliest Little Town in Southeast." Union workers were suing the sawmill operators, charging them with trying to break the union. The majority of the businessmen supported management. Letters to the editor intensified the divergence of community opinion.

To cut their costs, the Bunches found a cheaper location for the *Sentinel*. They entered into local disputes personally, which eroded their support in the community. They finally decided to leave Wrangell but keep the paper running by hiring editors. They went through several of those until they ran out of money and filed for bankruptcy in 1995.

Persily still was owed a substantial sum, the largest creditor in the bankruptcy. He flew to Wrangell to get out one edition of the newspaper to keep it in the market and began frustrating dealings with the bankruptcy court.

The publisher of the *Ketchikan Daily News*, Tena Williams, loaned one of her reporters, Tom Miller, who flew to Wrangell each week for more than a month to collect ads and stories. The paper was produced in the *News* plant. The typesetting equipment the Bunch editors left behind was inoperable. Williams is the granddaughter of Lew and Winifred Williams who published the Sentinel for twenty-five years starting in 1939, and the oldest daughter of Lew and Dorothy Williams.

After six weeks, Persily had the paper back in his name and sold it to a *Sentinel* staffer, Seanne Gillen Saunders, who had worked for the paper for nine months during the Bunch years and then returned to help Persily through the bankruptcy. She had worked at the *Ketchikan Daily News* in 1976 and was with the news departments for radio stations in Ketchikan for six years before returning to Wrangell in 1991.

Saunders was born in Wrangell to Jim and Madge Gillen and educated in Wrangell schools. She took college courses for two years while in Ketchikan. Her husband, Terry, operates a road construction company.

While the *Daily News* staff produced the *Sentinel*, Persily and Saunders were able to get it reequipped and restaffed. Saunders found larger, cleaner quarters on Main Street than those to which the Bunches had moved the plant. The paper was well supported by the community despite an economy depressed by the timber shutdown.

The *Sentinel* was ninety-seven years old on November 20, 1999. To observe that and remind readers that the paper will be the first Alaska newspaper to have printed continuously for one hundred years in 2002, the paper printed two extra pages in each of the last nine weeks of 1999. Each two-page section had pictures and stories from Sentinel files about one of the nine decades of the twentieth century.

One of the major debates covered by Saunders's staff in 2000 was where and how big a museum the city should build with help of a grant from the estate of James and Elsie Nolan, longtime local business owners. Nolan also served in the Territorial and State Legislatures. The project was finally approved and building opened in July 2004.

Among the museum artifacts are the *Sentinel*'s old Campbell drum printing press and one of its old Mergenthaler Linotypes.

The *Sentinel* is the oldest continuously printed newspaper in Alaska. The *Nome Nugget*, tracing its beginnings to January 1, 1900, is an older newspaper. But it suspended on occasion, the last time being from November 1942 until October 1943 during World War II.

The *Sentinel* went through another major change in early 2004 when it was purchased by Ron and Anne Loesch of the *Petersburg Pilot* and newspaper presswork switched from Ketchikan to the *Pilot*.

Chapter 43

The Pilot Succeeds in Petersburg

Petersburg and Wrangell newspapers provide studies on how small newspapers in Alaska fail or succeed.

The *Wrangell Sentinel* failed in 1995 and the owners, the Alvin Bunches, filed for bankruptcy. The paper had operated successfully for ninety-three years before the bankruptcy. The trouble occurred when the Bunches decided to move back to Idaho and hire editors to run the *Sentinel*. The paper was too small to support such an operation and ran out of money.

The former publisher, Larry Persily, the major creditor, reclaimed it from the bankruptcy court without missing an issue. He resold it to a Wrangell resident who had worked for the paper, Seanne Gillen Saunders. The *Sentinel*, restored to good health, observed its one hundredth anniversary, November 20, 2002 and was sold to the Petersburg publishers, Ron and Anne Loesch.

The *Petersburg Press* suspended operation in 1974, when the publishers, the Glenn Luckies, said it was no longer profitable enough to meet their needs. They closed up and took their printing equipment to Juneau.

Jamie Bryson of the *Wrangell Sentinel* started the *Petersburg Pilot* a week after the *Press* folded. He sold it later to Von Braschler and Braschler sold it in 1976 to Ron Loesch, who became, along with his wife Anne, Petersburg's longest-serving and most successful publishers.

Loesch was a pressman at the *Ketchikan Daily News* when he bought the *Petersburg Pilot* from Braschler on July 14, 1976. In the twenty-nine years that Loesch and Anne have owned the paper, the *Pilot* has won fifty-six awards for editorial, photographic and design excellence. Their twenty-nine years as publishers is longer than any other journalists have published a single newspaper in Alaska except for Robert Atwood who led *The Anchorage Times* for fifty-four years, C. W. Snedden who headed the *Fairbanks News-Miner* for thirty-nine years and the Thad Poulsons, editors and publishers at Sitka for 37 years in 2005.

Circulation of the *Pilot* has grown to almost 2,000 from 1,400 for the *Petersburg Press* in its last year. That indicates that the *Pilot* has earned greater community support and proven that a newspaper can operate successfully in Petersburg.

It takes more than an economically stable town to operate a successful newspaper, as the demise of the *Press* and the soaring success of the *Pilot* proves. Although the town's economy was hurt by the shutdown of the timber industry, the *Pilot* prospered.

Loesch says some of his success is attributable to the people who trained him on the job before going to Petersburg. He also says he has been lucky in attracting good people. He started with a staff of one, himself, and now has seven. For the first three years he did all of the work, writing, selling ads, printing, distributing, working ninety-hour weeks until he could "get his financial feet on the ground."

He installed his own newspaper press in 1985, the only Alaska weekly with its own press, and expanded it to four units by 1999. That enables him to print full color photos. In 1995, he purchased the building the plant occupied after renting it for ten years. This was the first time a Petersburg newspaper owned its own building. He capped his expansion by purchasing the *Wrangell Sentinel* in 2004 and printing it in his Petersburg plant.

Loesch emulates other successful small town publishers. He is active in everything – chamber of commerce, Rotary, planning commission. And he says, "We donate to everyone who knocks on the door."

The *Petersburg Press* had gone downhill in its last six years, ending in '74. Conversely, in nine consecutive years in the 1990s, the *Petersburg Pilot* prospered and won awards given by the National Newspaper Association and the Alaska Press Club., and still does in the new century.

Some stampeders sought silver

Petersburg's start differs from other Alaska towns. While the gold stampeders were mushing over the trails of '98, creating settlements as they sought gold, a handful of Norwegians were happily catching "silver," – salmon – starting a cannery and cold storage, a sawmill and building homes on the site of today's City of Petersburg.

Unlike many gold rush towns, Petersburg was never one of shacks, tents, log cabins and rough characters hoping to make a quick fortune and leave. The Norwegians brought their families, built nice homes. They came to fish and stay.

Situated on the north end of Mitkof Island and Wrangell Narrows, thirty-two miles northwest of Wrangell, Petersburg owes its birth to Peter Thams Buschmann, a native of Norway, who settled in the Pacific Northwest in 1891. In 1897, he began construction on a cannery for Icy Straits Packing Co. at the north end of what now is Petersburg's Main Street. Buschmann managed it when completed in 1900. He sold it in 1902, and it went bankrupt and through various owners until 1929 when Pacific American Fisheries acquired it.

A group of local fishermen and processors formed Petersburg Fisheries in 1965 and bought the plant from PAF. They changed the corporate name to Icicle Seafoods. They expanded throughout Alaska, becoming one of the North Pacific's largest seafood processors. Icicle's plant, incorporating Buschmann's original cannery, is the largest in a town that hosts several other major processors.

Petersburg was incorporated on April 20, 1910, with a year-around population of six hundred. Its corporate seal consists of a woodman's axe crossed with a halibut hook. By 2001, population was over 3,200, although some families left in the late '90s from the cutback in Tongass National Forest timber operations.

The Progressive first

Petersburg welcomed its first newspaper on January 18, 1913, when Jeffrey E. Rivard and J. Frederick Johnson launched the weekly *Petersburg Progressive.*

Rivard was a prospector on the beaches of Nome in 1900 and from there he moved to Chena as a newspaper reporter. Later, he reported for the *Seward Gateway.* Rivard became sole owner of the *Progressive* after a few months. Then he moved the plant to Ketchikan in October 1914, deciding it would be a more lucrative market.

Petersburg was not long without a newspaper. Lynn W. Miller, formerly of Tacoma, Washington, started *The Petersburg Weekly Report* on December 5, 1914. He had been mechanical foreman at the *Alaska Dispatch* in Juneau for the previous four years.

The *Report* was a six-column, four-page tabloid, with generous advertising patronage. He also installed an up-to-date job printing shop.

Miller opposed statehood because of the deplorable condition of the two major political parties in the territory – as a state, Alaska would be "a rotten borough exploited by unscrupulous tricksters."

Miller sold the paper to Martin S. Perkins in June 1918. Perkins had been on the staff of the *Alaska Daily Empire* after selling *The Morning Mail* in Ketchikan

Perkins supplemented his newspaper income by serving as U.S. commissioner in Petersburg from 1919 to 1922. He was also the paid secretary of the chamber of commerce and recording secretary of the Pioneers' Igloo.

A front-page editorial in 1920 described "Prosperous Petersburg" with its sawmill and its salmon, halibut and shrimp processing plants. There was also a picture of the new Model 8 Linotype, which made possible expansion of the paper from four to six pages.

Petersburg also was the center of a fast growing fur farming industry. There were twenty-five farms located on neighboring island raising mink and foxes.

Perkins sold the paper to Sid Charles in January 1924 and went fox farming on the Barrier Islands.

Sid Charles next in Petersburg

Charles changed the newspaper's name to *Petersburg Herald*. This was the fifteenth Alaska news organ with which Charles had been affiliated. He began attacking the issues of the day in his usual highly emotional style. He was not sympathetic to the idea that the Indians had been "robbed of their inheritance of fish and game by the white man. In fact, they had been pampered and accorded special considerations beyond that of the white citizen." That was different from his later support for settling Natives claims.

When Charles moved to Ketchikan in the fall of 1925, he assigned his interest in the *Herald* to several stockholders who backed him in his takeover of the *Report*. The *Herald* suspended publication in February 1926, when its shop foreman, Henry Phillips, left for Skagway to dismantle the remaining equipment of the defunct *Daily Alaskan*. That equipment was shipped to Petersburg to start a new newspaper, the *Alaskan*, owned and operated by the Alaska Native Brotherhood Publishing Co. Some of the equipment went to Ketchikan where William L. Paul started the *Alaska Fisherman*.

Press rises from Herald

A fourth weekly paper, the *Petersburg Press*, appeared on August 27, 1926, just a month after the *Alaskan*'s debut. John W. Schoettler, a Juneau printer, and Albert O. Elstad, a Petersburg businessman, bought the suspended *Herald*'s equipment and organized the Viking Publishing Co.

Schoettler relinquished his interest to Elstad in 1930.

Elstad operated an insurance business out of his newspaper office until 1933 when he moved to Juneau. During the time he ran the *Press*, he participated in heated political debate with the Paul brothers and their *Alaskan*. That continued until the *Alaskan* was forced out of business by foreclosure on debts to general merchants Hogue & Tveten in October 1932. Shortly after that, Elstad leased the *Press* to Chris Tveten's sons and moved to Juneau to become Alaska agent for his insurance companies.

The Tveten brothers, sons of one of the owners of what was then a major Petersburg store, lasted only fourteen months before deciding the newspaper business was not for them. So Elstad sold the *Press* to Hazan Brough and his wife.

Press loses forty advertisers

Petersburg was a one-paper town again after the *Alaskan* closed but the *Press* was losing money due to the poor economy and because of the personalities of the new owners. Forty businesses discontinued advertising.

After the Broughs had taken over on April 4, 1935, the paper acquired a tone of dullness that endured throughout their six-year tenure. Local news was scarce and their long-winded editorials dealt mainly with philosophical approval of the Roosevelt administration's New Deal welfare programs.

Claire and Ethel Wilder purchased the *Press* from the Broughs in 1941 and made it one of Southeast's most influential weeklies, proving for the first time in Petersburg that a successful newspaper that supports its town, wins support of the town. Claire later was elected several times as mayor of the Petersburg.

Claire had worked as a printer for *The Alaska Daily Press* in Juneau for the previous three years. He had worked on newspapers in Montana, Oregon and Washington from 1920 until he moved to Juneau.

The *Petersburg Press* had a circulation of about five hundred when the Wilders took over. Even that small run involved a lot of manual labor on decrepit equipment. With a great deal of effort, the Wilders survived the shortages of the war years. Then new equipment was purchased and the circulation grew to eight hundred.

Ethel handled the news and editorial departments, while Claire was in charge of the mechanical operations. The printing quality of the paper improved greatly.

The Wilders placed a political cartoon in the middle of the front page each week, copying the practice of Col. Robert McCormick with his *Chicago Tribune*.

The Wilders also ran an editorial comment column, "Random Thoughts," on the front page, similar the *Wrangell Sentinel*'s "Through the Sentinel Periscope," and Sid Charles's "Grins and Groans" in his Ketchikan paper. Within a couple of years, joining the front-page editorial practice in Southeast was a column called "Veatchcombings" on the front page of the *Sitka Sentinel* by publisher Harold Veatch.

The Claire Wilders ran the *Press* for seven years and then turned it over to their son William (Bill) Wilder and their son-in-law, Edward L. (Bud) Clemons, whose wife was the former Betty Mae Wilder. Bill and Bud were World War II veterans. Bud had grown up in Juneau. He took over the editorial duties and Bill tended to the business end.

The senior Wilders went to Las Cruces, *New Mexico*, where Claire was shop foreman and Ethel was society editor on *The Sun-News*.

Bud's editorial policy

On the first anniversary of his and his brother-in-law's *Press* ownership, Clemons explained to his readers why he wrote so few editorials:

> We find it rather difficult to get up a rich lather of perspiration over any of the issues that face the nation or face the world. There have been issues for many years and there will be issues long after we have passed into the world where nobody writes editorials. Why should we worry over what somebody else thinks about our opinions, much less other matters.
>
> The human race is an ancient institution. It has been bedeviled by wiser writers than this scribe. It has gone its way. So be it. All that we ask is the privilege of going our own way, with those who may choose to come along and without those who prefer going in some other direction.

Three months after making the above confession, Clemons quit the newspaper and bought into a local dime store.

Jack Zimmerman, a native of The Dalles, Oregon, succeeded Clemons as editor with Bill Wilder as publisher. Zimmerman had a university degree in journalism and had worked as a reporter on a Longview, Washington, paper.

On February 27, 1950, Bill Wilder was injured accidentally in the right eye and flown to Seattle for medical treatment. He was standing in front of a skeet trap when someone tripped the trigger. Wilder was hit by a clay pigeon and fragments of his glasses were driven into his eye. His father flew north to take charge of the *Press* until he recovered.

The Zimmermans returned to their former home in Oregon and Claire and Ethel Wilder were back in the same desks they had left two years earlier. Claire resumed his "Random Thoughts" column and editorialized more vigorously than he had previously. He made a strong pitch to get the Methodists to locate their proposed Alaska University in Petersburg, with the city offering as much free land for the campus as was desired.

Claire opposed immediate statehood for Alaska, echoing the sentiment of most of his Southeast colleagues. In an edition welcoming a National Editorial Association delegation, he wrote that they should not think that "all Alaskans were beating their breasts in sorrow because we remain a territory." He went on to write that most Alaskans favored statehood as an ideal but it was like wishing for a fur coat, "it would be fine to have if we could afford it. But until we can see our way clear to pay for the mink of statehood we hesitate to 'buy it.'"

He was equally opposed to commonwealth status for Alaska as an alternative to statehood. "We are Americans in every sense of the word and in due course of time we should be the forty-ninth state," he wrote.

Publisher to marshal

During the 1952 presidential election campaign, Wilder departed from his usual position of not dabbling in partisan politics. He had adhered to that position to avoid a family feud. His wife was as staunch a Democrat as he was a Republican. Through the years, they had learned to respect each other's opinions and to vote according to their individual conscience. In their united opinion in 1952, it was the man (Dwight Eisenhower) and not the party that really mattered.

Also, Claire Wilder felt compelled to tell his readers that he was voting Republican because of the numerous charges of "corruption, crime and collusion" among the Democratic holders of high office.

Wilder was rewarded for his forthright Republicanism by being appointed U.S. marshal for the First Judicial Division. He took his oath of office on December 1, 1953, and served in that post for the next seven years.

Bill Wilder never returned to newspapering after his accident because of impaired eyesight. He and his family moved to Juneau where he first was a fisherman and later was employed with the Employment Security Commission.

Bud and Betty Mae Clemons bought the *Press* from the Claire Wilders when Claire became U.S. marshal. Bud had taken advanced courses at the Southern School of Printing in Nashville, Tennessee, since he had last been with the *Press*. He served as business manager of the paper and hired George Megrath to run the news and advertising departments. Megrath stayed only seven months and then returned to Oregon. Betty Mae Clemons became editor.

The Clemons ran the paper for three years and then sold it to Lew Williams Jr. and his wife, Dorothy. The Clemons moved to Seattle where he worked as a Linotype operator.

The Williams years

Lew Williams Jr. was born in Spokane, Washington, on November 26, 1924. He graduated from Wrangell High School in 1942.

He started his newspaper career on January 1, 1936, as a carrier for the *Daily Alaska Empire* in Juneau, where his father was a reporter, editorial writer and editor. He moved from carrier to printer's apprentice on the *Wrangell Sentinel* after his parents bought the *Sentinel* in 1939.

After a three-year stint as an army paratrooper during World War II, Lew Jr. returned to Wrangell to assist in the operation of the family paper.

In 1953, a young teacher, Dorothy Baum of Mitchell, Nebraska, arrived in Wrangell to teach commercial courses in the high school – typing, shorthand and bookkeeping. She had earned a bachelor's degree at Nebraska State College at Kearney.

When the Williams arrived in Petersburg in May 1956, the couple had two infant daughters, Christena and Kathryn. Their son, Llewellyn (Lew) Morris III, was born in Petersburg the next year. The children later followed their parents into the Alaska newspaper business as owners of the *Ketchikan Daily News*.

Williams gave zip and content to the *Press* – qualities which were diminishing under the Clemons. Williams continued Claire Wilder's "Random Thoughts" column and used his dad's "Periscope" column from the *Wrangell Sentinel*. He introduced a third column, "News from Norway," to please his many Norwegian subscribers.

Williams supported the statehood movement despite the anti-statehood stand of some prominent local community leaders. Fishermen were generally in favor of statehood because it would get rid of fish traps and the bureaucratic control by the federal Fish and Wildlife Service, viewed as biased in favor of the salmon packers.

Dorothy and Lew Williams employed several talented teenagers as apprentices, to help in the business after school and during school vacations. One was James A. (Jimmy) Smith, who learned to run the Linotype and to cover evening meetings of the city council (especially when Lew was mayor) and the chamber of commerce.

Another was Tom Johnson, who lost his parents in a tragic murder-suicide and dropped out of high school. He was sleeping in

Before Offset—Lew and Dorothy Williams prepare their newspaper. Dorothy is setting type on a Model 8 Linotype while Lew readies galleys of type for proofreading. - *Photo courtesy of the Petersburg Press.*

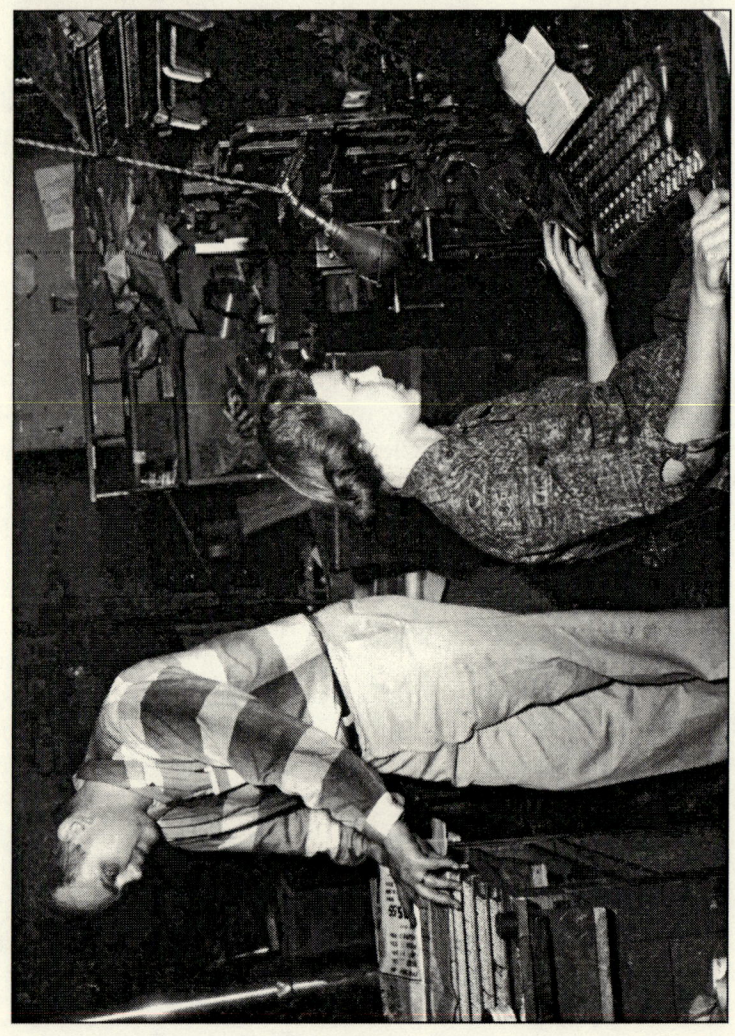

his old car when Williams hired him, got him back to high school and through one year of college at Fairbanks.

Later, when Johnson was twenty-five, Williams sent him to Wrangell to run the *Wrangell Sentinel*. Illness, personal problems and a fire on the second floor of the *Sentinel* building ended Johnson's newspaper career.

Smith, late in his high school senior year, exhibited a talent for writing and reporting in an offbeat manner that caused a stir in Petersburg but was enjoyed by many. More readers paid attention to the council and chamber meetings stories than usual. He later went on to Oberlin College and a successful career as a concert musician and educator.

Prior to statehood, the *Petersburg Press* was one of the pro-statehood newspapers that employed a Washington correspondent, A. Robert Smith. So Petersburg's Smith adopted the byline for his special reporting of J. Allen Smith.

To lead the first of his new style city council reports, Smith explained:

"We have decided to change our style of writing about the Petersburg City Council. Or at the least, I have – the boss isn't much of a partner in 'such foolishment.' I have been threatening to do this for nearly a year now. It is a style of writing employed by 'Sir' Douglas Welsh, controversial reporter for the *Post-Intelligencer* in Seattle. He reports on an esteemed board entitled the park board. He uses his wife in many reports – Greeneyes – and so that we will not be a carbon copy, our wife will be left out. This is fun!

"The council met as usual last Monday at 7:30 in the council chambers – shortly after the spectacular fifth-round knockout of heavyweight world boxing champion Ingo by the Stars and Stripes' own Patterson. However, that fight was short and sweet compared to some of which came before our governing board during their two and one-half hour meeting."

And so the story went on for two more columns.

The chamber of commerce received similar treatment. Smith's report on a meeting of Canadian and Alaska highway officials included details of the banquet menu and entertainment. The headline tells it all.

"Chamber Prexy Tells of Victoria Meet; Dancing Girls, Food, Roads."

Chapter 44

Petersburg Press Switches to Offset

Petersburg residents of Norwegian extraction – the majority, hence the name Little Norway – inaugurated a gala celebration in May 1958, still being held in 2005. It was initially a threefold festival commemorating Norway's Independence Day, May 17, Armed Forces Day, and the season's first halibut landings.

Townsfolk dressed in the traditional red, white and black Scandinavian folk costumes. A pageant depicting Norway's history is a major part of the observances. Throughout the festival, a group of costumed Vikings "raid" Petersburg and neighboring communities. They wear horned helmets, long beards, swords and all the trappings, and frolic through the streets "terrifying" maidens.

The "terrified maidens" in Petersburg wear specially designed Viking blue costumes with Alaska wildflowers embroidered on the bodice and long, full skirts.

One year, the Vikings raided the state capitol building in Juneau, "kidnapping" Gov. Keith Miller. They flew him to Petersburg where he became famous in Petersburg for his country Western singing.

Following ancient designs, the townspeople built a full-size replica of a Viking longboat and sailed it in Wrangell Narrows during the celebration. It is a major float in community parades.

Statehood supported, celebrated

Lew and Dorothy Williams, publishers of the *Petersburg Press*, 1956-66, were strong backers of statehood and opposed to any alternative. Lew, a World War II vet, wrote in one editorial:

> When we hear talk of commonwealth form of government for Alaska we get that same sinking feeling we had during wartime when standing on a troopship, we watched the U.S. coastline fade to the stern – you really stop and think how great it is to be an American and wish you could stay on U.S. soil.
>
> Commonwealth to us is the first step away from American citizenship and towards complete independence – witness the history of the British Empire. As one Alaskan, that's not what this editor wants.... We'll settle for statehood – NOW!

Petersburg residents celebrated passage of the statehood act June 30, 1958, along with the rest of Alaska, under the auspices of the chamber of commerce of which Williams was president. Congress had passed the act earlier that day. A Fourth of July aerial bomb was set off behind the *Press* building in downtown Petersburg to alert the town to the event.

Mayor Ernie Haugen declared a holiday, as did mayors throughout Alaska. A recording of the Alaska Flag Song blasted over Main Street from the Coliseum Theatre's amplifying system. The chimes of the Lutheran Church sent the strains of "America" all over town. Mayor Haugen pinned a new star on a large American flag displayed on Main Street. The *Press* printed a special "I was there" certificate. It was handed out so celebrating residents could collect signatures of their friends attesting to their presence in Petersburg, Alaska, on that historical date.

The big switch

Since 1930, the *Press* had been printed on a drum cylinder press manufactured in the 1890s by C. B. Cottrell & Sons in Rhode Island. It printed eight full-size pages. The *Press* went to the new photo offset method of production July 1, 1964, with page size reduced to tabloid, eleven by seventeen inches, a size it has continued since, as have most Alaska weekly newspapers.

Although the *Petticoat Gazette* at Seward was Alaska's first offset printed newspaper when it rolled off an offset press in 1959, the *Petersburg Press* was the first hot-metal Alaska newspaper to convert to offset. Its new equipment consisted of a Chief 22 offset press and a Kenro vertical camera. Williams described the new process to his readers:

> In offset, a photograph is made of the material to be printed. An aluminum or paper plate is made from the negative just as a picture is printed from a negative. The plate, when put on the press, transfers an inked image to a rubber blanket which prints – offsets – on to the paper page. In letterpress, type is set, inked and the image is transferred directly to the paper.

The first offset edition featured an aerial view of Petersburg that was later reduced and included in the front-page flag.

The following year, Dorothy and Lew Williams took two additional giant steps in their journalistic career. After thirty-three years of publication from offices on a street known by the picturesque name of Sing Lee Alley, the *Press* moved up the hill to the new Stokke Building on F Street. They also bought the *Wrangell Sentinel* from his parents, who were retiring after thirty-year Alaska newspaper careers. Both newspapers were printed in Petersburg after Tom Johnson's failed attempt at running the *Sentinel* on its own equipment in Wrangell.

Lew and Dorothy Williams and three children moved to Ketchikan in November 1966. They had purchased a minority interest in the *Ketchikan Daily News*. Lew became managing editor and Dorothy became business manager of that newspaper.

Gregory and the hippies

The Williams had several editors for short stints at the *Press* and then hired veteran journalist Albro Gregory, who had just left the Juneau *Empire*. Gregory introduced himself and his wife and complimented the local residents on the cleanliness of the town.

"We have seen no junk-cluttered yards such as those to be found in virtually every other Alaska city," he wrote, "no cast-off vehicles rusting at the roadsides and in vacant lots. The neat lawns, gardens, fresh paint on the houses – all that shows the people have a pride in their town's appearance."

Gregory produced an interesting paper. His editorial comments were relevant and pungent and his story headlines challenging. One headline "Don't Rock the Boat" commended the state on its ten-year tax incentive for new businesses, and another dealt with the high salaries that the legislators voted for themselves, of which he approved because of the horrendous expenses of living away from home during the sessions

For a man who generally rejected The Establishment's opinions, which got him in trouble at the *Empire*, Gregory's censure of "hippies" surprised some of his readers:

> The hippies are unwanted in Alaska. Let them remain in their little ghettos to the South. Let them demonstrate all they want but keep them out of Alaska. Let them keep their marijuana in their self-made hovels. Let them not spread their stench to the environs of the Great Land.
>
> Alaska is an emerging land. We do not want the hippie type hanging to its coat tails. Alaska opens its arms to the skilled in all forms but it must not allow itself to be slowed by the influx of a bunch of ragtag urchins, sometimes called the Flower Children.

Lew and Dorothy Williams sold both the *Press* and the *Sentinel* in September 1967 to the Nome Nugget Publishing Co. headed by Charlie Willis, president of the Alaska Airlines.

Gregory bid adieu to his Petersburg readers on Christmas Day 1968, announcing that he was leaving for "the land of the Golden Sands, reindeer, malemutes and snowmobiles" – where he was to be the editor and manager of the *Nome Nugget* for Nome Nugget Publishing.

Weaver and enviros

Robert (Bob) Weaver was transferred from the *Wrangell Sentinel* to succeed Gregory at the *Press*. Weaver continued the spirited style of his predecessor's editorials and added a couple of weekly columns. "From the Weaver's Loom" reflected his humorous responses to happenings of the week and "Petersburg: the Past" recalled significant events in the town's history as chronicled in past issues of the *Press*.

The paper ranged from twelve to eighteen pages, with lots of ads and syndicated features.

When the environmental groups advocated terminating the logging industry, Weaver reminded them that people also were a natural resource deserving of protection.

The paper was beset with problems beyond Weaver's ability to resolve. The Nome Nugget Publishing Co. was behind in its payments to Lew and Dorothy Williams and the latter threatened to place both the *Press* and the *Wrangell Sentinel* on the auction block. An out-of-court settlement was reached, canceling the scheduled public sale.

The *Press* moved to less expensive quarters, a four-bedroom house on Sing Lee Alley.

Weaver resigned in January 1971 to become press secretary to Alaska's U.S. Sen. Ted Stevens, in Washington DC. Before he and his wife, Carol, and their four children left Petersburg, he wrote that he wished that the "little horse and buggy town would move a little faster."

Nugget Publishing then succeeded in unloading what was then a money-losing paper onto its pressroom foreman, Glenn Luckie. Under the new ownership, the masthead listed Luckie as publisher and pressman, Gary Oines as editor, and Molly Luckie as business manager.

Luckies' luck runs out

The paper improved under the Luckies – the type was cleaner and the pictures clearer. It had lively local editorials. Longtime residents were interviewed and biographical profiles narrated, together with their pictures. Editor Oines was a local man, son of Mr. and Mrs. Willmer Oines of Petersburg.

A local gossip column titled "Blarney 'n' Buoyline" was introduced. The high school paper, *Riptide*, occupied two pages in many editions.

In supporting Cannikin, the proposed nuclear test on Amchitka in the Aleutian Islands, editorialist Oines argued:

> The Russians have more intercontinental ballistic missiles than does the U.S. We don't trust the USSR. The Communist Chinese are rapidly developing their missile capacity. We don't trust the Chinese either.
>
> We believe that only a strong America will survive to help insure the precarious world peace. We believe that the safeguard antiballistic missile system is essential if America is to remain strong. We believe that the Cannikin test is necessary if the safeguard system is to be perfected.

Although Luckie wanted Native land claims settled so a land freeze could be lifted and development of Alaska's resources resumed, he opposed what he termed an excessive land grant of forty million acres and a cash settlement of $1 billion to the Natives. Luckie lost the argument when the Alaska Native Land Claims Settlement Act passed Congress and was signed in 1971.

After three years, the Luckies suspended publication of the *Press*, declaring it a hopelessly unprofitable enterprise.

"We lose money seven months of the year, break even two months and make a modest profit during the last three months of each year. We can't operate that way and I don't think anyone else can either," Luckie concluded.

The Luckies moved to Juneau – along with the press on which they had been printing the paper – where they opened a commercial printing shop.

Pilot flies into slot

Jamie Bryson, who purchased the *Wrangell Sentinel* from Nome Nugget Publishing about the same time Luckies bought the *Press*, launched the *Petersburg Pilot* a week after the Luckies' departure. Bryson owned a flying school with several aircraft so he would fly to Petersburg, collect copy and ads, and assemble the pages in Wrangell. Both newspapers were printed in the *Ketchikan Daily News* plant.

On March 5, 1975, a year after its founding, Bryson suspended publication of the *Pilot*, blaming transportation and weather problems. He insisted that the newspaper had the potential of being "a dandy, little moneymaker. All it takes is enthusiasm and lots of hard work and dedication," he concluded.

Lew Williams of the *Ketchikan Daily News* alerted Von Braschler, a former *News* ad manager, of the availability of the Petersburg paper. Braschler resigned his job at an Anacortes, Washington, newspaper, and flew north to resume publication of the *Pilot* on April 11, 1975, with typesetting and printing done in Ketchikan. The paper had been grounded only four weeks.

Pilot grounds council

Braschler wrote few local editorials for the *Pilot*. However, when the city council began formulating a budget in secret meetings, he vowed that "if freedom of information continues to be flaunted in

Petersburg, this fledgling newspaper stands ready to carry its banner for the public and its guaranteed right to know."

That editorial comment resulted in a jam-packed public hearing on the budget. Irate citizens forced the council to modify its budget from requiring a 25.5 mill tax rate down to a budget supported by eighteen mills.

Braschler also pushed for stepped-up jet air service and hydroelectric power expansion. Petersburg was in danger of losing its reputation as a fish processing center because of power and transportation deficiencies.

Loesch arrives for longest stay

Braschler sold the *Pilot* to Ronald J. Loesch, 24, on July 15, 1976, after Braschler's estranged wife, Marlene, and their son refused to join him in Petersburg.

Loesch was a pressman at the *Ketchikan Daily News*, where his father, C. F. (Budd) Loesch, was shop foreman. A native of Ashtabula, Ohio, Ron had worked as a reporter and photographer on a paper in Oshkosh, Wisconsin, where again his father was in charge of the mechanical department.

Ron gained a partner in the *Pilot* when he married Anne Marie Tice of Oshkosh a year after he became a newspaper owner.

The *Pilot* of 1977 carried no world news – just local and state news identified with Petersburg. Loesch established a commercial printing shop but the newspaper was printed in the *Ketchikan Daily News* plant.

Loesch was active in community affairs and did not hesitate to take sides editorially in numerous municipal squabbles. Lengthy letters to the editor reflected feuding among council members and firing of city staff. There were eleven city managers over a ten-year period. Loesch observed that "the city manager needs a set of ballet shoes and an umbrella, and a safety net wouldn't hurt, the way he has to walk the tightrope."

He criticized the council for its frequent executive sessions behind closed doors:

> In our society, public officials are elected, not consecrated or ordained. If they let their election go to their heads and believe they are above or smarter than their

constituents, they can be un-elected. That's provided for in the law to protect the people.

Two council members were recalled in a record voter turnout after that editorial was published June 11, 1980.

Loesch pushed for construction of the Tyee Lake hydroelectric dam to provide more power for the cities of Petersburg and Wrangell. The state had worked out a plan, with the leadership of Rep. E. J. Haugen, R-Petersburg, for financing construction of four dams to provide power for six communities – Tyee Lake, serving Petersburg and Wrangell; Swan Lake, serving Ketchikan; Terror Lake, serving Kodiak; and Solomon Gulch, serving Valdez and Glennallen.

Loesch fought state and won

The Alaska Power Authority ran into stiff opposition when it began holding secret meetings with the individual community councils involved in the Four-Dam pool. Faced with the prospect that electricity would cost twice as much as what residents were already paying for diesel, the Petersburg voters were the first to reject signing a power contract with the state by a vote of 588 to 288.

The state administration, under Gov. William Sheffield, 1982-86, threatened that if Petersburg reneged on its promise to sign up for the electrical power, other state capital projects would be withheld from the region. Other towns also objected to the state's price proposal.

Recognizing that the communities needed the additional power, Loesch stepped into the breach in an effort at arbitration. He organized a media group to protest the secret meetings, threatening a court suit if the state agency did not allow the press to attend its meetings. The newspapers involved were the two Anchorage dailies, the *Ketchikan Daily News*, the *Wrangell Sentinel*, the *Petersburg Pilot*, the *Valdez Vanguard* and radio stations KFSK in Petersburg and KSTK in Wrangell. Reporters had been expelled from meetings held in Anchorage and Seattle.

Eventually, the meetings were opened to the press and long-term power contracts were signed in 1985 by the six communities. They gained reasonable power rates after four years of negotiations.

Petersburg's daily aircraft service got a boost when the Civil Aeronautics Board ordered that subsidized service to Wrangell and Petersburg, and to other Alaska small towns, be continued. Subsidized

Longest Serving Publishers

–Ron and Anne Loesch have published the Petersburg Pilot since 1976, longer and more successfully than other Petersburg publishers, winning many awards. They also publish the Wrangell Sentinel and print it in their modern plant. *-Photo courtesy of Petersburg Pilot.*

service was being phased out nationally, but Sen. Ted Stevens, R-Alaska, kept the program alive in Alaska, and it still is in 2005. It also assured that fish processing continued at high levels in Petersburg.

The threat to Petersburg's modes of transportation wasn't over. In the late 1990s the state decided to modify ferry routes. It had been proposed that Petersburg be dropped from direct service to and from Prince Rupert. The state backed down from this so that fish vans could get to a road head without switching ferries en route.

The Loesches purchased a building and their own newspaper printing press and upgraded other commercial printing and typesetting equipment over the years. By the 1990s, they were competing with other printers rather than having their press work done in Ketchikan or Juneau.

They also were winning awards. Ron was a community leader. With Anne, they are experts in operating a successful Alaska weekly newspaper, thus increasing the value of the newspaper to the community as well as its publishers.

Chapters 45-48

Kodiak, Seward, Valdez

and Cordova Journalists

Record Recoveries

> *I saw people running, with no place to go. It was just ghastly. They were just engulfed by buildings, water, mud and everything.*
>
> – Capt. Stewart of MS *Chena* in the *Valdez Earthquake Bugle* after March 27, 1964, earthquake

A Busy Editor –Mildred Kirkpatrick worked at the Seward Seaport Record when it burned in 1954, leaving Seward without a newspaper. Then the Seward Business and Professional Women's Club, with Mildred as president, founded the Petticoat Gazette, with Kirkpatrick as editor, to serve the community until a "real" newspaper appeared. That took 11 years. She served on the city council and school board. She was the first executive secretary of the Alaska Municipal League and a founder of the Association of Alaska School Boards. At the end of her career, when she was a guest in the Anchorage Pioneer's Home, she founded and edited the Home's newspaper. -*Photo courtesy of Wilma Kirkpatrick.*

Chapter 45

Kodiak Disasters Hit on Sunny Days

Good Friday, March 27, 1964 was a bright, sunny, crisp day in Kodiak. The *Kodiak Mirror* was off the press and being picked up by the delivery boys.

Suddenly, the earth began shaking like a bowl of Jello. Paper carriers and everyone else scattered, heading for high ground. A series of tsunamis (tidal waves) roared as they crashed through Kodiak. They hurled boats and floats from the small boat harbor up onto the downtown district, demolishing everything in their path.

The Alaska Packers' razor clam cannery was washed into the bay. It looked like a huge Mississippi riverboat with all smokestacks still belching. The *Kodiak Mirror* building was lifted off its concrete foundation and deposited about thirty feet toward the hillside. After the waves subsided, a large commercial fishing boat rested amid the rubble of what had been the *Mirror* plant.

With the town's newspaper plant wiped out, there were no *Mirror* reports on the quake at that time.

The *Mirror* was able to report the Exxon Valdez oil spill and its aftermath on another Good Friday twenty-five years later as oil drifted toward the Kodiak shoreline. But it printed only The Associated Press dispatches in its first two editions after the spill. Its staff was too busy working on a local feature: "Kodiak remembers twenty-five years after disaster." It was complete with pictures of what Kodiak looked like after hit by the tidal waves. The small staff could handle only one disaster at a time!

Kodiak's first disaster

It had been a bright, sunny day June 6, 1912. But not for long. A natural disaster – a volcanic eruption – threatened Kodiak.

George A. Learn, superintendent of the Baptist Mission at Wood Island near Kodiak, reported in the *Orphanage News Letter*, Kodiak's only newssheet, that he had been hearing loud reports all day, like the firing of cannon. He assumed the Coast Guard was target practicing.

About 3:30 p.m. he and the boys helping him in the mission garden saw strange clouds forming back of the Three Sisters Mountains. Then "the ugly black pall was spreading out north and south and coming east toward us."

They were sitting down to dinner when one of the boys came into the dining room covered with ash. It got so dark that lamps had to be lit. Learn went to the army radio station at Kodiak to find out what was happening. It was so dark that he needed a lantern to get home. That was less than two weeks before the longest day of the year, when it usually is daylight most of the night in Kodiak.

For two days it was dark as ash fell. He reported in his *News Letter* that they heard only rolling thunder and the "thumping on the windows of some little birds that had been attracted by the lamplight, trying to find refuge from the storm."

During the ash storm, a bolt of lightening hit the radio station, destroying it in an uncontrolled fire. By the afternoon of June 8, the sky lightened and they found eighteen inches to two feet of ash on the ground and on the roofs of buildings. Kodiak was only 110 miles from the eruption. Creeks, ponds and lakes were covered with ash. Drinking water was scarce.

Other newspapers reported that the Katmai eruption lasted sixty hours and was noticed worldwide. Ash fell in Juneau, 750 miles away. Juneau's *Dispatch* reported that the University of Washington recorded four quakes.

The *Dispatch* headlined on June 10: "Belching fire, volcanoes bring death. Fishing villages may have been wiped out. Shelikof believed to have perished. *Dora*'s decks covered with a foot and a half of ash.

"The volcanoes in eruption are the Katmai, the Redoubt and the Illiamna," it reported.

Fortunately that early report was inaccurate. Only three deaths were finally confirmed, mainly from heart attacks or accidents attributed to the ash fall. The villages weren't wiped out but people were evacuated for a while.

By June 17, the news was better. One hundred people had been rescued near Katmai and taken to Afognak, fifteen nautical miles from Kodiak. Ash was three-feet deep on mainland beaches. Cattle were dead, crops ruined but people had supplies and drinking water, thanks to the crews of the Coast Guard cutters Manning and McCulloch.

On June 11, the *Dispatch* reported ash was falling more than 1,500 miles south, at Victoria, British Columbia, and east at Dawson City, Yukon Territory. A few days later the volcanic cloud passed over Washington DC.

On August 3, 1912, almost two months after the eruption, the *Seward Gateway* printed a dispatch from the *New York Times*: "Volcanic dust containing cinders and molecules coming from the recent eruption in Alaska has arrived above the Alps ... and has been observed as far north as the observatory at Heidelberg (Germany)."

On September 15, the *Valdez Weekly Miner* reported that the volcano was still "belching vast quantities of vapor." And a geologist at the site said that the unusually heavy rain at Valdez during the summer, accompanied by lightening storms, might have been a precipitation of volcano vapors.

University of Alaska Fairbanks science writer Ned Rozell explained the eruption in a column for Alaska newspapers in 2001:

> Mount Katmai was a handsome mountain with three peaks poking more than 7,000 feet into the moist air of the Alaska Peninsula on June 5, 1912. Three days later, after the largest volcanic eruption of the 20th Century, the summit had disappeared. In its place today is an aquamarine lake rimmed by canyon walls 300 feet high. Mount Katmai's transformation from mountain to a crater lake is still a mystery to scientists because it imploded rather than exploded.
>
> During the eruption that created the Valley of Ten Thousand Smokes, Mount Katmai collapsed into itself like an ice cream cone left in the sun. At the same time, about 10 kilometers to the west, a volcano named Novarupta

spewed seven cubic miles of blistering rock and ash over the landscape.

The theory advanced by one scientist is that Katmai sat on a pocket of molten lava that somehow moved west to Novarupta, which caused Novarupt to explode, and Katmai to implode.

The fifty-six-square-mile Valley of Ten Thousand Smokes is now Katmai National Park and Preserve. More than ninety years later, twelve fissures still emit steam, gas and smoke.

National and world news coverage would have been more extensive at the time except for Alaska's distance from population centers, its sparse population, weak communications and few newspapers. In addition, the world's journals and journalists were occupied at that time on follow-ups of a more deadly disaster occurring two months before – the sinking of the *Titanic* on the night of April 14-15, 1912.

The lives of 1,500 passengers and crewmen were lost. Investigations continued through the summer on the loss and on the construction of the so-called unsinkable liner. The investigations were even headlined on front pages in Alaska, above and below banners on Katmai.

Russians move to higher ground

Kodiak is Alaska's oldest European settlement, established in August 1784 by Grigor Ivanovich Shelikof as the Russian-American fur trading center. A Russian colony was established first at Three Saints Bay on the south side of Kodiak Island with the arrival of a two-ship fleet of Russians, headed by Shelikof. It was moved sixty miles north in 1789 to St. Paul's Harbor on the northeast coast of the island, site of today's City of Kodiak. That became administrative headquarter for the Russian America Company from 1792 until the company moved headquarters to Sitka in 1808.

The name Kodiak was derived from the Innuit word *kikhtak* meaning island. During the 1800s, many spellings were used, including Kadiak. It was changed to its present spelling in 1901, adopting popular local usage.

Kodiak Island measures roughly one hundred by fifty miles, the second largest island in the United States, and is due north of Hawaii, the largest U.S. island, and due west of Juneau. It is about one hundred miles southwest of the tip of the Kenai Peninsula and 252 miles southwest of Anchorage.

By the early 1900s, the town of Kodiak had grown to a population of seven hundred to eight hundred people, still engaged in fishing, hunting sea otters and working for the Alaska Commercial Company, but no newspaper except for the *Orphanage News Letter*.

Mirror edit warns of threat

On June 15, 1940, as Paris was falling into German hands and Italian troops were taking the French town of Nice, the *Kodiak Mirror* was born on the other side of the world. Gene Dawson, a newcomer to town, came out with a twelve-page typewritten weekly, calling for a strong Alaska defense.

It was mimeographed at the naval station. He wrote a three-page editorial on the threat of an attack on Kodiak. The lead story was a report from Nome that the Soviets were constructing "a large airbase and wireless station on Big Diomede Island."

He immediately editorially supported incorporation of Kodiak as a first-class city, noting that it would then be eligible for nearly $10,000 annually in refunds of business licenses that currently went into the federal treasury. The court approved incorporation on July 1, 1940.

In January 1941, Dawson bought a flatbed press to handle his circulation that was nearing two thousand. The March 7, 1941, issue was the first to be mechanically printed on newsprint.

On December 6, 1941, Dawson sold his eighteen-month-old *Kodiak Mirror* to a newly arrived young couple, Bill and Lillian Lamme. The next day, the Lammes put out Kodiak's first "extra," carrying the headline: "U.S. Declares War on Japan."

Boy Scouts, taxi drivers and other volunteers distributed the one-page flyer throughout Kodiak. General Corlett, commander of Fort Greely near Kodiak, ordered nightly blackouts. Windows of all buildings were boarded up. Air raid wardens patrolled at night to enforce the blackout. Women and children at the military base prepared for evacuation by boat on a four-hour notice. Stores restricted the amount of food available to each customer.

After Japanese bombers hit Dutch Harbor and its navy base in the Aleutian Island June 3-4, 1942, Kodiak residents steeled themselves for an attack by the Japanese. Their military bases were

EXTRA!!

Kodiak Mirror

"News of America's Last Frontier"

VOL. 1   KODIAK, ALASKA, DECEMBER 7 1941   NO. 1

U. S. Declares War

the closest to enemy forces and stood between those forces and the Alaska mainland. Kodiak news reports were heavily censored.

Mrs. Lamme had been working for the *Mirror* when she and her husband purchased it from Dawson.

Twenty-eight-year-old Bill Lamme had arrived in Kodiak with his bride on September 8, 1940. He was a recent graduate of the University of Oregon School of Journalism. His wife came from a family of newspaper people and was welcomed immediately to a job in the *Mirror* office.

Kodiak as a war base

The town of Kodiak in the 1940s had sloping, crooked, mud streets. All of the buildings were one-story and "of cheapest frame construction, jerry-built with a view to quick profits, fast turnover and a first-class fire some day," according to Joseph Driscoll in his book, *War Discovers Alaska*, published in 1943.

During the World War II years, the army base of Fort Greely was at Bushkin River, four miles south of town. The navy submarine base and air station was at Women's Bay, six miles south of town and Fort Abercrombie, an observation post, was four miles north of town on Miller Point, now a state park. The sparsely populated fishing village of Kodiak became a military hub.

The army put out a newspaper called *The Kodiak Bear* at Fort Greely and the navy put out one called *The Willawaws*.

Running a paper while a war was going on presented innumerable challenges for the Lammes. They had no telephone and were constantly running out of supplies. Once when they ran out of ink, they concocted a substitute that made the print spread and spread. The first few hours you could read it, but then it became one big blur.

Because the paper was heavily in debt when they bought it, the Lammes were never able to turn it into a profit-making venture. The paperboys were the only ones who got rich. A couple of brothers stood in one spot on the navy base and sold enough papers to buy their parents a bathroom.

The Lammes had some exciting stories. The Japanese bombed the Dutch Harbor base at Unalaska in the Aleutians as a prelude to landing their troops on Kiska and Attu on June 7, 1942. Kodiak was the closest major Alaska town, 530 miles east of Dutch Harbor.

Being the North Pacific army and navy headquarters with twenty-five thousand soldiers and sailors, Kodiak and its bases were on a high alert for weeks.

It was almost a year – May 29, 1943 – before the U.S. Army drove the Japanese off of Attu, 1,200 miles west of Kodiak. Then Japan quietly evacuated Kiska, 1,080 miles west, reducing the threat to Kodiak and the rest of Alaska.

Look out for 100-foot wave!

Kodiak was alerted to look out for a tidal wave after a wave estimated at one hundred feet high wiped out the Scotch Cape lighthouse on Unimak Island, 455 miles west of Kodiak on April 1, 1946. The *Mirror* reported only five Coast Guardsmen killed because the usual complement of ten was reduced by personnel changes.

A report to the *Mirror* from Seattle said scientists recorded forty-five earthquakes in a twenty-four-hour period, centered on the southeast side of the Aleutians. There were tidal fluctuations but no damage in Kodiak and only minor damage at Dutch Harbor. More than 150 people perished when tidal waves hit Hawaii.

In a *Mirror* column, the newspaper's editor wrote, "Everything would have been fine if it hadn't been for the erroneous report, originating in Anchorage, that a definite one hundred-foot wave was a few minutes from Kodiak."

Then chaos as people ran to higher ground.

The report was from United Press, the competitive wire service to The Associated Press. The AP couldn't confirm it. Soon, the navy commander at Kodiak determined it was a false report and the navy radio station broadcast a correction all evening.

The *Mirror* editor wrote, "We felt like wiring back (to UP) that we hoped the erroneous wave as reported in Anchorage would wipe out the erroneous Rasputin as reported from Anchorage but we couldn't bring ourselves to be that catty."

After seven years of long hours, hard work, and bomb and tidal wave threats, the Lammes sold the paper to Mr. and Mrs. Melton L. Crawford.

The Crawfords sold the paper to James and Patrick Bennett in January 1954, and a year later, James Bennett sold his interest to Sig and Bertha Digree.

The Digrees modernized the plant with a Linotype and a faster press. Its logo read: "Kodiak, the Island Terrific in the North Pacific."

The paper opposed statehood, contending that Alaska was not yet ready for such a momentous step.

The Digrees also printed the *Mailboat Monitor*, which was started in June 1956 by Capt. Niels P. Thomsen, owner and skipper of the M. V. *Expansion*. Thomsen ran the mailboat from Seward to Kodiak and out the Aleutian Chain. Lacking newspapers, residents at each port flocked to the dock to ask for the latest news.

Thomsen didn't have time to stay in port and talk so he established the newspaper. He had correspondents in each town send him news that he could print so each town's residents would know what those in other towns were doing. The *Monitor* lasted almost eight years, until the *Mirror* plant was obliterated by the 1964 tidal wave.

In April 1956, two months before the *Monitor* started publication, Richard Whittaker – a former editor of the *Ketchikan Alaska Chronicle* – started the daily *Kodiak Islander* using Gestetner mimeograph equipment. He had worked in Kodiak for a year as a diver to raise enough money to buy the equipment and a year's supply of paper.

On the front page of his first edition was a letter from ex-President Harry Truman. Both were Democrat activists. Whittaker later became a successful lawyer in Ketchikan and represented Ketchikan in the Alaska Legislature. But his Kodiak venture failed after three months because the wrong paper had been shipped by the Gestetner Company, causing extra expense and unusually high waste.

Old friends bent, broken

Then came the tidal wave, in the aftermath of the great Alaska earthquake of March 27, 1964, that destroyed the *Mirror* plant along with the rest of downtown Kodiak.

A post-wave edition was typed and mimeographed at the high school and distributed by volunteers from the elementary school. Sig Digree wrote:

> We at the *Kodiak Mirror* saw several years of work brought to naught. The machinery such as the Linotype and press, by which we published each week, had a

sentimental value and seemed part of us. They were like dead bodies of lost friends when we looked at them afterwards, broken, twisted, bent and unusable.

The next week a temporary office was set up in the relatively unaffected Sears store. Arrangements were made with the *Cheechako News* in Soldotna to use its printing facilities. The writing and editing were done in Kodiak and then hand-carried by foreman S. Wayne Kotula to Soldotna on Wednesdays. The paper was printed and returned to Kodiak Saturday for distribution, weather permitting.

Digree suffered delays getting reestablished when the City of Kodiak and Urban Renewal officials could not agree on where the new plant should be located. After six months of frustration, the Digrees sold the paper to Wayne and Nancy Kotula.

The Kotulas published the *Mirror* as a triweekly or weekly until January 1976 when they changed it to a Monday through Friday daily in tabloid size.

The switch to a daily was made mainly because of the uncertain air service. In the winter, it was not unusual for the town to be without a plane for several consecutive days, hence without current printed news.

Meanwhile, the Kodiak economy was booming, helping it recover from the tidal wave. The king crab industry reached an all-time high in 1966, with 90.5 million pounds processed in twenty plants. Shrimp and halibut became major hauls in the 1970s. Kodiak shrimp trawlers landed an estimated 62.4 million pounds in 1970, more than twice the combined landings from the rest of Alaska, Washington, Oregon, and California. Kodiak's borough population jumped to seven thousand.

After the Magnuson-Stevens Fisheries Act of 1976 extended the United States seaward limit to two hundred miles, a major groundfish industry developed at Kodiak. The Coast Guard took over the World War II navy base. The town prospered and so did the newspaper, to the point it attracted competition.

Chapter 46

Mirror Sparkles with Native Editor

Karl Armstrong, a Kodiak Native, was the *Mirror*'s flamboyant editor from 1963 until 1975, during the time the Wayne Kotulas were publishers. He was fond of using two-inch high black headlines to shock his readers into thinking some dire catastrophe had occurred. His stories were rife with lusty phrases.

When the Russian crab fleet arrived in Kodiak waters, his headline read: "Pirates Return." The story told how the "marauding fleet of high seas pirates" were "looting and running amok smashing and slashing" Kodiak crab pots before the 200-mile limit.

Armstrong had fished for a number of years and wrote feature stories for the *Mirror* in the early 1960s about marine life. He took a six-month leave of absence from the *Mirror* in 1967, four years after being named editor, to serve as state director of information and special assistant to Gov. Walter Hickel.

Armstrong was a promoter of big plans and big dreams. He fit in well with Hickel, promoter of big ideas. Armstrong used to quote Daniel Burnham, a Chicago architect, who counseled in 1909: "Make no little plans; they have no magic to stir men's blood. Make big plans, remembering that a noble idea, once recorded, will never die."

Armstrong campaigned vigorously for a bridge to Near Island, for a Terror Lake hydroelectric project, for a full-time judge and district attorney's office in Kodiak, for more boat harbor space, for the two hundred-mile fishing limit, for a local community college and for a fisheries technology complex in the Trident Basin at Near Island. All materialized.

He wanted Kodiak to become a railhead, with a monorail encircling the island. When the state ferry *Tustumena* began its operation, he fought hard to have the name changed to *Kodiak Islander* and he pushed for a larger ship to serve Kodiak.

He enjoyed using overkill to awaken the community. In a weekly column titled "Outrageous," he would present extravagant ideas with tongue-in-cheek. Once he recommended that Kodiak become a separate state and thus become eligible for direct federal funding. A week later he went a step further, imagining the benefits if the island became the Republic of Kodiak, eligible for all sorts of foreign aid.

When the U.S. Navy threatened to close its base near Kodiak, Armstrong led a campaign in support of the defense department's proposal to store nerve gas at the abandoned installation. That editorial aroused the biggest controversy during his years as *Mirror* editor. During the height of the excitement, thirty-three "anti-gassers" staged a protest march into his office.

Armstrong made frequent trips to Washington DC lobbying for Native causes. He had friends in high places. He was one of the few Kodiak residents ever invited to tea in the White House Rose Garden. He was interviewed by Washington columnist Jack Anderson, successor to Drew Pearson of the Washington Merry-Go-Round column.

Armstrong lobbied for the Alaska Native Claims Settlement Act. He was especially proud of his role in gaining acceptance of a land exchange with the federal government whereby the Koniag Native Corp. acquired 280,000 acres of timberland on Afognak Island.

Over the years, he held executive positions with the Koniag Corp., the Leisnoi Village Corp., the Alaska Native Foundation, the Alaska Federation of Natives and the Kodiak Area Native Association. He was vice president of the *Tundra Times* corporation for six years.

Pro-environment paper emerges

The *Mirror*'s media monopoly was challenged briefly when a newly arrived couple, Fred and Pauli Kahrl, together with veteran pilot Gil Jarvela, launched the weekly *Island Times* September 12, 1970. It was produced in the Kahrls' commercial offset print shop, resulting in a clean, sharp text and pictures. It carried a generous portion of advertising at first. The first edition of 1,100 copies was an immediate sellout. Its editorial tone was pro-environmentalist, a contrast to the *Mirror*'s pro-development position.

Kahrl took a strong stand against the Atomic Energy Commission's plan to test a five-megaton nuclear bomb on Amchitka Island in the Aleutians. He helped organize the Kodiak Citizens Against the Amchitka Test to stage a welcoming banquet for the Canadian protest ship *Greenpeace* when it visited Kodiak preceding the atomic blast.

Decrying the President's willingness to "let the AEC out to play with its nuclear toy on Amchitka," he focused his attention editorially on the "gargantuan gamble" taken without the people's consent "despite our democratic form of government":

> The possibility of future radioactive leakage will live with us for up to 200,000 years, according to erudite commentary by a national columnist on ABC. Every person on the Pacific Rim will have been pawns in a gamble over which they had no control.
>
> Thus, if *Cannikin* does detonate without immediate adverse effects, we will still be victims of a more insidious type of contamination – the adulteration and compromise of our governmental ideals by a federal agency that has outgrown the controls engineered to regulate its activities.

Alan Austerman, a local businessman, succeeded Jarvela as assistant publisher of the *Island Times* in the summer of 1971, when the latter became manager of the Kodiak airport.

Kahrl's espousal of rigid regulations for waste treatment for fishing vessels in Kodiak Island harbors alienated him with the fishermen who were the lifeblood of the community. Pleading inability to live up to his ideals of journalistic objectivity and fearing becoming paranoid about it, Kahrl chose to suspend publication with the January 7, 1972, edition and left Kodiak. He said he was departing with "no small baggage of remorse, damaged pride and wounded ego."

Jack Clark next at Mirror

The Kotulas sold the *Mirror* in March 1975 to David and Nancy Stanchfield and Nancy's father Jack Clark, a veteran newspaperman from Idaho.

Clark and the Stanchfields organized the Kodiak Publishing Co., Inc., and Clark assumed the role of editor-publisher. Nancy operated the stationery store that was part of the new firm, and Dave fished for the Pacific Pearl Seafoods Co. The Stanchfields had been Kodiak residents for the previous six years.

Clark was with the Scripps-Hagadone newspaper chain for years, with his headquarters in Coeur d'Alene, Idaho. Nell Waage, who had just replaced Armstrong as managing editor of the *Mirror*, continued in that post with Clark as publisher.

Four months after Kotulas sold the *Mirror*, Roger Page of Page Photo and Printing started the weekly *Kodiak Fishwrapper and Litterbox Liner*. The paper emphasized local news and used features written by local notables. And its graphics displayed Page's talent as a graphic artist. He continued the paper until 1979, when he folded it because, he said, he had accomplished his goal, encouraging more local news and media in Kodiak. He cited the *Mirror* putting more emphasis on local news, the establishment of a radio station and establishment of the *Kadiak Times*.

A year after Kotulas sold the *Mirror* and the *Fish Wrapper* began circulation, Kodiak had three newspapers. Karl Armstrong had come back in the field. He launched the weekly *Kadiak Times* on May 6, 1976, together with Alan Austerman, former assistant publisher of the *Island Times*. Robert Middleton was hired as editor. One thousand copies of the first edition of May 6, 1976, went on sale for twenty-five cents at local grocery stores.

Armstrong sold his interest in the *Kadiak Times* to Austerman after four months and Middleton became general manager with Nancy Freeman, a former *Mirror* editor, as the new editor.

There was a rapid turnover of *Times* editors during the next five years, including Kent Brandli, Dennis Johnson and Nell Waage. In January 1981, Austerman sold the paper back to Armstrong, although it continued to be printed in Austerman's commercial print shop.

Armstrong assumed the editorial responsibilities with his usual flashy literary style. He resurrected his "Outrageous" column that he had written as editor of the *Mirror*. The *Times* format resembled a magazine more than a newspaper; it varied from thirty to fifty pages of local news and advertising. It issued an annual *Summer Visitors' Guide*.

When Armstrong succumbed to cancer September 11, 1983, Clara Helgason and Martha Fox became co-publishers of the *Times*, with Mike Rostad as editor. Rostad taught journalism at the newly established St. Herman Seminary and was faculty adviser to the student publication *The St. Herman Seminary Star*.

Fast editor turnover at Mirror

Meanwhile, the *Mirror* also underwent a fast turnover of editors. Kent Brandli started the merry-go-round, resigning after only a week to go south for medical attention.

He returned to Kodiak as editor of the *Kadiak Times*. Then in March 1979, he became a newscaster for the local KMXY radio station briefly, and then returned to the *Mirror* as associate editor.

Other successive editors at the *Mirror* included Kris Capps, Charles Spencer, Craig Bartlett and Scott Anderson. The paper was sold to Duane and Nancy Freeman on October 19, 1982.

The Freemans were twelve-year Kodiak residents, Duane having held administrative and teaching positions in the local school system.

Nancy Freeman had worked on newspapers in three Western states before arriving in Kodiak, where she served intermittently as editor on both the *Mirror* and the *Times*. In assuming the responsibilities of editor-publisher, she promised to emphasize the things that made the island unique.

"The *Kodiak Daily Mirror* should smell like a fish and scratch like a bear," she said.

Rather than editorialize on controversial issues, she presented summaries of arguments on both sides without editorial comment. Spirited letters to the editor were a substitute for staff editorials as controversial issues reached fever heat. For example, when the borough assembly suggested closing the bars at three instead of five o'clock in the mornings, a loud protest arose from the fishermen who arrived in port at all hours of the night. One wrote to the editor:

> Kodiak is harbor for 1,300 permanent vessels, 900 skiffs and a multitude of transient domestic and foreign vessels and fifty airplanes. The only entertainment available to the fishermen for socializing are the bars. Fishermen who have trod the decks will agree we don't punch clocks and work

fixed hours of the day or week. We catch the fish or crab or shrimp whenever the fishing is good. No eight to fives for us. We expect the same flexibility from this community we serve and make prosper.

We do not want the bars closed when we arrive. We are not outcasts, we deserve our R and R. You who do not want to go to bars until 5 a.m., do not have to. Those who want to, let them.

Another rash of letters to the editor appeared when the local residents became alarmed about the takeover of a seafood processing plant by the followers of Sun Myung Moon and the Unification Church. They feared the newcomers were bent on taking control of the whole community economically, politically and spirtually.

Mirror sold to chain

The *Kodiak Mirror*, an eight-page tabloid with a circulation of three thousand was sold by the Freemans in September 1998 to the owners of the *Fairbanks Daily News-Miner*, Richard Scudder and Dean Singleton. The new owners also own the *Denver Post* and a number of other newspapers in the Lower 48.

There followed a quick turnover of publishers at the paper. In January 1999, Asa Cole succeeded Freeman as publisher. Before going to Kodiak, Cole had been managing a string of thirty-seven small publications in eastern Massachusetts. Kay Cashman from the *Petroleum News* in Anchorage replaced Cole in June 2000. She returned to Anchorage and the *News* three months later and Amy Willis was named acting publisher. The "acting" was dropped in April 2001

Willis is the daughter of Duane and Nancy Freeman, former *Mirror* owners. She had worked at the newspaper in various positions from the time that she was in high school.

She earned a degree in journalism at the University of Alaska Anchorage in 1992, and returned to Kodiak, and to the *Mirror*, as advertising manager until promoted to acting publisher and then publisher.

The *Mirror* converted to a standard broadsheet under the new owners and expanded to ten to sixteen pages a day, with twenty-

Kodiak Daily Mirror Stars

–Karl Armstrong, left above, was a Native leader and colorful editor of the Kodiak Daily Mirror from 1963 until 1975 and later a director of the Tundra Times. The Mirror was sold in 1982 to a new publisher, Nancy Freeman, left, who sold the newspaper to a chain in 1998 that appointed Freeman's daughter, Amy Willis, above, as publisher in September 2000. -*Photos courtesy of the the Kodiak Mirror and the Armstrong family.*

eight to thirty on Friday when it includes the television log. By 2000, circulation had climbed to 3,900 a day.

Mirror policy continues

The *Mirror* has continued a policy of few editorials, covering its opinion page with letters to the editor and local and national opinion pieces, and a syndicated cartoon. It encourages local commentary and has several regular contributors on fisheries and outdoor subjects.

A Monday feature called the Fish Wrap covers Kodiak's commercial fisheries. That it reports on fisheries is expected for Kodiak, but its presentation is unusual. It is broadsheet size but the back sheet of the paper is printed on a web that is wide enough to fold around the regular pages and present a narrow two column sheet over the front page. It wraps around the main part of the paper so Fish Wrap is an apt name. The only other newspaper with a weekly page dedicated to waterfront activities, mainly fisheries, is the *Ketchikan Daily News*. Its "Waterfront" page appears on the front of its B Section in its weekend edition.

Another newspaper in the rich fishing area of the North Pacific is the *Dutch Harbor Fisherman* at Unalaska, a community of 4,300, about 530 air miles west of Kodiak.

The *Fisherman* is one in the chain of six rural newspapers published by Alaska Newspapers, Inc., which is owned by the Calista Native Corp., with headquarters and a printing plant in Anchorage.

Judging by their news coverage, both the *Mirror* and the *Fisherman*, in the words of retired *Mirror* publisher Freeman, "smell like a fish."

Chapter 47

Seward's Fortunes Rise with WWII

Seward's waterfront was booming in 1940, necessitating expansion of the dock. Supplies and equipment arrived steadily for construction of military bases at Anchorage and Fairbanks as World War II threatened. From then until *The Seward Phoenix Log* rose from economic ashes of the Great Alaska Earthquake of 1964, Seward residents read newspapers that varied in quality from a negative "icky" sheet to a newspaper that printed only "the news that's fun to print."

It started when the thirty-one-year-old *Seward Gateway* plant was destroyed by fire in November 1941. John Ballaine, a Seattle newspaperman, had founded the *Gateway* the same time he founded Seward and started its first railroad. The *Gateway* never recovered.

The Moose Pass Miner

The only other newspaper in the area at that time, the *Moose Pass Miner*, was at Moose Pass, twenty-eight miles north of Seward.

While some journalists had big dreams, especially those publishing Seward's early newspapers, a few settled for just informing their friends and neighbors. One of those was Lois Allen. She tried it successfully at Skagway before moving to Moose Pass.

The little mountain village of Moose Pass, on the shore of Upper Trail Lake, came into existence as a construction camp for the Alaska Northern Railroad in 1912. According to legend, it got its name because a mail carrier driving a dogteam had trouble gaining the right-of-way from a moose. Through the years, the local population ranged from 130 to two hundred.

In the summer of 1938, Allen, who had been editor-publisher of the *Skagway Cheechako* for two years, arrived in search of adventure. She liked what she saw and on November 7, she distributed a mimeographed newssheet, announcing that she was ready to provide the village with a weekly news organ and invited the townsfolk to suggest a name for it.

The following week's issue listed seven suggested names with *Moose Pass Miner* winning the most votes. It comprised four legal size sheets of paper, printed on one side and sold for twenty-five cents a copy.

In addition to local news happenings, Allen included gleanings from the radio news reports. Her friendly, informal style mirrored the neighborliness of the villagers. Hielo's Roadhouse ran a weekly ad about its Saturday night soiree. Those attending a "Hard Times Dance" were instructed to wear their raunchiest attire:

> A prize will be awarded the most poverty stricken cuss and another prize to the cussee (the latter being intended to represent the feminine form of cuss) who wears the most Cinderella-like collection of rags and patches.

When a local man became ill before finishing a cabin, which he had been building all summer, the men of the town staged an old-fashioned "help-your-neighbor" bee:

> The day was bitter cold but everybody worked with a will. A partition was built, the gables were lined, chinking of the cabin was completed, a good supply of wood cut. The ladies served a bountiful dinner of chicken and bear roast.

Under the title "Land Is for the People," the *Miner* echoed the sentiment of Kenai Peninsula residents protesting any kind of wildlife reservations on the Peninsula:

> If a reservation for wildlife were set up, the increase in the number of bears, wolves, coyotes and lynx would be horrible to contemplate and these predatory animals would do just what they are doing in the wildlife reservation of Mount McKinley Park – destroy the moose, sheep and

feathered specie which are such a Godsend in the way of food (for people).

Everybody on Kenai Peninsula should write a protest to Delegate Dimond in Washington and beg him to be on the alert that no wildlife reservation is set aside on Kenai Peninsula.

Mrs. Allen folded her newspaper in the fall of 1942 and moved to Ninilchik, where she taught school.

'Icky' sheet loses suit

After the *Gateway* plant burned, Seward was without a local paper until February 19, 1942. Then Lester Busey launched *The Seward News*, an eight-page tabloid, printed in *The Anchorage Daily Times* plant. The problems involved in relaying news and ad copy and printed papers between Seward and Anchorage proved so frustrating that Busey suspended publication on November 21, 1942 and moved to Anchorage.

Seward was again without a local newspaper until July 11, 1944 when Harold (Hal) and Nellie Hunt started the *Seward Polaris*. It proclaimed Seward to be "The Capital of the Kenai Peninsula, where Alaskans Meet the Oceans' Steamers." It was an eight-column, four-page, standard size paper that appeared twice-weekly and sold for a dime a copy. It subscribed to the United Press news service.

Polaris editorials were mostly negative. It opposed statehood on the grounds that "Big Money" wanted it so that the Morgan and Guggenheim interests could exploit it to their advantage. It opposed the city administration, accusing it of being in hock to a privileged bloc that sought to dominate the town.

Mayor Clarence Keating called the *Polaris* "an 'icky' sheet run by communists and possibly spies." Don Carlos Brownell, a former nine-term mayor and four-term territorial senator, won a libel suit against the paper.

In July 1947, the newspaper's name was changed to *The Seward Polaris & Kenai Peninsula & Aleutian Chain News* as a gesture in expanding its coverage to the west side of the peninsula and to the Aleutian Islands.

The Hunts sold the paper to John M. Coleman on September 1, 1948. The name was changed to *Seward Seaport Record*, with Frank

THE SEWARD POLARIS

Col. Tully of Signal Corps To Arrive Here Saturday

The Seward Polaris
KENAI PENINSULA-ALEUTIAN CHAIN NEWS

Seward Seaport Record

Laws of City To Be Brought Up to Date

Annual Battle with Moose and Snow Begins for Alaska Railroad's Workers

Slide Halts Trains; Wires All Down

DeLoughery as editor. Its new motto: "The Only Newspaper in the World That Gives a Hoot about Seward, Alaska."

Both Coleman and DeLoughery were newcomers to Alaska. They took up the fight to keep the railroad's coastal terminus at Seward rather than have it moved to Portage Bay (Whittier) as former railroad manager Col. Otto F. Ohlson recommended.

In 1949, the paper led an unsuccessful campaign to entice the location of Alaska Methodist University in Seward. The Methodists were already well-represented in Seward, operating the Jesse Lee Home for Children and the Seward General Hospital and Tuberculosis Sanatorium. The university went to Anchorage and is now Alaska Pacific University.

The official opening of the Anchorage-Seward Highway in 1951 was celebrated at Girdwood with a luncheon attended by federal and territorial officials. The 127-mile link was financed by the U.S. Department of Interior. For the first time, the Kenai Peninsula became part of the Alaska Highway system, including the Alaska Highway to the States.

Seward's population increased from 949 in 1940 to 2,114 in 1950. The paper published three times a week in the early 1950s. Its front page was filled with Associated Press world news dispatches. It ran a thirty-part series on the history of Seward authored by local historians. The paper enjoyed healthy advertising and circulation patronage.

The *Record* experienced short-lived competition when Onnolee O'Brien published the weekly *Seward Advertising Bulletin*. It was printed in the *Cordova Times* plant and lasted from October 30, 1952, until March 26, 1953. It was well edited but Seward could not support two newspapers.

The *Seaport Record*'s plant was destroyed by fire in May 1954. Harold (Skip) Bonser, publisher of the *Cordova Times*, bought Coleman's interest and resumed publication the following September. After four months he suspended publication, convinced that the community could not support even one printed newspaper.

Petticoat Gazette debuts

Casting about for a money-raising project, Seward's Business and Professional Women's Club decided to publish a newspaper, thus fattening the club treasury and at the same time performing a

PETTICOAT GAZETTE

RESURRECTION BAY. SEWARD'S ALL WEATHER HARBOR
PUBLISHED BY BUSINESS AND PROFESSIONAL WOMEN'S CLUB OF SEWARD

IX NO 45 EVERY THURSDAY SEWARD, ALASKA 15¢ PER COPY APR. 9,1

ALL AMERICA CITY

SEWARD IS STILL THE ALL-AMERICA CITY!

The red, white and blue All-America City banners still fly around town—and the spirit of the people is still the same. Be patient—we'll have that celebration yet...

REPORTS PROGRESS ON RECONSTRUCTION
City Hall, Apr. 8, 1964, 4:45 p.m. In absence of Mayor Perry Stockton, who is in ington, D.C., with the Governor, appearing re Senator Anderson's Federal State Com- e on Alaska Relief Legislation, the City ying to bring you up to date on what has red.
telegram was received yesterday (Tues.) Mayor Stockton, and also a tel...

MRS. SWETMANN RECEIVES "WHO'S WHO IN AME CITATION FOR LIBRARY PHILANTHROPY
Mrs. Viola T. Swetmann's outstanding to the Seward Community Library have bee nized by a Who's Who in America Citation Library Philanthropy, which appears in t Twenty-third Biennial Edition of "Who's published this month.
Selection of the two major award cita recipients is determined by size of gift tive to beneficiaries' resources, by the fice involved, or by unique circumstance rounding benefactions. Mrs. Swetmann's tion for the Library gifts was selected b Board of Editors as both unique and outs ing. Jackson Martindell, Chairman of Mar Who's Who, Inc., the publisher of "Who's said that the purpose of the citations is encourage educational philanthropy in all ramifications, as well as to honor the in dual donor.
Mrs. Viola Swetmann resides in Riversi Calif., in the winter, but comes back to Alaska, every summer. She is now a Honor Member of the Library Board.

community service. It was intended to span the supposedly brief period before a "real" newspaper arrived.

The first issue of the *Petticoat Gazette* came out on June 11, 1955, with the creed that the paper would print "all the news that's fun to print" and avoid controversial subjects, leaving those to *The Anchorage Daily Times* and the *Anchorage Daily News*.

Club president Mildred Kirkpatrick was editor. All club members were enlisted as reporters. During its first year, the staff was entirely voluntary. Thereafter, token salaries were paid to those who regularly assumed the tasks of collecting advertising, preparing layout, editing and typing the news stories.

Printing was done on a Multilith machine at the Seward Sanatorium as part of its patient rehabilitation program. The body of the news was typed. Because there were no fonts of headline-size type, heads and much of advertisements were sketched by hand. Each issue consisted of seven sheets of eight and a half by fourteen-inch paper with typewriting on both sides. At the top of the front page was a drawing of the harbor with a freight ship, labeled "Resurrection Bay, Seward's All Weather Harbor." At first it came out on flashy pink paper and sold for a dime a copy.

Kirkpatrick was a widow when she and her youngest son, Richard, then fifteen, arrived in Seward on May 7, 1947, to join her two older sons, Jim and Gene, who had arrived a year earlier. Mildred was born in Canada in 1903, the daughter of an evangelist, who moved his family to the United States when Mildred was five. She earned a librarian's degree at Drexel University in Philadelphia. During her first year in Seward, Mildred served as managing editor of the *Seaport Record*.

Kirkpatrick busy

Kirkpatrick was very active in local and state affairs. She was a charter member of the Seward Business and Professional Women's Club in 1952 and served as its president for the first three years. At various times she was a member of the city council, the school board and the Selective Service Board. She was the first executive secretary of what is now the Alaska Municipal League and was one of the founders of the Association of Alaska School Boards.

In 1959, she and her son, Gene, established the Kirkpatrick Printing Co., equipped with an offset press, and took over printing the *Gazette*, making the *Gazette* Alaska's first offset printed newspaper. Gene was also an electrician and photographer for the Alaska Railroad. Son Richard was elected mayor and son James served as chief of police.

The *Petticoat Gazette* started out with the idea of publishing the social, club and personal items of interest to women. After a few issues, it became clear that businessmen needed visual advertising space so it was expanded to allot 30 percent of its space for advertisements. It started with a circulation of four hundred and by the end of the second year it was seven hundred.

The ads had a feminine touch to them, such as Werner's Furniture Store:

> What every woman knows: It gives you a wonderful mental lift to have something new in the house. If you are sick and tired of this dull winter routine – drop in at Werner's Furniture and pick up an inexpensive pair of kitchen curtains! Advice from women to women.

Or the Seward Cleaners:

> Spill some gravy on your new suit? Leave it at Seward Cleaners, where Ginger and Bill Kane will clean it up for you in a jiffy. Fast one-day service if you ask for it.

News stories also were written in a cozy, informal style:

> Attention, All Hunters! The record polar bear killed last year by Pete Kesselring, local guide, has just arrived from the taxidermists, prepared in a full-head mount rug. This is displayed at the Seward Community Library this week. The polar bear has been recorded by the Boone and Crocket Club as 27 15/16 points which places it as the fourth largest polar bear on record. Be sure and stop in at the library to see this unusual sight.

The women were also interested in the Bradley Lake hydroelectric project, the city manager form of government, and getting Seward's main streets paved. It discussed those issues in the *Gazette*. The paper promoted scholarships at the University of Alaska for needy Seward students.

When the *Gazette*'s editor, Kirkpatrick, moved to Anchorage in the summer of 1966, the club's executive board decided to suspend publication of the paper.

Kirkpatrick served seven years as assistant director of the Anchorage chapter of the Alaska Tuberculosis Association, before moving into the Anchorage Pioneers' Home. There she was elected president of the residents' council for 1985-86. Ever the newswoman, she edited the Home's newspaper, *Mukluk*, before she died there July 5, 1991.

Phoenix rises

Seward suffered severely in the 1964 earthquake. The quake and seismic waves crumbled half of Seward's waterfront into the bay. Before the mud had settled, almost all of the town's 1,800 men, women, and children had pitched in to clean up and rebuild. New railroad and marine docks were built, including a small boat harbor, and its voters passed a bond issue for further harbor improvements.

Seward won the All-America City award for a second time in 1966, for its valiant rebuilding efforts after the quake. That same earthquake had interrupted the community celebration of its first award in 1964. The *Gazette* put out a twenty-two-page special edition celebrating the second award on April 29, 1966.

When Kirkpatrick moved to Anchorage, she sold her print shop equipment to Willard and Beverly Dunham and Joan Hoogland. The weekly *Seward Phoenix Log* made its debut on October 6, 1966, with Beverly Dunham as editor. It was printed in the Dunhams' basement.

Later, like most small offset newspapers, the Dunhams had their newspaper printed in Anchorage on a newspaper press, which could print and fold the entire paper at one time. They used their small offset press for commercial printing.

The paper's name came from the Russian ship built by Alexander Baranov on the shores of Resurrection Bay in 1793. It was the first ship built on the West Coast of North America. "Phoenix" was the name of the legendary bird who, according to fable, burned itself upon the altar every five hundred years and rose again young and beautiful. "Log" represented the chronicle of the historic ship. The paper's name thus was symbolic of Seward's resurrection following the earthquake.

Beverly Dunham was born in Seattle in 1932, the only child of Norwegian immigrants. Her father was a seafarer and fisherman. The family lived on an island in the Aleutians during the first seven years of her life. She didn't attend school until she was more than eight years old and living in Seattle.

When her father died in 1945, she and her mother moved to Seward. The town had a bustling economy at that time, serving as the supply point for the Aleutians, Kodiak, the Alaska Peninsula, Anchorage and Fairbanks.

Beverly learned to operate a Linotype machine while in high school. She worked three years for the *Seward Seaport Record* and one year with *Jessen's Weekly* in Fairbanks. In the late 1950s, she edited "60 *Speaks*," the newsletter of the cannery workers' ILWU Local 60.

She married Willard Dunham on Christmas Eve 1951. He managed the Seward office of the State Employment Service and later the Alaska Skill Center at Seward.

The *Log* was published for four years out of the Dunhams' home. In 1970 the plant moved downtown. On its fourth anniversary, the whole town was invited to a "whing-ding of a mortgage burning party." The Dunhams had bought out Hoogland in 1968.

The earthquake and tidal wave ended Seward's days as the transportation hub of Alaska. It had been the main point of entry for most of the goods and supplies destined for Southcentral and Interior Alaska. By virtue of the importance of the transportation industry, the community was at its mercy. If longshoremen "hung the hook" for any reason, regardless of who was at fault – management or labor – the town felt the impact. The effects of the crippling marine strikes of the late 1940s were felt for many years. The comeback after the earthquake was slow – so slow that many businesses failed and many townspeople moved away. Anchorage developed its own port so Seward and the Alaska Railroad lost a large volume of business.

The turning point toward a more secure future occurred in 1970, when a Petersburg firm, Icicle Seafoods, purchased the old Halibut Producers Co-op and expanded it into the largest halibut processing plant on the West Coast. In addition to halibut, it processed scallops, salmon, herring roe, shrimp and crab. Other factors contributing to the town's resurgence were location of a Coast Guard base and the Marine Science Institute of the University of Alaska in Seward. In the 1980s, coal and timber were exported through Seward.

The state established the Alaska Skill Center at Seward. Disadvantaged Alaskans, mostly Natives, received vocational training there. A state prison was constructed at Seward. The Seward Sealife Center was established after a second major disaster hit the Southcentral Alaska coast in 1989, the Exxon Valdez oil spill. Funds from the spill settlement helped fund the center.

Dunham's dialogue strong

Beverly Dunham did not hesitate to tackle controversial issues. She believed it was the duty of the local newspaper to stimulate dialogue. For example, even though her husband was a state employee, she editorialized against the state employees asking for an 8 percent pay raise in 1973 when the federal land freeze was still in effect, holding up construction of the oil pipeline. The state faced economic disaster if the pipeline was not approved and she suggested that the state's future depended on unselfishness from its residents.

"It will mean a pinch perhaps lasting for several years," she wrote, "but certainly a tight belt is preferable to losing one's trousers!"

Her two personal columns titled "Rocking the Boat" and "Flotsam and Jetsam" replaced the usual editorial page. She was pro-development and favored multiple uses of all lands. She joined most other Alaska editors in denouncing the Alaska National Interest Lands Conservation Act's proposed land withdrawals by the federal government.

She wrote in the April 19, 1973 *Log*:

> We are constantly reminded by those who resent being called "Outsiders" that Alaska belongs to ALL the people of the U.S. and THAT is the real problem. IT IS NOT SUPPOSED TO! Alaska should have been allowed to make its land selections (under the Statehood Act) BEFORE "national interest" lands were set aside. Perhaps it is time to form "Cold December" groups to let the rest of the U.S. know the needs, wants and RIGHTS of Alaskans! We have our RIGHTS!

A forty-eight-page Progress Edition was published in June 1975 to prove to the rest of Alaska and the outside world that Seward was alive and growing. It included the first full-process color cover ever published in *The Seward Phoenix Log*. It was the trading center of an area with a 3,500 population, including the communities of Cooper Landing, Hope, and Moose Pass.

The *Log* promoted Seward's celebration of its seventy-fifth anniversary in 1978. The two daughters and the son of the original founder, John Ballaine – Sephronia Kalin, Florence Andrews,

New Equipment & New Officers –Lew Williams, left, shows Willard Dunham how to operate a new offset press moved from the Wrangell Sentinel to Dunham's basement to print their new Seward Phoenix Log. Later the Alaska Newspaper Publishers' Association met in Seward with Beverly Dunham, left in the right photo, re-elected as president. Skip Snedden of the Fairbanks Daily News-Miner was elected vice president and Christmas Cowell of the Cordova Times and Valdez Vanguard was elected secretary. Beverly also was National Newspaper Association representative for Alaska for five years in the 1970s. –*Photo courtesy of Willard and Beverly Dunham.*

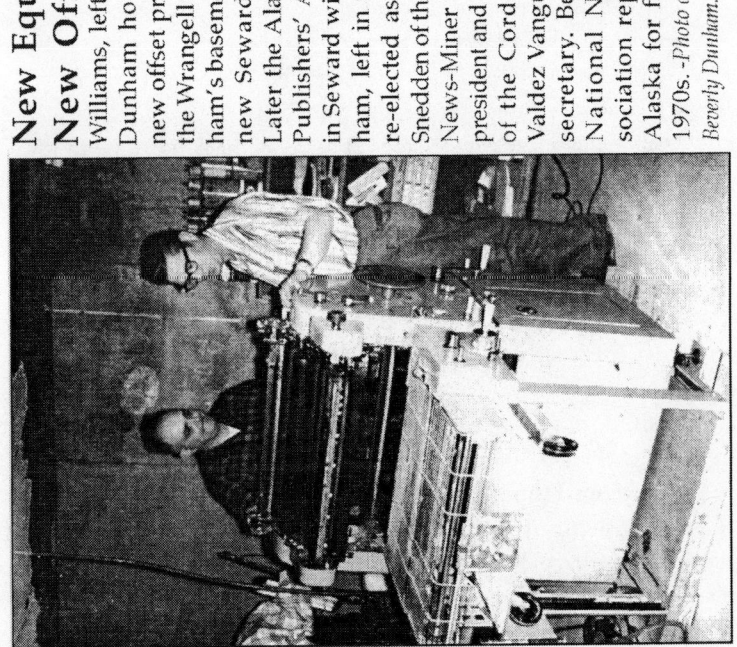

and Jerrold Ballaine – came from Seattle for the festivities. A monument was dedicated to their father, an old newspaperman. Seventh Avenue was renamed Ballaine Boulevard.

Atwood condemned, thanked

A favorite *Log* editorial target was Anchorage, blaming it for Seward's meager economy. A *Log* editorial on December 31, 1980, said:

> It is long past the time when the Kenai Peninsula and Matanuska and Susitna Valley people got together to impress upon Anchorage the need for economically strong satellite cities. It might even impress upon those in power in Anchorage, that it does not make sense to be constantly taking away every crumb it can from these smaller and less powerful areas.
>
> A case in point would be shipping. It seems more than a coincidence that within weeks of the time that the publisher of *The Anchorage Times* comes to Seward on a special train to "commemorate" or "observe" an arrangement for pipe or some other product to be shipped through Seward – we find that the arrangement has been modified, and part, if not all, of that product will instead be shipped through Anchorage.
>
> It gets downright spooky. When we hear Mr. Atwood is coming to Seward, we cringe and wonder what we are about to lose this time! It seems nothing is too small for Anchorage to cage from us. Other Anchorage satellite communities have felt the same greed.

However, four years later Atwood was a hero to the *Log*'s editorialist when his advocacy was credited with having secured the state's maximum security correctional institution for Seward, a facility sought by five other communities. He was invited to speak at the dedication ceremonies and was applauded when he told his audience:

"Don't be ashamed or doubtful about welcoming another government industry. It can do nothing but grow – more bureaucrats, more offices! Anchorage found that out."

Edgar Blatchford, right, was a sports reporter for The Seward Phoenix Log while in high school. After completing higher education, he took over Log ownership in February 1984. He purchased The Cordova Times and The Valdez Vanguard from the Fairbanks Daily News-Miner in 1990. Then he negotiated a merger with Calista Native Corporation's newspapers in 1992 to form Alaska Newspapers, Inc., the first successful Alaska-owned newspaper chain. Blatchford has served as a cabinet officer for Gov. Walter Hickel and Gov. Frank Mukowski. Between cabinet assignments he taught journalism at the University of Alaska Anchorage.
-*Photo courtesy of Alaska Department of Community and Economic Development.*

The *Log*'s editorialist approved: "Mr. Atwood's advice is well worth listening to. After all, the growth of Southcentral Alaska is due in large part to his leadership through his newspaper. In fact, many give him credit for leading Alaska to statehood. It's time we look at Anchorage as a partner, not as just a competitor."

Blatchford takes over

After sixteen years of publication, the Dunhams "developed a massive case of burnout" and negotiated the sale of the newspaper to Edgar Blatchford. Blatchford arrived in Seward from Nome in 1960, with his Inupiaq Eskimo parents, Ernest and Lena Blatchford, when he was in the third grade. His sister Rosemary, and brothers Mike and Tom, already were Seward residents.

Blatchford was a sports reporter for the *Log* while in high school and once told the Dunhams that he'd like to own the *Log* someday.

He took over *Log* ownership on February 1, 1984. He purchased *The Cordova Times* and *The Valdez Vanguard* from the *Fairbanks News-*

Miner in 1990. Over the next two years he negotiated with Calista Native Corp. to merge the corporation's newspapers with his, add several more, and form Alaska Newspapers, Inc., the first successful Alaska-owned newspaper chain.

Chapter 48

Valdez, Cordova Stagger and Recover

Merrill D. Stewart, captain of Alaska Steamship Co.'s freighter SS *Chena*, dramatically described for *The Valdez Earthquake Bulletin* the horror and havoc laid upon Valdez by the 1964 Good Friday earthquake and tidal waves:

> The *Chena* arrived at Valdez at 4:12 p.m. March 27. About 5:31 o'clock, while discharging cargo, we felt a severe earthquake, followed almost immediately by tidal waves. There were very heavy shocks about half a minute apart. Mounds of water were hitting at us from all directions.
>
> I was in the dining room. I made it to the bridge (three decks up) by climbing a vertical ladder. God knows how I got there.

The *Chena* was 10,800-ton freighter 440 feet long; much larger than the state ferry *Kennicott*, 382 feet long and seven thousand tons, which calls at Valdez.

> The Valdez piers started to collapse right away. There was a tremendous noise. The ship was laying over to port. I had been in earthquakes before, but I knew right away that this was the worst one yet.
>
> The *Chena* raised about thirty feet on an oncoming wave. The whole ship lifted and heeled to port about 50

degrees. Then it was slammed down heavily on the spot where the docks had disintegrated moments before. (Thirty-three people standing on the docks were killed.)

I saw people running, with no place to go. It was just ghastly. They were just engulfed by buildings, water, mud and everything.

I could see the land (at Valdez) jumping and leaping in a terrible turmoil. We were inside of where the dock had been. We had been washed into where the small boat harbor used to be. There was no water under the *Chena* for a brief interval. I realized we had to get out quickly if we were ever going to get out at all. There was water under us again. The stern was sitting in broken piling, rocks and mud.

I signaled to the engine room for power and got it very rapidly. I called for "slow ahead" then "half ahead" and finally for "full." In about four minutes, I would guess, we were moving appreciably, scraping on and off the mud (bottom) as the waves went up and down.

A big gush of water came off the beach, hit the bow and swung her out about 10 degrees. If that hadn't happened, we would have stayed there with the bow jammed in a mudbank and provided a new dock for the town of Valdez!

We broke free. The bow pushed through the wreckage of the cannery. We went out into the bay and stopped.

Two stevedores were killed by falling cargo in the No. 3 hold of the ship as it was rocked by the tidal wave, and one of the ship's officers went into shock and died of heart failure the next day.

The chaos following the 1964 Good Friday earthquake demanded some way in which individuals and organizations could communicate with one another in Valdez. A three-page, mimeographed sheet called *The Valdez Earthquake Bulletin*, appeared on April 10, 1964, with Ed and Frances Walker as publishers. Captain Stewart's report in the *Bulletin* was its dramatic lead story.

However, before the Good Friday Earthquake, World War II took its toll of Alaska newspapers. Four suspended publication because of conditions during World War II – *The Anchorage Weekly Times* and the *Forty-Ninth Star* in Anchorage, the *Nome Nugget*, and the *Valdez Weekly Miner*. The principal reasons for the suspensions were newsprint

FAIRBANKS Daily News-Miner

"America's Farthest North Daily Newspaper" ... Member of The Associated Press

VOL. XLII — 15¢ Per Copy — FAIRBANKS, ALASKA, SATURDAY, MARCH 28, 1964 — Fourteen Pages

FOURTH EXTRA

☆ ☆ ☆ ☆ See First Exclusive Disaster Photos - Pages 8 & 9 ☆ ☆ ☆ ☆

SOUTHCENTRAL CITIES STRICKEN

The Fairbanks Daily News-Miner published four extra editions to report on the March 27, 1964 Good Friday Earthquake. It even printed a special edition with the flags of The Anchorage Times and the Anchorage Daily News for those newspapers as they battled to recover from plant damage. Only two newspaper plants were completely destroyed by the earthquake and its tidal wave, the Kodiak Mirror and the Valdez News. The News never resumed publication. The Kodiak Mirror plant was rebuilt at a new location. The newspaper was printed in the Cheechakoo News' Soldotna plant until the Mirror's plant could be rebuilt. No Alaska journalists were among the 131 killed. Anchorage Times publisher Robert Atwood was practicing his trumpet when his log home on a bluff was shaken into sticks around him. Times managing editor Bill Tobin lost his car when the exterior wall of J. C. Penny building collapsed on it. Atwood found an emergency generator that enabled the Times to be on the street with an 8-page special edition on Sunday afternoon. The Daily News was able to publish a few days later. The Times staff tied up The Associated Press wirephoto lines for four hours transmitting the first pictures of damage taken by Alice Puster and Joe Rychetnik. For that the Times won an award from the Associated Press Managing Editors' Association.

and manpower shortages, mounting costs of labor and materials, and decreased advertising revenues as businesses experienced shortages.

Valdez editor hurting

Valdez and its aging editor-publisher Hal Selby were in low spirits in the early forties. The town's five hundred residents were missing out on the wartime boom enjoyed by its westward neighbors and its veteran editor was feeling the pangs of old age.

The minimal advertising patronage made the *Valdez Weekly Miner* a one-man operation. Its contents were limited to items clipped from the newspaper exchanges. Yet, the weekly printing reached 1,738, with many going to nonresidents who had lived in Valdez previously.

Selby ran unsuccessfully for a seat in the territorial House. His campaign ads espoused: less interference by the federal government; Alaska workers for Alaska jobs; lower territorial governmental expenditures; and opposition to increased taxation on gold production.

Valdez suffered a serious economic blow when its courthouse and jail burned to the ground at midnight on December 13, 1940. It had been built in 1904 when Valdez was designated headquarters for the Third Judicial Division. A prisoner set his mattress on fire and the fire spread rapidly. The court system immediately moved its headquarters to a new building in Anchorage.

Selby had suffered a heart attack earlier in the year and was confined to his home the greater part of the time, although he wrote some editorials, while his wife, daughter and son Tom ran the paper.

Selby died at his home on March 10, 1942. Funeral services were held at the Episcopal Church and the body was interred in the Valdez cemetery. His family continued publication through June 11, 1943. Then Tom took the equipment to Juneau where he opened a job printing shop, Miner Publishing Co.

Valdez was without a local newspaper for the next eleven years, except for a couple of sporadic ventures, each of which lasted only a few months.

Breeze bows to another News

Then a group of community volunteers founded and funded the *Valdez Breeze* in 1954. After nine years of continuous publication by volunteers and free distribution to local residents, the *Breeze* had a

Anchorage Daily Times
PRUDHOE WELL: 1,152 BARRELS
Kennedy Hints He May Run Against LBJ
Student Pilot Killed In Crash
Decision Due In 10 Days, Aides Report
Gas, Oil Flow 'Encouraging' To Two Firms

Fairbanks Daily News-Miner
Sale Nears $1 Billion
Unattached Natives Demonstrate
National Oil Sale Records Tumble in Alaska Bidding 
Names, Amounts Of High Bidders

Fairbanks Daily News-Miner
'Oil-laska' Now Financial Giant
First Pipe Shipment
Money From Leases Draws $45,000 in Interest Daily

Valdez Vanguard
"Where the news you want to know comes first."

Valdezans celebrate
—There's oil in that thar pipe!—

By PAT JONES
Staff Writer

It finally happened. A moment in history that set Valdez on its heels this weekend.

Thursday night at 11 p.m. official time, the city hall siren went off announcing that the long and anxiously awaited festivities off with an informal get-together at the Sheffield House inaugurating "The Black Crude", a drink specially conceived for oil arrival.

Saturday arrived wet and cloudy, but no one noticed as the official celebration kicked off with a fly-in breakfast at the airport.

Valdez was more than ready to accommodate them.

One of the most exciting crowd pleasers planned by the city was the Harbor Drive bed race. Every entry represented a theme. The dock workers from the terminal camp, dressed as rats, pushed a cheese to first place in the beginning heat.

celebration, introduced Dr. William Darch, president of Alyeska, Harry Mowell, vice president in charge of operations, Cmdrs. Purdy and Smith from the Coast Guard, City Manager Bill Merrice, Mayor Lynn Chrystal and other honored guests, inside the council chambers.

circulation of 550 copies in July 1963, with 235 going to locals and the remainder mailed to elsewhere in Alaska, to the States, and even to foreign countries.

When a commercial publication, the *Valdez News*, appeared on July 3, 1963, the volunteer staff of the *Breeze* gladly retired.

There are four publications named *Valdez News* in the community's history. The first was printed 1901-07; the second, 1950-61; the third, 1963-64, and the fourth 1978-79. They were related only by title.

The first editors and publishers of the third *Valdez News*, which replaced the *Breeze*, were pioneer Valdez residents Robert and Dorothy Clifton.

By the July 18, 1963, issue, only a few weeks after the paper started, Walter and Gloria Day, also Valdez pioneers, were the editors.

The *News* came to an abrupt end with the 1964 earthquake. The Days announced suspension of the *News* permanently as there were no advertisers and their equipment was badly damaged.

The chaos following the quake demanded some media, which is why *The Valdez Earthquake Bulletin*, appeared. It helped to quiet people's fears and assure them of future assistance. It served as a newssheet in which various agencies could issue instructions on what cooperative action was required. The military, the American Red Cross and The Salvation Army were first on the scene to provide security and health protection. Temporary water and sewer systems were installed. Then came state and federal representatives to devise reconstruction strategy.

Through the *Bulletin*, the people learned where they could get food, clothing, shelter and other assistance. They learned that Urban Renewal would purchase their damaged property and that the Small Business Administration would lend them money to reestablish in the new townsite. The municipal, state and federal governments would provide the infrastructure.

A variety of gifts poured into the devastated community from Outside individuals and organizations. One that brought some merriment was twenty dozen brassieres, foundation garments and garter belts from the Lovable Garment Mfg. Co. That gift of the famous "Action" bras was publicized on the national television networks.

On behalf of the women of Valdez, the *Bulletin* thanked the Lovable Company for its thoughtful donation. Mayor Bruce Woodford received a new car from the Volkswagen Co.

Helen Long's community-owned *Valdez Breeze* reappeared on May 22 to replace the *Bulletin* and the suspended *News*. The mayor and city council thought it would serve as a "symbol of more normal days." Two hundred and fifty copies were deposited at a central spot for residents to pick up at their convenience.

The feature story in the initial edition told of how the heirs of Valdez pioneers, Andrew Jackson Meals and George Cheever Hazelet, had donated 115 acres of land in the new townsite for residential rebuilding.

The *Breeze* ceased publication again on September 12, 1969 when the Days reentered the field with the weekly *Valdez-Copper Basin News*.

Cordova Times to triweekly

Times were tough in Cordova during and after World War II. Publisher Everett Pettyjohn converted the *Cordova Daily Times* to a triweekly in 1947, dropping the word "daily" from the title. Pettyjohn was active in community affairs, serving on the city council and as president of the school board. The town kept shrinking as salmon runs dwindled under federal management.

He suspended publication in 1949. The following year, he leased the plant to Harold and Marian Bonser and their son, William. The Bonsers bought the plant in 1951, including the three-story *Times* building, which housed fifteen rental units.

Harold "Skip" Bonser was born in Woodland, Washington, in 1897 and served in the U.S. Navy in World War I. He was a captain in the Merchant Marine during World War II. He had owned and published a newspaper in West Newbury, Massachusetts, and the *Carrol County Pioneer* in New Hampshire.

When the Bonsers arrived in Anchorage in 1947, he landed a printer's job at *The Anchorage Daily Times* for a year and moved to the *Anchorage News* for the next two years. When the Bonsers moved to Cordova in 1950, their son William joined them in restarting *The Cordova Times* as a weekly.

The Bonsers suspended publication with the April 2, 1956, issue because the town's businessmen reduced their advertising in his lackluster editorial product, short on news and lacking editorials. They continued to operate the commercial printing department.

Also Doing Job Work –After Harold (Skip) Bonser bought the weekly Cordova Times in 1951, he suffered through an economic turn down, a fire that destroyed his building, the 1964 earthquake and another economic shock when a fire destroyed Cordova's waterfront. Like most small town publishers, he did commercial printing to supplement the newspaper's income, as he is doing at a job press when this photo was taken. *-Photo courtesy of the Cordova Historical Society.*

They resumed newspaper publication on June 6, 1957, with a seven-column, four-page paper. A front-page editorial expressed appreciation to the advertisers who made the resumption possible.

Fires, quake strike Cordova and Times

A fire destroyed the main part of Cordova's business district in 1963, including the newspaper plant and its three-story building. The Bonsers built a new modest building large enough for just the printing plant and continued to publish a weekly more as a community service than as a profitable commercial enterprise.

Then came the 1964 earthquake that disrupted the sea floor causing the disappearance of two of the Cordova's major seafoods – dungeness crab and razor clams. It also inflicted damage on the salmon spawning streams. The earthquake wrecked sixty miles of the Copper River Highway.

Four years later, fire destroyed a major portion of Cordova's waterfront. Urban renewal funds had repaired the harbor following the earthquake. The burning of the docks posed a new economic disaster, as the town was wholly dependent on the sea for its survival. Cordova's physical isolation from the rest of the state made these disasters particularly acute. It could be reached only by plane or steamer.

Environmentalists sued the state in 1972 when reconstruction of the Copper River Highway was underway, insisting that an environmental impact statement must be filed before construction could proceed. *The Cordova Times*, the highway department and the City of Cordova took numerous polls. All were overwhelmingly in favor of the road completion except for one that was close to a tie. By the time the EIS was complete there was enough opposition that state politicians were able to find other places to spend highway funds that were less controversial.

News-Miner buys in

The Bonsers sold their Cordova paper, print shop and office supply store to the *Fairbanks Daily News-Miner* on December 19, 1973. Bonser entered a nursing home in Anchorage in the spring of 1974 and died there on September 7.

The Bonser Co. became a wholly owned subsidiary of the *News-Miner*. Two *News-Miner* employees, Fuller and Christmas Cowell, were dispatched to Cordova as publisher and assistant publisher respectively.

Fuller Cowell began his newspaper career as a teenager working for the Fairbanks Daily News-Miner. He met his wife Christmas at the News-Miner. They later ran The Cordova Times and started The Valdez Vanguard in 1975. Fuller worked in newspaper equipment sales and as a consultant and then joined McClatchy headquarters in 1981. He helped design the Anchorage Daily News' new plant, 1985 - 86. In 1993 he was named publisher of the Daily News but had to retire in 1999 to concentrate on a successful battle against leukemia. -*Photo courtesy Anchorage Daily News.*

As an incentive, C. W. Snedden offered the couple a stock option to purchase the Bonser Co. at a fixed price.

Fuller was born in Fort Knox, Kentucky, on April 21, 1952. His father was in the army and the family moved to Fairbanks when his father was assigned there in 1959. He attended Lathrop High School and the University of Alaska Fairbanks.

Fuller began his journalism career as a carrier for the *News-Miner* and worked in circulation. He was later apprenticed in the press, camera and plate-making departments.

Fuller met his future wife, Christmas Tripp, when she was working in the *News-Miner*'s circulation department. Christmas was born and raised in Fairbanks, in a family that operated sternwheelers on the Tanana and Yukon River systems. She became a journeyman printer in the *News-Miner*'s composing room and took journalism and editing classes at the University of Alaska before the couple moved to Cordova.

Fuller and Christmas converted *The Cordova Times* from letterpress to offset printing. A new ATF Chief 22 offset press was installed. The first edition the Cowells published contained the first full process color picture ever published in the *Times*. It showed the young couple accepting the keys to the newspaper from Harold (Skip) Bonser.

In 1975, Snedden was implementing an Employ Stock Ownership Plan at the *News-Miner*. He offered to trade the Cowell's Bonser Co. stock options for stock in the *News-Miner*. The Cowells accepted and became stockholders in the *News-Miner*. The joint operating agreement meant that Bonser Co. employees shared in the growth and earnings of the merged corporation.

Valdez wins pipeline terminal

In May of 1969, five years after Valdez was devastated by the Good Friday earthquake and tidal wave, Gov. Keith Miller announced that the consortium of oil companies that struck oil on Alaska's North Slope had selected Valdez as the coastal terminus for the eight hundred-mile trans-Alaska oil pipeline from Prudhoe Bay.

Pipe began arriving from Japan for the proposed pipeline. The piles grew higher and higher while the oil companies waited for right-of-way permits. Even as the pipeline was announced in 1969, Congress was preparing to implement the National Environmental Policy Act on January 1, 1970. An environmental impact statement was required before a project could be started on federal land. Environmental groups filed a suit against the oil companies, charging that officials were requesting excessive right-of-way width in violation of the Mineral Leasing Act of 1920.

To complicate matters further, the Natives had decided the time was right to push their aboriginal land claims. Secretary of Interior Stewart Udall had ordered a freeze on the public domain in 1968 until Congress could settle those claims.

It was not until January 1974 that President Nixon signed legislation from Congress that authorized the pipeline right-of-way permit. Construction started the following spring. Thus, for five more years – totaling ten years after the earthquake – the economy of Valdez had been uncertain as the pipeline permit was debated.

The Walter Day's *Valdez-Copper Basin News* complained about the delay:

> Are we to remain in a state of constant turmoil, constant restriction, suffering from the wave of conservation sweeping across the nation?

Alaska is rich in natural resources and a well-regulated development of those resources can provide a good livelihood for Alaskans, and their sons, and THEIR sons. If each developer faces a court battle with conservationists, new developers will take a strong look before entering into any project.

Alaska has a great promise, not as a playground for the Lower 48 states, but as a state which can provide a stable economy for its citizens, now and in the future.

Delay shrinks Basin News

The *Basin News* had shrunk from sixteen twelve-by-eighteen-inch pages to twelve nine-by-twelve-inch pages in 1972, as merchants reduced their advertising while the pipeline was in limbo. Once the right-of-way permit was issued, the oil companies purchased land for the tank terminal – 160 acres from the Day family and some from the state. Then the town's population jumped from 550 in 1970 to 2,500 in 1974 and to eight thousand in 1976. The Alyeska Pipeline Co. had 3,500 workers in Valdez at the peak of construction for the tank farm and docks.

By July 1974, the newspaper was twenty-eight pages with full-page ads for Alaska Airlines, Western Airlines and wholesale liquor firms.

The Days sold the *Basin News* in December 1974 to John and Mertice Nelson, recent arrivals from Portland, Oregon.

The boom enticed Fuller and Christmas Cowell to launch the weekly *Valdez Vanguard* on December 1, 1975. Christmas named the *Vanguard*, which was incorporated together with *The Cordova Times* as part of the Bonser Co., the *News-Miner* subsidiary. It was printed in the Cordova plant and flown to Valdez on Wednesdays, weather permitting, or transported via state ferry.

Oldtimers complained that their town was being ruined by crime, prostitution and drugs. Editor Nelson called the complainers "selfish and very foolish" and suggested that if they didn't like what was happening they "might pack their belongings and leave or keep their mouths shut."

This editorial brought charges that he had sided with the oil companies as opposed to the townspeople. He readily admitted that perhaps that was true as he firmly believed the pipeline had brought numerous advantages to the town that otherwise would not have been available:

> I myself am not a big city boy, and dread going to Anchorage or Fairbanks to receive services that at present do not exist here. I do believe that Valdez will, within the near future offer most everything desired, and most everyone will appreciate the fact that they can stay at home and save the expense of leaving town to get a tooth pulled. Think about it.

Nelson asked the local residents to support him instead of an out-of-town outfit, but when he didn't get the support he thought he was entitled to, he packed up and left after suffering a heart attack. The Bonser Co. purchased the assets of the *Valdez Copper Basin News* after it ceased publication in March 1976.

The first gush of oil through the forty-eight-inch pipeline arrived in Valdez on July 29, 1977, amid great celebration – boat races, a wiener roast, a fish fry – all the goodies of a small town whoop-de-do.

The *Vanguard* outgrew the capacity of the Cordova press in less than a year and had to be printed on the *News-Miner*'s larger high speed offset press in Fairbanks until the Bonser Co. could obtain and install a faster press in Cordova. A new Goss Community web press was ordered and installed at the Cordova plant in 1976.

From its first publication, *The Valdez Vanguard* was more than twice as big as *The Cordova Times*. From an operational standpoint the "tail was wagging the dog." So land was purchased and a new building constructed to house the presses and production operation in Valdez in 1981. The Goss press was moved from Cordova to Valdez.

After three years, the Cowells moved to Anchorage and then Seattle where he was a newspaper production consultant until 1981. Then they moved to California and Fuller joined McClatchy Newspapers at the *Sacramento* (California) *Bee* as plant and production director. Three years later, he became administrative director and in January 1986, was promoted to operations director.

Cowell became publisher of Gavlin Newspapers in 1987, a division of McClatchy, which published two dailies and a weekly in

California's South Santa Clara Valley. In 1991, Cowell was promoted to operations director at McClatchy corporation headquarters in Sacramento. In June 1993, he returned to Alaska as publisher of the *Anchorage Daily News*, a post he left in 1999 to successfully battle cancer.

C. F. (Budd) Loesch, production manager for the *Ketchikan Daily News*, followed Cowells as managing editor of the *Times* and the *Vanguard*. He was the first of a series of managing editors and others who kept the papers running during an economic downturn after pipeline completion.

Vanguard opposes Permanent Fund dividend

Under the Bonser Co. management, the *Vanguard* editorially opposed distribution of dividend checks to private citizens from the Alaska Permanent Fund. "It's poor public policy to spend public dollars on private needs when public needs go unfunded," it contended.

A lengthy editorial recommended a controlled harvest of sea otters in Prince William Sound area before the otter feasted on the crab to the point of crab extinction. Gillnetters also experienced damage to their nets as sea otters became tangled while pursuing salmon.

In April of 1987, the *News-Miner* leased the Bonser Co. to Lynn and Linda Wolf for three years with option to buy.

The Wolfs had lived in North Pole since 1984 and had started a weekly there in their North Pole Printing plant, along with three other families. At North Pole they also produced the *Gold Panner* for Eielson Air Force Base and the *Yukon Sentinel* for Fort Wainright.

The Wolfs were from Texas where Lynn had graduated from East Texas State University and then taught and coached football. He served as a Church of Christ pastor before moving to Anchorage in 1976.

The Wolfs' editorial policies lost them subscribers and they declined to act on their option by January 1, 1991, so the *News-Miner* took the property back and sold the papers to Edgar Blatchford. Blatchford already owned *The Seward Phoenix Log*. A year later he merged his three papers with papers owned by Calista to form Alaska Newspapers, Inc.

The Star rises

Pat and Jean Lynn moved from Anchorage to Valdez in 1988 to manage, and later buy, radio station KVAK, unaware that one year later they would be caught up in one of the most momentous events in Alaska history.

On Good Friday 1989, the tanker *Exxon Valdez* impaled itself on Bligh Reef after leaving Valdez and dumped 11.3 million gallons of crude oil into Prince William Sound – the worst oil spill in the nation's history.

The resulting cleanup effort brought thousands of workers and millions more dollars to the Valdez economy. It made "spillionaires" out Valdez and Cordova fishermen and other boat owners who charted their boats to Exxon for cleanup duties.

Lynn said the economic boost helped him rebuild the outmoded radio station and made it possible for him to go back into the newspaper business.

"My voice may have been on the radio but my heart was in the newspaper," he was fond of saying.

Pat Lynn began his newspaper career as a reporter in California. He and his wife, Jean, met and married in San Francisco in 1962. Pat went to work there on a weekly newspaper, the *Tribune*, in nearby Pacifica. Later he moved up to editor of the *Herald & News*, a daily newspaper serving Livermore, California. The Lynns moved across country to Florida in 1971 where Pat was an editor at the *St. Augustine Record*, in the nation's oldest city.

In 1975 he became executive editor of the *Columbus* (Mississippi) *Commercial Dispatch* during the height of the civil rights unrest in the Deep South.

It was from Columbus that Pat and Jean journeyed north when Pat accepted a news anchor job with Augie Hiebert's Northern Television at KTVA in Anchorage.

Seeking something of their own, the Lynns moved to Valdez to manage and later buy the radio station.

In 1989, a few months after the Exxon Valdez spill, John Lindauer, a former University of Alaska Anchorage chancellor, approached Lynns about going into the newspaper business with him in Valdez. They agreed and started the *Valdez Pioneer*.

With the demise of the Lindauer newspapers, the Lynns created a replacement, the *Valdez Star*, in October 1992.

Pat and Jean Lynn founded the Valdez Star in 1992 and were its editors and publishers until selling to one of their employees, Lee Revis, in July 2004. Pat still writes occasional items for the Star in his retirement. They bought out the competition, The Valdez Vanguard, and closed it in January 2004 after a 12-year competitive struggle with the Alaska Newspaper, Inc. publication. -*Photo courtesy of the Valdez Star.*

Lindauer sued the Lynns, claiming they took his customers from the *Pioneer* to start their *Star*. The suit went no place because the *Pioneer* lacked any assets by the time it folded.

The Lynns sold their Valdez radio station in 1996 to concentrate on the *Star*. Although the Lynns failed to become "spillionaires" from of the oil spill, they do credit its economic boost to Valdez with making the *Star* possible.

For Valdez and its newspapers, it had been quite a recovery from the deadly earthquake and tidal wave that wiped out the town, some of its residents and its newspaper, the third *Valdez News*.

Chapters 49-51

Southeast Journalists

Engage Bureaucrats,

Environmentalists,

Lawmakers and

the Court System

Due to an engagement with a special investigating committee of the House of Representatives, this column is abbreviated today.

– Bob Kederick, columnist
Daily Alaska Empire, 1957

Crimson Bears best Kayhi Kings, Page 6

Blizzard pounds northeast U.S., Page 5

Today's Trivia: How many justices sit on the Alaska Supreme Court? Answer, Page 2

Yushchenko sworn in, Page 14

KETCHIKAN DAILY NEWS

75 CENTS   MONDAY, JAN. 24, 2005   KETCHIKAN, ALASKA   VOL. 77 NO. 19 (USPS 293-940)   14 PAGES

Ambassador: Serious problems ahead of Iraq election

Kayhi defeats Juneau, Page A-6

PFD cheat gets prison time, Page 2

Today's Trivia: What competition features the ear pull, one-foot high kick and the greased pole walk? Answer, Page 2

Palestinian police deploy, Page A-10

KETCHIKAN DAILY NEWS WEEKEND EDITION

$1.50   SATURDAY/SUNDAY, JAN. 22-23, 2005   KETCHIKAN, ALASKA   VOL. 77 NO. 18 (USPS 293-940)   30 PAGES

BOLT THOSE ROCKS

Cold storage group hopeful
Awaits possible reconsideration

Trinidad mission completed
see page 3

Kenyon addresses Alaska Press Club
see page 3

Merchants Spring Market
see page 6 & 7

petersburg pilot
PETERSBURG, ALASKA

April 29, 2004   Vol. XXX, No. 18   www.petersburgpilot.com   16 Pages   One Dollar

Scott Newman survives brown bear attack

Member of the Associated Press

THE DAILY SENTINEL

Sitka Alaska

Monday, January 24, 2005   Volume 66 No. 15   50¢

NE Digs Out After Weekend Blizzard

One Dollar

Wrangell Alaska
January 27, 2005

WRANGELL SENTINEL

Volume 103, Number 4   Oldest Continuously Published Newspaper in Alaska   12 Pages

GCI seeks to provide exchange service

Chapter 49

Newspapers Battle Bureaucrats, Seattle

William L. Baker, the new owner of the *Ketchikan Alaska Chronicle*, wrote an editorial for his September 30, 1944, edition criticizing federal treatment of Alaska Natives.

Although Baker and his *Chronicle* disagreed with Sid Charles's *Ketchikan Daily News* on Gov. Ernest Gruening, on whether to abolish fish traps and on whether Alaska needed statehood, they both agreed to disagree with Washington DC bureaucrats. Republican Charles usually disagreed because they were New Deal Democrats. Democrat Baker, a statehood supporter, disagreed with federal management of Alaska affairs.

Baker wrote that the "dewy-eyed dreamers" in the Bureau of Indian Affairs and the Public Health Service spent money traveling Alaska to find out what is wrong with the poor Alaska Natives.

"They spent enough money taking surveys that several tuberculosis sanitariums could be built to serve the Natives. Instead, they return in six months, or a year or two years, and ask Natives to fill out more forms."

He compared Alaskans to Oklahomans – Okies and Alaskies – and said maybe John Steinbeck, who chronicled the Okies' migration west, could come to Alaska and chronicle the Alaskies suffering from "The Great Plan – Poverty Enforced from four thousand miles away."

Almost from the day the United States took over Alaska from Russia, Alaska newspaper editors, especially those in Ketchikan, have been vocal against federal policies, some usually enacted at the behest of conservationists, now called environmentalists, some at the behest of executives of mining, timber or fish processing companies headquartered in the Lower 48.

A. P. Swineford, in a lengthy editorial in the *Ketchikan Mining Journal* of September 8, 1904, took on federal Judge James Wickersham for a speech in Fairbanks in which Wickersham threw out the following feeler for public reaction:

> It is intended, as in the case of the Philippines, that Alaska shall not be permanently annexed as an integral part of the United States.

In response, Swineford threw out his own feeler:

> Shall the people of Alaska be required to organize here a sovereign independent nation ... shall the Republic of Alaska be divided into four or more states.... Sitka with its capital at Juneau; Alaska, with its capital at Valdez; Sumner with its capital at Nome; and Tanana, with its capital at Fairbanks?

Swineford was ridiculing Wickersham's idea, which died quickly.

Alaskans Shout 'No' to President

When President William H. Taft visited Seattle September 30, 1909, his remarks were "a sad disappointment to the hundreds of Alaskans and the thousands of Alaska sympathizers who heard him," the *Ketchikan Miner* reported.

Taft said he opposed territorial government for Alaska.

"When he said so his remarks were received by stony silence. The audience was shocked and their disappointment could only find expression in silence. Then when he went on to say that Alaska wasn't ready for self-government, he was interrupted by shouts, 'no, no, you are mistaken.'"

Taft went charging on to say there should be a federal bureau in charge of Alaska affairs based in Washington to represent the district's interests and advise the delegate to Congress.

When Taft was made an honorary Past Grand Chief of the Arctic Brotherhood, he repeated his remarks. Noting the protests of the Alaskans, he said, "If the Arctic Brotherhood is sorry it has conferred the honorary title on me, they can take it back."

The *Miner* reported that the day after Taft's remarks, Walter E. Clark, a Seattle newspaper editor, was sworn in as governor of Alaska. Taft appointed him. Clark said Alaskans should concentrate less on civil matters and more on resource development. However, the federal government had shut down that idea by withdrawing forest lands in 1902 and followed by withdrawing coal and other minerals from availability.

Governor Clark Snubbed

Later, the Taft-appointed Clark visited Fairbanks, accompanied by his wife, where, the *Valdez Miner* headlined: "Governor Clark Gets Cold Reception in Fairbanks." Clark had appointed someone from Nome to a Fairbanks post. The *Miner* subhead read: "People of Fairbanks Extended but Few Courtesies to the Governor of the Territory – Newspapers Reprove Him for His Political Methods."

The extent of the snub was reported in the final paragraph of the story: "While here, Mrs. Clark suffered a nervous breakdown and was accompanied down the river by a trained nurse. Reports since received (from St. Michael) are that Mrs. Clark is much improved."

J. E. Rivard, wrote in his *Ketchikan Daily News* in 1922:

> Alaska has been reserved to death. Alaska has been going downhill for these many years due solely to its management. As rich as the resources of the territory are, they cannot be developed unless these excesses of righteousness by government bureaus are recast and fool laws be made workable. We don't need charity, but we do need a fair deal.

That was an earlier *Ketchikan Daily News*, unrelated to today's paper with that name. But Rivard could have written the same thing for today's *Daily News*, especially if he were writing about management of Tongass National Forest in the 1990s when Ketchikan lost its pulp mill and several thousand timber jobs.

After statehood, the theme continued.

Despite Alaska having three influential members of Congress, the federal government still owned and managed almost two-thirds of Alaska's 365 million acres. The national environmental movement opposed use of Alaska lands and resources.

Seattle was still getting pounded by Ketchikan and other Alaska newspapers as recent as March 2001, when today's *Ketchikan Daily News* ran a column citing Seattle's slight of Alaska in the previous century:

> Seattleites opposed granting Alaska a nonvoting delegate to Congress in 1906 and lost. They lost again in opposing territorial status and a legislature in 1912. In 1946, the Seattle Chamber of Commerce raised $250,000 to lobby against a direct airline route between Anchorage and Chicago. They lost. Seattle interests opposed Alaska Statehood and lost. They opposed the trans-Alaska oil pipeline and lost.
>
> Washington state members of Congress dictated salmon regulations in Alaska through the federal Fish and Wildlife Service during territorial days. The salmon lost. Washingtonians destroyed their own salmon runs by over-fishing and sided with Canada against Alaska in recent international salmon treaty negotiations – and lost.
>
> So to have the *Seattle Times*, the *Seattle P-I* and the Seattle Establishment against Alaska on issues such as ANWR (oil drilling on the coastal plain of the Arctic National Wildlife Refuge) is encouraging. They usually lose.

Pat Charles in charge

Baker's *Chronicle* folded in March 1957. *Daily News* editor Gene Brice left in 1958. Then publisher Sid Charles died in January 1959.

That quick change in newspaper leadership in Ketchikan ended with Sid's daughter-in-law, Patricia Charles, becoming editor and co-publisher of the *Daily News*, the town's only newspaper. Pat's husband, Paul (Bud) Charles, assisted in production of the newspaper and wrote a few columns but he had been bitten by the boat bug like his father. So he bought and operated a succession of boats.

In those hot-metal production days, there were more staffers in production than in editorial, pressing a small editorial staff to fill up the pages. The editorial staff on the *News* was assisted by an unusual production man, William L. Weiss. He had arrived in Ketchikan in 1951 from his home in Pennsylvania and went to work as a printer and pressman for the *Daily News*.

First Daily Editor—Robert (Bob) N. DeArmond, above left, was the first managing editor of the Ketchikan Daily News when it switched to daily and dropped its old Alaska Daily Fishing News title in 1947. DeArmond, historian and book author, had joined the Ketchikan paper in 1944 when it was the tri-weekly Alaska Fishing News. Later he was a legislative columnist and set up the state library's newspaper microfilm program. Hall Anderson, top right, joined the Ketchikan Daily News as a full time photographer in 1984 and worked with the newspaper and court system to work out rules for taking pictures in state courtrooms. Prior to employing full time photographers, the Ketchikan Daily News depended upon its mechanical superintendent, William (Bill) Weiss, right, for many pictures. Weiss, who joined the Ketchikan newspaper in 1951, also pioneered local sports coverage for which a ball field was named in his honor and 10 Alaska high schools awarded him an honorary varsity letter. -*Photos courtesy of the Ketchikan Daily News.*

His hobby was youth sports. He never married and had children of his own, but helped organize Little League in Ketchikan and several other youth sports leagues. He coached in the leagues and assisted high school coaches, especially in wrestling and basketball. He wrote a regular sports column and helped editor Charles make up the sports pages as an unofficial sports editor. He also was the paper's part-time photographer. For his high school sports coverage and assistance with housing and chaperoning teams, he was given an honorary varsity letter by Ketchikan and nine other Alaska high schools.

Upon his death in December 1995, the *Daily News* devoted four columns on the front page to pictures and eulogies from many in Ketchikan, with whom he worked. A ball field and an annual wrestling tournament were named in his honor.

The hot story

While Pat Charles was editor and publisher, the *Daily News* and Mrs. Charles were involved in a continuing "hot" story. A firebug was active in Ketchikan in the late 1950s and early sixties. He ended up burning down four business blocks of the downtown area. Some Ketchikan residents had a suspicion about who the firebug was, including the newspaper's reporter Al Parkins. He had noticed that fire department Lt. Bill Mitchell was always the first fireman at the scene.

The Charleses lived in an apartment on the second floor of the wood-frame structure housing the newspaper in the downtown area. So while police and fire officials investigated the arsons, Mrs. Charles sent their young children to stay with a relative until the firebug was caught.

As it turned out, it was Mitchell. He was arrested in May 1961, disguised as a woman in a failed effort to avoid detection as he tried to leave town. He admitted setting up to a dozen serious fires.

A problem the newspaper had for years after Mitchell's apprehension and conviction was differentiating between four Bill Mitchells, unrelated, who lived in Ketchikan at the same time. One was a city council member and respected leading businessman.

At another time a Fredrick Williams was arrested for some crime. It turned out there were four Fredrick Williamses in the community. One of those not arrested complained to the newspaper that he didn't want to be identified with the arrested Frederick Williams. A reporter called the jail to obtain middle initials and age to better identify the arrested person and heard a jail official wonder what the other Fredrick Williams was complaining about. He had been once a "guest" of the jail.

Similar names are common in the Ketchikan area. The Williamses outnumber the Smiths, Joneses or other common names in the telephone book. Occasionally the editor is called upon to print: "The John A. Doe, twenty-nine, listed in district court Monday is not to be confused with the John B. Doe, twenty-seven, of Metlakatla." The paper has no problem running the explanatory statement.

Colorful Gregory arrives in Ketchikan

After several years, the Charleses looked for a managing editor to assist Pat. In August 1961 they hired Albro B. Gregory, fresh from a five-month honeymoon in the "Lesser States," as he was fond of referring to the Lower 48.

Gregory didn't hesitate to express his personal opinions through lively editorials. One of his pet peeves was parking meters. He even blamed labor troubles at Ketchikan Pulp Mill on the harassment of workers fined for overtime parking. He urged discarding the meters altogether, thus recouping the town's former serenity. There are no parking meters in Ketchikan today.

Gregory also made a practice of calling public officials at home early in the morning to obtain comments on an event before they had time to become fully awake. It gave him some interesting stories and editorials, but the practice was not liked by his victims.

In March 1963, when the state's first ferry, the Malaspina, started scheduled operations, Gregory flew to Seattle to ride the vessel north to Juneau, where he covered the inaugural ceremonies. His weekly column in the *News* titled "Ferry Tales from Alaska Land" narrated humorous incidents experienced by ferry passengers, whom he interviewed whenever a ferry was in port.

When Sen. Lester Bronson, a Nome Democrat, introduced a bill in the 1963 Legislature demanding free space in newspapers to answer editorial criticism of legislators, Gregory called it a "press-bridling" bill, violating the U.S. Constitution.

Bronson's bill never came to a vote. Strangely, Bronson served as interim editor of the *Nome Nugget* later that year.

In July 1965, the Gregorys moved to Juneau, where he became managing editor of the *Southeast Alaska Empire*. Pat Charles reassumed the editorial reins of the *Daily News*.

Editorials pushed for funds for building Ketchikan International Airport while Mrs. Charles was editor-publisher. She also supported Republican candidates such as Walter Hickel for governor and local men, Bill Boardman and Pete Cessnun, an air service owner, for the Legislature.

Hickel, Boardman and Cessnun were elected. The airport was funded and opened in 1973.

Starts New Alaskan

In 1965, the Charles family joined Robert Pickrell in creating a monthly Southeast tabloid, the *New Alaskan*. The publication was inserted in the *Daily News* once a month for two years and then the Charleses sold their interest to Pickrell. It was then distributed free in southern Southeast and outside that area to those who subscribed. Pickrell sold the publication when he retired in 1992 but the new owners lasted only two issues.

Pickrell came to Alaska with his family in 1961 to take a job as executive director of the Alaska Loggers Association. He had worked for the *White Center News* in the Seattle area. So it was natural for him to go into newspaper publishing and to support the timber industry in the *New Alaskan*. He is famous for some of his editorial crusades.

Writer Louise Brinck Harrington described those crusades in an article in the *Alaskan Southeaster* magazine in August 2000. It was headlined: "Bob Pickrell: Don Quixote Reincarnated."

Pickrell battled against the city garbage dump at Wolff Point on Tongass Narrows, calling it "Pinkerton's Park" after Mayor Jim Pinkerton. The dump was moved.

He embarrassed the state troopers and the attorney general's office after his forty-four-foot boat was stolen in 1980. Officials were slow to act so he chartered a plane and found the boat en route to Canada and called troopers, Canadian police and the U.S. Coast Guard. The boat was recovered and he published a series of articles titled "Someone Stole My Boat."

He billed the state for the cost of finding his boat, which led to the Don Quixote label, fighting the state government. After the series of articles further embarrassed state officials, the attorney general called and paid the bill. Alaska's Quixote had won.

Over the years there have been other news publications in the Ketchikan area, but they lasted only briefly.

Offset and Williamses arrive

In April 1966, the *Daily News* began the shift from printing with hot metal to the more efficient photo offset method. The Duplex flatbed press was stripped, broken apart and buried in its pit under the floor of the pressroom. A three-unit Goss Community offset press and the related camera and plate-developing equipment were installed. Linotypes were replaced by Friden Justowriters and phototypesetting devices.

Lew and Dorothy Williams of the *Petersburg Press* arrived in December 1966 to take charge of the paper, he as managing editor and she in the composing room. Pat Charles remained as publisher. Lew Williams had twenty years of newspaper experience, Dorothy ten years. They had switched the weekly *Press* to offset two years before. Within a year, the newspaper capitalized on Dorothy's education and experience in business and moved her up to business manager.

The Williamses, who were minority shareholders in Pioneer Printing Co., which owned the *News*, bought the Charleses' majority stock in June 1976.

In addition to printing the six-day daily, the Williamses expanded the Pioneer Printing Co. business to print newspapers for other publishers and organizations. They also started the *Southeast Log*, a free circulation tabloid distributed throughout Southeast for 19 years until high distribution costs closed it.

In December 1981 they began printing the tabloid weekly *Island News* for William R. (Bill) and Colleen MacCannell at Thorne Bay on Prince of Wales Island, the only other newspaper in the Ketchikan area.

The *Daily News* followed a national trend in the newspaper industry by switching to morning publication in September 1986.

According to Evangeline Atwood, coauthor of this manuscript, Lew Jr.'s general attitude toward life's problems was one of good humor with a deft touch of satire. When he faced a particularly difficult situation, he found it helped to introduce a degree of levity, reminiscent of his father's widely read "Periscope" column in the *Wrangell Sentinel*.

Colleen and Bill MacCannell are publishers of the Island News at Thorne Bay on Prince of Wales Island. They started the weekly newspaper serving two dozen communities and settlements in December 1981. *-Island News photo by Kim Harrison.*

Lew Jr. saved some of his choicest dissertations for his Saturday "Publisher's Corner," later called "End of the Week."

According to Williams, the Southeast Alaska Conservation Council's idea of a viable Alaska timber industry, judging by its actions and statements, is "a hippie sitting on a beach log carving toothpicks."

Anchorage chided

Anchorage was often a target of Williams' good-humored satire. On one occasion he launched an imaginary statewide organization called SAAAPS, standing for "Save Alaska for Alaskans, Abolish Anchorage, Please, Society." In introducing his project, he listed the advantages that would accrue to the state were there no Anchorage:

Without Anchorage, the Legislature could be reduced by 22 members, dropping all those folks who now are obliged to speak for Anchorage constituents.

Without Anchorage, the Permanent Fund dividend would almost double for other Alaskans.

Without Anchorage, the state could ease the crunch on the state court system by making it possible to drop 22 judges and the entire Supreme Court from the payroll.

Without Anchorage, Spenard would once again become a respectable community instead of the place where tired Anchorage businessmen go for a massage after a hard day at the office ripping off the rest of the state.

Williams fought relentlessly for the public's right to know, taking government agencies to court to force them to open their records and meetings. His record of success was 100 percent, winning one suit each against the school board, the borough assembly and the city council.

Williams was an aggressive booster for Ketchikan's tourist business. The *News* pushed for expanded docking facilities to accommodate more and bigger cruise ships and construction of a convention center. Both projects were accomplished. Further dock expansion is being pushed by current *Daily News* co-publisher Lew Williams III, serving on the city council.

To prove the theory that a local newspaper can take the unpopular side in a local issue and survive as long as it otherwise promotes its town, Lew Jr. won first place one year in a national editorial writing contest for small dailies. The award was given by the William Allen White School of Journalism at the University of Kansas for a series of editorials supporting a property tax on boats based on boat value rather than the current comparatively small flat fee. Ketchikan voters disagreed and killed the idea.

During his time in Petersburg, Williams had been elected mayor three times. In Ketchikan, he began service on state commissions, serving eight years on the Board of Governors of the Alaska Bar Association, and eight years on the University of Alaska Board of Regents. He served on several other state boards and said that instead of being a conflict of interest, it led him to tips on important news stories. He also said he confined his service to public boards and posts, turning down service on boards of companies in the private sector.

The Williamses had a series of managing editors after buying out the Charleses when Lew Jr. moved up to publisher. Of the eight editors by 2002, six had moved up from other newsroom positions.

Editor heads jury

One editor, Heidi Ekstrand was promoted from reporter to editor of the *News* in time to end up in an unusual situation for a journalist. She had to take an eight-month break to serve on the jury of a sensational criminal trial and was elected jury foreman. Longtime reporter Nikki Murray Jones (Norma Stillman) moved up to be acting managing editor.

Salmon fishing boat crewman John Kenneth Peel was charged with murdering eight people at Craig aboard the seine boat Investor and then burning the boat over the Labor Day weekend in 1982. He went on trial in January 1986 and three *Daily News* employees were called for jury duty. Only Ekstrand had to serve.

The Ketchikan jury failed to agree on a verdict. A retrial was held in Juneau and Peel was acquitted.

In 2002, longtime reporter Terry Miller was promoted to managing editor. Her husband is a senior reporter with the newspaper.

Third generation takes over

A third generation Alaskan journalistic dynasty (the only one in the state) developed at the *Daily News*. All three Williams children and Sid Charles's grandson, Douglas, were on the *Daily News* staff at 2000. Lew III, Christena and Kathryn Williams bought out their parents in 1995. Lew Jr. continued to write an occasional column for the *News*, which was sometimes reprinted in "The Voice of the Times" page in the *Anchorage Daily News* and in the *Juneau Empire*.

Doug Charles, son of Bud and Pat Charles, worked in commercial printing plants in Juneau and Anchorage from 1967 until 1983. He returned to the *Daily News* in 1984 as wire editor. He completed a special project for the Ketchikan Museum because of his skill in photography and interest in Alaska history. After the museum project, he rejoined the *Daily News* in 1998, running its commercial printing department. He also was a consultant to the authors of this manuscript

Ketchikan Daily News–2005

Newspaper Owners and Publishers: Lew Williams III, co-publisher, top left, Tena Williams, co-publisher, right, Kathy Williams, business manager, left. -*Ketchikan Daily News photos by Hall Anderson.*

on hot-metal printing equipment until moving to India several years later.

While attending Ketchikan High School, Lew III, Christena (Tena) and Kathryn (Kathy) Williams, worked as interns in various departments of the *Daily News*. They then attended various colleges and worked for publishers and printers in other states. Tena also worked on the news desk at *The Anchorage Times* and briefly as vacation relief for The Associated Press in Anchorage.

In the 1980s, the three returned to the *Daily News* and subsequently bought out their parents. Kathy became business manager; Lew III and Tena as co-publishers.

Tena and her brother editorially support economic development for Ketchikan. Both back it up with public service. Tena has been president of the chamber of commerce and serves on the hospital board and on a committee seeking an aquarium for Ketchikan. Gov. Frank Murkoski appointed her to the Alaska Judicial Council in 2005. Lew III has served four terms on the city council.

Although the pulp mill closure in 1997 adversely affected the business community and cost the newspaper three hundred of its five thousand subscribers, the Williamses expanded operations. They operated a low-power television station for seven years until local economics forced suspension in 2002. New printing equipment was added to boost the commercial printing department.

The younger Williamses continue the Alaska newspaper tradition of defending Alaska from abuse by federal bureaucrats.

In an editorial entitled, "A great idea," they supported Gov. Walter Hickel's plan, offered in a facetious manner: "Buying Alaska from the federal government is the cheapest thing the state could do." Then citing the problems Alaskans have with federal management, the editorial concludes:

"Governor Hickel says the Russians have told him they want Alaska back. He tells them that Alaskans want to get it first. Perhaps a sale is the way to go."

In 2003, Kristie Williams, a recent college graduate, joined the *Daily News* advertising department. She is the oldest daughter of co-publisher Lew III and Vicki Williams and is a fourth-generation Alaska newspaperwoman.

Chapter 50

Empire Upholds Privilege

The *Daily Alaska Empire* was so solidly entrenched in the business community in the 1940s, and had been since 1912, that it was overwhelming competition for the four-year-old *Alaska Daily Press*, successor to *Stroller's Weekly*.

The *Press* tried to compete more effectively by becoming a morning paper in December 1940. A year later, however, it was reduced to a weekly. Wartime conditions had made it even more difficult to survive, so E. S. (Bill) Evans sold his *Press* to the *Empire* in April 1947. The *Empire* tried to discourage further competition by keeping the *Press* operating as a weekly.

The *Press* was leased to Spencer and Ann DeLong on May 1, 1947. The DeLongs arrived in Juneau originally in 1935 and worked at both the *Press* and the *Empire*. They leased and edited the *Wrangell Sentinel* in 1944-45 and then moved to Fairbanks, where they worked for both the *News-Miner* and *Jessen's Weekly* before returning to Juneau in 1947.

The *Press* became the *Alaska Sunday Press* on June 29, 1947, with Ann as editor, Spencer as business manager and son David as circulation manager. The *Sunday Press* was printed Saturday nights, ready to appear at the Sunday morning breakfast tables. It comprised twelve regular size pages, plus a tabloid insert of eight pages of colored comics. It subscribed to the United Press news service and was delivered by carriers.

The DeLongs attempted to make it a Southeast newspaper with news correspondents in various Southeast towns. However, collecting news and advertising, and even distributing papers outside of Juneau, was expensive. Subsequent attempts at a newspaper covering all of Southeast – the *Southeast Log*, the *New Alaskan* and the *Southeast Empire*, for example – also failed because of the cost of communications, news and ad collection, and newspaper distribution.

Only the twenty-thousand-circulation *Capital City Weekly*, more of a shopper, was prospering after twenty-four years of publication as a free circulation weekly throughout the Panhandle when it was sold to the *Empire* in 2004.

The DeLongs were statehood advocates. *Empire* publisher Helen Monsen was not. DeLongs supported Gov. Ernest Gruening and his proposed tax reforms. Monsen did not.

DeLongs lose to 'Bobbsey Twins'

DeLongs criticized the "long-winded editorials" full of misleading statements by Austin E. (Cap) Lathrop's "high-powered editorial import from Chicago" (Bill Strand at the *Fairbanks Daily News-Miner*) blaming all of Alaska's ills on the present governor. Reference was made to anti-statehood speeches delivered in Seattle and Washington DC by Lathrop's secretary, Miriam Dickey, and by Mrs. Monsen:

> Other editorial buds which have popped with spring may be viewed in the statements by those Bobbsey Twins from the old Lathrop-Troy menage, Miriam Dickey and Helen Monsen. Having stabbed the statehood movement in the back from the relatively safe positions offered by distant Seattle and distant Washington, D.C., both dollar darlings wisely chose refuge in Europe rather than return to Alaska where their opinions are at variance with the majority vote.

So said an editorial April 19, 1948, in the *Sunday Press*. A month later, the DeLongs were gone and Dorothy H. Pegues, wife of a former *Empire* editor John E. Pegues, was the editor of the *Alaska Sunday Press*.

Mrs. Pegues was born Dorothy Elaine Haley in Juneau on January 12, 1900, the daughter of Edward J. Haley, a placer gold miner at Pine Creek near Atlin, British Columbia

After graduating from the University of Washington, Dorothy Haley's first newspaper job was as a reporter for *Stroller's Weekly*. Later, she was a reporter for *The Anchorage Daily Times*.

The Pegueses were living in Fairbanks, where John was on the staff of *Jessen's Weekly*, when the *Sunday Press* job was offered to Dorothy. When she took over the *Sunday Press*, John did some editorial writing for it until his death on September 21, 1949.

After the *Press* lost money for several years, the *Empire* replaced Dorothy Pegues in August 1950 with Lew M. Williams Jr. from Wrangell. Being skilled in both newspaper production and commercial printing – and with the help of Russell G. Maynard, who had similar experience from the time that his family owned the *Nome Nugget* – Williams improved the paper's finances.

Mrs. Pegues worked a few years at Miner Publishing Company, the former Tom Selby job printing shop in Juneau owned by Jack and Jean Gucker. In 1960, she became society editor for the *Fairbanks Daily News-Miner*.

Williams held the *Sunday Press* position for only six months. Then he was obliged to move back to Wrangell to take charge of the family-owned *Sentinel* from his ailing sister, Jane. Maynard succeeded Williams at the *Press*.

Three months after Maynard took over, the paper folded with the May 15, 1951, edition.

The Independent appears

The *Empire* had the Juneau newspaper field to itself only briefly. Folding of the *Press* encouraged competition. A weekly tabloid, the *Juneau Independent*, made its debut on September 4, 1952, with Jack E. McFarland, editor, Ervin H. Jensen, associate editor and John C. (Jack) Doyle, business manager. The paper was printed by Gucker's Miner Publishing Company.

McFarland and Jensen were disgruntled former *Empire* reporters. Doyle had been an assistant in the office of Gov. Ernest Gruening before Gruening was replaced by the Eisenhower Administration.

The *Empire* forecast the *Independent*'s demise in three weeks and when that did not happen, the *Empire* suggested that its survival was due to the governor's financial backing, whereupon the *Independent* responded:

We actually do have the governor's backing. Governor Gruening coughed up his five dollars for a year's subscription with a smile. The fiver and the smile were both welcome, although I personally suspect the smile was one of relief. With the pack after him for so long (with lead dog *Empire* snatching fangs full of pants week after week), he probably felt even a starving new pup might be a diversion.

The *Independent*'s support of Gruening's programs countered the criticism by the *Empire*. After the libel suit filed against the *Empire* in 1952 by Gruening, Henry Roden and Frank Metcalf, and after the national election that swept Republican Dwight Eisenhower into office, the volume of the *Empire*'s editorial rhetoric lessened.

President Eisenhower appointed B. Frank Heintzleman, the Forest Service's Alaska regional forester, as Gruening's successor in April 1953. There was no more Gruening over whom to debate.

With the change in Alaska and national politics, with Juneau's slumping economy and with internal problems at the *Empire*, and the pending libel suit, Mrs. Monsen and her sister, Dorothy Lingo of Anchorage, sold the Empire Printing Co. on June 1, 1955, to William Prescott Allen, of Montrose, Colorado.

Allen immediately made changes. In a front-page box notice on June 7, the *Empire* announced an increase in advertising and circulation rates. "Heavy losses over the past five years are forcing the change."

Allen had published the *Montrose Press* for twelve years and the *Laredo* (Texas) *Times* for over thirty years, together with his son, William Prescott Jr., and his nephew, Allen K. Tish.

For the three years that Allen owned the *Empire* his management contrasted sharply with the more conservative Troy-Monsen years.

Empire publisher claims privilege

In February 1956, eight months after purchasing the *Empire*, a Fort Worth, Texas, judge ordered publisher Allen to jail and fined him $100 for contempt of court. Citing reporter's privilege, he had refused to tell a grand jury the source of an editorial, charging that gambling flourished in Fort Worth.

The distinguished-looking, sixty-year-old publisher was released after a night in jail. The fine was lifted after he agreed to appear before the grand jury. He told jurors that his editorial was based on an anonymous letter.

While he was testifying before the grand jury, a quick cleanup of gambling ensued and the Fort Worth City Council outlawed all types of coin-operated games. It could be said that Allen made his point.

Texas Gov. Allan Shivers said he was "shocked" at Allen's overnight jailing because, he said, a newspaperman was bound by the ethics of his profession to "protect his sources of information."

The Fort Worth incident was the lead story in the press section of the March 3, 1956, edition of *Time Magazine*.

Charles makes early privilege claim

Alaska journalists from early days have claimed reporter's privilege and have been alert to the threat of prior restraint. In 1905, pioneer Alaska newsman Sid Charles was the first Alaska reporter to claim reporter's privilege. He was working for the *Fairbanks News*.

Charles refused to reveal the source for his story about the Blue Parka Bandit. The bandit was robbing gold miners carrying gold dust to town from the creeks. He was garbed in a blue parka with the hood drawn about his face.

Charles wrote that he had seen the bandit in Fairbanks, whereupon he was subpoenaed to appear before a grand jury to reveal the background of his story. He appeared, refused to reveal his sources and was charged with contempt. When he appeared before Judge James Wickersham, the judge rapped his gavel and said, "One dollar and costs. Court dismissed." That ended it.

Modern journalists should be aware that Judge Wickersham moved to Alaska from Tacoma, Washington. In his diaries, he wrote that after he arrived in Alaska he received a letter from an old friend, Edward Miller, business manager of the *Tacoma Daily News*. Miller asked Wickersham to extend a hand of friendship to young Charles, a new arrival in Alaska from Tacoma.

Journalists are advocating a federal reporter shield law, especially after *New York Times* reporter Judith Miller was charged with contempt of court in 2005 for not revealing a source. She served 85 days in jail. Alaska has a shield law covering more than journalists. Under current Alaska law, Sec. 09.25.300, "a public official or reporter may not be compelled to disclose the source of information procured or obtained while acting in the course of duties as a public official or reporter."

However, there are exceptions, so it is a conditional privilege that can be challenged in court. The court may modify the privilege if, in the opinion of the court, the privilege would result in a miscarriage of justice or the denial of a fair trial, or to be contrary to the public interest. Privilege can be claimed in testimony before any state or local agency

Juneau prior restraint nixed

Prior restraint is another threat to journalists. One of the notable Alaska cases, while it occurred in Juneau in 1979, it did not involve a reporter.

An employee of the Legislature, Sharman Haley, appeared at a rally on the Capitol steps and made a speech critical of multinational corporations. She refused her supervisor's request to refrain from giving further speeches and was fired. The Alaska Supreme Court ruled in 1984 that her firing was wrong because her boss's ultimatum "constituted an impermissible prior restraint on Haley's anticipated speech."

The famous Pentagon Papers case involving the *New York Times* and the *Washington Post* was cited by the court. It said that lacking "justification for imposition of such a restraint" it was a violation of the First Amendment protecting free speech. In the Pentagon Papers case, the federal government unsuccessfully sought to keep the newspapers from printing documents from a classified study on Vietnam War policy.

Nebraska newspapers were successful in a case similar to one later faced by Alaska reporters. The Nebraska case was decided by the U.S. Supreme Court in favor of the newspapers. A man was charged with murdering six people in Sutherland, Nebraska, in 1975. (That's two fewer victims than when a fishing boat was burned at Craig in 1982.)

A district court judge in Nebraska in 1976 prohibited reporting or commentating on judical proceedings held in public (the Sutherland murder trial) until after a jury was empaneled. The Nebraska Press Association took the matter to the Nebraska Supreme Court, which modified the order only slightly. So the press association went to the U.S. Supreme Court that issued an opinion June 30, 1976. The justices acknowledged there is a conflict between two constitutional rights, a right to an impartial jury and freedom of the press. It decided for the press association.

Like reporter privilege, freedom from prior restraint is not absolute. The U.S. Supreme Court decision in the Pentagon Papers said "only governmental allegation and proof that publication must inevitably, directly, and immediately cause the occurrence of an event kindred to imperiling the safety of a transport already at sea can support even the issuance of an interim restraining order" against publication.

So the government must have exceptional reason for prior restraint, which it lacked in the *State of Alaska vs. Haley* and the *New York Times Co. vs. the United States*. However, it is implied that there might be an occasion for such justification.

The almost case and a Web site

In 1999, the *Juneau Empire* was involved in a legal action that could have led to a prior restraint case. However, a judge defused the threat by not acting on a motion to delay publication of a story based on a public document.

The controversy stemmed from the newspaper's attempt to obtain details of a lawsuit filed by Halter Marine Group of Mississippi against the state. Halter Marine built the Alaska ferry *Kennicott* for $77 million and delivered it in 1999. The Mississippi company's lawsuit sought an additional $46 million from the state. Halter Marine said that change orders issued by the state drove up the cost.

In July 1999, the *Empire* filed a Freedom of Information request with the state, seeking records of the vessel's construction costs. Halter Marine went to court to stop the state from releasing the information, saying that release of labor cost figures would undermine its ability to compete with other ship builders.

On a Friday morning, Juneau Superior Court Judge Patricia Collins ruled in favor of the newspaper and ordered the material released. The story missed that Friday afternoon's publishing deadline, so it was posted on the newspaper's Web site.

Later in the day, Halter Marine asked Collins to stay the order while the company considered an appeal of her order to the Alaska Supreme Court. It claimed that labor rate information in the documents was proprietary. Before the situation developed further, Halter Marine withdrew its motion.

John McKay, an Anchorage attorney who specializes in media law, said at the time that the stay order probably would have been invalid because the paper had already legally obtained the documents and published a story on the Web, making the information available to a wide audience.

Allen's Antics, they were called

Those Alaskans who expected the change in ownership of the *Empire* to Allen to be an improvement were in for a disappointment. During the three years of his ownership, Allen's bizarre antics and irrational comments netted him national headlines and an unflattering image. He promoted the idea that Alaska should seek commonwealth status instead of statehood.

He is given credit for raising the commonwealth issue in Alaska. However, three months before he purchased the *Empire*, Mrs. Monsen's editorial quoted a *Collier's* magazine article suggesting commonwealth and concluded, "Frankly, as of now, we'll take commonwealth."

And two months before Allen bought the *Empire*, another editorial listed the results of a poll of Juneau residents taken by KINY radio. It showed commonwealth status favored by 185 compared with 175 for statehood now, 104 for statehood later and thirty-seven for staying as a territory.

The *Ketchikan Alaska Chronicle* warned that stories involving Allen should not be taken lightly because Allen had confided to some Alaskans that he hoped to be appointed governor of the territory. Allen said he was a personal friend of U.S. Sen. Lyndon Johnson, D-Texas, Senate majority leader, who could help him get the appointment.

Allen's seemingly off-the-cuff editorial comments lacked coherence. There were a series of vindictive personal slurs against Alaska Tennessee-Plan U.S. senators Gruening and Bill Egan, who Alaskans sent to Washington to lobby for statehood. Allen labeled them "phonies."

On another occasion, he called Gruening "the most able politician ever to come to this great territory." Then he switched back to relegate the former governor to a "minority lunatic fringe." Still later, when

Gruening visited Juneau, Allen honored him with a breakfast in the Gold Room of the Baranof Hotel, inviting one hundred civic leaders.

Sundborg to Independent

Despite the *Empire*'s disfavor in some circles in Juneau, there wasn't enough dissatisfaction that the *Juneau Independent* could attract sufficient advertising. Most business people were as conservative as the *Empire* publishers, and they needed the advantage of more frequent publication of a daily over a weekly.

So an ownership reorganization took place at the *Independent* on September 1, 1954, with George Sundborg taking over as managing editor and as one of the owners.

Sundborg had been a victim of the change of administration to Eisenhower. Sundborg, a Democrat, was replaced in the governor's office by a Republican, R. N. (Bob) DeArmond, former *Ketchikan Daily News* managing editor.

Sundborg was city editor of *Gray's Harbor Daily Washingtonian*, Hoquiam, Washington, until December 1938 when he moved to Juneau as a reporter and editorial writer for the *Empire*. He replaced Lew M. Williams Sr. who, with his wife, Winifred, bought the *Wrangell Sentinel*.

The Sundborgs moved to Portland, Oregon, in 1942 where he held a variety of government positions. Then it was back to Juneau in 1946 to be general manager of the Alaska Development Board, 1946-47, and later assistant to Governor Gruening.

Sundborg said the field for journalists in Juneau was limited in 1953. So he took the offer to buy into the *Independent* "not as a way to make my fortune but rather as giving me a voice to champion statehood and other issues."

Under Sundborg's management, the *Independent* became a lively and interesting paper. Jack McFarland continued writing his "Cabbages & Kings" colum. It was full of political gossip. The paper won the 1953-54 Outstanding News Coverage award from the Alaska Press Club.

On February 20, 1955, the *Independent* became a Sunday morning paper and free copies were delivered on every doorstep in town. It carried United Press news in its twenty-page edition, plus eight pages of colored comics. The *Independent* purchased the Assembly of God

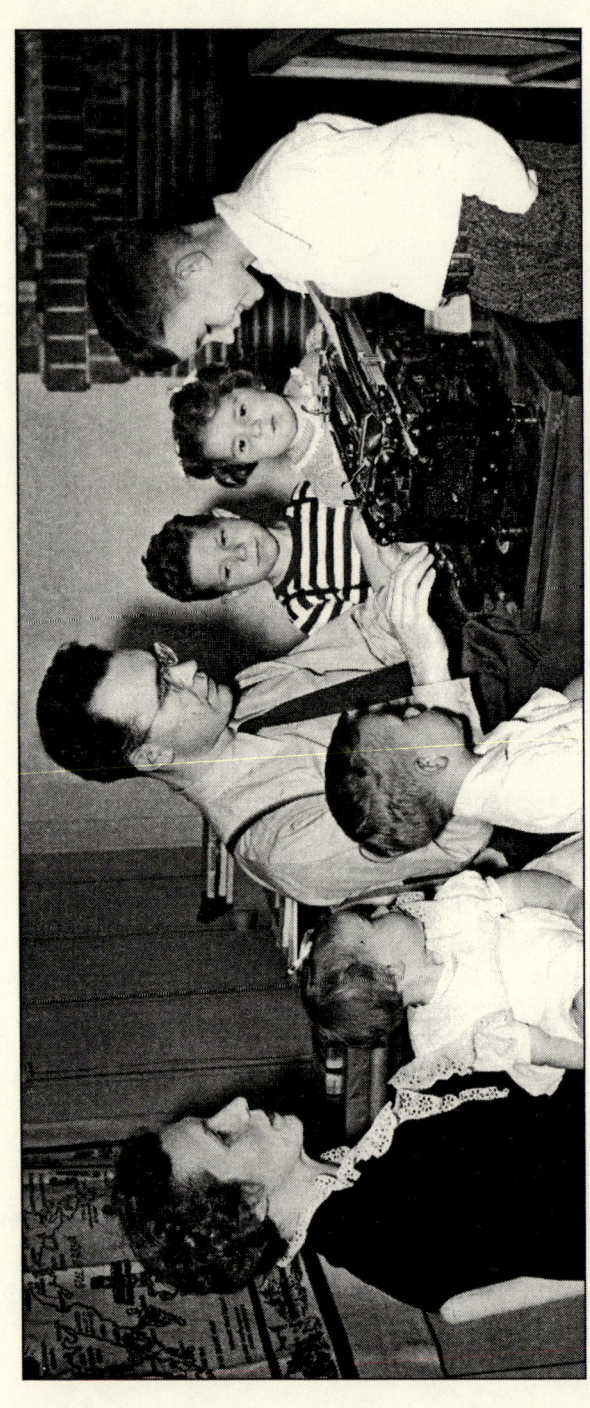

The Sundborgs—George Sundborg at the typewriter early in his extensive Alaska newspaper career is watched by his wife Mary and their children, left to right, Sarah, Stephen, George Jr., Rosemary and Pierre. Sundborg was editorial writer for the Juneau Empire, 1938-41; editor of the Juneau Independent, 1951-56; and editor of the Fairbanks Daily News-Miner, 1957-58. He also was a delegate to the Alaska Constitutional Convention, served as assistant to Gov. Ernest Gruening, as general manager of the Alaska Development Board and as administrative assistant to U.S. Senator Ernest Gruening. –*Photo courtesy George Sundborg.*

building at Fourth and Franklin, together with $18,000 in new equipment so it could typeset and print its own product instead of farming it out.

Money was tight for the new owners, Sundborg, McFarland and Doyle. They cut their wages to $75 a week in order to pay their three backshop staffers. They had some volunteer help. Vern Metcalfe wrote a weekly sports column called "Speaking of Sports." That was later changed to "Speaking of (just about everything except) Sports."

Metcalfe was a Democratic activist who served in the House in the 1951 and 1955 Territorial Legislatures. Metcalfe also was editor of the paper during the winter of 1955-56 when Sundborg was in Fairbanks as a delegate to Alaska Constitutional Convention.

Other volunteers included attorney Tom Stewart, later a state judge. He also was the constitutional convention secretary. Jane McMullin, who became Stewart's wife, was an *Independent* volunteer, along with Doris Anne Bartlett, daughter of Delegate and Mrs. Bartlett, and Mrs. Simon Helenthal, widow of a U.S. district court judge.

After McFarland left to teach school in Hoonah, Sundborg continued the "Cabbages and Kings" column for five years, although he didn't like the plagiarism of the title from O. Henry. The column broke a few important stories. Sundborg says that for years afterward oldtimers identified him with the column.

Sundborg sold the *Independent* in 1957 to an Anchorage corporation, First Alaska Investment. After he sold the *Independent*, Sundborg went to Fairbanks as managing editor of the *News-Miner*.

After four editors in two years, the *Independent* was sold to the Trans-Alaska Corporation of Seward. It suspended publication on April 29, 1959.

Legislature challenges reporter

Despite publisher Allen's publicized antics, the *Empire* produced a weak editorial page during his ownership. A front-page story February 7, 1957, described the visit of Interior Secretary Fred Seaton to the Alaska Legislature during its session in Juneau. On the editorial page the lead editorial was headlined, "Encouraging Visit." But the visit was about that of the British defense minister to the United States, not about Seaton's visit to Alaska. The second editorial, "Stand Together," encouraged European nations to stand together against Russia.

Seaton, a Kansas-Nebraska newspaper publisher, might have wondered after reading the *Empire*, should he finish his visit to a territory managed by his department, or run to warn the Swedes about Russia.

The *Empire* did have a colorful reporter, Bob Kederick, who wrote a column, "All Around Alaska." In one column he wrote: "*Most Unpleasant Rumor of the Year.* It's being wagged around that some of the boys are trying to get close to some of the legislators with that green folding stuff. Rumor (and that's all it is, as far as I know) has it that one particular bill now pending in the Legislature is such a plumb to somebody, that $$$$ in four figures is offered."

Rep. Richard Greuel, House speaker from Fairbanks, responded the next day that the "rumor was totally irresponsible and without basis in fact," and that printing it was "irresponsible." He appointed a committee to investigate.

Kederick got in another dig the next day with a brief column on the front page: "*The House and I* – Due to an engagement with a special investigating committee of the House of Representatives, this column is abbreviated today.

"The committee and I will chat about rumors that have been – and still are – floating around the night spots, corridors, ante rooms and sidewalks of Juneau.

"After the investigation, which was ordered by the Speaker of the House, I assume the lower legislative chamber will be permitted to return to work on such incidental matters as budgets and taxes."

Kederick didn't plead reporter privilege, possibly enjoying the notoriety and publicity for his column. He met with the House committee for forty minutes. Afterward, Committee Chairman Rep. Robert Ziegler said in a report, "although the rumor was worthy of publication as legitimate news, the manner in which it was written was irresponsible."

Kederick continued to write his political gossip column, needling lawmakers. In one paragraph a few weeks later, he inserted: "Now mind you, this is only a rumor."

Chapter 51

Reynolds, to Morris, to Courtroom Photos

William Prescott Allen suffered a series of strokes in 1958. After he regained his ability to walk and talk in 1959, he sold the *Daily Alaska Empire* on January 1, 1960, to Donald W. Reynolds. Also, Allen's idea of commonwealth status for Alaska had died when Alaska became a state on January 3, 1959.

Reynolds headed the Donrey Media Group that published thirteen newspapers in Arkansas, Oklahoma, Texas, Nevada, Washington, and Hawaii. Donrey also had television and radio stations.

Robert L. Brown, a news executive with the Reynolds chain, replaced Joe Kirkbride as managing editor of the *Empire* and also succeeded Morgan Coe as general manager. Brown moved to Juneau from Rogers, Arkansas, where he had been editor and general manager of Donrey's *Rogers Daily News* for the previous eighteen months. He was the first of nine editors Reynolds employed at the *Empire* in the ten years he owned it.

Empire goes offset with new name

On July 22, 1964, the name of the paper appeared as *Juneau Alaska Empire* instead of *Daily Alaska Empire*. (It had changed in 1926 from *Alaska Daily Empire* to *Daily Alaska Empire*.) On this same date the new offset newspaper press went into operation. The *Empire* was the first Alaska daily paper to go offset.

On August 1, 1965, Albro Gregory became managing editor of the *Empire*. He had just finished four years with the *Ketchikan Daily News*.

Gregory exhibited a journalistic self-confidence that had been missing at the *Empire*. The frequent turnover of editors had weakened the paper's influence on local issues. Lacking competition after the *Independent* folded, the *Empire* could proceed at a lackadaisical pace.

It also was stifled because the editorial staff waited constantly as the mechanical staff fought problems of setting type on the early, unreliable Justowriter typesetters used by small offset newspapers. The quality of printing suffered.

Despite production problems, with Gregory at the helm, the *Empire* was outspoken in local affairs. On the capital relocation issue, Gregory was as adamantly opposed as his fellow Southeast colleagues but he warned that if adequate housing was not provided for the legislators and their families, the issue would not die.

Photographer, magistrate collide

Gregory became embroiled in a freedom of the press incident in which he was not an original participant. While he was covering the Amchitka nuclear test, two *Empire* employees were threatened with contempt charges by a local magistrate. Photographer Lael Morgan, later a journalism professor at the University of Alaska Fairbanks, took a picture of a defendant charged with assault with a deadly weapon, while he sat in the public corridor outside the courtroom. He had given his consent.

Magistrate Thomas Schulz told Morgan that the picture could not be published. Acting editor Chuck Hoyt telephoned the magistrate to say that the picture would be published unless he received a written order forbidding it. No order arrived and the picture was published.

Morgan and Hoyt were ordered to appear in court to explain why they should not be punished for contempt of court. Thereupon, Augie Hiebert, president of the Alaska Broadcasters' Association, said the radio-television group, representing the entire Alaska news industry, opposed Schulz's action and would come to the defense of the accused.

Schulz dropped the contempt charges but simultaneously issued a written order banning all forms of photography or broadcasting in the corridors outside the courtrooms during the course of any judicial proceedings.

On his return to Juneau, Gregory wrote an editorial on "Throttling the Press," labeling Magistrate Schulz's action "capricious and arbitrary," and without foundation in law or judicial prerogative.

In the next session of the State Legislature the lawmakers made it unlawful for any government agency to prohibit or restrict public access to, or movement in, a public corridor of a public building; unless access or movement was prohibited by statute or ordinance.

The legislators might dictate guidelines for reporters' conduct in public buildings but their guidelines did not extend to the governor's office, which had its own policy. Gov. Walter Hickel disapproved of the *Empire's* handling of news stories emanating from the governor's office. Gregory was fired a couple of months after Hickel took office in December 1966. Gregory wrote *Jessen's Weekly* editor Jerome Sheldon that the firing occurred because "Hickel didn't like me."

William James, business manager of the *Empire*, told a different story on why Gregory was fired. It was alleged that Gregory was being paid by some businesses to assure they got favorable mention in news columns. That was a practice of some news editors in the early days of journalism before there was an emphasis on ethics.

Gregory was an old-time United Press journalist, but there was no indication he followed the payoff practice at Ketchikan, Juneau, Petersburg or Nome where he edited. He simply loved to skewer the local establishment, which created a problem for publishers.

Gregory's successor, Hoyt, a former editor of the *Juneau Independent*, also experienced an involuntary abrupt departure from the *Empire's* editorial staff. His feisty style of writing was unacceptable both to the governor and to the *Empire's* James. He antagonized both the legislators and members of the chamber of commerce – "the establishment."

In a departing editorial titled "Juneau to Prague," Hoyt discussed his entanglements with the Juneau "establishment." He said he was besieged by delegations from "various establishment power blocs" every time his editorials touched on "something other than Mom, Apple Pie and Country."

They pressed him to modify his views in accordance with theirs. He concluded it was "the way we might have to respond if we were in Prague." He returned to the *News-Miner* in April 1968 for the last time as sports editor and columnist. He died there in 1974 at age forty-nine.

Allan Adasiak, twenty-seven, a staff writer on the *Empire*, was promoted to editor. One of his first acts at the *Empire* was to change the paper's name again from *Juneau Alaska Empire* to *Southeast Alaska Empire*.

During the years Reynolds owned the *Empire*, he made overtures to buy the *Ketchikan Daily News* to build an Alaska operation large enough to attract more experienced management. The *Empire* alone was not a moneymaker, and in fact, lost money. Reynold's efforts failed. The Paul (Bud) Charles family had agreed to sell their *Ketchikan Daily News* to Lew and Dorothy Williams, formerly of the *Petersburg Press*. The Williamses also owned the *Daily Sentinel* at Sitka at that time.

The Williamses asked to buy the *Empire* but Reynolds sold it instead on March 20, 1969, to the Southeastern Newspapers Corp., of which William S. Morris III, of Augusta, Georgia, was president. William H. James, general manager of the *Empire*, was elevated to vice president. Southeastern Newspapers is now Morris Publishing Group.

First out-of-state paper for Morris

The Augusta-based Morris Corporation owned and operated six Georgia newspapers. The *Empire* was the first newspaper purchased outside of Georgia. By 2005, Morris had nine newspapers in Alaska: the *Empire*, the *Capital City Weekly*, the *Peninsula Clarion* at Kenai, the *Homer News*, the *Alaska Journal of Commerce*, the *Alaska Star*, the *Alaska Oil & Gas Reporter*, the *Alaska Military Weekly*, and the *Alaskan Equipment Trader* in Anchorage. It also owned *Alaska Magazine*, *The Milepost* and *Anchorage Best Read Guide*, and six Anchorage radio stations. Other Morris properties in Alaska included SignPro and Smart Target Marketing in Anchorage.

The Morris family owns forty newspapers nationwide and special publications in England. It also is active in book and magazine publication, outdoor advertising and computer services.

William III, sometime called Billy, is chairman and chief operating officer of Morris Publishing. His family has been in the newspaper business since 1929.

The Morris children are active in the privately held corporation. William IV is president. Susie Morris Baker was vice president in charge of Alaska newspapers, until moving back to Georgia. For a while she also was publisher of the *Clarion* and lived in Kenai and Anchorage. She has been replaced by *Clarion* publisher Stan Pitlo as director of Alaska communications. Tyler Morris is vice president in charge of Cowboy Publications.

Billy Morris picked Jeff Wilson, one of his advertising salesmen in Georgia, to go to Juneau in 1975 as advertising manager for the *Empire*.

Wilson joined the *Augusta Chronicle* in sales at age nineteen. He arrived in Juneau in April 1975. Forty-five days later, he replaced John Stringer, a Juneau man, as general manager when Stringer was beset with personal problems.

Stringer started his own weekly newspaper in Juneau, the *Juneau Independent*, not related to the earlier *Independent*. It lasted from July 1975 until March 1976.

Morris, Wilson, Sampson bring stability

Kim Elton, later a state legislator representing the Juneau area, took over as editor from March 1976 until June 1978. He was followed by Carl Sampson who was a graduate of the University of Alaska Fairbanks.

Sampson attended two years of college in Beloit, Wisconsin, and then went to Fairbanks, where he graduated from UAF in 1975. He ran the *Wrangell Sentinel* for five months and returned to UAF to help with a bicentennial project in 1976. After two years at *The Anchorage Times*, Sampson was hired by the *Empire* as city editor.

Wilson and Sampson epitomized the stability Morris ownership brought to the *Empire*. Wilson was business manager and later publisher for one month short of twenty years, April 1975 to March 1995, the longest term of any *Empire* manager except for founding publisher John Troy. Sampson was with the *Empire* first as city editor but most of the time as managing editor for fourteen years, longer than any other *Empire* managing editor.

When Sampson stepped into the editor's job he stepped into one of the longest and most heated statewide issues – moving the capital from Juneau. Sampson editorially echoed the vehement opposition to moving the capital from Juneau while the townspeople girded themselves for an assault in the 1978 and 1982 referendums. The issue was to rise again and be defeated in the 1990s and in 2002.

A visiting reporter from the *Los Angeles Times* summarized his impressions of the virulence with which the issue was attacked:

> Seven years ago, the people of Alaska voted to move their capital out of this soggy city on the Southeast peninsula, a place distant from Alaska's booming population centers.

Morris Publishing Group

publishes 27 daily, 13 non-daily and numerous free community newspapers in the United States. Head of the company is William S. Morris, III, at the microphone. Morris operates 7 newspapers and six Anchorage radio stations plus the Alaska Magazine, the Milepost and several other business in Alaska from headquarters (Morris Alaska) in Anchorage. The first Alaska acquisition for Morris was the Juneau Empire for which Morris built a new building in 1987, pictured below. *-Photos courtesy of Morris Publishing Group.*

Stability for the Empire

— William S. Morris, III, left above, bought the Juneau Empire in 1969. He brought stability to the Empire with Jeff Wilson, right above, as business manager and later publisher for almost 20 years, the longest term of any Empire manager except for founding publisher John Troy. Also hired was Carl Sampson, right, who was with the Empire as city editor and managing editor for 14 years, longer than any other Empire managing editor. -*Photos courtesy of the Juneau Empire.*

It is clear here only 44 days of the year. The rest of the time it is either rainy, snowy or cloudy. One time, years ago, the governor had to use the Coast Guard to round up the Legislature, which was marooned by bad weather on scattered airstrips.

The capital move has divided this state like nothing else. The battle over moving the capital is in many ways a struggle between two men: *Anchorage Times* publisher Robert Atwood, relentlessly editorializing and building public opinion for the move, and Juneau State Senator Bill Ray, wielding legislative power and wheeling and dealing to keep it where it is.

"It's a remote, inaccessible place, way off the beaten path," Atwood said of Juneau. "The legislators go down there and they're out of touch with the people. I call it the Juneau Syndrome. They aren't reflecting the will of the people."

"I fought that sumbitch with his newspaper right to a standstill," Ray said. "I've threatened, I've promised, I've cajoled – everything. Atwood and his cronies all have a vested interest, man! They've got people who have invested in that whole (Willow) area in real estate. There isn't anyone with a lick of sense in Anchorage who deep in his heart wants to move the capital."

Oil pumps prosperity

Even after Alaska gained statehood in 1959, Juneau and Alaska's economy limped along. Military base construction slowed in northern Alaska. Oil had been discovered at Swanson River on the Kenai and a momentary boom came with discovery of oil at Prudhoe Bay and the subsequent sale of leases on state land in 1969 for $900 million. The Legislature quickly spent that money and construction of the trans-Alaska oil pipeline to Valdez was delayed over environmental concerns until 1974. At one time in the early seventies, the state was close to going broke for lack of revenue.

After the pipeline was completed in the fall of 1977, oil production jumped from sixty-seven million barrels in 1976 to 448 million barrels in 1978 and continued up, bringing the state increased revenue, from a little over $1 billion in 1979 to as high as $4.5 billion in 1982.

That increased revenue led to increased state government spending, which boosted the economy of the state capital and its businesses, including the *Empire*.

A measure of that is that in 1970, the *Ketchikan Daily News* and the *Empire* each had a circulation of about 3,900. The *Daily News* was in a town with a stable timber economy and over the next twenty years saw a growth to five thousand in circulation. By contrast, the *Empire* circulation boomed to 8,800. The number of *Empire* employees grew from fourteen full-time and six part-time in 1969, to thirty-three full-time by the time the *Empire*'s new building was dedicated November 19, 1987, on its seventy-fifth anniversary.

Prosperity attracts competition

The capital's prosperity also brought competition for the *Empire*. Patrick McCarthy, operator of shoppers in Washington State, moved into Alaska in 1980 and began shoppers in Juneau, Valdez, Anchorage, and Fairbanks. They went by titles of *Penny Saver* or *Thrifty Nickel*. In Juneau it was *Thrifty Nickel*.

Among the sales people he hired was Renda Heimbigner, who was born and raised in Juneau, the daughter of Janis and Graham Roundtree. She had earned a degree in marketing at the University of Alaska Fairbanks and with her husband had returned to Juneau. After six months, McCarthy sold all of his shoppers. David and Renda Heimbigner bought the Juneau *Thrifty Nickel*. The name was changed to *Nickel Weekly* and later to *Capital City Weekly*, its current title.

David left the business after a year to go into another business and Renda began expanding the shopper operation. She and Chuck Auchberger printed the *Southeast Alaska Business Journal* for a few years. She later bought the *Boat Broker* and started another shopper, the *Hot Sheet*.

Meantime, the *Capital City Weekly* had expanded into a free circulation weekly newspaper serving all of Southeast.

Empire moves with growth

The *Empire*'s growth led to two location changes under Morris ownership. Morris bought the Alaska Electric Light and Power building on Franklin Street across from the Baranof Hotel in 1977 to acquire more space. The *Empire* quickly outgrew that so Morris began looking for a new location in 1983.

He selected the present site at 3100 Channel Drive, three miles north of downtown Juneau. He moved the *Empire* into a new $10 million building there in February 1987. The building housed new press units to boost its capacity. It was fully computerized with a custom-designed system by Compudat, a subsidiary of Morris Publishing.

Larry Persily and his wife, Leslie Murray, had moved to Juneau after selling the *Wrangell Sentinel* in 1984. Persily worked in Juneau for *The Anchorage Times*, The Associated Press, and as a state ombudsman investigator. Murray was editor of the *Empire's* seventy-fifth anniversary edition and had most of it together when she was killed in a car crash near the *Empire* on September 30, 1987.

Larry Persily joined the *Empire* in 1990 as city editor and moved up to managing editor when Sampson left in 1992. He stayed until 1995 when he started his own weekly, *The Paper*.

He started the paper with almost $300,000 from investors and personal savings. He called it a job opportunity for several journalists who had left the *Empire* after a new publisher changed the news focus to short, spot news reporting at the expense of in-depth articles.

The first issue of *The Paper* was published in November 1995 and the last in January of 1997. It was a thirty-two-page tabloid most of its life, reaching a circulation high of about two thousand. In its good months, it grossed $25,000 but still lost $8,000.

The Paper disclosed an illegal property tax break the city assembly had granted owners of a local mine. Exposure ended the break. And it revealed the city's effort to grant a no-interest loan to a developer who was years behind in his property and sales tax payments. The city retracted its loan offer.

"As with many new businesses, I started out undercapitalized and finished the same way," Persily said. "I should have turned over the business operation to someone else and not tried to run the business and the news pages."

After *The Paper* folded, Persily went to work for the state and was deputy commissioner of the Department of Revenue in the final years of the administration of Gov. Tony Knowles. In 2004, he became Juneau correspondent and government affairs editor for the *Petroleum News*, and in 2005, legislative reporter for the *Anchorage Daily News*. In October 2005 he was named editorial page editor for the *Daily News*.

Agnes the cat supervises or enjoys the warmth of a computer while co-editor Larry Persily works on an issue of the Wrangell Sentinel. The cat was named by his late wife, Leslie Murray, right, after a character in "Auntie Mame." Larry and Leslie published the Wrangell Sentinel 1976-84 and then moved to Juneau. Larry has worked as a capital correspondent for The Anchorage Times, The Associated Press, Petroleum News and Anchorage Daily News. He also was a managing editor for the Juneau Empire and owned and operated a weekly newspaper, The Paper, in Juneau 1995-1997. Leslie was a reporter for the Juneau Empire and editing its 75th anniversary edition in 1987 when she was killed in an auto accident near the Empire. The edition was dedicated to her.-*Photos courtesy of Larry Persily.*

Juneau Empire–2005

Robert Hale
Publisher

Lori Thomson
Managing Editor

Juneau Empire Photos

Empire management after Wilson

The *Empire* began a Sunday edition in September 1991 and started a weekly shopper early in the nineties, the *Southeast Empire* with fifteen thousand in circulation throughout the Panhandle outside of Juneau.

In March 1995, Wilson was promoted in the Morris chain to publisher of the thirty-four thousand-circulation *Athens Daily News* in Wilson's home state of Georgia. He was replaced in Juneau by John Winter.

Winter was promoted from the *Augusta Chronicle*'s Washington DC bureau chief in 1992 to publisher of the *Empire*. In the fall of 2000, he was named business manager of the twenty-five thousand circulation *Grand Island Independent* in Nebraska.

Before going to Nebraska, Winter hired Steve Reed, a widely experienced newsman, as managing editor of the *Empire*. Reed moved to Juneau after five years as publisher of a Colorado weekly, the *Gunnison Country Times*. Prior to that he spent eight years as Dallas bureau chief for the *Houston Chronicle*, and before that spent fourteen years with United Press International in Texas, London and Moscow.

The *Empire* started 2001 with a new publisher, Don Smith, fifty. He had been manager of Morris's Colorado holdings for the previous five years including as publisher of the 5,500-circulation *Glenwood Post*. He also managed five weekly publications. He had been publisher in Yankton, South Dakota, before going to Colorado.

In 2004, there was another switch with Robert O. Hale named publisher when Smith transferred to Grand Island, Nebraska. The new publisher came to the *Empire* after ten years as publisher of a paper in Monroe, Georgia. At the same time, Lori Thomson was promoted from design editor to managing editor when Reed left for the Pioneer Press in St. Paul. She graduated from Duke University with a bachelor's degree and from the University of Illinois with a master's. Thomson reported for the *Petersburg Pilot* before joining the *Empire*.

Photo emphasis, court collide

The photo offset method for printing, which swept the Alaska daily newspaper industry starting with the *Empire* in 1964, enabled newspapers to print pictures more easily, especially for the *Empire* after it moved into its new, well-equipped building on Channel Drive. Full color local photos appeared daily.

The *Ketchikan Daily News* also added press units to allow it to more easily produce color pictures and advertisements. As a result, both newspapers for the first time began employing full-time photographers in the 1980s. Before then only the larger publications, such as those in Anchorage and Fairbanks, could afford a full-time photographer.

Mark Kelley joined the *Empire* in August 1979 as its first full-time photographer. He took time off from the *Empire* in 1984-85 to earn a master's degree at Ohio University. Brian Wallace, one of four photographers Kelley trained at the *Empire*, filled in while he was in school. Kelley had been allowed to hire photographer interns to ease the work load.

Kelley had several conflicts with the legal system while a news photographer. He succeeded in obtaining State Sen. George Hohman's picture when the senator was on trial in 1983. And in another case, the *Empire* succeeded in quashing a subpoena to obtain Kelley's film.

Mark Kelley, left, was the first full time photographer for the Juneau Empire after the newspaper's switch to offset made picture publishing more practical. He trained his successor, Brian Wallace, and runs his own photography business. -*Photo courtesy of Owen Kelley.*

Wallace was born in Juneau December 20, 1960, the son of a prominent Tlingit family. He learned photography and practiced it in Juneau-Douglas High School, from which he graduated in 1980, and started working part-time for the *Empire*.

In 1990, after Kelley left the *Empire*, Wallace went full-time until 1995, when Michael Penn joined the staff to share the job with Wallace.

Penn had worked for the McClatchy newspaper chain at the *Sacramento Bee* in California and moved to Alaska as a photographer on McClatchy's *Anchorage Daily News*.

After *Empire* reporter and photographer Morgan and acting managing editor Hoyt tangled with Magistrate Schulz over taking pictures in the halls of the capitol – it also served as the court building at that time – more situations arose. Those led to agreements between the court system and newspapers over photography in court buildings, courtrooms and in the surrounding area.

The *Ketchikan Daily News* had employed several photographers for short terms until Hall Anderson joined the newspaper in 1984, and was still there after twenty years. Anderson attended the University of Oregon and earned a bachelor's degree in psychology in 1981 and also studied photography.

Anderson quickly was thrown into the controversy between the court system and the newspaper over photographic reporting, and again it involved Schulz.

Peel case forces guidelines

At the end of Anderson's first week of full-time work at the *Daily News*, he photographed murder suspect John Kenneth Peel, accused of murdering eight people aboard a fishing boat. Anderson took the picture while Peel was being transported in a patrol car near the Ketchikan court building. Anderson was immediately taken by an Alaska State Trooper to the chambers of Superior Court Judge Thomas Schulz.

Schulz had moved up from magistrate since his run-in with the *Empire* over photographing a suspect in a hallway of a state building. Anderson's camera and film were confiscated. Anderson was released while the judge pondered his next move and listened to an appeal by the *Daily News* attorney, Geoffrey Currall.

Judge Schulz had ordered that no photos be taken on court property but Anderson's photo had been taken from across the street. After two hours, Anderson's camera and film were returned to him. The photo, a picture of Peel through the rear window of a trooper's car, was published. However, the incident led to guidelines on news coverage before Peel's trial started in 1986.

Peel was charged specifically with murdering eight people aboard the seine boat *Investor* at Craig, and then attempting to burn the boat and the bodies. The *Investor* owner, Mark Colthurst, and his wife and two children and four crew members were salmon fishing in Alaska from their homes in Bellingham, Washington. Peel, who had worked on the *Investor* in a previous season, also was from Bellingham. So there was heightened interest outside of Ketchikan in the case.

Peel was to be tried in Ketchikan, the nearest superior court to Craig. News media representatives flocked to Ketchikan. *Daily News* photographer Anderson was inundated with requests for pictures.

Judge Schulz called a meeting with court personnel, attorneys and Ketchikan media representatives to agree on ground rules for photography. By that time, Schulz was the presiding judge for Southeast Alaska. That meant that the agreement also would have impact in all Southeast state courts.

The agreement ironed out in November 1984, shortly after the incident with Anderson, was later adopted statewide by the state court system, and with minor changes, became part of the Alaska Court System's media plan.

The court system had experimented with cameras in the courtroom in Anchorage in 1978 and adopted its first Electronic Media Plan in 1979. It was modified again in 1982. Between 1982 and 1984 only ten requests for media camera coverage were granted out of twenty-two requests because defendants had to give permission to be photographed.

University of Alaska Fairbanks journalism professor Dean Gottehrer appealed to the Alaska Supreme Court outlining reasons for broadening camera rules. So with the high profile case coming up in Ketchikan, and Gottehrer's appeal, the plan was changed in March 1985 to eliminate the defendant's consent.

Peel's arraignment came in 1984, before the March 1985 rule change. So the newspaper and Peel counsel worked out an agreement whereby the newspaper wouldn't photograph Peel outside the court if the newspaper was granted permission to photograph in court.

The complication was that part of the case against Peel was based upon witnesses identifying him. So *Daily News* photographer Anderson refrained from photographing Peel in court except when he appeared in a ski mask. He confined his photography to counsel and witnesses.

Judge Schulz extended the agreement worked out by the *Daily News* and Peel to all media covering the trial. For the Peel case, the media was assigned its own room to conduct interviews and take pictures to encourage them from blocking the small hall and lobby. Extra copies of all public papers filed in the case were produced for the media. Television cameras were allowed but could be moved only during recesses.

After the trial, a long-term agreement was developed for coverage of court proceedings in Ketchikan and the points are included in the statewide media plan. Most of the requests by the media for coverage are made in Anchorage courts but the high-profile mass murder in the Ketchikan area emphasized the need for the new statewide plan.

That plan is Alaska Court Rule 50, Media Coverage of Court Proceedings. It requires applying for permission to cover a case, protects jurors from being photographed, and limits coverage in divorce, domestic violence, sexual offenses or custody hearings unless the participants agree. It allows the judge to deny coverage to insure a fair trial and prevent distractions. So the guarantee of court coverage, like reporter privilege and protection from prior restraint, is not absolute.

The jury deadlocked on the first Peel case so he was retried in Juneau. The state court system agreement on photography was ineffective there because the case was tried in a federal court building because of space requirements. Federal rules applied even though the presiding judge was State Superior Court Judge Walter Carpeneti. Under federal rules that meant absolutely no pictures.

However, thanks to the pioneering actions of the *Juneau Empire* and the *Ketchikan Daily News*, the appeal of a university journalism professor, and cooperation of Southeast judges and lawyers, an agreement is in effect statewide. It protects the freedom of the press, the decorum of the courts, the rights of the accused and victims, and the public's right to know.

Chapters 52-54

Peninsula Journalists Lead Fight on Public Records and Meetings

Newspapers shouldn't play with their credibility too often.

– John Marrs, editor
Peninsula Clarion, 1985

HOMER NEWS
Celebrating 40 years as Homer's news source

Homer, Alaska • Vol. 31, No. 49 — Thursday, December 9, 2004 — 75 Cents

Counting the costs of alcohol abuse
Troubled families, birth defects, health-care expenses all part of the price

SOUTHEAST ALASKA'S
Island News

25¢ Copy

Week of January 31, 2005 — SERVING PRINCE OF WALES SINCE 1981 — Volume 24, Number 5

| Cape Pole | Coffman Cove | Craig | Edna Bay | Hollis | Hydaburg | Kasaan | Klawock | Meyers Chuck |
| Naukati | Point Baker | Port Protection | Saltery Cove | Thorne Bay | Waterfall | Whale Pass |

Federal Subsistence Board approves changes to fisheries regs

The Federal Subsistence Board's adopted new fisheries regulations for Southeast Alaska, including a regulation to establish a subsistence fishery for steelhead trout throughout Southeast. The Board adopted these regulations at its January 11-13 meeting in Anchorage. The new regulations are effective April 1st, 2005 through March 31st, 2006.

Under the new Southeast steelhead regulation, qualified rural residents possessing a subsistence fishing permit may harvest steelhead from January 1st thru May 31st. The daily household harvest and possession limit is one fish, with an annual with data about harvest locations. In addition, Federal fishery managers, in consultation with the Alaska Department of Fish & Game, will have the authority to limit harvest & provide special protection on streams where there are conservation concerns. The new regulation won't affect the existing Federal subsistence steelhead fishery on POW Island.

The Board also adopted regulations modifying harvest limits for trout, Dolly Varden, and grayling in Southeast. Under these new regulations, the daily household harvest & possession limit is 20 Dolly Varden, 20 grayling and 20 brook trout. The

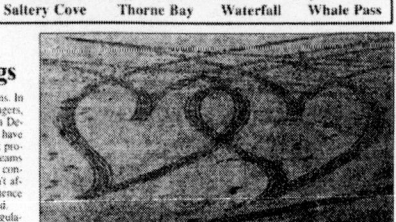

Hearts in the snow anyone?
This hearts pattern was seen in the snow at the Klawock Heenya parking lot in Klawock. It was sent with this note: thought this was different, a sign of hope, a fluke? Who knows, but I enjoyed it.

ICY PASSAGES $1.50

Volume 12 Number 4 — The Newspaper of GUSTAVUS — APRIL 2005

| New counseling director hired - page 3 | School vandal pleads guilty - page 6 |

Serving Haines and Klukwan since 1966

Chilkat Valley News

Volume XXXV Number 31 — Thursday, August 11, 2005 — $1

New arrivals bolster sales of land, houses

Chapter 52

Peninsula Journalists First at Seldovia

Kenai is the oldest town on the west side of the Kenai Peninsula but the first newspapers along that Cook Inlet shore were at Seldovia. That community had several newspapers serving the area before the *Homer Homesteader* appeared in 1944 and *On the Kenai* appeared in 1957.

One of the Seldovia newspapers established the name *Frontiersman* that was later carried by its publisher to Palmer to become today's *Frontiersman*.

The Seldovia Herald appeared January 16, 1930, with Lester Busey as editor-publisher. It started as a semimonthly and became a weekly from December 13, 1930, through June 17, 1933.

Seldovia, located across Kachemak Bay from Homer, derived its name from the Russian word "seldovoi" meaning herring. The Russian surveyor Lt. Mikhail Tebenkov named a five-mile-long estuary on the southwest shore of Kachemak Bay, Seldovia Bay in the 1800s.

In the 1880 U.S. census, the village consisted of "68 Kodiak Natives and three Creoles. They were sea otter hunters and lived in log houses and had a small chapel." The 1890 census gave the population as ninety-nine. A post office was established in 1898. The 2000 census credited Seldovia with 286 people.

Busey started as a printer's devil in 1905 on the *Astorian* in Oregon. He was more of a "writing newspaperman" than an aggressive reporter. He had a sensitive appreciation of poetry. His nuances in words and the force of phrases reflected his personality. A friend once remarked,

THE CHITINA LEADER

...pments From Copper River Valley Are Over $2,000,000 Eacl...

CHITINA, ALASKA, TUESDAY, AUGUST 24, 1915.

- TERM OF COURT SET FOR VALDEZ SEPT. 14
- SEWARD RAILWAY LITIGATION DISMISSED
- MANY BUILDINGS GOING UP AT ANCHORAGE
- FAMOUS WRITER ON VISIT TO ALASKA
- SCARCITY OF WATER FOR SLUICING PURPOSES

WHAT CORDOVA

The Seldovia Herald

A COOK INLET ENTERPRISE

VOL. 1 NO. 29.   SELDOVIA, ALASKA, SATURDAY, AUGUST 15, 1931.   PRICE 10 CENTS

ROAD MEETING ON FRIDAY NIGHT

Plans Meeting Endorsement-Organization to be Program Sought Friday

A community meeting, called for the purpose of discussing the proposed Seldovia-built thoroughfare, to effect organization and adopt ways and means for going ahead with the plan, will be held the evening of Friday, the 21st. Hour, 8:30 o'clock.

The public is urged to be present where every chance will be given everybody to express views, and to thresh out all points that may need explaining.

Plans for the roadway have achieved the point when its perfect feasibility is generally admitted. The general view is that the thoroughfare can be quickly built, once the people get down to business and through competent organization go after an actual construction

Seldovia Guide Takes Florida Hunter In Hand for Hunt

Tony Martin and Zenas Beach departed for Anchorage a few days ago, traveling on the former's gas boat Halcyon, and timing their going to reach the Inlet City by the 15th, there to meet Jas. T. Swann, big game hunter from Florida. Mr. Martin as guide, assisted by Mr. Cesch, packer, will conduct Mr. Swann over a wide stretch of territory during the next two months.

Homer Draw From Chica

Families On Way to Se To Catch Boat f Cook Inlet

A number of families ar es route from Chicago to H Alaska They are traveling automobile to Seattle, and coming with the definite pu of making their homes in famed agricultural and fox ing area.

They are friends of the M sons, who came from Seat

The Daily Nome Industrial Worker

This Paper is Owned, Controlled and Operated by Local 240 of the W. F. of M.

IS TO STATE PEACE TERMS TODAY

WORLD'S EYES TURN TO GERMAN TERMS

OFFICERS DIFFER AS TO SERVIAN FIGHTING

"I really believe that Lester could write a poem to Tchaikowsky's 'Concerto in B Flat Minor' that would make sense and that would interpret that masterpiece's true meaning."

Busey suspended publication in 1933 to join the staff of the *Seward Gateway*.

Daniels starts at Seldovia

Viola Daniels, an energetic young woman in her twenties, arrived in Seldovia and started *The Frontiersman* on November 20, 1946. It was a twice-weekly mimeographed, three-column tabloid of six pages.

In explaining why she chose the paper's name, Daniels said the word "frontier" suggested a young country peopled by active vigorous pioneers with vision for the future.

Reocurring maritime strikes at Pacific ports resulted in frequent newsprint shortages. At one point she was reduced to using typing paper for several issues. Even the post office ran out of stamps so she could not mail the paper to her subscribers.

Daniels refrained from taking editorial positions on local issues for the first few months, but once she gained self-confidence, she came out strong on issues. She was named city clerk. In that capacity she was privy to the numerous problems with which the city council had to deal.

Many divisive issues led mayors and councilmen to resign frequently in disgust. There was a citizen element that opposed change, however beneficial it appeared. Daniels usually found herself siding with the more progressive element.

She urged a reliable utility system to insure a stable economy.

She explained the simple formula to her readers thusly: "No water and power, no canneries operating, no fish needed, no money for next winter's food and clothing."

Her critics threatened loss of advertising and subscribers. To that she responded that as much as she needed "to sell enough papers and advertising to pay the rent and eat three times a day, it was more important to help Seldovia become a better city."

Daniels sold the paper to Patrick and Lee O'Brien, Seldovians, in September 1947, and moved to Palmer where she started *The Valley Frontiersman*, now published out of Wasilla as *The Frontiersman*.

The October 8, 1947, edition of the Seldovia paper is the last one on file in state archives. It is unknown how long the O'Briens published the paper.

First railroad, street lights at Homer

Homer's beginnings are sketchy. During the late 1880s and early 1890s, substantial coal mining supported eight miles of standard gauge railroad built from the mines to the beach. Historical data indicates this was the first railroad in Alaska.

Coal oil lamps lighted the boardwalks, also an Alaska first. Soon, federal leasing restrictions made the mining effort commercially unprofitable so the coal fields near Homer lay dormant. Local residents picked up pieces of coal for domestic fuel. Government geologists estimate that about four hundred million tons of coal lies in the Homer district.

A gold mining miniboom occurred in Cook Inlet in the 1890s. In the spring of 1896, Homer Pennock, a native of Michigan, set up camp on the end of Coal Spit, a narrow peninsula of land extending four miles into Kachemak Bay. It is known today as Homer Spit. Four hundred men were living on the spit at one time.

Pennock's campmates voted unanimously to name both the spit and the town for their leader. When word came of the Klondike gold strike in 1898, most of the inlet miners headed for the new gold fields.

In 1946, a number of World War II veterans homesteaded in the Homer area, following a scattering of earlier homesteaders in the 1930s. A town developed on a bench of land varying in width from a quarter-of-a-mile to two miles, below a 1,400-foot bluff overlooking the spit. The population in 1940 was 325, and by 2000, 3,946. Annexation could boost Homer population but the State Local Boundary Commission reduced the recommended annexation to 4.5 square miles from the city's requested twenty-five square miles. Regardless of the size of the city, about six thousand people live in the area, providing a substantial market for competing weekly newspapers, the *Homer News* and the *Homer Tribune*.

Fishing and seafood processing are the most stable sectors of the economy. This also attracts sport fishermen and tourists encouraged by roads extended into the area from Anchorage. Homer has a large colony of artists. There is a cold storage. A sawmill provides lumber locally and wood chips are shipped through the port to Japan.

Homesteader appears in '44

Homer's first commercial newspaper was the two-page, mimeographed weekly *Homer Homesteader*, established on April 14, 1944, by William R. Benson. He operated a real estate and insurance business, as well as a variety store that sold washing machines, heaters, ranges, furniture, gasoline and oil.

Benson's weekly editorials radiated optimism about Homer's future. He urged the acquisition of an electrical system and the digging of deep wells for safe and bountiful water. He pushed for development work to prove up coal veins for a local fuel supply.

His continuous prodding for the amenities of modern living met with a degree of negative criticism from some of his readers, which he resented:

> The writer has felt the sting many times from those poor hapless souls, who spend their idle hours picking to pieces someone who is trying to do something constructive.
>
> The mail we get from people who have reached the top rungs of the ladder, commending our efforts, more than compensates for the little adverse criticism locally from people who should be our most consistent backers.

Irregular and unreliable steamer schedules caused constant newsprint and supplies shortages. When Benson suspended publication of the *Homesteader* in December 1949, Homer had an electrical and water system, two cold storage plants, a hotel, two restaurants, three general stores and airmail service four times weekly. The 175-mile highway to Seward was completed.

Benson felt good about the role his paper had played in promoting these developments. One goal he failed to realize, however, was a railroad from Homer to Anchorage.

Homer News next

The first of a series of weeklies titled the *Homer News* appeared briefly in 1931, according to the Alaska State Library. No copies of that first effort are available. The next *Homer News* appeared March 1950 with Harry and W. M. Hegdahl as editor-publishers. It appeared at irregular intervals before ceasing.

Harry Hegdahl reactivated it on June 10, 1954, with Bill Raver as his editor. Raver had been a reporter for the *Anchorage Daily News* the previous year. He was born in Jerome, Idaho, on November 26, 1919. He was a World War II veteran and a graduate of the San Jose State College School of Journalism.

His wife, Dorothy, assisted him on the Homer paper.

In his introductory editorial, Raver promised that he would faithfully publish a paper every Thursday as he was aware that his predecessors had annoyed their readers by their erratic publication:

> Lots of folks have asked us what we intend to use for news here in Homer. Well, there's a lot more news in and about Homer than most people think. Lots of things happen here just the same as they happen in any other small town. Businesses change hands or expand, social, fraternal and business groups do things, people take trips and have visitors from out of town, people get married, babies are born and people die here just like anywhere else.
>
> Politically speaking, the *News* will be Democratic in its editorial columns. However, news of both political parties will be treated equally.

The *News* was a mimeographed tabloid. By the end of the first month, the circulation was more than 225 copies a week. On August 5, it inaugurated a radio program that was broadcast from 5:30 to 7 p.m. daily except Sundays.

On August 18, 1955, the name of the paper was changed to *Kenai Peninsula Pioneer* to identify its expanded coverage to all of the peninsula communities. The publication day was changed from Thursday to Monday because both Bill and Dorothy Raver held part-time jobs in the school system. They worked on the paper during the weekends and had it in the mail on Monday morning.

The Ravers suspended publication on February 27, 1956, due to a variety of problems. Also, they had competition from Bob Norman's weekly *Homer Herald*, started in 1955.

The *Herald* also was a mimeographed tabloid. It accompanied the weekly *Shopping News* that Norman launched the previous year. It was mailed free to all post office boxholders in Homer, Anchor

Point, Ninilchik, Clam Gulch, Kasilof, Cohoe and Soldotna. Both papers were packed with community news.

The *Herald* became *The Homer Journal* in March 1959 just before all of Norman's publications suspended. That left the town without a local newssheet.

Courier fills vacuum

Unlike Seldovia, Homer's population had grown. It was more than 1,200 in 1959, when James and Marie McDowell, publishers of the weekly *Knik Arm Courier* in Chugiak, filled the news vacuum around Kachemak Bay. They launched the weekly, five-column, sixteen-page tabloid *Cook Inlet Courier* on August 19, 1959. Based on their twelve years of Alaska residence as pioneering entrepreneurs, the McDowells had little sympathy with conservationists who "want to keep Alaska a vast wilderness park."

The *Cook Inlet Courier* was "dedicated to the Manifest Destiny of the Cook Inlet Ports" and its slogan read: "Only newspaper in the world that gives a damn about Homer."

By a two-to-one margin, Homer voters decided to incorporate eleven square miles into a first-class city in March 1964 in order to protect their interests within the newly established Kenai Peninsula Borough. Letters to the editor reflected general discontent with the whole borough concept and some individuals suggested seceding from it. The paper cautioned against such rash action.

Separate editions of the *Courier* were published in Homer and in Kenai, from October 19, 1967, through March 8, 1968. Then the McDowells moved to Kenai and issued a combined Homer-Kenai weekly.

Homer News resurrected

A weekly *Homer News* was reactivated in 1964 with H. A. and Marion Thorn as editor-publishers. It was the third newspaper in the area with that name. It was printed rather than mimeographed and ran twelve and fourteen pages.

Thorn opposed the imposition of a borough form of government just as the McDowells did with their *Cook Inlet Courier*, calling it "premature and a little bit stupid."

The borough assembly levied a 3 percent sales tax that was supposed to raise $350,000 and then be terminated. After a two-year interval, Thorn demanded that an accounting be made to the taxpayers and it was found that $536,000 had been raised. His continued protests led to an eventual termination of the tax as other sources of revenue developed. The Thorns suspended publication of the *News* with the June 8, 1967, edition.

Then the Thorns' associate editor, G. Lucille Billings, reactivated the title *Homer News* for the fourth time on July 6, 1972. The paper was printed in Herb Rhodes' Anchorage Printing Co. plant.

Billings sold the paper in March 1973, to Louis and Linda Gjosund of Homer. They changed the name to *Homer Weekly News* and they identified their first edition on April 5, 1973, as volume I, number 1. Instead of having it printed in either Anchorage or Kenai as had been done previously, the Gjosunds contracted the printing with Jim and Al Clymer, owners of the Fritz Creek Studios in Homer. They ran twelve to fourteen pages weekly.

Letters to the editor reflected bitter feuding between special interest groups – old-timer versus newcomer, developer versus conservationist, liberal versus conservative, and socialist versus capitalist – a big hubub over a new city ordinance requiring mandatory sewer hookups!

The individualist homesteader was being supplanted by the individualist environmentalist, who frowned on economic development. A letter to the editor from the chairman of the local advisory planning committee portrayed the anti-growth philosophy.

Another long letter opposed oil drilling in Kachemak Bay because it would destroy Homer's relaxed lifestyle – turn it into another Kenai!

The competitive oil and gas lease sale of tracts in Kachemak Bay on Dec 13, 1974, brought a total high bonus bid of $24,824,845.55. Fishing interests protested so loudly that the deal was canceled. Then the Legislature authorized the governor to buy back the acreage from the oil companies.

Ironically, it was the oil companies that caused the turnaround. An oil drilling barge got stuck in the mud just off Homer Spit and an oil slick appeared in the bay during the two months it took to free the barge by use of explosives. That led the *News* to question the technological expertise of the oil companies in regard to "the sanctity of the environment."

A church without sermons?

Gary Williams, a longtime Peninsula resident, bought the *News* from the Gjosunds in June 1974, three months after "weekly" was dropped from the name and it was simply the *Homer News*, the fifth publication with that name. Williams said he would avoid editorial comment, leaving the pro and con arguments to writers of letters to the editor. This brought a vociferous negative response from a reader:

> Editorials are the lifeblood of a newspaper; they give it its meaning. As a church without sermons would certainly lose some of its appeal, so would a newspaper without editorials. To deal solely with reporting the news turns your back on a journalistic tradition and responsibility that have been fought for since the beginning of the country.
>
> As issues become increasingly complex, commentary and editorials become an even more important part of a newspaper's task, especially in areas like Homer where coverage by other media is sparse.

Meanwhile, the McDowells continued to publish a lively, interesting newspaper. Gov. William Egan appointed Marie McDowell to the state board of education in 1972. She died of cancer on July 10, 1973, and was interred in the Memorial Cemetery in Homer. With Marie gone, the *Cook Inlet Courier* folded in July 1974, after fifteen years of publication.

With his competition gone, Williams prospered and sold the *News* to Howard and Tod Simons of Cambridge, Massachusetts. The new owners took over on January 1, 1978.

Simons was an editor for the *Washington Post* when he was attracted to Alaska journalism and Homer in 1977 while on a bird watching trip. During that trip, he attended an Alaska Newspaper Association meeting in Anchorage. Tom Gibboney, managing editor of the *Anchorage Daily News*, was a friend of Williams and mentioned to Simons that the paper was for sale. Simons bought it and hired Gibboney as editor and general manager. Gibboney also was a 20 percent stockholder in the operation. The other major stockholders were Martin and Nancy Cohen of Washington DC.

Gibboney was a graduate of the University of Florida. While stationed at Fort Richardson in 1967, he was a part-time sports editor for the *Anchorage Daily News*.

Gibboney stayed with the *Homer News* until 1988. The paper profited and expanded under Gibboney. It enjoyed generous advertising patronage.

Environmental leanings

Editorials under Gibboney and the new owners leaned more to the environmental than to the developmental sector. When state conservation officials lowered the pollution requirements for Tesoro Alaska's North Kenai refinery – in order to save the company $2.4 million when it expanded its facilities to handle high sulfur North Slope crude – the *News* called it "a lousy deal for anyone who has to live and breathe on the Kenai Peninsula."

The *News* urged the state to scuttle the sale of North Slope crude to the company. The editorial raised the possibility of Tesoro's sulfur dioxide blowing up Cook Inlet, mixing with the foul air over Anchorage, and being blown back down the peninsula as acid rain.

Gibboney left Homer in August 1988 to accept a Knight Fellowship at Stanford University. Shelley Gill, former successful publisher of *The Frontiersman*, replaced him as editor. And when Gill went on maternity leave in March 1989, her former editor at Wasilla, T. C. Mitchell, took her place as editor. He was on leave from a job in California. When he returned to California, Allen Baker moved up from reporter to editor and manager.

'No' to nukes

Baker was in charge during the year-long "great debate" and election on whether Homer should, by ordinance, declare itself a nuclear-free zone. In an editorial on September 28, 1989, just before the election, Baker's editorial advised: "Nuclear free Homer – Yes. It may be only a gesture, but this proposition is a chance to go on record against the insanity of nuclear proliferation."

Letters to the editor dominated two pages of the *News* before the election, both for and against the ordinance. Voters in the community that editorialists frequently describe as "The Cosmic Hamlet by the Sea," adopted the ordinance by a close 321-293 vote.

When Baker left after a year and one-half for a job in Washington state, a nationwide search for a new editor attracted seventy applicants. Mark Turner, a new resident of Homer, accepted the job in early 1991. He had vacationed twice in Homer and had moved there to do freelance writing a month before the post opened. He had the newspaper background for the job, nine years with the *Arizona Star* in Tucson.

Gibboney was in Menlo Park, California, when Howard Simons, the major stockholder and publisher of the *News*, died. The other owners, the Cohens and Gibboney, chose to sell the 4,400 circulation weekly to Morris Publishing in February 2000. Morris already owned the nearby *Peninsula Clarion* at Kenai. That common ownership enables the two newspapers to share news of the peninsula and take advantage of the *Clarion's* extensive printing equipment.

Turner remained as editor and became publisher under Morris ownership until January 2002. Then Morris moved him to Anchorage as general manager of Alaska publications. In that position, he is responsible for the *Alaska Star*, the *Alaska Journal of Commerce*, the *Alaska Oil and Gas Reporter*, the *Alaskan Equipment Trader* and Morris's Alaska military publications.

Replacing Turner as publisher of the *Homer News* was Gary Thomas, who had lived in Homer since 1979 and was a strong advocate for local community involvement in issues. He moved to Homer after graduating from St. Lawrence University in Canton, New York, and was general manager of KBBI public radio between 1980 and 1990.

Prior to being named publisher of the *News*, Thomas headed the marketing division of the *News* for four years. Before that he was president of Bodett & Company, Inc. and managed the talent of Tom Bodett, made famous nationally in Motel 6 radio commercials: "We'll leave the light on for you."

Pascall's Tribune emerges

The *Homer Tribune* runs in its flag the statement: "The only locally owned and operated Homer newspaper." James Hornaday, a state court judge, started the paper as a newsletter in August 1991, about five months after Turner took over as editor of the *News*.

The *Tribune* was started and has survived as a counter to the liberal views of the *News*, especially under Simons's ownership. It started

Jane Pascall
Editor/Publisher
Homer Tribune

Tribune Photo

publication less than a year after Homer voters approved the controversial nuclear-free zone ordinances.

Shortly after Hornaday started the *Tribune*, a recent graduate of the University of Alaska Fairbanks, Jane Pascall, joined the operation. A year later she became a partner and then the sole owner of what is now a successful 3,500-circulation tabloid weekly.

Pascall was born in England but is a naturalized citizen who grew up in southern California. She majored in business, with a emphasis on marketing, at UAF.

Pascall writes few editorials but has a large volume of opinion in the letters columns. The editorials she does write are usually for some special event.

Both the *News* and the *Tribune* gave front-page play to the annexation problem at Homer in 2000 and 2001 and to the court cases filed over it. Both papers picked the annexation story as the top local story of 2000.

Homer city memos withheld

The newspapers editorialized in support of the lawsuit to open to the public municipal memos on the annexation. Superior Court Judge Harold Brown ruled Homer municipal officials had a right to hold confidential certain deliberative memos. The outcome of the legal action was a concern to all Alaska media, so the Alaska Newspaper Association entered the case. It filed an appeal brief in the Alaska Supreme Court over Judge Brown's January 2001 decision.

Brown had based his decision on a federal case denying a newspaper reporter access to internal memos in *Quarles vs. Department of the Navy*, and on two state decisions: *Gwich'in Steering Committee vs. State of Alaska* and *Capital Information Group vs. State of Alaska*. Capital Information is a news organization.

The Homer case began when the city council petitioned the Local Boundary Commission to add twenty-five square miles of surrounding land to the city, noting that the 2,700 people in the area already were enjoying city services. Some residents protested and asked for disclosure of memos between department heads and the city manager. Those memos were denied on the basis they were part of the give and take in making a decision and not especially factual. The final financial documents were public record.

Brown extended to the city, and by precedent, to other Alaska municipalities, an Alaska Supreme Court decision allowing state agencies, such as the governor's office, to keep predecisional memos confidential. The Gwich'in had sought documents exchanged between Gov. Tony Knowles and consultants hired to promote oil exploration on the coastal plain of the Arctic National Wildlife Refuge. The Alaska Supreme Court ruled in October 2000 that the public's interest in those documents did not outweigh the governor's interest in a free flow of information within his administration, so the documents remained confidential.

The state high court had ruled similarly for the state in August 1996 when the news organization, Capital Information, tried to obtain memos exchanged between state commissioners and the governor's Office of Management and Budget.

Brown also cited the Quarles decision by the U.S. Court of Appeals in Washington DC when it denied a reporter access to the navy's analyses of homeports for 130 ships.

Attorney John McKay told the *Anchorage Daily News* that Brown's decision could encourage officials in other municipalities to hold back from the public many documents now considered accessible, such as background memos about municipal tax needs.

The newspaper association was not involved in the proposed annexation by the city of Homer, only in whether memos involved in the case can be held confidential. But again, the Alaska Supreme Court sided with the government unit, and in 2004 upheld Brown's decision to keep the memos confidential.

Chapter 53

Frontiersman Triggers '94 Meeting Law Change

Before the Alaska Newspaper Association filed an action to open municipal memos in Homer to public scrutiny, *The Frontiersman* in Wasilla went to court accusing Matanuska-Susitna Borough Assembly members of violating the state's Open Meetings Act. The result was that Superior Court Judge Beverly Cutler in 1987 enjoined three or more members of the assembly from meeting to discuss business.

Their downfall was the habit of a majority of the assembly members meeting in a Palmer coffee shop prior to the meeting to line up their votes. They always quit discussing business when reporter Brian O'Donohue showed up. So publisher Shelley Gill sent a new reporter, Eric Troyer, who assembly members wouldn't recognize, and photographer Linda Cordel, to the coffee shop. They reported and photographed the assembly members acting on assembly business outside of the regular public meeting.

Judge Cutler even strengthened her ban to say assembly members could not have telephonic conversation among themselves to arrive at a decision.

The lawsuit that ate Cordova

Judge Cutler's ruling was followed by an even stricter interpretation of the open meeting law by a judge in Fairbanks. That ruling made it almost impossible for two members of the city council to speak to each other on the street or anyplace else. Then came "The Lawsuit That Ate Cordova."

Triggers Meeting Law Change –Shelley Gill, shown here with her horse Adak, was publisher of the Frontiersman 1983-86. She sent a reporter and photographer to a Palmer coffee house to witness an unofficial meeting of a majority of the borough assembly who were arranging their votes secretly before a public meeting. The story and lawsuit brought by the newspaper resulted in a court decision in 1987 that affected elected bodies statewide and a rewriting of the open meeting laws by the Alaska State Legislature. Gill retired as publisher to her homestead near Homer to write children's books. She had 21 in print by 2004.-*Photo courtesy Shelley Gill.*

Following the *Exxon Valdez* oil spill in 1989, Cordova councilwoman Connie Taylor complained that city business was being carried on in secret and filed a lawsuit against three of her council colleagues.

Twenty months later the suit was settled. A judge ruled in her favor – city officials had violated the open meeting law. The judge ordered the city to pay legal bills of more than $1 million, which ate up all of the current city funds and reserves.

That forced the city to cut back on snow removal and other operations. It also used up the $200,000 set aside for parking improvements and for harbor operation.

Superior Court Judge Peter Michalski found the city guilty of three violations of the Open Meeting Act, but dismissed a dozen other charges leveled by Taylor. The city and Taylor agreed not to appeal the $1 million decision but Cordova officials joined those of Fairbanks, Ketchikan and other Alaska municipalities in seeking to have the Open Meeting Act amended to a more reasonable interpretation.

The Cordova suit was expensive, according to Anchorage-based media attorney John McKay, because the city employed a four-lawyer defense in an effort to scare Taylor out of her action. "Right or wrong, they decided to go to war with this woman."

The animosity the suit stirred up cost Taylor her seat on the council. She was recalled.

The Ketchikan City Council tried the same tactic – "going to war" – with the *Ketchikan Daily News* in the late eighties and failed. The settlement cost Ketchikan only a little over $100,000, plus the time of its own attorney.

Then the Open Meeting Act, AS 44.62.310, was amended by Legislature in 1994 in subsection h(2)(A) to describe a meeting of a government body as being when more than three, or a majority of the members of the body, whichever is less, is present.

Between Anchorage and Fairbanks

The City of Palmer, forty-two miles northeast of Anchorage on the Glenn Highway, is the heart of the Matanuska Valley. In the 1960s, the area became the Matanuka-Susitna Borough, the link between Alaska's two largest cities, Anchorage and Fairbanks.

The city took its name from George Palmer, who operated trading posts in the valley at the turn of the century. Homesteaders settled in the valley when the Alaska Railroad was completed in the 1920s. In 1935, the federal government transplanted 202 farm families from the drought-stricken Midwest to the valley – the Matanuska Project.

Within days of the arrival of those 202 families at Palmer, a daily news bulletin was posted on the outside wall of the tent occupied by the Presbyterian minister, Bert J. Bingle. *The Palmer Daily* first appeared on May 14, 1935. It was typewritten on two pages of yellow copy paper, presenting both world and local news.

The daily bulletin was discontinued when the Alaska Rural Rehabilitation Corporation, the government agency running the colony, started the *Matanuska Valley Pioneer* on August 22, 1935. It was a four-page mimeographed weekly tabloid put out in a little ten-by-twelve-foot tent and distributed free to all the colonists. Jack Allman was its editor.

Valley's First Weekly—A federal agency, the Alaska Rural Rehabilitation Corporation, started the weekly Matanuska Valley Pioneer in August 1935 to serve the 202 families moved to the valley from the Midwest. It's editor, Jack Allman, stands before his office.
 -*Photo from the Lulu Fairbanks collection, 68-69-140a, Jack Allman, Archives, University of Alaska Fairbanks.*

Allman arrived in Alaska at age seven, joining his mother in Skagway in 1903. She married Tom Marquam in 1910 in Fairbanks. He was an attorney and former editor of the *Fairbanks Times* (1907-08).

Allman served with the U.S. Army Corps of Engineers in Europe during World War I. After his discharge, he was a correspondent in Paris for several years for the *Chicago Tribune*. Later in New York, he had a daily radio program on a national network and became a popular writer of ice and snow fiction for such magazines as *Argosy*, *Blue Book*, and *Adventure*. He returned to Alaska when the Matanuska Project started.

Allman's journalistic expertise was evident in the professional product that he put out for the colony, especially his editorials. As the *Pioneer* was more of a house organ than a commercial newspaper, it was incumbent on the editor to answer criticisms of the project. Disgruntled colonists wrote letters to friends and relatives that were published in their hometown papers in the States. Negative criticism appeared in the Alaska press as well.

For example, the *Cordova Times* called the colonization project "the product of idealism steeped in the sordid slime of rapacious commercialism, where political favoritism and a desire to grab while the grabbing is good have taken all but a tithe of the billions appropriated in a worthy cause." One of Harry Steel's last hoorahs, to which Allman replied:

> Has the writer ever visited this project? Does he speak with authority or does he know only what he has heard in the biased reports of the disgruntled few who have quit the colony because the jaundiced streaks down their backs couldn't be hidden, and as a result found themselves ostracized by those with guts enough to take a few disappointments and still carry on?
>
> Why is the successful rehabilitation of 175 families called "idealism steeped in the sordid slime of rapacious commercialism," as he so sophomorically puts it?

Private paper started

If there had not been a newspaper to kill some of the ill-founded rumors, there would have been chaos. Allman resigned as a corporation

MATANUSKA VALLEY POST

A Message From The Governor

Hospital Funds Are Boosted; Fine Community Cooperation

Valley FRONTIERSMAN

School District, City Government Plans Are Weighed

Sorry, No Paper Next Saturday

MATANUSKA VALLEY RECORD

How Anchorage Got Its Name

The Growth of the Anchorage Schools

employee on December 15, 1935, and put out the *Pioneer* as a private enterprise. He moved to a sixteen-by-thirty-foot tent formerly occupied by the timekeeper.

In the front section of the tent was the reception room with a "powder horn" into which individuals were invited to drop news items, queries or complaints. The center section housed the publishing equipment and the rear was Allman's living quarters. It was something of a nuisance to be just twenty feet from the mess hall to which workers were summoned to a six o'clock breakfast by the clanging of a beaten railroad iron.

On October 26, 1936, the *Pioneer* came out with its first printed edition. Allman bought an antique press from Jim Virdin of Ketchikan, who had acquired it on a gambling debt. It went to Skagway originally from Tacoma for M. L. Sherpy, who started Skagway's first newspaper, the *Skaguay News*, in the fall of 1897. As a newsboy in Skagway from 1903 to 1907, Allman sold papers printed on the same machine.

Unfortunately, the press collapsed under the pressure of regular publication. In an editorial titled "It Can't Be Done," Allman announced the suspension of the paper on December 19, 1936. Not only was his mechanical equipment falling apart but so was his circulation, with the departure of the workers as construction was completed for the project.

The Valley Settler was the next weekly newssheet to appear on the streets of Palmer. It was a mimeographed tabloid issued by the Matanuska Valley Farmers' Cooperating Association. It started on December 2, 1937. However it failed, as did the *Valley Post* that followed it.

Frontiersman, "Lion's Den' appear

On September 17, 1947, Viola Daniels, former *Anchorage Daily Times* reporter and former editor-publisher of *The Frontiersman* in Seldovia, launched the twice-weekly *Valley Frontiersman* in Palmer. It was a more professional publication than the *Settler* or *Post*. It was a five-column, twelve-by-nineteen-inch, eight-to-ten-page tabloid. It had generous advertising from Anchorage merchants. Her personal opinion column was titled "Daniels – In the Lion's Den."

Daniels was irritated by a local habit of nonsubscribers grabbing papers off the newsstand without paying a dime for them. They would then gather around in a restaurant and discuss the day's news and point out errors. She labeled such groups "Let's-Give-the-Paper-Hell" clubs. She revealed her frustrations through her "Lion's Den" column on Valentine's Day 1948:

> Club policy in regard to newspapers is whole-hearted non-support. "Don't advertise, don't subscribe, and don't ever be caught giving any authentic information" is the club's motto.
>
> There is probably no more satisfied group of readers anywhere in the Valley, than the "Let's-Give-The-Paper-Hell" club membership at the conclusion of a meeting. They're the boys who get ten cents worth of enjoyment out of every issue printed. The fact that the dime's worth of pleasure is at the expense of someone else, makes it doubly enjoyable.

After ten months, Daniels was forced to quit:

> Today I write "thirty" to my hitch as editor-reporter, circulation manager and office boy for the *Valley Frontiersman*. There'll be a new reporter at my typewriter, a new voice answering my telephone.
>
> I shan't be leaving our Valley, or our town, so I'll not be saying goodbye. It is just a farewell to *The Frontiersman*. I shall be a Valley correspondent for an Anchorage newspaper.
>
> My heart is heavy as I pull the door of the "Den" closed and snap a padlock into place.

DeJulio from News to Palmer

Alvin J. DeJulio became general manager and editor of *The Frontiersman* shortly after Daniels closed her "Den." He was a former part owner of the *Anchorage Daily News*.

Civic history was made when Palmer voted to become a first-class incorporated city on April 10, 1951. Newspaper history was made when the *Valley Frontiersman* put out an election "extra," having it on the streets within minutes after voting returns were officially recorded by the city council – 254 yes votes to 113 no votes. That was Palmer's first newspaper "extra."

DeJulio died in 1959 and his widow, Billie, carried on until October 1961, when she sold the paper to Theodore Schmidtke, whom she later married. He was a former printer with the *Anchorage Daily News*.

As the Anchorage Bowl filled up and real estate prices skyrocketed, Anchorage workers established homes in the Matanuska-Susitna Valley, in which Palmer and Wasilla were the principal towns.

Schmidtke expanded *The Frontiersman* to a seven-column, ten-page, standard size newspaper. Valley was dropped from the name. Special correspondents provided news columns from Wasilla, Willow, Big Lake and Talkeetna.

When Schmidtke was killed in a one-car accident in December 1973, Billie DeJulio Schmidtke was a widow again. She advertised the paper for sale. Jerome Sheldon, former editor of *Jessen's Weekly* in Fairbanks, wrote her from Palo Alto, California, offering to buy it. He and his wife took over the operation on April 1, 1974.

The Sheldons sold *The Frontiersman* after four years to Skagit Alaska, Inc., owned by Scripps-Wood Newspapers of Mount Vernon, Washington. Leighton P. Wood was president of the company. It also published the daily *Skagit Valley Herald* in Mount Vernon and the weekly *American* in Anacortes, Washington.

Wood was attracted to the area because there was a strong move by Alaskans in Southcentral to move the capital of Alaska from Juneau to a site at Willow, in *The Frontiersman's* circulation area. When that didn't occur, Wood sold the newspaper in 1993 to Michael and Patricia Lindsey and they sold it in 1996 to Wick Communications.

Wasilla overtakes Palmer

Palmer residents were inclined to withdraw the welcome mat to an onrush of newcomers from Anchorage who disrupted their slow-paced lifestyle. So newcomers directed their feet to Wasilla, located eleven miles southwest of Palmer. Wasilla had developed into a trading center for the gold miners roaming the nearby Talkeetna mountains following construction of the Alaska Railroad. It derived its name from the Knik Indian Chief Wasilla, also known as Chief Vasili.

Despite the voters' rejection of relocating the capital in the 1982 referendum, new residents continued to pour into the Wasilla area. In due time, Wasilla displaced Palmer as the nucleus of the Matanuska-Susitna Borough that had grown to over twenty-five thousand by 1980. Borough population in 2000 topped sixty thousand.

Sun comes out

Jack and Katherine Sorgenfrei started the weekly *Valley Sun* in Wasilla on June 7, 1978. Sorgenfrei arrived in Anchorage in 1967 to work for Alaska Advertisers. The Anchorage Printing Co. printed the *Valley Sun* while its editorial offices were in Wasilla.

Sorgenfrei sold the *Sun* to Skagit Alaska, Inc. in August 1979, the same firm having bought *The Frontiersman*.

There was a succession of editor and publishers of the two papers until Shelley Gill was named publisher in 1983, and exposed the borough assembly's secret meetings. She had worked for the paper previously as a reporter in 1979 and for the *Tundra Times*. *The Frontiersman* started twice weekly publication in July 1984. It had offices in both Palmer and Wasilla but moved its main office to Wasilla with the June 25, 1986 edition.

Third valley paper debuts

The Mat-Su Valley welcomed a third newspaper on April 4, 1984, when longtime Wasilla resident and former mayor, Harold Newcomb, launched the weekly *Valley Press* in Wasilla. Fifteen thousand, five hundred copies were distributed free throughout the borough.

Newcomb arrived in Wasilla in the early 1950s, and for years operated a general store. He promised that the *Press* would fill a void left by *The Frontiersman* and *Valley Sun*:

> I hope to make money but that's not my driving force. I feel like there are things that need to be done that have not been done. Coverage of issues by the other two papers has often been inaccurate or poor. It's sensationalism to sell papers to make money, and it's not in the best interests of the community.

Newcomb's optimism was shortlived. The *Valley Press* folded two years after its debut. Skagit Alaska changed the *Valley Sun* to a shopper in 1985, leaving the newspaper field to *The Frontiersman*.

Sutton has its Siding

Jim and Mary Bauer's biweekly *Sutton Siding* made its debut in January 1985, providing a cluster of villages about fifteen miles northeast of Palmer with their own local newssheet. It reached about 450 subscribers in the settlements of Sutton, Jonesville, Eska, and Chickaloon strung along the Glenn Highway. It is a coal-rich region, first tapped by the Alaska Railroad in 1917 as a source of fuel for its operation.

The Bauers moved from Anchorage to Sutton in 1979 because they liked the slower pace. Editorially, they tried to tread a line between the extremely reclusive element of Sutton society and the development-oriented faction. When the state was considering placing a maximum security prison in the area in 1985, the paper helped crystallize local sentiment against it so the idea was dropped. After two years the publication suspended.

Talkeetna gets two papers

Talkeetna, a little village on the Alaska Railroad, eighty miles north of Anchorage, had its beginning before the railroad was built. The meeting of three rivers, Talkeetna, Susitna and Chulitna gave the village its name. Trappers and miners built cabins along the riverbanks as early as 1909. Three years later, the Army Engineers platted a townsite. Population remained around the 10-mark until the 1970s. A miniboom erupted when three nearby sites were in contention for possible location of Alaska's new capital city – Larson Lake, Mt. Yenlo and Willow.

Local residents were divided on the advantages of having "the spire of a Brazilia North emerge through the spruce trees as a beacon to democracy and the American way."

Two weekly newspapers were launched within months of each other in 1976 – *The Susitna Valley Chronicle* on January 13 and *The Susitna Sentinel* on May 12. Former *Anchorage Daily News* staffers started both. Some were encouraged that the capital would be moving to Willow. Some opposed the idea.

Slim and Pam Randles were the publishers of the mimeographed tabloid *Chronicle*. They were spokesmen for the element that opposed the incursion of civilization onto their doorsteps, as indicated in an editorial April 13, 1976:

> It is distressing to see the erosion of a way of life, the great "cop out" of not being able to fight city hall, the sale of our birthright for a mess of pottage.
>
> With the pressure to move the capital up here; the pressure to build the Devil's Canyon dams, the pressure to

expand existing parks and create new ones, the pressure to greatly curtail hunting, fishing and grazing in the mountains, we can no longer sit in our cabins, have another cup of coffee and think things are going to work out for the best.

Maybe we can't stop progress. Can't we make our voices heard sufficiently to at least guide the steamroller of progress in the least destructive paths? If a person doesn't speak now, he does not deserve to be heard crying in his beer later.

The Randles and their friends did make an exception of the modern art of television however, admitting that there was a time and place for such a recreational outlet to be enjoyed, even though "moose meat in every cache was still more important than an antenna on each cabin roof."

The *Chronicle* changed its name to *The Alaskan* in February 1977 and suspended after four editions.

Thor and Nancy Brandt-Erichsen's *Sentinel* was printed in Anchorage and delivered by truck along the highway to Talkeetna with newsstand stops at Palmer, Wasilla and Willow. The Brandt-Erichsens continued to live in Anchorage, delaying a move to their Talkeetna homestead until finances would permit. The final edition came out in the summer of 1979.

The capital-move proposal had caused a small boom in Mat-Su Borough area but was squelched when voters failed to approve it. The number of newspapers, at one time a half dozen, dropped to *The Frontiersman* alone.

Gill builds Frontiersman

Publisher Gill built *The Frontiersman* to more than five thousand circulation in her three years. She had increased publication from weekly to twice weekly and won many awards for news coverage from the Iditarod race to sexual abuse. Gill resigned as publisher to devote herself to being a full-time writer. Her fourth children's book was issued as she left *The Frontiersman* to move to Homer. The count was twenty-one titles in 2004.

Duncan Frazier, former managing editor of *The Anchorage Times*, went with Skagit-Alaska in March 1986, replacing Gill.

The Frontiersman–2005

Kari S. Sleight
Publisher

Mark Kelsey
Managing Editor

Frontiersman Photos

In seven years at *The Frontiersman*, Frazier led a successful editorial campaign to create a police department for Wasilla, which was outgrowing Palmer.

After Skagit sold the Palmer-Wasilla papers to Michael Lindsey, a Wyoming-based newspaper broker, Frazier stayed three months and rejoined Skagit Valley in Washington as publisher of its weekly *Anacortes American*.

Lindsey sold *The Frontiersman* to Arizona-based Wick Communications in January 1996. Wick owns newspapers in twelve states. Its president is John M. Mathew, formerly CEO of Boone Newspapers.

In November 1997, Kari Sleight was named publisher. She also holds the post of advertising director. Her managing editor is Mark Kelsey, who began his journalism career as sports editor on *The*

Frontiersman, 1995-97, then worked on other papers before returning to *The Frontiersman* in March 2005.

Sleight began her newspaper career in 1977 at the *Idaho Free Press* in Napa, Idaho, in advertising. She joined the *Argus* (Oregon) *Observer* where she was classified ad manager when she was named publisher of *The Frontiersman.*

Between stints at *The Frontiersman,* Kelsey worked on papers in Juneau, Kenai and Homer and on two newspapers in New Hampshire.

Publisher Sleight and editor Kelsey report that local governing bodies still are adhering strictly to Judge Cutler's court order.

Chapter 54

Clarion Wins Public Records Ruling

Alaska's newest daily newspaper, the *Peninsula Clarion*, had yet to observe its tenth birthday when it was involved in a public right-to-know case that set a standard in Alaska.

The Alaska Supreme Court took the issue raised in the lawsuit by the *Clarion*, combined it with a similar action by the *Anchorage Daily News*, and ruled that applications for top municipal offices are public records.

The real embarrassment for elected officials in Kenai and Anchorage occurred when the newspapers discovered that the people picked for top public positions, before applications were public, had lied on their resumes. After the newspapers obtained the names of the favored applicants, they checked, discovered and reported the inaccuracies. The applicants immediately decided not to accept the public employment offered.

First in Kenai

The seven thousand-circulation *Clarion*, founded in 1970, went to court in 1979 to obtain the list of applicants for city manager and their resumes. Superior Court Judge James Hanson agreed with the *Clarion* that those were public records. He gave the city council ten days to disclose the information. That allowed time for applicants to withdraw their names if they didn't want their applications made public. He also said his ruling did not block the city from appealing his ruling to the Alaska Supreme Court.

Among the applications released was that of a thirty-year-old Louisiana man that the Kenai City Council had offered the job of city manager. *Clarion* publisher Max Swearingen and editor Ron Chappell checked the man's references in Pensacola, Florida, where he had last worked. They learned that he had lied about his job experience and his education. The man said it was all a mistake; that he was on his way to Alaska to explain. He never arrived.

The city council went on to locate a city manager following Judge Hanson's rules – everything public – and appealed his ruling to the Supreme Court!

Then in Anchorage

A year later, Anchorage Mayor George Sullivan sought to hire a former New York and Pennsylvania police officer as Anchorage police chief. The *Anchorage Daily News* went to court to seek release of the names and resumes of applicants for the job.

Three hours before Superior Court Judge Karl Johnston issued a stay blocking the assembly from considering the recommendation for chief, the mayor announced his choice.

Managing editor Clay Haswell set his newsroom to work investigating the background of the mayor's choice. They found that he had left a major item off of his resume. It was that he had been fired three years earlier for drinking on duty and harassing women in the Pennsylvania department he headed.

The candidate got as far as the Anchorage airport where he saw the *News*' headline and took the next plane back east.

Began in Ketchikan

Seeking applications and resumes of candidates for top local government offices began in 1977, when the *Ketchikan Daily News* went to court to force the Ketchikan Gateway Borough to reveal applicants for borough planning chief and borough manager.

Superior Court Judge Thomas Schulz ruled that such information was public record and must be released. His ruling, early in 1978, limited the applications and resumes to only the top supervisory personnel, not union employees.

Shortly thereafter, he ruled similarly in Juneau when the *Empire* sought release of applicants for city/borough manager.

The Ketchikan and Juneau public bodies declined to appeal the Schulz decision to the Alaska Supreme Court. The City of Kenai and the Municipality of Anchorage, however, went to the high court, which combined the cases. The state's highest court ruled in 1982 that the local governments were entities of the state and must follow the public records laws of the state and that those job applications are public records.

Local governments have attempted to withhold similar records since and lost based on what is now called the Peninsula Newspapers decision, named after the *Clarion*'s corporate name.

Anchorage local officials tried to withhold records again in 1987 when the *Anchorage Daily News* sought a library board advisory committee employment performance report that it had sent to Mayor Tom Fink. The newspaper also sought release of the mayor's "Blue Ribbon Panel" economic report on Anchorage.

To defend its action of holding the reports confidential, city officials went on the offensive. They attempted to depose newspaper officials. The newspaper sought to have the depositions quashed. In a 1990 decision, the Supreme Court ruled that the two reports were public records and must be released. It further ruled that the newspaper staffers were improperly deposed as a stalling tactic.

In many of these cases, the newspapers were reimbursed part of their legal fees and court costs. The *Anchorage Daily News*, after successfully challenging the school board in court, sought to be declared a public interest litigant and entitled to all legal costs. The court gave the newspaper only half of its legal costs but did declare it a public interest litigant in that particular case.

Early in the 1970s, the Ketchikan Gateway Borough School board paid $4,000 in attorney fees for the *Ketchikan Daily News*. The newspaper successfully sued to make public the board's Hart Report on the performance of school principals and other middle management.

Kenai second settlement

The City of Kenai, located on the west shore of Kenai Peninsula, approximately sixty air miles and 150 auto miles from Anchorage, was founded by the Russians in 1791, seven years after they founded Kodiak and 179 years before there was a *Clarion* to watch over the public's right to know. So Kenai is the second oldest permanent European (white) settlement in Alaska.

Gregor Konovalov, commander of the Russian ship *George*, established Fort St. Nicholas in 1791 at the mouth of the Kenai River overlooking Cook Inlet.

Prior to the Russian settlement the area was occupied by the Kenaitze Indians and was a bustling community active in fishing, hunting, trapping and some farming. After the days of the Russians and the fur industry came the heyday of commercial fishing and canning of salmon. The town's population remained between two hundred and three hundred until 1959, when it rose to 778 following opening of a dirt road from Anchorage in 1951 and the discovery of oil at nearby Swanson River in 1957.

After World War II, a twin city named Soldotna developed nine miles from Kenai at the Sterling-Kenai Spur Road junction. Soldotna took its name from a nearby stream that flowed into the Kenai River. It was a derivative of either the Russian word *soldat* meaning soldier, or the Indian word *tseldatna* meaning stream fork. Homesteaders settled in the area using their veterans' preference for land. Soldotna became a trading center and a bedroom community for the oil industry.

The area's first local newssheet, titled *On the Kenai*, was an insert in the *Nosy News & Shopping Guide*, published in Anchorage and distributed free. Dick Hoblitzell was editor and general manager of the *Shopping Guide*. Jackie Sewell was editor of the Kenai insert, which first appeared on May 18, 1957.

In July, Sewell, a Kenai resident, split her publication away from Hoblitzell's, making it an independent commercial enterprise. The five-column, four-page tabloid continued to be printed by Herb Rhodes's Anchorage Printing Co., and sold for a dime a copy. She had correspondents in Kasilof-Cohoe, Ninilchik, Homer, Moose Pass, and Clam Gulch. A primary aim of the weekly was to alert residents of Anchorage and the surrounding areas to Kenai Peninsula's recreational attractions so they would spend their weekends there hunting and fishing.

Although the discovery of oil in July 1957 in the Swanson River area, just twenty miles northeast of Kenai, augured well for the economy, the difficulties of publishing during the winter months caused Sewell to suspend publication with the December 21 edition.

Cheechako arrives

It was two years before a second journalistic venture was launched. That same year, Union and Marathon Oil companies found gas in the Kalifonsky Beach area six miles south of Kenai. A pipeline was constructed to supply Kenai, Soldotna and Anchorage with natural gas.

Loren and Dorothy Stewart, longtime peninsula homesteaders, started the *Kenai Peninsula Cheechako News* in Soldotna on October 30, 1959. Loren had previous newspaper experience before coming to Alaska. They homesteaded in 1949 halfway between Kenai and Soldotna in the Big Eddy area.

The paper was first published twice a month in a sixteen-by-thirty-two-foot army surplus tent. It ran four to six pages and it, too, was printed at Anchorage Printing Co. The flag pictured a miner panning for gold, an oil derrick and a tourist reading a guide to Alaska with a motto: "News from the Oil Center of Alaska." The Stewarts worked on the paper during the day. At night they worked on the building that would eventually house the newspaper plant.

Among the big stories in that first edition were the incorporation of the Kenai and Soldotna city governments, the first hookup to natural gas, the opening of Soldotna's first school and the opening of the new Kenai Peninsula branch of the National Bank of Alaska.

Stewart's first editorial, titled "Voice in the Wilderness," was a nostalgic review of the changes that had taken place during his ten years of residence:

> We enjoyed knowing, and being a friend of every one of our neighbors. We liked having moose in our front yard, and catching as many eighteen-inch rainbow trout in Big Eddy as we could use.
>
> We particularly liked not having to lock our door when we left for a month or two on the fishing site, and we liked the low rate of direct taxes.
>
> Yes, we would have liked things to remain as they were. But this is not possible. Already most of these things are gone and the rest are going.
>
> We must give up one thing to gain another. The better roads we built brought tourists and sportsmen and cut into

our fish and game supply, and it increased our taxes. But who would give up our paved road?

We can grow and develop with Alaska or we can fight this development. If we choose to fight it we are fighting only a delaying action. We cannot win. We can only hold our tiny area stagnant while the rest of Alaska runs by us.

Less than a year after going into business, the Stewarts installed a Duplex newspaper press that they bought in Hoquiam, Washington. It had been used for years by the daily *Washingtonian*. One-half of their new building was shop, one-quarter office and one-quarter a private apartment.

Stewart came out for growth and development, which would remain the paper's stance. His editorials fought against reservation of Alaska land by the federal government under the Alaska National Interest Lands Conservation Act of 1980, reiterating the belief that multiple land use need not detract from the wilderness experience.

The tax man cometh

Between 1960 and 1964 discoveries of oil were made by the major petroleum companies offshore in Cook Inlet. There were fourteen drilling platforms, all with underwater pipelines taking the oil to the shipping docks for loading onto tankers.

Within thirty miles of Kenai and Soldotna was an oil refining complex. Union Chemicals, a division of Union Oil Co., produced ammonia and urea for fertilizer. Phillips' LNG plant shipped liquefied gas to Japan. Tesoro and Chevron USA refineries shipped thousands of barrels of gasoline and oil.

A migration reminiscent of the gold rush days of 1898 brought oil experts from all over the world to the Kenai Peninsula. Their families followed and the little towns of Kenai and Soldotna experienced a housing crunch as their populations skyrocketed

Kenai attracted industry besides oil and gas. Two large salmon canneries employed two hundred persons during the summer. To lengthen the fish processing season, a cold storage and new plants were built.

In the 1960s, the Kenai Peninsula's *Cheechako News* was published three times a week. It went daily in April 1968. It was a full-size, seven-column, four-page newspaper. Its style and content were breezy and fresh.

The Internal Revenue Service threatened to close down the paper in 1969, claiming it was delinquent in paying $13,676 in withholding and Social Security taxes. A Small Business Administration representative rescued the newspaper by posting a cardboard sign on the front door bearing the words "U.S. Government Property."

By taking "peaceable possession" of the property via its prior earthquake disaster loan, the SBA averted a shutdown by the IRS. This gave the Stewarts time to arrange for a loan to pay off the tax debt, without missing a single issue.

The *Cheechako News* experienced tough competition when John Nelson started the weekly *Peninsula Clarion* on August 27, 1970, a five-column, twelve-page tabloid, which sold for a dime. It also was sent free to all post-office boxholders and rural route patrons. It was printed in Clint Young's Kenai print shop.

Stewart promised for several years that he was going to the new, more efficient offset method of printing, even before papers like the *Petersburg Press* and *Juneau Empire* switched in 1964. But he never did. His competition, the *Clarion*, began as an offset publication.

Clarion features pictures

The *Clarion*'s front page featured large photographs of local scenes, thanks to the offset method of printing that makes pictures easier to produce.

The *Clarion* was born into a beehive of controversy. Residents were opposing zoning ordinances proposed by the borough assembly; the borough had appropriated insufficient funds for the school; the people opposed the schoolteachers' high salaries, and the city electrical workers were out on strike. Folks were complaining about an economic depression as the oil companies slowed down drilling and production.

During Nelson's management, the *Clarion*'s editorial tone was ultra conservative, leading to the accusation of it being aligned with the John Birch Society. He viewed the national scene as one in which the liberals had "declared war on our Christian traditions, constitutional concepts, free enterprise economics and old-fashioned Bible morals." Alaska's government, he wrote, was heading down the road toward socialism, Communism, and ultimate control by "power-hungry bureaucrats."

The conservative *Clarion*'s circulation soon exceeded the *Cheechako News* and exceeded that of James and Marie McDowell's *Cook Inlet Courier* in Homer, at that time an equally conservative area of the Kenai Peninsula. Nelson sold the *Clarion* to Clinton Young in August 1972. Young had been printing the paper for Nelson.

Charles Clinton Young was born in Michigan on April 26, 1906. His father homesteaded in Sheridan County, Montana, and Clint began his journalism career at age eleven, hand-setting type after school for the weekly *Antelope Independent*. He graduated from typesetter to flyboy on the press, the person who spread ink on the type. In a 1960 interview he said, "The type was mounted on an old butter churn. The hand-operated contraption could just get out the paper's two hundred circulation."

Young took the borough assembly to task for not putting print jobs out for competitive bid. The borough chairman responded, "Oh, we don't put them out to bid. We use them as a kind of political plum."

As a consequence, if an editor dared to criticize the administration, he was boycotted as a potential printing contractor, even if it cost the taxpayers more for a lesser product.

The *Clarion*'s editorial din against such a policy forced the assembly into competitive bidding. The *Clarion*'s new photo-offset operation could submit lower bids than the hot-metal typeset plants.

Young was a strong supporter of moving the capital from Juneau to "where it is accessible to the scrutiny of the greatest number of people. Let's get in and vote to move it and stop this senseless squandering of money on the Juneau landholders' rock pile."

Clarion goes daily

Young sold the paper in October 1975 to Kenai Peninsula Newspapers, Inc., a firm organized by Max Swearingen, Dick Morgan and Patrick O'Connell.

Swearingen, a Kansas native, and his family moved to Kenai in September 1974 when he was hired as the first general manager of the Peninsula Oilers Baseball Club in the Alaska League. During a newspaper career that spanned some twenty-three years, mostly in the circulation and promotion areas, Swearingen worked on newspapers in Kansas, Missouri, Arkansas and Florida.

O'Connell was a journalism instructor at Kenai Central High School, and Morgan was the owner of Morgan's Steel in Kenai.

The *Clarion* became Alaska's eighth daily newspaper on June 5, 1978, publishing five mornings a week and boasting the largest circulation of any peninsula paper. The decision to go daily was based on an overwhelming response to a *Clarion* survey conducted several months previous.

The *Clarion* joined the *Cheechako News* in supporting the developers in their battles with the conservationists

Harry V. Martin became managing editor of the *Clarion* in May 1977. He had been residing in Napa, California, while writing a book entitled *The Second American Civil War*, a conflict he predicted would take place following World War III.

Martin was born in San Francisco on March 26, 1939. He received a bachelor's degree from San Francisco State College and a master's degree from the University of New South Wales, Sydney, Australia.

Martin resigned as editor after a few months. *Clarion* owners alleged he had pocketed ad dollars for a promised newspaper supplement that was never printed. The *Clarion* began investigating Martin's past and he sued for libel. The case dragged on for three years and then the newspaper settled with Martin for $13,000, which his creditors immediately attached.

Ronnie Chappell succeeded Martin as the *Clarion*'s editor. Chappell had joined the paper in 1978, a week after it switched from weekly to daily. He was editor in 1979 when the newspaper successfully challenged the City of Kenai over applications of city manager applicants. Chappell was succeeded by Steve Rinehart in 1980 when Chappell became peninsula reporter for the *Anchorage Daily News*. He later went with the oil industry in public relations. Rinehart stayed only a year and moved to the *Homer News* as managing editor.

Dunsworth takes over

Swearingen, co-publisher with Dick Morgan, died of a heart attack on September 7, 1981, at age forty-six. Wayne Dunsworth, the business manager, moved up to take over publisher Swearingen's duties and became co-owner.

John Marrs, who was born in Nebraska in 1947, took over as managing editor and was popular because of his community activities. He became the *Clarion*'s editor-in-chief in 1983.

The *Clarion* enjoyed unprecedented growth during the 1980s as did the entire Kenai Peninsula. Population rose from 32,303 people in 1982 to 38,930 in 1984, central peninsula and Homer being the fastest growing regions of the state in that short span. Population was up to 40,802 in 1990 and was 49,691 in 2000.

The *Clarion* had offices in both Kenai and Soldotna. By 1985, it was running twenty-eight to sixty-four pages daily. Its Friday edition included an additional twenty- to twenty-four-page supplement titled *The Tides*, which carried the weekly radio and television logs and syndicated material from Copley and The Associated Press news services, plus local feature stories. Editor Marrs wrote thought-provoking editorials on controversial local issues. He supported relocation of the state capital from Juneau to western Alaska, Seward being favored.

The editorial page, titled "Opinions," offered an appetizing daily fare of imaginative opinions on timely issues. The *Clarion* joined the loud citizen outcry protesting the increase in retirement pay that legislators voted themselves in 1976. The act was repealed except for "grandfather" coverage for ten lawmakers already vested in the system.

When the voters rejected the multimillion-dollar price tag for relocating the capital to western Alaska, the *Clarion* suggested electing a capital every four years the same way we elect governors. Or, make the capital's site a retention election as we do our judges. Every four years the voters would say leave it or move it

The *Clarion* favored the state's purchase of the Alaska Railroad from the federal government but opposed giving the governor authority to appoint and dismiss members of the state's railroad commission. It favored instead that the authority be set up through constitutional amendments to insulate it from political influence.

Stewart continues criticism

Meanwhile, the Stewarts had continued to publish the *Cheechako News* weekly, after losing the daily market to the *Clarion*. They turned out vigorous editorial comment on state and local affairs. Bureaucrats came in for their share of negative criticism. Stewart likened them to chickweed:

> You can poison the chickweed. Plow, fertilize and plant the ground with profitable crops, but still the chickweed pops up from nowhere and overwhelms the highly desirable and beneficial crops that you so carefully planted and tended.

The *News* also was strong for moving the capital from Juneau.

The Stewarts sold the *Cheechako News* in March 1983 to Anchorage advertising executive Robert L. Grimm. After twenty-three years publishing the *News*, they wanted to enjoy more leisure at their Kenai River home and perhaps do some writing.

Grimm had been general manager for Alaska Advertisers Agency, which represented Carr-Gottstein interests throughout the state. He had previous newspaper experience in advertising with the Tribune Publishing Co. in Lewiston, Idaho.

A financial partner in the new ownership of the *News* was Kelly V. Roberts, a certified public accountant in Lewiston. Grimm's wife, Karyn, worked on the paper.

The paper's name was changed in October 1985 to the *Kenai Peninsula Soldotna Sun*. It also changed from a broadsheet, standard-sized newspaper to a modern tabloid design.

The *Sun* suspended publication in March 1986, when it fell victim to rising costs and declining revenue.

Morris invests in Clarion

William S. Morris III's Morris Publishing bought the *Clarion* in December 1991. It installed Ronnie Hughes as publisher, replacing Dunsworth who retired when he sold his interest in the paper. Morris invested $1 million in a larger press and seven thousand square feet of added building space for the operation. The bigger Goss Suburban press is sixty feet long and needed the added space. It also could produce twenty-eight thousand newspapers an hour with full color, twice the speed of its old Goss Community.

Hughes moved to the *Clarion* from Crescent City, Florida, where he was general manager of another Morris newspaper, the *Courier-Journal*. He left Kenai in mid-1994, after the newspaper switched from

Clarion Installs New Press

—Peninsula Clarion publisher Ronnie Hughes, center, Dick Westmoreland of the composition department, left, and assistant managing editor Jon Little look over one of the first newspapers to come off the paper's new Goss Suburban 1500 press in December 1992. The press was part of an expansion at the Kenai paper following its purchase by Morris Publishing Group of Augusta, Georgia. -*Photo by Roy Shapley courtesy of the Peninsula Clarion.*

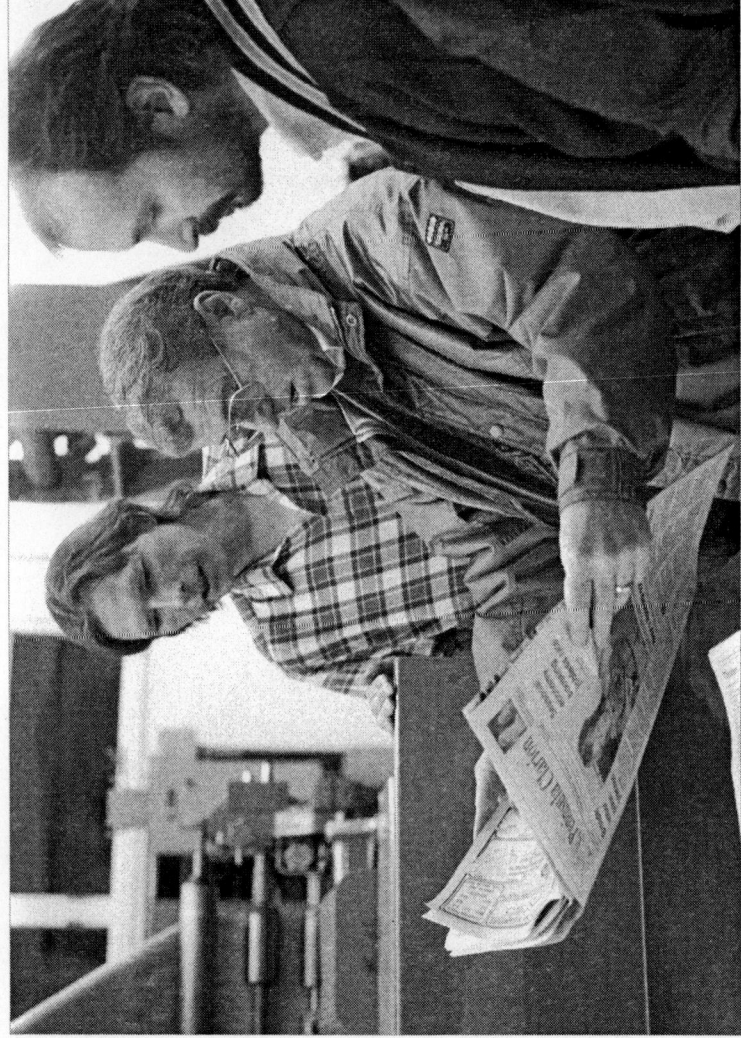

Dick Morgan, left, and Wayne Dunsworth stand outside the Peninsula Clarion's Kenai facility in 1990, shortly after announcing they had sold the newspaper to Morris Communications Corp. of Augusta, Georgia. *-Photo courtesy of the Peninsula Clarion.*

Peninsula Clarion–2005

Stan Pitlo
Publisher

Lori Evans
*Editor & Publisher
Homer News
Ex. Editor at the Clarion*

Clarion Photos by M. Scott Moon

tabloid to broadsheet. Susie Morris Baker, daughter of Mr. and Mrs. William Morris III, also an officer in the newspaper corporation, served as publisher for a year.

Stan Pitlo, current publisher of the *Clarion*, was named general manager of the newspaper in 1995 and publisher in 1999. After Baker returned to Georgia, he was named director of Alaska publications for Morris. His executive editor was Lori Evans, who joined the *Clarion* in February 1991 after eleven years as a reporter for the *Juneau Empire*. During their tenure, the *Clarion* began publishing a Sunday edition in June 1997.

Pitlo was born in Seattle in 1951, and earned a bachelor's degree in communications in 1974 at Washington State University. That same year he moved to Anchorage where he spent ten years in the advertising department of *The Anchorage Times*. He held a variety of media jobs in Alaska until he joined the *Clarion* as marketing director in 1993.

Evans was born in Alexandria, Louisiana, and grew up in New Orleans and Houston. Before going to Juneau, Evans earned a bachelor's degree with a major in English and a minor in journalism at Hardin-Simmons University in Abilene, Texas, in 1976. She worked on Florida newspapers, rising to editor at the *Englewood* (Florida) *Herald*. At the *Clarion* she worked up to managing editor and is now executive editor and editor-publisher of the *Homer News*.

The *Clarion*, which some described at its beginning in 1970 as a conservative political flyer, has developed into a leading seven-day Alaska newspaper in a relatively short time, compared with other Alaska dailies. The *Fairbanks Daily News-Miner* was one hundred in 2003, the *Empire* was eighty years old in 2002, the *Ketchikan Daily News* was seventy in 2004, and the *Kodiak Mirror* sixty-three, the same year. During its growing years, in addition to precedent-setting legal battles, the *Clarion* has had its share of amusing situations.

Marrs tells about a story published on the front page one April 1. It reported that a Korean contractor, Loo Flir Pa, had caught a world-record 101-pound king salmon while visiting Kenai. In a "Reader's Notebook" on page 2 of the same edition, Marrs advised that *Loo Flir Pa* is *April Fool* spelled backward. However, someone at the local radio station missed page 2 and broadcast the front-page story, which must have been a pronouncing problem for the announcer.

Marr's later wrote: "It was so successful we never tried to top it, probably for good reason. Newspapers shouldn't play with their credibility too often."

Chapters 55-58

New Publishers,

New Technology

Lead Newspapers

Into Twenty-First Century

Newspapers will continue to be the leading medium for the next fifty years.

– W. Dean Singleton, president, MediaNews Group, co-owner of the *Kodiak Mirror* and the *Fairbanks News-Miner*, 1992.

Fairbanks Daily News-Miner

The voice of Interior Alaska since 1903

WEDNESDAY, JANUARY 12, 2005

TODAY — SPILL CLEANUP

House gets update on gas line

ALCOHOL TAX — Governor mulls hike to deter kids, abuse — ALASKA

ANOREXIA — 'Sopranos' actress to share her story — LIFE

NFL HOPEFUL — Colony High grad wants spot in pros — SPORTS

WEATHER — It's so mild, it's wild — High of 35; low of 24

Anchorage Daily News

ALASKA'S NEWSPAPER

Tuesday, January 25, 2005

Charging moose kills lead dog of Iditarod musher

Juneau Empire

FRIDAY, Jan. 21, 2005 — 50 cents

The voice of Alaska's capital city since 1912

Bill cuts parties out of absentee ballot requests

Hostage — American pleads for life in video — World/A-8

Sumo — Foreigners dominate Japan's national sport — Sports/A-8

Taking off — Students learn about space in astronaut trainee's class — Schools/B-1

Mostly sunny 33/15

Peninsula Clarion

Vol. 35, Issue 101 — WEDNESDAY, JANUARY 26, 2005 — Soldotna-Kenai, Alaska

Up Front / In the news

School budget gets A for effort

Not perfect, but figures show district in better shape than past few years

Chapter 55

Gregory, McGuire Acquire Nugget

The *Nome Nugget* observed its one hundredth anniversary with a special edition on January 1, 2000. That was exactly one hundred years to the day after the first issue of the *Nugget*, a Special New Years Edition, came off the press.

The *Nugget* is Alaska's oldest newspaper but suspended production for nine months during World War II because of a shortage of manpower and supplies. When it resumed publication it went through several noncontroversial owners and editors until it was taken over by Albro Gregory, who had been an outspoken editor in Fairbanks, Ketchikan, Juneau, and Petersburg.

It was to be the end of the journalistic trail for the old wire service veteran. He had covered Alaska issues in Washington DC for the United Press during the campaign for statehood. In 1959, after statehood, he joined *Jessen's Weekly* in Fairbanks before dazzling Southeast Alaska.

When Gregory later retired to Fairbanks, he sold the *Nugget* to Nancy McGuire, an equally outspoken journalist, who blankets the Northwest with six thousand copies a week, more circulation than some Alaska daily newspapers.

Her success has discouraged competition, including that of Alaska Newspapers Inc., the successful Native-owned newspaper chain.

After suspension

But first, the heirs of gold rush journalist George Maynard sold the suspended *Nugget* in August 1943 to Wilfred and Emily Boucher who began with a circulation of about eight hundred. The Bouchers were the daughter and son-in-law of Antonio (Tony) Polet, pioneer Nome merchant.

Emily Polet was born in Nome and earned a bachelor's degree at the University of Washington in 1927. Her future husband, Wilfred Amide Boucher, was born in Coeur d'Alene, Idaho, and received an engineering degree from the same university in 1925.

When the Bouchers bought the *Nugget*, Wilfred served as editor-publisher and Emily as society editor. Their first issue of the revitalized *Nome Nugget* on October 1, 1943, was a twenty-page "Souvenir Edition" describing Nome and the northwestern region of which it was the trading center.

Emily Boucher moves up

By 1945, Emily was co-editor with her husband and six years later, she was managing editor, a role she held for the remainder of her association with the paper. Although she never carried the title publisher, those were her duties, especially after her husband's death in 1951. She was the third woman to publish a Nome newspaper.

Although the *Nugget* did not take a pro or anti stand on statehood, its readers were exposed to oft-quoted *Anchorage Daily Times* pro-statehood editorials and her father was an outspoken supporter.

Nome's community leaders were divided on the statehood issue. The Lomens, Nome businessmen, opposed it, fearing additional taxes. Howard Lyng, an independent gold mine operator, one-time Democratic National Committeeman and territorial senator, favored it.

The Bouchers editorialized against the plan to have Alaskans elect their governor instead of full statehood as being "a sop craftily conceived by the anti-statehood group, of which U.S. Sen. Hugh Butler of Nebraska was the mouthpiece, to head off statehood."

When legislators contemplated abolishing the Alaska Development Board, of which Tony Polet was a member, the *Nugget* suggested that "the goose, which had laid a golden egg for the people of Alaska, is about to be cooked." It urged its readers to tell their legislators that they want the board to continue its good work.

The paper urged construction of a seawall to protect Nome's shoreline during its annual storms that wiped out the homes and businesses adjacent to the beach line. It was pointed out that Nome was the commercial, communication, transportation and government center for the coastal area of about 147,000 square miles. The area had a population of 11,877, of which 1,559 resided in Nome. Congress approved construction of a $1.875 million seawall in 1948.

The *Nugget* circulated in most of the Eskimo villages of the Seward Peninsula. Many of the readers had little or no schooling so the language had to be kept quite simple. Some villages took only one subscription and everyone shared its news.

One subscriber paid with reindeer meat from his herd; another with a choice fifty-pound king salmon caught in the spring run at Unalakleet; still another picked a gallon of luscious lingonberries late in the fall. An Eskimo trapper at Pilot Point offered to exchange a couple of his pen and ink sketches for a subscription.

In addition to publishing the *Nugget*, Mrs. Boucher was a part-time city librarian. She also operated a real estate and insurance business.

The Seward Peninsula did not share in the revolutionary changes that swept Alaska following statehood. Its population of less than twelve thousand represented 5 percent of the total state population, of which approximately 80 percent were Eskimos living a subsistence lifestyle. Seven or eight months of the year Nome is accessible only by air.

Emily Boucher determinedly carried on as editor-publisher of the triweekly *Nugget* until September 1963 when she sold it to a group of Nome businessmen. Twenty years of publishing the paper, plus her other civic and business activities, had taken its toll physically.

Enter Phelps and Willis

State Sen. Lester Bronson filled in as interim editor. Though lacking previous journalistic experience, Bronson, fifty-six, enjoyed the trust and confidence of the community. He was a member of the Territorial House, 1955, of the State Senate, 1959-1964, and the State House, 1969-1970.

He was called "Tiger" Bronson because of a brief career as a prizefighter in his youth and because of his pugilistic behavior in the legislature. One time, he got so angry over newspaper coverage of his legislative conduct that he threatened to have the editors brought to trial before the legislature.

Al Phelps, a native of Las Vegas, New Mexico, and former publisher of weeklies in the Pacific Northwest, succeeded Bronson as the *Nugget*'s editor in November 1964.

In the fall of 1966, Charles F. Willis Jr., president of Alaska Airlines, joined with Phelps and Fairbanks banker Vernon Forbes to buy the *Nugget*. They formed the Nome Nugget Publishing Co. for the purpose of acquiring a chain of Alaska newspapers.

Gregory livens Nome

Phelps and Willis also purchased the Wrangell and Petersburg newspapers. They transferred Albro Gregory from Petersburg to Nome as *Nugget* editor in December 1968. Gregory introduced a journalistic sensationalism that Nome residents had not experienced since the gold rush days.

Gregory wrote his friend, Jerome Sheldon, a colleague from his Fairbanks newspaper days:

> Nome is a paradox. On the one hand we have the Swedish Covenant Church, which is against fun. On the other hand, we have the rugged individualists who were born of the gold rush, who believe in two-fisted drinking and fun, fun, fun.

A former editor of the *Nugget*, Bob Richardson, was a member of the former group. He refused to accept liquor ads.

Gregory, who liked his martinis at the Breakers bar, soon changed that policy.

Gregory purchased the *Nugget* in April 1971 after failure of the Willis-Phelps-Forbes chain. Gregory and his wife, Adelaide, lived in the rear of the newspaper office. She served as business manager of the paper and lab technician at the Nome hospital until she died of cancer in October 1973.

Gregory sported a long, bushy white beard on his ruddy, round face, and wore casual Bush garb, suggesting the prototype of an old Alaska "Sourdough," much to the delight of the visiting tourists. Alaska Airlines paid him $2 a head to escort tourists through the *Nugget* plant. The building was from the old army post. The equipment displayed was the old hot-metal plant idled by the switch to offset with press work done in Anchorage. Most of the visitors thought maybe Gregory was a dropout from Dyea and White Pass stampede days who had come to a final resting place in Nome.

One well-to-do widow became so enamoured with the bewhiskered newsman that she promoted matrimony. She had been a widow for ten years when she and a friend were tourists in a Nome coffee shop and spied the local editor at a nearby table. A conversation ensued that led to a correspondence and a wedding six months later. In sharing the happy news with his fellow journalists throughout the state, Gregory's special dispatch read:

> All the bars on Nome's Front Street emptied about 7 p.m. on January 22 when police cars, with lights flashing and sirens wailing sped toward the roadhouse. But crime wasn't the problem. It was just Nome's finest escorting Albro Gregory, editor of the *Nome Nugget*, and his bride to their wedding reception. Some fifty friends celebrated with them. A modern day fairy story.

Gregory filled the *Nugget* with pictures of his bride because, "sez" he, "she's a pretty lady." The marriage lasted only briefly.

Gregory helped shorten Nome's long winter nights by his unpredictable editorial stances. He wanted Nome to return to its gold rush flavor, so he railed against replacing the wooden sidewalks with concrete and against paving the streets.

In an editorial titled "Mud in Streets Is Our Business," he contended that "it seems to me that if we here in Nome want to wade through mud sometimes and get dust blown in our eyes at other times, it should be our own damned business." He recommended that Nomeites cover the concrete sidewalks with boards. When he lost his battle, he complained: "Next they'll be telling us to wear white shirts and ties to the office, just like in Anchorage."

Gregory vowed he would not allow outsiders to foist any more newfangled things on the town. Parking meters on Front Street would come only "over my dead body." Whereupon, Mayor George Sullivan of Anchorage sent a parking meter to Nome in June 1975. Nome City Manager Herb Hensley and Nome Mayor Robert Renshaw had it installed in front of the *Nugget* office, where Gregory's car was parked.

When Gregory returned to the office from the Breakers, he found a parking ticket on his car, the one and only parking ticket in Nome's history.

A snowplow swept the meter away with its blade in December 1978, and it was stolen once. Each time it was replaced and continued to stand in front of the *Nugget* office as a reminder of the hysterical past. After new sidewalks were installed, a good base for the meter was not possible so the current *Nugget* owner moved it inside for safekeeping.

Gregory's spicy language and outspoken editorials made some readers gasp in shock and others laugh uproariously. In the words of Stanton Patty, Alaska editor for the *Seattle Times*: "In print, he can be as burning as acid on an open sore – when necessary. Sometimes an editor has to use strong words to stick up for what he thinks is best for his town. Gregory never ducked an issue even though it cost him advertising and the *Nugget* was struggling to pay its bills."

His unconventional headlines aroused attention. In reporting a school board meeting, the headline read: "*All Hell Breaks Loose on School Finance*." Later when the board arrived at an acceptable solution, his headline read: "*Let's Quit Bitchin*." His lax attitude toward alcoholism was especially repugnant to the church-going element. The day came when a second paper was launched by a group who "were sick of the bar owners' point of view."

Straights start Straights

The Bering Straights made its debut on February 27, 1976, with Phillip Dunne, twenty-six, a disciple of the Baha'i faith, as its editor. Dunne, the son of a retired labor reporter for the *San Diego Evening Tribune*, wandered north "to find himself" after completing two years at Mesa Community College in Arizona. In his words, he was "confused and disoriented by the world in which he lived." The Baha'is wanted to start a community in Nome. Phil volunteered to lead a group of twenty-seven missionaries.

The *Straights* started as a mimeographed, twelve-page eleven-by-seventeen-inch tabloid. Editorials and news articles emphasized the need for curbing alcoholism. Religious meetings received generous coverage. Nome had eleven different church groups. Dunne had to rely on volunteer help to put out the paper as advertising revenue barely covered the cost of supplies, with nothing left for salaries, including Dunne's.

He alienated the town's major advertiser in one of his first editorials by criticizing the unsanitary toilet facilities at the Wien Airlines' airport waiting room. The airline boycotted the *Straights* throughout the paper's seven years of existence.

The *Nugget* boasted a circulation of about 1,500 so the new paper had difficulty securing ads. At the end of a year of tireless effort, Dunne announced his retirement only to retract it when Leo B. Rasmussen, local merchant and multitermed mayor, along with Mike Murphy and Richard Rusk, offered to guarantee a financial base for the operation. Dunne stayed on for another four years, transforming it into a printed publication.

Among the *Straights'* strongest supporters were John and Barbara Shaffer, the Methodist minister and his wife. She was a member of the city council and served as business manager of the *Straights*. The Shaffers were primarily responsible for promoting a referendum in August 1978 to determine whether or not Nome residents would vote the town dry as Bethel had done shortly before. The *Straights* campaigned for a yes vote while the *Nugget* urged a no vote. The result was 70 percent against prohibition.

Dunne relinquished the editorship in November 1980 in order to pursue his studies in elementary teaching at the University of Alaska Fairbanks. Robert A. Rawls, a native of North Carolina, offered to take Dunne's place.

Rawls had been an itinerant carpenter in Alaska since 1975. Although he lacked formal journalism training, his mild-mannered, people-oriented personality helped him do a creditable job. He did nothing to offend his readers and was content just to be performing a useful community service. However, psychological strain led to his resignation in December 1981.

Meanwhile, significant changes were taking place at the *Nugget*. Its crusty, seventy-year-old editor was again relaxing in the arms of romance and ready to retire from his lifetime career. On February 24, 1980, he married Jane Konicki, regional representative of the Social Security Administration in Fairbanks. The rites took place in the Breakers saloon, with Superior Court Judge William Sanders in his black judicial robes conducting the ceremony.

Then in June, Gregory sold the *Nugget* and announced his departure for Fairbanks to write his memoirs. Nome's city fathers declared "A Salute to Albro Gregory Day" and two hundred well-wishers attended a banquet in the editor's honor at the Fort Davis roadhouse. They established a $3,000 scholarship in his name to be awarded to a Nome area high school student who wanted to go to college and major in English or journalism. In his farewell remarks, Gregory promised that his successor would continue to help Alaska "despite meddling foot draggers like the environmentalists."

McGuire takes over

A local schoolteacher owned the *Nugget* briefly, hired interim editors and served as one himself until January 1, 1982, when Nancy L. McGuire became owner, editor and publisher of the *Nugget*. Nome's fourth woman publisher was a tough competitor to the *Straights*. It lasted only twelve more months.

In bowing out on December 21, 1982, the *Straights* people expressed satisfaction in having accomplished their primary purpose, namely, to make the *Nugget* a more respectable newssheet. At least they had bid goodbye to their nemesis, Albro Gregory, whose journalistic exploits were recounted for years in newsrooms from Ketchikan to Nome.

McGuire was born in December 1943 in Pittsburgh, Pennsylvania. As an infant she was taken to Mars, Pennsylvania, where she grew up. ("Now you have met someone from Mars," she says.)

She earned a bachelor's degree and a master's degree from Indiana University of Pennsylvania. She taught high school science for thirteen years. In 1978, she became director of the arts and science program with Northwest Community College in Nome. She also worked as a volunteer reporter for *Nugget*.

McGuire began providing comprehensive news coverage for the town and strong editorials in the tradition of former *Nugget* publishers. Like Gregory, she had the *Nugget* printed in Anchorage. She took advantage of the latest technology to provide full color photos and ads in the publication.

In 1998, she created a equally colorful Web site for the *Nugget* (http://nomenugget.com) and became Nome's first internet service provider. Her reporting and that of her eleven-member staff is fair and accurate, especially compared with early Nome editors and reporters. Circulation climbed toward six thousand.

Her success attracted the interest of Alaska Newspapers, Inc., a subsidiary of the Calista Corp., a Native corporation for the Yukon-Kuskokwim Delta area. It owned seven other small town newspapers. McGuire declined to sell out to ANI. The corporation ignored her

Two Outspoken Journalists

—Nancy McGuire, above, is the fourth woman to publish a Nome newspaper and the most outspoken. She bought the Nome Nugget from Albro Gregory, left, in 1982, who had owned it since 1971. Gregory was a controversial editor in Fairbanks, Ketchikan, Juneau and Petersburg before going to Nome. -*Photos courtesy of Peggy Fagerstom-Nome Photos and the Nome Nugget.*

success in defeating *The Bering Straights* in a year and started the *Bering Strait Record* to compete with the *Nugget*.

The idea was to force her to sell her newspaper so they could merge it with their *Record*, discontinue the *Record* and capitalize on the *Nugget*'s history and reputation. Rob Stapleton, who had been a photographer for the *Nugget*, was the first editor of the *Record* but lasted only a few months.

The *Record* and the *Nugget*, both weeklies, fought for advertising dollars and engaged in a sometimes tense battle for the news. However, their staffs were friendly.

On a Saturday morning that staffs of both papers were celebrating the *Record*'s third anniversary, ANI publisher Christopher Casati arrived from Anchorage to announce that the *Record* was being closed.

"It was definitely and always a cash thing," Casati said of the decision to close. "We threw the best people we could get at that job, and they did the best they could.

"The Nome marketplace just could not sustain two newspapers."

The *Record* employed four people when it closed, managing editor Tommy Wells, business manager Joe Nash and their wives.

Wells, who moved to Alaska from Texas with his wife, accepted a job at the *Nugget*.

McGuire's sharp editorial pen continues to attract supporters to the *Nugget* and on one occasion changed a local agency's policy. She wrote in her January 13, 2000, issue that Limburger "stinks" and "the same goes for the Nome Joint Utilities' fuel discount for board members and employees." Shortly after the *Nugget* reached its six thousand subscribers, the utilities board cancelled the discount.

Nome looks to future

When McGuire and her staff put out their centennial edition on January 1, 2000, rather than recite what occurred in an eventful one hundred years, the *Nugget*'s articles focused on the future of Nome with predictions written by community leaders.

Publisher McGuire herself editorialized in a whimsical manner reflecting in her Centennial Edition the boosterism of previous Nome publishers:

"What lies ahead in the next century? It's fun to speculate. Nome will expand so that Front Street will extend (twelve miles) as far east as Cape Nome, which will be covered with trees and expensive sea-view homes. Our westward boundary will be all the way to the Cripple River where the Mining Dude Ranch will still be looking for the illusive mother lode. The road to Teller will be dotted with tourist hotels and Pilgrim Hot Springs will be a world-class health spa catering to spiritualists and bird watchers on the lookout for the bristle-thighed curlew.

"Nome, Kotzebue, Barrow and Fairbanks will be connected by rail . . . Nomeites will continue to spoil their dogs and . . . . The *Nome Nugget* will still be Alaska's Oldest Newspaper."

And the newspaper's masthead will still proclaim: "There is no place like Nome."

Chapter 56

Mukluk Telegraph to Satellite

Opening The Associated Press correspondent's office in Juneau two years before statehood dramatically increased Alaska news volume. It was a long way from interviewing travelers in from the creeks or up from the States – the Mukluk Telegraph. The news volume was given another boost when a correspondent was placed in Anchorage in the early 1970s.

In 1949, AP members in Alaska agreed to pay for a correspondent in Juneau during the sixty-day legislative sessions, which occurred every other year. That whetted the appetite for more Alaska news, leading to full-time correspondent in 1956.

Prior to 1956, AP members in Alaska sent stories to the bureau in Seattle, which transmitted them north to all members. That is, members provided the stories if they remembered or had time.

Murlin Spencer, bureau chief in Seattle, was in charge of AP's Alaska news coverage when William J. Tobin was assigned as the first correspondent in Juneau in 1956. Spencer later said that assigning Tobin to Juneau "was the best thing The Associated Press had ever done when it came to assigning somebody to a new job."

Tobin put on the wire up to two dozen stories a day when the Legislature was in session. He also covered oil developments, such as the first oil strike on the Kenai in 1957. He did everything from filing stories for Alaska members, to rewriting Alaska stories for the national wire, to doing a weather roundup.

However, before coming north, Tobin had reservations about Alaska. He joined AP as a copyboy in Indianapolis while attending Butler University. After graduation and two years in the army, he returned as a writer until assigned to AP Newsfeatures in New York, followed by regional membership executive in Louisville, Kentucky.

The recently married young AP executive knew little of Alaska when assigned to Juneau. So he consulted the Louisville Library. He found that there was a Juneau Country Club. He informed his wife, Marge, and her mother that with a country club, Juneau couldn't be too primitive.

When the Tobins arrived in Juneau they discovered the Juneau Country Club was a typical Juneau bar and restaurant located at Salmon Creek, about three miles north of Juneau.

Tobin said the editors and owners of Juneau's two newspapers, the *Empire* and the *Independent* welcomed him. The *Empire* had only one reporter at that time, Bob Kederick. Tobin's arrival doubled its reporting staff.

Tobin set up Alaska's first election central, collecting returns and tabulating them – with the help of his wife and others – as they were phoned in from throughout the territory.

A Teletype had been installed in a new pressroom on the third floor of the Federal Building for use of the full-time correspondent. That speeded capital news to AP members.

The pressroom expanded as newspaper and broadcast members, enthused by AP coverage, sent their own correspondents to Juneau to supplement AP. The Legislature expanded in what became the State Capitol Building after statehood. So by 1992, AP was forced to find quarters a block away from the capitol. Other news correspondents found their own space.

Tobin moved up in AP in 1960 to assistant bureau chief in Baltimore and then bureau chief in Montana. Another assignment was imminent in 1963. By then, the Tobins had three children and wanted to settle down, preferably in Alaska. Tobin asked Bob Atwood at *The Anchorage Daily Times* if he had a job for him. The response was, "Managing editor beginning Monday."

It didn't happen quite that fast but did happen. After more than sixty years in the business, forty-two at the *Times* and "The Voice of the Times," Tobin is still active. His Sunday column, begun as a Saturday column on July 20, 1963, is the longest running in Alaska.

United Press first

United Press (UP) had a chance to sew up Alaska first in providing news to Alaska's editors. However, its on-again, off-again service ceded the Alaska market to the AP. The AP had previously provided news indirectly through the *Seattle Post-Intelligencer*. That newspaper provided stories to one or more of the independent news bureaus serving Alaska.

Before that, Alaska editors received Outside news by talking with steamship captains and passengers, who also brought newspapers from the States, or from interviewing those who mushed in over the trail.

The U.S. Army Signal Corps' system of connecting scattered military posts in the wilderness brought the first operational telegraph links. The system allowed public and commercial use as well as government business. By the fall of 1905, a submarine cable was completed from Seattle to Sitka, Juneau, Skagway, Valdez, and Seward, a length of 2,800 miles. It was the longest submarine cable built within the United States at that time.

The submarine cable, combined with 1,500 miles of landlines and 107 miles of the new wireless, formed what was known as the Washington-Alaska Military Cable and Telegraph System, later named Alaska Communications System, a part of the U.S. Army Signal Corps.

Skagway's *Alaskan* and Juneau's *Record-Miner* were the first newspapers to avail themselves of the WAMCATS system in 1902, before it extended westward. They provided their readers with a brief news budget from the AP, made up mornings at the *Seattle P-I*.

United Press north in '07

Ohio publisher E. W. Scripps founded United Press in 1907 by merging his news services. Scripps had founded the first major newspaper chain in the United States and created three news organizations to serve them. UP service was offered to Alaska in 1907. Signing up for it were Juneau's *Daily Alaska Dispatch*, the *Fairbanks News*, the *Seward Gateway*, the *Nome Gold Digger* and the Skagway's *Daily Alaskan*. UP discontinued the service to Alaska after two years.

After UP left Alaska, the papers received news dispatches from the Alaska News Bureau in Seattle, managed by Elmer Friend, former telegraph editor for the *Seattle Star* and later city editor of Juneau's *Empire*.

In the fall of 1910, five of the largest papers quit subscribing to Friend's service. They switched to a new one, Alaska Press Association, set up by Will Steel, who with his brother, Harry, was a former Dawson, Nome and Cordova newsman. According to a story September 1, 1910, in Juneau's *Daily Record*, the change was made after Friend agreed to serve the *Tanana Star* in Fairbanks, a James Wickersham campaign sheet, even though the *Fairbanks Times* had an exclusive contract with Friend.

Ochs brings AP to Alaska

Adolph Ochs, publisher of the *New York Times*, accompanied by his wife and their daughter, Iphigene, visited Skagway's *Daily Alaskan* office in August 1909, while their steamer was in port. As a director of The Associated Press, he promised to see that its services would be extended to Alaska. It was available five years later. The *Alaska Daily Dispatch* in Juneau, the *Seward Gateway*, and the *Cordova Daily Times* were the first to subscribe.

In those early years, the papers received what was known as a "pony" (small) report from Seattle amounting to five hundred words. It was a telegram sent in Morse code by WAMCATS operators. Mistakes in transmission were common. More mistakes were common in reconstructing the skeletonized message to make it read in normal English.

Sometimes so many verbs, prepositions and conjunctions were omitted to reduce transmission costs, which were by the word, that it was difficult to make sense out of the wire. A prizefight could be reported in such brevity that everything could be understood except who won. The wire might say, "Dokes knocked out Smith fifth." The newspaper rewrite man then had to take his choice to make it read, "Joe Dokes knocked out Bill Smith in the fifth round," or "Joe Dokes was knocked out by Bill Smith in the fifth." Quite a difference.

The pony cable continued for small weekly newspapers through the 1950s, after which the proliferation of media made reporting of national and international news unnecessary for weeklies.

One of the last major stories before the pony budget was dropped was the assassination of President John F. Kennedy in November 22, 1963, right on the Friday deadline of weekly newspapers in Kodiak, Wrangell and Petersburg.

Next came Teletypes

The Anchorage Daily Times and the *Fairbanks Daily News-Miner* were the first newspapers to subscribe to AP's direct Teletype service in January 1945. Juneau's *Empire*, the *Ketchikan Alaska Chronicle* and *Cordova Times* followed later that year. ACS (former WAMCATS) inaugurated timed wire press service whereby the papers could take regular Teletype service in multiples of thirty minutes or more. This speeded the flow and increased the quantity of news. The papers received two hours of wire time a day – about six thousand words.

The AP leased a twenty-four-hour circuit from ACS in 1954. It was a two-way circuit, extending three thousand miles. It provided a continuous link between Seattle and the papers in Anchorage, Fairbanks, Juneau, Ketchikan, and Sitka, and also served twelve radio stations and later five television subscribers. The fee was over $100,000 a year which the members shared according to size of their operation.

That twenty-four-hour circuit allowed the AP to provide a punched tape to Alaska that could drive typesetters automatically.

The twenty-four-hour circuit was divided, one-half the time for afternoon newspaper budgets and one-half for the morning papers. It interrupted transmission periodically for fifteen minutes to allow members to file copy to the AP and other members.

This worked fine in theory but was abused. Someone would type "foobash" or some other garble during the open time, interfering with anyone wanting to send a news item. Alaska's first state governor, William Egan, had a Teletype in his office and on occasion typed his complaint about a story. On other occasions, members carried on personal business over the circuit, even asking for spelling of words rather than using a dictionary. It got so bad that after a few years the Seattle bureau sent a technician through the state taking off all of the keyboards, requiring members to file stories by telephone.

UP back but loses suit

United Press came back to Alaska in the 1930s to serve the *Alaska Press* in Juneau and the *Alaska Fishing News* and its successor, the *Ketchikan Daily News*. It also served the *Anchorage Daily News* and the *Fairbanks Daily News-Miner*, the latter as a supplement to its AP service. But the AP dominated the market.

The *Fishing News* converted to daily publication in 1945 and changed its name to *Ketchikan Daily News* in 1947. The *Daily News* was in head-to-head afternoon competition with the *Ketchikan Alaska Chronicle*, the Ketchikan AP member. *News* owners, the Charles family, dropped UP service and joined the AP in 1954, alleging a disproportionate high price for less news volume from UP and the need to be competitive with the *Chronicle*. This change was possible because the AP had lost a lawsuit in 1945 challenging its ability to offer exclusive contracts – one AP newspaper per town.

The lawsuit had been filed against the AP by Marshall Field III, who owned the *Chicago Sun*, a new tabloid competing against Col. Robert McCormick's *Chicago Tribune*. McCormick was the AP member who held the AP Chicago franchise. The case went to the U.S. Supreme Court, which ruled against the AP's exclusive contract policy. That forced the AP to sell its news to any organization that could pay the cost. The ruling led to the downfall of UP. Its subscribers could then switch to the bigger news agency that had a better state and regional newsgathering network.

UP sued the Charles for dropping its service, alleging that there was an automatic five-year extension of the contract beyond its termination date of February 14, 1954. After a jury in Ketchikan decided for the Charles, UP took the case to the Ninth Circuit Court of Appeals and lost again.

In May 1958, United Press merged with Hearst's International News Service (INS) to become UPI.

UPI's last gasp

UPI opened an Alaska bureau in the *Anchorage Daily News* building shortly after statehood in 1959. In April 1961 an Arizona newsman, Gordon Evans, moved from a San Francisco assignment to staff the office. Evans had been a navy journalist stationed in Kodiak during the Korean War and traveled most of Alaska.

Evans left after two years to be managing editor at the *Daily News*. The Anchorage UPI office closed in 1967.

UPI was sold to Doug Ruhe and Bill Geissler, two members of the Baha'i Faith in 1982, leading to rumors it was purchased by the Rev. Sun Myung Moon's Unification Church. The Reverend Moon was not involved in that purchase but his *Washington Times* did buy UPI from later owners in 2000.

Paid to take it

The sale by the Scripps Foundation was unusual in that Scripps grandson, who ran Scripps by that time, paid Ruhe and Geissler

$7.5 million to take UPI off its hands. If Scripps had instead folded the wire service it had been subsidizing, it would have cost Scripps $50 million to cover pension funds and other obligations.

Under the new ownership, UPI opened an office in Anchorage in July of 1983 to enable it to brag it had operations in all fifty states. Two years later it placed a correspondent in Juneau, adding a second reporter during legislative session.

Ruhe and Geissler mismanaged UPI into Chapter 11 bankruptcy in 1985. Loss of UPI Alaska correspondents resulted. There was only one UPI newspaper subscriber in Alaska by then, *The Anchorage Times*, taking UPI and the New York Times Service to supplement its AP budget.

AP expands in Alaska

The Associated Press's first Alaska bureau chief was Tad Bartimus when the bureau was created in Anchorage in 1974, independent of Seattle. Kent Sturgis was the last Seattle bureau chief to be in charge of Alaska. Bartimus also was the AP's first female bureau chief. She had been an AP correspondent in the Vietnam War. She is now an author and syndicated columnist.

A correspondent, Ward Sims, was assigned to Fairbanks during construction of the trans-Alaska oil pipeline. That office was closed after construction was completed and Sims became bureau chief in Anchorage. When he retired he was replaced by Hal Spencer, who was replaced after three years by Dean Fosdick.

Fosdick became bureau chief in 1986 after spending three years in Juneau as correspondent. He had completed twenty-five years with AP in 2001 when he retired, eighteen of them in Alaska, a record for AP staffers in Alaska.

Larry Campbell from the *Anchorage Daily News* replaced Fosdick.

By 2005, the AP served fourteen newspapers and fifty-three radio and television broadcasters in Alaska with a staff of four and one-half, one assigned to Juneau full-time and one working only during legislative sessions.

Ex-AP people on Alaska papers

Alaska newspapers always had close relations with the AP. In addition to Tobin and Sturgis mentioned above, Tena Williams, co-publisher of the *Ketchikan Daily News* worked vacation relief for the AP in Anchorage one fall. Her father, Lew Williams Jr., had been legislative relief in Seattle in 1951. Sandy and Thad Poulson, publishers of the *Sitka Sentinel* had been Juneau correspondents. Larry Persily, *Anchorage Daily News* editorial page editor, former editor of the *Empire* and former publisher of the *Wrangell Sentinel* and *The Paper*, served as AP legislative correspondent. Dan Joling, correspondent in Anchorage and Juneau, is a former managing editor of the *News-Miner* and former reporter for *The Paper*.

Seattle bureau chief Murlin Spencer was with the *News-Miner* and *The Anchorage Times* after retiring from the AP. Rene J. (Jack) Cappon was on the AP's New York desk when he married Susan Brown, daughter of the Norman Browns, publishers of the *Anchorage Daily News*. Cappon was managing editor of that newspaper for the last two years of the Brown's ownership. Then Cappon returned to AP in New York in 1967 until he retired in 2002.

The Wire Service Guild struck the AP for nine days in 1969. Eleven executives from Northwest newspaper members moved to the desks of the Seattle bureau to keep the copy moving. Patricia Charles, then publisher of the *Ketchikan Daily News*, filled in from Alaska.

William Morris III, whose corporation owns newspapers in Juneau, Anchorage, Kenai, and Homer, was elected to three terms as a director of the AP, starting in 1976. W. Dean Singleton, who owns the *Kodiak Mirror* and *Fairbanks Daily News-Miner* with Richard Scudder, currently serves as an AP director.

Change in transmission

By 1977, Alaska newspapers were into computers and so was the AP. The key to changing the news service from leased wire to computers and satellites in Alaska was getting Bob Atwood of *The Anchorage Times* to agree to a contract accepting Datastream. His paper was paying the bulk of the leased wire charges.

Charlie Price, the AP communications chief in Seattle and Bill Barnard, western vice president in San Francisco, flew to Anchorage and met with Atwood. Lunch time was close so Atwood suggested going to the Whale's Tail at the Captain Cook Hotel.

As they were finishing lunch in the subdued light of the restaurant, an eager Barnard handed Atwood a contract and finished his sales pitch. Atwood said, "If I could see this thing, I'd sign it." Technician Price whipped out his troubleshooting penlight. Atwood signed and a new era of news delivery via satellite opened in Alaska in December 1982.

Chapter 57

Fairbanks Publishers Were Technical Pioneers

While Southcentral and Southeast Alaska newspapers were battling for the public's right to know, and protecting and expanding journalists' privilege under the law, Fairbanks publishers were continuing their leadership in newsgathering and production methods.

A newsprint shortage crippled the newspaper industry during the Korean War. Many newspapers narrowed their columns and reduced the width of their pages. C. W. (Bill) Snedden, who purchased the *Fairbanks Daily News-Miner* in 1950, opposed narrower pages. He believed it was a false economy.

He reasoned that a publisher bought a printing press to print the full width on a web of newsprint. To narrow the web meant that portions of the printing cylinders and ink rollers were paid for but unused. A wider page, using all of the press, allowed one more column to a page for ads and news.

His theory didn't change until new owners took over the *News-Miner* in 1992. The new owners were aware of the need to conserve newsprint and get the most out of it. They just approached it differently.

While Snedden was upgrading his new newspaper purchase in the 1950s, a fourth generation New Jersey newspaper publisher, Richard (Dick) Scudder, smelled up the family kitchen boiling old newspapers. He was working on a process for de-inking and recycling newsprint. It worked. He opened the first newsprint recycling plant in 1960, Garden State Paper Company in New Jersey. He followed that with similar plants in California, Illinois, Mexico and Georgia.

That was long before it became an economic necessity for the industry to recycle newsprint.

Scudder and his associate in the MediaNews Group, W. Dean Singleton, bought the *News-Miner* in 1992 from the Snedden estate and from the employees who held part of the ownership through an employees' stock plan.

So the *News-Miner*'s current owners follow a tradition of earlier Fairbanks newspaper owners and publishers: being leaders in methods and technology. From Robert McChesney's photo engraving equipment installed in the *Fairbanks Daily News* in 1905, to W. F. Thompson's eight-hour-day in '06 and aircraft delivery of papers in '24; to Lathrop's new cement buildings and new press in 1937; to Snedden's switch to offset in '65; to Chuck Gray's pioneering technique of color printing; to the recycling of newsprint, Fairbanks publishers have been leaders in developing improved methods.

39 years as publisher

Snedden was publisher of the *News-Miner* for thirty-nine years, far longer than any other Fairbanks publisher.

Charles Willis Snedden was born in Spokane, Washington, on July 20, 1913. He started in the newspaper business in 1926 as an apprentice printer at age thirteen on the *Portland* (Oregon) *Telegram*. He worked his way through the pressroom and composing room to become a master Linotype operator by age eighteen when he was ready for college. Later he joined Mergenthaler Linotype Company as a machinist and salesman.

After being rejected for military service during World War II, Snedden spent the war years at the Kaiser Shipyard in Portland, in charge of heavy equipment installations in Liberty ships. Afterward, he started a consulting business in which he assisted newspapers having financial problems. His fee was a percentage of the increase in profits the paper made after his recommendations were followed.

"It gave me an excellent income," he admitted modestly.

Snedden built a new building for the *News-Miner* in 1953, next to the existing one, to house a thirty-two-page Goss Straightline rotary press. The press was purchased from the *Sacramento Union*. It was capable of turning out up to twenty-five thousand papers an hour and dubbed "Alice." It was two stories high. It produced the *News-Miner*'s daily circulation of ten thousand in forty minutes. The

New Equipment, New Stand–C.W. (Bill) Snedden purchased the Fairbanks Daily News-Miner in 1950 and was publisher for 39 years. He changed its editorial policy from anti-statehood to a strong voice for statehood. He was a pioneer in the newspaper industry in adopting modern printing methods.-*Photo courtesy of the Fairbanks Daily News-Miner.*

press it replaced required up to eight hours to complete the multiple runs when more than eight pages were required.

On November 19, 1953, the *News-Miner* made Alaska newspaper history when it put out a 128-page Progress Edition, the biggest single edition of a newspaper ever published in Alaska and the first to be published in more than two colors. Twenty-one thousand copies were printed for distribution throughout Alaska and the Lower 48.

Snedden found he had a handyman in the shop who took a special interest in perfecting color printing, which through the years brought the *News-Miner* national recognition. The young man, Charles L. (Chuck) Gray, first started working at the paper in 1944 in the stereotyping department and advanced to the position of president and general manager in the 1970s. He later succeeded Snedden as publisher. Gray held seminars throughout the nation for newspapers interested in improving their color reproduction.

Snedden also made changes in his editorial department and the newspaper's editorial stands.

Editorial changes

After he purchased the *News-Miner* from the estate of Austin E. (Cap) Lathrop in 1950, Snedden retained Lathrop's editor, William Strand, only until February 1951. Then Strand returned to Washington DC, joining the staff of the *Washington Times-Herald* as executive city editor.

When the Republicans took the presidency with Dwight Eisenhower in 1953, Strand was appointed director of the Division of Territories & Insular Possessions in the Department of Interior, the federal czar of Alaska.

Statehood supporters were unhappy over Strand's appointment to Interior. At a cocktail party in his Washington home, Strand told a group of pro-statehood supporters that "Alaskans can huff and puff all they please about statehood," but he had it safely sewed up through three members of Congress – two in the House and one in the Senate – and the bill wasn't going anywhere.

Furthermore, he informed Alaska's Republican National Committeeman Walter J. Hickel that he, Strand, would take complete charge of all federal appointments in the territory. He didn't give a "tinker's damn" what Hickel thought and that Hickel should go home and tell his Alaskans the same.

Flying Good News to Washington
C.W. Snedden, publisher of the Fairbanks Daily News-Miner, with flight attendant Marita Sherer of San Diego, look over one of the 300 newspapers flown to Washington D. C. July 1, 1958 by Air Force jet, reporting Alaska's reaction to Congress approving Alaska statehood the day before. -*Photo courtesy of the Fairbanks Daily News-Miner*

Jack Ryan succeeded Strand as managing editor of the *News-Miner*. Ryan was a former managing editor of the *Anchorage Daily News* and former Anchorage correspondent for United Press International.

The statehood switch

Ryan wrote lively editorials and his weekly column titled "Sourdough Jack" was a popular feature. Another innovative feature was a weekly editorial by a prominent citizen.

Statehood was a hot political issue and Snedden felt the need of taking a strong editorial position on one side or the other. He rented an apartment where Ryan could hibernate while researching the pros and cons of the issue. After two weeks, Ryan reported that the facts convinced him that Alaska's economic future demanded that it change from a territory to a state.

On February 27, 1954, the *News-Miner* came out with a front-page editorial titled "Statehood NOW":

> Here in Alaska we live at the whim of federal agencies and exist according to the will of Congress. We are disfranchised, helpless American citizens, living under a form of oppression almost as disheartening and tyrannical as that which brought about the Boston Tea Party and the glorious American Revolution of 1776.

> The *News-Miner* has long advocated that we should try to build industry and develop the resources of Alaska before taking the long step to statehood. But we are disheartened with this waiting and waiting, while our destinies are twisted this way and that way by threats of filibusters, the whims of federal agencies and the uncomprehending attitude taken by many Congressmen.
>
> Alaska has a great destiny. We are going to be a prosperous valued state of the Union some day, through the toil, foresight and enterprise of our citizens here in the north. But we are not going to make substantial progress toward this destiny living under the supervision of a Congress that does not understand our problems or realize our possibilities.
>
> We say, turn Alaska loose from this deadly federal embrace. Give Americans in Alaska the full privileges of American citizenship. Turn Alaska's destiny over to Alaskans. Alaska citizens can meet the challenges of statehood, and they are eager to do so. Alaskans should demand statehood now.

The editorial came as a shock to Fairbanks readers who had been so thoroughly brainwashed under the Lathrop-Strand regime that nine out of ten residents agreed with those who contended that Alaska wasn't ready for statehood.

At the conclusion of the Alaska Constitutional Convention in 1956 at the University of Alaska in Fairbanks, the *News-Miner* put out an eight-page special edition describing the happenings at the convention and providing the full text of the constitution. The Alaska Statehood Committee paid for additional copies of the edition and distributed them through all Alaska newspapers.

Territorial Gov. Mike Stepovich, a Republican appointed by President Eisenhower, appointed Snedden as a tenth member of the Alaska Statehood Committee on October 17, 1957. That was six months after Bill Baker's *Ketchikan Chronicle* folded and Baker lacked personal funds to continue on the committee.

Alaskans approved the constitution. They elected a pseudo congressman, and two pseudo senators, and sent them to Washington as Tennessee had done to lobby for statehood.

Preceding the election of the Alaska-Tennessee delegation, the *News-Miner* campaigned on behalf of the Republican candidates. Snedden predicted a GOP national victory in the fall. It made no sense, he reasoned, to send Democrats back to Washington to argue the cause of statehood before a Republican Administration. But Alaskans elected three Democrats – Ernest Gruening and Bill Egan as senators and Ralph Rivers as congressman.

Ryan resigned as *News-Miner* editor in 1957 to become a freelance writer. George Sundborg, a Democrat and a dedicated statehood supporter, who had just sold his *Juneau Independent*, succeeded him. Together with Snedden, he made the *News-Miner* a strong voice for statehood.

Shortly after his arrival at the *News-Miner*, Sundborg had an opportunity to display his talents as an on-the-spot reporter when the plant was engulfed in flames. With smoke billowing around him and water streaming down from the ceiling, he sat at The Associated Press Teletype describing the harrowing incident.

Sundborg quit typing when the Teletype shorted out but continued his dramatic coverage by telephone to The Associated Press in Seattle.

While Sundborg kept the pro-statehood editorial campaign hot at home, Snedden, went on a speaking tour of the nation and spent months in Washington DC lobbying members of Congress, all at his own expense. *Anchorage Times* publisher Robert Atwood, chairman of the Alaska Statehood Committee, was doing the same, also at his own expense. The crusade of Alaska's two largest newspapers and their publishers was a major factor in gaining statehood.

Snedden was most effective working behind the scenes. He was able to enlist the help of influential publishers such as William Randolph Hearst Jr. A tactic Snedden used was to ghostwrite editorials for newspapers around the country in areas where congressmen opposed statehood. That changed the lawmakers' opinions on the issue. Alaska statehood wasn't that important to most of them so they were willing to go along with their local newspaper's opinion.

Although Snedden and Sundborg had a falling-out in 1958, Sundborg still maintained in 2000, "Bill Snedden deserves great credit for the role he played in Alaska's quest for statehood."

Interior secretary a publisher

President Eisenhower opposed statehood initially but his Secretary of the Interior Fred Seaton favored it. Snedden had sold Lintoypes to Seaton when Seaton published newspapers in Nebraska and Kansas. Together with a young solicitor in the Interior Department named Ted Stevens (whom Snedden recommended for the job), Snedden, Seaton, Atwood and Alaska's Alaska-Tennesee Plan delegation pressured Congress into putting the Alaska Statehood Act to a vote. It passed.

Stevens had been the *News-Miner*'s attorney when he first arrived in Alaska. After his Interior post and after statehood, Stevens served in the Alaska Legislature. He drew up the bylaws for the Alaska Publishers' Association, forerunner of the Alaska Newspaper Association, before he was appointed to the U.S. Senate in 1968 on the death of Sen. E. L. Bartlett.

After the statehood bill passed June 30, 1958, a special four-color, forty-page issue of the *News-Miner* was flown to Washington along with copies of Anchorage newspapers, to be on the desk of every member of Congress the following day. Snedden's crusading effort was noted in a story in the July 14 edition of *Time Magazine*.

Sundborg was asked by Snedden the first of August 1958 to leave the *News-Miner*. This was a month after the statehood bill passed, and a month after Snedden had telephoned to Sundborg the outline for an editorial referring to syndicated columnist Drew Pearson as the "Garbage man of the Fourth Estate." Snedden was upset over Pearson writing that Fairbanks resident and former Gov. Mike Stepovich was a "Johnny-come-lately" on Alaska statehood. Stepovich, a friend of Snedden's, was running against Gruening, a friend of Sundborg's, for U.S. senator.

Sundborg went on to manage Gruening's campaign for election as one of Alaska's first U.S. senators, beating the Snedden-backed Stepovich. He served as Gruening's administrative assistant throughout the senator's ten years in Congress.

Cliff Cernick, a former editor of the *Anchorage Daily News* and one of the founders of the Alaska Press Club and the Farthest North Press Club, succeeded Sundborg at the *News-Miner*. It was during his tenure that one of the most precedent-setting libel suits in Alaskan newspaper history was filed in October 1958.

Pearson sued the *News-Miner* for $176,000, charging that two editorials were "false, scandalous, defamatory and libelous," particularly the one labeling him as "the garbage man of the fourth estate." Pearson lost in state superior court and in an appeal to the Alaska Supreme Court.

'No' to capital move

The *News-Miner* opposed moving the state capital from Juneau, charging the proposal to be a "carefully organized Madison Avenue – type propaganda campaign centered in the civic greed of Anchorage."

Cernick resigned in February 1961 to become education editor for the *Santa Barbara* (California) *News-Press.* Then Charles Hoyt moved up from news editor to the top spot in the newsroom. David B. Galloway followed Hoyt as head of the newsroom in 1963 after Hoyt moved to Juneau. Galloway was executive editor and assistant to the publisher at the time of the switch from hot metal to offset printing and the dedication of the new offset plant.

Galloway had joined the *News-Miner* in June 1962. He started in journalism as a copyboy for the Office of War Information in Washington DC, his native city. He later was a reporter for the *Washington Post* and for California newspapers.

The big switch

"America's Farthest North Daily" converted to offset printing on August 30, 1965. Publisher Snedden exhibited courage in making this radical change because it meant constructing a new building equipped with temperature, humidity and dust controls. It meant scrapping all of the Linotype machines and their auxiliary equipment, dominant in the industry at that time. Time-tested methods and typesetting equipment were supplanted by the new. It was an expensive and lengthy procedure.

Offset printing represented a technology breakthrough, that could not be ignored by publishers who wanted to remain in the vanguard of newspaper publishing. Of the 1,763 daily newspapers published in the United States in 1965, with a combined circulation of sixty three million, only 159 were printed in offset. By 2000, the number of daily newspapers had dropped to 1,480 with a circulation of fifty-nine million. However, all were printed totally or partially by offset.

The reduction in the number of newspapers and circulation is attributed to expansion of new media and to the increased efficiency of newspapers in covering larger circulation areas.

Snedden had leased 2.4 acres of land from the Alaska Railroad making it possible to have a railroad spur next to his new plant to unload newsprint and supplies. He built a 24,500 square foot building to house his new Goss Urbanite web offset press. It was capable of producing forty thousand thirty-two-page newspapers an hour with full color pictures, especially with methods perfected by Chuck Gray, who at that time was in charge of the company's production.

Over one thousand people toured the new building following dedication ceremonies on November 7, 1965. U.S. Senator Bartlett was the principal speaker. Bartlett had been a reporter and editor on the *News-Miner* before going into politics in 1939.

"A newspaper should be fiercely independent," Bartlett said. "An editorial page that is neutral is harmful to the prestige of the paper, harmful to the community it serves, harmful to the highest requirements of journalism."

Among the guests at the dedication was Marion Bates, daughter of W. F. Thompson, the *News-Miner*'s first editor-publisher and one of its most outspoken editorial writers.

After the offset switch, Snedden expanded his business. A second story was added to the plant, incorporating a rooftop penthouse for Snedden and his wife, and commercial office space.

In addition to the *News-Miner*, the publishing firm operated the Commercial Printing Co.; the Snoball Express, a rural trucking service; two weeklies, the *Valdez Vanguard* and the *Cordova Times*; and the monthly *Northland News*, distributed free in the northern Bush villages. *Northland News* reached 8,800 households from Tok to Barrow and from the Canadian border to St. Lawrence Island.

AP veteran steps in

Veteran Associated Press Bureau Chief Murlin Spencer became the *News-Miner*'s executive editor in 1968 after Galloway moved back to California. Spencer had been The Associated Press bureau chief in Salt Lake City, Sacramento, San Francisco, Seattle, Honolulu, Tokyo, and Melbourne, Australia, over a period of thirty-one years.

Spencer was born in Fort Morgan, Colorado, on November 11, 1909. He starting newspapering on his father's *Fort Morgan Times* after graduating from the University of Nebraska.

Spencer spent World War II in the Pacific area for The Associated Press. Most of the time, he was at General Douglas MacArthur's headquarters. He reported from Guam early in August 1945 when the first atomic bomb devastated Hiroshima. He witnessed and reported on MacArthur accepting the Japanese surrender aboard the battleship *Missouri* on September 2, 1945.

At the conclusion of the war, Spencer became AP bureau chief in Seattle, covering Washington, Alaska, and British Columbia. He toured Alaska annually.

When Spencer neared the end of his Seattle AP tour, he told his successor, Wick Temple, later an AP vice president in New York, "I hated that damned ship," referring to the *Missouri* in mothballs in Bremerton. That was because every year for the twenty-odd years he was in Seattle, the New York bureau insisted that he go to Bremerton and do yet another retrospective on the surrender. The USS *Missouri* is now a floating museum, permanently moored in Pearl Harbor.

Spencer took early retirement from AP in 1968 to accept the *News-Miner* editor post.

The coded story

It was during Spencer's tenure that the *News-Miner* experienced a unique journalistic perfidy. Kent Brandley (sometimes he spelled it Brandli) was sportswriter and columnist for the *News-Miner* from 1960 to 1969. He quit seven different times but was never fired until the end. He was born in Salt Lake City in 1937 of pioneer Mormon parents and had roamed the major countries of the world.

He inserted a cryptogram in his weekly column titled "Our Fairbanks" in the May 11, 1969 edition in the following paragraph:

> How a person spends Sundays in Alaska depends whether outside conditions permit an after breakfast bicycle ride or, if happening to have skis, he may now find them to be more practical. If he moved elsewhere, the time spent inside might be more voluntary. It's necessary perhaps to have a climate that can only bring strong types to Alaska,

your home. Weather brings your own private fence. The green grass is nice but a party should be exclusive.

Questioning the reason for inclusion of the paragraph that appeared to make no sense, revealed that interpretation was by utilizating a simple code. Select each fifth word in sequence. From that emerged: "Sunday's outside breakfast happening may be moved inside. It's a bring your own grass party."

Snedden fired Brandley on the spot, saying that such conduct "violated the basic principles of journalism and reflected adversely upon the integrity of the *News-Miner*. Our readers have a right to expect an accurate account of daily events and happenings, without hidden innuendo."

Spencer resigned in April 1971 because of ill health and had a leg amputated. After he recovered, he served as editor of the *Port Angeles* (Washington) *Evening News* and as managing editor of *The Anchorage Times* briefly before finishing out his journalism career at the *Register-Guard* in Eugene, Oregon. He died back home in Fort Morgan, Colorado, in 1992 at age eighty-five.

Don Dennis was thirty-one and had been wire editor at the *News-Miner* for three years, when he was promoted to managing editor replacing Spencer. He graduated from Pueblo College and was sports editor on the *Chieftain* and the *Star-Journal* in Pueblo and on the *Grand Junction* (Colorado) *Sentinel* before going to Fairbanks.

In May 1975, Dennis took charge of the editorial page and G. Kent Sturgis, twenty-eight, became managing editor. A native-born Fairbanksan, Sturgis began working at the *News-Miner* while a student at Lathrop High School and at the University of Alaska Fairbanks. He did his last two years of study at the University of Washington in Seattle. During that time he worked part-time at the *Seattle Times* and at The Associated Press bureau.

In 1970, Sturgis opened the AP's first office in Anchorage, the second in Alaska. The first full-time AP office in Alaska had opened in Juneau in 1956 with Bill Tobin as correspondent. After two years in Anchorage, Sturgis became AP bureau chief in Seattle until joining the *News-Miner*. While Sturgis was bureau chief in Seattle, a separate bureau was created for Alaska with offices in Anchorage. Prior to that, Alaska was under Seattle jurisdiction.

Sturgis left the *News-Miner* in 1986 after eleven years to form Epicenter Press, based in Kenmore, Washington, near Seattle, a publisher of Alaskan books. He and his associates in Epicenter, Lael Morgan and B. G. Olson, had about sixty titles in circulation by 2000.

In 1976, at age sixty-three, publisher Snedden, long suffering from heart trouble, decided to live a more leisurely life. He bought himself a larger boat on which he and his wife, Helen, cruised around Southeast Alaska during the summer months. He made Gray president and general manager of his Alaskan business interests, primarily the *News-Miner*, retaining the title of chairman of the board and publisher.

Snedden dies, N-M sold

Snedden died in August 1989. Gray took over as publisher until Scudder and Singleton purchased the paper in February 1992. Gray managed the sale of the *News-Miner* and continued to serve as an advisor and publisher emeritus after the sale.

After Scudder and Singleton bought the *News-Miner*, they decided to seek another managing editor. So in 1993, they moved the editorial page editor, Sue Mattson, into the post replacing Dan Joling and brought in a Singleton acquaintance, Jack Neece, as assistant managing editor.

Joling, with a master's degree in journalism from the prestigious University of Missouri, had moved up to managing editor of the *Fairbanks News-Miner* in 1988, replacing Ken Noblit, who had replaced Sturgis. Joling had been with the paper ten years, starting as a reporter

After leaving the *News-Miner*, Joling worked for the *Juneau Empire* and for Larry Persily's *The Paper*, a short-lived Juneau weekly. He taught journalism for a year at the University of Alaska Fairbanks before settling in Juneau where he worked for The Associated Press.

Sue Mattson held a journalism degree but began at the *News-Miner* as a dispatcher in the advertising department. She moved to the newsroom when an opening occurred before following Joling as managing editor. However, Mattson didn't care for the responsibility and was replaced after nine months by assistant managing editor Neece, Singleton's friend from Oakland, California. Neece stayed

Fairbanks Daily News-Miner–2005

Marilyn Romano
Publisher

Kelly Bostain
Managing Editor

News-Miner Photos

only six months and then went to South Carolina and was replaced by Kelly Bostian in 1995.

Bostian was a popular outdoor editor for the *News-Miner* before becoming managing editor. He was born in Toledo, Iowa, and held degrees in journalism and fish and wildlife from Iowa State University. His first job in 1982 was with the *News-Miner* as a feature writer and then general assignment and police reporter before going to the outdoor beat.

Bostian brought stability to the newsroom after the frequent change of managing editors. He was still managing editor in 2005.

New, non-owner publishers

The new owners named Paul Massey, fifty-eight at the time, as *News-Miner* publisher. Massey and his wife, Jane, moved to Alaska from Ohio where Paul had been president of Sun Newspaper for four

New Owners, New Publisher–After Richard Scudder and W. Dean Singleton bought the Fairbanks Daily News-Miner in 1992, they named Paul Massey, left, as publisher replacing Charles Gray, center. With them is Singleton. -*Photo courtesy of the Fairbanks Daily News-Miner*

years. Before that he was a newspaperman in Dedham, Massachusetts, where he merged three weekly newspapers into one daily.

Massey was active in civic organizations in Fairbanks. He was president of Rotary in 1998 and served on the board of directors of the Fairbanks Chamber of Commerce and four other organizations.

Massey retired as *News-Miner* publisher in June 2000 and moved back to the East Coast.

Marilyn F. Romano moved up in the *News-Miner* organization and was named publisher to replace Massey. Romano arrived in Fairbanks in April 1992 from Houston, Texas, where she began her newspaper career. She was advertising director for the *News-Miner* from 1992 until 1998, when she was promoted to general manager and then publisher on Massey's departure.

The new publisher of the *News-Miner* is president of the board of United Way in Fairbanks. She sits on the boards of Big Brothers-Big Sisters, the Midnight Sun Council of the Boy Scouts and the Greater Fairbanks Chamber of Commerce. She is on the advisory boards of the University of Alaska, the Fairbanks International Airport and Alaska Airlines.

Scudder, the originator of newsprint recycling, turned eighty-six in 2000. He is chairman of MediaNews Group that owns fifty-one daily newspapers with almost two million in circulation, through four or more different corporations in ten states.

Scudder's family has been in the newspaper business for more than one hundred years. He is a fourth generation newspaper publisher. Until 1972, Scudder was publisher of the Newark Evening News, New Jersey's major daily newspaper, founded by his grandfather in 1882.

Scudder was chairman of the board of the Garden State Paper Company when he and Singleton bought the *News-Miner*. Garden State is the largest producer of 100 percent recycled newsprint. It uses the process he invented.

How to get a job

Singleton, forty-eight in 2000, owns one-third of MediaNews Group and is its president and chief negotiator in buying newspapers. He began his newspaper career as a part-time newspaper reporter at the age of fifteen in his hometown of Graham, Texas. He held positions in the news departments of several Texas papers, including the *Dallas Morning News*, *Tyler Morning Telegraph* and the *Wichita Falls Record News*.

In 1976, Singleton joined Albritton Communications Company owned by Texan Joe Albritton. He became president of that company's newspaper division in 1978, building the company through a series of newspaper and broadcast acquisitions.

In December 1983 Singleton teamed with Scudder to begin buying newspapers throughout the United States. MediaNews Group was created as the umbrella operating company for the various newspaper holding companies owned by the two men.

National publications have run features on Singleton and the rapid rise of newspaper ownership by MediaNews, by 2000 the nation's seventh largest newspaper chain. Its flagship newspaper is the *Denver Post*. Singleton told the *All-Alaska Weekly* that "his appetite for buying newspapers is fueled by his belief that newspapers will continue to be the leading medium for the next fifty years"

In an interview with Fairbanks' *Pioneer All-Alaska Weekly*, Singleton recounted how he had been turned down for a job at the *Dallas Times Herald* in 1970 because he was too young and inexperienced. After he purchased the *Times Herald* sixteen years later, he ran an advertisement in the trade publication *Editor & Publisher* headlined "How I got a job at the *Dallas Times Herald*."

Chapter 58

Dominance Shifts from Times to News

Norman Brown's *Anchorage Daily News* debuted May 1, 1948, two years after its founding as the weekly *Anchorage News*. A second Anchorage daily meant keener competition for *The Anchorage Daily Times*. By the spring of 1951, the *News* claimed a circulation of 7,500, second in size to Alaska's largest newspaper, Robert (Bob) Atwood's *Times*, with twelve thousand circulation.

Brown's wife, Blanche, and their son, Cole, worked full-time on the *News*. Daughter Susan had worked part-time at the *Daily News* from the time that she was ten years old, but she joined The Associated Press in New York City after graduating from the University of Washington.

Dueling editors

The *Times* and *News* usually took opposite sides on controversial issues, especially statehood. The *News* was absolutely opposed while the *Times* was unequivocal supportive. George Sundborg, editor of the weekly *Juneau Independent*, commented on the squabbling in his column titled "Cabbages & Kings":

> Norm Brown and Bob Atwood fight over such things as whether or not starving moose are menacing householders and whether or not a bunch of Japanese laborers are about to move on to the beaches of the Aleutians to start picking abandoned military installations to pieces.

The *Times* did carry an interesting comment – of a sort – on the relationship last week. It noted that it was lending the *News* ten rolls of newsprint at the request of Brown, who said his stocks were depleted and he would have to have help if his paper was to continue publication until a new shipment arrived.

Up at Fairbanks, the *News-Miner* commented that it assumed the *News* would now soften its policy toward the *Times* because "it would hardly be cricket to call a concern names on its own newsprint."

New Anchorage papers

After statehood, Anchorage media expanded. During the 1960s, three weeklies shared the field with the two dailies. Two weeklies folded after a few issues but the third lasted into the 1980s.

The *Alaska Journal Express* appeared on August 28, 1960. A. E. Fortier was publisher. Suspension came on October 16, 1960, after the staff received no paychecks for five weeks.

Alaska Business first appeared on November 26, 1969, with Frank Martone as publisher and Ot Hampton as editor. Its termination date is unknown.

The Greatlander Shopping News, with Herb Rhodes as editor – publisher, rolled off the presses at his Anchorage Printing Co. in 1969. It lasted the longest.

Rhodes was born in Hoquiam, Washington, and earned a journalism degree from Washington State College after navy service in World War II.

He and his wife headed north in July 1947 where Herb became a reporter for *The Anchorage Daily Times*. Two years later, he went to work for the Alaska Railroad as publicity and advertising agent and edited *The Railbelt Reporter*.

In 1951, Rhodes established Anchorage Printing Co. in Spenard after buying the commercial printing department of *The Anchorage Daily Times*.

The Greatlander Shopping News's ads were interspersed with Alaska feature stories and how-to-do-it articles, like insulating homes in Alaska. Rhodes wrote fiery front-page editorials on controversial issues. Some accused him of practicing yellow journalism.

Shopping News publication ceased on June 11, 1985, at the height of the newspaper war between the *Times* and the *Daily News*. Rhodes substituted the less-costly *Greatlander Bush Mailer*, a weekly shopper circulated in rural villages. Rhodes said the *Shopping News* was a money-losing publication in competition with the town's warring dailies, offering ridiculously low ad rates.

Lee Jordan, whose parents taught printing in Alabama, worked for *The Anchorage Times* before opening his own shop in 1958 and starting the weekly *Chugiak-Eagle River Star* in January 1971. He editorialized strongly for moving the capital from Juneau and for forming a borough in his circulation area independent of the Anchorage Borough. He was elected the new borough's mayor in 1974. However, the Alaska Supreme Court immediately ruled the borough illegal. He sold the *Star*, now the *Alaska Star*, to the Morris Publishing Group in 2000.

The Alaska Advocate

After the *News* won its first Pulitzer Prize in 1976, three of its staffers – Howard Weaver, Mark Weaver, and Andy Williams – and two Associated Press writers – John Greely and Rodger Painter – launched a weekly, *The Alaska Advocate*. It was a twenty-page tabloid that aimed at being an all-Alaska journal of opinion and political commentary.

The *Advocate* staff envisioned an antiestablishment, *Rolling Stone*-type publication. They delighted in radical rhetoric and psychedelic layout and shunned a business orientation. Howard Weaver was executive editor. They claimed 825 subscribers and $5,000 in operating capital when they started.

Bob Atwood was the cover story of the first issue on January 6, 1977. The six-page expose of his private and public life was rife with errors. But Atwood had declined a personal interview, so the authors depended upon hearsay to present an unflattering profile. The cartoon illustration on the cover page depicted three men (different portraits of Atwood) playing "Media Monopoly," with the caption "Bob Atwood and the Alaska Information Game." Justifying their use of Atwood as their introductory drawing card, they wrote:

> He owns the biggest newspaper in Alaska, and it may soon be the only one in town. What he thinks, how he acts and why, become public questions because he's built a life and fortune around changing what the public thinks.

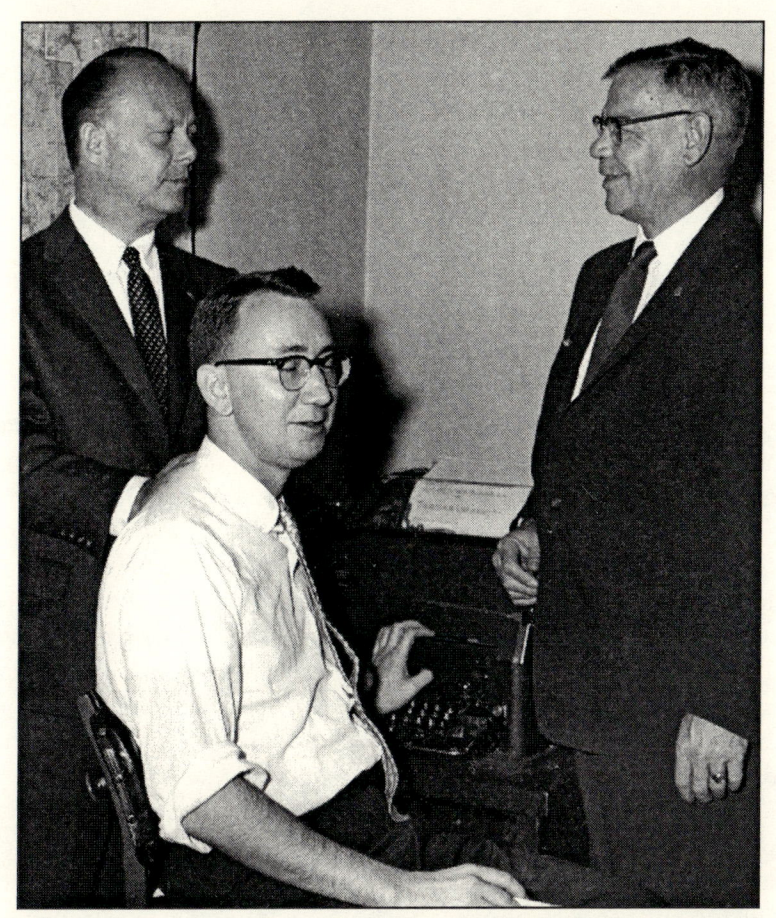

The Morning After Alaskans Ratified Statehood
In an Aug. 27 1958, photograph, Interior Secretary Fred Seaton, left, AP correspondent William J. Tobin, seated at the Teletype, and Alaska Delegate E.L. (Bob)Bartlett, who became one of Alaska's first U.S. senators, enjoy election returns after Alaskans approved statehood. Seaton also was publisher of a chain of newspapers in Kansas and Nebraska at the time. Tobin was the first fulltime correspondent for The Associated Press when he opened an AP office in Juneau in 1956. Bartlett was an associate editor and reporter for the Fairbanks Daily News-Miner before he went into politics. -*Photo courtesy of William J. Tobin.*

> That he uses his newspaper to shape and influence public opinion is beyond question.
>
> The paper is a booster, a witting partner of the chamber of commerce, Babbitt's bible in broadsheet. He has campaigned tirelessly and effectively to build Anchorage into the kind of city he wants. Anyone with his clout demands examination. Today, with his only competitor struggling on the ropes of financial collapse, that examination becomes critical.
>
> The *Times* is the dominant voice in the state's dominant city, and when it thunders, there's likely to be rain.

When the weekly folded after 113 issues, Weaver claimed that "no other story ever approached 'Media Monopoly' for generating comment or controversy and I'm confident that a lot of people never read another issue; it angered many merchants."

In support of their motto "Sacred Cows Make the Best Hamburger," those political activists and social reformers spent two years trying to create their version of society, what they accused Atwood of doing. They were anti-big oil, anti-Teamsters' union, anti-Atwood, anti-capital move. They supported environmentalists and the lockup of 131.4 million acres of Alaska's federal land by Congress, which it did later with the Alaska National Interest Lands Conservation Act of 1980.

The rambunctious weekly won several national and state awards but failed to attract readers and advertising to support its style of journalism. It folded in the March 1979.

Howard Weaver, born in Anchorage and graduated from East Anchorage High School and Johns Hopkins University, went back to work at the *News* as an editorial writer. He rose to editorial page editor, then managing editor in '81 and editor after Kay Fanning left in '83. He participated in or directed each of the two series that won Pulitzers for the *Daily News*.

After the *News* won the newspaper war, Weaver spent a year in school in England and returned briefly to the *News*. He transferred to McClatchy headquarters in California and became editorial page editor of the Sacramento Bee and later vice president for news for McClatchy.

John Greely went to work for public radio and TV in Juneau from which he retired in 2001. Painter became a lobbyist representing an aquaculture organization. Williams remained in Fairbanks and Mark Weaver attended the University of Alaska Anchorage.

The *Advocate*'s managing editor was Pat Dougherty. He joined the *Anchorage Daily News* where he rose to editor in 1998.

Rhodes prints others

Gregg Rhodes, one of the Rhodes' sons, took over management of Anchorage Printing Co. in the 1990s. The company prints a number of newspapers for other publishers. Among them is the *Anchorage Press*, that Nick Coltman and two others started in 1992, the year *The Anchorage Times* and John Lindauer's chain of weekly papers suspended publication. Coltman was sales manager for Lindauer.

Coltman and two other Lindauer staffers, Barry Bialik and Bill Boulay, started what they first called the *Anchorage Bypass*. After a year and one-half they changed the name to *Anchorage Press*. Coltman and his wife, Maggie Balean, bought out Bialik and Boulay after a couple of years.

In its masthead, the *Press* says it is "an Anchorage-wide art, entertainment, recreation, news and metro feature newspaper." It comes out on Thursdays in tabloid format of forty or more pages.

Coltman and his wife have expanded operations into publishing monthly magazines. And in 2000 they won the contract to publish the fifty-six-year-old *Sourdough Sentinel* for Elmendorf Air Force Base. They won that contract from Morris Publishing Group that publishes the *Alaska Journal of Commerce* and the *Alaska Star* in the Anchorage area.

The *Turnagain Times*, a twice-a-month tabloid newspaper, appeared in the Anchorage area in June 1998. Co-founders Kent Smith and Ken Osuna started the newspaper to cover news of the Turnagain Arm and western Prince William Sound areas.

In its initial issue, Osuna wrote, "All too often, unless it's a major wreck on the Seward Highway, or a quirky story about those quaint people along the Turnagain Arm, the world according to the Anchorage news media ends at Potter Marsh."

Osuna and Smith came from the broadcast side of media to found the free circulation *Times* at Girdwood. Both had worked for station KTKN in Ketchikan. Smith later worked at public station KCHU in Valdez and Osuna for station KENI in Anchorage. Smith left the publication after two years for a broadcasting job in Boston.

Alaska Newspapers, Inc. added an eighth newspaper to its chain of weeklies in July 2002 when it introduced the *Anchorage Chronicle* with an initial press run of 10,500. The newspaper sold for twenty-five cents on newsstands in the Anchorage area. ANI editor-in-chief Alex DeMarban said the newspaper stresses local news and some state news.

The newspaper was relatively inexpensive for ANI to start because it already had its own printing plant and a staff of seventy-five to print its other publications. It had to add only five people to get the *Chronicle* on the street. At the end of 2004, ANI had seen enough in the Anchorage market and suspended publication of the *Chronicle*.

The editors

But before the newcomers and new publications arrived in Anchorage, Atwood and Brown battled it out for the daily market. Atwood and Brown remained editors-in-chief of their respective papers, but they hired managing editors along the way. The *News* had Jack Ryan, Cliff Cernick, Joe Rothstein, Lynn Thomas, Gordon Evans, and the Brown's son-in-law, Jack Cappon. The *Times* had Bernie Kosinski, and Bill Tobin. Both had Clint Andrews and Bob Kederick. Tobin stayed the longest in Anchorage journalism, still an editor of the "Voice of the Times" in 2005.

Tobin held various Associated Press assignments before joining the *Times* in 1963. He was managing editor for ten years and then associate editor. After Kosinski lost his life in a drowning accident in Hawaii, the title of general manager was added.

Tobin played an active role in community affairs, serving as president of the Anchorage Chamber of Commerce, the Alaska World Affairs Council, and the Alaska Press Club. He served on the boards of directors of the Alaska Mutual Savings Bank, the Providence Hospital Association, and Commonwealth North. His quick wit made him a favorite as the master of ceremonies at community events.

Capital move issue

After the achievement of statehood, Atwood shifted his attention to moving the state capital from Juneau. The population majority had shifted to Southcentral Alaska. Atwood started writing editorials, noting the advantages in bringing the governing process closer to the people.

The *Anchorage Daily News* opposed moving the capital. It was too expensive and the money was needed for more worthwhile programs.

Both newspapers viewed with concern the foisting of a borough form of government on Anchorage's suburban area.

On December 3, 1963, the Greater Anchorage Area Borough was born. It took twelve more years of acrimonious bickering between two competing governments – city and borough – to finally unify into one government.

During those twelve years, reams and reams of editorials tried to delineate the arguments. Four votes were held before residents agreed to the merger.

News supports Natives

One major issue on which the two Anchorage daily papers differed was on Native land claims settlement legislation. The *Times* contended that the land claims had no legal basis, but if Congress chose to give the Natives land and financial payment, it was a federal commitment.

As the debate dragged on for two years, the *Times* pushed for a settlement so that resource development could resume, especially after Interior Secretary Stewart Udall froze state land selections in 1968.

News editor-publisher Brown more fully supported the Native claims, believing that the Natives deserved land allotments, although he thought the money settlement seemed excessive.

Brown's staff, under editor Rothstein, ran a series on Native issues in 1965 entitled "Village People." Later, under the new publisher, Larry Fanning, a second series on Native issues, "The Emerging Village People," began in December 1967. Bob Zelnick, a *News* reporter, wrote a series in 1968, "Justice in the Bush."

Zelnick's series won the *Daily News* the national Gavel Award, but it cost them a libel suit. A Nome taxi operator objected to the accusation that his taxis were delivering illegal booze.

Brown wrote about meeting Willie Hensley, the young Native activist, after passage of the Alaska Native Claims Settlement Act in 1971. Hensley said, "Thank God for the *Anchorage News!*"

That support for Native causes helped the *Daily News* when it was in the middle of its most severe financial crisis in 1976. Publisher Kay Fanning declared in a front-page story that she would have to close the paper unless she received new resources immediately. The Bristol Bay Native Corporation responded with a loan of $70,000 to keep the paper afloat.

The offset switch

The *Times* converted to offset with a new Goss Metro press on May 12, 1969. A three-story wing was added to the *Times*' Fourth Avenue building to house the press, a $2 million upgrading project. It also added the UPI news service, offering readers three of the world's leading news organizations, the AP, UPI, and the *New York Times*. Still later, computers replaced typewriters and Linotypes.

Atwood's youngest daughter, Elaine, became assistant publisher, after going through the slots of reporter, society editor, and city editor.

After graduating from West High School in Anchorage, she graduated from Mills College, Oakland, California, with a major in history and government. She spent her junior year at the University of Geneva, Switzerland, and then was director of the World Affairs Council's information center in Boston. She returned to Anchorage in 1964 and was later chosen the first woman president of the Anchorage Chamber of Commerce.

Starting with the January 2, 1976, edition, the word "daily" was deleted from the *Times*' flag.

Fannings arrive

In June 1967, the Browns sold the *News* to Larry and Kay Fanning, recently arrived from Chicago, where they had been associated with the *Chicago Sun-Times*. Mrs. Fanning was a former wife of Marshall Field IV, publisher of the *Sun-Times*.

Lawrence Stanley Fanning was born in Minneapolis, Minnesota, in 1914. He attended the University of San Francisco and spent twenty-one years on the *San Francisco Chronicle*, the last twelve as managing editor. Then he joined the Marshall Field Enterprises in Chicago where he became executive editor of both the *Chicago Daily News* and the *Chicago Sun-Times*.

Katherine Woodruff Fanning was born in 1927 in Joliet, Illinois, where her father, Frederick W. Woodruff, was a bank president. She graduated from Smith College in 1949. The following year, she married Marshall Field.

Kay and Field divorced in 1963. Two years later, she visited two of her former college classmates living in Anchorage, Mrs. Lowell Thomas Jr. and Mrs. George Wichman. She took a job as librarian at the *Anchorage Daily News* and later was promoted to reporter. On September 13, 1966, she married Fanning.

When the Fannings bought the *News,* they also bought a seventy-five-year-old letterpress. With antiquated letterpress equipment and with Linotypes that were not automated, the *Anchorage Daily News* was becoming a financial loser competing with the *Times'* new offset plant.

The Fannings had asked successful Oregon newspaper publisher and newspaper consultant Robert (Bob) Chandler his advice on buying the *Anchorage Daily News.* He had recommended against it. The Fannings went ahead anyway.

One of Larry Fanning's early editorial stances was unpopular with Alaskans. When Fanning editorially supported gun control he met vociferous opposition and quickly backed off. It took him a while to learn that Alaska is different from Chicago.

Fanning was accused of opposing construction of the oil pipeline from Prudhoe Bay to Valdez on the grounds that it would damage the environment. Kay Fanning said the *News* was not opposed but "wanted it built right and it ultimately was."

However, through the years, the *Daily News* has tended to support environmentalists' stands, opposing logging in Southeast Alaska's Tongass National Forest and opposing aerial wolf hunting as part of predator control in northern Alaska.

The paper was subsidized for almost ten years by Mrs. Fanning's son Frederick (Ted) Field, who had inherited one-half of the voting stock of the $400-million-a-year Field Enterprises.

Larry Fanning approached Atwood on the prospect of a joint operation. But on February 3, 1971, before the deal could be completed, Larry suffered a massive coronary at his desk and died within minutes.

News earns Pulitzers

Although Mrs. Fanning was battling financial problems from the start, after taking over from her husband, she had encouraged investigative news reporting. In 1976 the paper won the Pulitzer Prize for public service for its series of articles, "Empire." The series analyzed the growing economic and political influence of the Alaska Teamsters' Union.

The Pulitzer for the *Daily News* was especially pleasing for Mrs. Fanning because it beat out a four-reporter team rushed to Alaska from the *Los Angeles Times* that attempted a blockbuster series on the same subject. The *Times* printed its series the week before the

First Alaska Pulitzer
Anchorage Daily News Editor and Publisher Kay Fanning, left, enjoys the moment when reporters for the newspaper receive word from Columbia University Feb. 4, 1976 that their story on Alaska Teamsters Union won the Pulitzer prize for public service. It was the first Pulitzer for an Alaska newspaper. The reporters are Jim Rabb, who later went into law, Bob Porterfield, on the phone, who went on to another Pulitzer winning team on the Boston Globe, and Howard Weaver, lead writer. By 1989, Weaver had moved to editor of the News and led the team that won a second Pulitzer for the newspaper.
-Photo courtesy of the Anchorage Daily News

Daily News and emphasized the Teamsters' stranglehold on Alaska. The *Times* series also entered in the Pulitzer competition.

"Our series wasn't as sensational as the *Times*," Mrs. Fanning said, "and we didn't use a lot of compromising but unprovable stuff. We worked hard to keep the series solid with documentation."

Writing the series for the *Daily News* were Jim Babb, who later went into law; Bob Porterfield, who went on to another Pulitzer-winning team on the *Boston Globe*; and Howard Weaver, the lead writer. He later was lead writer and editor of the series for which the *Daily News* won a second Pulitzer in 1989.

The second Pulitzer was for its series, "A People in Peril," highlighting the epidemic of alcoholism and suicide in Alaska villages.

Those were the first and only Pulitzers for Alaska newspapers in the twentieth century. It was the first time two Pulitzers for public service were won by a newspaper as small as the *Daily News*. The staff, whose average age was in the midtwenties, was the youngest winning team when it won its first Pulitzer.

Joint operating fiasco

Mrs. Fanning resumed negotiations with Atwood on a joint operating agreement after the death of her husband. She said she would have to suspend publication without the agreement because her family could no longer subsidize it. A contract was signed in December 1974 whereby both papers were printed in the *Times*' plant.

The *Times* assumed all responsibilities for advertising and circulation, but each paper maintained separate editorial departments. A wing was added to the *Times* building to house the *News* editorial office.

All of the *Daily News* production, advertising, and circulation employees were laid off. The *News'* twenty-person news staff moved into the new space adjacent to the *Times*. The two papers sold unit advertising, which meant an advertiser would get a slightly lower rate if he or she bought both papers rather than advertising in each independently. That arrangement was supposed to enhance total ad revenue and turn the *News* around. But in practice, the *News* continued to lose.

By the fall of 1976, the *News'* financial situation became more critical. Kay's son Ted Field, who had put in $5 million, said he could no longer subsidize the operation. Mrs. Fanning's two daughters had each put in $200,000. And even her mother had contributed $25,000.

That was when Mrs. Fanning went public about the newspaper's financial crisis and the Bristol Bay Native Corporation responded.

Several wealthy easterners concerned about the environment had made loans to the *News*. One, Patricia Hewitt, heiress of the John Deere Company, loaned $300,000. She did so after a cocktail party to help the cause given by Robert Redford at his New York apartment.

About fifty people convened at the *Daily News* office and formed a "Committee for Two Newspapers." It was co-chaired at first by Hugh Fleischer, a well-known environmentalist, and by Frank Reed, a prominent banker. (Reed resigned later when the *News* filed a lawsuit against the *Times*.)

Subcommittees were formed to encourage people to advertise in the *News* and to subscribe. Jeff Lowenfels, a stranger to Mrs. Fanning, attended the meeting and offered to write a garden column gratis. He was still writing that column in 2005, probably the longest-running garden column in the country.

Fanning hired Chandler, and a Lee Newspapers official as consultants in an effort to get the *Times* to change the joint operating agreement so that it worked to save the *News*. Atwood wouldn't budge so Fanning filed a lawsuit charging antitrust and breach of contract. She asked for $16.5 million. The *Times* filed a countersuit and invoked a clause in the agreement terminating it on one-month notice.

That would put the *News* out of business so the *News* obtained an injunction to force the *Times* to continue the agreement pending court-ordered arbitration. In September 1978, a settlement was reached. The *Times* would continue publishing the *News* for six months, or until April 1, 1979, and pay the *News* $750,000 plus attorney fees.

McClatchy Newspapers followed that three months later by purchasing 80 percent of the *Daily News* stock. Fanning remained as editor and publisher. Then there was a scramble to get a new plant running by deadline.

McClatchy sent scores of people to Alaska to aid in hiring, training and setting up advertising, circulation, accounting and production departments. The newsroom staff tripled. The newspaper was redesigned. It was all done in two and one-half months.

Unfortunately for the *Times*, it continued afternoon publication. The *News* had published mornings since editors Jack Cappon and Gordon Evans switched from afternoons in 1963. The trend nationwide was toward stronger morning papers and the demise of afternoon papers. The McClatchys were encouraged to buy the *News* by Atwood's insistence on remaining an afternoon publication, firm in his motto of providing "Today's News Today."

Real violence

There ensued a typical newspaper war for domination of the Anchorage market. The only violence in the war was from outside sources.

A well-armed, forty-one-year-old cab driver, Donald Lee Ramsey, entered the *Times*' front entrance October 26, 1986, carrying a semiautomatic rifle, a pistol, a large knife, a garrote and hand grenades. It was the middle of the morning, a few hours before the afternoon paper went to press.

The intruder chained the front door closed. Then he hurled smoke bombs into the first-floor front office area, causing a fire that bellowed great clouds of smoke upstairs to the offices of the Atwoods and their staffs.

After he charged into Elaine Atwood's office, the seventy-nine-year-old publisher joined his daughter and wrestled the attacker into submission and held him until help arrived.

Ramsey had intended to keep Bob Atwood hostage and force him to print what he wanted. He was frustrated over his inability to

Anchorage Daily News–2005

Mike Sexton
Publisher

Pat Dougherty
Executive Editor
Senior Vice President

Anchorage Daily News Photos

inspire a recall movement against Mayor Tony Knowles for not enforcing ordinances against his landlord over mice and vermin in his apartment.

After his apartment burned, the fire department said it was accidental. But Ramsey thought it was part of a conspiracy against him by his enemies, who he viewed as public officials and civic leaders.

He also said his grievance against the *Times* was that it had refused to run a full-page ad on the grounds that it libeled U.S. Sen. Frank Murkowski.

Ramsey told Elaine as he was being taken away, "Miss Atwood, I left you something here on your desk."

It was a backpack full of grenades.

"I survived the scuffle with only bruises to my face and hands," Bob Atwood said. "I was now almost eighty years old. While I still felt strong enough to subdue gunmen, I felt my battle with McClatchy slipping away. My problems compounded the next year when I suffered the grievous loss of Evangeline, my loyal wife and confidante. She died suddenly of cancer."

Death at the Daily News

About seven months later, the *Anchorage Daily News* plant was the scene of violence. A former mail-room machine operator, Derrick Green, entered the plant about 4:15 a.m. May 7, 1987, with a shotgun and killed Gerald Clarkson, a machine operator with whom Green had worked. Green fired four shots, missing other staffers. He was looking for his former supervisor when subdued by police.

Green had been laid off the week before his attack as part of a company-wide staff reduction. His supervisor, Mel Jones, said he had been counseled and did not appear upset.

Daily News management hired an armed guard to patrol the plant and increased security after the incident.

After Fanning

Kay Fanning left the *Daily News* in 1983 to become editor of the *Christian Science Monitor*. Business manager Jerry Grilly moved up to *News* publisher, and Weaver moved up from managing editor to editor.

Grilly started with Cleveland-based Sun Newspapers and then joined McClatchy in 1979. McClatchy sent him to Anchorage as business manager.

Weaver held the post of *Daily News* editor from 1983 until the *News* defeated the *Times* in the newspaper war.

After Grilly and Weaver left, Fuller Cowell was named publisher and Pat Dougherty moved up to editor.

Dougherty earned a bachelor's degree in journalism at Baylor University in Texas in 1974, and started his newspaper career in 1975 as a reporter for the *Alexandria Gazette* in Alexandria, Virginia. In addition to the *Gazette*, he worked for *The Anchorage Times*, the *Alaska Advocate* and joined the *Anchorage Daily News* in 1980 as editor of *We Alaskans* magazine. He was promoted to editor of the *Daily News* in the fall of 1998.

Cowell began his newspaper career as a teenager working for the *Fairbanks Daily News-Miner*. He later ran the *Cordova Times* and started the *Valdez Vanguard* with his wife, Christmas. He went into newspaper equipment sales and consulting and then joined McClatchy headquarters in 1981.

He helped design the *Daily News*' new plant in 1985-86. He returned to Alaska in 1993 as publisher of the *Daily News* but had to retire in 1999 to concentrate on a successful battle against leukemia.

Mike Sexton, president of Central Maine Newspapers, replaced Cowell as *Daily News* publisher. He had been a newspaper publisher for seventeen years, most of it in the Midwest on moderately sized newspapers.

Times' war editors

In January 1980, *Anchorage Times* managing editor Clint Andrews relinquished his post to become director of special projects and chief editorial writer for the *Times*. There followed a succession of editors to manage the *Times* newsroom during its war years with the *News*.

The first managing editor was Fred Dickey, forty-four, who had been with the *Oakland* (California) *Tribune* and other California newspapers. He resigned after seventeen months to become copy desk editor for the *San Diego Union*. Drex Heikes, twenty-eight, moved up from the news staff to succeed him.

Drex was the son of Marvin and Jenalee Heikes, owners of Burkeshore Marina at Big Lake, Alaska, and was a graduate of West Anchorage High School and the University of Oregon. He left after a year to become metro editor of the *Fresno* (California) *Bee*.

Sunday editor Lana Johnson, a thirteen-year *Times* staffer, became managing editor in September 1982. When she resigned her *Times* post after two years, city editor Duncan Frazier, thirty-three, former managing editor of the *Ketchikan Daily News*, was appointed acting managing editor.

Thomas Anthony (Tony) Durr, assistant managing editor of the *San Antonio* (Texas) *Express News*, took over as managing editor of the *Times* in February 1985 and Frazier left the *Times* in August to join Leighton Wood's Skagit Alaska, Inc. at Wasilla as publisher of *The Frontiersman* and the *Wasilla Sun*.

Durr was with the *Times* less than a year. He left for Kodiak where he was editor of the *Kodiak Mirror* briefly before his sudden death at a young age.

Following Durr, one of the University of Alaska Anchorage's Atwood Chair of Journalism professors, Wallace Allen, from Minneapolis, filled in as managing editor and then Carol Wood, a longtime *Times* staffer, moved up to the post from the copy desk.

In the meantime, Atwood hired several consultants to devise a way to overcome the *Daily News* in their newspaper war. One of the consultants, William Hofer, became general manager until Bill Allen bought the paper. Allen made Hofer president but fired him within a month. Wood went back to UAA to complete a degree in nursing.

Bill Allen brought in Hugh Cunningham, a Texas journalism instructor, as editor and hired Paul Jenkins from the Anchorage bureau of The Associated Press as managing editor. J. Randolph Murray, who had been with the *Orlando* (Florida) *Sentinel* and the *Chicago Tribune*, later replaced Cunningham.

Murray went back to newspapers in Florida and Alabama when the *Times* suspended publication.

Jenkins joined the three-member "Voice of the Times" staff with Tobin and Dennis Fradley.

Jenkins graduated in 1973 from the University of Central Florida, with honors in a double major, political science and journalism. He worked for The Associated Press in Anchorage for ten years. In 1990-92, he was *Anchorage Times*' managing editor when his staff of one hundred won the Blethen Award for outstanding news coverage.

Fradley earned a bachelor's in journalism at the University of Alaska Fairbanks in 1971. He began as a sportswriter with *The Anchorage Times*. In 1972-74 he was assistant city editor, political reporter, and resource editor at the *Fairbanks Daily News-Miner*.

He worked in Washington DC for Alaska's senators, Ted Stevens and Frank Murkowski, and returned to Alaska in January 1991 to be editorial page editor of *The Anchorage Times* and editorial writer for the *Times* page. He joined the governor's office when Frank Murkowski was elected governor in 2002.

Tom Brennan replaced Fradley on the "Voice of the Times." In 1967 Brennan joined *The Anchorage Times* for two years and then spent eleven years with Atlantic-Richfield Company. He operated his own communications consulting firm for twenty years before joining the "Voice of the Times" in November 2000.

FAREWELL!

Without warning, Anchorage newspaper readers were greeted the morning of June 3, 1992, with a shocking *Times* banner headline: "FAREWELL!"

There followed the subhead: "After seventy-seven years, The *Times* stops the presses – for good."

Assistant publisher Tobin, who had been a top executive with the newspaper for twenty-nine years, wrote the heads. "I wanted something short and classy as our last banner. And 'Farewell!' seemed to say it all, to me."

Alaska's biggest newspaper war was over.

The lead story, under the byline of Scott Reeves, reported: "After seventy-seven years of reporting and influencing events in Alaska, *The Anchorage Times* was sold Tuesday for an undisclosed price to McClatchy Newspapers, Inc. and will cease publication today."

Stunned *Times* staffers embraced, cried, or stood silently after editor Murray gave them the bad news. The staff photographer recorded the event for that day's pages.

Allen kept the negotiations secret until the morning the decision was announced, first to department heads, who then informed staff.

Managing editor Jenkins said the *Times*' local coverage had forced the *News* to improve its reporting of Anchorage events.

"They couldn't beat us – they had to buy us," he told staffers.

That last issue of the *Times* covered reaction from staff, readers and civic and political leaders in the state and from former publisher Atwood. The history of the *Times* was outlined from its start in 1915 as the *Knik News*.

The *Times* editorial that day touched on the key problem that allowed the *Daily News* to overtake the *Times* and convert old-time Alaska newspaper journalism to corporate journalism: "The *Times*, too long in adhering to its traditional afternoon roots, let itself fall too far behind to recover."

Epilogue

Journalism Education

Advances in Alaska

With the large number of Alaskans being trained as journalists by UA, it's probable that the university some day will welcome another Alaska journalist as a regent.

Started Journalism Program–Dr. Saradell Ard, left, headed the Humanities Department at the University of Alaska Anchorage when her long time friends Robert and Evangeline Atwood, above, encouraged her to start a journalism program at UAA. They backed up that encouragement with grants to bring prominent journalist north to teach, but insisted that UAA hire a full-time professor to head the program. The first Atwood Professor of Journalism and Dr. Sylvia Broady, the first professor and chair of the newly created department, arrived on campus September 1980. -*Photos courtesy of Atwood Estate and Saradell Ard.*

Epilogue

Atwoods Promote Journalism Education

The personal friendship of Robert B. Atwood and his wife Evangeline with Dr. Saradell Ard led to creation of the University of Alaska Anchorage School of Journalism and Public Communications in the late 1970s and early eighties. Twenty-five years later, Robert and Evangeline Atwood are gone. But the school they promoted, and still support through grants from their foundation, has thrived and educated dozens of journalists now working in newsrooms across the state.

In the early 1970s, Dr. Ard headed the Humanities Division at University of Alaska Anchorage. The Atwoods published the state's largest newspaper, *The Anchorage Times*. Dr. Ard sought to establish a new department of public communications at UAA, her interest piqued when the Atwoods asked why something wasn't being done toward educating journalists within Alaska.

Dr. Ard talked with nationally known journalism educators and reviewed programs at other universities. She formed an advisory committee of communication professionals to ascertain the needs of the Anchorage media. That led to formation of the JPC Professional Advisory Council, still active today.

Through Dr. Ard's work, the University of Alaska Board of Regents approved the degree requirements for a Department of Public Communications in 1976. No funding was provided for the next four years. Some classes were offered by hiring adjuncts from the local communications field and using existing faculty. By 1979, the need for a full program was established when sixty-nine students declared majors in journalism and public communications.

During weekends at the Atwood's Girdwood A-frame in those unfunded years, Dr. Ard and the Atwoods frequently discussed the struggling state of the program. From those discussions came the offer by Bob Atwood to provide the initial funding for a chair of journalism with the stipulation that the university would hire the program's first full-time professor of communications. That launched Public Communications as a full department in the university and created the Atwood Chair of Journalism.

Atwood also asked that journalism be given greater recognition in the title by changing the name from Public Communications to Journalism and Public Communications. In the years since, and in recognition of the Atwood's continuing financial support of the program, some have suggested that it be renamed again, this time as the Robert B. Atwood School of Journalism and Public Communications.

Financial donations by Robert and Evangeline Atwood also kept the doors of the Alaska Pacific University open during an APU financial crisis. That led to the naming of the Student Center at APU after the Atwoods. The couple received honorary degrees from both UAA and APU.

The Alaska Legislature in 1998 named a twenty-story state office building in Anchorage after the deceased publisher in recognition of his contributions to Alaska. The building had been the Bank of California building before purchase by the state.

Other newspapers contribute

Although the Atwoods have been major financial contributors to university education in Alaska, other newspapers also have been generous. McClatchy's *Anchorage Daily News* has contributed between $200,000 and $100,000 to the University of Alaska, Alaska Pacific University and Sheldon Jackson College at Sitka, although neither APU nor SJC provide a major or minor in journalism.

The *News* also has been giving $1,000 journalism scholarships to each of the journalism schools since McClatchy Newspapers purchased the *News* in 1979.

Fairbanks Daily News-Miner publisher Marilyn Romano says her newspaper contributes to the university but not specifically to the

Endows UAF Chair

–Helen Snedden, right, widow of long time Fairbanks Daily News-Miner publisher C.W. (Bill) Snedden, announced early in 2004 that she is endowing the C.W. Snedden Chair of Journalism at the University of Alaska Fairbanks. As this book was published, details on the program were still being organized. *-Photo courtesy of the Fairbanks Daily News-Miner.*

journalism department. She serves on the University of Alaska Fairbanks advisory board.

A current major *News-Miner* contribution is more than $100,000 in cash and services toward expansion of the University museum. The athletic department receives about $20,000 of the $200,000 a year in grants and services for campus programs.

The *News-Miner* also has an intern program in which it not only helps train journalists, it also trains people in other newspaper departments. Many are offered full-time jobs after they graduate.

Journalism courses started at UAF

Journalism courses in Alaska began at the University of Alaska Fairbanks in the early 1960s when Charles Keim was an instructor in English and writing courses. A minor was obtainable in journalism. At that time, too, the Fairbanks campus was the only campus of the University of Alaska. The Anchorage campus was a community college. It and other community colleges did not become part of the university system until 1963.

The Alaska Press Club named Keim as "Alaska 49er" in 1963, one of the first of a group of forty-nine Alaskans honored for their

First Department Heads–Robert Rhodes, above, Atwood Professor of Journalism at UAA 1989-91, and the journalism department's first chairperson 1980-1995, Dr. Sylvia Broady, stand before pictures of former Atwood professors Cleve Mathews, Mort Stern, B. Dale Davis, Wallace Allen and John Strohmeyer (bottom row). Jimmy Bedford, lecturing below, was the first journalism department chairman at UAF, 1967-1981. -*Photos courtesy Dr. Sylvia Broady, the Historical Collection, 72-2-11, Jimmy Bedford, Archives, University of Alaska Fairbanks.*

"significant endeavors for the growth and cultural advancement of their state." Keim died in 2000 at his retirement home on Fox Island, Washington.

In the 1966-67 UAF catalog, it was announced that a major in journalism was coming under Dean Keim. It became a full program in 1967-68, with James (Jimmy) Bedford as chair of the department. His first graduate with a bachelor's degree in journalism and English in 1968 was Richard Arab. He took a job at the *Ketchikan Daily News* after graduation.

Bedford was born in 1927 at Columbia, Missouri, home of the University of Missouri's famed journalism program. There he earned bachelor's degrees in economics and journalism, followed by a master's degree in journalism.

He joined the staff at the University of Alaska Fairbanks in 1965, teaching journalism and photojournalism before heading the department.

He wrote a weekly column for the *News-Miner*, "Journeys on the Planet Earth," and took on a variety of freelance writing and photography assignments following his retirement in 1981.

Bedford served as treasurer on the board of the *Tundra Times*. He belonged to the Farthest North and Alaska Press clubs, the National Press Photographers Association, and the Society of Professional Journalists.

In 1986, it was discovered he had a brain cancer. He died at his home in Fairbanks in July 1990 at age sixty-three. On his death, a Bedford Scholarship Fund was started for journalism students at UAF.

B. G. Olson next

After Bedford, the UAF department was headed by prominent communications people. Included among them was B. G. Olson. He was hired as an assistant in university relations by Dr. Sylvia Broady and moved up to head university relations when Broady resigned in 1966 to go to Europe with her husband. Olson stayed until 1968 as director of university relations and assistant to University President William Wood. Prior to that, Olson had worked for the *Alaska Sportsman* magazine in Ketchikan and at the *Juneau Independent*.

Olson left UAF to earn a law degree and returned in 1974 to resume teaching in the journalism department, specializing in communications law. Wood and Olson also helped organize the Alaska Public Broadcasting Commission, which hired UAF broadcasting professor

Dr. Charles Northrip as executive director. Olson served on the commission for ten years in the 1980s.

Olson and Bedford co-chaired the journalism department after Bedford's retirement in '81 and until his death. They were followed as chairs by George M. Winford, 1986-87; Dean M. Gottehrer, 1987-90; Bruce L. Smith, 1990-92; Jerry Brigham, 1992-94; Lael Morgan, 1994-96; Charles Mason, 1996-2001; and the current head, Dr. Joy Morrison.

Gottehrer also was instrumental in helping the Alaska Newspaper Association work out rules for use of cameras in the courtroom, which led to Alaska Court Rule 50. He personally appealed to the Alaska Supreme Court and won endorsement of the new rule.

Later, financed by the Alaska Newspaper Association, Gottehrer worked with the Alaska bureau of The Associated Press to produce the "The Associated Press Stylebook for Alaska," published by Epicenter Press.

Winford's newspaper experience had been on weeklies in Louisiana. Smith was manager of the university's station KUAC while in charge of the department. Brigham also was a radio man and left the university to manage a small station in the Southwest.

Morgan, a former Alaska newspaper reporter and photographer, is an author of books and articles. Her work has appeared in the *Los Angeles Times* and *National Geographic*. Following thirty years researching history of the north, she authored "The Good Time Girls of the Alaska-Yukon Gold Rush" and "Art and Eskimo Power; The Life and Times of Howard Rock."

When she left as chair of the department, she formed a publishing house, Epicenter Press, with Kent Sturgis, former *News-Miner* managing editor and former AP bureau chief in Seattle. Their partner and chairman of their board is the retired university administrator and journalism instructor, Olson, who lives in Sitka.

Mason worked for the *News-Miner* 1984 to 1987 as a photographer and worked up to chief photographer. He earned a master's degree in documentary photography at Illinois State University in '88. Then he returned to the *News-Miner* as photo editor before joining the journalism department at UAF in 1990.

Tenured at UAF, he also continues as a stringer photographer for such prominent organizations as *Time* magazine, Black Star Publications in New York, the AP and the *Anchorage Daily News*.

Dr. Morrison, head of the department since July 2001 and an instructor in mass communications, joined the UAF faculty in 1990 when Smith was acting department chair. She is a native of South Africa and began her education there but earned her bachelor's and master's degrees at the University of New Mexico. She was awarded her doctorate in mass communications at the University of Iowa in 1991.

She has been a leader among Alaska educators who have assisted journalism programs in Russia.

Broady first at UAA JPC

The first head of the University of Alaska Anchorage Journalism and Public Communications program was Dr. Sylvia Broady. She earned a bachelor's in journalism at Michigan State University where she was on the staff of the college paper. She earned a doctorate at MSU and taught there as an assistant professor.

She first joined the University of Alaska in 1963 when it was a single campus in Fairbanks. Then she and her husband were overseas until 1977 when they returned to Anchorage. She ran a public relations firm for three years. During that time she was a lecturer in the public communications program. In 1980 she established the Department of Journalism and Public Communications at UAA under Dr. Ard's Humanities Department.

Broady retired as professor emeritus of JPC in 1995 after fifteen years as chairman but continues to work with the department. The Alaska Press Club recognized her in 1995 for "a life time of dedication to journalism education in Alaska." The Alaska Press Women named her Communicator of Achievement in 1991, and awarded her the 1990 Golden Nugget Award as a "champion for women in journalism, and most of all a champion for excellence in our field."

She was replaced from within the department by Larry Campbell, who was with the *Anchorage Daily News* before joining UAA. He was one of the members of a team that won a Pulitzer Prize for that newspaper in 1988. He grew up in Anchorage and graduated from Dimond High School and the University of Oregon. In 1982, he joined the staff of the *Daily News* until joining the UAA in 1994.

Campbell resigned from the UAA in 1998 to return to the *Daily News* but didn't stay there long. He was tapped by the AP to be Alaska bureau chief in Anchorage after Dean Fosdick retired in May 2001.

Jim Avery served as chair of the UAA JPC department for a year and then accepted a position at the University of Oklahoma. The current chair of the department followed Avery. He is Dr. Frederick W. Pearce, a specialist in broadband communications and technologies, with experience in both commercial and public broadcasting. He is director of the Alaska Telemedicine Project that provides medical support throughout Alaska and the Russian Far East.

He earned his bachelor's degree in radio, television, and film at Iona College in New York; and a master's and a doctorate at the University of Pittsburgh. He joined UAA in 1991 after teaching mass communications at Wheeling (Virginia) College and at the University of Scranton.

Pearce has served on local, state, and university committees dedicated to improving communications to rural areas, and has been a consultant to local broadcasters and small businesses. His consulting included projects in the Russian Far East.

The UAA Faculty

The UAA hired Edgar Blatchford as an assistant journalism professor in 1995. Blatchford is an Inupiaq Eskimo, born in Nome. He was publisher of newspapers in Seward, Cordova, and Valdez before merging his operations with Alaska Newspapers, Inc. He later joined the cabinet of Gov. Frank Murkowski as commissioner of community and economic development, similar to a post he held under Gov. Walter Hickel in 1990-1994.

UAA gained a wire service veteran when Roseanne Pagano left the AP bureau in Anchorage in 1999 to accept a professorship. Pagano has wide experience in newspaper, wire service and magazine writing.

Among the many consulted on organizing the JPC program was broadcaster Mel Kalkowski. He arrived in Anchorage in 1968 with Armed Forces Radio. From there he went to stations KTVA, KFQD, and KIMO using the on-air name of Mel Carter.

He now teaches part-time in JPC and is in charge of the summer journalism program financed by an *Anchorage Daily News* grant.

Atwood chairs are prize-winners

The Atwood Chair professor at UAA brings an experienced, practicing journalist to the campus for a year (some stayed for two or three) to instruct and lecture.

The program began in 1979 with the initial gift of $100,000 from the Atwoods.

The first Atwood professor hired was Cleve Mathews, professor of journalism in the Newhouse School of Communications at Syracuse University. Beginning in September 1980, he helped Dr. Broady organize the journalism program. Mathews wrote the bylaws and operating procedure for the first student newspaper and served as advisor. Other Atwood professors served as publications advisor until 1998 when others in the department assumed the responsibility.

The second Atwood professor was Mort Stern, Ph.D., former executive editor of the *Denver Post* and the third, in 1983, was B. Dale Davis, former executive editor and vice president for the *Philadelphia Bulletin*. Davis stayed two years.

The fourth Atwood professor was Wallace Allen, assistant managing editor of the *Minneapolis Tribune*. He served two years and then became managing editor of *The Anchorage Times* for two years.

Richard Smyser, editor of the *Oak Ridger* in Oak Ridge, Tennessee, was the next Atwood professor. He was by that time also past president of both the American Society of Newspaper Editors and the Associated Press Managing Editors' Association.

John Strohmeyer, former vice president and editor of the *Bethlehem Globe-Times*, followed Smyser as Atwood professor. He won a Pulitzer for editorial writing and is a Harvard Nieman Fellow. He served two years as an Atwood professor and stayed in Alaska after the professorship as a successful writer of books.

The seventh Atwood professor was Robert Rhodes, executive editor of the *Corpus Christi Caller-Times*. He also stayed two years.

James D. Atwater, a former dean of the University of Missouri School of Journalism and senior editor for *Time* magazine, became an Atwood professor in 1991 for two years.

The first woman Atwood professor was Tad Bartimus. She also had been the first Alaska bureau chief for the AP when she opened the Anchorage bureau in 1974. In the intervening years she was an AP national correspondent and a nationally syndicated columnist. Bartimus stayed three years as the Atwood professor.

Terry Wimmer, science and technology editor of the *Orange County* (California) *Register* followed Bartimus. He had headed a Pulitzer Prize winning team for investigative reporting while at the *Register*.

He was followed by a third Pulitzer winner, Byron Acohido, business reporter for the *Seattle Times.*

Carol Rich, author of nationally acclaimed textbooks on news writing, and the use of the World Wide Web in the newsroom, was the next Atwood professor. She not only stayed two years in the post but became a professor of journalism at UAA.

A year was missed in hiring an Atwood professor but the thirteenth person to hold the post, for the 2001-2002 school year, was a fourth Pulitzer Prize winner, Gary Cohn, an investigative reporter from the *Baltimore Sun.*

Stars boost enrollment

The star-studded program at UAA has attracted an average of 250 students annually. More than 240 alumni are listed working in their field, two dozen on Alaska newspapers. Many of the rest are in Alaska broadcasting, public relations or education. Among the Alaska trained journalist some are in top positions. Alaska-born Andy Hall, editor of *Alaska Magazine*, received his bachelor's degree from the UAA JPC program. He worked at the *Peninsula Clarion* and *Kodiak Mirror* before becoming editor of Alaska's largest magazine. Amy Willis, publisher of the *Kodiak Mirror*, received her bachelor's degree in the UAA journalism program.

The future

A pioneer Alaska newspaper editor, L. Frank Shaw, served on the University's first board of regents. He was appointed in 1917 by Gov. J. F. A. Strong, another pioneer publisher. At that time the school was known as the Agricultural College and School of Mines and the regents were called trustees.

Shaw had edited newspapers in Valdez, Seward, Anchorage, and Fairbanks. He was editor of the *Cook Inlet Pioneer and Knik News* when he and gold rush journalist Ted Needham moved it from Knik to Anchorage in 1915, where it became *The Anchorage Daily Times.*

Fairbanks newspaper and radio-TV station owner A. E. (Cap) Lathrop served on the board of regents between 1932 and 1950 under appointments by Governors George Parks, John Troy and Ernest Gruening.

The third regent with newspaper experience was Gordon Evans who served 1983-1991 and was president 1989-90. He came to

Alaska in 1961 as UPI correspondent in Anchorage. He moved to managing editor of the *Anchorage Daily News* and then to Juneau as special assistant to Gov. Bill Egan. He attended law school and practiced in Juneau from 1970 until he retired in 2003.

The fourth regent with newspaper connections was Lew M. Williams Jr., who was appointed to the post by Gov. Walter Hickel for a 1991-99 term after Williams retired in 1990 as publisher of the *Ketchikan Daily News*.

Although the Atwoods contributed generously to the university, none served on the board of regents. Mrs. Atwood's brother and nephew, Elmer and Edward Rasmuson – both past presidents of the National Bank of Alaska – served on the board. The UAF library is named for Elmer Rasmuson for his contributions. However, with the large number of Alaskans being trained as journalists by UA and staying in the state to practice their profession, it's probable that the university some day will welcome another Alaska journalist as a regent.

There might be among them another Bob Atwood, Bill Snedden, Wrong Font Thompson, Major Strong, Stroller White, John Troy, or Sid Charles.

There should be another Karl Armstrong, Howard Rock, Cy Peck, or Louis Paul.

There will be another Marie Coe, Mildred Kirkpatrick, Marie McDowell, Jackie Lindauer, or Sarah Pritchett.

Appendix

Index

Acohido, Byron, 688
Adams, Capt. Charles, 116
Adasiak, Allan, 559
Agnew, J. P., 94
Alaska:
 Court System, 15, 333, 572
 First Judicial Division, 178, 462
 First Territorial Legislature, 184, 289, 299
 Historical Library, 20
 Public Broadcasting Commission, 683
 State Library, 581, 729, 730
 Statehood, 14, 27, 194, 291, 325–338, 348, 370, 371, 394, 412, 442, 534, 645–649
 Supreme Court, 186, 191, 192, 195, 550, 551, 572, 589, 590, 605, 607, 650, 684, 738, 739
 Territory of Alaska, 23, 735
 Third Judicial Division, 206, 232, 515
Alaska Advocate, The, 660, 671, 672
Alaska Airlines, 270, 333, 399, 402, 403, 449, 469, 523, 626, 656
Alaska Appeal, 23
Alaska Broadcasters' Association, 558
Alaska Bulletin, 23
Alaska Business, 16

Alaska Citizen, The, 69, 70, 136, 140, 141, 190, 261, 274, 389
Alaska Daily Capital, 263, 320, 345
Alaska Daily Dispatch, 47, 289, 637
Alaska Daily Empire, 68, 86, 183, 227, 248, 257, 273, 289, 333, 345, 458, 557
Alaska Daily Press, The, 352, 354, 460, 545
Alaska Daily Record, 179, 188, 282

Alaska Dispatch, 59, 182, 216, 262, 292, 346, 458, 636
Alaska Examiner, 362
Alaska Fisherman, 362, 407, 409, 459
Alaska Fishing News, 71, 121, 323, 333, 356, 364, 366, 367, 412, 638
Alaska Forum, 252, 253
Alaska Free Press, The, 49, 53, 185
Alaska Herald, 31, 52
Alaska Journal, 51, 52
Alaska Journal Express, 659
Alaska Journal of Commerce, 16, 560, 587, 663
Alaska Labor News, 318
Alaska Monthly, The, 204
Alaska Magazine, 16, 352, 367, 560, 688

Alaska Military Weekly, 560
Alaska Miner, The, 56, 59, 61, 278, 396
Alaska Mining Record, 53, 54, 57, 58, 81
Alaska Native Brotherhood, 40, 299, 356, 362, 407, 415, 426, 459
Alaska Native Sisterhood, 355, 409
Alaska Native Claims Settlement Act, 409, 413, 490, 665
Alaska National Interest Lands Conservation Act, 405, 507, 610, 662
Alaska News, The, 52, 54, 56
Alaska Newspaper Association, 585, 589, 591, 649, 684
Alaska Newspapers, Inc., 251, 407, 496, 511, 525, 630, 663, 686
Alaska Oil and Gas Reporter, 587
Alaska Pacific University, 326, 501, 680
Alaska Pioneer, 275
Alaska Press, The, 348, 350, 638
Alaska Press Club, 456, 553, 649, 664, 681, 683, 685
Alaska Press Women, 685
Alaska Prospector, 202, 244
Alaska Railroad Record, 318
Alaska Record-Miner, The, 61, 62, 161, 215
Alaska Sentinel, The, 89, 166, 169, 171, 179, 297
Alaska Searchlight, 54
Alaska Spokesman, 290
Alaska Sportsman, 352, 367, 369, 683
Alaska Star, 16, 560, 587, 660, 663
Alaska Statehood Act, 14, 291, 649
Alaska Statehood Committee, 325, 336, 348, 370, 371, 647, 648

Alaska Sunday Morning Post, 289
Alaska Sunday Press, 440, 545, 546
Alaska Syndicate, The, 203, 204, 207, 209, 214, 215, 221, 236, 239, 242, 243, 273, 301, 312
Alaska Transcript, 178
Alaska Times, 22, 23, 234–237
Alaska Truth, The, 57, 59, 157
Alaska Weekly, The, 265, 319, 320, 324, 346, 392, 393
Alaska Weekly Dispatch, 319
Alaska Weekly Miner, 250
Alaska Weekly Post, The, 247, 248
Alaska Weekly Transcript, 180
Alaskan, 182, 235, 236, 296, 298, 302, 317, 321–323, 362, 396, 407–411, 426, 459
Alaskan, The, 25–33, 40–52, 83–89, 156, 214–220, 287, 300, 423, 602
Alaskan Equipment Trader, 560, 587
Alaskan and Herald Combined, The, 32
Alaskan Southeaster, 305, 538
Alaskan World, 138
Allen, Bill, 13, 15, 674, 675
Allen, Eugene C., 68, 107, 108, 215
Allen, George, 68
Allen, June, 282
Allen, Lois Hudson, 299, 300, 497, 498, 499
Allen, Wallace, 673, 687
Allen, William Prescott, 357, 548, 549, 552–555, 557
Allman, Jack, 382, 593
American Missionary Association Missionary School, 41
Anchorage Alaskan, 250, 320, 322
Anchorage Best Read Guide, 560
Anchorage Bypass, 663
Anchorage Chronicle, 419, 663

Anchorage Daily Alaskan, 321, 322, 382, 390, 396
Anchorage Daily News, 9, 13–15, 190, 239, 276, 304, 338, 355, 406, 453, 502, 525, 542, 566, 570, 582, 585, 586, 589, 598–601, 605–607, 613, 638-641, 646, 649, 658, 662, 664–667, 672, 680, 684–686
Anchorage Daily Times, The, 41, 56, 85, 68–70, 237, 242, 247–250, 262, 317–326, 329, 345, 352, 353, 358, 363, 392, 396, 403, 444, 499, 518, 547, 635, 637, 658, 659, 688, 689
Anchorage Hi-Life, 331
Anchorage News, 331, 370, 518, 658, 665
Anchorage Press, 663
Anchorage Times, The, 8, 13, 304, 319, 320, 327, 330, 419, 420, 444, 452, 456, 509, 544, 561, 566, 602, 618, 640, 641, 653, 663, 672–675, 679, 687
Anchorage Weekly Democrat, 318
Anchorage Weekly Times, The, 513
Anderson, Capt. L. B., 125, 126, 130
Anderson, Hall, 570, 571, 572
Anderson, Jack, 193, 490
Anderson, Oscar, 321
Anderson, Roy, 364, 365, 367
Anderson, Scott, 493
Andrews, Clint, 664, 673
Arbuckle, George (Buck), 70, 120, 134, 136, 252, 255–257, 263
Arctic Weekly Sun, The, 68, 98
Ard, Dr. Saradell, 679
Armstrong, Karl, 489, 490, 492, 493, 689

Arrowhead, The, 427
Associated Press, The, 29, 99, 146, 193, 247, 270, 287, 291, 317, 330, 350, 351, 367, 369, 419, 432, 437, 479, 486, 544, 566, 614, 634, 637, 640, 648–654, 658, 674, 684, 687,
Atwater, James D., 687
Atwood Chair of Journalism, 673, 680, 686
Atwood, Elaine, 666, 670, 671
Atwood, Evangeline, 7, 8, 239, 352, 539, 679, 680, 689
Atwood, Robert Bruce (Bob), 13–15, 41, 323–341, 352, 370, 392, 456, 509, 510, 564, 635, 641, 649, 658–675, 679, 680, 687–689
Aurora Borealis, 94
Austerman, Allan, 491, 492
Avalanche, The, 224
Avery, Jim, 686

Babb, Jim, 418, 668
Baker, Allen, 586, 587
Baker, Susie Morris, 560, 618
Baker, William L. (Bill), 276, 333, 336, 367–376, 428–430, 531, 534, 647
Balean, Maggie, 663
Ball, Col. Mottram D., 25, 28
Ballaine, Frank, 244, 247, 248, 251
Ballaine, John Edmund, 234, 244, 245, 247, 251, 497, 507
Ballinger, Richard, Sec. of Interior, 62, 164, 218
Baranov, Alexander, 20, 243, 505
Barnette, Elbridge Truman and Isabelle, 116–119, 125–130
Barnard, Bill, 641

Bartimus, Tad, 640, 687
Bartlett, Craig, 493
Bartlett, Delegate E. L., 429, 555
Bartlett, Doris Anne, 555
Bartlett, E. L. (Bob), 175, 194, 271, 390, 391, 437, 439
Bartlett, Sen., E. L., 325, 649, 651
Bauer, Jim and Mary, 600, 601
Bayles, Ike, 322
Beard, James, 356
Becker, Frank E., 135, 136
Beddoe, William A., 54–59
Bedell, Edgar L. (Ted), 320, 322
Bedford, James (Jimmy), 683, 684
Bell, Arthur G., 134, 139
Bell, Lt. Edward, 94
Bellows, George Lafeyette, 69, 117–120, 136, 190,
Belt, George, 94
Bender, Helen, 352, 353,
Bender, Robert W., 350, 436,
Bennett, Elbert, 360
Benson, William R., 581
Bering Straights, The, 628, 632
Bering Strait Record, 632
Bernard, Raleigh (Los), 127, 128, 129, 352, 358
Bettles, Gordon Charles, 37, 38
Bialik, Barry, 663
Billings, G. Lucille, 584
Birkinbine, Lt. Henry P. M., 88, 301
Blatchford, Edgar, 510, 525, 686
Blahut, Emil, 385
Blethen, Col. Alden J., 287
Blethen, C. B., 111
Blum, Sam, 215, 219
Boat Broker, 565
Bohi, Heidi, 420
Bone, Gov. Scott C., 111, 231, 363

Bonser Company, The, 520–525
Bonser, Harold (Skip) and Marian, 501, 518–522
Bostian, Kelly, 655
Boucher, Emily and Wilfred, 115, 623–625
Boulay, Bill, 663
Bourke, Joseph, 202
Bouse, J. B., 94
Bradner, Tim, 382
Brady, Commissioner John G., 25–28
Brady, Gov. John G., 41–46, 57, 59, 86, 104, 156–159, 164, 182, 189, 206, 269
Brady, William Jeffrey (Jeff), 297, 303, 306–308
Bramble, Earl, 331
Brandley, Kent, 652, 653
Brandli, Kent, 492, 493, 652
Brandt-Erichsen, Thor and Nancy, 602
Braschler, Von, 449, 455, 471, 472
Brazil, Herb and Patrice, 383
Bremer, Arthur S., 393, 394
Brennan, Tom, 674
Brice, Gene, 369, 534
Brigham, Jerry, 684
British Colonist, The, 21
Broady, Dr. Sylvia, 683–687
Bronson, Sen. Lester (Tiger), 537, 625
Brough, Hazan, 459, 460
Brown, Beriah, 25, 287
Brown, Cole, 658
Brown, Edward H., 25
Brown, Fred M., 217
Brown, Judge Harold, 588–590
Brown, Judge Melvin C., 61, 160, 161, 163, 178

Brown, Norman Cole and Blanche, 14, 239, 329, 331, 370, 641, 658, 664–666
Brown, Robert L., 557
Brown, Susan, 641
Bryson, Jamie, 448–450, 455, 471
Buell, Arthur, 68, 99
Bunch, Alvin, 452
Bunch, E. Struthers, 70, 127, 131
Bunnell, Charles, 228, 273
Busey, Lester, 250, 251, 499, 577, 579
Bushell, Richard, 45, 88, 89, 161–163, 171, 172, 188, 272, 274, 297

Calhoun, William C., 22
Calista Native Corporation, 407, 419, 496, 511, 525, 630
Callaham, A. B., 270, 289, 290
Callahan, Sam, 70, 252, 254, 255, 256, 260, 264
Calvin, Jack and Sasha, 427, 429
Camp, F. B., 248
Campbell, Larry, 640, 685
Capital City Weekly, 185, 546, 560, 565
Capital Information Group vs. State, 589
Capital move, 184 322, 564, 602, 650, 662, 664
Cappon, Rene J. (Jack), 641, 664, 670
Carmack, George W., 64
Carpenter, George A., 52–54, 68, 98, 99
Caribou Sun, 57
Carpeneti, Judge Walter, 573
Carruthers, Charles, C., 383
Casati, Christopher, 420, 632
Cashman, Kay, 494
Caskey, Judson Harmon, 69, 127, 134, 136, 140, 143, 146,147, 190

Castle, Neville H., 111
Catalla Drill, The, 208, 209
Cernick, Cliff, 649, 650, 664
Chamberlain, Edward C., 28, 29, 32, 33
Chamberlin, Rep. Art, 351
Chandler, Bob, 667, 669
Chappell, Ron (Ronnie), 606, 613
Charles, Douglas, 542
Charles, Mildred Sutter, 366
Charles, Patricia, 369, 534–539, 641
Charles, Paul S. (Bud), 366, 376, 534, 560
Charles, Sydney (Sid) Dean, 70, 121, 122, 130, 131, 217, 276, 319, 323, 345–347, 356, 361–370, 374–376, 412, 423–425, 458, 460, 531, 534, 549, 639, 689
Cheechako News, 609–615
Cheek, C. F., 187
Chena Herald, 119
Chena, SS, 512
Chena Times, 69, 119
Chicago Tribune, 371, 393, 460, 595, 639, 674
Chickaloon News, 407, 419
Chilkat Post, The, 301
Chilkat Valley News, 303, 304, 305
Chilkoot Post, The, 301
Chitina Herald, 222
Chitina Leader, The, 220, 221
Choquette, Buck, 168, 208
Choquette, Georgiana, 168
Chugiak-Eagle River Star, 660
Chung, Hi (China Joe), 48
Clara Nevada, SS, 286, 287
Clarion, 16, 560, 587, 605–607, 611–619, 688
Clark, Jack, 491, 492

Clark, Gov. Walter D., 220, 533
Clark, Willoughby, 168, 208, 209
Clemons, Edward L. (Bud) and Betty Mae, 460–463
Cleveland, Cynthia, 24
Cleveland, Pres. Grover, 24, 25, 32, 33, 156
Clifton, Robert and Dorothy, 517
Coe, Cassius and Marie, 97, 98, 103, 104, 201, 689
Coe, Curtis P., 41
Coe, Morgan, 557
Coffey, John F., 318, 319
Cohn, Gary, 688
Colby, Robert L., 186–188
Cole, Asa, 494
Cole, C. E., 85
Cole, Dermot, 193–195
Cole, Frank and Mary, 224, 364, 425
Coleman, John M., 499, 501
Collins, Rep. Ernest B., 184, 289
Collins, Judge Patricia, 551
Collins, Sally Jo, 383
Coltman, Nick, 663
Committee for Two Newspapers, 669
Committee of 101, 73, 82
Commoner, The, 228–230, 299, 315
Cook Inlet Courier, 583, 585, 612
Cook Inlet Pioneer & Knik News, 68, 247, 311, 314
Copper Bee, The, 224
Cordel, Linda, 591
Cordova Alaskan, 87, 108, 181, 188, 207, 211
Cordova Daily Alaskan, 69, 234, 314
Cordova Daily Herald, The, 237, 320
Cordova Daily Times, 240, 322, 329, 518, 637
Cordova Times, 46, 231, 237, 239, 242, 250, 317, 319, 363, 396, 501, 510, 518–524, 595, 651, 672
Corson, John W., 134, 216, 297
Cotter, Frank J., 70, 346
Council City News, 68, 107, 110, 111, 167
Court photography, 570–573
Court proceedings, media coverage, 572
Coutant, Walter S., 88, 160–163, 178–182
Cowell, Fuller and Christmas, 9, 520–525, 672, 673
Coyne, Cyril A. (Cy), 303, 306
Coyney, Weston, 83
Cramer, John C., 289
Crary, Will H., 202–206
Crawford, Melton L., 486
Cunningham, Hugh, 674
Currall, Geoffrey, 571
Curtis, W. C., 165
Cutler, Judge Beverly, 591, 604

Daily Alaska Dispatch, 59, 182, 262, 636
Daily Alaska Empire, 8, 176, 333, 374, 436, 463, 545, 557
Daily Alaskan, The, 74, 83, 85, 86, 235, 296
Daily Alaskan, 317, 321
Daily Evening Record and Weekly Mining Journal, 58
Daily Miner, 128, 163, 274
Daily Morning Alaskan, 44, 57, 71, 83, 102
Daily Progressive Miner, The, 274, 275
Daily Sentinel, 423, 433, 435, 560
Dalton, Jack, 52, 76, 87
Daly, James J., 23

Index

Daniels, Viola, 579, 597, 598
Davis, B. Dale, 687
Dawes, Harold F., 171, 172
Dawson Daily News, 83, 96, 102, 105, 120, 123, 126, 136, 324
Dawson News, 65, 96, 112, 127, 146
Dawson Nugget, 105
Dawson, Gene, 483
Dawson World, 324
Day, A. J. (Bert), 262
Day, Charles M., 230
Day, Ray G., 226
Day, Walter and Gloria, 517, 522, 523
DeArmond, Robert N. (Bob), 9, 84, 347, 369, 371, 553
Dech, Claud H., 180, 244
DeJulio, Alvin, 331, 598, 599
Delaney, Judge Arthur K., 178
DeLong, Spencer and Ann, 439, 545, 546
DeLoughery, Frank, 501
Delta Midnight Sun, 385
Delta Paper, 385, 386
Delta Weekly Gazette, 385
Delta Weekly News, The, 384
Delta Wind, 386
DeMarban, Alex, 663
Dennis, Don, 653
Denny, John B., 178, 179
Denny, L. C., 105
DePew, Lucy, 201
Derry, Charlie, 260
DeSucca, George W., 83
DeVane, Thomas, 262
Devine, E. C., 105, 106
Diamond Drill, 209, 212
Dickey, Fred, 673
Dickey, Miriam, 546
Digree, Sig and Bertha, 486–488

Dikeman, William A., 257
Dimond, Anthony (Tony), 175, 318, 392, 429, 437, 439, 499
Dodge, William Sumner, 21, 22
Dougherty, Patrick, 662, 672
Douglas City Miner, 56
Douglas Island News, 59, 62, 146, 161, 182, 187, 188, 263, 290, 346, 347
Douglas News, 56, 179
Doyle, John C. (Jack), 547, 555
Dumar, Leo, 109
Dunbar, Oscar W., 83, 85
Duncan, William, Fr., 41, 157
Dunham, Sam, 38
Dunham, Willard and Beverly, 505–510
Dunn, George, 94
Dunne, Phillip, 628, 629
Dunsworth, Wayne, 613, 615
Durr, Thomas Anthony (Tony), 673
Dutch Harbor Fisherman, 419, 496
Dyea Press, The, 59, 80
Dyea Trail, The, 58, 59, 77
Dynes, W. M., 276

Eagle City Tribune, 383
Eagle Eye, 304, 305
Eagle Gee Pole, 383
Eagle Reporter, 383
Eagle View, 384
Eagle's Eye, 383
Earle, B. B., 94
Earle, F. E., 94
Earthquake, Good Friday, 286, 385, 512, 513, 522
Echols, E. S., 94
Edelman, Carolyn, 306
Edes, William C., 312
Edmunson, Sarah Eleanor, 174

Edwards, William R., 252, 253
Egan, Alaska, 232, 382, 383
Egan, Frank, 383
Egan, Gov. William A. (Bill), 232, 383, 689
Eielson, Carl Ben, 148
Eisenhower, Pres. Dwight, 14, 325, 341, 373, 462, 548, 645, 647, 649
Ekstrand, Heidi, 542
Elstad, Albert O., 410, 459
Elton, Kim, 561
Endelman, Max, 53
Eskimo Bulletin, 41
Estus, Paul, 447, 448
Esquimaux, The, 19, 20, 107
Evans, E. S. (Bill), 348, 351, 545
Evans, Gordon, 639, 664, 670, 688
Evans, Lori, 618, 619
Exxon Valdez, 479, 506, 526, 592

Fairbanks Daily News, 69, 131, 134, 297
Fairbanks Daily News-Miner, 7, 16, 65, 68, 69, 114, 116, 118, 134, 142, 175, 189, 191, 202, 274, 322, 324, 326, 330, 333, 336, 373, 385, 388, 389, 393, 396, 398, 401, 406, 415, 416, 439, 446, 448, 494, 520, 546, 547, 619, 637, 638, 641, 642, 672, 674, 680
Fairbanks Daily Times, 70, 126, 139, 220
Fairbanks Evening News, 120, 123, 125
Fairbanks Facts, The, 138, 139
Fairbanks Gazette, The, 118
Fairbanks Miner, 117, 118
Fairbanks News, 65, 69, 70, 105, 120, 345, 389
Fairbanks Times, 37, 69, 105, 126, 129, 256, 321, 381, 595, 637

Fairbanks Weekly News, 69
Fairbanks Weekly Palladium & Local Regulator, The, 135
Fairweather Reporter, 306
Fanning, Larry and Kay, 14, 15, 662, 665–672
Farthest North Press Club, 405, 649
Ferguson, Valentine (Tiny) and Jane, 440
Ferney, Julius H., 430, 431, 440
Field, Marshall, 15, 639, 666
Field, Ted, 667, 669
Filbin, Jack, 70, 136, 260, 261, 262
Findley, G. C., 85
Fink, Tom, 607
Fires
   Anchorage, 670
   Cordova, 520
   Fairbanks, 126, 147, 398
   Fort Seward (Haines), 302
   Hyder, 278
   Juneau, 55
   Katalla, 213
   Ketchikan, 536
   Kodiak, 480
   Nome, 112, 114, 115
   Seward, 497, 501
   Sitka, 431
   Tok, 388
   Valdez, 230, 515
   Wrangell, 170, 441, 445
Fischer, Sec. of Interior Walter L., 213, 218
Fisk, Charles J., 322, 323
Fitz, Albert H., 110, 111
Fitz, Frances E., 110, 111
Fleischer, Hugh, 669
Flesser, Sid, 385
Florske, John, 304

Flynn, James, 234
Forbes, Dr. Henry, 416
Forbes, Vernon, 626
Fort Seward News, The, 301
Fort Wrangel News, 59, 168
Fortier, A. E., 659
Fortier, Edward J., 332
Forty-Ninth Star, 231, 317, 318, 332, 513
Fosdick, Dean, 640, 685
Foster, Rep. Frank H., 360
Fox, Martha, 493
Fradley, Dennis, 674
Frame, Arthur, 363
Frame, John Wesley, 62, 69, 177–182, 188, 215, 216–219, 225–231, 235, 250, 265, 280, 289, 299, 315–318, 361–363, 376
Frazier, Duncan, 602, 603, 673
Fredericks, Karen, 382
Freeman, Nancy and Duane, 492, 493, 494, 496
Fremming, Dave, 305
French, Peter, 27
Free Press, The, 140
Friend, Elmer E., 302, 350, 636
Frontiersman, The, 579, 586, 591, 597–604, 673
Furnival, F. J., 276

Galloway, David B., 650, 651
Garwood, George, 70
Gates, Hal, 331
Gaustad, Ole Peter, 137, 142
Gaustad, Violet Marie (Vide), 175
Gay, Alfred (Al), 193
Gibboney, Tom, 585–587
Gill, Shelley, 586, 591, 600, 602
Gillam, Harold, 365

Gillette, Louis T., 178
Gilmore, Tom, 117
Gilmore, William A., 138, 226
Gjosund, Louis and Linda, 584, 585
Glacier, The, 40
Glenora News, 128, 167
Gold Panner, 525
Gold Rushes
    Barnette's Cache (Fairbanks) (1902), 117
    Birch Creek (Circle city), (1893), 38
    Cassiar (Wrangell) (1874), 167, 168
    Hyder (1919), 278
    Iditarod (1908), 257
    Juneau, (1880), 33
    Klondike, (1898), 13, 34, 41–44, 53, 65, 85, 300, 303, 308, 315
    McGrath, 382
    Nome, (1900), 43, 105
    Ruby (1911), 260
    Tenderfoot (1917-18), 384
Golden North Airways, 189
Gottehrer, Dean, 572, 684
Gottstein, J. B., 321
Gough, E. H.. 61
Granduc Mine, 277, 278, 281
Grant, Allan X., 68, 70, 105, 257, 260–264, 314
Graves, Wallace, 331
Gray, Charles L. (Chuck), 7, 643, 645, 651, 654
Gray, Latimer (Dolly), 348
Greatlander Bush Mailer, 660
Greatlander Shopping News, 659, 660
Greely, John, 660, 662
Green, Derrick, 672
Gregory, Albro B., 282, 371, 399, 400,

468, 469, 537, 538, 557–559, 623, 626–630
Greuel, Richard J., 400, 556
Griffin, E. W., 127
Grigsby, George, 293
Grilly, Jerry, 672
Grimm, Robert L. and Karyn, 615
Gruening, Dr. Ernest, 232, 353
Gruening, Gov. Ernest, 194, 331–338, 354–357, 367–371, 374, 392–394, 439, 440, 441, 531, 546–548, 552, 553, 648, 649, 688
Gruening, Sen. Ernest, 195, 325, 377
Gucker, Jack and Jean, 233, 547
Guggenheim-Morgan, 179, 203, 204, 212, 215–218, 247, 273, 278, 499
Gwich'in Steering Committee vs. State of Alaska, 589

Haines Herald, 302
Haines Sentinel, The, 303
Haines Pioneer Press, 88, 300, 301
Haley, Dorothy, 546, 547
Haley, Sharman, 550, 551
Hall, Annie Hall Strong, 75
Hampton, Ot, 403, 659
Hanlon, Margaret, 424
Hanlon, Victor, 427
Hanlon, William Richter, 424
Hanlon, Williams Jr., 424
Hanson, Judge James, 605, 606
Hanson, Louis, 360, 367
Harding, Pres. Warren G., 111, 147, 174, 382
Halter Marine Group, 551, 552
Harper, Arthur, 37, 75
Harrais, Martin, 138, 226
Harrington, John J., 19

Harrington, Louise Brinck, 538
Harris, Beth Kay, 74
Harris, Dick, 33, 48
Harrison, Pres. Benjamin, 30, 50
Harrison, W. F., 261
Haswell, Clay, 606
Hatcher, Cordelia, 146
Hayne, Joseph T., 85
Hazelet, George C., 214–219, 231, 236, 246, 518
Hearst, William Randolph Jr., 194, 392, 639, 648
Heath, E. A., 272, 273
Heckey, John S., 231, 316–318
Heckman, J. R. (Bob), 161, 172, 272, 359, 360
Hedrick, Bonnie, 304
Heeter, Samuel E., 254
Hegdahl, Harry and W. M., 581, 582
Heikes, Drex, 673
Heilig, Frederick, 37, 134, 139
Heimbigner, David and Renda, 565
Heintzleman, Gov. B. Frank, 373, 548
Helgason, Clara, 493
Heney, M. J., 76, 199, 204, 207, 212, 214, 215, 244
Henning, Robert (Bob), 352
Henry, George Hinton, 35, 37, 140, 141, 254, 255
Hepp, Judge Everett, 195
Herron, Charles, 237, 247, 316–321, 345, 346
Hewitt, Patricia, 669
Hickel, Gov. Walter J., 489, 538, 544, 559, 645, 686, 688
Hickman, Zack, 108, 134
Hiebert, Augie, 526, 558
Hielscher, J. F., 201

Hildreth, H. H., 43–45, 202
Hill, George M., 56, 65, 69, 117–119, 257
Hillary, Tad, 215, 244
Hirschberg, Max R., 108
Hoben, Harry V., 248
Hoblitzell, Dick, 608
Hodge, Judge Walter, 357
Hofer, William, 674
Hoggatt, Gov. Wilford B., 46, 47, 62, 131, 133, 164, 170, 171, 179–182, 216
Homer Herald, 582
Homer Homesteader, 577, 581
Homer Journal, 583
Homer News, 16, 560, 580–587, 613, 619
Homer Tribune, 580, 587
Homer Weekly News, 584
Hopp, Charles, 59–62, 149, 161, 163, 168, 169, 179, 187, 188
Hornaday, Judge James, 587, 588
Hornsby, Dr. J. Allan, 74, 83
Hot Springs Echo, 255
Hot Springs Post, 70, 255
Howdeshell, Bert, 270, 272, 298, 299
Howells, A. J., 83
Howard, Arthur, 49
Howard, Frank, 49, 53, 55
Howard, George T., 37
Howard, J. C., 49, 50
Hoyt, Charles (Chuck), 558, 559, 570, 650
Hubbard, O. P., 137
Hubbard, Samuel, 94, 253
Hubrick, J. P., 224
Hughes, Ronnie, 615
Hull, W. R. (Rube), 278, 280

Hunt, Harold (Hal) and Nellie, 499
Hunter, Robert R. (Gravy Bob) and Hazel, 231, 315, 316, 317
Hutmacher, E. J., 119
Hyder Alaska Miner, 278
Hyder Silver Dollar, The, 280
Hyder Weekly Herald, The, 280
Hyder Weekly Miner, The, 280

Ickes, Sec. of Interior Harold, 232, 353, 411, 412
Icy Passages, 305, 306
Iditarod Nugget, The, 68, 257
Iditarod Pioneer, The, 257, 260
Industrial Worker, 105, 106, 111–113, 180, 262
Ingersoll, Charles, 272
Ingram, Rep. Hunter, 184
Interloper, The, 45, 88, 89, 171, 297
Investigative Reporters and Editors, 193
Irwin, the Rev. George M., 61, 62
Island News, 539
Island Times, 490, 491, 492
Islander, SS, 287

Jackson, Dr. Sheldon, 28, 57, 59, 156
Jackson, the Rev. Sheldon, 40
Jacobs, George and Beth, 388
James, William, 559, 560
Jarvela, Gil, 490, 491
Jameson, Earle, 345
Jeffrey, George A., 118
Jenkins, Paul, 419, 674, 675
Jensen, Ervin H., 547
Jensen, Ingvard M. (Ed), 85, 289, 295, 296
Jessen, Ernest F. and Catherine, 249, 250, 321, 396–404

Jessen's Daily, 402, 403
Jessen's Weekly, 396–403
Johnson, Carl C., 289
Johnson, Dennis, 492
Johnson, Rep. Frank, 370, 373
Johnson, J. Frederick, 457
Johnson, Lana, 673
Johnson, Thomas C., 445, 463, 465, 468
Johnston, Capt. John J., 179
Johnston, Judge Karl, 606
Joling, Dan, 641, 654
Jonas, Dan H., 131
Jones, Charles W., 319
Jones, Mel, 672
Jones, Nikki Murray (Norma Stillman), 542
Jones, Williams E., 23
Jordan, Lee, 660
Joslin, Falcon, 119, 301
Jump, Robert, 304, 305
Juneau Alaska Empire, 557, 559
Juneau City Mining Record, 31, 32, 50
Juneau Daily Capital, The, 345
Juneau Empire, 16, 185, 191–195, 287, 452, 542, 551, 573, 611, 618, 654
Juneau Independent, 357, 547, 553, 559, 561, 648, 658, 683
Juneau Journal, 157
Juneau Record-Miner, 348
Juneau Spirit, 346

Kadiak Times, 492, 493
Katalla Herald, The, 68, 207, 209, 211, 214
Kalkowski, Mel, 686

Katmai Eruption, 41, 480,482
Kederick, Bob, 556, 635, 664
Keen, Charles, 191, 192, 195
Keim, Charles, 681, 683
Keller, Dr. Lester S. and Martha, 85, 86, 187, 188, 296–299
Keller, Jack, 298, 299
Kelley, Mark, 569, 570
Kelly, Williams A., 28
Kemp, Randall H., 244
Kenai Peninsula Cheechako News, 609–615
Kenai Peninsula Newspaper, Inc., 615
Kenai Peninsula Pioneer, 582
Kenai Peninsula Soldotna Sun, 615
Kenealy, Maurice Edward, 29, 30
Kenyon, Rick and Bonnie, 224
Ketchikan Alaska Chronicle, 276, 322, 333, 336, 352, 358, 363, 366, 369, 370, 412, 430, 487, 552, 638
Ketchikan Daily News, The, (1922-1923), 359, 360, 533
Ketchikan Daily News, (1947-present), 7, 9, 16, 71, 121, 193, 276, 281, 333, 338, 364, 369, 375, 400, 401, 412, 432, 433, 449, 453–455, 463, 468, 471–473, 496, 525, 531, 534, 553, 557, 560, 565, 569–573, 593, 606, 607, 619, 638, 640, 641, 673, 683, 689
Ketchikan Miner, 164, 165, 172, 179, 270–274, 286, 298
Ketchikan Mining Journal, 88, 244
Ketchikan Mining News, The, 88, 163
Ketchikan Times, 68, 271, 276, 358
Ketchikan Tribune, 364
Kilroy, George, 265
Kinney, Claud, 87, 209, 215

Kinney, O. M., 209, 212, 215
Kinzie, Robert A., 179
Kirkpatrick, Mildred, 502–505, 689
Kirkwood, Ann, 452, 452
Klondike Nugget, 65, 68, 107, 108, 123, 136, 146
Klondike News, 215
Klopsch, Louis, 138, 139
Knapp, George and Gertrude, 189
Knapp, Gov. Lyman F., 30–33
Knight, E. W., 346
Knik Arm Courier, 583
Knik News, 312, 313
Knowles, Gov. Tony, 566, 589
Kodiak Baptist Orphanage, 41
Kodiak Bear, The, 485
Kodiak Daily Mirror, 16, 493
Kodiak Fish Wrapper and Litterbox Liner, 492
Kodiak Mirror, 338, 479, 483, 487, 494, 619, 641, 673, 688
Kosinski, Bernie, 664
Kotula, Wayne and Nancy, 488–492
Kurtz, Walter C., 99
Kusko Courier, 383
Kusko Times, 264, 382

Ladd, Annette Steel, 241, 242
Ladue, Joseph, 64, 65
Lamme, Bill and Lillian, 483–486
Lampson, F., 23
Lane, Franklin K., 64, 65, 142, 143, 247, 251, 294, 311, 314
Latimer, J. M. (Kirk), 130
Lathrop, Capt. Austin E. (Cap), 151, 202, 250, 322, 326, 336, 389–400, 546, 645, 688
Lattin, M. V., 224

Leach, Gus B., 57, 58, 81
Learn, George, 480
LeMasters, Clarence and Kelmar, 425, 426
Leslie, Frank, 76
Leslie's Magazine, 76
Leslie's Weekly, 111
Lewis, Capt. Charles H., 287
Lewis, Lena Morrow, 290
Libby, Capt. Daniel B., 19
Libel, 37, 82, 106, 108, 128, 185, 191, 194, 195, 331, 346, 356, 357, 374, 375, 499, 548, 613, 649, 650, 665, 671
Libel, civil, 189–191, 195
Libel, criminal, 51, 53, 129, 140, 143, 180, 185–188, 296
Lien, Paul, 390, 391, 403
Lincke, Clarence J. (Jack), 320, 321, 322
Lindauer, John and Jacqueline, 386, 406, 526, 527, 663
Lindsey, Michael and Patricia, 599, 603
Lingo, Dorothy, 354, 548
Loesch, C. F. (Budd), 525
Loesch, Ronald J. (Ron) and Anne, 454–456, 472–475
Long, Helen, 518
Lord-Jenkins, Linda, 418
Lott, Paul and Trilby, 385
Loussac, Z. J., 322
Lowenfels, Jeff, 669
Luckie, Glenn and Molly, 449, 455, 470, 471
Lynell, Gus, 262
Lyng, Howard, 624
Lynn, Pat and Jean, 526, 527

Lynn Canal News, 303
Lynn Canal Weekly, The, 302
Lyons, Thomas R., 179, 230

MacCannell, William R. (Bill) and Colleen, 539
Mailboat Monitor, The, 487
Mainhart, Benjamin, 427
Maloney, John, 53, 180
Marquam, Tom, 134, 139
Marrs, John, 614, 619
Marston, Janis, 303, 304
Martin, Fred, 318
Martin, Harry V., 613
Martone, Frank, 659
Marx, Walter John, 108
Mason, Charles, 684
Mason, Frank, 69, 117, 119, 120
Massey, Paul, 655, 656
Matanuska Valley Pioneer, 382, 593
Mathew, John M., 603
Mathews, Cleve, 687
Mattson, Sue, 654
Maynard, George and Mary, 68, 105–115, 265, 623
Maynard, Mildred, 115
Maynard, Russell G., 115, 547
McBride, Angus G., 59, 168, 169
McCafferty, John, 29
McCarthy, Patrick, 565
McCarthy Weekly News, The, 224, 425
McChesney, Robert J. (Bob), 69, 120–126, 130, 217, 225, 226, 234, 643
McClatchy Company, 14–16, 525, 570, 662, 670–672, 675, 680
McClatchy Newspapers, Inc., 524, 670

McDowell, James and Marie, 583, 585, 612, 689
McFarland, Jack E., 547, 553, 555
McGrath Bulletin, 383
McGrath, Jack, 261
McGrath Weekly, The, 383
McGuire, Nancy, 623, 630, 632
McIntyre, William, 64, 65, 83, 120, 324
McKay, Sec. of Interior Douglas, 373
McKay, John, 552, 589, 593
McKean, Edward G., 360
McKeand, J. H., 128, 168
McKenzie, Alexander, 98
McKinley, Pres. William, 98
McRoberts, Theodore, R.. 382, 383
Mears, Lt. Frederick J., 312, 316
Media Coverage of Court Proceedings, 572
MediaNews Group, 16, 621, 643, 656, 657
Megrath, George, 462
Menaker, Raymond R., 303, 304
Mergenthaler Linotype Company, 85, 127, 130, 131, 136, 174, 179, 260, 262, 276, 292, 314, 322, 323, 327, 350, 360, 364, 366, 369, 394, 398, 428, 440, 454, 458, 462, 463, 487, 506, 539, 643, 650, 666
Metcalf, Frank, 356, 357, 548
Metcalfe, Vern, 555
Metlakahtlan, 41
Mexican Mine, 282, 283
Michalski, Judge Peter, 592
Milepost, The, 16
Miller, Clarke, 49
Miller, Edward, 122, 549

Miller, Joaquin, 38
Miller, Judith, 549
Miller, Lynn W., 458
Miller, Terry, 9, 542
Miller, Tom, 453
Miner Publishing Company, 233, 547
Miners' Union Bulletin, 137
Mining Journal, 57, 155, 157–163, 166, 171, 178, 269, 272
Mitchell, T. C., 586
Modern Methods, 272
Monthly Mining Review, 118
Monsen, Helen, 302, 353–357, 546, 548, 552
Moore, William Alfred, 222
Moose Pass Miner, 300
Moran, Bernard B. (Casey), 70, 123
Moran's Weekly Alaskan, 124
Moreno, Harry M., 111
Morgan, Dick, 612, 613
Morgan, H. M., 94
Morgan, Lael, 558, 570, 654, 684
Morning Bulletin, 118
Morning Mail, The, 273, 274, 458
Morning Transcript, The, 180
Morning Pioneer Press, 105
Morris Communications Corporation, 560
Morris Publishing Group, 16, 560, 566, 568, 587, 615, 663
Morris, Tyler, 560
Morris, William S. III (Billy), 16, 560, 615, 618, 641
Morris, William, IV, 560
Morrison, Dr. Joy, 684, 685
Morrissey, Edward G., 69, 276, 358, 363, 364, 565
Mukluk, 505

Mukluk News, 386, 388
Mukluk Telegraph, 38, 108, 386, 388, 634, 636
Murphy, Thomas, G., 21–23, 48
Murray, J. Randolph, 13, 674, 675
Murray, Leslie, 450, 566
Myers, Frank, 31, 50, 51

Nash, Joe, 632
Nash, Will A., 87
National Editorial Association, 300, 429, 461
National Newspaper Association, 456
National Press Photographers Association, 683
Neece, Jack, 654
Needham, Theodore R. (Ted), 54, 56, 68–71, 120, 126, 168, 172, 246, 247, 251, 275, 276, 312, 313, 316, 688
Nelson, Adrian Clough, 222, 223
Nelson Daily Miner, The, 128
Nelson, James A., 242
Nelson, John, 611, 612
Nelson, John and Mertice, 523, 524
Nelson, John T., 388
Nelson, Philip Clough, 222
Nenana News, 312, 321, 381
Nenana Valley Roadrunner, 382
Neubert, Walter T., 364
New Alaskan, 538, 546
Newcomb, Harold, 600
New York Herald, 83, 203
New York Times, 192, 287, 311, 481, 549–551, 637, 640, 666
Nilsson, W. Don, 385
Noble, Nellie Mulrooney, 137
Noblit, Ken, 654

Nome Chronicle, 68
Nome Daily Chronicle, The, 99
Nome Daily Gold Digger, 99
Nome Daily Nugget, 93
Nome Gold Digger, 68, 102–106, 111, 201, 262, 280, 636
Nome News, 68, 96, 99, 102, 105–110
Nome Nugget, 68, 99, 105, 111, 112, 115, 160, 262, 265, 314, 338, 402, 446, 454, 469, 513, 537, 547, 623, 624, 627, 633
Nome Weekly Gold Digger, The, 88, 97, 98
Nome Nugget Publishing Company, 445–448, 469–471, 626
Nordale, Hjalmar, 149–151
Norman, Bob, 582, 583
North Star, 40
North Wind, 303
Northern Light, 130, 131, 406
Northern Printing Company, 331
Northern Publishing Company, 190
Northern Star, 427
Northland News, 651
Northrip, Dr. Charles, 684
Nosy News & Shopping Guide, 608
Nowell, Thomas, 50
Noyes, Judge Arthur H., 98, 99

O'Brien, A. R. (Gloomy Gus), 60, 62, 187–189, 296, 297
O'Brien, Onnolee, 501
O'Brien, Patrick and Lee, 579, 580
Ochs, Adolph, 637
O'Connell, Patrick, 612, 613
O'Donohue, Brian, 591
Ohlson, Col. Otto F., 232, 251
Oines, Gary, 470

Olson, B. G. (Wally), 382, 654, 683, 684
On The Kenai, 577, 608
Open Meeting Act, 592, 593
Ormasen, Peggy, 304
O'Ragen, Barney, 21
Oregonian, The, 15, 212
Orphanage News Letter, 41, 480, 483
Orr, Edward S., 106
Osuna, Ken, 663

Pagano, Roseanne, 686
Painter, Rodger, 660, 662
Palmer Daily, The, 593
Paper, The, 566, 641, 654
Parks, Gov. George, 688
Parkins, Al, 536
Pascall, Jane, 587, 588
Pathfinder, The, 250, 318
Patton, Cassia, 31, 41–47
Patty, Stanton, 628
Paul, Frederick. L., 411
Paul, Louis, 407, 410, 411, 425, 689
Paul, William (Bill) L. Sr., 407–413, 425, 459
Pearce, Dr. Frederick W., 686
Pearson, Drew, 192–195, 336, 367, 490, 649, 650
Peck, Cyrus, Cyrus Jr. and Ray, 413, 689
Pedro, Felix, 117
Peel, John Kenneth, 542, 571–573
Pegler, Westbrook, 194
Pegues, John Edouard and Dorothy Elaine 347, 350, 399, 546, 547
Pender, Jane, 382, 385
Peninsula Clarion, 16, 560, 587, 605, 611, 688

Penn, Michael, 570
Penny Saver, 565
Pentz, Linden B., 175
Peratrovich, Elizabeth and Roy, 355, 356
Perkins, Martin S., 273, 458
Persily, Larry, 9, 450–455, 566, 654
Petersburg Herald, 363, 407, 458, 459
Petersburg Pilot, 296, 449, 454–456, 471–473, 569
Petersburg Press, 338, 375, 410, 437, 441–449, 455, 456, 459, 460, 465–467, 471, 539, 560, 611
Petersburg Progressive, 457
Petersburg Weekly Report, 425, 458
Petroleum News, 453, 494, 566
Petticoat Gazette, 467, 501–505
Pettyjohn, Everett Howard, 242
Petroff, Ivan, 23
Phelps, Al, 402, 446, 625, 626
Phillips, Carol, 382
Phillips, Henry E., 407, 459
Phillips, Nelson, 445
Photography in court, 570–573
Pickrell, Robert, 538
Pilz, George, 33
Pinchot, Gifford, 212, 218, 221, 292
Pitlo, Stan, 560, 618
Pioneer All-Alaska Weekly, The, 403, 657
Pioneer Printing Company, 367, 539
Pioneer Scout, The, 108, 109
Platt, Sen. Orville H., 162
Poling, Bert and John, 300
Porcupine Nugget, 87
Porcupine Quill, 87
Porter, Brian
Porter, Orville T., 30, 32, 53

Porter, Walter, 30, 31, 32
Porterfield, Bob, 668
Portland, S.S., 63
Poulson, Thad and Sandy, 16, 432, 433, 435, 640
Pracht, Max, 51
Praetor, J. B., 54
Pratz, Fred C., 23
Premier Mine, 278
Preston, Charles and Keren, 384
Prevost, the Rev. Jules L., 34, 37–39
Price, Charles (Charlie), 641
Princess Sophia, SS, 285, 286, 293
Prior restraint, 549–551
Pritchett, James Wesley and Sarah, 173, 174, 175, 176
Privilege, reporter, 549, 550
Progressive (Ketchikan), 273–275
Prospector Daily Bulletin, 204
Pugh, John, 293
Pulitzer Prize, 15, 660, 667, 685, 687, 688
Public meetings (Open Meetings Act), 591–593
Public records, 605–607
Railbelt Reporter, The
Railroads:
    Alaska Central Railroad, 206, 244, 314
    Alaska Home Railway, 205
    Alaska Midland Railroad, 301
    Alaska Northern Railroad, 245, 247, 312
    Alaska Railroad, 64, 114, 232, 243, 245, 250, 251, 275, 293, 314, 321, 328, 381, 401, 503, 506, 593, 599, 601, 614, 651, 659

Alsek & Yukon Railroad, 301
Chilkoot Railroad, 77
Copper River & Northwestern Railway, 74, 179, 199, 200, 204, 211, 220, 221, 234–236, 242, 250, 273, 301
Copper River Railroad, 207, 215
Copper River & Yukon Railroad, 203
Haines Mission & Boundary Railroad, 300
Homer Railroad, 1890, 580
Tanana Mines Railroad, 117, 119
Tanana Valley Railway, 142
Valdez & Yukon Railroad, 204
White Pass & Yukon Railroad, 74, 76, 80, 89, 207, 214, 299, 302, 306
Ramme, Richard A., 427
Rampart Forum, The, 253
Rampart Miner, The, 253
Rampart Whirlpool, The, 253
Ramsey, Donald Lee, 670, 671
Randles, Slim and Pam W., 287, 601, 602
Rasmuson, Edward A. and Jenny, 8, 41, 321, 326, 327, 352
Rasmuson, Edward, 8, 689
Rasmuson Elmer, 8, 689
Raver, Bill and Dorothy, 582
Rawls, Robert A., 629
Record-Miner, 45, 47, 60–62, 133, 161, 178, 179, 215, 636
Reed, Frank, 669
Reed, Steve, 568, 569
Reeves, Scott, 675
Reid, Frank H., 73, 74
Reynolds, Donald W., 557, 560
Reynolds, Henry D., 46, 205, 226, 234, 245
Rhodes, Gregg, 662
Rhodes, Herb, 584, 608, 659–662
Rhodes, Robert, 687
Rice, James (Jake), 160
Rich, Carol, 688
Richards, Tom Jr., 418
Riggins, George E., 157
Riggs, Gov. Thomas C. Jr., 293, 294, 312, 347
Rinehart, Steve, 613
Ritchie, Elmer E., 206, 226–230, 245
Rivard, Jeffrey E., 273–276, 359, 360, 361
Riverside Mine, 278
Riviera, Dan, 195
Roadrunner, 382
Roberts, Kelly V. and Karyn, 615
Robertson, Frank G., 74
Robertson, R. E., 361
Robinson, Williams H., 46, 47
Rock, Howard, 401, 405, 407, 415–418, 684, 689
Roden, Henry, 69, 119, 120, 134, 265, 356, 357, 439, 548
Roediger, Capt. Richard, 64, 65, 83, 96, 120, 136, 324
Romano, Marilyn F., 656, 680
Roosevelt, Pres. Franklin D., 329, 348–351, 394, 439, 459
Roosevelt, Pres. Theodore (Teddy), 46, 47, 86, 138, 159, 161, 182, 209, 212, 273, 292
Rostad, Mike, 493
Rothstein, Joe, 664, 665

Rousseau, Albert M., 83
Ruby Citizen, The, 261
Ruby Record, The, 261
Ruby Record-Citizen, The, 260, 261, 264
Russell, Edward Crawford, 59–62, 80, 81, 87, 112, 177–182, 186–188, 216, 290–292, 319, 346
Rustgard, John, 189, 410, 411
Ryan, Jack, 646, 648, 664
Rybachek, Rose, 191

Sampson, Carl, 449, 561, 566
Sandford, Charles F., 280
Saportsa, Billie, 74
Saturday Mail, The, 274
Saunders, Seanne Gillen, 454, 455
Sawyer, E. O. Jr., 247, 248
Schaap, Christian H., 30–32, 43
Scheffler, Charles, 45, 46, 88, 89, 234, 235
Schmidtke, Theodore (Ted) and Billie, 599
Schoettler, John W., 459
Schooley, Loretta, 385, 386
Schultz, Judge Thomas, 606, 607, 738, 739
Schulz, Magistrate Thomas, 558, 570–572
Schwankl, Jim, 420
Scripps, E. W., 636
Scripps League, 305, 335, 492, 599, 639, 640
Scudder, Richard (Dick), 16, 494, 641–643, 654–657
Seaton, Sec. of Interior Fred, 325, 555, 556, 649
Seattle Post-Intelligencer (P-I), 23, 25, 63, 94, 111, 231, 248, 276, 287, 351, 392, 534, 636
Seattle Times, 15, 37, 111, 287, 534, 628, 653, 688
Selby, Hal B., 230–233, 249, 348, 515
Selby, Tom, 233, 249, 515, 547
Seldovia Herald, The, 577
Settlemier, Charles, 65, 265, 323, 324, 326, 327, 392, 393
Seward Advertising Bulletin, 501
Seward Gateway, 68, 136, 206, 231, 244, 245, 248, 250, 312–315, 320, 348, 396, 457, 481, 497, 579, 636, 637
Seward News, The, 499
Seward Phoenix Log, The, 419, 445, 497, 505–510, 525
Seward Polaris & Kenai Peninsula & Aleutian Chain News, 499
Seward Seaport Record, 499, 506
Seward Tribune, The, 247, 312
Sewell, Jackie, 608
Sexton, Mike, 673
Shackleford, Louis P., 179, 180, 186, 235
Shattuck, Allen, 163, 355
Shattuck, Henry, 187
Shaw, Chauncy Dunn, 45, 178
Shaw, L. Frank, 68, 71, 206, 245, 246, 313, 316, 319, 320, 688
Sheakley, Gov. James, 33, 42
Sheldon Jackson College
    Museum, 30
    School, 40, 42, 429, 431, 680
    The Rev. Dr. Sheldon Jackson, 28, 40, 57, 95, 156
Sheldon, Jerome Fife, 559, 599, 626
Sherman, A. W., 366

Sherpy, M. L., 72, 83, 85
Shield law, 549, 550
Simons, Howard and Tod, 585, 587
Singleton, W. Dean, 16, 494, 641, 643, 654, 657
Sims, Ward, 640
Sitka Cablegram, The, 46, 47
Sitka Alaskan, 88, 178, 179
Sitka Post, The, 23
Sitka Progress, The, 425–427
Sitka Sentinel (also see Daily Sentinel), 338, 367, 423, 428, 430, 440, 460, 641
Sitka Shopping News, 427
Sitka Sun, 423, 424, 426
Sitka Times, The, 20–22
Sitka Tribune, 363, 364, 424, 425
Sitka Weekly, The, 427
SJC Adventures, 40
SJC Today, 40
Skagit Alaska, Inc., 599–602, 673
Skaguay-Atlin Budget, 85
Skaguay News, 70, 72, 82–84, 308
Skagway Alaskan (also see Alaskan), 87, 130, 160, 169, 173, 179, 181, 182, 187, 215, 244, 248, 272, 289, 299, 300, 302
Skagway Cheechako, 299, 498
Skagway News, 201, 248, 296, 297, 303, 306, 308
Sleight, Kari, 603, 604
Smith, Alfred L., 118
Smith, Bruce L., 684
Smith, the Rev. E. Otis, 32, 43, 51, 52, 54
Smith, James Allen, 463, 465, 569
Smith, Jefferson (Soapy), 72, 74, 83, 168, 308
Smith, Kent, 663
Smith, Maurice V. (Maury), 399
Smith, Thomas K., 364
Smyser, Richard, 687
Snapp, Thomas Aubrey, 401–406, 415, 416
Snedden, Charles Willis (Bill), 194, 195, 336, 338, 394, 395, 402, 456, 521, 522, 642–654, 689
Snow, Chester Kingsley, 70, 260, 262
Snyder, A. V. R. and George, 166, 169–171, 179
Spieler, 388
Socialist Press, The, 140
Society of Professional Journalists, 683
Solka, Paul Jr., 118, 390, 391, 394, 399
Sorgenfrei, Jack and Katherine, 600
Sourdough Sentinel, 663
Southeast Alaska Business Journal, 565
Southeast Alaska Empire, 445, 538, 546, 559, 568
Southeast Log, 539, 546
Southworth, Roy Gratton, 70, 130, 131, 134, 139, 140, 321–324, 381, 382, 396
Spencer, Charles, 493
Spencer, Hal, 640
Spencer, Murlin, 634, 641, 651–653
Spute, Chris, 305
Stahl, Eugene C., 53, 54
Stamm, Albert Gustavus, 256, 257
Stanchfield, David and Nancy, 491, 492
Stanhope, Paul, 172, 173, 275
Stapleton, Rob, 632
Star, 137, 147, 217, 225
Star of Bengal, 286

State of California, SS, 287
Steel, Harry, 68, 69, 96, 102, 105–108, 134, 217–221, 231–240, 248–251, 317, 319, 329, 363, 595, 637
Steel, Will, 68, 69, 96, 107, 108, 134, 217, 220, 234–236, 251, 263, 345–347, 637
Stepovich, Gov. Mike, 194, 195, 325, 647, 649
Stern, Mort, 687
Stevens, Mort, 139
Stevens, S. H., 104, 106
Stevens, Sen. Theodore (Ted), 326, 418, 470, 475, 488, 649, 674
Stewart, Elliott, 206, 226, 230, 244, 245
Stewart, Loren and Dorothy, 609–611, 614, 615
Stewart, Capt. Merrill D., 512, 513
Stewart, Judge Thomas (Tom), 555
Stikeen River Journal, 120, 128. 168
Stone, Bernard M. (Bernie), 68, 69, 105, 111, 247, 248, 251, 271, 276, 312, 316, 321, 358, 382, 390–392, 396
Strand, William C. (Bill), 370, 373, 393, 394, 546, 645–647
Stringer, John, 561
Strohmeyer, John, 687
Stroller's Weekly, 70, 84, 346
Strong, Gov. John Franklin Alexander, 68, 71–75, 82, 83, 86, 96–99, 102–107, 144, 145, 160, 177, 182–184, 209–213, 228, 257, 260, 289, 293–295, 319, 688, 689
Sturgis, G. Kent, 640, 653, 654, 684

Sulzer, Charles, 272, 276, 293
Summers, Clem M., 179, 186, 187
Sundborg, George, 194, 195, 553, 555, 648, 649, 658
Sunday Capital, The, 345, 346
Sunday Chronicle, 375
Sunday Democrat, The, 318
Sunday Observer, The, 402
Susitna Sentinel, 601
Susitna Valley Chronicle, 287, 601
Sutton, Larry, 191
Sutton Siding, 600
Swearingen, Max, 606, 612–614
Swineford, Gov. Alfred P., 24–31, 49, 50, 57, 59, 71, 82, 88, 155–166, 172, 179, 182, 269, 272, 355, 532
Swinehart, George B., 53, 57, 58, 68, 98, 99, 118
Sylvester, E. O., 32, 51–55

Tabor, Hale, 429, 430
Tacoma Daily News, 64, 121, 122
Tacoma Ledger, 29, 75, 436
Tacoma News, 64, 142
Tacoma Tribune, 65
Taft, Pres. William Howard, 182, 212, 218, 235, 532, 533
Tanana Citizen, The, 37, 255
Tanana Daily Miner, 127–130, 255
Tanana Daily Star, 137
Tanana Daily Tribune, 65
Tanana Leader, 255, 256
Tanana Miner, 69, 120, 134, 255, 389
Tanana Star, 637
Tanana Teller, 70
Tanana Tribune, 65, 70, 131, 134
Taylor, Councilwoman Connie, 592, 593

Teller Musher, The, 108
Teller News, 68, 107, 108
Temple, Wick, 652
Tewkesbury, David (Tewkes), 68, 98, 99, 265, 319, 392, 393
Thlinget, The, 40
Thomas, Gary, 587
Thomas, Lynn, 664
Thomson, Lori, 569
Thompson, William Fentress, 69, 114, 120, 126-137, 141-151, 167, 175, 255, 389, 391, 643, 651, 689
Thomsen, Capt. Niels P., 487
Thorn, H. A. and Marion, 583, 584
Thrifty Nickel, 565
Timmins, John, 54, 55
Tobin, William (Bill), 9, 14, 634, 635, 640, 653, 664, 674, 675
Tok Bugle, 388
Torkelson, Sewald, 180
Towne, George S., 85
Troy, Gov. John Weir, 71, 82, 85, 86, 160, 162, 164, 179, 184, 189, 228, 270-273, 289-296, 299, 345, 347, 350-354, 399, 546, 548, 688, 689
Truman, Pres. Harry S., 334, 336, 338, 371, 374, 394, 412, 413, 430, 441, 487
Truth, The (Cordova), 219, 220
Truth (Valdez), 226
Tundra Times, 405, 407, 415, 418, 490, 600, 683
Turnagain Times, 663
Turner, Mark, 587

Ullrich, Will C., 180, 187
Ulmer, Charles D. Sr., 77, 80
Ulmer, George T., 58, 59, 77, 80, 81
Ulmer, George T. Jr., 59, 77, 80
Ulmer, Ralph, 77, 80
Underwood, John Jasper (Jack), 109-111, 167, 169, 265
United Press, 139, 248, 350, 366, 369, 371, 393, 399, 427, 486, 499, 545, 553, 559, 623, 635, 636, 638, 639
United Press International, 453, 569, 639, 646, 689
University of Alaska Anchorage, 7, 224, 494, 526, 662, 673, 680
University of Alaska Anchorage School of Journalism and Public Communications, 326, 679, 685
University of Alaska Fairbanks, 7, 35, 71, 118, 273, 295, 338, 406, 449, 481, 506, 521, 541, 558, 561, 565, 572, 588, 629, 647, 653, 654, 656, 674, 681, 683
University of Alaska Southeast, 413, 420, 423

Valdez Breeze, 233, 515-518
Valdez-Copper Basin News, 518
Valdez Daily News, 204
Valdez Earthquake Bulletin, The, 517
Valdez Miner, 226
Valdez News, 201-203, 226, 517, 527
Valdez News Letter, 226
Valdez Pioneer, 526, 527
Valdez Prospector, 203, 204, 226
Valdez Star, 526, 527
Valdez Vanguard, The, 473, 510, 523-525, 651, 672
Valdez Weekly Miner, 226
Valdez Weekly Prospector, The, 206, 245

Valley Frontiersman, 579, 597, 598
Valley Post, The, 597
Valley Press, 600
Valley Settler, The, 597
Valley Sun, 600
Veatch, Harold and Ernestine, 367, 428–433, 460
VECO, 15
Verstovian, The, 40
Voice of the Brotherhood, 413
Voice of the Times, The, 14, 15, 419, 542, 635, 664, 674

Waage, Nell, 492
Wade, Patricia, 407, 419
Wahl, Robert A. (Bob), 428, 429
Walker, Ed and Frances, 385, 513
Walker's Weekly, 385
Wall, Sam, 69, 122, 123, 297
Wallace, Brian, 569, 570
Ward, Frank H., 52–54
Ward, James Wilbur, 69, 70, 126, 131, 137, 237, 247, 251, 255, 320, 345
Ward, William W., 23
Washington Post, 550, 585, 650
Weaver, Howard, 660, 662, 668
Weaver, Mark, 660, 663
Weaver, Robert C. (Bob), 446, 447, 469, 470
Weekly Alaska Dispatch, 59
Weekly Alaskan, The, 231, 315
Weekly Capital, 270
Weekly Fairbanks News, 56, 69, 117–120, 136, 217, 257
Weekly Times, The, 139, 318, 331
Weiss, William L. (Bill), 432, 534
Wells, Tommy, 632
White, Al, 226, 318

White, Elmer John (Stroller), 60, 61, 70, 82–85, 123, 146, 180, 189, 252, 263, 308, 346–348, 689
Whitehorse Star, 60
Whittaker, Richard L., 367, 487
Whittren, F., 105, 106
Wick Communications, 599, 603
Wickersham, Judge James, 34, 35, 64, 88, 89, 104, 106, 117, 118, 120, 122, 125, 126, 131, 134, 137, 138, 160, 171, 173, 180, 183, 215–218, 226, 228, 231, 237, 272, 273, 290–294, 297, 363, 383, 391, 411, 532, 549, 637
Wilcox, Charles Herbert, 231–235
Wilder, Claire and Ethel, 437, 460–463
Wilder, William (Bill), 460–462
Willawaws, The, 485
Williams, Andy, 406, 660, 662
Williams, Christena (Tena), 453, 454, 542, 544, 640
Williams, Gary, 585
Williams, Jane, 440, 547
Williams, Kathryn (Kathy), 542, 544
Williams, Kristie, 544
Williams, Lew M. III and Vicki, 541, 542, 544
Williams, Lew M. Jr. and Dorothy, 7–9, 16, 192, 193, 338, 432, 433, 441, 442, 445, 446, 454, 462–471, 539–542, 547, 560, 640, 688, 689
Williams, Lew M. Sr. and Winnie, 176, 336, 338, 352, 436–445, 454, 553
Williams, Steve, 304
Willis, Amy, 494, 688
Willis, Charles F. Jr., 402–404, 446, 448, 469, 625, 626

Wilson, Jeff, 561, 568
Wilson, Lavelle and Catherine, 388
Wilson, T. G. (Tug), 168
Wilson, Pres. Woodrow, 64, 136, 144, 145, 182, 184, 228, 245, 301, 311, 318
Wimmer, Terry, 687
Winde, H. W., 94
Winford, George M., 684
Wingate, James B., 252, 253, 254
Winter, John, 568
Wishaar, E. B., 68, 102
Wolf, Lynn and Linda, 525
Wolfgram, William A., 249
Wood, Carol, 673, 674
Wood, Leighton, 599, 673
Woodward, G. Carlton and Harry, 117
Wrangell Sentinel, 89, 169, 171, 246, 272, 275, 336, 338, 352, 412, 431, 445–456, 460–465, 468–473, 539, 545, 547, 553, 561, 566, 641
Wrangell Standard, 169
Wrangell St. Elias News, 224
Wright, Mrs. Clara E., 253
Wyatt, Walter A., 160, 163, 178, 244, 245

Young, Alexander C., 290
Young, Charles Clinton, 611, 612
Young, the Rev. Dr. S. Hall, 40, 75, 124
Yukon Midnight Sun, 58, 98, 105, 129
Yukon Morning Sun, 120, 129
Yukon Press, 34–39, 140
Yukon Sentinel, 525
Yukon Sun, 65, 129, 146, 202
Yukon Valley News, 70, 254, 256, 257

Zelnick, Bob, 665
Zimmerman, Jack, 461

Books and Other Sources of Information

This book, *Bent Pins to Chains*, is based on a manuscript by Evangeline Atwood, "A History of One Hundred Years of Newspapering in Alaska, 1885-1985." Her manuscript was updated to 2005, and this book was completed after extensive research of newspaper files in the microfilm department of the Alaska State Library. Information and help also was provided by more than one hundred individuals contacted by authors, Atwood and Williams, and by various Alaska newspapers and individuals who provided photos.

Other sources of information are credited in the manuscript, such as that from articles in magazines, especially *Alaska Southeaster*, and including *Time*, *Alaska Life*, *Alaska Monthly*, *Frank Leslie's Weekly*, *Alaska Journal*, the *Quill* at University of Alaska Fairbanks and the *New York Times Magazine*.

Books and other sources that provided information include:

A Bibliography of Alaskan Literature, 1724-1924 by James Wickersham; Vol. 1, Miscellaneous Publications of the Alaska Agricultural College and School of Mines, printed in 1937 by *Cordova Daily Times*.

A History of One Hundred Years of Newspapering in Alaska,1885-1985, by Evangeline Atwood; unpublished manuscript in the archives of the Alaska State Library, Juneau, and the University of Alaska archives in Fairbanks and Anchorage.

Adventures in Alaska Journalism Since 1903, by Paul Solka Jr.; Commercial Printing Co., Fairbanks, 1980.

Alaska, an Empire in the Making, by John J. Underwood; Dodd, Mead and Company, New York, 1913.

Alaska Department of Community and Economic Development Web site for information on Alaska communities.

Alaska, Its History, Climate and Natural Resources, by A. P. Swineford; Rand, McNally & Co., 1898.

Alaska Newspapers on Microfilm, 1866-1998, compiled by Mary C. Nicolson, assisted by Mary Anne Slemmons, for the Alaska State Library Newspaper Project, University of Alaska Fairbanks and the Alaska State Library, 1998.

Alaska – Our Northern Wonderland, by Frank G. Carpenter; Doubleday, Doran & Company, Inc., New York, 1928.

Alaska State Library archives.

Alaska, the Great Country, by Ella Higginson; MacMillan Co., New York, 1908.

Alaska, the Last Frontier, by Henry W. Clark; Grosset & Dunlap, New York, 1930.

Alaska's Kodiak Island, by George C. Ameigh and Yul M. Chaffin; Anchorage Printing Co., 1962.

Allied Daily Newspaper Association records. Now the Pacific Northwest Newspaper Association, Sacramento, California

Anchorage Daily News archives.

Anchorage Museum of History and Art.

Anchorage, Star of the North, by Evangeline Atwood; Continental Heritage Press, Oklahoma City, 1982.

AP, the Story of News, by Oliver Grambling; Farrar and Rinehart, New York, 1940.

Biography of Alfred Peter Swineford, by Katheryn A. Marriott, Santa Barbara, California, an unpublished manuscript.

Bob Atwood's Alaska, an unpublished manuscript.

Carrie M. McLain Museum, Nome.

Central District Museum and Historical Society.

Citizen Hearst, the Biography of William Randolph Hearst, by W. W. Swanberg; Scribner's, New York, 1996

Continental Dash, the Russian – American Telegraph, by Rosemary Neering, Horsdal & Schubert Publishers, Ganges, British Columbia, 1989.

Cordova Historical Society.

Cyclopedia of American Biography, D. Appleton & Co., New York, 1898.

Dawson Historical Complex NHSC, Dawson City, Yukon Territory, Canada

Dictionary of Alaska Place Names; Geological Survey Professional Paper 567, by Donald J. Orth; United States Government Printing Office, 1971.

Down to the Wire; UPI's Fight for Survival, by Gregory Gordon and Ronald E. Cohen; McGraw-Hill, New York, 1990

Early Newspapers on the Upper Yukon Watershed: 1894-1907, unpublished 1963 master's thesis at the University of Alaska Fairbanks by Dora Elizabeth McLean.

Fairbanks Daily News-Miner archives.

Farthest North College President: Charles E. Bunnell and the Early History of the University of Alaska, by William R. Cashen, University of Alaska Press, December 1972.

Fortunes from the Earth; An History of the Base and Industrial Minerals of Southeaast Alaska, by Patricia Roppel; Sunflower University Press, Manhattan, Kansas, 1991.

Frontier Politics: Alaska's James Wickersham, by Evangeline Atwood; Binford & Mort, 1979

Geology and Coal Resources of the Homer District Kenai Coal Field, Alaska, United States Government Bulletin No.1058-F by Barnes and Cobb; United States Government Printing Office, about 1900.

Hall Young of Alaska, by S. Hall Young; Revelle Co., New York, 1927.

History of Alaska: 1730-1885, by Hubert Rowe Bancroft, reprinted by Antiquarian Press, New York, 1959.

History of American Journalism, by James Melvin Lee, Houghton Mifflin Co., New York, 1917.

In Days Primeval, by Bernard Moore; Vantage Press, 1968

Institute of Social, Economic & Government Research, University of Alaska Fairbanks, 1970.

Jerome Sheldon Papers, University of Alaska Anchorage archives.

Ketchikan Museums.

Ketchikan Public Library.

Klondike Newsman: Stroller White, by R. N. DeArmond; Lynn Canal Publishing, Skagway, 1992.

Lomen Collection by E. D. Evans, University of Alaska archives, 1919.

Lost Frontier; the Marketing of Alaska, by John Hanrahan and Peter Gruenstein; W. W. Norton & Co., New York, 1977.

Milltown; A Social History of Everett, Washington, by Norman H. Clark; University of Washington Press, 1970.

Morris Newspaper Group archives.

National Cyclopedia of American Biography, a series published annually between 1980 and 1985 by James T. White Company.

Newspaper Association of America, Reston, Virginia, records and publications.

Newspapering in the Old West, by Robert F. Karolevitz; Superior Publishing Co., Seattle, 1965.

Nome and the Seward Peninsula, by E. S. Harrison, Seattle, 1905.

Old Yukon; Tales – Trails – Trials, by James Wickersham; West Publishing Co., St. Paul, Minnesota, 1938.

Parks Canada, Dawson City. Yukon Territory, photo archives.

Pulitzer's Prize Editor; a Biography of John A. Cockerill, by Homer W. King; Duke University Press, Durham, North Carolina, 1965.

Railroad in the Clouds; The Alaska Railroad in the Age of Steam, 1914-45, by William N. Wilson; Pruett Publishing Co., Boulder, Colorado, 1977.

Resurrection Bay Historical Society archives.

Soapy Smith, King of the Frontier Con Men, by Frank G. Robertson and Beth Kay Harris; Hastings House, 1961.

Stroller White; Tales of a Klondike Newsman, by R. N. DeArmond; Mitchell Press, Vancouver, Canada, 1969.

Strong and Bunnell papers, University of Alaska Fairbanks archives.

Strong Papers, letters from J. F. A. Strong to Charles Herron, 1913-17, University of Alaska Fairbanks archives.

Tacoma Headlines, by Paul W. Harvey; *Tacoma News-Tribune,* 1962

Tacoma; Its History and Its Builders, by Herbert Hunt, 1916.

The Adventurers of an Alaska Printer in the Panhandle, by Richard Bushell and published in 1997 by distant relative Alice Large of Atascadero, California

The Associated Press.

The Arizona Project, by Michael F. Wendland; Sheed Andres and McMeel, Mission, Kansas, 1977.

The Associated Press Stylebook and Briefing on Media Law, Norm Goldstein, editor; Perseus Books, Reading, Massachusetts, 1998.

The Associated Press Stylebook for Alaska, Dean M. Gottehrer, editor; Epicenter Press, Fairbanks, 2000.

The Chicago Manual of Style, 15th edition, The University of Chicago Press.

The Copper Spike, by Lone Janson; Alaska Northwest Publishing Co., 1975.

The Destiny of Russia America, by the history department of the University of Alaska Fairbanks; Limestone Press, 1990.

The Firecracker Boys, by Dan O'Neill, St. Martin's Press, 1995.

The Founding of Juneau, by R. N. DeArmond.

The Nugget, a periodical by William Marx; Cedarlea Press, Edgewater, Md. 1982.

The Scandalous Mr. Bennett, by Richard O'Connor; Doubleday & Company, Garden City, New York, 1962

The Story of Alaska, by Clarence L. Andrews; Caxton Printers, Caldwell, Idaho, 1947.

The Story of Sitka, by Clarence L. Andrews, Lowman & Hanford, Seattle, Washington, 1922.

The Trail of the Goldseekers, by Hamlin Garland; Reprint Services Corp. 1999.

Then Fight for It, a paper on early Alaska land claims activist William L. Paul Sr., delivered by Professor Stephen Haycox of the University of Alaska Anchorage at a conference November 2003 at the University of Victoria.

Through the Yukon and Alaska, by T. A. Rickard; Mining and Scientific Press, San Francisco, 1909.

Travel and Adventure in the Territory of Alaska, by Frederick Whymper, John Murray; Albermarle Street, London, 1869.

Two Years in the Klondike and Alaskan Gold Fields, 1896-98 by William B. Haskell; Hartford Publishing Co., 1898; reprinted by University of Alaska Press, 1998, with preface by Terrance Cole.

University of Alaska Anchorage and University of Alaska Fairbanks journalism faculty.

University of Alaska Fairbanks archives.

University of Washington Libraries.

Voyage Around the World, 1803-06, by I. F. Lisianskii; F. Drekhsler, St. Petersburg, Russia, 1812.

War Discovers Alaska, by Joseph Driscoll; J. B. Lippincott, Philadelphia, 1943.

We are Alaskans, by Mary Lee Davis; W. A. Wilde Co., Boston, 1931.

Who Was Who in America; 1607-2000, published by Marquis Who's Who.

Who's Who in Alaska Politics; a Biographical Dictionary of Alaskan Political Personalities, 1884-1974 compiled by Evangeline Atwood and Robert N. DeArmond; Binford & Mort, Portland, Oregon, for the Alaska Historical Commission.

Wickersham Diaries, by James Wickersham; University of Alaska Fairbanks archives.

What is a Newspaper?

What is a newspaper of general circulation? That description is important because legal advertisements are recognized in some laws as an official notice only when published in "a newspaper of general circulation."

Alaska foreclosure law requires publication in a newspaper of general circulation and describes it. This does not bar publication of legal notices in publications other than newspapers of general circulation. Some local and federal notices, such as timber sales, are published in the weekly *Island News* on Prince of Wales Island although the *Island News* does not qualify under state foreclosure law, under state court decisions and under postal regulations as a newspaper of general circulation.

Federal regulations do not describe a newspaper of general circulation as specifically as does Alaska law. Federal regulations for the Forest Service requires only that each year the regional foresters publish in the *Federal Register* a list of the principal newspapers to be utilized for publishing notices required by law. The Forest Service has designated the *Island News*. That is practical because there is no other publication on Prince of Wales Island.

Representatives of free circulation newspapers and shoppers have occasionally asked the state legislature to broaden state law to give them access to legal advertisements. Newspapers have protested that by arguing that only their paid subscription lists prove that a broad section of the public has been informed of a government action.

Newspapers in Alaska also face competition for the legal advertising dollars with the increased popularity of the Internet. Some state agencies now run only a boxed notice in newspapers saying that a regulation is being changed and that the full text is available on a state Web page.

State officials say use of the Internet is a way to cut advertising costs. Newspaper representatives say that instead of cutting costs, it means hiring more state workers to put the information on a Web page, and that not everyone is computer literate.

Some states, such as Nebraska, set the rate newspapers can charge for legal advertisements, supposedly to control expense. But Nebraska law also specifies what must be advertised in a newspaper. The list is lengthy – minutes of public meetings, financial reports of government entities, even cemeteries. That might be why the state sets the legal advertising rate.

There is no law in Alaska setting legal rates and Alaska newspapers oppose the idea. However, Alaska publication requirements are less stringent for public agencies – fewer items need to be published.

Under Sec. 09.35.140 of Alaska law, a newspaper of general circulation is described as one printed in a newspaper format; distributed at least once a week for 50 weeks; has a paid circulation of at least 500 copies; holds a second class mailing permit from the U.S. Postal Service; is not published primarily to distribute advertising; and is not intended primarily for a particular professional or occupational group.

To retain its second class mailing permit, a newspapers of general circulation must print a statement each Oct. 1 listing how many papers it delivers to paid subscribers in each postal zone. Postal inspectors periodically make unannounced audits of a newspaper's circulation records.

The publication must be issued regularly – daily, weekly, – and at least 50 percent of its circulation must be distributed to paid subscribers. A second class publication must contain no more than 75 percent advertising in each issue.

The Alaska Supreme Court has been liberal for newspaper publishers in interpreting what constitutes a newspaper of general circulation and how much it must distribute in a specified area. In one instance in 1976, fishermen based in Homer, along with the owner of a lodge on Kachemak Bay, challenged the sale of oil and gas leases, alleging that proper notice was not published in a newspaper of general circulation. They alleged that *The Anchorage Times* was not a newspaper of general circulation in their area.

Superior Court Judge Thomas Schulz of Ketchikan, hearing the case in Anchorage, sided with the state that the *Times* was a newspaper of general circulation in that area. The fishermen and lodge owner appealed. On July 9, 1976, the Alaska Supreme Court upheld Judge Schulz's decision, adding that "a newspaper which contains news of general interest to the community and reaches a diverse readership is one of general circulation."

The state's high court added: "At the time the notice was published, the population of Homer area was approximately 3,500. The paid circulation of *The Anchorage Times* in the area was approximately 130. The number of readers, albeit small, was not so insignificant that the newspaper would fail to reach a diverse group of people in the community. Therefore, it must be said that *The Anchorage Times* was a newspaper of general circulation in the Homer area."

In September 2000, the Alaska Supreme Court went further in stating that the *Tundra Drums* was not a newspaper of general circulation in the City of St. Mary's because there was no proof of subscribers. One hundred copies were offered for sale at the town's two stores.

However, there are negative aspects to being a newspaper of general circulation with a second class mail permit. It is against postal regulations to send lottery tickets or advertisements for lotteries or bingo games through the mail.

Section 1302 of postal regulations covering lottery tickets or related matter says that any newspaper inserted in the mail "containing any advertisement of any lottery, gift enterprise or scheme of any kind offering prizes dependent" upon chance and payment for a chance, "shall be fined not more than $1,000 or imprisoned not more than two years or both; and for any subsequent offense shall be imprisoned not more than five years."

This has been a problem for Alaska newspapers for years trying to report on Alaska's famous Nenana Ice Classic or local organizations' bingo games.

With the proliferation of state lotteries, federal regulations have relaxed enough to allow newspapers to print winning lottery numbers of states that border the state in which the newspaper is published. The *Ketchikan Daily News*, for example, prints the Washington State winning lottery numbers.

Names of winners of lotteries or the ice pool (after the fact) are reported without problem.

In the above paragraph "the newspaper shall be fined . . . or imprisoned?" Shades of 1906 Tanana. See Chapter 3.